PRESIDENT ROOSEVELT
AND THE
COMING OF THE WAR
1941

A STUDY IN APPEARANCES
AND REALITIES

By

CHARLES A. BEARD

ARCHON BOOKS
1968

SBN: 208 00265 0
LIBRARY OF CONGRESS CATALOG CARD NUMBER: 68-8012
PRINTED IN THE UNITED STATES OF AMERICA

PREFATORY NOTE

THIS volume is a sequel to my *American Foreign Policy in the Making, 1932–1940* (Yale University Press, 1946), to which reference is made in the following pages as Beard, *op. cit.*

Since a considerable part of this sequel is based upon the documentation provided by the Joint Committee on the Investigation of the Pearl Harbor Attack of the Congress of the United States, I have used for convenience abbreviations of my citations of that authority. CJC, *Report* refers to the Joint Committee's unnumbered volume which embraces the views of the majority, the additional views of Mr. Keefe, and the minority views of Mr. Ferguson and Mr. Brewster (see Chap. XII). The volumes of the Joint Committee containing the hearings are numbered Parts 1–11 and the Exhibits, Parts 12–39. The reference to "CJC, Part—" is to the volume indicated by the number that follows. In a few cases references are made to mimeographs of documents presented to the committee and the public before the series was formally published; for example, extracts from Secretary Stimson's *Diary* and his supplementary statement. Several papers placed in the committee's hands were not included in its published volumes and so I have occasionally referred to its unpublished materials. The transcripts of the committee's hearings and documents, unprinted as well as printed, have been transferred to the National Archives where they may be examined by citizens in quest of the complete record.

To Miss Ella Holliday, of the Yale Press, I am deeply indebted for her skill and invincible patience in connection with the typing and checking of the manuscript.

CHARLES A. BEARD

New Milford, Connecticut,
Spring, 1947.

CONTENTS

PART I

APPEARANCES

CHAPTER I

Moral Commitments for the Conduct of Foreign Affairs in 1941

PRESIDENT ROOSEVELT entered the year 1941 carrying moral responsibility for his covenants with the American people to keep this nation out of war—so to conduct foreign affairs as to avoid war. Those covenants, made in the election campaign of 1940, were of two kinds. The first were the pledges of the Democratic party to which he publicly subscribed while he was bidding for the suffrages of the people. The second were his personal promises to the people, supplementing the obligations of his party's platform.[1]

The antiwar covenants of the Democratic party, to which President Roosevelt had committed himself unreservedly during the campaign, were clear-cut: "We will not participate in foreign wars, and we will not send our Army, naval, or air forces to fight in foreign lands outside of the Americas, except in case of attack. . . . The direction and aim of our foreign policy has been, and will continue to be, the security and defense of our own land and the maintenance of its peace."

In supplementing the pledges of the Democratic platform, President Roosevelt had also been unequivocal in his personal declarations. At Philadelphia, October 23, 1940, he had branded as false a Republican charge that "this Administration wishes to lead this country into war," and proclaimed that he was "following the road to peace." At Boston on October 30, he was even more emphatic, for there he declared: "I have said this before, but I shall say it again and again and again: Your boys are not going to be sent into any foreign wars. . . . The purpose of our defense is defense." At Buffalo, Novem-

1. For the record, see Beard, *American Foreign Policy in the Making, 1932–1940*, pp. 312 ff.

ber 2, his vow was short and unqualified: "Your President says this country is not going to war."

It is true that the Democratic platform of 1940 pledged to liberty-loving peoples wantonly attacked "all the material aid at our command, consistent with law and not inconsistent with the interests of our own national self-defense." It is true also that during the campaign President Roosevelt reiterated, reinforced, and enlarged upon this promise. But neither Democratic party leaders nor President Roosevelt at the time construed the pledge to extend, conditionally, material aid to liberty-loving peoples as canceling the conditions and their antiwar covenants. And indeed it would require more than casuistry to show that an indefinite and conditional pledge in fact obliterated *ex vi termini* definite and unequivocal pledges to the contrary made simultaneously and subsequently.[2]

On their part, the Republicans and their candidate, Wendell Willkie, likewise committed themselves to definite promises that they would keep the United States out of war. The antiwar plank of the Republican platform read: "The Republican party is firmly opposed to involving this nation in foreign war." While expressing a real fear that the Administration was heading for war, Mr. Willkie reiterated again and again and again during the campaign a solemn promise that if elected President no American boys would be sent to fight in any European or Asiatic war.[3]

Whatever secret reservations President Roosevelt and Mr. Willkie may have cherished when they made their antiwar commitments to the American people, there can be no doubt

2. Even the Committee to Defend America by Aiding the Allies did not claim in 1940 or until late in 1941 that the promise of such aid authorized the President to take the country into war in seeking to extend aid to liberty-loving peoples wantonly attacked. Walter Johnson, *The Battle against Isolation* (Chicago, University of Chicago Press, 1944). Moreover, nothing said by President Roosevelt or sponsors of the measure authorizing this aid, namely, the Lend-Lease Act, while it was pending, lent the slightest countenance to the claim that lend-lease canceled all antiwar pledges and empowered the President to wage war in executing the law that provided for the extension of the aid. See below, Chap. II.

3. For Mr. Willkie's antiwar speeches during the campaign of 1940, see Beard, *op. cit.*, pp. 296 ff. For statements on limited aid to the Allies in the Republican platform and Mr. Willkie's speeches, see *ibid.*, pp. 295 ff.

about the unequivocal nature of their covenants to keep the country out of war if victorious at the polls.[4] Nor could there be any doubt that the overwhelming majority of the American people were then convinced that the United States should stay out of war in Europe and Asia. That conviction had long been maturing, in a large measure as the result of experiences during and after World War I.

As leader of "the great crusade" in 1917–18, President Wilson had held up before the American people a noble dream of a new and better world. In moving speeches and summary statements, he had told them that they were fighting a war for democracy, a war to end wars, a war to crush German military despotism, a war to close the old era of secret diplomacy and imperialism, a war to establish permanent peace among the war-weary peoples of the earth. But the war had scarcely come to a close when stark events began to dissolve the dream. Even in the so-called settlement at Versailles only two or three of President Wilson's Fourteen Points for an ideal peace were realized. For the American people the years that followed were years of deepening disillusionment.[5]

With regard to foreign policy, no trend in American public opinion between 1919 and 1941 was more marked than a diminishing confidence in the peace promises of the League of Nations and a growing resolve to keep the United States out of the next war in Europe. If the trend was especially marked at first among Republicans, it became powerfully evident among Democrats at their national conventions in 1924 and 1928.[6] It reached a high point in 1932. In February of that

4. *Ibid.*, Chap. X.

5. Among the many books that contributed to American disillusionment about how war came in 1917 and about President Wilson's lofty principles for a new world order and to the triumph of isolationism in the United States after 1918, few, if any, were more widely read or more powerful than *Road to War: America, 1914–1917* (Houghton, 1935) by Walter Millis, editorial writer on the *New York Herald Tribune*. On the jacket this book was advertised as an account of "the Frenzied Years of 1914-1917 when . . . a peace-loving democracy, muddled but excited, misinformed and whipped to frenzy, embarked upon its greatest foreign war. . . . Read it and blush! Read it and beware! Read it and renew, your youth!"

6. Beard, *op. cit.*, pp. 45 ff.

year Franklin D. Roosevelt, then seeking the Democratic nomination for President, publicly declared that he was opposed to American membership in the League of Nations and was in favor of nonentanglement in the political quarrels of Europe; and in November of that year, after making a nationwide campaign mainly on domestic issues, Governor Roosevelt was elected President of the United States.[7] The trend of Democratic opinion against involvement in the next European war came to a climax in 1935 when Congress, completely dominated by Democrats, passed the first Neutrality Act—a law deliberately designed to keep the United States out of the next European war, already on the horizon, by forbidding a number of specific practices identical with or akin to the practices that had prevailed in 1914–17 and had resulted in "shooting" incidents on the high seas prior to the declaration of war on Germany in April, 1917. Although President Roosevelt dissented from some features of the Neutrality measure he signed it, endorsed the design of Congress to keep the United States out of the next war, and praised the purpose of Congress in his campaign for reëlection in 1936.

Only once during the years from 1933 to 1940 did President Roosevelt apparently make an open break with the policy of neutrality for the United States in European wars. That was in his "quarantine speech" at Chicago in October, 1937; but almost immediately he declared in effect that his speech really meant no breach with the Neutrality Act, no intention on his part to intervene by arms in a European war when it came.[8] Furthermore, if, despite his subsequent denials, the quarantine speech was to be taken at the moment as indicating that President Roosevelt had actually shifted from neutrality to the doctrine of armed intervention, that indication was explicitly canceled in 1939 and 1940 by his various public promises to maintain the neutrality of the United States.

Had President Roosevelt been privately convinced in 1940 that the United States should enter the war, he knew, as well

7. *Ibid.*, pp. 72 ff.
8. *Ibid.*, pp. 188 ff.

as Mr. Willkie did, that the sentiment of the Democratic party, and of the country, was almost solidly against that view. Only a small proportion of the delegates at the Republican convention at Philadelphia in June dared to reveal opinions veering in the direction of war for the United States and all such opinions were quickly overridden by the resolute majority of noninterventionists.[9] At the Democratic convention in Chicago a few days later the antiwar sentiment among the delegates was even stronger, if possible, than it had been among the Republicans at Philadelphia; President Roosevelt and his agents bowed to that sentiment.[10]

Indeed, in respect of foreign policy, the striking feature of the political campaign of 1940 was the predominance of the antiwar sentiment among Democrats and Republicans—the overwhelming majority of the American people. At no time during that contest did President Roosevelt or Mr. Willkie or any other responsible party leader venture to propose openly that the United States should become involved in foreign wars or should adopt measures calculated to result in war. On the contrary, as far as the two great parties were concerned, the only choice before the voters was between two candidates, President Roosevelt and Mr. Willkie, both engaged in outbidding each other in the solemnity and the precision of their pledges to maintain the neutrality and peace of the United States.

Nor must the circumstances in which their pledges were made be forgotten. Before the campaign of 1940 got into full swing France had fallen a victim to Hitler's conquering hordes, British armed forces had suffered disaster at Dunkirk, Germany seemed triumphant in western Europe, and Great Britain was beleaguered, daily expecting a German invasion. In other words, the peril of Britain seemed greater in the summer and autumn of 1940 than it did after June, 1941, when Hitler plunged into a war with Russia. Yet it was in those months of Britain's desperation in 1940 that President Roose-

9. *Ibid.*, pp. 276 ff.
10. *Ibid.*, pp. 282 ff.

velt and Democratic candidates for Congress, pleading for the suffrages of the American people, promised that, if victorious, they would maintain the security and peace of the United States.

If the processes of popular election and responsible government had any meaning or validity, the antiwar covenants with the American people, freely entered into by the Democratic party and President Roosevelt during the campaign of 1940, were specific commitments to be fulfilled after their victory at the polls in November. Those covenants were explicit mandates for the President in the conduct of foreign affairs in 1941. They were equally explicit mandates for the Democratic Senators and Representatives, who had indubitable control of Congress, in the enactment of legislation relative to all issues of peace and war.

Those covenants were no mere incidents or practical jokes of the campaign. They were, in fact, major promises of the campaign, extensively and definitely expounded in documents and speeches, and were binding in honor and good conscience after the election. In short, unless deceiving the people in matters of life and death is to be regarded as a proper feature of the democratic politics and popular decisions at the polls are to be treated as chimeras, President Roosevelt's peace pledges of 1940 were imperatives for him in 1941; and only by spurning the peace pledges of their party could Democratic Senators and Representatives dominant in Congress enact into law measures calculated to take the United States into war.

To this principle of representative government, admittedly, exceptions are allowable, for example, where a drastic and unexpected alteration in the posture of affairs calls for a change of policy after an election. If, however, President Roosevelt came to the conclusion in 1941 that his antiwar commitments of 1940 had been rendered obsolete by changed circumstances in 1941 and that the United States should engage in war, he was under constitutional and moral obligations to explain to the country the grounds and nature of a reversal in policy. It may be said, to be sure, and has been said by defenders of his course, that in many of his addresses in 1941 he declared that there was danger of war coming, danger of attacks upon the United States, and a growing need for more and more preparation for defense. Indeed he did assert publicly that Hitler had designs for conquering the world, suppressing all religions, destroying liberty, and subduing the American people. He did say, more than once, that Hitler intended to attack the United States and, after the "shooting war" had begun, that Hitler had attacked America.[11] In some addresses also he claimed that, in the election returns of 1940 [12] and the Lend-Lease Act, he had sanction for pursuing an almost unlimited policy in the conduct of foreign affairs; and such addresses could be and occasionally were interpreted by American advocates of war to be public announcements of his intention to push affairs to the extreme of war in support of the Allies if necessary to assure their victory over the Axis Powers.

But over against all his declarations about war dangers in 1941 and his claims to a sanction for pursuing an aggressive policy stood his other declarations in line with the antiwar pledges of 1940. Repeatedly, between January 1, 1941, and the middle of December, 1941, he represented his policy as a policy contrary to war, as a quest for the peace and security of the United States.[13] Once during those months, that is, on November 29, 1941, it is true, he did say that within a year American boys might be fighting, but this utterance was vague and gave no indication that the fighting would be due to a change in his policy as proclaimed in 1940.[14]

Nor at his press conferences during 1941, as reported in the *New York Times*,[15] did President Roosevelt make any

11. For a convenient collection of President Roosevelt's speeches and addresses for the year 1941, see *Roosevelt's Foreign Policy, 1933–1941* (Wilfred Funk, Inc., New York, 1942), pp. 318–616. Hereafter referred to as Funk.

12. For instance, his message to Congress, January 6, 1941 (Funk, pp. 320–321), where President Roosevelt made extravagant claims to such a sanction, which were in fact plainly contradicted by party platforms and campaign speeches in 1940. For the platforms and speeches, see Beard, *op. cit.*, pp. 265–323.

13. See below, Chaps. II, IV, V, VI, VII, and VIII.

14. See below, Chap. VII, pp. 201 ff.

15. Owing to the fact that the official minutes of President Roosevelt's press conferences for 1941 have not yet been published (1947) and that the reports of

statement to the effect that his antiwar policy of 1940 had been abandoned in favor of a war policy. On the contrary, for instance, at a conference on July 1, 1941, more than three months after the enactment of the Lend-Lease Law, the question of policy was put to him bluntly by a persistent reporter:

"Mr. President, back when the war first started, it was a popular question to ask you if you thought we could keep out of war. . . . You always said that we could." The President answered that he had not said so. He had stated that he hoped we could. Some observers saw in Mr. Roosevelt's remark a change in his position, since some time ago he expressed not only his hope but his belief that this country could avoid war. The President insisted, however, that *the matter of wording had not changed his position. He had been giving the same answer* to the question of whether this country could keep out of war *since Sept. 1, 1939, when hostilities started in Europe.*[16]

In other words, on July 1, 1941, President Roosevelt said that his position on the relation of the United States to the war had not changed; that he had been giving the same answer to the question of whether this country could keep out of war since September 1, 1939, when the war started in Europe. What had he been saying during the months from September 1, 1939, to December 31, 1940? The answer is in the official record of his public addresses, papers, and press conferences, for the years 1939 and 1940, prepared under his own direction. During those months he had said publicly and repeatedly that the United States should and would stay out of war.[17] Once in that period, December 29, 1940, he had indicated that there was risk in "any course we may take," but he had

press conferences taken by his stenographers, now in his papers at the Hyde Park Library, are not yet open to students (see below, p. 194, note), I have been compelled to rely upon the reports of press conferences in the *New York Times.* It is scarcely possible that such a revolutionary step by the President as an announcement of a reversal of his antiwar commitments of 1940 and the adoption of a contrary policy would have escaped the notice of the *New York Times* reporters and publication in the *Times.*

16. *Ibid.,* July 2, 1941. (Italics supplied.)

17. For analysis of this record, see Beard, *op. cit.,* pp. 234 ff.

countered this new note in his line of policy by saying in the same address: "You can, therefore, nail any talk about sending armies to Europe as deliberate untruth." [18] So ended the year 1940 in respect of his numerous antiwar pledges to the American people.

Whatever intimations of a possible shift in his position President Roosevelt may have intended to convey in the prolix language of his numerous speeches in 1941 on dangers of attacks, none of them signified in clear or definite words, or even implied, that he had actually made a change to a war policy. Moreover, if this had been his intent, his other utterances to the contrary in 1941 explicitly offset any connotation that he had abandoned his covenants of 1940 in favor of a direction of affairs toward war. In fact, on the day after the Japanese attack on Pearl Harbor, President Roosevelt declared that the United States was at peace with Japan on December 7, was engaged in conversations with the Japanese Government and Emperor "looking toward the maintenance of peace in the Pacific," and that Japan had sprung "a surprise offensive" on this nation.

To be sure, many of his critics alleged that he intended all along to take America into the war by a circuitous route, but the President and his supporters in Congress repeatedly insisted that his resolve and purpose were defense and security for the United States. Indeed, as Mr. Justice Frankfurter described the management of foreign relations in those troublous times, the President "so skilfully conducted affairs as to avoid even the appearance of an act of aggression on our part." [19]

Until war finally came with the Japanese attack on December 7, 1941, President Roosevelt maintained this appearance. When tension with Japan reached a danger point and a secret warning notice to American outpost military commanders was being framed by the War Department on November 27, 1941, a safeguarding clause was inserted in it at

18. *Ibid.*, pp. 321 f.
19. *Harvard Alumni Bulletin,* April 28, 1945. Memorial address in honor of President Roosevelt.

the direction of the President: "If hostilities cannot be avoided, the U.S. desires that Japan commit the first overt act." [20] Nor during subsequent days of strain, between November 27 and December 7, did the President call upon Congress for a declaration of war or for authority to commit any acts of war against any of the three powers which, in his numerous addresses and speeches on war dangers, he had designated as menaces to the United States.[21]

20. In his testimony before the Roberts Commission on Pearl Harbor, General Gerow, in explaining the phrasing of this sentence, said that "the President had definitely stated that he wanted Japan to commit the first overt act." CJC, Part 39, p. 85.

21. The subject of a message to Congress on war dangers was more than once mentioned in the President's "War Cabinet" during the period immediately preceding the Japanese attack. See below, Chap. XVII, pp. 528 ff. But the President refrained from sending such a message to Congress.

CHAPTER II

Representations of Lend-Lease Aid to the Allies

THE plank of the Democratic platform which promised material aid to liberty-loving peoples wantonly attacked contained no specifications respecting the fulfillment of the pledge. It was restricted by the conditional clause "consistent with law and not inconsistent with the interests of our own national self-defense" and also by the other planks of the platform that committed the President and Congress to the policy of keeping the country out of war: "We will not participate in foreign wars, and we will not send our Army, naval or air forces to fight in foreign lands outside of the Americas, except in case of attack. . . . The direction and aim of our foreign policy has been, and will continue to be, the security and defense of our own land and the maintenance of its peace." Hence, how to aid the Allies without violating the conditional clause and the unequivocal commitments to a foreign policy of security, defense, and peace for the United States was a difficult problem for Democratic leadership after the election of 1940, and the announcement of plans for solving it was awaited with expectancy as the year 1941 opened.

Instead of offering at once to the country and Congress a program for the solution of this problem, President Roosevelt began to discuss the subject, as if casually, with journalists, and he continued this practice after a bill providing for aid to the Allies had appeared in Congress and had been taken under consideration. On January 1, 1941, readers of metropolitan newspapers learned that the President had conversed with reporters on the matter of aiding the Allies, but the published accounts of the conversation contained nothing definite as to the nature of the project which the President had in mind. According to the version of the press conference printed in the *New York Times* on that day, the President "gave the impression to some of those present that he was still trying to think out his lend-lease scheme and had by no means completed its details." Indeed, he said to the reporters that "he wished some one could put into the English language details of the lend-lease plan which he had in mind."

The chief question for the President, at this press conference, seemed to be some method of enabling the Allies as beneficiaries of lend-lease to replace the munitions and goods they were to receive on loan or lease. He spoke, for example, of three antiaircraft guns that might be sent to Great Britain. One of them might never have to fire a shot, and it could be sent back to the United States "in time." Another might be extensively used in warfare; it could be repaired and sent back. But the third might be destroyed in the war by a bomb. "How to carry out the replacement of this one was the problem," he mused, "from a legislative standpoint." The matter of British finances came up. The President "indicated no concern. . . . He appeared perfectly certain that ways would be found. He did not fear, he said, that the British would be solvent on Monday and broke on Tuesday." Such was the nature of the information from the White House on lend-lease laid before the American people on New Year's Day, 1941.

Two days later, January 3, 1941, President Roosevelt told Senators Barkley, Harrison, and Byrnes that he would submit to Congress "a comprehensive plan for all-out aid to Great Britain 'short of war.' " He intimated to the Senators that the plan would involve creating a governmental corporation to handle the lend-lease scheme which "he roughly outlined a few days ago." [1]

On the day that President Roosevelt informed Democratic leaders in the Senate that he would submit a plan for "all-out aid to Britain 'short of war,' " that is, on January 3, 1941, he held a general press conference at which he spoke of sending Harry Hopkins as his personal representative to Great Britain. Reporters assumed that this move had some relation to aiding

1. *New York Times*, January 4, 1941, p. 1.

the Allies. But in response to requests for definite statements in respect of Mr. Hopkins' functions, he dismissed the affair lightly as if it had no particular significance.

The President was asked whether Mr. Hopkins would have any special mission. His reply was "No, no, no!" Any title? "No, no!" When asked whether Mr. Hopkins would be on the Government pay roll, the President replied: "I suppose they will pay his expenses—probably a per diem, not very large— either for you or Hopkins! (*Laughter.*)" He assured the journalists that Mr. Hopkins "will have no powers." One journalist persisted: "Will he have any mission to perform?" This the President parried: "No; you can't get anything exciting. (*Laughter.*) He's just going over to say 'How do you do?' to a lot of my friends. (*Laughter.*)" [2]

In his annual message on January 6, 1941, the President informed Congress and the country of a design to furnish enormous quantities of arms, munitions, implements of war, and other commodities to the Allies enlisted against the Axis Powers. These aids to "the democracies"—these implements of war—were to be supplied on loan, lease, or otherwise by the Government of the United States, not by private citizens and concerns of the United States; and they were to be paid for, at least temporarily, by American taxpayers, not by the foreign belligerents who received them. It is true that in this annual message the President said: "For what we send abroad, we shall be repaid within a reasonable time following the close of hostilities, in similar materials, or, at our option, in other goods of many kinds, which they can produce and which we need." But at the moment, American taxpayers and investors were to furnish the money, with such expectations of recompense as their experience with the debts of World War I might vouchsafe.

Under international law, as long and generally recognized, it was an act of war for a neutral government to supply munitions, arms, and implements of war to one of the belligerents

2: *Public Papers and Addresses of Franklin D. Roosevelt* (Macmillan, 1941), 1940 Volume, pp. 645 ff.

engaged in a war.[3] Private citizens and concerns could supply them, at the risk of capture and seizure by the other belligerent, according to well-known laws of war. A government, however, could not do this without committing an act of war under international law.

For this principle of international law, the United States had vigorously contended since the establishment of independence, never more vigorously than from 1914 to 1917. It had been the main point in a serious dispute between the United States and Great Britain during the American Civil War, when the United States stoutly maintained that Great Britain had committed a hostile act merely by permitting private shipyards in Great Britain to build war vessels for the Southern Confederacy and by allowing them to escape to sea where they preyed on the merchantmen and warships of the United States; Great Britain finally yielded to the contention and paid heavy damages. President Roosevelt admitted the gravity of his proposal in saying: "Such aid is not an act of war, even if a dictator should unilaterally proclaim it so to be"; in other words, a dictator might treat it as an act of war and meet it by an attack on the United States.

On January 7, 1941, the day after his annual message proposing aid to the Allies, President Roosevelt held another press conference. Near the close of the session a journalist remarked: "Reuters is carrying a dispatch out of Stockholm that American troops are occupying Greenland, or have occupied it." The President dismissed the news with the retort: "New one on me! must have been while I was asleep. (*Laughter*.)" [4]

At a press conference, January 10, 1941, President Roosevelt called for swift action on the Lend-Lease Bill, "utmost speed," but he left "the method of obtaining it" to Congress.[5] Although the press conference was long, the actual nature and purposes of the bill were apparently not discussed at all. One

3. For Secretary Henry L. Stimson's attempt to provide some sanction of international law for the Lend-Lease Act, see Hearings before the Senate Committee on Foreign Relations, Lend-Lease Bill, 1941, Part 1, pp. 89 ff.

4. *Public Papers*, 1940 Volume, p. 689.

5. *New York Times*, January 11, 1941.

point of major significance for foreign policy, however, seems to have been considered. The bill provided that its terms, which conferred enormous powers upon the President, were to be effective, "notwithstanding the provisions of any other law." Evidently questions were raised at the conference about this sweeping clause which was to repeal all other legislation that stood in the way of the bill's authorizations; but the President specifically denied that the Johnson Act, barring loans to belligerents, and the Neutrality Act would be nullified by the repealer. Thus he assured Congress and the country that American neutrality as provided by the Neutrality Act would not be abrogated by the enactment of the Lend-Lease Bill. So far, the antiwar covenants of 1940 appeared to be reaffirmed.

In the meantime, Burton K. Wheeler, Democratic Senator from Montana, had begun to inquire about the logic of the lend-lease scheme and to criticize its principal features. On January 4, he called "idiotic" the project outlined by President Roosevelt at his press conference on January 3, and declared: "If it is our war, how can we justify lending them stuff and asking them to pay us back? If it is our war, we ought to have the courage to go over and fight it, but it is not our war." [6]

About a week later, in a radio broadcast, Senator Wheeler criticized the Lend-Lease Bill at length. "Never before," he said, "has the Congress of the United States been asked by any President to violate international law. Never before has this nation resorted to duplicity in the conduct of its foreign affairs. Never before has the United States given to one man the power to strip this Nation of its defenses. Never before has a Congress coldly and flatly been asked to abdicate." Moreover, the Senator declared: "The lend-lease-give program is the New Deal's triple A. foreign policy; it will plow under every fourth American boy." [7] Approval of the lend-lease

6. *Ibid.*, January 5, 1941.

7. January 12, 1941; *Congressional Record*, 77th Congress, First Session, Vol. 87, Part 10 (Appendix), pp. A 178-179. In the administration of the Agricultural Adjustment Act (AAA) the cotton crop had been reduced by "plowing under" a certain proportion of the rows in each field.

project by Congress, the Senator asserted, "means war, open and complete warfare. . . ."

At his press conference two days later, January 14, 1941, President Roosevelt remarked: "I don't think I have any news. Anybody got any news?" A reporter evidently thought that the lend-lease discussion was news, for he asked the President whether he would care to comment on the proposition to put a time limit on the bill. The President replied: "Oh, no; because if I start commenting on one [proposed limit], you boys will be asking me about two or three every Tuesday and two or three every Friday; and you merely start a chain. Don't let's start one of those chains now."

But the issue of peace or war was already before the country and the probable consequences which would flow from the enactment of the Lend-Lease Bill into law were being discussed with great anxiety. As if expressing this popular interest, a reporter inquired: "Mr. President, do you have any comment on the label that has been put on the lend-lease bill as a 'blank check' bill?" The President replied in tones of anger: "Yes, I suppose so; the easiest answer is: 'Write me another that you would not put that label on but which would accomplish the same objective.' That is a perfectly good answer to all these people. That is not an answer at all, however, to those who talk about plowing under every fourth American child, which I regard as the most untruthful, as the most dastardly, unpatriotic thing that has ever been said. Quote me on that. That really is the rottenest thing that has been said in public life in my generation."

At this point a reporter wanted to know where that statement about "plowing under" had been originally made. The President answered: "I read it in the paper; it has been quoted by several people. . . ." He was then asked: "You say you don't remember who said it?" The President brought the interview to a conclusion with the words: "No; it was said by three or four people. In other words, it's a good time to kill a proposed slogan, at birth." [8]

8. *Public Papers*, 1940 Volume, pp. 710 ff. The editor of the volume noted, in brackets, that the President was referring to a remark made by Senator Burton

At a press conference on January 17, President Roosevelt characterized as verging on the "absurd" numerous suggestions for limiting the powers to be given to him by the bill. Some of these suggestions he discussed with the derisive raillery he had often displayed on such occasions. It had been said that under the terms of the bill, the President could give away the American Navy or buy the British Navy. As to giving away the American Navy, he said: "The bill did not prevent the President of the United States from standing on his head, but the President did not expect to stand on his head." As to buying the British Navy, he remarked that supposedly Congress might authorize him to buy the German Navy, too. "And didn't the reporters think that this was awful cow-jumping-over-the-moon stuff?" Asked whether he had discussed the bill with a representative of the Vatican, "Mr. Roosevelt leaned back in his chair and roared with laughter. Maybe he was trying to buy the Vatican Navy, he suggested."

Taking seriously the issue of limitations which the President thus dismissed with laughter, many members of Congress on both sides of the party line insisted that several of the powers conferred on the President by his plans were too sweeping; and in fact certain of the bill's provisions were materially amended in this respect before it was passed. Evidently aware of this primary and practical objection to the original Lend-Lease Bill, a reporter at the press conference on January 17 inquired whether, since the President did not intend to use some of the powers in question, he had any objections to putting limitations on them. In response, "Mr. Roosevelt reiterated that the bill did not restrict him from standing on his head, implying that such limitations were unnecessary." When the reporter persisted, the President said that things were changing from day to day and that the proposed legislative grant of power represented "just a precautionary measure for continuing American defense." [9]

Among the other grave issues raised in Congress and outside

K. Wheeler. *Ibid.*, p. 712. On January 13, 1941, Admiral Stark, Chief of Naval Operations, wrote secretly to Admiral Kimmel at Hawaii, "we are heading straight for this war." See below, Chap. XIV.

9. *New York Times*, January 18, 1941, pp. 1, 4.

in relation to the Lend-Lease Bill was the question of using American naval vessels to convoy supplies to Great Britain. On this point it had been said in various quarters that it would seem strange for the United States to manufacture huge quantities of supplies for Great Britain, turn them over to British ships in American harbors, and then quietly allow German submarines to send them all to the bottom of the sea, instead of assuring delivery by convoying supply ships into British waters or to Iceland. Moreover, it had been contended that since convoying was an act of war under international law, a resort to that practice by the United States would inevitably lead to "shooting," if not immediately to war.[10] At a press conference on January 21, a reporter asked President Roosevelt about his intentions with regard to convoys. The President replied that he "had never considered using American naval vessels to convoy ships bearing supplies to Great Britain." He also said that "the suggestion was new to him and asked what about the Falkland Islands [in the South Atlantic], the Celebes [in the Dutch East Indies], or the Andamans [in the Bay of Bengal]."

Another question brought up in public discussions of the bill pertained to the broad provision of the measure allowing the President to transfer equipment and materials of war to Great Britain. In this connection fear was expressed that he might transfer to foreign powers ships of war that were needed for the defense of the United States in the Atlantic and in the Pacific, as he had done in 1940. This point was also raised at the press conference on January 21, 1941; and the President "described as cow-jumping-over-the-moon, Old Mother Hubbard stuff assertions that he would transfer American naval ships to Britain or any other foreign power. He also reiterated that he had no intention of standing on his head." [11]

Commenting, February 4, on a statement recently made by Senator Wheeler to the effect that five sixths of the American

10. See below, p. 30, and Chap. III.
11. *New York Times*, January 22, 1941, p. 1.

airplane output was going to Great Britain, the President remarked that, of course, one could work out all kinds of things with figures and these figures must be very satisfactory to the Reich dictator. Asked what he would do first if the Lend-Lease Bill passed, he responded that "he would go out into the middle of Pennsylvania Avenue and stand on his head, since that would not be prohibited." Thereupon a reporter inquired: "How would that aid beleaguered democracies?" The President's reply was that "it would result in some publicity." [12]

While the discussion of the Lend-Lease Bill was "dragging along" in Congress, Jesse Jones, head of the Department of Commerce and the Reconstruction Finance Corporation, went before the House Committee on Banking and Currency and asked for the speedy passage of a bill allowing the Federal Housing Administration to insure mortgages up to the amount of $100,000,000. In the course of his testimony, Mr. Jones exclaimed: "We're in the war; at least we're nearly in the war; we're preparing for it; when you do that, you've got to throw money away." Bethinking himself, Mr. Jones had the official stenographer strike the words from the committee's formal record. [13] But his words were given publicity by the press.

After Mr. Jones' blunt declaration to the House Committee on Banking and Currency became known, "President Roosevelt described the statement as a lot of words that do not mean anything. He said that he did not mean for his remarks to apply particularly to Mr. Jones, but to the press or anyone else who expressed himself in a similar manner." [14] The form of the President's characterization was somewhat cryptic, but it seemed to deplore the use of such words as "we are in the war," or "nearly in it," or "preparing for it." Taken in connection with the numerous antiwar statements he had previously made, it implied that he disapproved of introducing into public dis-

12. *Ibid.*, February 5, 1941.
13. *Ibid.*, February 19, 1941.
14. *Ibid.*

cussions the idea that the United States was going into the war or preparing for it while the Lend-Lease Bill was under consideration.

Before the Lend-Lease Bill passed, a letter directed to President Roosevelt in the name of the League of Women Voters informed him that the League favored the measure but made some inquiries as to his intentions. Replying to this letter on March 5, 1941, the President said: "In acknowledging my appreciation of the League's position, I am glad to reiterate the assurance that the policy under which the measure would be operated would not be a war policy but the contrary." [15]

When President Roosevelt's public comments on the Lend-Lease Bill during its course through Congress are reduced to substantial elements respecting the foreign policy implicit in the measure, they amount to the following statements:

The law did not nullify the Neutrality Act designed to assure the neutrality of the United States in foreign wars.

The idea of using the United States Navy to convoy ships to Great Britain or Iceland had not been considered and was to be dismissed as irrelevant, as if beyond consideration or merely amusing.

Senator Wheeler's assertion that the lend-lease program would "plow under every fourth American boy" and meant open and complete war was "the most dastardly and unpatriotic thing ever said," "the rottenest thing that has been said in public life in my generation."

Jesse Jones' declaration that "We're in the war; at least we are nearly in it; we're preparing for it" was a lot of words that did not mean anything.

The Lend-Lease Act was to be administered not as a war measure but the contrary; that is, as a peace measure.

Hence it was to be concluded or inferred that President Roosevelt's public statements on this occasion were in line with his antiwar covenants of 1940.

15. *Commercial and Financial Chronicle*, March 8, 1941, Vol. 152, p. 1517; Beard, *op. cit.*, p. 197.

WHAT powers, in fact, did the Lend-Lease Bill, as originally introduced "into" Congress, confer upon the President? Without any limitation as to time or cost or quantity or number, it authorized the President to do the following, among other things: (1) to designate as a beneficiary of its provisions any country in the world, "whose defense the President deems vital to the defense of the United States"; (2) to manufacture or otherwise procure any weapon, munition, aircraft, boat, or other article of defense; (3) to sell, transfer, exchange, lease, lend, or otherwise dispose of any such implements, articles of defense, and machinery or tools for the manufacture of the same to any government so designated by the President; (4) to repair, outfit, and recondition defense articles for such designated government; (5) to communicate to such government any defense information pertaining to such defense articles; and (6) to determine the terms and conditions of receipt and repayment by such foreign governments, or any other direct or indirect benefit which the President deems satisfactory. And all these things the President could do at his pleasure and on his own motion, "*notwithstanding the provisions of any other law.*" (Italics supplied.)

So far as the specific language of the bill was concerned, the President could do all these things as he pleased until Congress saw fit to repeal the law, perhaps over his veto by a two-thirds vote. Nor was he required to report to Congress in any way anything he did under the law. Within the broad sweep of the Lend-Lease Bill, if passed, his own decisions were to be law. And as to final settlement for such aids to other governments designated by the President, he could make any arrangements whatever which he *deemed* satisfactory, that is, satisfactory to himself.

During the hearings and debates on the Lend-Lease Bill in January, February, and March, 1941, many controversial points were raised and discussed. Among them four questions had direct bearings on the intentions behind the bill and the foreign policy which it implied—peace or war:

By whom was the Lend-Lease Bill conceived and drafted?

Are the ships carrying munitions to the beneficiaries to be convoyed by American naval vessels or left to the mercies of the swarming Axis submarines?

If these ships are to be convoyed by American naval vessels, is not this convoying itself an act of war on the part of the United States?

Is the bill really calculated to fulfill the Administration's pledges on maintaining neutrality and keeping the country out of war or is it to be regarded as authorizing the President to set out boldly on the road to war?

AUTHORSHIP OF THE BILL

WHO drafted the bill? On this question, immediately asked in Congress and outside, neither the President nor anybody authorized to speak for him furnished to the American public any definite information.

In his note to his message of January 6, 1941, as reprinted in his *Public Papers*, 1940 Volume, the President gave no clue as to the origins of the measure; he merely said: "Pursuant to these recommendations [in his message], the 'Lend-Lease Bill' was introduced into Congress on January 10, 1941." Secretary Hull was equally cryptic. In the State Department's volume *Peace and War: United States Foreign Policy*, *1931–1941* (July, 1943, ed., p. 100) it is simply stated: "Early in January 1941 there was introduced in Congress a bill to enable the Government to furnish aid to nations whose defense was deemed by the President to be vital to the defense of the United States."

At hearings before the House Committee on Foreign Affairs and before the Senate Committee on Foreign Relations, and during the debates in the House and Senate, a persistent search was made for the author or authors of the Lend-Lease Bill who could assume responsibility for its terms and explain the purpose of the project in general and the purposes of its several provisions in detail. But from the beginning to the end, from the day the bill was presented to Congress until it was finally passed, this search was fruitless. The Administration leaders who introduced the bill in the House and in the Senate assumed responsibility for introducing it, and undertook to expound it as they understood it. Yet even they were unable, or unwilling, to name the author or authors of the bill, so that the designer or designers of the measure could be questioned as to the meaning which he or they alone knew and intended, as the bill was drafted, section by section and line by line.

From the documents, official papers, and congressional speeches pertaining to the origin and passage of the bill a volume could be written on the search for the authorship, general purposes, and specific intentions of the measure. But as far as the hearings of the House Committee and the debates of the House were concerned, the situation was described on the basis of documentation by Representative Karl E. Mundt, of South Dakota, on February 4, 1941. While it is true that Mr. Mundt was speaking as a Republican and introduced critical observations of his own, he had records to support him when he said that Secretary Hull, Secretary Morgenthau, Secretary Stimson, and Secretary Knox disclaimed personal responsibility for the authorship of the Lend-Lease Bill.

Although some of Mr. Mundt's animadversions may be discounted on grounds of opposition partisanship, the views he expressed represented opinions widely held in the House and, therefore, with justification deserve quotation at length:

Mr. Chairman, we are confronted with a very strange and a very unique situation—a situation in which the Secretary of State, Mr. Hull, charged with the responsibility of maintaining the peaceful neutral relations of America, refuses to admit that he had anything to do with drafting the legislation now before us. We are confronted with a situation in which the Secretary of the Treasury, who had been charged with initiating the bill, who is charged also with the responsibility of rescuing this country from bankruptcy, if he can, disclaims any authorship of the bill. Stranger than that, we are confronted with a situation in which the Secretary of War, Mr. Stimson, a man certainly who by his belligerent advocacy of quick and vigorous steps, shorter and shorter of war, marks him as a man who would not disclaim any responsibility in this respect, the Secretary of War charged with defending these United States, a Secretary of War who must operate under a bill labeled "for purposes of national defense" repeatedly states he had nothing to do with drafting the bill. He said he did not see it until its draft was completed—and so it goes, Secretary after Secretary testified in that fashion.

It may be that those portions of the bill which say "for other purposes" have some well-known consultants who helped draft the bill; but insofar as the other portions of the bill at least are concerned, and insofar as its national-defense purposes are concerned, we find this strange piece of legislation disclaimed by the Secretaries of the President's Cabinet. We find this piece of legislation—surreptitiously conceived, individually disclaimed, of unknown parentage—placed before us, like a baby in a basket on our doorstep, and we are asked to adopt it.

I think it is mighty important, Mr. Chairman, that we pause to wonder a bit why this legislation, containing so many powers that the President says he did not ask for and that the President did not want, was drawn in such a unique manner, because it is kind of stimulating to contemplate what person or what power put into this bill those undesired and undesirable powers, since they are definitely found in the legislation. We are asked to violate all pretenses of neutrality; we are asked to disregard the remaining vestiges of international law; and the Secretary of State, charged with the responsibility of maintaining our peaceful relations, disclaims authorship.

I have said that this bill is a very important piece of legislation and that it was conceived in a most unique manner. I think that the vast delegation of powers taking place in this bill, enormous as they are, probably are equaled and excelled only by the anonymity of their enormity. I think it is amazing that we are confronted with a situation of this type in a bill of this importance, when Secretaries testifying before this committee, members of the President's Cabinet, argue that the bill may be necessary but answer as few questions as they possibly can concerning whether or not the bill is wise.

If this bill is designed primarily, as I am afraid it is, for "the other purposes" aspect of this act, this evasiveness is understandable; but if the bill is devised primarily for the national-defense purposes of this act, it seems to be uncommon strange that those charged with administering it should disclaim any responsibility for initiating this particular legislation.[16]

The search conducted by United States Senators for the author or authors who could explain the purpose and meaning of the Lend-Lease Bill was no more successful. When Secretary Hull came before the Senate Committee on Foreign Relations he refused to discuss certain vital matters except in camera, under the seal of secrecy. In his testimony before the House Committee in charge of the bill, he had referred to it as "a Treasury bill," and when he appeared before the Senate Committee he declined or "preferred" not to discuss the matter of authorship.[17]

When asked by Senator LaFollette whether there was someone who could give the Senate Committee a broad outline of the powers intended to be conferred by the bill, Secretary Morgenthau answered "No." Under further questioning, Mr. Morgenthau disclaimed ability to deal with any save the financial aspects of the measure, and gave only a general account of its history. At his first appearance before the Senate Committee on January 28, 1941, Mr. Morgenthau made the following statements:

Several weeks ago the President asked me to come over to his office after he had had a talk with the Speaker of the House, and he asked that the Treasury get into touch with the Speaker, who, in turn, would put us into touch with Mr. Beaman [Congressional draftsman]. . . .

We worked very hard on this. But there have been a number of other people also. To get the impression that the Treasury wrote

16. *Congressional Record*, 77th Congress, First Session, Vol. 87, Part 1, p. 611.
17. Hearings before the Senate Committee on Foreign Relations, Lend-Lease Bill, January 27 to February 3, 1941, Part 1, p. 34.

the bill I think is incorrect, because I attended at least a half-dozen conferences with the Democratic leaders both in [the] Senate and the House, and last night with the minority leaders.

I might point out that at no time has any meeting taken place in my office. They have always been either at the White House or at the State Department. . . .

SENATOR JOHNSON of California. So you cannot tell us the genesis of the bill or who was the principal scrivener who wrote it.

MR. MORGENTHAU. That is correct. I think it was a product of many brains.[18]

Further inquiries failed to disclose any person prepared, by knowledge of the bill's origin and purposes, to explain its provisions. At length, Senator Alben Barkley declared that he was the sponsor of the bill in the Senate and prepared to explain it as best he could and as he understood it. Thereupon Senator Bennett Clark made the following proposition:

That that portion of the Secretary of State's remarks before the House committee on foreign affairs, in which he said this was the Treasury, and also the remarks of the Secretary of the Treasury this morning, in which he said it was not the Treasury, and also the remarks of the distinguished Senator, and I hope the next Justice of the United States Supreme Court, Mr. Byrnes, in which he said it was Congress, be printed together as an exhibit to the Senator's testimony.[19]

To this proposition, Senator Barkley replied:

I certainly have no objection to that. I wish merely to state that regardless of who wrote the bill, whether it was written by a taxi-cab driver or the Attorney General of the United States, the language speaks for itself. It is plain enough for anybody to understand, it seems to me, regardless of who had anything to do with the writing of this bill.[20]

As the House and Senate Committee hearings and the debates on the bill in Congress revealed again and again, Senator

18. *Ibid.*, pp. 34 ff.
19. *Ibid.*, p. 58.
20. *Ibid.* The Senate Hearings alone embrace 914 pages. As to what the act really proved to mean in the hands of the Administration, see below, Chap. XVII. Secretary Stimson's explanation of 1946.

Barkley and his colleagues who sponsored the bill did not in fact find the language of the measure plain enough for everybody to understand. On the contrary they were often unable to answer accurately questions as to the meaning of the bill in general or specific clauses of the bill; and any person willing to spend several months comparing the explanations offered by the sponsors of the bill with the actions of the President under the bill can discover numerous discrepancies between what was said about the meaning of the bill and what was done under its authority.[21]

However, amid the disputes about the authorship and purpose and meaning of the bill, Secretary Morgenthau made certain points "plain enough for anybody to understand," even if, as Senator Barkley remarked, the bill "was written by a taxicab driver." The first point was that "several weeks" before January 28, 1941, apparently in December, or perhaps November, 1940, President Roosevelt was talking with the Speaker of the House of Representatives about the proposed bill and he called Secretary Morgenthau to the White House for a conference on the measure. Secretary Morgenthau's second point was that meetings of persons concerned in preparing the bill were "always" held "either at the White House or at the State Department." Yet the President refrained from assuming authorship of the bill and from explaining it by means of a special message to Congress when the bill was introduced by Mr. McCormack, the Democratic majority leader in the House and by Mr. Barkley, the Democratic majority leader in the Senate.

So much for Secretary Morgenthau's information to Congress and the public in January, 1941, when the Lend-Lease Bill was pending. But about six years later, Mr. Morgenthau told what purported to be the truth about the genesis of the bill—in *Collier's* for October 18, 1947. There he printed an extract from a letter ("now published for the first time")

21. For a striking example, see Hearings before the House Committee on Foreign Affairs, 78th Congress, First Session on H.R. 1501, January 29 to February 23, 1943, on the "Extension of Lend-Lease Act," particularly the statement of the Honorable Dean G. Acheson, Assistant Secretary of State, pp. 81 ff.

from Mr. Churchill to President Roosevelt, dated December 7, 1940, proposing a form of American aid to Great Britain free from what President Roosevelt called "the dollar sign." There Mr. Morgenthau stated that President Roosevelt approved and developed Mr. Churchill's idea and that "the Lend-Lease bill was born" in the White House, December 30, 1940, at a conference attended by the President, Mr. Morgenthau, and Arthur Purvis, head of the British-French purchasing commission. The hour of the "birth" was about noon that day. According to Mr. Morgenthau's account in 1947, the Lend-Lease Bill was drafted on January 2, 1941, by "Ed Foley, my crack general counsel, and his bright assistant, Oscar Cox," and some changes were later made by them on suggestions from other departments. The bill so drawn was approved by Secretaries Hull, Stimson, and Knox. Mr. Morgenthau also related in *Collier's* in 1947, that there was opposition to the bill on the part of subordinates in the State Department and printed a colloquy between Secretary Knox and himself in 1941 as follows: Secretary Knox, "Let's organize a hanging bee over there someday and hang the ones that you and I pick out." Mr. Morgenthau, "We won't leave many people over there."

THE QUESTION OF CONVOYING MERCHANT SHIPS [22]

AMONG the arguments brought up against the Lend-Lease Bill was the contention that it would be folly for the United States to send billions of dollars worth of munitions on the way to Great Britain only to be sunk by German submarines, that the American Navy would be used to convoy or protect such shipments, and that this convoying of merchant ships loaded with munitions across the Atlantic would be an act of hostility or aggression—an act of war on the part of the United States. This matter was brought to the attention of Secretary Knox during the hearings on the Lend-Lease Bill. Senator Nye said to him: "You stand very much opposed to the idea of convoy-

22. See below, Chap. III.

ing merchantmen across the Atlantic?" Secretary Knox replied: "Yes." To the question: "You look upon it as an act of war?" Secretary Knox responded: "Yes." But in answer to other questions, the Secretary said that, if the President ordered a convoy, he would obey the orders as a subordinate of the Commander in Chief.[23] In other words, Secretary Knox was prepared to commit an act of war against Germany in obedience to the President's orders.

Although Secretary Knox, head of the Navy Department, whose business it would be to convoy merchant ships bearing munitions across the seas if this policy was decided upon, expressed opposition to convoying and declared it to be an act of war in itself, Mr. Stimson, Secretary of War, took a different view. At the Senate Committee hearings, he was quoted as declaring himself in favor of sending munitions to Great Britain "if necessary in our own ships and under convoy."[24] He was not sure whether convoying would actually put the United States into the war. On the basis of the Kellogg Pact of 1928 and some resolutions adopted at a meeting of the International Law Association at Budapest in 1934, Secretary Stimson claimed that everything authorized by the Lend-Lease Bill was justifiable "by international law itself, as that international law has been interpreted in the light of a great treaty which this country initiated." The governments which had signed the Kellogg Pact in 1928 had not recognized or accepted the interpretation of international law put forward by professors at Budapest in 1934, but, in Mr. Stimson's opinion, neither convoying nor anything else authorized by the Lend-Lease Bill would constitute an act of war or violate international law.

What were Administration supporters in Congress to do in this dilemma? Opponents of the bill demanded an amendment prohibiting the use of convoys on the ground that, as Secretary

23. Hearings before the Senate Committee on Foreign Relations, Lend-Lease Bill, 1941, Part 1, p. 211.

24. *Ibid.*, pp. 159, 115, 89 ff. In fact Mr. Stimson had justified convoying munition ships in June, 1940, prior to his appointment as Secretary of War, and held exalted notions of Executive power. See below, pp. 566 ff.

Knox had said, it would constitute "an act of war." If, the critics asked in substance of the majority, you want to avoid war, as you claim, and convoying is an act of war, why not add a safeguard in the interest of peace by incorporating in the bill a provision to that effect? Over this pointed question a sharp contest was waged, partly in public and partly behind the scenes. Counterquestions were raised by sponsors of the measure: Has Congress the power under the Constitution to forbid the President as Commander in Chief to employ the Navy for convoying purposes, even though convoying is generally regarded as an act of war? Shall we strike down with one hand all we grant with the other? Why pass the bill if we nullify it by a destructive prohibition?

Entangled in logical and moral difficulties, advocates of the bill in Congress evolved a formula that appeared to be in line with the idea of keeping the United States out of war by aiding the enemies of the Axis Powers. The formula took the shape of two paragraphs which were added to the original bill as amendments. These paragraphs read: "(d) Nothing in this Act shall be construed to authorize or to permit the authorization of convoying by naval vessels of the United States. (e) Nothing in this Act shall be construed to authorize or to permit the authorization of the entry of any American vessel into a combat area in violation of section 3 of the Neutrality Act of 1939."

The language of these amendments was apparently explicit. Nothing in the act was to be construed by the President as authorizing or permitting the use of convoys or as authorizing him to send American vessels into combat areas. Nor was there in existing legislation any provision authorizing him to take such actions in the circumstances contemplated by the Lend-Lease Act. Furthermore, such actions were, to all appearances, explicitly forbidden by another amendment attached to the original bill, namely, Section 10. It read: "Nothing in this Act *shall be construed to change existing law relating to the use of the land and naval forces of the United States, except* in so far as such use relates to the manufacture, procurement, and repair of defense articles, the communication of information, and *other noncombatant purposes* enumerated in this Act." (Italics supplied.)

In other words, Congress declared that the Lend-Lease Law conferred on the President no power whatever to use the armed forces for combatant purposes, that in executing the law he could not order the armed forces to commit acts of war. This provision was designed to meet the charge made by many Democrats and Republicans that otherwise President Roosevelt could treat the measure as authorizing him to wage an undeclared war under color of "aiding the Allies." Indeed, it is doubtful whether Congress would have passed the bill if provisions against convoying and committing "combatant," or fighting, acts had not been written clearly in the bill.

SEARCHES FOR THE MEANING OF THE BILL AT HEARINGS OF CONGRESSIONAL COMMITTEES

IN HIS public statements before the House and Senate Committees in charge of the Lend-Lease Bill, Secretary Hull took a definite line. He represented the bill as based on the principle that the United States should give immediate aid to Great Britain "and other victims of attack" in the interest of self-defense for the United States. The keynote of his persistent argument was "defense"—the bill provided the machinery for the effective use of our resources "in our own self-defense." [25] This formula he recited again and again. If he regarded the measure as constituting an act of war or as leading inexorably to war on the part of the United States, he gave no indication of that opinion in his published testimony.

Speaking as head of the Department of the Navy, Secretary Knox sought to convince the members of the House Committee that the Lend-Lease Bill was a necessary measure of

25. Hearings before the House Committee on Foreign Affairs, 77th Congress, First Session on H.R. 1776, 1941, pp. 6–7.

national defense, intended to gain time in which to make military and naval preparations to maintain the "essential interests" of the American people "throughout the world":

To keep our land secure we must prevent the establishment of strong aggressive military power in any part of the New World. We can keep non-American military power out of our hemisphere only through being able to control the seas that surround our shores. Once we lose the power to control even a part of those seas, inevitably the wars of Europe and Asia will be transferred to the Americas.

We need time to build ships and to train their crews. We need time to build our outlying bases so that we can operate our fleets as a screen for our continent. We need time to train our armies, to accumulate war stores, to gear our industry for defense.

Only Great Britain and its fleet can give us that time. And they need our help to survive.

If we fully organize the mental and material resources of the American people, we can give Britain that help and simultaneously can build a strong military defense for ourselves. The cost to us in money, effort and sacrifice will be great—but that cost will be far greater even in the immediate future, should we now stand aside and let Britain fall.

We are a strong Nation, though our military strength is still largely potential. I believe that the American people have what it takes in character, courage and wisdom to guard this country and to guard this hemisphere. But to keep from engaging in a desperate struggle in American territory, they need time to make ready their arms. They can get time to make ready, and can maintain their essential interests throughout the world, only so long as Britain and its fleet survive. With our unstinted help, I firmly believe that Britain cannot be defeated.

We will act in our best national interests, therefore, if, while increasing our naval power as fast as we can, we provide the British Commonwealth with the means that will bring her through this tragic crisis.[26]

In his testimony before the House Committee, Secretary Stimson followed in general the line taken by Secretary Hull.

26. *Ibid.*, p 158

He stood firmly by the bill exactly as it was written, laid stress on defense, opposed limiting amendments, and categorically denied that, in case the aid given to Great Britain and China failed to sustain them in Europe and Asia, the consequence of the Lend-Lease Bill, if enacted into law, would necessarily be the sending of American manpower to fight in Europe and Asia. The following passages from the Hearings before the House Committee give his views on the bill as a "peace" measure and on efforts to calculate the probable consequences of the actions to be taken under it, if duly passed:

MR. FISH: . . . have you any objection if the Congress inserts a provision in the bill prohibiting the President from giving away any part of the Navy?

MR. STIMSON: For myself I submit that question is one which should be asked of the Secretary of the Navy. But on the knowledge that I have of the situation I should object to it, because I can well conceive that a portion, or some of the Navy, might be transferred under conditions that might be very advantageous to meet a situation that might develop. . . .[27]

MR. FISH: Is not our outer defense our Navy? Has not the Congress appropriated for a two-ocean Navy?

SECRETARY STIMSON: No sir; only in one sense. Our first line of defense is our diplomacy, if you will permit me to say it, by which we try to keep as many enemies away from us, and to get as many friends on our side as we can throughout the whole world. Then the Navy is another line, and the line of bases is another line. The Army is the last line to be used, the continental Army, in a situation which will never occur, I hope; namely, when an enemy has got its foot on our soil and is ready to do to us what the Germans did to the countries of Europe last spring.

MR. FISH: Mr. Secretary, if our Navy is not our first line of defense, then some foreign nation must be our first line of defense, and if Great Britain is our first line of defense, then it is our war, and it would be craven not to be in it. But I believe the American Navy is our first line of defense, and always will be, and we do not have to depend on anyone else.

THE CHAIRMAN: Do you wish to reply to that, Mr. Secretary?

27. *Ibid.*, p. 93.

Secretary Stimson: I do not see any question there. I heard a statement of Mr. Fish's opinion.

Mr. Fish: I will ask you point blank if Great Britain is our first line of defense, are you in favor of going to war?

Secretary Stimson: I am in favor of assisting Great Britain to maintain her fleet. I am in favor of that. At present, she, being at war, is providing for the defense of the North Atlantic, and we are vitally interested in that defense.

Mr. Fish: Is it not rather cowardly of us, if England is fighting our battle, not to go into the war?

Secretary Stimson: I am not going to pursue this line of argument. We are not concerned with it in this bill. . . .[28]

Mr. Tinkham: May I ask you if that is your fixed opinion, that there should not be put into this bill a clause which would forbid our warships going into belligerent waters?

Secretary Stimson: Yes; that is my opinion, most certainly. No one can foresee what situations might arise that will make it most essential, in the light of our defense—not offense—for our country to send its warships into what you call belligerent waters.

Mr. Tinkham: May I ask you under what conditions, as you conceive them, we should send warships into belligerent waters without that being an offensive action?

Secretary Stimson: Well, I do not think I care to indulge in speculation. That is too broad a field. But I say the thing might happen. I do not believe that this country should in any circumstances tie its hands behind its back.

Mr. Tinkham: Even to keep out war?

Secretary Stimson: I think it would be perhaps one of the surest ways of getting into war, or, at any rate, of getting into a position where we could be safely attacked, and attacked under disadvantages. . . .

Mr. Tinkham: You are in favor of the United States remaining at peace, if possible, are you not?

Secretary Stimson: I am, certainly. But I am in favor also of its remaining in a state of complete readiness in case, contrary to its desire, it should be forced to defend itself by military action.

Mr. Tinkham: . . . Now still in relation to warships, do you think that our warships should convoy American ships to England?

28. *Ibid.*, pp. 101–102.

SECRETARY STIMSON: Let me say first that nothing in this bill touches upon that question at all. . . .[29]

MR. TINKHAM: . . . May I put the question in this way, Mr. Secretary: If, under this bill, our resources are put behind England and behind China, which means in Europe and in Asia, and they are not sufficient, and China seems to be falling and England seems to be falling, is it not inherent, once having committed ourselves with all our resources, to send our manpower in order to maintain our dignity and our position?

SECRETARY STIMSON: I do not see that it would be from anything now before me at all a consequence that would necessarily follow from that. I think, on the contrary, it is the best bet we can make to save us from sending our manpower. That is my view. I may be mistaken. But I am very strongly and clearly of that view.

MR. TINKHAM: I take exactly the opposite position, Mr. Secretary. Now, if there is nothing in the bill to prohibit cargo convoys, would you object to having an amendment in the bill which forbade convoys by the American Navy to Great Britain or to other countries?

SECRETARY STIMSON: I think the bill should stand as it does.

MR. TINKHAM: In other words, you object to any such limitation?

SECRETARY STIMSON: I prefer the bill as it is, on the same principle that I said before. I think this Government of ours, the United States, should not tie its hands, or even its finger, in the face of the emergency that exists now; and all of these little things are in the nature of shackles which you would have put on this Nation in a great emergency. No one can foresee whether or not that might not be very dangerous to it in an unforeseen emergency.[30]

Among the other expositions of the Lend-Lease Bill before the House Committee that of William C. Bullitt was regarded as having especial significance. Mr. Bullitt had been the American Ambassador at Paris during the fall of France and had made speeches which, as reported in the press, sounded like a call for the United States to take up arms in the European war. But before the committee he represented the bill as a measure of defense, intended to "buy time" for the United

29. *Ibid.*, pp. 113 f.
30. *Ibid.*, p. 115.

States, by aiding Great Britain, and to prepare against a probable invasion of this hemisphere that would menace American liberties. Mr. Bullitt said:

We are not prepared today to meet an attack by the totalitarian states that are leagued against us. We must buy time in which to prepare.

We can buy that time only by making certain that the British fleet will continue to hold the totalitarian forces in Europe while our fleet watches in the Pacific. . . .

Should the British Navy be eliminated and should the Panama Canal be blocked before we are prepared, invasion of the Western Hemisphere would be almost certain. It is entirely certain that the shipbuilding facilities in the hands of the totalitarian dictators would be at least four times as great as our shipbuilding facilities. . . . We should have to organize our American life on a military basis from top to bottom and maintain it on a military basis throughout years of misery and years of totalitarian propaganda directed against our democratic form of government. How long, under those conditions, we could maintain the liberties that have been the birthright of every American since the birth of our Nation, no man knows.

These would be to us the consequences of British defeat. We must, therefore, for our own self-preservation, try to see to it that Great Britain is not defeated.

We are determined not to be drawn into this war. We leave out of discussion, therefore, the policy of going to war, although we know that the most certain way to insure against risk of British defeat would be for us to go to war. We set two limits on our support of Great Britain: First, we will not declare war; second, we will not ourselves initiate military or naval hostilities.

We can diminish the danger to ourselves only by supplying promptly to the British and the other states that are now holding the totalitarian war machines away from our shores every material, munition and arm that they need. . . .[31]

Mr. Johnson: The charge has been made by some of the opponents of this bill that it is a war bill, that it is a bill designed to get us into war. I would like to have your opinion on that.

Mr. Bullitt: In my opinion, the bill will provide means for

31. *Ibid.*, pp. 582 f.

effectively aiding Great Britain. There is only one result of this war that can make certain that we will come into the war, which is that Great Britain shall be beaten, because if Great Britain is beaten, we will be attacked in this hemisphere—not probably first directly by an attack on us, but by a movement through South America. . . .

MR. JOHNSON: Do you believe, then, that this bill, instead of being designed to get us into war, would be calculated, if it passes, to aid England and prevent its fall, and therefore keep the war out of America?

MR. BULLITT: I believe exactly that. . . .[32]

Opponents of the Lend-Lease Bill before the House Committee, whatever their differences of opinion as to details of the project, were agreed on one thing: This is a war bill which grants to the President almost dictatorial power over the human and material resources of the United States and will, if enacted, lead inevitably to participation in the war on a world scale. Colonel Charles Lindbergh declared it to be "a major step to getting us into war." [33] Norman Thomas maintained that it would eventuate in a "total war on two oceans and five continents; a war likely to result in stalemate; perhaps in such a breakup of western civilization, that Stalin, with his vast armies and loyal Communist followers, will be the victor. . . ." Mr. Thomas charged President Roosevelt with wanting to take a gamble with the lives and destinies of the American people, or "to put us in war gradually, knowing that we would refuse to go into it all at once." [34] Dr. Brooks Emeny characterized the bill as "definitely a step in the direction of war," and stated that he would oppose the bill "until it has become apparent that the American people are fully aware that the probabilities are that the bill as proposed is not a measure short of war." [35]

Insofar as the central issue at stake in the Lend-Lease Bill was concerned—peace or war for the United States—the testi-

32. *Ibid.*, pp. 594 f.
33. *Ibid.*, p. 430.
34. *Ibid.*, p. 320.
35. *Ibid.*, p. 466.

mony before the Senate Committee on Foreign Relations practically duplicated that offered to the House Committee, except
that the emphasis on the pacific intentions of the bill was, if
anything, more positive in tone. What Secretary Hull said to
the Senate Committee at a secret hearing remains unknown,
but at the public hearing he offered the statement he had
presented to the House Committee.[36]

When asked at the House hearings whether the bill, if
passed, was likely to get the country into the war, Secretary
Hull said that for a long time he had agreed with countries
that relied primarily on neutrality as a way of keeping out of
trouble, but as things developed he had reached the conclusion
that "the surest way to keep out of trouble [is] to prevent an
invasion of this hemisphere. . . . I think that is the safest
course. I want you to know that in my view there is danger
in any direction." [37] In short, Secretary Hull refused to accept
the view that the bill marked a sure step on the road to war;
while granting that there was danger in any course, he repeatedly emphasized defense of the United States in this hemisphere.

The Secretary of War, Henry L. Stimson, stated to the
Senate Committee that through the Lend-Lease Bill the United
States was buying time to prepare for its own security and
buying this time from "the only nation that can sell it," Great
Britain. Yet, in response to a question from Senator LaFollette
about the possibility of getting into war, Secretary Stimson
said: "As Secretary of War, I became a subordinate of the
President and was directed to follow out his policies, and those
policies, as I understand them, have always been, as shown by
many, many occasions, a desire, if possible—if possible—to effect the safety of this country without becoming involved in
any warlike or forcible or military measures. Now, so long as
I remain his Secretary of War I shall endeavor loyally to follow out his policies. . . ." Still later Senator Pepper remarked

36. Hearings before the Senate Committee on Foreign Relations, Lend-Lease
Bill, 1941, Part 1, pp. 3 ff.
37. Hearings before the House Committee on Foreign Affairs, 1941, pp. 12–13.

to Mr. Stimson: "So that this is a method toward the peace of this country and not a step toward getting this country into war?" Mr. Stimson replied: ". . . it is about the last call for lunch on that kind of procedure. This is an effort to do just as you say—to carry out, by nonviolent methods, the protection of our own country through aid to Great Britain. It may be the last." [38]

The testimony of Secretary Knox was plainly and indisputably in favor of neutrality, peace, and keeping out of the European war. In 1940 Mr. Knox had declared: "With the wisdom that comes from experience, we know that the phrases, 'a war to preserve democracy,' or 'a war to end all wars' were afterthoughts—rhetorical incitements to our war spirit. We will not fall for this form of incitement so readily again. . . . We must keep out of this war. . . . We must keep out. It finds expression in the columns of the newspapers, on the air, and from the rostrum. This cry knows no partisanship." [39]

In his testimony before the Senate Committee on July 10, 1940, when ratification of his appointment as Secretary of the Navy in President Roosevelt's Administration was under consideration, Mr. Knox had declared that he "would not favor sending any of our boys to Europe under any circumstances in the present crisis." Mr. Knox added that "my position has consistently been from the first that we ought to aid them [Great Britain and her allies] in a moral and economic way, never in manpower." Asked whether, if the moral and economic way was not sufficient for them to win, he "would feel that we should go the rest of the way," Mr. Knox had said simply, "No." The questioner had repeated: "You do not?" Mr. Knox had again replied: "No." [40]

When on January 31, 1941, Mr. Knox, as Secretary of the Navy came before the Senate Committee on Foreign Relations to support the Lend-Lease Bill, he testified that his mind had not changed with respect to keeping "our sons out of the

38. Hearings before the Senate Committee on Foreign Relations, Lend-Lease Bill, 1941, Part 1, pp. 115, 125.
39. Quoted in *ibid.*, p. 208.
40. Quoted in *ibid.*, p. 209.

European war." He said that we should have to fight in case the vital interests of the United States were at stake, but that "this I conceive to be the only way that we can preserve ourselves from that necessity—to help Britain. That is the only way that I can see to save our boys from going to war." [41]

Although Secretary Morgenthau declined to comment on the proposition that it might be necessary to go beyond financial and material aid to Great Britain, he stated at one point in the Senate hearings: "My chief interest in this bill is to gain us time to get ready so that we will be strong enough so that nobody would dare jump on us. The best way I know to gain time is to keep England fighting. Now, I am interested in our own security, first, last, and foremost." At another point in the Senate hearings, this colloquy occurred:

SENATOR JOHNSON OF CALIFORNIA. Now there is just one thing that I want, and that is to keep this country out of war.
SECRETARY MORGENTHAU. You and me both.
SENATOR JOHNSON. . . . Do you, too?
SECRETARY MORGENTHAU. Most fervently.
SENATOR JOHNSON. . . . Well, I will shake hands across the table, because there are a great many people in this audience and in this city and in this country at present who want nothing better than to stick us into some war and with all of its bloody consequences.
SECRETARY MORGENTHAU. No; it is my most fervent prayer that we stay at peace.
SENATOR JOHNSON. . . . Well, we will play ball together. [42]

None of the Administration's officials who spoke for the Lend-Lease Bill at the committee hearings of the House or Senate and none of the private citizens who favored it took the position that the bill was intended to be an act of war or a deliberate step on the road to war. A few supporting speakers at the hearings admitted that actions under it might eventuate in war or that, if it proved to be insufficient to save Great Britain, war might follow. But as against opponents of the bill

41. *Ibid.*, p. 209.
42. *Ibid.*, p. 73, also pp. 49, 67–68.

who repeatedly called it an act of war or an act leading to war, advocates of the measure usually went on record to the contrary. To summarize hundreds of passages in a single formula justified by the expressions used, the Administration's case for the bill was this: It is a law that will provide additional security for the United States and keep the country out of war or at all events it is the best hope of security and noninvolvement for the United States.

It is impossible to discover by a minute examination of the questions they asked and the statements they made during the hearings just what the majority of the Democratic Senators who supported the Lend-Lease Bill actually thought of its nature or of the consequences that would flow from the actions taken by President Roosevelt in carrying out the powers granted to him. Did they regard it as primarily a peace measure? Did they think that the risks of war, which some of them admitted, were so slight as to be negligible?

In respect of such questions some of the Democratic Senators openly expressed definite opinions. For example, Senator Walter George, chairman of the Senate Committee, used precise language when he said to General Robert Wood, National Chairman of the America First Committee: "I can assure you that I no more want to see this country in war than you do, and I agree with your statement that the vast majority of our people do not want to go to war, and so long as they keep that state of mind we will not go to war." [43]

On the other hand, it is not clear just what conception of the business in hand Senator Alben Barkley had in mind, for instance, when he questioned Dr. James B. Conant, president of Harvard University, who had earlier declared that "this is in essence a religious war—a war to my mind between good and evil." When his turn came to examine the witness, Senator Barkley asked:

Dr. Conant, while it is true so far as I am able to recall historically there has never been precisely the same situation existing in the world during any war or at the conclusion of any war which

43. *Ibid.*, Part 2, p. 395.

now exists in Europe and throughout the world, looking at the matter from a historical standpoint, do you recall any incident or any occasion in history when there has been a just negotiated peace as a result of overwhelming conquest by either side in a war having conquest or any other particular purpose as its basis?

Evidently somewhat puzzled by the Senator's inquiry, Dr. Conant replied:

I think those words are very difficult to define, Senator, and my knowledge of history is by no means competent to handle that in the broad range of affairs. But I have the distinct impression that if you and I had been living, let us say, in England, in the eighteen hundreds, the defeat of Napoleon, while I do not think it is of the order of magnitude as the present struggle, would have eventuated in a much better peace, from the point of view of England and [than] the success of Napoleon.

Pursuing this line, Senator Barkley then inquired whether Germany had not imposed peace on France in 1871 and whether that did not usually happen when there was a one-sided victory in war. Dr. Conant replied in the affirmative and Senator Barkley thereupon closed the colloquy.[44]

Opponents of the Lend-Lease Bill who appeared before the Senate Committee on Foreign Relations likewise duplicated the general argument against the proposal that had been advanced before the House Committee. Their case may be concisely stated as follows: This is a war measure; it will confer upon the President practically unlimited power to wage undeclared wars wherever and whenever he chooses; it will inevitably lead the country into another world war on a larger scale; and the consequences to the United States of such a war will be frightful to contemplate at the end of the conflict.

THE LEND-LEASE BILL EXPOUNDED IN CONGRESS AS A MEASURE FOR DEFENSE AND PEACE

During the debates in the House of Representatives and the Senate, supporters of the Lend-Lease Bill repeatedly based

44. *Ibid.*, Part 3, pp. 835, 844 f.

their case on the ground that it was a measure calculated to provide defense and peace for the United States. Several speakers admitted that there were risks of war in such action; and the proposition was given many turns and qualifications; but the following extracts from the debates on the bill at various stages indicate the general nature of the argument on this side.

Representative John W. McCormack, Democrat of Massachusetts:

The present bill is a peace measure for our people. It is based on the necessity for our own self-defense, and our country has a right—and it is. our duty to do so when danger exists—to provide for our self-defense, international law to the contrary notwithstanding. The real warmongers are those who oppose action, and in their blind opposition are attempting to divide our people. This is no time for division. This is the time for unity. Division at this time will result in harm. It might result in destruction. . . .

Suppose, in the papers of tomorrow or later on, the people of America should read of the defeat of Britain, what do you suppose will be their feeling? Will it be one of calmness, of safety and security, or will it be one of alarm, one with the feeling of fear, or impending danger? Would not their feelings be properly summed up in the words "we are next?" That is the reason why this is a defense measure and a peace measure so that "we will not be next."

It is amazing to me how many people think in terms of keeping our country out of war. Every one of us by nature and at heart is a pacifist. I do not want to resort to violence. . . . We do not want trouble. We do not want war. Our inclination is to run away, to do everything we can to avert it. But sometimes the law of self-preservation stares us in the face as individuals and the same law of preservation at times stares a nation in the face. In the face of a greater danger—destruction in all probability—we are compelled then to react in a contrary direction to what our natural instincts prompt us to do. That is why there are two aspects involved, one of which is to keep our country out of war—that is the easiest thing we have to do. All we have to do is nothing, but if we do nothing, does your judgment tell you that we are keeping war from our shores later? In order to keep our country out of war, as I see it, in the face of the imminent danger that confronts us, to prevent that danger from becoming actual we have to take affirmative steps of some kind to prevent the war later coming to our shores.

The purpose of the pending bill is to keep our country out of war, and to keep war from coming to our shores later on. That can only be done by preventing an Axis victory. It is unfortunate that the present world situation exists that requires us to consider legislation of this kind. That condition was not brought about by us, but it exists just the same. . . .

The argument has also been advanced that this bill will lead us into war. I cannot agree with that view. It is my opinion that this bill is the safest course that we can take to keep us out of war and to lessen the chances of war coming to our shores later on.

No matter what course we take, inaction or action as proposed in the pending bill, certain risks are involved. The question in this respect is whether by inaction we take a greater risk than we will take by proper judgment and action that we deem necessary for our welfare. . . .[45]

Representative Luther Johnson, Democrat of Texas:

Of course, no one can tell whether or not we are going to be involved in war in the future. In this changing world, with conditions changing overnight, it is a mere guess as to what will or will not happen.

I assert that there is nothing in this bill by which Congress surrenders its war-making powers. . . .

I am as much opposed to war as any opponent of this bill, but we are dealing with realities. . . . Hitler, as head of the Axis Powers, will likely declare war whenever in his judgment it is best for him to do so, and nothing that we have done in the past, or what we propose to do under this bill, will affect his decision. . . . In my judgment, there is nothing in this bill which will hasten or accentuate our involvement in war. . . .

This bill will do what is needed now by England, and we say it is a peace measure. Why? Because if England falls we know that we will likely be involved in war both from the Atlantic and the

45. *Congressional Record*, 77th Congress, First Session, Vol. 87, Part 1, House of Representatives, pp. 592 f.

Pacific, but if this bill passes and England stands, which God grant that she may, and I believe she will, then there is no danger of invasion here, because as long as the Atlantic Ocean is controlled by the British Fleet, I think our Navy can take care of the other side, and we are in no danger. . . .[46]

Representative Anton F. Maciejewski, Democrat of Illinois:

The lend-lease bill seeks to insure us against involvement in the wars now taking place in foreign lands by authorizing the President to give material aid to those friendly nations whose continued independent existence is necessary for our vital defense.[47]

Representative James P. Richards, Democrat of South Carolina:

Mr. Chairman, I do not guarantee, I do not even assert that this bill will keep us out of war. God grant that it may. I do believe that taking this step to forge another link in the proper defenses of the United States will have a tendency to keep us out of war. I do not know what the future will reveal. I do not know what legislation we shall be called upon to enact in behalf of the defense of our beloved country, I do not know where or when our boys may be called to go in defense of the Nation. Some have said our frontier is the Rhine. I do not agree with that. . . . It is, however, my humble opinion, my sincere belief, that the first defense lines of the United States are today anywhere on this earth where occasion requires that we exert our influence or where we should place our feet, or where we should shed our blood in defense of this country, the only remaining great free democracy left on the face of the earth.[48]

Representative Malcolm Tarver, Democrat of Georgia:

I am . . . in favor of aid to England, every ounce of aid we can furnish short of sending our own boys to European battlefields. . . . I do not want to tie up that aid with hampering restrictions. If we are going to help Britain at all, let us make our aid effective and let the world know that we are going to give it without stint. I do not know whether to do so will keep us out of

46. *Ibid.,* p. 499.
47. *Ibid.,* p. 516.
48. *Ibid.,* pp. 525 f.

war or not. Nobody knows. I believe there is a chance it may . . .

The surest way of "keeping war out of America" is to aid Great Britain, without stint, to the fullest extent of our resources. If we deny aid to Great Britain it is possible that the Axis Powers will prevail. Then will come the real test for America. Aid for Britain is our strongest insurance against actual warfare.[49]

Representative E. V. Izak, Democrat of California:

I predict if this bill is not passed you will see a negotiated peace, which in no way will curb the onward march of Hitler and the totalitarian nations. . . .

They say it may mean war. My friends, you cannot tell, and I cannot tell, whether the passage of this bill means war or peace. We do not know. But I want to say that it is not in your power, and it is not in mine, to prevent war. I lost all patience with my people when they came to me during the last campaign and said: "Please don't get us into war." I said, "Don't look at me. I am not getting you into war, but there is one man who has the power to do that, and that is Mr. Hitler. Look at him." [50]

Representative Stephen Young, Democrat of Ohio:

I am determined to do my utmost to keep war 3,000 miles distant from our shores. Let us strengthen, not weaken the hands of the Commander in Chief of our Army and Navy so that no dictators will dare attack us.[51]

Representative John Dingell, Democrat of Michigan:

. . . The bill will permit counter moves to circumvent German and Japanese threats whenever they may appear to menace our American rights and interests, whether in China, in Europe, or in the Western Hemisphere. The bill will save the lives of American boys and girls. . . .

If we are to stand by our oft-repeated declarations of policy, if we are to defend the flag as long as it waves over the Philippines, if we are to protect our vital far eastern trade routes, our missions, and our rights, then we must be prepared for any eventuality. The yellow peril of the Pacific, stimulated by the poison of

49. *Ibid.,* pp. 551 f.
50. *Ibid.,* p. 575.
51. *Ibid.,* p. 577.

German cohesion and phobia, each day threatens America with ever-increasing boldness. . . . Japan will not fight the United States only because she cannot do so successfully at this time. She will attempt to gain every advantage she can, and we must act in concert with Great Britain and Holland to stop her in her tracks; there is no time to lose. Not a shot will be fired, not a single life will be lost if we act with determination and promptness, if with courage, we act now.[52]

Representative W. R. Poage, Democrat of Texas:

Let it not be said that we were unwilling to use American money and American munitions now as a means of saving American lives later on. Let us pass H.R. 1776 as the only effective method of protecting the liberty we gained in the year 1776, and of preserving the peace that we enjoy in 1941.[53]

Senator Alben Barkley, Democrat of Kentucky:

I do not pretend that there are not risks, no matter what we do or fail to do. It may be a choice of risks. If we do nothing, we run the risk of being hemmed in and fenced off as a sort of unilateral concentration camp. We run the risk of seeing the rest of the world overrun, and then being compelled to fight a hostile world or be overrun ourselves.

On the other hand, if we take action which is contemplated in the legislation now before us, while that course is not free from risks, the chances are that the foul aggressor, who now boasts that he has his eyes upon us, may be stopped in his tracks. . . .

This measure is not based on any design on our part to attempt to secure a contract in advance as to what the terms of peace shall be. This would be a manifest impossibility. The basis of this bill is our own national defense, and that defense is to be accomplished by affording aid to those who are attempting to stop this international marauder in the hope that we may never have to undergo the vandalism which his victims are undergoing today in Europe. You might with equal propriety ask a peaceful citizen who is under the heel of a highwayman with a knife at his throat what use he will make of his life if you help him to preserve it.

52. *Ibid.*, p. 633.
53. *Ibid.*, p. 647.

This measure does not surrender the right of Congress to declare war. . . .

This measure does not confer upon the President the right to convoy ships across the ocean.

It does not confer upon him the right to send American troops to Europe. . . .

We do not want war. We hate war. Most of us here have seen the ravages of war, and we have seen the devastation and the suffering which it has always entailed. We do not want these ravages and this suffering to come to our shores. We believe that this measure offers the surest method by which we can avoid participation actively in this war and at the same time help those nations which are heroically grappling with a universal enemy and to preserve the doctrines of our fathers and the aspirations of our own hearts.

. . . The course which we chart is not without risk. Our liberties were not won in the first instance without risk. Our glorious history as a nation has not been written in golden letters upon the immortal page without risk of life or property or safety.

Are we less willing to assume those risks than were our forefathers? Are we cowed into submission by the fear of sacrifice or physical discomfort? Are we content to see others give up life and limb and home and comfort and peace itself while we fear to give even a portion of the wealth with which a generous God has blessed us? [54]

Senator Claude Pepper, Democrat of Florida:

We have had to come to the decision that one or the other shall live, totalitarianism or democracy, tyranny or freedom, and that it is as impossible for the two to live in the same world as it is for darkness and light to inhabit the same space at the same time. One of them must be crushed and the other live triumphant, and there can be no peace, and there will be no peace, until Hitlerism is crushed . . .

It is asked, "Why do you not declare war on him?" The answer is, because we do not choose to, and if we do, we will, and if we do we will make the choice and not he.

Ah, they say, this is a step to war. This is the only way possible to stay out of war. If this will not keep us out, nothing will. If

54. *Ibid.*, pp. 1037 ff.

this fails many months will not pass before we will be making a decision very much more fateful than that we make now as to the destiny of the people and the sons of America.

Mr. President, I venture to lay down the statement that not the American Congress, but the American people, will not let England fall, and whether we like it or not, let England totter, and they will drive us into action under the lash of their demands. Call it war or do not call it war—lay it down as a premise, America will not let England fall to Hitler. If the action now proposed will not save England, we will save it anyway. Watch American opinion, and see if what I say is not true.

Those who are trying to save us from having to make that terrible decision—which God forbid we shall ever have to make—have offered this alternative which contains some hope of success. Our Army leader, our Commander in Chief, our Secretary of the Navy, our Secretary of War, the Chief of our General Staff, tell us it will save England, and by saving England will save us from a horrible decision between peace and war. I favor trying it, therefore, and on bended knee, praying that it will save us from war. . . .

I said a moment ago, and I say now, that those who offer this bill are trying to keep a brave country, a people who love life, from ever having to decide whether they will give up their peace, or whether they will give up the means of preserving their security.[55]

Senator Tom Connally, Democrat of Texas:

This bill, I submit, is not intended to get the Nation into war, but it is intended to keep it out of war. It is the purpose of the bill by aiding Great Britain and by giving succor, aid and assistance to those who are struggling against the aggressors, to keep the war in Europe, and keep the invaders away from our own land.

If Britain, without our assistance, cannot resist the tide of aggression, we might as well prepare for an endless struggle over the years, because if Britain is defeated and overwhelmed, and if her navy is conquered, just so surely as the earth circles around the sun, sooner or later the conquering armies, and new navies built from the resources of conquered lands, will sweep across the ocean and attack the people of the United States.

55. *Ibid.*, pp. 1057 f.

Mr. President, when the Colonies gained their independence and established the United States of America, and later when the Monroe Doctrine was proclaimed, there was created a great zone of the earth's surface known as the Western Hemisphere, dedicated to free governments and democratic institutions. The purpose of this bill is to make secure forever that hemisphere as a sanctuary of freedom into which no alien conqueror shall ever set his accursed footsteps.

. . . The cold-blooded dictators, intoxicated by conquest . . . await only the moment of their choice to strike down free government and democracy wherever it lives. This bill is America's answer to their challenge. We propose to keep the war away from our shores. We propose to preserve our own freedom and that of the western world.[56]

Senator J. W. Bailey, Democrat of North Carolina:

The American people, with every opportunity to decide and to protest, have given assurance that they desire that their country, for their sakes, shall resist the totalitarian powers with material aid to Britain and other nations.

It becomes me to say that in following this course we may not win. We cannot have any assurance of victory in the fortunes of war; but on the other hand, in this course lies the only hope of escaping war, and our best hope of escaping what is worse—defeat in war! . . .

Some say what is proposed by the bill is intervention. It is. I think that is what my friend, the senior Senator from Montana, wishes me to say. It is intervention. It is not neutrality. It is the reversal of the policy which we laid down in the neutrality act. . . . It is intervention. We may not regard it as war, and intervention is not necessarily war. There is a difference between intervening and being an armed belligerent. . . .

I am hoping that intervention may not mean war, but I am ready if intervention does mean war . . . I am not holding back. I abhor the idea of war. I am not one of those who will hold out the flattering hope that we can fight a war of limited liability. I think it might be well for Mr. Hitler and Mr. Mussolini, and the war party in Japan to know that there is a country in the world

56. *Ibid.*, Part 2, p. 1158.

left that will not stop short once the gage of battle is thrown down—not short of the last dollar and the last man. . . .

It is said that the passage of the bill will lead to war. I do not know whether it will or not. I think those who predict that it will lead to war are in a pretty safe position, because there is a great deal of probability that war is coming, either course we take, and, when it comes, those who say it will come on account of this proposed act will say, "Now it has come on account of the act." Those who take the affirmative have to take the responsibility for events. The man who takes the opposition side is always in a fortunate position; he is not responsible for anything; he can always say, "I did not advocate it." I question whether the passage of the pending bill will lead to war, and I say its object is to head off war. We hope to enable England to win the fight with ships and men and planes, and what is more, up to now it is a war which so far as England and Germany are concerned, is not dependent upon the foot soldier. I agree again that, in the last analysis, the foot soldier cannot be dispensed with; he cleans up and he occupies, but, so far, this is a war of air and of sea and a war of diplomacy and of morale.[57]

Senator James E. Murray, Democrat of Montana:

Mr. President, this bill, as I see it, relates solely to the defense of our country and defines the policies which will guide us in a war-mad world. I can see no design in it to drag the United States into war. Regardless of the provisions of the measure, there is no way that we can get into this war unless we deliberately decide to enter it, and that can be accomplished only by a declaration of war. We are justified, in our own defense, to protect our country from the threat of the tri-partite agreement of the dictators representing Germany, Italy and Japan. We are, therefore, entitled to contribute aid to England and thus block the Axis scheme to dominate the world.

. . . I think the pending measure is a sound solution of our defense problems. By stopping the war in Europe we shall keep it out of America. It is the judgment of the great majority of this body that it offers the best chance of avoiding war. . . .

This measure will not, as has been charged, take the United States into war. On the contrary, it will keep war away from the

57. *Ibid.*, p. 1162.

United States because, as I have pointed out, the successful defense of England, the strengthening of her air forces, and the awakening of the democratic spirit of the world will start a chain of events that will accomplish the ultimate defeat of Hitler. . . . We are seeking here only to protect the interests of the United States and save our people from the dangerous consequences of totalitarianism. The measure declares a sound American policy. It creates no dictatorship and it does not involve us in war. I have full faith in the pledge of the President of the United States to keep us out of war.[58]

Senator A. B. Chandler, Democrat of Kentucky:

I do not think any of us know that our efforts will be short of war. I think all of us hope they will be. But as between sending $2,000,000,000 worth of aid to Britain, which will be short of war, and may result in a British defeat, and may result in the future in our becoming involved and having a great deal more trouble, and doing what is proposed to be done under the pending measure, I prefer that we pass the bill and give the President authority to give Britain all-out aid, so that she will have a chance to win.

Mr. McCarran. And thereby create the avenue for trouble? Is that what the Senator means?

Mr. Chandler. We are faced with the proposal of giving affirmative aid and the possibility of getting into trouble or of doing nothing and facing the possibility of getting into trouble, and between the two I would choose the giving of affirmative aid.[59]

Senator Morris Sheppard, Democrat of Texas:

It is my opinion that this measure enables us to gain the time necessary for the development of our own defensive armament. The struggling democracies need aid; we need time . . .

In view of the international situation that confronts us today, time is of the essence in the promotion of our national defense. We cannot afford to wait until the aggressor has accomplished his purpose, or started his advance into new areas. Such help, therefore, as America may render to Great Britain or any other nation

58. *Ibid.*, pp. 1352 ff.
59. *Ibid.*, p. 1473.

which the President may consider to be fighting the cause of democracy in a way vital to our own interest must be rendered as speedily as possible. . . . We are threatened with pagan barbarism, the rule of the sword, the denial of individual liberty. We are threatened with tyranny, oppression, persecution, and economic enslavement.

The measure before us enables us still to stop this threat without the necessity of war on our part . . .

. . . Because, therefore, this measure purposes to aid the nations now opposing aggressors and to provide for our own future needs through the stimulation of our defense industries, and, above all, because it is an act to promote the defense of the United States and may save us from war, it is my opinion that it should pass.[60]

Senator Scott Lucas, Democrat of Illinois:

No, Mr. President, I repeat that H.R. 1776 is a peace measure and not one of war. I submit it is a step in the direction of peace, and if I thought for one moment that it was a step toward war, I would be standing here opposing it with all the power and force that I command. . . .

We who support this bill are the real guardians of the peace. We are the realistic, hard-boiled avoiders of war. We advocate the only practical method of making America first in naval power, first in national power, first in power of the ideals which guarantee life, liberty, and the pursuit of happiness.[61]

THE LEND-LEASE BILL ATTACKED IN CONGRESS AS A WAR MEASURE

REJECTING the bill, either in its original or amended form, as a design for peace and defense, opponents were equally firm in denouncing it as a war measure.

Representative Thomas A. Jenkins, Republican of Ohio:

From the speech of the gentleman from Massachusetts, Mr. McCormack, I have been strengthened in my belief that there is

60. *Ibid.*, pp. 1493 f.
61. *Ibid.*, p. 1615.

something in connection with this bill that has not yet been brought out. At first we were given to understand that this bill was drafted as the free handiwork of Congress. That is not true. This bill has been cautiously and clandestinely put together. Ostensibly the physical drafting of it was done by a group of Congressmen, but its genius was in the heart and mind of someone aside from the active membership of Congress. Its genius comes from those who want the United States of America involved in this world conflict. There are powerful influences in the United States of America that would not stop in their determination to involve us in war, regardless of how dire the consequences might be. The cry of American mothers against another war that would rob them of their sons is not heard by this group. The prospect of the loss of lives and the loss of property and the bankruptcy of the Nation do not deter this group. They want Hitler destroyed for a different reason than what most of us have for his destruction. That this bill had all been thought out is proven by the President's message to Congress delivered on the sixth of January. . . . In this message he said that he would be compelled to ask Congress for money and materials that he might transfer them to the belligerents in this war. Through all these debates and through all these hearings I have been seeking to locate the real genius of this bill. Can it be the insatiable ambition of the President to want to have a hand in the domination of the world? Can it be in moneyed influences against whom Hitler has committed some special act which they resent? Or can it be as the result of fear of world domination from Hitler and his followers? I must confess that I do not know the answer, but I have a strong conviction that, as I have already stated, this bill has behind it and back of it some motives the purposes of which have not yet been disclosed. . . . There are some who think that the President wants this bill so that he may then be able to take from Great Britain, or at least to share with Great Britain, the active management of the war. If the President could, under threat of withholding money and supplies, demand that the war be carried on along certain lines, he would be in a position to have his demands recognized. If he assumes a position of collaboration and co-generalship with the war leaders of Great Britain, we are then actively in the war.[62]

62. *Ibid.*, Part 1, pp. 596 f.

Representative Bartel Jonkman, Republican of Michigan:

Mr. Chairman, we do not know and we cannot know where we are going under this bill, and we cannot know what situation we will be in when we get there. This bill not only undertakes to bring order out of chaos in Europe, including the Russia, Poland and Latvia tangle, but its objective is to set the whole world in order for our own defense and safety . . . this will mean war, bankruptcy, dictatorship, and, I may add, failure.[63]

Representative Usher Burdick, Republican of North Dakota:

All-out aid to Britain may mean anything. To sell her supplies is one thing—that we are doing now— . . . To sell her supplies and convoy them to England is another thing; to have these convoys sunk by German submarines and mines is another thing; to have actual war is the last thing. But the first thing and the last thing are in close proximity—the last thing is inevitable from the first thing. This means, therefore, if we grant these dictatorial powers to the President war is inevitable. A war for what? The last war was fought "to make the world safe for democracy." Did it make it safe? Is democracy safe now anywhere in the world, even including our own country? What will we enter this war for?[64]

Representative Hugh Peterson, Democrat of Georgia:

This is no defense measure.

It is a measure of aggressive warfare.

If it is enacted into law and its provisions are really made effective the inevitable result will be the sending of the armed forces of this nation—the sons of this Republic—to stand guard or do battle even unto the uttermost parts of the earth. Only a miracle could save us from such a sad fate. And no one can predict what the final outcome would be.

One of my prime purposes in making these remarks here today is to warn my constituents as well as all the people of this Republic as to the consequences which they must expect from the passage of this measure. I predict that with its passage the armed forces of

63. *Ibid.*, p. 530.
64. *Ibid.*, p. 539.

this Republic will be marching into actual battle before any other more formal declaration of war is made by Congress. . . .

This legislation, cloaked in the robes of peace, is in its naked form a cowardly declaration of war.

It is clear to me that there are those who know that the American people do not want to go to war. They know that the American people do not want their sons to die on the far-flung battlefields of Europe and Asia and Africa for the cause of world empire. So with shrewdly designed legislation such as this they pose as angels of peace even as they swiftly drag us down the dark and bloody pathway of warfare and destruction.[65]

Representative James O'Connor, Democrat of Montana:

I want to say this also: that the mandate we received from the American people, including the President of the United States, was to keep this country out of war. Stimson and Knox did not run for office. They did not receive a mandate. . . .

. . . I gather from this legislation that supply ships will be convoyed to Europe in some fashion to get supplies there. That will start the shooting, President Roosevelt said, and when the shooting starts the Congress can say nothing more. Therefore, this may be the last time we will have a chance to go on record in this House to get this country into war or keep it out of war. My considered judgment is that this bill, if enacted into law, will lay the foundation for our entry, and that when England calls for convoys and troops she will get them.

. . . I cannot and will not by my vote pass a bill that, to me, ignores the will of the American people, namely; to keep us out of this war—that puts this nation on the brink of disaster such as was never known.[66]

Representative Melvin Maas, Republican of Minnesota:

To aid Great Britain by permitting her to purchase war supplies here is one thing; but for the United States Government, as such, to actually furnish those supplies is to become an active participant in England's war. Once in the war, it will not be very easy to get out.[67]

65. *Ibid.*, pp. 542 f.
66. *Ibid.*, p. 548.
67. *Ibid.*, p. 557.

Representative Richard Gale, Republican of Minnesota:

Without question the people of the United States are sympathetic toward England and sincerely would like to see Hitler defeated, but let us not confuse "sympathy" with a desire to sacrifice untold wealth, personal liberty, and priceless lives in a long, bitter war.

H.R. 1776, if passed, may be the declaration of such a war and probably the only declaration that Congress will be called upon to make. Stripped of high-sounding phrases, of timid misconception, stripped of reluctance to face the truth, the issue before the country is not merely the lend-lease bill but whether we shall have war.[68]

Representative Martin Sweeney, Democrat of Ohio:

I have a mandate from the voters of the Twentieth Congressional District of Ohio . . . to vote against this vicious war-involving measure known as H.R. 1776 . . .

We now predict that the lend-lease, give-away measure would invest in the Chief Executive the power to involve us in actual participation in the war. . . . I care not how sincere or patriotic any President of the United States may be, such power must be kept within the Congress. We are actually in the war once this bill is passed.[69]

Representative Dewey Short, Republican of Missouri:

There is one question I believe every member of this body should ask himself before he votes for this bill. Am I willing to go the whole way? You cannot be half way in war and half way out of war. You cannot insult people, spit in their faces, slap their jaws, kick them on the shins and then say "we do not want to fight." There is no such thing as what is expressed by that sham slogan of "methods short of war. . . ."

. . . You can dress this measure up all you please, you can sprinkle it with perfume and pour powder on it, masquerade it in any form you please with these innocuous and meaningless amendments that have been offered, but it is still foul and it stinks to high heaven. It does not need a doctor, it needs an undertaker. We do

68. *Ibid.*, p. 568.
69. *Ibid.*, p. 580.

take not one or two but several other steps nearer the brink, nearer the precipice of active involvement, and if you cannot kill this bill, then I would like to see you offer an amendment that the Members who vote for this vicious thing will, the day war is declared or we become involved, resign their seats and go in the front contingent. That of course will never happen.

This bill is a war bill, it is a dictatorship bill, and it is a bankruptcy bill. . . .[70]

Representative Clifford Hope, Republican of Kansas:

The American people have a right to express their opinions, and Members of Congress the right to vote their convictions as to whether or not we become a belligerent. The present bill will put us in the war in the end just as surely as if Congress had voted a declaration of war. We will be in for all purposes and to the finish. We will be in without any vote in Congress on the question and without the great majority of our people having any idea that this momentous step has been taken.[71]

Representative Philip Bennett, Republican of Missouri:

Yes, Mr. Chairman, if we want to help the oppressed let us do it in compliance with our Constitution and international laws. Let us do it short of war, which phrase is ominously missing from recent utterances of the President. The conclusion is inescapable that the President is reconciled to active military intervention if such intervention is needed to defeat the Axis in this war.

"But our boys are not going to be sent abroad," says the President. . . .

Nonsense, Mr. Chairman; even now their berths are being built on transport ships.

Even now tags for identification of the dead and wounded are being printed by the William C. Ballantyne Co., of Washington. . . .[72]

Representative George H. Tinkham, Republican of Massachusetts:

Mr. Chairman, the bill now under discussion, with its delegation of limitless powers to the President to intervene in war anywhere

70. *Ibid.*, pp. 600 f.
71. *Ibid.*, p. 608.
72. *Ibid.*, p. 618.

in the world with all the resources of the United States, is a war bill of monstrous implications. The passage of this bill means the adoption by the United States of a policy of unrestrained, brutal, naked power policies for the domination of the world. This policy is imperialism gone mad. . . .

The politicians in Washington in their misleading and mendacious representations of policies and purposes are being as false to the American people as the French politicians recently were false to the French people. The consequences will be as disastrous.

It is patently disloyal to the American people to involve them in war against their will, and that is precisely what the enactment of the bill H.R. 1776 will do. The bill does not empower the President to declare war, but it does empower him to make war. In these days, war is seldom formally declared. . . .

The United States will unquestionably become actively engaged in war if this bill is enacted.[73]

Representative H. Carl Anderson, Republican of Minnesota:

Our job as Congressmen is to prevent a recurrence of our troops again being used abroad. Yes; we will always protect our own, but I cannot but feel that H.R. 1776, backed up by the glaring headlines of the warminded eastern press and the propaganda ground out in the movies, owned in large part by the same group who dominate this press; I cannot but feel that all of this, together with the wrapping of our flag about this so-called lend-lease bill, is but a prelude once more to brass bands again accompanying our brothers and perhaps our sons on a march to a war of destruction in a foreign country, a war which we had no part in starting. No; neither were we consulted with by Britain at Versailles nor at Munich. I sympathize with the poor people in Europe today, . . . but the clammy, cold hand of death accompanies the convoying by our warships of supplies going to their aid.[74]

Representative Gerald Landis, Republican of Indiana:

I believe a majority of our people who are advocating aid short of war do not desire us to enter the war. We are being edged into

73. *Ibid.,* pp. 626 f.
74. *Ibid.,* p. 638.

the war without the masses' knowledge. The course we are pursuing is bound to involve us in war. If we aid Britain short of war and beyond the limits of the Neutrality Act, it ultimately means war.[75]

Representative Vito Marcantonio, American Labor party of New York:

Mr. Chairman, I am opposed to this bill because I am opposed to converting this country into an arsenal, not an arsenal for democracy, if you please, but an arsenal in pursuance of a policy which would catapult the American people into a war which is not a war for democracy but a war for the maintenance of the present British imperialist interests, a war between two gangs of imperialistic bandits, one gang who stole yesterday and one gang who is trying to steal today.

You who are asking us to follow a policy which will inevitably plunge us into actual conflict, not plunge us into war, because we are in that war from the standpoint of armaments—from the standpoint of having put our country on a war-economy basis we are actually in war—you are asking us to go further into that war, and inevitably, for now that you have become this arsenal and this military reservoir, you are bound to engage in actual conflict. . . .

. . . The great question is, what is short of war? Who knows what short of war is? I think short of war means that we should stay home here, attend to our own business, and stay out of Europe. That is my idea of short of war. . . . I say now before Almighty God and this Congress that I am going to do everything to keep America out of war. I promise that. I do not care what the people in my district think. If I received a telegram tomorrow from everybody in my district wanting me to vote for this bill, I would resign my job in Congress before I would vote for it. I would not do it, because this bill is going to lead the American people into war. . . .

. . . it is my belief that this bill will lead us into war and will cause us the greatest anxiety and trouble this country has ever had. I am sure the only way we can keep out of war is to defeat this bill.[76]

75. *Ibid.*, p. 653.
76. *Ibid.*, pp. 656 ff.

Senator Bennett Clark, Democrat of Missouri:

This is not a defense bill; it is a war bill. We pledge ourselves to assuring, guaranteeing military victory of one belligerent over another. We all know that we will have to follow that up by any means that may be necessary. We all know that that is equivalent to a declaration of a state of war ourselves, and must be followed up by sending our warships, our planes, our guns, and, ultimately, the men, the boys of this country of the coming generation who are the hope and heart of the future of the United States, across the seas. Once committed, Mr. President, we cannot turn aside. . . .

Mr. President, we are facing a situation in which, if we pass this bill, we are taking certainly the next to the last step leading to our involvement in war. It may be that we are taking the last step, because under the powers given in this bill steps may be taken which will create a state of war.[77]

Senator Pat McCarran, Democrat of Nevada:

If this bill is enacted into law, Mr. President, it is war—war under the ignominious circumstance of never having been declared by the Congress of the United States.

First of all, this is the President's bill. The present President of the United States gave his O.K.—to use the common vernacular of the street—to the bill. What does he want, and what do we yield?

First of all, he wants and we yield power in his own discretion, on his own terms, and as he may see fit, to conduct undeclared war anywhere in the world. . . .

I say we are weakening the Executive Office when we grant that power. We make the Executive Office a mere messenger boy for carrying on war abroad.[78]

Senator Burton K. Wheeler, Democrat of Montana:

Actually once we are committed to the course laid out by this bill, the die is cast.

The momentum forcing us along the primrose path to our fatal rendezvous with war will dictate sheeplike approval of each ap-

77. *Ibid.*, pp. 1100 f.
78. *Ibid.*, pp. 1268 f.

propriation requested and meekly obedient extension of the time limit, just as Hitler's powers and Mussolini's powers were extended by the docile representatives of the people. . . .

Are we again to be just marionettes to dance when our ruler pulls the strings, just Charlie McCarthys to utter words that the ruler puts in our mouths? . . .

There is no fairer test of democracy than the right of the people, through their chosen representatives, to determine between peace and war. This is the issue which, above all other issues, is important to them. More than any other, it has to do with their inalienable rights to life, liberty and the pursuit of happiness.

We may talk about the right of free assemblage and the right of free speech, but the most important thing to a people anywhere is the question whether or not they shall be dragged into war. The choice between sending millions of their boys to be killed and maimed, and keeping them at home to engage in productive employment, contributing to the happiness and wealth of the country . . . the choice between terrible total war with its ravages on women and little children, and the blessings of peace—this choice belongs to them. The loosing of the Four Horsemen of the Apocalypse should not depend on the whim or caprice of any one man, be he wise and good, or vindictive and power crazy. "War's a game that were their subjects wise, kings would not play at."

To the extent that the people, through their chosen representatives, have surrendered control over this choice to one man, to that extent they have sacrificed democracy. Oh, I know that in some cases neither people nor ruler can make the choice; there are times when they are subjected to unprovoked attack by the invading armed forces of another country. Everyone in his right senses will grant that power must reside in someone to take the necessary immediate measures to meet and beat back such assaults. But everyone else knows that such cases have nothing to do with the underlying premise of H.R. 1776, namely the fantastic claim that our frontiers are no longer our two seacoasts; that they are no longer even in the Western Hemisphere, but lie along the Rhine, or on the English Channel, or at Salonika, or at Singapore. The people have a right to pause and think and choose for themselves before they plunge into war on any such theory. And as we mention H.R. 1776, it may not be amiss to recall one of the injuries and usurpations charged against the King of Great Britain in our Declaration of Independence:

"He has affected to render the military independent of, and superior to, the civil power." [79]

Senator David Walsh, Democrat of Massachusetts:

First and foremost, in purpose and effect it gives blanket approval to policies and a course of conduct that I most earnestly and regretfully believe will lead the United States into war in Europe or in Asia, or perhaps both. Indeed, in my judgment, this bill when viewed in the perspective of all the attendant circumstances is an absolute committal of the United States to war as Britain's ally in her life and death struggle with Nazi Germany and Hitler's associated partners and pawns. I say this fully conscious that the proponents of this legislation, when it was first presented to Congress and to the country . . . , loudly proclaimed it a measure to keep the United States out of war. Such a claim is entirely specious. Such a belief is a delusion. The proponents of this legislation, it seems to me, refuse to face the realities of the course which they advocate. If they do face them and perceive them, they have not acquainted the country with the implications.

But it is only fair to say that as public debate and consideration of this legislation have advanced, less is heard of the claim that this is a peace measure. There is now a tacit admission even from many of the proponents that this bill does in fact take us down the road to war. [80]

Senator Arthur Vandenberg, Republican of Michigan:

My greatest fundamental objection to it is that it invites and authorizes the President of the United States to enter the continental arena of "power politics," which has been the curse of the Old World and the cradle of its incessant wars for a thousand years, invites and authorizes him to become power politician No. 1 of this whole, mad world. . . . I am opposed to any of these policies, Mr. President, which would needlessly threaten to drag us into war, when we are still officially saying that we intend to stop "short of war" and when this very legislation is being

79. *Ibid.*, pp. 1597 ff.
80. *Ibid.*, Part 2, p. 1625.

labeled "peace." I freely concede that our whole status today is precarious, but that is no reason why we should make it more so. Yes; the ice is thin at best. We chose thin ice when we abandoned neutrality. We chose the risk. We have taken the risk ever since . . . when I speak of policies that would needlessly drag us into war, which is to say, would precipitate us into it, I am not speaking of our international engagements, although I could wish that some great power might keep these lamps trimmed and burning. I certainly am not speaking of threats that may be hurled at us—as in the Axis challenge of last fall—in an effort to coerce us by intimidation. Intimidation acts adversely upon us. I am speaking, rather, of policies which would needlessly be likely to expose us to physical attack which could be met only by armed resistance, thus precipitating war. I find such exposure in this bill. I cannot approve. I repeat that if we are going to war—which God forbid—I would go all the way to war, deliberately conscious of our decision, and not drift in or back in, deliberately pretending to be unconscious of anything but peace in our hearts.[81]

Senator C. Wayland Brooks, Republican of Illinois:

This bill is a war bill. It asks for the same powers that would be asked for if we were actually fighting, shooting, marching, defending our own shores . . .

I have heard distinguished Senators on the floor of the Senate talking about crushing Hitler and grinding him into the ground, and I wonder if they have honestly translated to the people of America what this means.

This means arming to the teeth; giving one man complete and full authority to lease, lend, or otherwise dispose of our military resources to engage in every present or possible conflict in the whole world if he believes that it is for the best interests of America to do it. . . .

When this power is voted to one man, I predict today that it will—sooner than we expect—involve us in active, personal fighting participation in war; and you cannot shirk your responsibility by turning over this authority to any one man. The blood of the American boys will be on your hands whether they wear khaki, forest green or navy blue.

81. *Ibid.*, pp. 1103 ff.

Mr. President, this is a war bill, with war powers, with the deliberate intention to becoming involved in other people's wars. . . . We do not need any declaration of war. All we need to do is carry out the intended provisions of this bill and we will be in the wars.[82]

Senator Robert M. LaFollette, Progressive of Wisconsin:

Mr. President, every Senator who votes for the bill has now been warned what some administration Senators themselves really believe the bill means. It means war. And all America should also know that it means war.

As for myself, I am opposed to our entering the war. I will not give my vote for any bill which is one step nearer another blood bath for our youth, one step nearer totalitarianism for the United States. I am not willing to add my vote to help in any way a course of action which I am convinced can end only in the same bitter disillusionment and futile disaster of the last war.

For the bill means war. Whatever fine trappings it is decked with, it hides the skull and bones of death on Old World battlefields and death on the seven seas. Who will assume to limit where the graveyards of this war will be? . . .

The full implications of this measure are not to be found by reading the bill itself. You judge a man not by one act alone but by the sum total of his acts. So the bill must be judged against the background of other statements by the President, as recently as his radio address to the Nation on December 29, 1940, and his message to Congress on January 6, 1941. The bill is a blank check to permit him to make good the reckless assurances he gave the world when he overdrew on his authority to speak the convictions of the American people. His assurances to the world were: First, the United States will guarantee a smashing victory for the British Empire; and second, the United States is committed to the establishment of the "four freedoms" everywhere in the world.[83]

Senator Robert A. Taft, Republican of Ohio:

Mr. Taft: The important thing about this bill, it seems to me, is that its provisions in effect give the President power to carry on a kind of undeclared war all over the world, in which America

82. *Ibid.*, p. 1250.
83. *Ibid.*, p. 1300.

would do everything except actually put soldiers in the front-line trenches where the fighting is.

MR. WHEELER: I think that is true.

MR. TAFT: I do not see how we can long conduct such a war without actually being in the shooting end of the war as well as in the service-of-supply end which this bill justifies.[84]

After prolonged and prolix debates, the Lend-Lease Bill, amended in several respects, was finally passed by large majorities in both houses of Congress. Although there were some defections from party ranks, the main support for the measure came from Democrats, and Republicans supplied by far the major portion of the opposition votes. In the House of Representatives the vote was 260 for and 165 against; in the Senate it was 60 for and 31 against. The bill, entitled "An Act to Promote the Defense of the United States," became a law on March 11, 1941, with the signature of President Roosevelt. Time would tell of its meaning and consequences. Was it in reality an act authorizing the President to wage undeclared wars, as critics alleged, or was the measure, as Senator Tom Connally declared, "intended to keep it [the Nation] out of war"?

84. *Ibid.*, p. 1588.

CHAPTER III

Patrolling as Appearances

AMONG the many criticisms of the Lend-Lease Bill as it came to Congress in its original form, few were more pointed than the objection that if enacted a next step would be a presidential order instructing the commanders of American naval forces to convoy British and other ships bearing military supplies to the beneficiaries of the act—a step certain to result in shooting, attacks, and war.[1] The original bill (Section 3) was silent on the subject but in response to protests from the opposition Congress amended the section by a provision that nothing in the act should be construed to authorize convoying.

Nevertheless, the matter of convoys remained embarrassing for Administration supporters who, out of conviction or expediency, insisted that the Lend-Lease Act was a peace measure or at all events, if involving war risks, was, as Senator Pepper phrased the argument for it, "the only possible way to stay out of war." [2] That British shipping was in dire need of protection against German submarines was well known; the transfer of American destroyers to Great Britain in 1940 had advertised the fact to the people of the United States; and news of sea warfare since that action had apparently confirmed it.

At the same time it was obvious that if American naval forces convoyed British ships or patrolled the sea lanes for the purpose of warding off German or Italian submarine attacks, a "shooting war" was almost certain to ensue. Thus lend-lease, despite its appearances as a peace measure, might easily become in reality a war measure, as its foes were contending. In such circumstances, advocates of aid to the Allies were hard pressed to find arguments which squarely met the assertion of their opponents that lend-lease meant American convoys and that

1. See above, p. 30.
2. See above, p. 50.

convoys meant sending American boys to fight in Europe and Asia, notwithstanding all the promises to American mothers and fathers in the campaign of 1940.

When a reporter had brought the issue immediately to the attention of President Roosevelt at a press conference during the discussion of the Lend-Lease Bill, by remarking that, according to one suggestion, the Navy might convoy ships into British waters where the British Navy would take them over, the President had dismissed the idea as if beneath consideration.[3]

The President's supporters in Congress, however, had not been able to dispose of the troublesome issue so easily and to brush off questioners with a laugh. At hearings on the Lend-Lease Bill Secretary of the Navy Frank Knox had been driven into a corner and compelled to say just where he stood in respect of convoying. On that occasion, Mr. Knox had declared that he was very much opposed to the idea of convoying merchantmen across the Atlantic and that he looked upon it as "an act of war."[4]

Of all the controversial issues relative to President Roosevelt's promises to keep the country out of war, the question of using American naval vessels to convoy British or other merchant ships on their way to British waters or elsewhere to war zones was about the hottest that appeared during the days subsequent to the enactment of the Lend-Lease Act, March 11, 1941. Opponents of involvement in war, Democrats and Republicans alike, repeatedly raised it in Congress and outside as the acid test of the President's sincerity, and the sincerity of the Senators and Representatives who had supported that measure in Congress. Amid the disputes over convoying, which raged from March 11 to December, 1941, these opponents of war continued to recite various pledges which had been made by sponsors of the Lend-Lease Bill while it was pending to the effect that convoying would not be undertaken, in particular

3. See above, p. 20.
4. See above, p. 31.

President Roosevelt's statement that "Convoys mean shooting and shooting means war." [5]

On their part, even frank and open advocates of war were for a time in a dilemma with regard to convoying. They knew that Democrats and Republicans in Congress, owing to the peace pledges they had made to their constituents and/or their convictions, would not vote for a declaration of war; and they knew also that convoying was the most effective means likely to edge the country indirectly into war, for convoying would probably bring on shooting and shooting might easily end in a full-fledged war. But owing to continued popular hostility to involvement in war, it was inexpedient for frank and open advocates of war to represent convoying to the public as a way of maneuvering the United States into the armed conflict. For them it was, temporarily "good strategy" to acclaim convoying as merely another device for defending America by aiding the Allies—and advocacy in this guise was among the liberties they enjoyed as citizens.

On the other hand, President Roosevelt, bound by his anti-war pledges and his commitment that lend-lease would not be administered as a war policy, was in a different position with reference to convoying, when he began to act under the statute; and, judging by the appearances reflected in official statements from the White House at the time, he claimed no authority under that law to order convoying and he did not contemplate commanding the American Navy to engage in it. On the contrary, he made public statements to the effect that, while he approved lawful "patrolling," he was not intending to use the Navy for convoying. Meanwhile advocates of war or strong action worked hard to stir up public sentiment in favor of convoying as aid to the Allies for the defense of America.

The stages in the development of the controversy over convoying during the second half of March, 1941, are illustrated by the following brief outline of events:

March 15. President Roosevelt, in a radio address, declared

5. See below, p. 75.

that he would maintain a bridge of ships to Great Britain and Greece.

March 16. Senator Carter Glass announced that he favored convoys if the President intended to imply in his "bridge-of-ships" speech that this measure was contemplated.

March 17. The Committee to Defend America by Aiding the Allies announced support for convoys.

March 18. President Roosevelt parried questions on the subject of convoying.

March 19. Representative Sauthoff's amendment to forbid convoying was opposed in the House of Representatives by supporters of the Administration.

March 20. Secretary Knox declared before a Senate Committee that he had no plan for convoys.

March 27. Senator Glass again announced himself in favor of convoys.[6]

At the end of March, a joint resolution to bar resort to convoys came up for consideration in Congress and was used to challenge the sincerity of members who had hitherto declared themselves against convoying. In the House of Representatives, it was sponsored by Harry Sauthoff, of Wisconsin. In the Senate, where the resolution was presented by Charles W. Tobey, of New Hampshire, the question of convoys was briefly reviewed on March 31, with Senator Tobey taking the lead. During the debate Senator Barkley seemed to maintain that convoying ships, which Congress had declared to be unauthorized by the Lend-Lease Act, would not in itself necessarily result in war, any more than some other actions specifically authorized by the law.[7] The state of opinion on the

---

6. For each item in the list see the *New York Times* for the following day.

7. Later, on April 2, Senator Tobey charged Senator Barkley with having said in effect that he could see no difference between convoying ships and repairing British ships in American harbors. Mr. Barkley replied that what he had meant to say was: "if Germany desires an excuse to wage war against us, the mere convoying of ships would be a mere incident so far as Germany is concerned. . . . If it were to their interest to do so they would not require such an incident even." *Congressional Record*, April 2, 1941, p. 2856. To Mr. Tobey this was another sign that Mr. Barkley was gradually shifting the position which he had taken when the Lend-Lease Bill was before Congress.

subject in the Senate is indicated by the following extract from the *Congressional Record* of March 31, 1941:

MR. TOBEY. Mr. President, in this historic Chamber an earnest and historic debate was recently held, culminating in the passage of the so-called lease-lend bill. That debate was conducted by Members of the Senate in a spirit of sincere and earnest presentation of the facts as they understood them. Many of those who spoke for the lease-lend bill in this Chamber during the several weeks of debate took the position that they were voting for the bill because in their conscientious judgment it was the best means to keep us out of participation in the World War.

In contradistinction, those of us who voted against the bill held that we should vote against it because we honestly believed that it was fraught with the grave danger of making us a participant in the World War. So, sincere men on each side voiced their contentions, the majority prevailed, and the bill became law upon being signed by the President. But from this statement of mine it becomes apparent that all of my colleagues on both sides of that question had in their hearts a hatred of war, a bitterness toward war, and a fear that this Nation might be drawn into the war, that they were opposed to our being drawn into war. As the debate progressed toward taking the final vote on the lease-lend bill, there was but one Senator in this Chamber who came out definitely in advocacy of the United States' forthwith going into war.

The gravest issue now before the country is the question of whether or not we will be involved as a participant in this World War. Dr. Gallup, who has been quoted from one end of the country to the other, recently took a poll, as a result of which he certified, I believe, that 83 percent of the American people were opposed to the United States becoming involved as a participant in the foreign war.

With that background I make bold to state that the gravest issue now before the country is the issue of whether we shall go into that war or not.

The factor which in my judgment is most certain to involve us in that war is the issue of whether or not we shall adopt the policy of using our ships and planes as convoys to merchant ships carrying materials to the aid of belligerents.

In section 3, subsection (e) of the lend-lease bill is the following language:

"(e) Nothing in this act shall be construed to authorize or to permit the authorization of the entry of any American vessel into a combat area in violation of section 3 of the Neutrality Act of 1939."

Section 3, subsection (d) contains this language:

"(d) Nothing in this act shall be construed to authorize or to permit the authorization of convoying vessels by naval vessels of the United States."

While the lend-lease bill was being considered before the House Foreign Affairs Committee and before the Senate Committee on Foreign Relations, there appeared before us many noted witnesses, not the least of whom was the present Secretary of the Navy, the Honorable Frank Knox. He was asked by one of the Senators, "You stand very much opposed to the idea of convoying merchantmen across the Atlantic?" His answer was tersely and definitely, "Yes."

"You do look upon it as an act of war?"

"Yes," he said.

He made a similar statement before the House committee, in answer to a question from Mrs. Bolton, a Representative from the State of Ohio. His statement there was that he was very much opposed to the idea of convoying merchantmen across the Atlantic, that he looked upon it as an act of war.

The President himself in a recent statement given to the press made a similar statement. I think his words were:

"Convoying means shooting, and shooting means war."

In confirmation of that I read from a feature article by Frank L. Kluckhohn, appearing in the New York Times for January 22, 1941, in which he says:

"Sources close to the White House said it is obvious that if the United States Navy convoys ships, either under an American or other flag, into a combat zone, shooting is pretty sure to result, and shooting comes awfully close to war."

Mr. VANDENBERG. Mr. President, will the Senator yield at that point?

Mr. TOBEY. I am very glad to yield to the Senator from Michigan.

Mr. VANDENBERG. In connection with the authorities which the Senator is quoting on the subject, I think he has overlooked probably the most persuasive authority of all, so far as the Senate of the United States is concerned. If he will permit me to do so, I should like to call attention to the unequivocal statement made by the distinguished chairman of the Senate Foreign Relations Committee on March 6, 1941, as reported at page 1892 in the Record. The very distinguished Senator from Georgia [Mr. George], the chairman of the Foreign Relations Committee, who piloted the lend-lease bill through the Senate, was speaking:

"As plainly as I can, I have always stood against convoying vessels by the American Fleet, and will stand against convoying vessels by any unit of the American Fleet until and unless the point shall come when I shall be willing to vote for war, because, in my judgment, convoying would lead us into actual war."

Mr. Tobey. I thank the Senator. That is a powerful indictment of convoys.

Mr. President, if it is our conviction that convoys mean war—and we have the eminent authority just cited, as well as the President of the United States and Secretary Knox and many other notable men in this country—we of the Congress having assured the American people that we will keep out of the war, as has the President and as has the distinguished candidate who opposed him in the recent election, then it logically follows that we of the Congress should take every step possible to keep us out of the war as a participant, and should use the powers vested in us by the Constitution to prohibit the use of our ships as convoys.

Mr. Connally. Mr. President, will the Senator yield?

Mr. Tobey. I yield to the Senator from Texas.

Mr. Connally. Does the Senator from New Hampshire mean that the simple act of convoying would be war, or does he mean that the adoption of such a policy would result in acts of war by the other side? Which does he mean?

Mr. Tobey. I will take as my authority the President's own words, when he said, "Convoys mean shooting, and shooting means war."

Mr. Connally. Evidently the Senator does not care to answer my question.

Mr. Tobey. I have answered it; I have quoted an eminent authority, and no man should be more obedient to that authority than the Senator from Texas.

Mr. Connally. The Senator did not answer my question. I wanted him to answer the question.

MR. TOBEY. What is the question?

MR. CONNALLY. The question is, Does the Senator contend that it would be an act of war if we should adopt the policy of convoying vessels; or does he mean that the adoption of such a policy would inevitably result in acts of war by an enemy?

MR. TOBEY. I will answer the Senator by saying that, in my judgment, it is an act of war for a neutral country to convoy ships carrying supplies to a belligerent.

Mr. President, I should like to have the attention of the Senator from Texas, who propounded the question.

MR. CONNALLY. I beg the Senator's pardon.

MR. TOBEY. The Senator asked a question and then turned his back. Does he desire to have an answer to his question, or not?

MR. CONNALLY. I thought the Senator had answered the question.

MR. TOBEY. The answer to the Senator's question had been only half completed. More than that, with an abhorrence of war in my heart, an abhorrence which I hope is shared by the Senator from Texas, I think war will be a direct result of such convoying. As the Senator from Georgia, the chairman of our great committee, said, "If we convoy these ships, it means shooting, and that is tantamount to a declaration of war."

MR. BARKLEY. Mr. President, will the Senator yield?

MR. TOBEY. I yield.

MR. BARKLEY. I am not attempting to pass upon the wisdom of attempting to convoy; but it seems to me that the mere act of convoying would not result in shooting unless the other side did some shooting. Regardless of what the President said, the shooting would depend entirely upon whether the other side wanted to shoot at the convoy, would it not?

MR. TOBEY. Let me answer by propounding a question. Does the Senator agree with the President in his expressed utterance to which I have just referred?

MR. BARKLEY. I may or may not. I am attempting to ascertain whether the Senator can elucidate what the President meant by mere shooting. The mere convoying of a ship does not mean shooting unless somebody shoots at the convoy. The convoy would not shoot at something just for the pleasure of having target practice.

Does the Senator mean or does he think the President meant

that the mere convoying of a ship or of a group of ships across the ocean would automatically result in shooting?

MR. TOBEY. No. In answer to the question asked by the Senator from Kentucky, the distinguished majority leader, I will put it this way: It seems to me that what the President had in mind—and it is apparent to all of us—was that if we convoy a group of ships carrying supplies to a belligerent, obviously the enemy of that belligerent is going to take steps to put those convoys out of business; and when, as, and if that occurs, the shooting begins, and our ships are sunk, there will be a wave of wrathful indignation that will go over this country and that will arouse the people passionately and earnestly and perhaps necessarily to cry out and to say, "We will go to war and lick those fellows over there."

MR. BARKLEY. I will say to the Senator that I think that is a deduction that is not far-fetched; but when it comes to technical acts of war, the mere fact that one peaceful nation permits a belligerent nation to repair its vessels in its own shipyards would be regarded under what used to be international law as an act of war, the mere lending or leasing or furnishing of equipment for war use might be so regarded. But we recognize the fact that all international law has been thrown out, and, judging by recent events, we see that it is difficult now to draw a comparison between one act of war that occurred when international law had some force and another act of war. So what is the difference, except that one may be more provocative than the other? In legal effect, what is the difference between convoying a ship on the ocean in order to safeguard transport of facilities and supplies to another nation, and permitting that nation's warships to come into our harbors— as we have done by law—and permitting our Government to buy equipment and to furnish equipment and supplies to a belligerent nation, which we have done by law? What is the difference in international law between those two operations?

MR. TOBEY. May I ask the Senator from Kentucky a question?

MR. BARKLEY. I should like to have the Senator answer my question first.

MR. TOBEY. I will be glad to answer it if I understand the Senator correctly, but I will put it this way: The convoying of ships, in my judgment, is the greatest single factor which would bring us into war by its results. There are others that could do so, as I stated on the floor of the Senate when speaking against the lease-lend bill. I felt then, and still hold—I do not know whether the Senator recalls my statement at that time—that when we open our yards to repair belligerent ships, that might well involve us in war, as other things might, but standing out preeminently as a war danger, the danger of involving us in war, in my judgment, is the matter of convoys.

MR. BARKLEY. Mr. President, will the Senator yield further?

MR. TOBEY. Yes.

MR. BARKLEY. I do not want to take the time of the Senator from New Hampshire or of any other Senator, because we have not as yet completed the morning hour and we are anxious to secure action on a couple of appropriation bills, but I wish to ask the Senator a question. Of course, it all depends on whether the nation against whom the operations are directed regards them as a sufficient breach of its rights to make an attack upon us or to declare war. It would have a technical right to declare war on us for allowing a British war vessel to be repaired in the United States; there is no doubt of that, and, under the old conception of international law, they would have the right to declare war against us because we loaned money to one of the belligerents in opposition to that particular country or do any of the things that we can do under the lease-lend bill we have authorized to be done and which are going to be done now—

The ACTING PRESIDENT pro tempore. The Chair will state that the hour of 2 o'clock having arrived, morning business is closed. The Senator from New Hampshire has the floor.

MR. BARKLEY. What I was trying to elucidate for the Senator from New Hampshire when the gavel rapped and disturbed the continuity of my thought was that if a nation sees fit to take advantage of the technical violation of what used to be international law to declare war against us or any other nation similarly situated, it could have done so already on the basis of what we have already done in aid of England or Greece or China. Is not that true?

MR. TOBEY. I cannot say that is true. Everything is relative in this world, as Mr. Einstein says. Let me ask the Senator is he defending convoys?

MR. BARKLEY. Oh, no; the Senator knows that I am not.

MR. TOBEY. I am asking the Senator in good faith.

Mr. Barkley. And I am answering the Senator in good faith; if we have violated international law in such a way as could result in a declaration of war against us by Germany, we have already done that, and the convoying of ships would be only an incident.

Mr. Tobey. As I said a moment ago, the matter of convoys is the preeminent danger, in my judgment.

Mr. Barkley. It may be so.

Mr. Tobey. And the President felt so when he made the statement to which I referred, and Frank Knox also said so.

Mr. Barkley. If Germany wants an excuse to declare war against us, she has already had it, and we know from her history with other nations that if it was to her interest she would have done it without any excuse. . . .

Mr. Tobey. Does not the Senator feel that the matter of convoys presents a greater danger of involving us in war than anything else?

Mr. Barkley. It may be; I am not disputing that; but what I am trying to ascertain is whether the Senator from New Hampshire thinks that Germany would wait if Germany saw it was to her interest to declare war, or whether Hitler would wait, for I do not really like to associate Hitler with Germany, because I have great respect for the German people; I have none for Hitler, and I hope the time will come when they will themselves recognize the difference between the German people and Hitler.

Mr. Tobey. Let me say to the Senator that in that respect I agree with him 100 percent, but let me say further with reference to our colloquy here that there is always a straw that breaks the camel's back, and that straw, in my judgment, will be when, as, and if we send convoys to transport goods to belligerent nations.

Mr. Barkley. That will depend upon events that we cannot now foresee.

Mr. Tobey. Does not the Senator feel so, too?

Mr. Barkley. I will express my views upon that subject when the occasion has arisen.

Mr. Tobey. In the words of the advertisement, "If eventually, why not now?"

Mr. Barkley. I do not think it is possible for anybody today, even including the wise Senator from New Hampshire, to foresee conditions that may exist.

Mr. Tobey. Of course, the Senator is a past master of sarcasm that has no place in this Chamber, in my judgment. So I will proceed, if you please.

Mr. Barkley. The Senator has my permission to proceed, but did the Senator suggest that I was a psychiatrist?

Mr. Tobey. No; and neither did I say that the Senator need[s] a psychiatrist.

Mr. Barkley. I am willing to acquit the Senator from New Hampshire of any such need.

Mr. Tobey. I said the Senator indulged in sarcasm and possibly that that might be out of place at this time.

Mr. Smith. Mr. President, will the Senator allow me to interrupt him?

Mr. Tobey. I am glad to yield to the Senator from South Carolina.

Mr. Smith. With reference to the point made by the Senator from Kentucky that these acts in contravention of what was once international law have given the opportunity to certain nations to declare war against us, and they have not done so, let me say that when we send our vessels into the belligerent zone it is going to make us declare war against them.

Mr. Tobey. I quite agree with the Senator.

Mr. Smith. That is what I am trying to avoid. It is not a question of their declaring war against us but it is the doing of those things which will force the American people to declare war against certain nations.

Mr. Tobey. I quite agree with the Senator; and the Congress and the President having assured the American people they were going to do all they could to keep out of war, then it logically follows that the Congress should take every step to keep this Nation out of war and use all the powers vested in it by the Constitution to prohibit the use of our ships of peace for war purposes. To that end I am introducing a joint resolution, which I will take the liberty of reading. It is as follows:

"Joint resolution prohibiting the use of the armed forces of the United States and American vessels and aircraft for transporting, delivering, or convoying articles or materials to belligerent countries

"*Resolved, etc.*, That, except in time of war, hereafter no part of the land or naval forces of the United States, and no vessel documented, or aircraft registered or licensed, under the laws of the United States, shall be used, directly or indirectly, beyond the limits of the territorial waters of the United States and its Territories and possessions, to transport or deliver, or in connection with the transportation or delivery of, or for convoy purposes in connection with the transportation or delivery of, any articles or materials to or for the use of any foreign country with respect to which the President has issued a proclamation under section 1 of the Neutrality Act of 1939, or which is engaged in actual hostilities with one or more foreign countries, even though a state of war has not been declared or recognized in any such proclamation."

MR. VANDENBERG. Mr. President, may I ask the Senator a question?

MR. TOBEY. I am glad to yield.

MR. VANDENBERG. I call the Senator's attention to the language he has used in the joint resolution, "that except in time of war." Of course, this is a time of war. I assume that the Senator means a war in which we are associated?

MR. TOBEY. The Senator is correct. I may advise him that I raised that question with the drafting agency of the Senate that helped draft the resolution this morning. They said it was the proper language to use, but I questioned it then, and will be very glad to change it.

MR. VANDENBERG. It does not seen to me quite definite enough.

MR. TOBEY. I thank the Senator, and I will change it.

Mr. President, since both groups in the Senate protest that they are opposed to our entry into the war, and since it is undisputed that convoying will definitely take us into the war, this joint resolution provides a means of affording Senators a vehicle to translate their public statements into specific legislation to keep the country from taking this fatal step into war. It presents the issue directly and without equivocation. The people have an opportunity to see whether the administration and the Members of the Senate mean business when they say that they are opposed to our country entering the war.

The ACTING PRESIDENT pro tempore. Without objection, the joint resolution introduced by the Senator from New Hampshire will be received and appropriately referred.

"The joint resolution (S.J. Res. 62) prohibiting the use of the armed forces of the United States and American vessels and aircraft for transporting, delivering, or convoying articles or materials to belligerent countries, was read twice by its title and referred to the Committee on Foreign Relations."

During the first two weeks of April, the issue of convoying loomed large in the press and Congress, while President Roosevelt again parried questions on the subject. Charges and countercharges flew thick and fast.[8]

In a dispatch dated Washington, April 16, published in the *New York Daily News*, April 17, John O'Donnell stated: "Charges that battlecraft of the Navy and Coast Guard are now giving armed escort to munition-laden British merchantmen leaving Atlantic ports for the European battlefront exploded in the capital tonight." Mr. O'Donnell said also that "detailed information" respecting the nature of this convoying or escorting had already been placed in the hands of Senators and would become a matter of public record in a Senate debate on Friday, April 18.

Concerning this "information" and the controversy over it, Mr. O'Donnell made the following additional statements. Late at night, April 16, the Navy Department authorized the issuance of an announcement credited to Admiral Stark, Chief of Naval Operations, which denied that the Navy was convoying British ships on the high seas. Senators opposed to convoying, Mr. O'Donnell continued, were not inclined to quibble over words but insisted that, whatever the word for it, American naval vessels were in fact giving to British ships all assistance of information, patrol, and reconnaissance for hundreds of miles outward from American ports; these

---

8. President Roosevelt turned aside a question on convoying; Senator Taft and a group opposed to convoying held a conference on the question. *New York Times*, April 2. President Roosevelt reported in conference with Secretary Knox and Admiral Stark on convoying. Senator Tobey sought action on his resolution, claiming that Secretary Knox favored convoying; Senator Barkley denied the allegation that Secretary Knox had been correctly reported. *Ibid.*, April 3. Report that British and American officers had held a staff conference on joint convoys. *Ibid.*, April 4. Report respecting the British-American conference on convoys denied by President Roosevelt. *Ibid.*, April 5. President Roosevelt reported as saying, after a conference with Admiral Stark, that the law required the United States Navy to protect ships in nonbelligerent zones. *Ibid.*, April 16.

Senators maintained also that American naval vessels, flying the Stars and Stripes, were sailing between opposing enemies on the high seas and daring one side to shoot.

Allegations of this kind had already come to President Roosevelt's attention and, according to Mr. O'Donnell's report, he had answered them through his secretary, Stephen Early. The President, speaking through Mr. Early, said that he was required by law to protect American shipping against attack outside the declared combat zones; and the President was very much "amused" by the newspaper stories. Mr. Early added: "The President suggested that he might startle the world in a few days with a sensational announcement that if New York City were attacked by an enemy it will be defended."

The following day, April 17, the President, through his secretary, again took note of the convoy charges. Mr. Early declared that American naval vessels were operating far out in the Atlantic "on neutrality patrol" and flashing news of alien ships in uncoded messages that anyone could listen to. He stated that American naval vessels were carrying out their original instructions "to observe and report" and were "keeping war from our front doors." Referring evidently to Mr. O'Donnell's dispatch of the previous day, Mr. Early added: "The President of the United States, after reading a morning paper, said that he thought the author of the story had very closely woven the long-time and historic policy of the United States into a story which was a deliberate lie." [9]

The nature of the relation between the historic policy of the United States and the policy of convoying the merchant ships of a foreign belligerent in April, 1941, the President did not indicate. Nor did he explain its connection with the charge that American naval vessels were convoying or otherwise giving armed protection to British ships on the high seas. As reported the President's statement conveyed the idea that Mr. O'Donnell's story was false.

In a front-page dispatch from Washington, dated April 18,

9: *Ibid.*, April 18, 1941.

the *New York Times* gave an extended account of the convoy controversy. The report stated that a message on the question from Senator Tobey had been received by Secretary Early "and referred to the Navy Department"—the head of which, Secretary Knox, had two days before declined to discuss the issue and had passed it on to the President. In response to an inquiry from a reporter, the President said that he had not read Senator Tobey's message. From "some quarters" the author of the *Times* dispatch learned that the Navy Department had perfected plans for convoys and was ready to put them into effect whenever the President reached his decision.[10]

As Mr. O'Donnell had predicted in his story of April 16, Senator Tobey raised the question of convoys in the Senate on April 18:[11]

MR. TOBEY: Mr. President, . . . I have authoritative information that today in the White House there are thousands upon thousands of letters from the rank and file of the American people demanding to know what the President's policy is on convoys and where the administration stands on this issue.

Because of the word-twisting phrases of avoidance and indirection employed by the Executive and his spokesmen in the Congress, and because it is only a matter of plain honesty for the White House to give the people a frank statement in the matter, I addressed last night to the President a telegram which I now read to the Senate:

"THE PRESIDENT,

"*The White House, Washington, D.C.:*

"The people of America are aroused on the issue of convoys. The time has come for a frank, unequivocal, and complete statement from you on this vital matter.

"For several weeks word-twisting phrases of avoidance and indirection have been used to conceal rather than reveal the policy of the Chief Executive on the matter of convoys.

"Please review in your mind the events of the past several weeks. During the period when the administration was soliciting support of the people for the lease-lend bill the question of con-

10. *Ibid.*, April 19, 1941.
11. *Congressional Record*, April 18, 1941, pp. 3176 ff.

voys came up, and you stated that convoys mean shooting, and shooting means war, thereby implying to the people that you were opposed to convoys.

"Your Secretary of the Navy expressed his opposition to convoys in public testimony before the House and Senate committees at their hearings on the lease-lend bill, but added that he would change his mind in favor of convoys if you gave the word.

"During the first week of April reliable newspapers reported that Secretary Knox was in favor of convoys. When queried by the press as to whether he had, in fact, changed his mind, he replied, 'I have no comment.' Thus the American people were not enlightened.

"Then the Associated Press reported your statement to legislative leaders that suggestions for convoys were 'too absurd to talk about at this time.'

"The next step was a New York Times report of conferences between British and American naval representatives to determine how a joint convoy system could be operated. The Christian Science Monitor and other leading papers reported that detailed plans for the use of convoys had already been drawn up and submitted to you.

"During this time you, Members of the Senate and House, and I were receiving thousands of letters from the American people seeking definite assurance that the Navy was not going to convoy.

"Then the chairman of the House Military Affairs Committee sounded the note for convoys.

"Then you in a press conference admitted that the plan for convoys was under consideration.

"Then your spokesman, Representative Sol Bloom, chairman of the Foreign Affairs Committee, issued a public statement denying the right of the Congress to prohibit convoys and asserting that you and you alone had the unrestricted authority in the matter.

"Then your White House Secretary, Mr. Stephen Early, said that you were very much amused at newspaper reports that American ships would be convoying.

"During this time the American people in increasing numbers were continuing to write to Washington for information as to your policy on convoys.

"Then in your latest press conference you stated that on the convoy question more nonsense was being written and more statements made by people who did not know a hill of beans about it than you had ever seen before. You stated that you knew more about it than the writers and orators, but that you were not talking about it. Thus again the American people were left unenlightened because you did not care to discuss the subject.

"Yesterday reports persisted that the Navy is already being used to escort merchant vessels carrying war materials to belligerents. This morning your Secretary of the Navy said that there was not a syllable of truth in the report. Later this morning your White House Secretary, Mr. Stephen Early, branded the report as a deliberate lie, and still, regardless of these conflicting reports, you are silent in the face of the people's justified desire for direct, complete information from you.

"On different days of the past 3 weeks you have alternately advised the people that the suggestion of convoys was too absurd to talk about, that a plan for convoys was under consideration, and, finally, that you know more about the subject than anyone else but do not care to discuss it.

"Is not this issue of vital concern to the millions of American people? Have you not stated that convoys mean shooting and shooting means war for this country? Are not the people entitled to frank and honest dealing on this vital issue? Is this the kind of maneuvering that builds up the faith of the people in their Government?

"I recall to your memory your statement made to the American people over a Nationwide radio broadcast in which you said to them, 'You are, I believe, the most enlightened and the best informed people in all the world at this moment. You are subjected to no censorship of the news, and I want to add that your Government has no information which it has any thought of withholding from you.'

"In this hour when the men and women of the United States are asking for a statement from you, their national leader, in this hour when it is imperative in the national interest that the people be enlightened, and informed on the vital issue of convoys, which holds in the balance the question of our involvement in the war, I respectively urge that you give me at this time a frank, informative, and unequivocal statement of your position on the issue of convoys.

"I further ask for direct replies to the following questions:

"1. At any time during the past several weeks have United States aircraft or naval vessels or Coast Guard cutters been used to convoy, escort, or otherwise used in conjunction with merchant vessels carrying goods to belligerent countries?

"2. Are any such aircraft or vessels now being so employed?

"3. Is there contemplation of such use of such aircraft or vessels in the near future?

"4. What instructions have been given to the officers of any such aircraft or vessels with regard to action in the event that any of these merchant vessels carrying goods to belligerents are attacked?

"A few weeks ago on another matter of importance to the people you were asked for a statement of your position and you replied to me in a letter marked 'personal and confidential.' I emphasize at this time that this is an issue vital to the people of America on which they are entitled to information, and I therefore respectfully request that your reply be of such a nature that I may give the people the assurance which they are entitled to.

> "CHARLES W. TOBEY,
> "*United States Senator.*

"APRIL 17, 1941."

Mr. President, you will recall that more than 2 weeks ago I addressed a telegram to Secretary Knox, calling upon him to state frankly to the people his policy regarding convoys, in view of his reported change of heart. The day after I sent the telegram to him, he was interviewed by the press as to whether the reports were true, and he replied:

"I have no comment."

I advise the Senate at this time that to date Mr. Knox has given no reply to that telegram, and the people are still in ignorance on a matter for which they have a justified thirst for knowledge.

On March 31 I introduced a joint resolution (S.J. Res. 62) to prohibit convoys. Later on that day, a man who has close contacts with the Government came to my office and asked me if I would be surprised to learn that United States convoys were already being employed. I replied that I could not believe that the President would for a moment permit this practice, in view of his statement that:

"Convoys mean shooting and shooting means war."

This man left my office, and from then on I receive a series of persistent reports that convoys were being employed.

A few days ago Admiral Land, Chief of the Maritime Commission, came out in favor of convoys. Only yesterday, a Government investigator, well known to me, advised that he had information from within the Maritime Commission that convoys are being secretly employed at this time.

Why is it that the President has been unusually uninformative, in the face of the public demand for information, in the face of reports of reliable and reputable members of the press that plans had been drawn up for a joint enterprise of convoys between the United States and Great Britain; in the face of the report in Secretary Knox's own newspaper, the Chicago Daily News, made several weeks ago, that a plan for convoys was in the offing, although nobody, least of all the President, is saying so openly, in the face of the President's statement that he knows more about convoys than most others in the country, but that he was not going to tell the people about it; in the face of persistent reports that the Navy is already being used to convoy merchant vessels carrying war goods to belligerents?

Mr. President, these persistent rumors have come to me repeatedly in the past few days from various sources, and yesterday I received a letter, the contents of which I feel forced, as a public duty, to bring to the American people, and to the Congress. It comes from the Atlantic Seaboard, and reads as follows:

"APRIL 15.

"MY DEAR SENATOR TOBEY: I know you are against convoying by our Navy. Some information has come to me which has shocked me. I think I should pass it on to you.

"A young relative is in the Navy. He has been at sea on service. He was taken ill and put ashore in order to go to a hospital. I cannot tell you the name of the port. In fact I should not write this at all, but I think you should know.

"He tells me that the United States Navy has been convoying ships for about 1 month. His ship was one of the convoys. If I tell you the name of the ship or the lad's name I would perhaps get him in trouble. He has been worried and thinks someone should know.

"He says that they in the service know that the President's delay on the subject of convoying—the 'put off' as he expresses it, is because it is secretly going on.

"I trust you to use this information as you see fit, and only wish I could have given more details."

There, Mr. President, is a sincere, fair, frank statement through this relative, the testimony of a United States naval man, who is now in the hospital, and has been for a month on a ship which was part of an American convoy. Yet the President of the United States calls the suggestion that convoys are being used absurd, and laughs it off; and the American public, asking for information, are turned down cold. What price democracy? What has become of it in this country?

Because this naval man has had the courage and honesty to report a situation which holds in the balance the lives of millions of Americans, and because a revelation of the name of his relative who wrote this letter would, in all likelihood, lead to a revelation of this young man's identity, with the possibility of prejudice to his position in the Navy, I am keeping faith with the woman who wrote the letter by eliminating her name and address from the letter. If a committee of the Senate desires to hold hearings to investigate this matter, and will give assurances that this man's identity will not become known to his superiors, I shall be very glad, under such an arrangement, to turn the letter over to the committee or to make it available to them. . . .

Mr. President, it is a serious thing when the responsible officials of our Government, including our national leader, remain uninformative on this matter, which is so pregnant with danger to millions of American people. It is a danger to the American people when the convoy plans are drawn up in secret and there are hidden maneuverings to conceal from the people actions which are of such grave importance to the people. It is an incredible attitude for the President to laugh in the face of the people's justified request for information—for him to say, in the first instance, that convoys mean shooting and shooting means war, and in the second instance that the subject is too ridiculous for him to talk about—and in the third instance that he knows more about the subject than the rest of the people but does not choose to enlighten them.

Mr. President, press conferences are held, I believe, on Tuesday and Friday of each week. I hold in my hand a copy of the New York Herald Tribune, the issue of Thursday, April 17, and therein appears an article by Mark Sullivan, than whom there is no newspaper correspondent or writer more esteemed or trusted in the United States of America. Mark Sullivan, writing under his own name, made the feature of his article yesterday morning the press conference of the President held last Tuesday, and I shall read a portion of it. A question was asked the President which had nothing to do with the subject I have been discussing. Mark Sullivan's article then proceeds:

"That question was meant, by allegory, to bring up the subject of use of our naval power to protect British cargo ships carrying supplies from us, in short, the question of convoy. This is a subject which Mr. Roosevelt does not like. Whenever it was brought up in this press conference, as it was in several forms, Mr. Roosevelt bridled. On this subject he said there has been more nonsense, more printer's ink wasted, more oratory by people who don't know a hill of beans about it than on any other subject in modern times. Having thus designated comprehensive ignorance as the state of others who speak on the subject, Mr. Roosevelt reassured us by saying that he knows something about the subject. While we were reassured by this, we were not enlightened in detail, for Mr. Roosevelt said he did not care to discuss the subject.

"From this momentary interlude of irritation Mr. Roosevelt was brought back to his high enjoyment of the occasion by one who asked whether he was going to take a scheduled trip to Warm Springs, Ga."

I quote that testimony from Mark Sullivan, bringing us a word picture of the press conference held last Tuesday, at which Mr. Sullivan says when the question of convoys was brought up, the President bridled, and irritation was manifest in the President's voice and manner. Why? Is it remarkable that on a question of such supreme importance the people want to know what is going on today? Their lives, their property, the lifeblood of their children is at stake in this matter. The President has said that "convoys mean war." Then why should not the people ask about these things, and why should the leader of this country, chosen in the last election for a third term, bridle up and become irritable because people ask him what the administration has been doing about convoys? A classic statement which I have hidden in my heart is—

"The truth will bear the test."

So I say to the Senate of the United States, and to the President, and to the people of this country, "Let us have the truth wherever it leads us. Keep faith with the people who put you there, Mr.

President, and who put us here in the Senate." Let us measure up to their great trust in us, a trust that we shall keep faith with them and keep them out of war and in the paths of peace, if it is humanly possible, and that we will not resort secretly, if you please, to a policy of convoys, the use of which was confirmed by the eloquent testimony of this boy who is now in the hospital and who was on a warship which was engaged in convoy work a month, which the President says will mean war.

"Convoys mean shooting, and shooting means war. . . ."

In response to Mr. Tobey's charges, Senator Barkley made two significant statements of a definite nature: (1) that in none of his conferences with the President had there been any discussion of convoys or any intimation that the problem of convoying was being considered; and (2) that on the authority of Secretary Knox and Admiral Stark no convoys had been used or were being used. Senator Barkley's statements and his exchange of views with Senator Tobey follow: [12]

Mr. President, a few days ago when the matter of convoys was under discussion in the Senate, I was interrogated by the Senator from New Hampshire, although not on the floor but in my seat. I responded, and in that colloquy said that all I had ever heard about the convoy of American ships or British ships or any other ships carrying materials of war from any place to any other place was what I had read in the newspapers and what I had heard on the floor of the Senate. While I am not at liberty to reveal what takes place in private conferences between me and executive officers, including the President of the United States, I think I am at liberty to say that in no private conference in which I have participated has there been any discussion of convoys or any intimation that the problem of convoys was one that was being given consideration. What has happened in other conferences to which I was not a party I am not, of course, at liberty to say, for I do not know.

In view of the discussion and the publicity which have revolved around the subject during the last few days, I took the liberty this morning to confer with the Secretary of the Navy, Mr. Knox, and the Chief of Naval Operations, Admiral Stark, both of whom unequivocally and emphatically authorized me to say for them,

12. *Ibid.*, pp. 3183 ff.

if I thought it necessary to make any statement whatever about it on the floor of the Senate, that not a single ship, American or foreign, carrying any war materials from any place to any other place, had been convoyed or was being convoyed from any place to any other place, and that no orders had been received from anybody in authority to give such orders for convoying any ship of any kind from any place to any other place anywhere in the world.

I take it for granted that the statement of the Secretary of the Navy and the statement of the Chief of Naval Operations, Admiral Stark, in both of whom I believe the American people have implicit confidence, are entitled to credit by the American people and by Members of the Senate over the rumors and backstairs gossip of people whose names are not revealed, who, apparently, are willing to write letters, or of some unidentified officer somewhere in a department of the Government, whose name is not revealed, to the effect that they have a suspicion that the President of the United States, under his oath of office and in the exercise of his judgment in a great crisis in our history and in the world's history, is deliberately undertaking to deceive the American people and by connivance and under cover to bring about the convoying of ships, a suggestion which he publicly denounces as absolutely untrue.

I suppose there are persons in this country who do not give full faith and credit to the statement of any public officer, including the President of the United States; but I am confident that the American people, without regard to politics, Mr. President, believe that the President of the United States is earnestly seeking to preserve the interests of the United States, to carry out his obligation which he took on the 20th of last January to support the Constitution and to administer the Presidential office to the best of his ability, and I am firmly of the opinion that the American people do not believe, no matter from what source the insinuations may come, that Franklin D. Roosevelt is deliberately attempting to deceive them or that he is secretly carrying out some policy or purpose or course which he publicly and emphatically denies he is carrying out or that he issued any orders to anybody else to carry out.

In all frankness and with the utmost kindness, for I have for the Senator from New Hampshire the utmost personal affection and kindliest feelings and I know how earnest and intense he is in advocating anything in which he believes or which he discusses, I do not believe any man in a responsible position, here or elsewhere, renders the American people any service by trying to create widespread suspicion that the President of the United States is not acting in good faith in all that he does or says upon this delicate subject. . . .

Mr. Tobey. Mr. President, let me say to the distinguished majority leader—and I heartily reciprocate, as he knows, the feelings of good will he has expressed toward me—that it is about time those in authority in this country at the head of the Navy, either the bureaucratic head or the actual head, or the man in the White House spoke and enlightened the people on this burning issue of the hour.

I have not created suspicion or cast suspicion. The suspicion abroad in the land was generated from the inner circles of the administration of the United States Government when, if you please, the President called the suggestion of convoys absurd; when a few days later he said, "We are considering convoys"; when a youth from New England writes, "I am on a convoy ship, and have been on it for a month."

Suspicion! If anyone with any perspicacity or understanding is not suspicious under these circumstances, he ought to go to a school for feeble-minded, in my judgment. There is ground for suspicion and incredulity all the way down through; and let me ask the Senator a question on this matter of convoys.

Mr. Barkley. That is what I thought the Senator rose to do. . . .

Mr. Tobey. Let me ask the Senator one other question. Does not the Senator from Kentucky believe that the American people should have first-hand information and reassurance from the Executive and from the Secretary of the Navy and from Admiral Stark that convoys are not either being used or being considered? Does he not believe that?

Mr. Barkley. I have stated to the Senator from New Hampshire, and, if my words get into the press, to the country, that the Secretary of the Navy and Admiral Stark, the Chief of Naval Operations, have stated unequivocally and emphatically that convoys are not being used and have not been used in a single instance. The President of the United States has stated in the press, and it has gone all over the country, that statements to the contrary are absolutely untrue. What further can any of these gentlemen do to enlighten the American people?

Mr. Tobey. I will say to the majority leader that it is unfortunate that it takes a campaign over the radio and public addresses in the Senate to smoke out some of the persons in authority to tell the American people about these things.

Mr. Barkley. There was nothing to smoke out except the bugaboo the Senator himself has raised over the radio and elsewhere.

Mr. Tobey. The Senator from New Hampshire did succeed in getting the Secretary of the Navy on record, and also Admiral Stark, the first time that was done.

Mr. Barkley. The Secretary of the Navy has stated repeatedly—

Mr. Tobey. What has he stated?

Mr. Barkley. Practically what I have stated here today.

Mr. Tobey. I will tell the Senator what he has repeatedly stated—that he is against convoys, because convoys mean war.

Mr. Barkley. All right. The Senator has quoted that statement time after time.

Mr. Tobey. Yes; and I shall continue to do so.

Mr. Barkley. I have not the slightest doubt about it. [Laughter.]

Mr. Tobey. Now, let me ask the Senator another question. Does he agree with me that, if American ships are sunk, it means war?

Mr. Barkley. The Senator and I discussed that question 2 or 3 weeks ago.

Mr. Tobey. I ask the Senator the question again.

Mr. Barkley. I will stand upon the statement I then made. Whether convoys mean war or do not mean war, nobody now can prophesy.

Mr. Tobey. Does the Senator believe they do?

Mr. Barkley. I do not know whether they do or not. I do not believe they necessarily do. Nobody can prophesy what the future will bring forth; and for that very reason I think it is unfair to the American people to conjure up imaginary situations which do not exist and never have existed.

Mr. Tobey. May I enlighten the Senator by reading to him the words of three patriots of the Congress—and I use that word advisedly?

Mr. Barkley. Did the Senator say "patriots" or "patriarchs"? [Laughter.]

Mr. Tobey. Patriots. They are synonymous in this case.

I now read the words of the Senator from New York [Mr. Wagner]:

"There is only one realistic course for America to follow if it wants to avoid the causes of war and at the same time maintain its dignity and self-respect. This course is for the American Congress absolutely to prohibit American ships from carrying American passengers or American goods of any kind to any belligerent nation, or to proceed through any combat areas."

Those are the words of the distinguished senior Senator from New York.

What did Representative Sol Bloom, of New York, say on the same subject?

"Where a part of the world has gone mad, where laws and rights are trampled upon, it is folly for the United States to expect its ships and citizens to be safe in exercising their rights. They will not be safe. They will be slaughtered. The United States would go to war as a consequence, and in that war thousands of other lives would be sacrificed."

Now listen to what the Senator sitting behind the majority leader, the distinguished James F. Byrnes, of North Carolina, said about the danger of convoys.

Mr. Barkley. South Carolina, if the Senator please.

Mr. Tobey. South Carolina; I beg the Senator's pardon.

Mr. Byrnes. Mr. President, it is the State south of North Carolina.

Mr. Tobey. I realize that. I also remember what the Governor of North Carolina said to the Governor of South Carolina. [Laughter.]

The Senator from South Carolina is speaking:

"Under the administration proposal we sacrifice our right to sail the seas. By the cash requirement we sacrifice the right even to send American property on the ships of other nations into the zone of war. By this sacrifice we remove the cause of our entering the World War and the cause most likely to result in our entering another war."

And President Roosevelt gave us the following solemn assurance:

"This Government clearly and definitely will insist that American citizens and American ships keep away from the immediate perils of the actual zones of conflict."

I ask the majority leader, How can we convoy without entering the war zones?

Mr. Barkley. Mr. President, nothing has been done by the American Government since the war was declared in 1939, or since the passage of the lend-lease bill which is inconsistent with what the Senator from New Hampshire has read from the speech of the Senator from South Carolina [Mr. Byrnes].

Mr. Tobey. I now call the attention of the majority leader to his own words. I know he likes to hear them.

Mr. Barkley. That is a good speech, too. If the Senator from New Hampshire would quote from me oftener, he would make better speeches than he does. [Laughter.]

Mr. Tobey. I thank the Senator. In other words, in the opinion of the majority leader, the oracle has spoken, "thus saith the Lord," when he speaks. [Laughter.]

Mr. Barkley. My opinion of myself is almost as good as the Senator's opinion of himself, although not quite. [Laughter.]

Mr. Tobey. I shake hands with the Senator on that statement, sir. I now read his own words to him:

"If we had intended to include the Navy in the Neutrality Act, we certainly would have said so, and would not have limited the interpretation of the words 'American vessel' by the provision for American registry—"

And so on.

Mr. Barkley. All right. I said that.

Mr. President, that is all I have to say on the subject of convoys. The Senator from New Hampshire has made this dissertation on numerous occasions here in the Senate and over the radio, and I presume he will do so again in the future; so it is not necessary to indulge in a running debate with him now on the subject; but I did feel that the American people and the Senate were entitled to the emphatic statements of the Secretary of the Navy and the Chief of Naval Operations with respect to this entire situation. . . .

While the controversy over convoying, accompanied by charges, denials, and no little equivocation, was in progress, the issue had been obscured, if not complicated, by President Roosevelt's announcement on April 10, that on the previous day an agreement had been signed with the Danish Minister in Washington which included "Greenland in our sphere of coöperative hemispheric defense." This action necessarily involved naval protection of American forces in Greenland and shipping to and from that occupied territory, but it was accompanied by no official statement respecting the actual measures of patrol to be employed.

About two weeks after the occupation of Greenland the Administration began to prepare the country for the use of American armed forces in assuring the delivery of lend-lease materials to the beneficiaries. In an address on April 24, 1941, Secretary Knox, without mentioning convoys by name, declared: "We cannot allow our goods to be sunk in the Atlantic—we shall be beaten if they do [are]. We must make our promise good to give aid to Britain. We must see the job through. All of this is needed for our own safety and our future security. This is our fight." [13] On the same day, Secretary Hull said as much in other words in a public address before the American Society of International Law. The declared policy of Congress and the President, he asserted, "means in practical application that such aid [to Great Britain and other countries] must reach its destination in the shortest of time and in maximum quantity. So ways must be found to do this." [14]

The following day, April 25, 1941, President Roosevelt, at a press conference, referred to the addresses of Secretary Knox and Secretary Hull on expediting the delivery of materials to the beneficiaries of the Lend-Lease Act. He denied that the Government was considering naval escorts for convoys and stated that warships and airplanes were engaging in "patrol" work. For the instruction of the reporters he explained the difference between convoy and patrol. To emphasize his dis-

13. *New York Times*, April 25, 1941. This, of course, meant convoying which Mr. Knox had recently called "an act of war." See above, p. 31.
14. *Ibid.*

tinction, he said that there was the same difference between the two operations as between a cow and a horse and then added that calling a cow a horse, while all right with him, did not make it a horse.[15] The *New York Times* report of the President's press conference on convoys and patrols follows:

Washington, April 25, 1941: At his press conference on April 25 Roosevelt expressed the following views on the subject of convoys:

1. Secretaries Hull and Knox spoke for a great many American people and for the President, as well as for themselves, when they said in speeches yesterday that ways must be quickly found to send the fullest possible aid to nations bearing the brunt of the Axis attack, and that the American people have irrevocably committed themselves to see that a victory of the aggressor nations should be prevented.

2. The Pan-American neutrality patrol was operating to protect the Western Hemisphere and advise shipping of danger in the same way that it had operated for a year and a half. Because the danger to the Western Hemisphere was growing greater, the patrol was operating farther at sea and would operate still farther as need to do so developed.

The patrol, made up of warships and planes, will go as far in the waters of the seven seas as may be necessary for the protection of this hemisphere. There never has been a 300 mile "safety" belt around the Americas as reported, it was insisted.

3. This was a patrol, however, and not a convoy.[16] A convoy meant escorting merchant ships traveling in a group and protecting the ships from attack by fighting off an assailant. A patrol is a reconnaissance in certain areas to detect any aggressor ships which might be coming to the Western Hemisphere. It was indicated that ships could avoid areas reported to be dangerous. *The patrol*

15. Patrol is a military term. As a verb it means to send out troops in advance of the main body to reconnoiter the country, to go the rounds, and to gain information of the presence and movements of the enemy. To convoy is to accompany, escort, or guide. It is especially applied to ships of war accompanying merchant vessels for the purpose of protecting them against enemy forces.

16. As a matter of fact, the United States Navy was then and had been for some time secretly engaged in coöperating with the British in maintaining "escorts" to keep "convoys" moving in the Atlantic. CJC, Part 16, pp. 2162 f. See below, Chap. XIV.

would report the presence of any aggressor to the President, and he would decide what to do.

4. This government has no idea at this time of escorting convoys. There was no discussion of whether this action would be undertaken later.

Mr. Roosevelt recalled that while wagon trains going westward in pioneer days had armed guards, they also had scouts. It was sensible to keep the trains more than two miles from where the Indians were, he added. The clear implication was that the neutrality patrol would do the same for ships crossing the Atlantic and operating elsewhere.

Whether this meant that Mr. Roosevelt thought the convoy system ineffective and that he was prepared to supply the British with an information service could not be ascertained.

Aides have privately maintained, however, that the President was reluctant to provide naval escorts for shipping unless public demand for such action was overwhelming.[17] It was regarded in some quarters as significant that he coupled his remarks on convoys with a denunciation of appeasers and defeatists.

He remarked that a minority of Americans said out of one side of their mouths that they did not want dictatorships and out of the other that the dictatorships were bound to win the war. This was un-American and opposed to the views of most of the people, the President declared. He was willing to fight for democratic processes, and so were a great majority of Americans. . . .

After warning reporters to be careful in interpreting the speeches of Secretaries Hull and Knox, the President gave the following explanation of the patrol and convoy situation:

In September, 1939, the whole question of hemispheric defense came up. This was because of conditions at the outbreak of the war—the complete failure to adhere to international law and the surprise invasion followed by other attacks. At that time this and other nations of the Western Hemisphere started a patrol of the seas on all sides of the Americas. Some geographers said it extended 300 miles off the shores, but the President asked, off what shores?

17. The Committee to Defend America by Aiding the Allies, which worked in close touch with the President and his Administration in creating "public demand" was already campaigning for convoys. Johnson, *The Battle against Isolation,* pp. 210 ff.

As a matter of fact the American Navy and vessels of other American nations patrolled up to reasonable limit, whatever that was. A lot of careless people called it 100 miles, but off the eastern shore of Maryland, for instance, the patrol always had extended 1,000 miles at sea.

The patrol was extended from time to time at different places and pulled in at others, depending upon day-by-day conditions. *This had continued for a year and a half.* From time to time the patrol has been extended and it will be extended farther as the protection of this hemisphere requires.

But these were patrolling operations, not convoying. There is the same difference between the two operations as between a cow and a horse. If one looks at a cow and calls it a horse that is all right with the President, but that does not make a cow a horse. The President does not think they are the same.

After defining in sea terms, as well, the difference between patrols and convoys, the President said that, by the rule of common sense, back in 1939 the area patrolled in the Atlantic was nearer to shore because there did not seem to be as much danger of attack as now. Bermuda, Newfoundland, Greenland or Brazil appeared safe.

Events in the war show attack to be more possible now than in 1939. Moreover, the United States has valuable American property and lives to protect now that it did not have then. In Newfoundland, Bermuda, the Bahamas, Antigua and, in fact, all the West Indies where this country has acquired bases, as well as in British Guiana, the United States has property where it did not have it a year and a half ago.

The President remarked that he had talked today to a Senator from the West. In the old days, the Senator recalled, wagon trains had some guards around them, but they did not move across the plains unless they had reports from scouts. It was not safe to wait until the Indians got two miles away. It was advisable to ascertain whether the Indians were 200 miles away.

It was at this point that Mr. Roosevelt denied the government was considering naval escorts for convoys.

"Has any better system been devised?" a reporter asked.

The reporter was told to read Bairnsfather, the cartoonist, creator of the World War's *Old Bill*, who sought "a better 'ole!"

What, the President was asked, was the relation of all this to British aid? That, said Mr. Roosevelt, was a new one.

The President thought reports that 40 per cent of American supplies going to Britain were being sunk was far too high. He did not, however, say how many supply ships were being sunk, or what percentages were involved.[18]

In distinguishing between convoys and patrols and ruling out "at this time" the use of convoys, the President at his conference on April 25, 1941, appeared to be adhering to the policy which he had announced on March 5, 1941, namely, he would not operate the Lend-Lease Act as "a war policy but the contrary." [19] American patrols would detect aggressor ships "coming to the Western Hemisphere"; they would report "the presence of any aggressor to the President, and he would decide what to do." The nature of the decisions he might make after receiving such reports was left unsettled but there was no indication that he then contemplated the ordering of American patrols to fire at sight on aggressor ships.[20]

During the weeks that immediately followed President Roosevelt's exposition of patrolling, as distinguished from convoying, on April 25, Washington reverberated with charges that, in spite of his assurances, the American Navy was convoying British ships, and with counterassertions that, at all events, convoying is likely to be, or must be, the next step, no matter what had been declared in the Lend-Lease Act or by

18. *New York Times*, April 26, 1941, pp. 1, 4. (Italics supplied.)

19. See above, p. 22.

20. Descending for a moment from the high realm of appearances, it is appropriate to note here briefly the actual plan which had been promulgated April 21, 1941, "at the direction of the President" and which had gone into effect on April 24, 1941—the day before he made his public statement on patrols. This plan, disclosed at the Pearl Harbor hearings more than four years later, ordered the American Navy to trail naval vessels and aircraft of the belligerent powers, other than the powers which had sovereignty over territory in the Western Hemisphere, and to "broadcast [not report to the President] in plain language their movements at four-hour intervals, or oftener if necessary," and to "prevent interference with United States flag shipping," without intervening in armed engagements of belligerents. The plan also stated: *"The execution of this plan shall give the appearance of routine naval exercises* where the departure of units from ports are being made." CJC, Part 5, p. 2293. (Italics supplied.) See Chap. XIV below, "Secret War Decisions and Plans."

its Democratic sponsors of the act in Congress while the measure was pending. Indeed, on April 25, Representative Clare Hoffman of Michigan referred to newspaper reports that convoying was already in progress and declared that experience forced him to go along with reporters rather than official spokesmen in matters of truthfulness. Mr. Hoffman said that he had not believed President Roosevelt when the President avowed the intention of keeping the country out of war, "but millions of American citizens ignored his previous record and took him at his word." [21] From day to day, such allegations flew to and fro in the Capital.

April 29, Senator Tobey quoted passages from the *Washington Times-Herald* asserting that the Administration was putting heavy pressure on the Foreign Relations Committee of the Senate for the purpose of smothering the resolution against convoying which was in the hands of the committee, and that the chairman of the committee, Senator George, was "strictly on the spot." The newspaper report cited by Senator Tobey called attention to the fact that Senator George had been against convoying during the discussions of the Lend-Lease Bill, and quoted Senator George as having said at that time: "I insisted at the White House that it be made clear that we are not undertaking to convoy shipments to Britain." [22]

April 30. The Senate Committee on Foreign Relations killed the anticonvoy resolution by a vote of ten to thirteen.

May 6. Secretary Stimson made a radio broadcast urging the adoption of measures to insure the delivery of supplies to Great Britain and saying that the Lend-Lease Act was not enough. While careful in his use of words, Mr. Stimson implied that convoying must be undertaken systematically. (Report of broadcast in *New York Times*, May 7, 1941.)

May 7. Representative D. E. Satterfield of Virginia declared himself in favor of convoying. (*Congressional Record*, May 7, 1941.) Other Democratic members of Congress soon followed

21. *Congressional Record*, April 25, 1941.
22. *Ibid.*, April 29, 1941.

this example and made similar declarations of sentiments with regard to the subject.

May 9. Representative R. O. Woodruff charged Secretary Stimson with openly advocating the use of American naval vessels to convoy supplies to Great Britain. Mr. Woodruff stated that President Roosevelt's secretary, Mr. Early, had been asked by reporters whether the President had approved Mr. Stimson's address in advance and that Mr. Early had replied: "They might properly and safely assume Mr. Stimson had talked the speech over with the President in advance." (*Congressional Record*, May 9, 1941.)

May 15. Senator Tobey discussed in the Senate reports then in circulation to the effect that President Roosevelt had resolved to deliver a "sensational" speech openly advocating convoys but had at the last moment shrunk from taking the risk in view of popular hostility to war. Senator Barkley insisted that Senator Tobey had no right to make such claims. (*Congressional Record*, May 14, 15, 1941.)

May 26. Senator Harry Truman inserted in the *Congressional Record* a vigorous and outspoken address by Senator Joseph Guffey in favor of convoying even though war might result.

If in fact, at this time, President Roosevelt contemplated announcing in a public address the use of American naval vessels to convoy merchant ships to Great Britain, he refrained from the adventure. When, on May 27, he made a national broadcast relative to his proclamation of an unlimited national emergency, President Roosevelt gave a special explanation of the troublesome word "attack" [23] and referred to the extension of the American "patrol" in the Atlantic, as if still clinging to the distinction which he had drawn at his press conference, April 25. He informed the country that the delivery of supplies to Great Britain "is imperative. . . . It will be done," leaving undescribed the exact methods he intended to employ, or was employing. With regard to "attack" and "patrol" the President declared:

23. See above, Chap. I, and below, Chap. V.

I have said on many occasions that the United States is mustering its men and its resources only for the purpose of defense—only to repel attack. I repeat that statement now. But we must be realistic when we use the word "attack"; we have to relate it to the lightning speed of modern warfare.

Anyone with an atlas and a reasonable knowledge of the sudden striking force of modern war, knows that it is stupid to wait until a probable enemy has gained a foothold from which to attack. Old-fashioned common sense calls for the use of a strategy which will prevent such an enemy from gaining a foothold in the first place.

We have, accordingly, extended our patrol in north and south Atlantic waters. We are steadily adding more and more ships and planes to that patrol. It is well known that the strength of the Atlantic Fleet has been greatly increased during the past year, and is constantly being built up.

These ships and planes warn of the presence of attacking raiders, on the sea, under the sea, and above the sea. The danger from these raiders is greatly lessened if their location is definitely known. We are thus being forewarned; and we shall be on our guard against efforts to establish Nazi bases closer to our Hemisphere.[24]

In respect of patrolling, with its probability of warlike "incidents," these lines from the President's address of May 27 were sensational. The area of "defense" was widened indefinitely and the word "attack" defined to include actions other than assaults on American territory, possessions, or ships. But, as far as public information was concerned, nothing more than patrolling was in process: "We have, accordingly, extended our patrol in north and south Atlantic waters. We are steadily adding more and more ships and planes to that patrol."[25]

Many implications could be read into the President's announcement of May 27, notwithstanding his restriction of actions to patrolling and reporting, and watchful observers discovered in the address signs of an intention to proceed rapidly

24. Thirteen days earlier, May 14, 1941, Admiral Stark issued a memorandum to the commandants of fifteen naval districts in which he stated: "Plans and machinery for convoy are pretty well in hand." See below, Chap. XIV, "Secret War Decisions and Plans."

25. Funk, *Roosevelt's Foreign Policy, 1933–1941*, pp. 399 ff.

with operations likely to result in hostilities. For example, Senator Robert A. Taft, in a broadcast the following evening, reviewed the campaign pledges of 1940 and charged President Roosevelt with threatening to take warlike, aggressive action at his own discretion in defiance of Congress and the Constitution. Senator Taft said:

There is only one way in which this question ought to be determined under a democratic form of government. The Constitution provides that only Congress can declare war, and rightly so, because the Members of Congress are the most direct representatives of the people whose vital interest is at stake; rightly so, because no nation should go to war unless a majority of the people approve that action. The President has no right to declare war whether a national emergency exists or not. It follows inevitably that he has no right to engage deliberately in military or naval action equivalent to war except when the country is attacked.

There is another reason why this great issue today must be submitted to the people. Less than 7 months ago the President gave his pledge, "We will not send our Army, naval and air forces to fight in foreign lands outside of the Americas except in case of attack." The Republican candidate was equally emphatic. He said: "The American people do not want war. They have no idea whatever of joining in any conflict, whether on the Atlantic or the Pacific. They are determined to keep America at peace. In this determination I stand with them. I am for keeping out of war." We now face the fundamental question whether we shall abandon the position of both political parties in the last election. Surely that cannot be done without submitting the question directly to the representatives of the people.

The President's broadcast last night was a disappointment to millions of people because it still avoided the basic issue. It still indicated *an intention on his part to push further and further toward war without consulting the people.* In recent months there has been a tremendous growth of public sentiment against war and against convoys. *Because the President sensed that feeling, he carefully avoided any direct advocacy of convoys or of war. He talked of patrols and defense and freedom of the seas.* His arguments with regard to Hitler, if they are valid at all, are arguments for war, but he did not dare to advocate war itself because the people are opposed to it. *His speech contains vague threats of aggressive, warlike action to be undertaken in his sole discretion.* He hints that the term "defense" will be interpreted by him to mean the occupation of islands 3,000 miles from our eastern shore, within 400 miles from Africa, belonging to a neutral nation. In short, he is suggesting that he may, in dictator style, take warlike action without submitting to the people whose vital welfare is concerned the question whether or not we shall go to war. That is not democratic procedure.[26]

Whatever may have been known in official circles during June and July, 1941, about realities of patrolling, the American public knew little or nothing about them. Indeed, as late as July 30, 1941, the *New York Times* reported that the Secretary of the Navy, Frank Knox, had declared "there was no truth in the other newspaper stories that naval units were convoying or escorting ships at sea or dropping depth charges on German naval units." The release of the statement made by Secretary Knox could not fail to leave the impression on the public that convoying was not in effect.[27]

As to what was really going on at sea, according to the form of action described by President Roosevelt in his public statement of April 25, 1941, as "patrolling" and "reporting,"

---

26. *Congressional Record*, May 29, 1941 (Appendix). (Italics supplied.)

27. A secret defense plan issued by the Navy at the direction of the President on July 11, 1941, after the occupation of Iceland, was broad in scope, especially as applicable to shipping to and from Iceland, Greenland, and the northern portion of North America. Orders to the American Navy instructed it to "protect United States and Iceland shipping against hostile attack by *escorting, covering, and patrolling*, as required by circumstances, and by destroying hostile forces which *threaten such shipping*." Since the President, on April 25, 1941, had defined convoying as "escorting," the Navy was by this order of July 11, 1941, actually directed to engage in convoying and to wage war on hostile forces that threatened such shipping. Furthermore the Navy was ordered to "escort convoys of United States and Iceland flag shipping, including the shipping of any nationality which may join such convoys between United States ports and bases and Iceland." Other orders issued to the Navy on July 25, 1941, August 13, 1941, August 25, 1941, and September 3, 1941, broadened patrolling, escorting, and convoying to wider areas and authorized hostile acts against Axis craft. An order of August 28 extended similar operations to waters in the Southeastern Pacific. CJC, Part 5, pp. 2294 ff. (Italics supplied.) See below, Chap. XIV, "Secret War Decisions and Plans."

no definite information was issued to the public by the White House.

On June 9, 1941, the *Washington Post*, a journal that supported the President's foreign policy, carried on its first page a story by two prominent columnists, Alsop and Kintner, which charged the Administration with pursuing a strangely equivocal course in its war program and failing publicly to disclose episodes in the Atlantic patrol. They asserted that more than a month earlier there had been some kind of encounter between American and German warcraft and that slightly more recently an American destroyer had made an attack on what was believed to be a German submarine. The columnists also declared that "the President, all his important advisers, and the War and Navy Departments hope . . . that the patrol will produce an incident to serve as the pretext for really effective action by this country . . . the chances are strong that an incident will eventually occur. . . ." [28]

On the same day, June 9, 1941, Senator Burton K. Wheeler read into the *Congressional Record* passages from the Alsop and Kintner story and, as he read, commented on them:

Today, on the front page of the Washington Post, is another story by Alsop and Kintner:

"Nothing better illustrates the strangely equivocal position in which present war policy places this country than the undisclosed episodes of the Atlantic patrol. In one case, rather more than a month ago, an encounter between German and American warcraft at sea very nearly terminated in an attack by the Germans. In another, slightly more recent, an attack on what was believed to be a German submarine was actually made by an American destroyer.

"No details of the first episode are available, but the basic facts of the second are known."

Known to whom? Known to these columnists, who get inside

28. This was a circuitous way of alleging that the President was seeking to provoke the attack that would enable him to take advantage of the "escalator clause" of the Democratic platform and put the country into the war. See below, Chap. V.

information from the War Department and from the Navy Department—facts which are denied the Members of the United States Senate.

"The destroyer, the name of which cannot be ascertained, was picking up survivors from a British vessel sunk not far from the coast of Greenland. While the operation was in progress the destroyer's detecting device announced the approach of a submarine. The submarine could only have been German. It was virtually certain to use its torpedoes, as semidarkness concealed the nationality of the American ship. And the commander of the destroyer accordingly dropped three depth charges.

SHOOTING ALREADY

"Thus, although the President is waiting for the Germans to shoot first, the truth is that there has been shooting already." In other words, here on the front page of the Washington Post is an article by these men saying, "Now you have an excuse. Shooting has already started. You ought to go into the war, and you ought to start shooting in a shooting war."

"The truth may be denied—indeed, it is likely to be. The outcome of the episode is a mystery, since the light was too poor for the commander of the destroyer to make certain that the submarine really was nearby, or to guess whether the depth charges had taken effect. But official denials cannot alter either the episode's basic facts or its broad meaning."

What nonsense. One minute they say shooting has already taken place, and the next minute they say they do not know whether the submarine was a German submarine or not; they do not know how close it was; they do not know anything about it. . . .

The article goes on to say:

"The episode's meaning is pretty obvious. The Atlantic patrol in itself is not effective. Even now it has not been extended to cover the most dangerous waters, yet four British ships have recently been sunk in the part of the ocean it supposedly guards. The President, all his most important advisers, and the War and Navy Departments hope, however, that the patrol will produce an incident to serve as the pretext for really effective action by this country. The interest of the Germans is to avoid such an incident. It is perfectly possible that the submarine was in fact sunk, and that the Germans have suppressed all public complaint in order to keep public opinion here in its present lulled condition. Nevertheless, as the episode described above pretty clearly demonstrates the chances are strong that an incident will eventually occur. . . ."

If what Alsop and Kintner say about the President is not true, then they are doing the President of the United States a very great disservice. If what they say is true, then the American people should know it. Whether it is true or untrue I do not know, but it is inconceivable to me that a man who has been elected President of the United States for three consecutive terms, who has been given the greatest honor the American people could bestow upon him, would be anxious to take the country into war; I cannot believe he is praying for an incident which would make it possible for him to take us into war.[29]

At his weekly press conference, June 11, 1941, the Secretary of the Navy denounced the depth-bomb story, without denying it. The following account of the conference appeared in the *New York Times*, June 12, 1941:

Frank Knox, Secretary of the Navy, served notice on some forty newspaper correspondents who attended his weekly press conference today that he expects them to print only such news about Navy operations as his office considers proper.

He denounced a printed report that an American destroyer had depth-bombed away an approaching German submarine, but declined either to confirm or deny the report.

"You can get news of anything that is true and that ought to be printed," the Secretary said. . . .

Secretary Knox was then asked what had been done or would be done about publication on Monday morning in several newspapers of a syndicated story detailing reports of an alleged near-encounter between an American destroyer and a German submarine.

"I don't know anything about it," Mr. Knox replied. "I did not get any information about it. But I think it was a terrible thing to print."

"Is the story true?" the Secretary was asked.

"I am not discussing it. There is no comment," Mr. Knox said.

29. *Congressional Record*, 77th Congress, 1st Session, Vol. 87, Part 5, Senate, June 9, 1941, pp. 4861–4862.

A reporter remarked that the public records show that J. W. Alsop, Jr., co-author of the story, was commissioned as an officer in the Naval Reserve on June 2, one week before the story was printed.

"He is not in the Navy," Secretary Knox said. "He will not get a line of news that you don't get."

He went on to denounce what he called a growth of "backstairs-gossip" reporting by some newspapers.[30]

Taking up the Alsop and Kintner story again and referring to other newspaper accounts of convoying or patrolling, Senator Wheeler submitted to the Senate on June 30, 1941, the following resolution which was referred to the Senate Committee on Naval Affairs:

Whereas on June 2, 1941, Joseph W. Alsop was sworn in as a Naval Reserve Officer by the Secretary of Navy Frank Knox; and

Whereas the said Alsop, as coauthor of a syndicated newspaper column—on June 9, 1941, 1 week after he had taken the oath as a Naval Reserve officer—stated in that column [for statements, see above, p. 107]: . . .

Whereas on June 23, 1941, Drew Pearson and Robert S. Allen in their syndicated newspaper column charged

"A group of American naval vessels has just returned from its first experience at Atlantic patrol, or convoying, whatever it is called—they helped to get about 80 British merchantmen safely most of the way to the west coast of Africa. There the British took over.

"Three United States airplane carriers, six destroyers, and three cruisers accompanied the convoy across the Atlantic—but never within sight of the 80 British merchantmen.

"One airplane carrier steamed ahead of the merchantmen, another to the rear, another to the north. Each carrier was protected by two destroyers, zigzagging constantly. The carriers performed the most important part of the patrol, keeping their airplanes constantly scouring the sky.

"Once a plane sighted a German surface raider and radioed its position to British warships, which rushed up and sank her. The

30. *New York Times*, June 12, 1941.

battle took place so close to American vessels that they could hear the fighting, though they never saw the ships. United States radio operators picked up the distress message sent to Berlin by the Nazi vessel saying that she was sinking.

"On another occasion, an airplane carrier detector picked up the vibrations of a submarine, and signaled it to come to the surface. When there was no answer, United States destroyers immediately dropped depth charges. After that the detector picked up no more vibrations.

"When the patrol reached its meeting place with the British, near Cape Verde Islands off the African coast, it turned north, and shortly after this, the 12 United States naval vessels headed home"; and

Whereas on June 23, 1941, Gen. Hugh S. Johnson in his syndicated column stated:

"To an experienced eye there can be small doubt, after reading innocent but censored letters from young naval officers, that we have already sunk Nazi submarines. A submerged sub isn't so hot with the radio. A depth bomb leaves no trace. If this is an incorrect conjecture—and it can be no more than conjecture—there is little doubt that our Navy spots German subs and guides British ships to them.

"It seems to be quite generally believed that the seizure of great passenger liners and recent shifts of the Navy from the Pacific (not through the Panama Canal, but around Cape Horn) are preparatory to an attack on Dakar in west Africa, or other key Atlantic positions.

"What's the difference between that and outright war?" and

Whereas other reports circulate to the effect that some of our ships have sunk German ships; and that American sailors are in London servicing American planes; and:
Therefore be it

Resolved, That the Committee on Naval Affairs or any duly authorized subcommittee thereof is authorized and directed to make, and to report to the Senate the results of a thorough and complete investigation of the charges that American naval units are convoying or escorting ships or that American naval units have destroyed by shooting or by dropping depth bombs on German naval units; and be it further

Resolved, That the Committee on Naval Affairs, if it finds that our naval vessels are doing such acts as above described in violation of law that it ascertain at whose direction and upon what authority such acts were committed. . . .[31]

Two days later, July 2, 1941, Secretary Knox, who had previously been noncommittal on the subject, positively denied that American naval vessels had been engaged in encounters with German craft while on patrol missions, and declared untrue the assertion that the Navy was actually convoying vessels. The *New York Times* gave the following account of the press conference at which the Secretary's denial was made:

Secretary Knox denied categorically today that naval vessels had been engaged in encounters with German craft while carrying out patrol missions in the Atlantic Ocean.

On previous occasions the Secretary had replied to inquiries concerning such reports with the words, "No comment."

When reporters asked again today, in view of new reports of encounters recently as told in syndicated columns, the Secretary was positive in his reply.

"Can you tell us," a reporter asked, "whether any American vessel has been engaged in any encounter with a belligerent craft?"

"Most decidedly not," Secretary Knox replied.

He was equally emphatic in stating that the American Navy has lost no lives and has lost no property in carrying out its patrol functions.

"Then what is the basis," an inquirer asked, "for these stories of shooting?"

"There has been a leak somewhere," Mr. Knox said. "Some one has talked unwisely and incorrectly."

"How about the suggestion that the Navy actually is convoying vessels?"

"That is absolutely untrue," Mr. Knox replied.[32]

A momentous step in respect of patrolling was taken early in July, 1941, when American armed forces were landed in

31. *Congressional Record*, 77th Congress, 1st Session, Vol. 87, Part 5, Senate, June 30, 1941, p. 5700.
32. *New York Times*, July 3, 1941.

Iceland "in order to supplement, and eventually to replace, the British forces which have until now been stationed in Iceland in order to ensure the adequate defense of that country," as President Roosevelt explained it to Congress in his message of July 7, 1941, announcing the *fait accompli*. In his explanation, the President also expressed the view that he had authority to use the armed forces of the United States in about any way he deemed necessary to keep the sea lanes open for "the steady flow of munitions to Britain."

The process of reasoning by which the President arrived at this conclusion was definitely stated in his message to Congress.[33] The occupation of Iceland by Germany, he declared, would constitute "a serious threat in three dimensions":

The threat against Greenland and the northern portion of the North American continent, including the islands which lie off it.

The threat against *all shipping in the North Atlantic.*

The threat against the *steady flow* of munitions to Britain—*which is a matter of broad policy clearly approved by Congress.*[34]

It is, *therefore, imperative* that the approaches between the Americas and those strategic outposts, the safety of which this country regards as essential to its national security, and which it must *therefore* defend, shall remain *open and free from all hostile activity or threat thereof.*

As Commander-in-Chief I have *consequently* issued orders to the Navy that *all necessary steps be taken to insure the safety of communications in the approaches between Iceland and the United States, as well as on the seas between the United States and all other strategic outposts.*

This government will insure the adequate defense of Iceland with full recognition of the independence of Iceland as a sovereign state.

Many members of Congress were excited by the reports that a "shooting war" had begun. Republicans charged that the occupation of Iceland was an unlawful step toward an undeclared war and that hundreds of American workmen were

33. Funk, *op. cit.*, pp. 428 ff. (Italics supplied.)
34. See above, p. 9. By July 31, Admiral Stark had concluded that the Iceland situation "may produce an incident." See below, Chap. XIV.

constructing another naval base in northern Ireland. Far and wide, concern was expressed over President Roosevelt's declaration of July 7 that he had ordered the Navy to insure safety of communications in the approaches to Iceland and elsewhere, and restless members of the Senate Committee on Naval Affairs were at last moved to act. They voted to call Secretary Knox and Admiral Stark before them in an executive session. The chairman, Senator David Walsh, announced that he intended to ask Secretary Knox for clear answers to the reports that the Navy had already engaged in a "shooting war." [35]

Just what transpired at the secret session of the Senate Committee on Naval Affairs on July 11, 1941, was not made public. The following day the *New York Times* reported that Secretary Knox and Admiral Stark had denied that the American Navy had engaged in combat with German naval units while patrolling the North Atlantic; but the *Times* account also indicated some uncertainty as to whether the denial was categorical after all. Here is the exact language of the account:

Categorical denials of published reports that the American Navy had engaged in combat with German naval units in patrolling the North Atlantic were made by Secretary Knox and Admiral Harold R. Stark, Chief of Naval Operations, during three hours of secret questioning today by the Senate Naval Affairs Committee.

Some of the committee members said, however, that they could not conclude from the testimony of the two officials that there had been no "shooting" of any kind by our ships. Some of them understood Mr. Knox to confirm in effect that on one occasion an American destroyer had dropped a depth bomb when its detecting instruments indicated the nearness of a submarine as the destroyer was picking up survivors from a sunken British vessel in semi-darkness.

In the main, however, Mr. Knox and Admiral Stark repudiated all suggestions that the Navy had been engaged in aggressive activities against Nazi ships. . . .[36]

Rumors persisted to the effect that, despite the alleged denials of Secretary Knox and Admiral Stark, shooting of

35. *New York Times*, July 11, 1941.
36. *Ibid.*, July 12, 1941, p. 1.

some kind had occurred and was occurring in the North Atlantic. At last on July 29, 1941, the Senate Naval Affairs Committee released an extract from a statement made by Secretary
Knox at a secret hearing which purported to give an official
account of one alleged incident. This extract, including direct
and indirect quotations from the Secretary's testimony, appeared in the *New York Times* of July 30, 1941, in part, as
follows:

One United States destroyer, said Colonel Knox, operating off
Greenland heard the SOS of a steamer and proceeded to the location and picked up sixty of the survivors of the steamer. While
engaged in this act of mercy, the operator of the listening equipment reported to the captain that he thought he heard a submerged submarine.

The captain immediately turned toward the direction indicated
and dropped three depth charges. In doing so he very prudently
exercised the right of self-preservation, for had there been a submarine there his destroyer might have been sunk.

There was no other evidence that a submarine was there and it
is quite possible no submarine was there. The equipment echo
might have been received from a whale or a large fish, or a cold
current, instead of a submarine.

Aside from this one incident, which was disclosed by two members of the crew of the destroyer after they returned to Boston,
there was no truth, Secretary Knox said, in the other newspaper
stories that naval units were convoying or escorting ships at sea
or dropping depth charges on German naval units. . . .[37]

Thus as far as official appearances were concerned, the
month of July, 1941, closed with official assurances that "there
was no truth . . . in the other newspaper stories that naval
units were convoying or escorting ships at sea or dropping
depth charges on German naval units." It seemed then that
President Roosevelt's statement on April 25 to the effect that
there was patrolling and reporting, but no convoying or escorting, was still as valid as when he made it. Secretary
Knox had, indeed, conceded that an American destroyer had

37. *New York Times*, July 30, 1941. This was a false "appearance," for on July
11, the President had ordered the Navy to engage in convoying. See above, p. 106.

dropped three charges in response to indications from its listening equipment; yet he had added that this had been done in the interests of self-preservation and that "the equipment echo might have been received from a whale or large fish, or a cold current, instead of a submarine." [38]

According to the appearances of words and actions by the Roosevelt Administration in July, 1941, Greenland and Iceland had been occupied by American forces and the President had issued orders to the Navy to insure the safety of communications between the United States and "strategic outposts." These orders could be construed to mean that every kind of step was being taken, including convoying and shooting as well as the patrolling announced by the President on April 25, to keep the seas open to all the outposts which he deemed "strategic." But Secretary Knox declared "absolutely untrue" on July 2 the suggestion that the Navy was actually convoying vessels and, later in the month, he denied that naval units were convoying or escorting ships at sea.

American newspapers, however, by unearthing and publishing news, made the official appearances look dubious, if not deliberately deceptive. The insistence of the Senate Committee on Naval Affairs that the public and Congress had a right to know what was going on, to know whether President Roosevelt was clandestinely pushing "aggressive activities" against Nazi war vessels toward open hostilities and full-fledged war, brought out facts that had been suppressed or denied. Consequently, President Roosevelt, Secretary Knox, and Admiral Stark were embarrassed by "leaks," charges, and reports to the effect that they were making "complicated moves" which had all the grim reality of acts of aggression. Affairs had reached such a stage by the middle of June that Secretary Knox sought to impose a peacetime censorship on the newspapers—he served notice on them that he expected them "to print only such news about Navy operations as his office considers proper." What of President Roosevelt's prom-

38. For the further development of "patrolling" into a "shooting war," see below, Chap. V.

ise in March, 1941, that the policy under which the Lend-Lease Act would be operated would not be a war policy, but "the contrary"? [39] Was there, after all, as much difference as he had claimed in April between patrolling and convoying as between a cow and a horse? [40]

39. See above, p. 22.
40. *Ibid.*, p. 100. Writing on the state of American naval assistance to British merchant shipping, Edgar McInnis, British historian of the war, said that in June, 1941, "the United States was not ready to engage openly and admittedly in the work of convoying. But her patrols were sweeping half way across the Atlantic. . . ." *The War: Second Year* (Oxford Press, 1941), p. 217.

CHAPTER IV

The Atlantic Conference—Appearances

EARLY in August, 1941, alert journalists discovered that on the 3d of the month President Roosevelt had embarked on the warship *Potomac* for what was officially called a private cruise, and that the British Prime Minister, Winston Churchill, and Harry Hopkins, the President's "observer," had disappeared from London. Immediately it was suspected that an important conference was to be held somewhere in the Atlantic. But not until August 14 was the veil of secrecy lifted. On that day a statement was issued by the White House giving the American public an official report on the Atlantic meeting, which apparently covered the subjects discussed, the policies adopted, and the decisions reached. The first sentence of the document read: "The following statement signed [1] by the President of the United States and the Prime Minister of Great Britain is released for the information of the Press."

The official statement of August 14, given out in Washington and London, consisted of two parts: a report on the transactions of the conference and a joint declaration of general principles, soon to be known as the Atlantic Charter. In the first part it was disclosed that the President and the Prime Minister had met at sea; that they had been accompanied by officials of their two governments and by high-ranking officers of their respective armed forces; that the problem of the supply of munitions as provided by the Lend-Lease Act for the powers engaged in resisting aggression had been further examined; that Lord Beaverbrook, British Minister of Supply, would proceed to Washington to discuss additional details

---

1. For President Roosevelt's statement in 1944 that the Atlantic Charter had not been formally drawn up in a single document and duly "signed," see *New York Times*, December 20, 1944.

with appropriate officials of the United States Government; and that these conferences would also deal with the supply problems of the Soviet Union.

The first part of the official statement, relative to the trans-actions of the Atlantic meeting, also reported that the President and the Prime Minister had held several sessions. It stated: "They have considered the dangers to world civiliza-tion arising from the policies of military domination by con-quest, upon which the Hitlerite government of Germany and other governments associated therewith have embarked, and *have made clear the steps which their countries are respec-tively taking for their safety in the face of these dangers.*" (Italics supplied.)

Presumably by the words "made clear," the President and the Prime Minister meant that they had made clear to each other the steps which "their countries" were taking for their safety; for in no official communiqué did the President and the Prime Minister make clear to the public the steps which they had actually taken at the Atlantic Conference in respect of safety for the United States or Great Britain.

The second part of the official release on August 14 opened with the announcement that the President and Prime Minister "have agreed upon the following joint declaration: . . . be-ing met together, [they] deem it right to make known certain common principles in the national policies of their respective countries on which they base their hopes for a better future of the world."

Immediately following came their declaration of principles:

First, their countries seek no aggrandizement, territorial or other;

Second, they desire to see no territorial changes that do not accord with the freely expressed wishes of the peoples concerned;

Third, they respect the right of all peoples to choose the form of government under which they will live; and they wish to see sovereign rights and self-government restored to those who have been forcibly deprived of them;

Fourth, they will endeavor, with due respect for their existing obligations, to further the enjoyment by all states, great or small, victor or vanquished, of access, on equal terms, to the trade and to the raw materials of the world which are needed for their economic prosperity;

Fifth, they desire to bring about the fullest collaboration between all nations in the economic field with the object of securing, for all, improved labor standards, economic advancement, and social security;

Sixth, after the final destruction of the Nazi tyranny, they hope to see established a peace which will afford to all nations the means of dwelling in safety within their own boundaries, and which will afford assurance that all the men in all the lands may live out their lives in freedom from fear and want;

Seventh, such a peace should enable all men to traverse the high seas and oceans without hindrance;

Eighth, they believe that all of the nations of the world, for realistic as well as spiritual reasons, must come to the abandonment of the use of force. Since no future peace can be maintained if land, sea, or air armaments continue to be employed by nations which threaten, or may threaten, aggression outside of their frontiers, they believe, pending the establishment of a wider and permanent system of general security, that the disarmament of such nations is essential. They will likewise aid and encourage all other practicable measures which will lighten for peace-loving peoples the crushing burden of armaments.

(Signed) Franklin D. Roosevelt.
(Signed) Winston S. Churchill.

August 15, 1941, the White House released to the press copies of a joint message from President Roosevelt and Prime Minister Churchill to Josef Stalin offering to provide Russia with supplies in the war against Hitlerism and proposing a conference in Moscow on the apportionment of joint resources in this enterprise.[2]

The next day, August 16, when President Roosevelt greeted representatives of the press at Rockland, Maine, on his return from the Atlantic meeting, he was in excellent humor but rather uncommunicative. As if anticipating requests

2. Texts of releases in Funk, *Roosevelt's Foreign Policy, 1933–1941*, pp. 450 f.

for information more definite than that given in the White House releases, the President told the reporters that he and Mr. Churchill had spent "more than a day together" and had discussed the situation on every continent and in every section of every continent. A reporter called his attention to the fact that the eight peace aims set forth in the official statement of August 14 said nothing about how Nazi tyranny was to be destroyed. The President remarked that this was a narrow way to look at it; and added that the discussions were "primarily" an interchange of views on the present and the future. Had he and Mr. Churchill reached a complete understanding on all aspects of the war situation? The President said that he thought so.

Then came three questions which went to the roots of foreign policy and the heart of the business. "Are we any closer to entering the war?" While declining to permit a direct quotation, the President said that he should say no. How were the conferences with Mr. Churchill to be implemented? The President answered that there would be further exchanges of ideas. Would Russia be asked to subscribe to the eight points? The reply was that no one had suggested it until the reporter raised the issue.

The following passages are from the *New York Times* account of the Rockland press conference on August 16:

The President said that he had been with Mr. Churchill for more than a day—he would be no more specific than that—and that at one time or another they had discussed the situation on every continent. Every continent you ever heard of, he added facetiously. There wasn't a single section of a single continent that hadn't been discussed, he said.

He said the idea of the conference had been jointly that of Mr. Churchill and himself, that it had been talked about since February, but because of the Greek and Crete campaigns had been delayed for three months beyond the intended date.

The President was reminded by a reporter that the eight peace aims jointly announced on Thursday said nothing about how the "Nazi tyranny" was to be destroyed.

The President replied that this was a narrow way to look at it. The conferences, he said, were primarily an interchange of views on the present and future—a swapping of information that was eminently successful.

Mr. Roosevelt was asked whether it could be assumed that he and Mr. Churchill had reached a complete understanding with regard to all aspects of the war situation. He replied: Yes, he thought so.

Some one asked: "Are we any closer to entering the war?"

The President replied that he should say no. He declined, however, to permit direct quotation of this answer when a reporter asked whether it might be enclosed in quotation marks.

On how the Churchill conferences would be implemented, the President would only say that there would be further exchanges of ideas.

"Will Russia be asked to subscribe to the eight points?" the President was asked.

He replied that no one had suggested it until the reporter asked the question.

The President added, however, that the conferees had discussed fitting Russian needs into the existing production program.[3]

Two days later, August 18, President Roosevelt met congressional leaders in Washington and, it was said, gave them a detailed account of the Atlantic conferences with Mr. Churchill. If press reports of what he told them were comprehensive, he told them little. He did, however, "repeatedly" assure them that he had made no *new* commitments for the United States in his conversations with Mr. Churchill. Apparently he did not explain to the members of Congress what he meant by the word "new." Apart from his reassuring declaration as to commitments, the most significant feature of his report to congressional leaders was his statement that the chief dangers of early involvement in a "shooting war" lay in the Far East where the chances were even that Japan would start new aggressions.

In substance, the President's accounting to congressional

3. *New York Times*, August 17, 1941.

leaders, as described in a special dispatch to the *New York Times*, scarcely went beyond a denial of new commitments and a warning against dangers in the Far East. Such at least seemed to be the chief upshot as gathered by Turner Catledge, the author of the dispatch:

In a detailed report to Congressional leaders on his meeting at sea with Prime Minister Churchill, President Roosevelt today described Russia as the key to the immediate situation in Europe and raised the hope that the Soviet would hold out indefinitely against the Nazi military machine.

The President told the Capitol spokesmen who conferred with him at the White House to encourage their colleagues not to become alarmed at the early German progress on the Eastern Front.

Russian resistance had probably already precluded an attempt by Germany to invade Great Britain this year, he told them, expressing meanwhile, a British view, which he seemed to endorse, that a decisive German defeat would require an invasion of the Continent by Great Britain and her Allies. Apparently he could see nothing but a long war.

Mr. Roosevelt assured his visitors repeatedly that he had made no new commitments for the United States in his conversations with Mr. Churchill. He said all phases of the international situation had been explored, and that possibilities of action in view of likely developments had been discussed.

The chief danger of the early involvement of the United States in a "shooting war" as he saw it, lay in the situation in the Far East, where, he intimated, chances were about even that Japan would start new aggressions.

The President evidently convinced the conferees that Russia was a long way from being routed, despite the German advances of the last few days. Though he said the eventual and final defeat of Germany would undoubtedly require the invasion of the Continent of Europe by Britain and such allies as she had at the time, he left no impression that an attempt to take troops across the English Channel was being planned.[4]

The next day, August 19, at his first press conference in Washington after his return from the Atlantic meeting, Presi-

4. Dispatch by Turner Catledge, *ibid.*, August 19, 1941, pp. 1, 4.

dent Roosevelt seemed to be in a mood to tell the American people that they were already at war and that they must quickly realize the serious nature of the struggle they had on their hands. Yet he intimated that he did not intend to take the issue to Congress or the people; for he said that the "accurate reporting" of the Atlantic meeting "made it unnecessary for him to make a fireside chat explaining the event to the American people."

Extracts from the account in the *New York Times* of the August 19 press conference follow:

President Roosevelt emphasized today that it was imperative for the American people to realize they had a major struggle on their hands if the fight of the democracies against nazism was to be won. He said this fight would go through 1943 if necessary.

In his first press conference since his return to Washington after his meeting at sea with Prime Minister Winston Churchill, the President read a statement that Abraham Lincoln made to Mrs. Mary A. Livermore of Chicago in 1862, in which Lincoln was quoted as having said the people "have no idea that the war is to be carried on and put through by hard, tough fighting." There was a parallel in the situation today, Mr. Roosevelt emphasized.

The President said flatly, in reply to questions, that he thought many people in the United States had not awakened to the danger to this country and that people all over the world had not realized the world danger.

The primary result of his meeting with the British Prime Minister, the Chief Executive emphasized, was that it had brought a better meeting of minds on the fight the democracies are putting up against nazism.

It seemed clear to his auditors that Mr. Roosevelt had come back to Washington with a grim determination that the United States should play its part effectively in assuring the overthrow of Hitlerism, with all it represents, and that he was chiefly concerned now with the state of American public opinion. Asked whether he had any comment on the fact that the House of Representatives had agreed to extend the period of service of selectees for eighteen months by only one vote, the President replied that this illustrated what he meant.

The President read the following excerpt of President Lincoln's conversation with Mrs. Livermore as reported in "Abraham Lincoln: the War Years," by Carl Sandburg. The passage from the book read as follows:

" 'I have no word of encouragement to give,' was the slow, blunt reply. 'The military situation is far from bright; and the country knows it as well as I do.' . . .

"The President went on: 'The fact is the people have not yet made up their minds that we are at war with the South. They have not buckled down to the determination to fight this war through; for they have got the idea into their heads that we are going to get out of this fix somehow by strategy. That's the word—strategy! General McClellan thinks he is going to whip the rebels by strategy and the Army has got the same notion. They have no idea that the war is to be carried on and put through by hard, tough fighting, that it will hurt somebody; and no headway is going to be made while this delusion lasts.' "

It was a rather interesting parallel, President Roosevelt remarked, referring specifically to Lincoln's belief that this country had not awakened to the fact we had a war, although it had been going on a whole year.

A reporter asked whether the Chief Executive could disclose whether Mr. Churchill thought that Great Britain could win the war without American help. The President—who said last week after coming ashore in Maine following his Atlantic conferences that this country was no closer to war than before—said that he did not think this was the kind of question that should be answered since it was "headliny" and without substance.

The President prefaced these assertions by paying tribute to the manner in which the American press had handled rumors of his meeting with Mr. Churchill before the official announcement had been made, and after danger to Mr. Churchill and himself had passed, and the President said that the subsequent accurate reporting had made it unnecessary for him to make a fireside chat explaining the event to the American people. There were one or two highly imaginary accounts of the meetings from London, Mr. Roosevelt asserted, but he thought they were recognized in this country as imaginary.

The President read a letter from a friend, whom he declined to name, saying that the important fact was that Mr. Roosevelt and Mr. Churchill had met and that talk of press releases and like details constituted "trivia."

A reporter asked who would determine what was trivia, and the Chief Executive replied to his auditors: "You fellows." [5]

The methods followed by President Roosevelt in reporting to the country and congressional leaders on the actions taken at the Atlantic Conference, coupled with the slight information he saw fit to impart, aroused dissatisfaction among interventionists no less than among opponents of involvement in the armed conflict. The eminent publicist Walter Lippmann, eager to get on with the war, while praising the President for his eloquent addresses on the gravity of "our position," deplored the "smart-aleckisms and wisecracks" which deflated his solemn warnings.

The situation in Washington from the interventionist point of view was described in a dispatch from that city, dated August 21, to the London *Times*. This dispatch quoted Mr. Lippmann's strictures on Congress and the President and added a note of anxiety that the mass of the American people were "utterly unaware of the brute reality that they are in fact at war." It also expressed the opinion that the President and other leaders might be at fault in failing to awaken Americans from "the delusion that they are at peace."

An extract from the dispatch follows:

. . . The President had not thought until last night that it would be necessary thus to address Congress, and through Congress the American people. On the present state of Congress, the voice of Mr. Walter Lippmann, as an American, will perhaps carry a greater weight than that of any non-American observer and he says that an "appallingly dangerous and demoralizing and humiliating situation" has developed within that body during the past fortnight.

It is due to the fact (he continues) that in default of high seriousness in the President's leadership of the people, Republican opposition in Congress had decided that it was free to play at partisan

5. Dispatch by Frank Kluckhohn, *New York Times,* August 20, 1941, pp. 1, 2.

politics, even at the risk of disorganizing the army, repudiating its commander, demoralizing the people, and shattering the influence of the United States throughout the world.

No more need be said, and no less can be said of the Republicans. Mr. Lippmann's reference to the President he extends by declaring that the addresses in which Mr. Roosevelt has truthfully, profoundly, and eloquently described "the gravity of our position," have been punctuated and deflated by the subsequent "smart-aleckisms and wisecracks," as though one listened to epoch-making news and appeals to patriotism over the wireless "interspersed with advertisements for soft mattresses and efficient laxatives."

These are hard words, but Mr. Lippmann is not the only American who believes that they are justified. Does the present state of the public mind give them added validity? Certainly it does if the accumulating evidence of conditions in the army camps can be taken as a touchstone—but can they? It would be bitterly unfair to say that to-day they can. What is clear, however, is that in the mass the American people are utterly unaware of the brute reality that they are in fact at war, because in the world of our day they cannot stay out and at the same time save either their material possessions or their freedom of spirit.

They are arming themselves and others; they are deploying their immense economic strength and wide political influence; and they are doing all this in order to defeat a declared enemy. But because they have not fired a shot or dropped a bomb the vast majority of them cling to the delusion that they are at peace. Whether this be the fault of the President and their other leaders, or whether the trouble goes deeper none can say with certainty. . . .[6]

Either on his own motion or stirred to action by criticism, President Roosevelt had in fact let it be known on August 20 that he had resolved to address Congress and the American people on the state of foreign affairs. The report aroused great expectancy. At last, it seemed to journalists, a full account of the commitments at the Atlantic Conference might be forthcoming, accompanied by a solemn warning to the people, on the impending perils of war. All such expectations proved to be unfounded.

6. London *Times*, August 22, 1941.

The message [7] which President Roosevelt presented to Congress on August 21 added nothing whatever to the statements which he had previously made as to the understandings and commitments of the Atlantic Conference. In his first paragraph he said that "over a week ago" he had held several conferences with Mr. Churchill at sea and that on grounds of safety no prior announcement could properly be made. In the second paragraph he referred to the official statement which had been issued on August 14 and commented, "I quote it for the information of Congress and for the record." Then came a reproduction of that official statement. [8]

In a few brief paragraphs, the President then brought his message to an end. He referred to the Lend-Lease Act and said that the military and naval conversations at the Atlantic meeting had made clear gains "in furthering the effectiveness of this aid"—to the democracies waging war against dictators East and West. He spoke of arrangements for conferences with Soviet Russia on matters of aid in its defense against Germany. In his fifth paragraph he dwelt on the merits of the principles set forth in the Atlantic declaration, said that it "presents a goal which is worth while for our type of civilization to seek," and maintained that it could not be opposed in any major particular without admitting a willingness to compromise with Nazism or to accept Nazi domination. His sixth paragraph dealt with the untrustworthiness of the written or spoken words of the Nazi Government. He concluded: "It is also unnecessary for me to point out that the [Atlantic] declaration of principles includes of necessity the world need for freedom of religion and freedom of information. No society of the world organized under the announced principles could survive without these freedoms which are a part of the whole freedom for which we strive."

Such was the official information given, at the time, to the American people by President Roosevelt in respect of the Atlantic Conference. Apparently, according to his accounts

7. Funk, *op. cit.*, pp. 453 f.
8. See above, pp. 118 ff., for the official statement.

of the transactions at sea, the President and Mr. Churchill, aided by their civil and military advisers, had considered operations under the Lend-Lease Act, agreed on condemning Hitlerite Germany and her satellites, arranged for conferences on aiding Russia, and formulated, in a statement of principles, their hopes for a better world to come after the overthrow of Nazi tyranny. Apparently also, according to his reports to the public, the President had made no "new" commitments at the Atlantic Conference and had reached no understandings that brought the United States nearer to war.

More extended and in some respects more explicit than President Roosevelt's report to Congress, August 21, on the Atlantic meeting was Mr. Churchill's explanation to the people of Great Britain, broadcast to the world on August 24, 1941.[9] The primary importance of the meeting, Mr. Churchill said, lay in the fact that "it symbolizes, in a form and manner which everyone can understand in every land and in every clime, the deep underlying unities which stir and, at decisive moments, rule the English-speaking peoples throughout the world." With regard to origins of the Atlantic Charter, "we had the idea when we met there, the President and I, that without attempting to draw final and formal peace aims, or war aims, it was necessary to give all peoples, and especially the oppressed and conquered peoples, a simple, rough-and-ready war-time statement of the goal towards which the British Commonwealth and the United States mean to make their way, and thus make a way for others. . . ."

In his message to Congress on August 21, President Roosevelt had included the reference of the joint report on the "steps" which the two countries were "respectively taking for their safety in the face of these [Axis] dangers." Mr. Churchill spoke more boldly: "You will, perhaps, have noticed that the President of the United States and the British representative, in what is aptly called the Atlantic Charter, have jointly pledged their countries to the final destruction of the Nazi

9. Full text in *Voices of History, Great Speeches and Papers for the Year 1941* (New York, Franklin Watts, Inc., 1942). Franklin Watts, ed.

tyranny. That is a solemn and grave undertaking. It must be made good. It will be made good. And, of course, many practical arrangements to fulfil that purpose have been and are being organized and set in motion."

Premier Churchill was also more precise and clear on the subject of the Japanese negotiations, although he did not put them first on the program of the Atlantic meeting. In his broadcast, he spoke at length of "the carnage, ruin, and corruption" brought about in Asia by the Japanese armies. He said that "they menace by their movements Siam, menace Singapore, the British link with Australasia, and menace the Philippine Islands under the protection of the United States." Then Mr. Churchill struck a resounding note:

It is certain that this has got to stop. Every effort will be made to secure a peaceful settlement. The United States are labouring with infinite patience to arrive at a fair and amicable settlement which will give Japan the utmost reassurance for her legitimate interests. We earnestly hope these negotiations will succeed. But this I must say: that if these hopes should fail we shall, of course, range ourselves unhesitatingly at the side of the United States.

Going beyond the text of Mr. Roosevelt's message to Congress three days earlier, Mr. Churchill declared that there were two distinct and marked differences in this joint declaration and the war aims announced at the latter part of the last world war. "No one should overlook them," he said. "The United States and Great Britain do not now assume that there will never be any more war again. On the contrary, we intend to take ample precaution to prevent its renewal in any period we can foresee by effectively disarming the guilty nations while remaining suitably protected ourselves."

The second difference between the war aims, Mr. Churchill explained, "is this: that instead of trying to ruin German trade by all kinds of additional trade barriers and hindrances, as was the mood of 1917, we have definitely adopted the view that it is not in the interests of the world and of our two countries that any large nation should be unprosperous or shut out from the means of making a decent living for itself and its people by its industry and enterprise."

Near the end of his broadcast on August 24, Mr. Churchill came to the supreme issue that was uppermost in the minds of the British people: When is the United States coming into the war for the destruction of Nazi tyranny? He took cognizance of it by saying: "The question has been asked: 'How near is the United States to war?'" In answering the question he intimated that the United States was already in action: "There is certainly one man who knows the answer to that question. If Hitler has not yet declared war upon the United States it is surely not out of his love for American institutions. It is certainly not because he could not find a pretext. He has murdered half a dozen countries for far less." In closing, the Prime Minister exclaimed: "I felt that hard and terrible and long-drawn out as this struggle may be, we shall not be denied the strength to do our duty to the end."

Although Mr. Churchill's exposition of the transactions at the Atlantic Conference was cautious, it implied that President Roosevelt was committing enough acts of hostility against Germany to warrant Hitler in making war on the United States. But the President's own statements on the conference lent little countenance to the view that the United States was already at war or in the war. He referred to Japanese aggressions as possible auguries of war; and, as if by analogy, in quoting President Lincoln's lines on Civil War times, he hinted broadly that Americans in August, 1941, had better recognize the fact that they were in the war. But the President also said that the country was no closer to war as a result of decisions at the Atlantic Conference and that no new commitments had been made at the meeting. Accordingly, it appeared, late in August, 1941, that apart from arrangements for lend-lease operations, agreement on the noble principles of the Atlantic Charter, and discussions of numerous world issues, nothing had been done at the conference which bound the United States to take more vigorous actions definitely pointed in the direction of war.

American advocates of immediate war on Hitler, unless they had inside information about the conference, derived small comfort from President Roosevelt's statements on its transactions. Nor were American opponents of war in any better position, however deep and inveterate their suspicions. They could find in his words no evidence that he had entered into agreements with Mr. Churchill in the nature of an alliance for parallel diplomatic pressure on Japan or for military or naval coöperation against one or all of the Axis Powers. While adding to national bewilderment over patrolling and convoying, President Roosevelt's reports to the people after the Atlantic Conference allowed the undiscriminating to keep on cherishing the hope that he was or might be striving to keep the country out of war, with prospects of success.

There was, of course, the Atlantic Charter which, the President had said in his message to Congress, August 21, included of necessity the world need for freedom of religion and "freedom of information." In imposing appearances it seemed to be the most meaningful statement that had emerged from the conference. But in British opinion it was no substitute for an American Expeditionary Force to be employed in the invasion of the Continent; and to Americans eager to have the President move quickly in the direction of an all-out war on Hitler it offered little promise. If invincible optimists could see in the Charter a splendid plan for a beneficent world order to come, informed skeptics with memories going back to World War I could recall the unhappy fate of President Wilson's Fourteen Points and were more inclined to jeer,[10] or at least discount, the Charter than to applaud the new pronouncement in respect of blessings to be conferred on mankind after World War II. In net result, therefore, the appearances of the Atlantic Conference did little to free the President from his peace covenants of 1940 and to promote national unity for participation in the war, if such had been his purpose in planning and advertising his meeting with Prime Minister Churchill.

10. Harold Nicolson, *Peacemaking, 1919* (Houghton, 1939).

CHAPTER V

"In Case of Attack" in the Atlantic

ACCORDING to President Roosevelt's reports to Congress and the Press, no new commitments had been made at the Atlantic Conference, nor was the country any closer to war. Not even an appearance of retreat from the peace and neutrality pledges of 1940 had been indicated by the President's public announcements on his return home. Americans eager to have their country get into the fight at once were dissatisfied. Clark Eichelberger, distinguished advocate of world peace, speaking for the Committee to Defend America by Aiding the Allies, expressed disappointment "that a plan of action against Hitler had not been made," and then he declared: "We must point out with all possible vigor that the United States will have a right to participate in the building of the future world peace if it will make its full contribution to the defeat of the aggressors. Consequently our participation in the conflict should be speeded up." [1]

THE TROUBLESOME "ESCAPE" CLAUSE

IT IS possible that Mr. Eichelberger, in demanding that "our participation in the conflict be speeded up," was speaking in the name of President Roosevelt; for, during the previous months managers of the Committee to Defend America by Aiding the Allies had covertly kept in touch with the Administration and, with its approval, had acted as propaganda agents in creating favorable public sentiment for its projects in advance of official announcements respecting them from Washington.[2] In other words, when President Roosevelt wished to

1. Johnson, *The Battle against Isolation*, p. 218.
2. The inside story of the committee's secret relations with President Roosevelt, Secretary Hull, and other members of the Administration in "softening up" the people for participation in the war is told with gusto by the historian of the committee, Walter Johnson, *op. cit., passim.* In advertising this work, the Uni-

make one of his "complicated moves" he sometimes privately cooperated with this committee in the business of stirring up an agitation for the move before he deemed the time ripe to make an official acknowledgment of it.

President Roosevelt, however, was not free to make a public demand, in Mr. Eichelberger's style, for speeding up "our participation" in the conflict. The antiwar plank of the Democratic platform, to which he had committed himself in the campaign of 1940, read: "We will not participate in foreign wars . . . except in case of attack." [3] Under this obligation, if such obligations publicly assumed had any moral force, President Roosevelt could call upon the country and Congress to "participate" in the war only in case of an attack. Of this covenant the President was poignantly conscious, for he repeatedly referred to the word "attack" in his public addresses and statements during the year 1941 and more than once he sought to interpret it out of existence as a restraint upon his powers, by giving it an illimitable definition.

To most members of the Democratic convention at Chicago who accepted and approved this conditional antiwar plank, and probably to most American citizens who read it, the plank had a plain meaning. It meant and could only mean to scrupulous minds that, if the Democrats were victorious in the coming election, they would not allow the United States Government to participate in foreign wars, unless American territory, shipping, or other possessions were made the object of an unwarranted, unprovoked attack by the armed forces of some foreign power. In case of such an attack, the President had power, on his own motion, to use the armed forces of the United States to repel the assault or invasion,[4] and could call upon Congress for a declaration of war. In the absence of such an attack, on the other hand, if he deemed war against a for-

versity of Chicago Press, as if in a novel interpretation of the functions of scholarship, declared: "Isolationism, which here stands condemned by its own lies, must not have another chance." See the jacket of the book.

3. For origin and nature of the antiwar plank, see Beard, *op. cit.*, pp. 291 ff.

4. See, for instance, the opinion of Mr. Justice Grier in the Prize Cases, 2 Black, 635 (1863).

eign government to be necessary and proper owing to changed circumstances or for any other reason,[5] he was bound by his commitment to the plank and by the Constitution to appeal to Congress for a legal sanction to employ the armed forces in war, inside and outside of the Americas.

It is possible, of course, that President Roosevelt entertained a disingenuous view of the conditional clause, "except in case of attack," when he bound himself to the antiwar plank during the campaign of 1940. The words had been added to the original draft of the plank on the insistence of his representatives at the Democratic convention and he may have then thought that thereby the antiwar part of the covenant would be or could be rendered innocuous by explication. In any case, however, during the campaign of 1940, the President made no public interpretation of the conditional clause which indicated that he might, after all, have some *arrière-pensée* in respect of it, that he contemplated reducing it to an absurdity by giving it a capricious definition hitherto unknown to lexicography, international law, or diplomacy.

If the President had in 1940 no reservations respecting the meaning of the term "attack," he acquired them sometime in 1941, certainly as early as May 27, for, in a public address on that day, he declared in effect that an attack calling for defensive action on the part of the United States did not necessarily mean a warlike assault by a foreign power on anything belonging to the United States but could "begin by the domination of any base which menaces our security—north or south":

I have said on many occasions that the United States is mustering its men and its resources only for purposes of defense—only to repel attack. I repeat that statement now. But we must be realistic when we use the word "attack"; we have to relate it to the lightning speed of modern warfare.

Some people seem to think that we are not attacked until bombs actually drop on New York or San Francisco or New Orleans or Chicago. But they are simply shutting their eyes to the lesson we

5. See above, Chap. I, pp. 3 ff.

must learn from the fate of every nation that the Nazis have conquered.

The attack on Czechoslovakia began with the conquest of Aus-
tria. The attack on Norway began with the occupation of Den-
mark. The attack on Greece began with occupation of Albania and
Bulgaria. The attack on the Suez Canal began with the invasion of
the Balkans and North Africa. The attack on the United States
can begin with the domination of any base which menaces our
security—north or south.

Nobody can foretell tonight just when the acts of the dictators
will ripen into attack on this hemisphere and us. But we know
enough by now to realize that it would be suicide to wait until
they are in our front yard.

When your enemy comes at you in a tank or a bombing plane,
if you hold your fire until you see the whites of his eyes, you will
never know what hit you. Our Bunker Hill of tomorrow may be
several thousand miles from Boston.

Anyone with an atlas and a reasonable knowledge of the sudden striking force of modern war knows that it is stupid to wait
until a probable enemy has gained a foothold from which to attack.
Old-fashioned common sense calls for the use of a strategy which
will prevent such an enemy from gaining a foothold in the first
place.

We have, accordingly, extended our patrol in North and South
Atlantic waters. We are steadily adding more and more ships and
planes to that patrol. It is well known that the strength of the
Atlantic fleet has been greatly increased during the past year, and
is constantly being built up. . . .[6]

Approaching the troublesome word "attack" more boldly
in July, 1941,[7] President Roosevelt attenuated the interpretation of it which he had given on May 27, 1941. As if recalling
the language of the antiwar plank and yet without mentioning
it by name, he spoke of the very idea as now obsolete. "There
was a time," he said, "when we could afford to say that we
would not fight unless attacked"; and he immediately added:
"Modern techniques of warfare have changed all that." Here
he seemed to be contending that the Democratic pledge

6. Funk, *Roosevelt's Foreign Policy, 1933–1941*, pp. 399 f. (Italics supplied.)
7. Introduction to *Public Papers*, 1940 Volume, dated July 17, 1941, p. xxxi.

against war "except in case of attack" was out of date when made in 1940 or had become untenable since that year or did not mean what it seemed to mean. The President's exegesis of July, 1941, read:

Modern warfare has given us a new definition for that word "attack." There was a time when we could afford to say that we would not fight unless attacked, and then wait until the physical attack came upon us before starting to shoot. Modern techniques of warfare have changed all that. An attack today is a very different thing. An attack today begins as soon as any base has been occupied from which our security is threatened. That base may be thousands of miles away from our own shores. The American Government must, of necessity, decide at which point any threat of attack against this hemisphere has begun; and to make their stand when that point has been reached.

Evidently, President Roosevelt did not in July, 1941, regard the word "attack" as necessarily implying an act of war at all against the United States—a physical assault in the form of shooting at or bombing the territory, shipping, or other possessions of the United States; for he said: "An attack *begins* as soon as *any base* has been occupied from which *our security* is *threatened*." (Italics supplied.) Since he added that this base might be thousands of miles away from our shores, he evidently meant that he could regard an attack on the United States as *beginning*, that is, as constituting an attack, if made on the territory of some foreign country thousands of miles away from the United States, not on any possessions of the United States. If this is what the word "attack," as used in the conditional clause of the Democratic antiwar plank, was actually intended to convey by its authors—representatives of President Roosevelt at Chicago—then it is noteworthy that no such explanation of the term was offered to the public by the President during his campaign of 1940 for the votes of the American people.

Although the interpretation of the word "attack" announced publicly by the President in July, 1941, seemed explicit in itself, the last sentence of his statement, bearing on action to be taken by the United States "in case of attack," was really open to diversity of constructions. There, he said, *the American Government* must, of necessity, decide at which point *any threat* of attack against this hemisphere has *begun,* and to *make "their" stand* when that point has been reached. In ordinary usage the words "the American Government" mean the Legislative, Executive, and Judicial Departments of the federal system. Under the Constitution this is the proper usage; for the Constitution, Article I, Section 8, so indicates in speaking of the "powers vested by this Constitution in the Government of the United States, or in any Department or Officer thereof."

Did President Roosevelt intend to include Congress in his conception when he thus spoke of "the American Government"? Or was he referring to the Executive alone? Did he intend to imply that a mere *threat* of an attack on *this hemisphere,* as distinguished from an attack, would, of necessity, bring about American armed action against the authors of the threat? The text of his statement afforded no answers to these pertinent questions. Not until some of his "complicated moves" in the autumn of 1941 had produced results did President Roosevelt give intimations of the realities covered by his conception of the word "attack."

APPEARANCES AND REALITIES OF THE ATTACK ON THE U.S.S. *Greer* (SEPTEMBER)

THE hopes of those who were working to speed up American participation in the war by aiding the Allies were raised to a high pitch in September, 1941, not by an Executive appeal to Congress for a declaration of war on Hitler, but by events at sea. On September 4, the Navy Department announced that a submarine of undetermined nationality had attacked the American destroyer *Greer* that morning in the Atlantic on its way to Iceland; that torpedoes had been fired at the vessel; that the *Greer* had counterattacked by dropping depth charges, with unknown results. The destroyer, the department explained, was operating as a part of the Atlantic patrol established during the summer by President Roosevelt and was carrying mail. Was this the "attack" [8] that would emancipate President Roosevelt from his commitment to the Democratic plank of 1940 against participating in foreign wars "except in case of attack"?

On September 5, cables from Iceland reported that the *Greer* had arrived safely, that the incident was described as a German attack, and that the destroyer had been aided in repelling the attack by British aircraft, coöperating in the reconnaissance. It was also announced in the press that President Roosevelt had issued orders to the Navy to search out and "eliminate" the submarine which attacked the *Greer*, and that he considered the attack as deliberate. The President hinted that it might have been the work of a German submarine.

From Berlin came a German official version of the affair. The German version asserted that the attack had not been initiated by the German submarine; on the contrary, it contended, the submarine had been attacked with depth bombs, pursued continuously in the German blockade zone, and assailed by depth bombs until midnight. The German statement concluded: "Roosevelt thereby is endeavoring with all the means at his disposal to provoke incidents for the purpose of baiting the American people into the war." The Navy Department quickly denied the German allegations and stated that the initial attack in the engagement had been made by the German submarine.

For days the war of words went on in the press, American and Axis, while anxious observers in the United States waited for an official statement by President Roosevelt. The statement came on September 11 in the form of a radio broadcast.

The *Greer*, the President said, "was carrying American mail to Iceland. She was flying the American flag. Her identity as an American ship was unmistakable. She was then and there attacked by a submarine. Germany admits that it was a German submarine . . . I tell you the blunt fact that the German submarine fired first upon this American destroyer without

8. See above, p. 3. The evidence on which this narration of events is based appeared in the *New York Times*, September 5, 6, 7, 9, 12, 13, 14, 1941.

warning, and with deliberate design to sink her"—at a point southeast of Greenland.

"We have sought no shooting war with Hitler," the President continued.

We do not seek it now. . . . In the waters which we deem necessary for our defense, American naval vessels and American planes will no longer wait until Axis submarines lurking under water, or Axis raiders on the surface of the sea, strike their deadly blow—first. . . . The aggression is not ours. Ours is solely defense. But let this warning be clear. From now on, if German or Italian vessels of war enter the waters, the protection of which is necessary for American defense, they do so at their own peril. The orders which I have given as Commander in Chief to the United States Army and Navy are to carry out that policy—at once. . . . There will be no shooting unless Germany continues to seek it. . . . I have no illusions about the gravity of this step. . . . It is the result of months and months of constant thought and anxiety and prayer. . . .[9]

But, while the President stated that the Navy would not wait for Axis vessels to strike first, he did not invoke the escape clause of the Democratic antiwar plank and call upon Congress to authorize war; he announced, in effect, that as Commander in Chief, he was directing affairs relative to shooting in the Atlantic. Nor, indeed, were signs in Washington propitious for an invocation of the clause; for alert journalists and members of Congress in the City of Rumors thought they had ground for believing that the President's account of the attack on the *Greer*, if not false, was lacking in exactitude and comprehensiveness. Stirred by the allegations and counter-allegations, the Senate Committee on Naval Affairs prepared to hold a hearing on the attack and sent a list of pointed questions to Admiral Harold R. Stark, Chief of Naval Operations, designed to secure a full official record of the *Greer* case.

In a letter to Senator David I. Walsh, chairman of the Senate Committee on Naval Affairs, dated September 20, 1941, Admiral Stark enclosed a statement giving what he believed

9. Funk, *op. cit.*, pp. 470 ff.

to be "a good picture of what happened" and answers to the questions. Although Admiral Stark's letter, statement, and answers were not made public until late in October, 1941, the tenor of his reply was immediately disclosed to some members of Congress and it added fuel to the fire of opposition to President Roosevelt's methods and policies. Had the President made use of the *Greer* case in an appeal to Congress after September 11 for a declaration of war to implement the escalator clause, these documents, it was known in congressional circles, would be used as ammunition by his critics. Indeed, after the President on October 9, 1941, called upon Congress for another step in legislation—an act to permit the arming of American merchant ships—Admiral Stark's papers on the *Greer* were inserted in the *Congressional Record* and thus made public before the next "case of attack." [10]

Admiral Stark's report to the Senate Committee, which filled several typewritten pages presented an account of the *Greer* affair which made the President's statement of the case to the nation on September 11 appear in some respects inadequate, and, in others, incorrect. The following summary gives the essential facts of the *Greer* incident as supplied by Admiral Stark to the Senate Committee:

While en route to Iceland with mail, passengers, and some freight, the *Greer* was informed by a British plane of the presence of a submerged submarine about ten miles directly ahead.

Acting on this information from the British plane, the *Greer* proceeded to trail the submarine, broadcasting its position.

This chase of the submarine went on for over three hours; the British plane dropped four depth charges in the vicinity of the submarine and departed, leaving the *Greer* to continue the hunt, zigzagging and searching.

The *Greer* thus had held contact with the submarine for three hours and twenty-eight minutes; the submarine fired a torpedo which crossed the *Greer* about 100 yards astern.

10. *Congressional Record*, 77th Congress, First Session, Vol. 87, Part 8, p. 8314. On September 22, Admiral Stark had written secretly to Admiral Hart: "We are now escorting convoys." See below, Chap. XIV.

Then the *Greer* "attacked the submarine with a pattern of eight depth charges"; to which the submarine replied with another torpedo that missed the *Greer*.

After losing sound contact at this time with the submarine, the *Greer* started searching for it, made contact again about two hours later, and "attacked immediately with depth charges," without discoverable results.

The *Greer* thereupon continued its search for about three hours more and proceeded to its destination, Iceland.

APPEARANCES AND REALITIES OF THE ATTACK ON THE U.S.S. *Kearny* (OCTOBER–NOVEMBER)

ABOUT six weeks after the attack on the *Greer*, while Congress had before it a measure to authorize the arming of American merchant ships on recommendation of President Roosevelt,[11] another serious attack on an American war vessel was reported in the news—an attack far more distressing in terms of death and suffering than the attack on the *Greer*. On October 17, 1941, the Navy Department announced that the U.S.S. *Kearny* "was torpedoed this morning while on patrol duty about 350 miles south and west of Iceland." Although the President declined to issue any statement on this new case until all the facts were in, he said that the *Kearny* was within the American defense zone when torpedoed and that orders to shoot on sight German and Italian raiders in waters vital to American defense were still unchanged. At a press conference, Secretary Hull described German attacks as acts of piracy and attempted frightfulness as a part of a general world movement of conquest.[12]

After a brief period of silence in Berlin, a German radio broadcast denied responsibility and declared that there was not a word of truth in the story that a German submarine had torpedoed the *Kearny*. October 19, the Navy Department announced that the *Kearny*, attacked by a submarine, undoubtedly German, had reached port, with eleven members of the

11. See below, Chap. VI.
12. *New York Times*, October 18, 1941, pp. 1–3.

crew missing and several men injured. When asked the next day about any plans for making an official protest to the German Government, Secretary Hull "remarked acidly that one did not very often send diplomatic notes to an international highwayman." [13]

On October 27, 1941, President Roosevelt delivered a long and vehement address [14] to the nation on the subject of Axis attacks on American ships, dwelling at length on the *Kearny* case, and defied the Axis Powers: "All we Americans have cleared our decks and taken our battle stations." After opening briefly with references to previous attacks, the President took up the new case:

Five months ago tonight I proclaimed to the American people the existence of a state of unlimited emergency.

Since then much has happened. Our Army and Navy are temporarily in Iceland in the defense of the Western Hemisphere.

Hitler has attacked shipping in areas close to the Americas in the North and South Atlantic.

Many American-owned merchant ships have been sunk on the high seas. One American destroyer was attacked on September 4. Another destroyer was attacked and hit on October 17. Eleven brave and loyal men of our Navy were killed by the Nazis.

We have wished to avoid shooting. But the shooting has started. And history has recorded who fired the first shot.[15] In the long run, however, all that will matter is who fired the last shot.

America has been attacked. The U.S.S. *Kearny* is not just a Navy ship. She belongs to every man, woman, and child in this Nation.

Illinois, Alabama, California, North Carolina, Ohio, Louisiana, Texas, Pennsylvania, Georgia, Arkansas, New York, Virginia—those are the home States of the honored dead and wounded of the *Kearny*. Hitler's torpedo was directed at every American, whether he lives on our seacoasts or in the innermost part of the Nation, far from the sea and far from the guns and tanks of the marching hordes of would-be conquerors of the world.

13. *Ibid.*, October 20, 1941.
14. Funk, *op. cit.*, pp. 512 ff.
15. See below, p. 147.

The purpose of Hitler's attack was to frighten the American people off the high seas—to force us to make a trembling retreat. This is not the first time he has misjudged the American spirit. That spirit is now aroused.

If our national policy were to be dominated by the fear of shooting, then all of our ships and those of our sister republics would have to be tied up in home harbors. Our Navy would have to remain respectfully—abjectly—behind any line which Hitler might decree on any ocean as his own dictated version of his own war zone.

Naturally, we reject that absurd and insulting suggestion. We reject it because of our own self-interest, because of our own self-respect, because, most of all, of our own good faith. Freedom of the seas is now, as it has always been, a fundamental policy of your Government and mine. . . .

After giving his version of the *Kearny* case and declaring that America had been attacked, President Roosevelt announced measures of retaliation:

Our determination not to take it lying down has been expressed in the orders to the American Navy to shoot on sight. Those orders stand. Furthermore, the House of Representatives has already voted to amend part of the Neutrality Act of 1937, today outmoded by force of violent circumstances. The Senate Committee on Foreign Relations has also recommended elimination of other hamstringing provisions in that Act. That is the course of honesty and of realism. . . . It can never be doubted that the goods *will* be delivered by this nation, whose Navy believes in the tradition of "Damn the torpedoes; full speed ahead!"

There was great rejoicing in the White House on the day after President Roosevelt's address on October 27. His secretary, Stephen Early, stated that a flood of messages was coming in and that they were favorable in a ratio of about eight to one. Evidently advocates of war for the United States were under the impression that the great day for which they had so longed had come at last.

"America has been attacked" were, indeed, electric words.

They were immediately taken by journalists in Washington and other close observers to mean that President Roosevelt had cast off the shackles of the antiwar and pro-neutrality pledges he had made to the nation. Arthur Krock, one of the best informed journalists in the Capital and a shrewd inquirer into the significance of White House announcements, said in his column headed "America Attacked," under the date line of October 28: "Four words in the President's Navy Day speech last night are being accepted here today as his own evidence in rebuttal of the charge that his present foreign policy violates the Democratic platform of 1940 and his antiwar campaign pledges in that same year. The words were: 'America has been attacked.' "

After referring to the President's radio address of September 11, 1941, and his assignment of the "first shot" to invaders of the American defense waters, Mr. Krock went on to say:

But not until his Navy Day speech [of October 27] did the President make use of phraseology which leads back to the 1940 Democratic platform plank and those campaign utterances his critics have since charged him with violating. Therefore the general conclusion is that last night the President made his official defense for the present generation and for the judgment of history. . . . The key to the historical importance of the utterance is identified here as the word "attacked."

Thereupon, Mr. Krock gave an inside history of the way in which Senator James F. Byrnes, "who was representing the President" in the drafting of the platform at the Democratic convention of 1940, held up the antiwar plank and procured the addition of the words "except in case of attack." [16] Mr. Krock added: "Now the President has officially declared that 'America has been attacked.' Therefore, by the very text of the platform pledge, the promise against dispatch of our armed forces 'outside the Americas' as well as the rest of the promise can be held to be automatically cancelled. In this view any

16. See Beard, *op. cit.*, pp. 288 ff., for the proceedings at the Democratic convention in Chicago in 1940.

further steps away from the remainder of the platform plank are consistent with the full text."

But there remained the President's pledge against participation in "foreign" wars. Mr. Krock took note of it and reported that this word was no longer deemed an obstacle: "As for the word 'foreign' Mrs. Roosevelt and others close to the President have already said that, since the European war is no longer 'foreign' to our interest, our activity in it would not be activity in a 'foreign' war."

Notwithstanding this authoritative explication by Mrs. Roosevelt and others close to President Roosevelt, there remained also for consideration certain outstanding and categorical peace pledges made by the President personally during the campaign. Mr. Krock cited two of them—the Boston pledge of October 30, 1940: "Your boys are not going to be sent into any foreign war"; and the fireside chat of December, 1940: "You can therefore nail any talk of sending armies to Europe as a deliberate untruth."

These statements, too, Mr. Krock declared, "can, on the basis of this reasoning [about attack and foreign war] and the complete platform text, be held equally consistent with steps since taken or any of their logical consequences."

In this presentation of the case, on October 28, Mr. Krock seemed to be supporting the President's "official defense for the present generation and for the judgment of history." He seemed to be saying likewise that the steps taken by the President in the direction of war since 1940 or "any of their logical consequences" (which certainly included a call upon Congress for a declaration of war) could be held "consistent" with the pledges and declarations of 1940.

Having applied his line of interpretation to other antiwar statements by the President, Mr. Krock said: "This reasoning can be disputed during the development of our anti-aggressor policy, just as it has been disputed up to now. The factual argument over what constitutes initiating 'attack,' as in the instance of the U.S.S. *Greer*, may continue over the U.S.S. *Kearny's* experience if the full report shall show a similar set of preliminaries"; that is, shall show that the American destroyer had chased or attacked the German submarine first.[17]

Mr. Krock closed his elaborate argument for President Roosevelt's strategy, as presented to his generation and the bar of history to come, with the words: "But it now appears that, when 'attack' is conceded in any episode, the challenge of the critics will be met by the five immensely important words ["except in case of attack"] Mr. Byrnes caused to be added to the 1940 platform."

The next day, October 29, while the words, "America has been attacked," were still reverberating in the country, Secretary Knox made public a formal report on the way in which the *Kearny* had been attacked. In his address of October 27 on the *Kearny* case, President Roosevelt had said: "We have wished to avoid shooting. But the shooting has started. And history has recorded who fired the first shot." The report by Secretary Knox two days later read:

On the night of October 16–17 the U.S.S. *Kearny* while escorting a convoy of merchant ships received distress signals from another convoy which was under attack from several submarines. The U.S.S. *Kearny* proceeded to the aid of the attacked convoy. On arriving at the scene of the attack the U.S.S. *Kearny* dropped depth bombs when she sighted a merchant ship under attack by a submarine. Some time afterward three torpedo tracks were observed·approaching the U.S.S. *Kearny*. One passed ahead of the ship, one astern, and the third struck the U.S.S. *Kearny* on the starboard side in the vicinity of the forward fire room. . . . The U.S.S. *Kearny* was forced out of action by the explosion.[18]

The rejoicing of President Roosevelt's supporters over what seemed to be a sure case of an attack that meant war for the United States, at long last, proved to be premature; for the Senate Committee on Naval Affairs, remembering its experiences in the *Greer* case, immediately gave attention to the

17. *New York Times*, October 29, 1941, p. 4. Perhaps Mr. Krock was not at the moment conversant with the "factual" phase of the incident, but he learned about it later and spoke bitterly about it. See below, pp. 150 ff.

18. Article by Charles Hurd in *ibid.*, October 30, 1941, pp. 1–5.

case of the *Kearny*, and managed to get some of the facts in that affair from Admiral Stark, Chief of Naval Operations. Although the committee made no public report on these facts at once, news of its findings "leaked" out and spread among members of Congress and their friends.[19] The leaks indicated that the *Kearny* was actually on convoy duty [20] at the time of the shooting and had been engaged at length in fighting a pack of German submarines before she was hit by a torpedo. Such facts were not released to the press by the committee until early in December,[21] but leaks and rumors in Washington completely dashed interventionist hopes that the *Kearny* attack would now bring full-fledged war in the Atlantic.

Other shootings and sinkings occurred in the Atlantic. Two of the most flagrant cases were those of the tanker *Salinas* on October 30, 1941, and the *Reuben James* on the night of October 30–31. But President Roosevelt did not make as much

19. See Arthur Krock's statement, below, pp. 150 ff.

20. Asked at a secret hearing of a Senate Committee, October 27, 1941, whether American vessels were convoying ships, Secretary Hull replied: "That is my guess." When Senator Wheeler made the charge that the Navy was convoying ships across the Atlantic to Great Britain, Secretary Knox declared: "That statement is not true." *Ibid.*, October 28 and November 20, 1941.

21. The following account of the Senate Committee's report to Congress was published in the *New York Times*, December 4, 1941:

"The destroyer *Kearny* fought nearly three hours against a pack of German submarines before she was hit by a torpedo, an official Navy report to Congress revealed today. . . .

"The Navy report—a letter from Admiral Harold R. Stark, Chief of Naval Operations, to Chairman David I. Walsh, Democrat, of Massachusetts, of the Senate Naval Affairs Committee—said the *Kearny* was on convoy duty, and 'a number' of merchant ships were damaged 'and some of them sunk during the battle.'

"Admiral Stark said that although United States vessels were in the convoy 'it may be stated . . . that no United States flag merchant ship was sunk at this time.'

"Senator Walsh, who had asked for answers to a series of questions on the *Kearny* incident, released Admiral Stark's report without comment, except to say that so far as the Senate's efforts to obtain information were concerned 'the *Kearny* incident is closed.'

"He said, however, that he had written Admiral Stark asking for similar information about the sinking of the destroyer *Reuben James*, which went down off Iceland with a loss of 100 officers and men.

"Senator Walsh had told Admiral Stark that information on the *Kearny* should be made public 'since it has become impossible to keep secret from the press the proceedings of committees of the Senate.' He waived replies that would reveal military or naval secrets. . . ."

of these two cases as he had made of the *Greer* and *Kearny* cases. When asked on October 31, 1941, whether the sinking of the *Reuben James* would lead to the breaking of diplomatic relations with Germany, he "indicated surprise." The reporter inquired: "Will this first actual sinking make any difference in the international relations of the United States?" The President replied that he "did not think so—the destroyer was merely carrying out its assigned task." Asked whether Berlin had cause to worry about some of its submarines that had encountered our Navy, "The President suggested that the reporter go to a good psychiatrist." [22] Thus the electric words "America has been attacked," instead of setting off the real war in the Atlantic, fizzled out in an anticlimax. If President Roosevelt had actually been seeking war in the Atlantic by exploiting German "attacks," he had apparently exhausted the possibilities of that expedient by November 1, 1941.

THE ATTACK IN THE ATLANTIC FAILS TO MATERIALIZE

ABOUT this point in the "series of complicated moves," in which President Roosevelt "so skilfully conducted affairs as to avoid even the appearance of an act of aggression on our part," many supporters of his "moves" and advocates of full participation by the United States in the war became dissatisfied with his conduct of affairs. Arthur Krock was among them. In his column of October 28, 1941, immediately after President Roosevelt had declared "America has been attacked," Mr. Krock had said: "Therefore the general conclusion is that last night the President [in his address of October 27] made his official defense for the present generation and for the judgment of history"; and Mr. Krock had added: "It now ap-

22. *Ibid.*, November 1, 1941. Later reports indicated: the *Salinas* and three American freighters were in a convoy accompanied by five American destroyers, joined on the voyage by thirty-eight British ships, most of them tankers; American naval vessels took up the task of escorting the convoy at a given point after British war vessels turned back; German submarines attacked the convoy and a general engagement ensued; the *Reuben James* came to the aid of the *Salinas;* later the *Reuben James* was sunk in an engagement. *New York Times*, November 1, 5, 6, 8, 1941.

pears that, when 'attack' is conceded in any episode, the challenge of the critics will be met by the five immensely important words Mr. Byrnes caused to be added to the 1940 platform"—except in case of attack.

As an informed and competent exponent of the foreign policy espoused by the *New York Times*, Mr. Krock evidently had been convinced on October 28, 1941, that President Roosevelt had secured the "attack" with which to make his war case for that generation and the judgment of history. But a few days later Mr. Krock became indignant at the President for not taking full advantage of the opportunity presented by the attacks, for obscuring the issues, and for failing to tell the truth. In an address before the alumni of Columbia College on November 5, 1941, Mr. Krock said:

. . . Lately the President and Hitler have had another argument. Some weeks ago the U.S.S. Destroyer *Greer* was the target of a German submarine torpedo that missed. Then the U.S.S. Destroyer *Kearny* was the target of a German torpedo that struck, but only wounded. More recently the U.S.S. *Reuben James* was the target of a German torpedo that killed. The argument is over who "attacked" whom.

An "attack" means an onset, an aggressive initiation of combat, a move which is the antithesis of "defense." Let's face it, Mr. President. Americans are grown up now. In that definition, all three of our destroyers attacked the German submarines. Like the British who went after Fuzzy-Wuzzy in the Sudan, the Navy can say: "Our orders were to break you, an' of course we went and did."

The U.S.S. *Greer* was informed by a British naval plane that a submarine lay ten miles ahead in her path. The British plane then went back and "attacked" the submarine. The *Greer* gave chase to the submarine, broadcasting its location on the way. The submarine, when the *Greer* came in range, then tried its best to sink the *Greer*.

The U.S.S. *Kearny* was on convoy duty in the same waters. She responded to a distress signal from a convoy which a pack of submarines had attacked. Her errand was to find the pack and destroy it. While so engaged, a submarine fought back; one torpedo hit the mark and eleven American Navy men were killed.

The U.S.S. *Reuben James* was with a convoy and went on call to the aid of another which German submarines had engaged. A submarine sank our destroyer, with what loss of American life is yet unknown. I believe the full log will demonstrate that as soon as the *Reuben James* came into the area infested by the submarines she tried to finish them. She, too, attacked. Certainly I hope so.

The Navy some time ago was ordered by the President to "shoot on sight." The Navy neither misunderstands the orders of its Commander in Chief nor is loutish in executing them.

So, in my opinion, Hitler can throw at us both the dictionary and the facts when he says we "attacked" him. Why should the American Government ever have attempted to obscure it? If the Navy had not done what it did the United States would have been guilty of the most heart-breaking bluff ever made by a great nation.

Yet our government did attempt to obscure it, as the record shows.

In his press conference of Sept. 5 (I quote from *New York Times* Washington dispatches, and I guarantee their accuracy): "The Executive made clear that he believed the attack on the American vessel (the *Greer*) was deliberate, and that he considered it no less serious because the destroyer had evaded destruction and answered with depth charges. The attempt to sink the *Greer* took place in daylight when visibility was good, the President declared, and more than one attack was made by the submarine."

From a Washington dispatch to the same newspaper, Sept. 6: "The Navy Department declined to comment on the German Government's charge that the submarine was merely trying to defend itself. A spokesman called attention to the Navy Department's original announcement: that the initial attack was made by the submarine on the *Greer*." From Berlin the same day, had come this: "The German contention is that the sub fired on the *Greer* only after having been pursued for two hours."

Then on Oct. 14 were disclosed the actual facts as I stated them before: The scout work of the British plane; its return to drop depth charges; the pursuit and broadcast by the *Greer*. How were these facts obtained? The Navy did not volunteer them, contenting itself with original statements which can politely be called misleading. They were obtained because a Senate Committee demanded them.

On Oct. 17 a *Times* dispatch carried another statement from the Navy about another destroyer. It announced that the U.S.S. *Kearny* was torpedoed while on "patrol duty." Three days later members of the same Senate committee that elicited the true story of the *Greer* told the press the *Kearny* was not on patrol, but on convoy duty. Seven days later, at a press conference, the President asserted that this was true. The *Kearny* was on convoy and not on patrol duty at all.

By the time the *Reuben James* was sunk the government had apparently come to the conclusion that the Navy should no longer be left in the position of obscuring the facts or giving out only part of the story. That time the truth was published at once, in the tradition of the United States Navy. I do not blame that great service for any of the faults of omission I have recounted.

The blame, as I see it, is at the door of the Administration. Perhaps the straightforward account of the sinking of the *Reuben James* opens a new and worthier chapter in the official book. . . .

When Senator Walsh's committee and a few inquisitive newspaper men finally elicited all the pertinent facts about the encounters of the *Greer* and the *Kearny*, some of those who seem to think that our foreign policy must be publicly justified by proving an unprovoked German "attack" shifted back to the sinking of the *Robin Moor*. That sinking was brutally done; those rescued owe their lives to chance, not to the Nazi commander; and certainly the *Robin Moor* was "attacked." But the attack was not unprovoked. Some weeks before the lease-lend bill had become law. From that moment, whatever the political quibblers may say, we were committed to the military defeat of Germany. . . .[23]

Now American men are giving their lives that this armament may reach its destination. To their memories, and to their brothers in arms who may die tomorrow, to the grown-up American nation they are defending, the Administration and Congress owe a solemn obligation: the truth. In wartime, for excellent reasons, it cannot always be the whole truth. But always it should be nothing but the truth.[24]

23. See above, Chap. II, *passim*.
24. *New York Times*, November 6, 1941.

Both explicitly and implicitly, Mr. Krock's line in his address of November 5, 1941, was clear and frank. It was the line taken by the *New York Times* and many other advocates of American participation in the war at various points in time after the Lend-Lease Act had been safely passed and signed, March 11. The line was that the act authorized the President to do anything he deemed necessary to inflict a military defeat on Germany, including a resort to open war, and that the measure committed the people of the United States irrevocably to such authorization.

Where can warrant be found for this interpretation of the act in the history of its passage, in President Roosevelt's own statements while it was up for consideration by Congress, and in the averments of its Democratic sponsors in Congress during the debates on it? If there was one thing that President Roosevelt and the Democratic leaders in Congress then categorically denied, it was the contention of critics that the loose language of the bill would allow the President to claim the power to wage war under its terms.[25]

In view of the history of the Lend-Lease Bill, if the act as finally passed in March, 1941, was a declaration of war or an

25. In 1944, Arthur Hays Sulzberger, president and publisher of the *New York Times*, interpreted the Lend-Lease Act as a warlike act by which the United States went to war. Speaking in New York City, January 31, 1944, Mr. Sulzberger said: "I happen to be among those who believe that we did not go to war because we were attacked at Pearl Harbor. I hold rather that we were attacked at Pearl Harbor because we had gone to war when we made the Lend-Lease declaration. And we took the fateful step because we knew that all we hold dear in the world was under attack and that we could not let it perish. That declaration was an affirmative act on our part and a warlike act, and we made it because we knew that freedom must be defended wherever it is attacked or we who possess it will lose it." *Washington Times-Herald*, February 1, 1944, p. 2. In reply to an inquiry, Mr. Sulzberger informed me, October 22, 1945, that the quotation is accurate.

In an address to the alumni of Brown University, June 19, 1944, Mr. Sulzberger stated: "I believe that we willed our participation in this war—that we went into it affirmatively when we signed the Lease-Lend Act; that we chose our course deliberately because we knew that our future could not be as we had mapped it unless we halted the aggressor as quickly as we could." *New York Times*, June 20, 1944. For what President Roosevelt and the Democratic sponsors of the Lend-Lease Bill in Congress told the people of the United States about the nature and intention of the measure, see above Chap. II. Nor did the *New York Times* in its editorial on the act, March 12, 1941, characterize the law as a warlike act by which Congress deliberately authorized war.

authorization of the President to inflict a military defeat on Germany by any acts of war he deemed fitting and proper, then efforts at intelligible communication as to the purposes of the law must be regarded as vain, unless, forsooth, the explanations and promises made by President Roosevelt and Democratic defenders of the measure are to be treated as intentionally deceptive. In any event, the Constitution confers on Congress the power "to declare war," not the power to authorize the President to make war when, where, as, and if he decides to make it; hence, only by flouting a plain provision of the Constitution could Mr. Krock, Congress, President Roosevelt, or anybody else claim that the Lend-Lease Act authorized the President to wage war at his discretion and pleasure in carrying out its provisions.

Furthermore, if in truth the Lend-Lease Act of March, 1941, had authorized President Roosevelt to go to war, had emancipated him from his peace pledges of 1940, why had Mr. Krock been at such pains a few days earlier, in his column of October 28, 1941,[26] to argue that when an "attack" was conceded in any clash at sea the President thereby escaped from the restraint of his public commitment to the antiwar plank of the Democratic platform of 1940? If the President had been set free and empowered to make war by the Lend-Lease Act of March 11, 1941, why did he need another liberation on October 28, 1941, seven months later? Apparently the answer to this riddle is: By November 5, 1941, Mr. Krock had come to the conclusion that President Roosevelt, by deceptive tactics in dealing with cases of "attack," had estopped himself from using such incidents as grounds for leading the country directly into war, and would henceforward have to seek in some other quarter authority for waging war on his own motion.

At all events, Mr. Krock, in his speech of November 5, charged the President with deception and with failure to take advantage of the Lend-Lease Act in pressing war on Hitler to the hilt—to the point of war under that act. But Mr. Krock

26. See above, p. 145.

failed to recognize the delicate position in which the President was placed at the moment. Amendments to the Neutrality Act of 1939 were then pending in Congress and had been for weeks; and Democratic sponsors of the amendments had denied and were denying that modifications were intended to make the country any less neutral or to commit the United States to war.[27] According to allegations and outward signs, the amendments to the Neutrality Act, like the Lend-Lease Act itself, were designed for the defense of the United States and not as an authorization of war.

Aware of the stout opposition in Congress to modifications of the Neutrality Act and of the fierce hostility to war expressed in the Senate and the House during the debates on the amendments, President Roosevelt was particularly constrained in November, 1941, to make his complicated moves so skillfully as to avoid even the appearance of an act of aggression. Politically and morally, it would have been difficult, if not impossible, for him to have used at the time either the Lend-Lease Act or the "attacks" in the Atlantic as full warrant for waging a lawful war in that area or for calling upon Congress to declare war. Nevertheless, Mr. Krock undoubtedly expressed accurately the sentiments and reasoning of war advocates in the United States, although he played into the hands of the opposition by charging the President with flagrant deception and concealment of the truth. In so doing, he must have increased, rather than diminished, President Roosevelt's embarrassment in the conduct of affairs in the Atlantic theater during the rest of November, 1941.

27. See below, Chap. VI. Late in 1947, after this chapter was in final proof, the Navy Department released a set of captured German documents in two volumes (*Fuehrer Conferences on Matters Dealing with the German Navy 1941*). The documents show that Hitler persistently held his Navy in check for the purpose of avoiding an act of overt war with the United States in 1941. With regard to disputes over "attacks," it may be noted that, under a treaty proclaimed February 25, 1929, the United States and Germany were bound to submit to "adjudication by a competent tribunal" any disputes between them unsettled by diplomatic proceedings, and "not to declare war or begin hostilities" before the report of the tribunal. Department of State, *Treaty Series*, No. 775.

CHAPTER VI

No Call for "Any Declaration of War"

IF President Roosevelt thought that the cases of "attack" in the Atlantic during September, October, and November, justified calling upon Congress for a declaration of war against Germany, he did not say so in any public pronouncement. Nor if he had desired to make such an appeal, did he have reason for believing that Congress would hear it gladly. On the contrary, the treatment accorded in the Senate to his allegations respecting those attacks and the vehement criticisms of his methods voiced on Capitol Hill indicated sharp hostility to a full-fledged involvement of the United States in the European war.

Besides, President Roosevelt was at the time entangled in a sharp controversy that was raging, in Congress and outside, over a demand for amendments of the Neutrality Act for the purpose of making it easier to render more effective aid to the Allies in the Atlantic area. Two sections of the act, in particular, it was alleged by Americans engaged in pressing for amendments,[1] hampered the delivery of such aid; the first forbade the arming of American merchant ships and the second prohibited American merchant and naval vessels from entering the combat zones. In advocating amendments, the President laid emphasis on the first; for, as everybody knew, the mere arming of merchant ships would be less objectionable to opponents of war than allowing merchant and naval vessels to enter war zones where they might become immediately engaged in shooting affrays.

The President's method of handling the ticklish issue of modifying the Neutrality Act and his fear of the opposition

1. Amending the Neutrality Act was a part of the program of the Committee to Defend America by Aiding the Allies, which by October, 1941, had thrown off the mask of neutrality and was definitely headed in the direction of war. Johnson, *The Battle against Isolation*, pp. 218 ff.

in Congress to war were illustrated at his press conference on September 23, reported as follows the next day by the *New York Times:*

Arming of the United States merchant ships and the supplying of arms for the vessels of other American republics is to be this government's answer to the German U-boat campaign in the North Atlantic, President Roosevelt made clear today.

No doubt was left by the President that Congress would be asked soon either to modify or repeal the Neutrality Act so that the arming of merchantmen would be possible. Congressional leaders are working upon a measure to effect this end.

Speaking out in his press conference less than twenty-four hours after the State Department had disclosed the sinking of the freighter *Pink Star* [under Panamanian registry], the Chief Executive made clear that the United States would do everything possible to protect Atlantic shipping and maintain the freedom of the seas. . . .

He said that the main issue was that the world is facing the most outrageous movement in all recorded history, an attempt by a certain group of people to conquer and hold the world. . . .

Congress, he stated emphatically, has made clear that United States policy is to help those peoples fighting the movement of conquest, and that is why America is trying to assure the transport of foodstuffs and military supplies to Great Britain. It is for protection against those who would dominate the world that American troops are in Greenland and Iceland; the dictators must be prevented from getting footholds for an attack on the New World.

A reporter asked whether it was not easier to defend ships by arming them.

The President said he thought we were heading toward the arming of United States merchant ships and those of other American nations. We are going to do everything we can to protect ships.

"Will there be just piecemeal changes in the Neutrality Act?" another reporter asked.

The reply was, that that was the problem. A decision would be made next week as to how much to ask in the way of repeal. . . .

The President emphasized that the arming of merchant ships

would not be in violation of international law, and noted that there were many precedents for providing American cargo and passenger vessels with arms to defend themselves.

But, President Roosevelt noted, specific legislation, the Neutrality Act, now forbids the arming of nonnaval vessels. It was then that the question was asked as to whether the law would be repealed outright or amended piecemeal.

Mr. Roosevelt agreed that the Neutrality Act would have to be revised, but said that he had under consideration the question of how much he should ask in the way of repeal. In saying that a decision might be made next week he did not disclose whether this would be revealed in a message to Congress or by some other means, such as the mere introduction of a bill which subsequently would receive his endorsement. . . .

In a message to Congress on October 9, President Roosevelt urged modifications in the Neutrality Act and recommended specifically the repeal of Section 6 of the act which prohibited the arming of American flag ships engaged in foreign commerce. "The revisions which I suggest," the President said, "do not call for a declaration of war any more than the Lend-Lease Act called for a declaration of war. This is a matter of essential defense of American rights." Then the President assured Congress: "The repeal or modification of these provisions will not leave the United States *any less neutral* than we are today, but will make it possible for us *to defend the Americas* far more successfully, and to *give aid* far more effectively against the tremendous forces now marching toward conquest of the world."

While he laid stress on the matter of arming merchant ships, President Roosevelt referred in his message to provisions forbidding American ships to enter war zones: "There are other phases of the Neutrality Act to the correction of which I hope the Congress will give earnest and early attention. One of these provisions is of major importance. I believe that *it is essential to the proper defense of our country* that we cease giving the definite assistance which we are now giving to the aggressors. For, in effect, we are inviting their control of the seas *by keeping our ships out of the ports of our own friends.*

It is time for this country to stop playing into Hitler's hands, and to unshackle our own." [2]

The House of Representatives acted quickly on the President's recommendation that the arming of American merchant ships be allowed; but the brief debate was marked by displays of militant hostility and the vote, hurried through under a "gag" rule, seemed to show that the opposition to this measure was stronger than it had been to the Lend-Lease Bill in March, 1941. In the Senate, there was less haste; with aid from a few Republican Senators and encouragement from the White House, sponsors of the bill, before it came to a vote, widened it in such a way as to riddle the whole Neutrality Act.[3] November 7, the measure passed the Senate by a vote of fifty for and thirty-seven against; six days later the House concurred by a vote of 212 for and 194 against.[4]

As thus adopted, the measure repealed the sections of the Neutrality Act which forbade the arming of merchant ships, and authorized the President to permit or cause to be armed such ships, during the unlimited national emergency proclaimed on May 27, 1941. It also repealed the sections relative to commerce with states engaged in armed conflict and to the exclusion of American ships from combat areas.

While this revision of the Neutrality Act was pending in Congress, the arguments that had been used in 1939 by members in discussing proposed modifications of the act in the autumn of that year [5] were repeated, with various shadings and qualifications. In October, 1941, supporters of the Administration in Congress were more hesitant in claiming that the revision was indeed likely to keep the country out of war.[6] But

2. Funk, *Roosevelt's Foreign Policy, 1933–1941*, p. 504 ff. (Italics supplied.)
3. George H. E. Smith, *Current History*, December, 1941, pp. 303 ff.
4. Johnson, *op. cit.*, p. 222.
5. Beard, *op. cit.*, pp. 238 ff.
6. For example, during the debate in the House on October 16, 1941, Representative Carl Curtis, Republican from Nebraska, asked Representative Pete Jarman, Democrat of Alabama, member of the Foreign Affairs Committee, whether Administration supporters in promoting the bill of repeal had as their objective "the keeping of this country out of war." On this subject the following colloquy took place:
"Mr. Curtis: The gentleman is a member of the Committee on Foreign Affairs, and the House always appreciates his opinion on these matters. In the nearly

the old contentions of 1939 were reiterated in October and November, 1941: on the one side, the bill to amend the Neutrality Act is not a war measure but is designed to provide for national defense; and on the other side, the bill means war for the United States.

The following extracts from the debates in the House and the Senate illustrate the manner in which supporters of the bill for amending the Neutrality Act, in one form or another,[7] represented that action as designed to keep the country out of war:

Representative Walter A. Lynch, Democrat of New York:

No one in this House is more opposed to war than I. It is because I am opposed to war that I have voted for every bill that would give us an adequate army for defense and a navy strong enough to defeat any combination of navies in the world. . . .

It is because I want to keep war from our land that I shall vote to arm American merchantmen. If an armed American merchantman, on the high seas, sinks a German submarine or surface raider in self-defense, war is not inevitable. If German submarines or surface raiders continue to sink unarmed American ships, war, in my opinion, is inevitable. . . .

Let me say we all want peace, but we can never have peace if unarmed American merchantmen are sunk, their crews drowned or left adrift on the ocean. War may not come if we permit American seamen to defend themselves. War will surely come, as

three years that I have been in this body, I have noticed that all of the measures that have been brought in by the committee have had as their objective the keeping of this country out of war. It has been so stated when these measures were presented to the floor. I ask the gentleman if that is still the objective in this legislation, or has the committee abandoned that objective?

"Mr. JARMAN: We absolutely have not abandoned that objective, but, as I have tried to show, the United States has recently set out on a program of all-out national defense, wherever we may best accomplish that in the opinion of the Congress.

"Mr. CURTIS: Then it is not necessarily offered as an effort to keep us out of war?

"Mr. JARMAN: I would not say absolutely; no. The main purpose is to get those goods over there to defeat Hitler."

House Debate, *Congressional Record*, 77th Congress, First Session. Vol. 87, Part 7, October 16, 1941, p. 7964.

7. No attempt is made here to show the distinctions drawn in the debates between arming American merchant ships and allowing American merchant and naval vessels to enter war zones.

it came before, when unarmed American ships were sunk without warning.[8]

Representative Martin F. Smith, Democrat of Washington:

Mr. Chairman, I am supporting and voting for the passage of House Joint Resolution 237 to repeal section 6 of the Neutrality Act of 1939, relating to the arming of American vessels. . . .

Unless our shipments of munitions and supplies reach their destination and are safely delivered to Britain and the democracies our aid will prove wholly ineffective. Obviously there would be no object gained in our manufacturing, producing, and shipping these articles and then have them sunk to the bottom of the ocean. This is only common sense. We are committed, in obedience to overwhelming public opinion, to a policy of national defense by furnishing aid to Britain and the democracies in order to thereby keep war away from the United States. We have fully embarked upon this policy and there can be no turning back now. . . .

We should continue to render every possible aid to Britain and the democracies by furnishing them with material and supplies, but not manpower. I am opposed to sending our boys to fight and die in the Red Sea, Greenland, Iceland, or any other foreign world outpost far distant—thousands of miles away—from our country.[9]

Representative James W. Mott, Republican of Oregon:

I said in the beginning that all are agreed that it is not only our right under international law but our duty in the interest of our own security to maintain and defend our natural right to use the seas, and to do that with every means we possess. This proposition seems to me to be fundamental; otherwise we would not be a free nation, free to enjoy our sovereign rights as a nation. We propose now to implement this right by the means of arming our merchant vessels for their own protection. This in itself, in my opinion, will not and cannot lead us into war. If I thought it would I certainly would not support it. This is not an aggressive action. It is a defensive action. I believe that, far from leading us into the

8. *Ibid.*, p. 7966.
9. *Ibid.*, pp. 7971–7972.

war, it will help to keep the war away from us, and that, I am sure, is what all of us desire.[10]

Representative W. O. Burgin, Democrat of North Carolina:

Step by step they say we are getting into war, but there is no evidence of it. We are still not in war. I have heard it said that 85 per cent of the American people are opposed to war. I am convinced that 100 per cent of the American people are opposed to war. I do not believe that there is a single Member of this House who thinks that the American people want to go to war or that this Congress wants to go to war. We all abhor war. . . .

We are considering today not a war resolution at all. I am not a Solomon and I am not attempting to advise any of you but may I say that this is simply a resolution affecting our domestic policy. . . .

We have heard considerable argument here on the subject of war. This resolution is not a declaration of war; it only provides for the arming of our merchant ships in order that they may be protected against the pirates of the sea. The adoption of this resolution and the arming of our merchant ships may not be 100 per cent protection but I cannot see for the life of me why arming our ships would involve us in war.[11]

Representative Luther Patrick, Democrat of Alabama:

Now it seems to me that if Germany should sink a merchant vessel that is unarmed, it will certainly be a greater aggravation and have a greater tendency to provoke us into war than if she were to tackle an armed merchant vessel, no matter what it does. Whatever justification there may be for the position of gentlemen on other things, I cannot see how they can logically say that this is a step to, because all on earth this is trying to do is arm merchant vessels. No other proposition is involved at all.[12]

Representative Homer D. Angell, Republican of Oregon:

While I believe that we should use every means at our command to build up our national defenses, to preserve the freedom of the

10. *Ibid.*, p. 7976.
11. *Ibid.*, p. 7982.
12. *Ibid.*, p. 7985.

seas, to uphold the Monroe Doctrine, and to protect our Western Hemisphere, I also hold the belief that we should not send our American troops overseas beyond the Americas to engage in this or any foreign war unless we are attacked. I do not believe, however, that the arming of our merchant ships—a right granted by international law and a right that we have always adhered to except when voluntarily surrendered—in any way imperils our peace and our security. It certainly does not join us as a belligerent in the war.[13]

Senator Tom Connally, Democrat of Texas:

So, Mr. President, I have concluded that it is our solemn duty to the American people to repeal sections 2, 3 and 6 and to revert to our rights under international law. We would simply reassume the status of other nations under international law.

Why are we doing these things? Why are we providing a two-ocean navy which, I hope, will be capable of controlling both the Pacific and the Atlantic? It is not for aggression. It is not because we covet an inch of the territory of any of our neighbors. It is because we propose to see that the interests of the United States, our territory, the lives of our people, and our institutions shall have security behind this wall of steel which the Navy will provide.

Mr. President, we want no war. I know there are those who charge those of us who want to repeal these provisions as wanting war. We have no desire to engage in the World War. We propose, however, to adopt every device and every measure which we can adopt to keep that war from coming to our own shores.[14]

Senator Claude Pepper, Democrat of Florida:

I agree that the issue involved is no less solemn than peace or war for this Nation; but I do not agree that the opponents of this proposal are the friends of peace. On the contrary, time will tell that those who are the advocates of this measure are those who have closest at heart the peace of their country.[15]

13. *Ibid.*, p. 8016.
14. *Ibid.*, Part 8, p. 8250.
15. *Ibid.*, p. 8284.

Senator Joseph O'Mahoney, Democrat of Wyoming:

This measure before us is not a measure to go to war. It is a measure to take away from our Government the shackles which were placed upon it in a law that was passed before the incredible Hitler plan of conquest had revealed itself to the world.[16]

Senator Theodore Green, Democrat of Rhode Island:

Mr. President, the people of this country do not want to go to war, and neither does the Congress, and neither do those who are in favor of amending the Neutrality Act. The question is not, however, Shall we go to war? The question is rather whether the war will come to us. In other words, if we do not want war here in America, we must make every effort to keep it away from here.

There had been a good deal of talk here about keeping out of war. Almost all of us want to keep out of war; yet here on the floor of the Senate, as well as elsewhere, anyone who disagrees with a proposal for keeping out of war accuses the proposer of trying to get us into war. There is no more reason for the so-called isolationists making this accusation against those who make such a proposal than there is for their opponents making the same accusation. In fact there is less reason, because in the present state of the World War we shall run a greater risk by doing nothing than by doing something to avert it.

The most effective means of keeping war away from America is to prevent Germany from completing her list of conquered European countries; and this can best be done by rendering aid to the countries that are fighting Germany on the other side of the Atlantic Ocean. So, we should give all material aid to any nation fighting Germany and her allies. That means not only producing war materials for them but also making certain that the materials reach them. It is no help to them and a loss to us if, after producing by the sweat of our brow these war materials, they are sunk in the Atlantic Ocean.[17]

Senator Chan Gurney, Republican of South Dakota:

I am convinced that the Neutrality Act of 1939 should be repealed in its entirety. This should be done now and without further delay. . . .

16. *Ibid.*, p. 8384.
17. *Ibid.*, p. 8402.

Complete repeal is the only honest stand we can take. Partial repeal is an obvious subterfuge, designed to placate those who have closed their eyes to the handwriting on the wall. It is designed to deceive our people into believing that a Neutrality Act still remains on our statute books, whereas in actual fact its remains might as well have been buried with the rest. . . .

. . . I am convinced that the Neutrality Act has not only prolonged and expanded the war but was largely responsible for starting it. Hitler was assured that we would not deliver the goods, and he knew he could prevent our friends from getting them. I am sure the act did not then, and does not now, express the underlying interests and convictions of the American people.[18]

The following extracts indicate the nature of the arguments against the proposed modification of the Neutrality Act as authorizing more steps on the road to war:

Representative George Holden Tinkham, Republican of Massachusetts:

With the declared policy of carrying contraband to belligerent governments, United States merchantmen under international law can be sunk as war vessels. Thus, if this bill is passed, it means the wholesale sinking of our merchant marine and the unlimited killing of our seamen and citizens. If our ships should go into belligerent ports, as suggested by the President, there would be more inflammatory incidents and the shedding of more blood. This would mean war, of course, and apparently this is what President Roosevelt and Secretary of State Hull desire. On the plea that constitutes a fantastic extension of the doctrine of the freedom of the seas under which they are proceeding to send contraband of war through combat waters to a belligerent, they have already declared naval warfare without seeking the consent of Congress, contrary to all historical precedent and to the constitutional provisions in relation to war.[19]

Representative Daniel Reed, Republican of New York:

I ask: How can any Member who desires to keep this country out of a foreign war vote to repeal section 6 of the Neutrality Act, as

18. *Ibid.,* p. 8419.
19. *Ibid.,* Part 7, p. 7958.

is now proposed, when he knows that such repeal will invite attack?

Armed merchant ships were sunk in wholesale lots in World War No. 1. The record shows that guns on merchant ships were no defense but only served to invite attack without warning. This proposal here today will do nothing more than to send out upon the high seas a suicide fleet to create an incident to plunge our country into war![20]

Representative Harold Knutson, Republican of Minnesota:

My countrymen, do not deceive yourselves or attempt to deceive those whom you represent by asserting that the passage of this legislation is calculated to preserve the peace of our country. No one in his right mind will contend that, and those of you who vote for this resolution will not be able to convince those whom you represent that you are today voting for another measure that is designed to keep America out of the war. This is another, and perhaps the last, step to war. Mark the prediction.[21]

Representative John M. Coffee, Democrat of Washington:

Mr. Chairman, I am opposed to this measure which would permit the arming of our merchant vessels. This is admittedly only a prelude to sending armed merchantmen into the combat zones. If we repeal section 6 of the Neutrality Act, which this bill proposes to do, we will be taking one of the last steps that will plunge this Nation into the war. It may be the last opportunity that the Congress will have to register its opposition against becoming actually engaged in war.

More than 80 per cent of our people are opposed to war, and I am confident the majority of the Members of this Congress are opposed to involving this Nation in the war. How inconsistent it is for Congress to oppose war and yet approve all of these steps that lead inevitably to war.[22]

Representative John M. Robsion, Republican of Kentucky:

We would have been in the war long ago but for the determined opposition of 80 per cent or more of the American people and a

20. *Ibid.*, p. 7979.
21. *Ibid.*, p. 7985.
22. *Ibid.*, p. 7986.

majority of Congress. This bill and others are mere subterfuges of the Administration to have the Congress give the President a green light for war. We should not sit supinely by and permit the President and his Cabinet to carry on these undeclared wars.[23]

Representative George W. Gillie, Republican of Indiana:

The issue as I see it is simple and clear-cut. It is war or peace. For who is to doubt that if we arm our merchant ships, load them with munitions, and send them into the Atlantic war zones, we will not be in the war before the start of another year?

The administration is seeking the destruction of this last safe-guard for peace in typical piecemeal fashion. Today we are asked to repeal section 6 of the Neutrality Act and permit the arming of American merchant vessels. If we do this in a few days we will be requested to repeal section 2 of the act and permit our armed ships to enter the European war zones [which was done].

The only reason repeal of section 2 is not sought at this time is the fear on the part of the war party that the American people have not been fully conditioned to take the final, shooting step.

Mr. Chairman, this is a typical administration trick. If the people will not take their medicine in one big gulp, give it to them in little sugar-coated doses. It all adds up to the same thing—active participation in a shooting war. . . .

Let us serve notice to the world by our vote on this amendment that the Yanks are not coming, that our sailors are not going to be sent to die in European waters, and that 80 per cent of the American people are still firm in their resolve not to become involved in a shooting war on foreign soil.[24]

Representative H. Carl Anderson, Republican of Minnesota:

Mr. Chairman, this legislation is, in my opinion, another step toward war and a definite advancement on the road to another A.E.F.

Any member of this House who is sincere in his pledge to his people back home that he would never vote to send American boys again into foreign wars cannot do other than to vote against the repeal of section 6 of our Neutrality Act.[25]

23. *Ibid.*, p. 7998.
24. *Ibid.*, p. 8000.
25. *Ibid.*, p. 8018.

Senator Arthur Vandenberg, Republican of Michigan:

Mr. President, I consider the pending Senate decision as substantially settling the question whether America deliberately and consciously shall go all the way into a shooting war, probably upon two oceans. The ultimate acknowledgment by Congress of a state of war, I fear, will be a mere formality, ratifying a precipitated fact if we approve the needless provocation and trend inherent in this proposed action. Therefore I consider that I am now facing the controlling issue so far as our own acts are concerned in respect to our entry into World War No. 2. It is in the presence of that grim and sinister specter, including a second A.E.F., without which the highest British command frankly says there cannot be an anti-Axis military victory on the continent of Europe, that I take my stand against the pending resolution.[26]

Senator Robert A. Taft, Republican of Ohio:

Mr. President, the adoption of the joint resolution now before the Senate would be direct authority from the Congress to the President to carry on an undeclared war against Germany, Italy and Japan on all the oceans of the world and in all the ports into which seagoing ships may sail. If the Members of the Senate intend to keep their pledges to the people of the United States, pledges made by themselves, by their leaders and by their parties, they can only vote "No" on the impending measure. . . .

It seems common sense to say that in the interest of all of us, Americans shall keep away from battlefields far from our own land. But more than anything else, the actual experience of the World War, the inevitable result of shipping contraband to a belligerent nation through such a zone, is conclusive proof of what will happen if we repeal this law.[27]

Senator Gerald Nye, Republican of North Dakota:

The resolution provides for the arming of American merchant ships, and removes any and all restrictions upon the movement of American ships. A surer way to get into war is not known than that of going out and looking and asking for war. That way invites incidents—not lone incidents but incidents by wholesale. . . .

26. *Ibid.*, Part 8, p. 8251.
27. *Ibid.*, pp. 8278 f.

Getting rid of whatever is left of fortification against American involvement is the continuing purpose embodied in the pending proposal. We are told that the laws of neutrality have proven a failure. Yes, Mr. President, they have proven a failure, a miserable failure, from the standpoint of such people as may have hoped that the United States would become involved in Europe's war in spite of the existence of such laws. But the laws of neutrality have been a huge success from the standpoint of the purpose which caused their enactment. They were intended to afford America a fortification against easy involvement in another foreign war, and so long as we have permitted those laws to function they have served their purpose exactly 100 per cent. But if we now repeal what we are asked to repeal by the pending proposal, we can put it down as pretty certain that we will be involved in the European war. . . .[28]

The pending question is this and bluntly this and no less than this:

Shall America, deliberately and consciously, go all the way into a shooting war, perhaps upon two oceans, or shall it not?

That question has no trimmings and no qualifying phrases to go along with it. It is a question of war or no war, war with its inevitable A.E.F. and its inevitable slaughter, or no war with an America pursuing the independent destiny which it can so readily achieve, beholden to no one, afraid of nothing.

The high command of Britain has made it plain that without an American A.E.F. there is no possibility of reentering the continent of Europe and forcing Hitler back into Berlin. How can anyone possibly doubt, at this point, that the first American ship manned by an American crew, under an American flag, loaded with American munitions designed for Britain and running a German submarine blockade, is simply the advance guard of an American transport loaded with troops for overseas duty and return voyages with our dead and wounded? [29]

Senator Robert M. LaFollette, Progressive of Wisconsin:

Mr. President, it is my contention that if we adopt the joint resolution which proposes the repeal of the three most vital sections of the Neutrality Act we shall have removed the last barrier

28. *Ibid.*, pp. 8306 f.
29. *Ibid.*, p. 8314.

which stands between the people of this country and actual involvement in war.

Therefore, I think that when Senators vote upon this issue they will be voting upon the issue of peace or war. I am convinced that if we repeal these essential sections of the Neutrality Act, if we send our merchantmen armed and in convoys through belligerent waters and have them discharge actual contraband of war in belligerent ports, our ships will be sunk and lives will be lost. In my opinion, this will be the final softening up process in an effort to bring a reluctant people to a willingness to accept actual hostilities.[30]

Senator C. Wayland Brooks, Republican of Illinois:

Each step that we have taken thus far has been taken with the insistent announcement that it was to keep us out of war. I say to you this is the last step. You cannot shoot your way a little bit into war any more than you can go a little bit over Niagara Falls.

Indeed, if we repeal the provisions prohibiting the arming of our merchant ships, and if we repeal the prohibition against their carrying contraband of war and sailing into belligerent ports of warring countries it is, in effect, a proclamation that "Here we come with war material in American ships, under the American flag, manned by American gun crews, shooting our way through as participants in the war."

I do not question the patriotic motives of men who sincerely desire to do that very thing; but I protest doing it while telling the American people, "We are doing it to avoid war."

I said before, the President has been at war; the Cabinet has been at war; but Congress has not been at war. In every action, Congress has definitely stated that it was not a war move, and that no act of war must be committed. Now, if this joint resolution passes, and we arm our ships and send them out to shoot under an act of Congress, by that action Congress goes overboard and is at war.

When the administration, the Cabinet, and the Congress are all at war, the country is at war; America is at war. Consequently, I am opposed to the passage of this joint resolution.[31]

30. *Ibid.*, p. 8321.
31. *Ibid.*, pp. 8377 f.

Senator D. Worth Clark, Democrat of Idaho:

There are in this body Senators who still insist that the step we are now called on to take will not mean war. But I do not very well see how any man can fail to perceive that even though this step may not mean war, this is the last spot at which we can stop short of war. We have been carried along swiftly and mercilessly by the fatal logic of our own actions. At each step it has become more difficult to resist that logic. If we take this one further step the power to resist war will be gone. We will be utterly at the mercy of two men—one of them Adolf Hitler, the other Franklin D. Roosevelt. Either one can put us into the war at any instant he may choose, if this measure is passed; the power of decision will have passed out of the hands of the American people and out of the hands of the Congress.[32]

Senator David Walsh, Democrat of Massachusetts:

I submit that although the resolution upon which we are soon to vote contains no words of war or words of peace, it is nevertheless the issue of war and peace, and history will rate this action by the Congress as tantamount to our concurrence in a shooting war which the President on his own authority has proclaimed.

We are being asked to proceed by indirection and by subterfuge to take our country into the war in Europe. The Neutrality Act, which was described as a law "to keep us out of war" is now being scrapped. The consequence is to serve notice upon the American people that Congress has removed all barriers to our actual participation in the war.[33]

Senator Burton K. Wheeler, Democrat of Montana:

Mr. President, the passage of the joint resolution now pending would give congressional approval to convoys; it would give congressional approval to naval warfare; it would give congressional approval to delivery of contraband of war to a belligerent, and it would place the stamp of congressional approval upon the orders given American destroyers to chase and destroy German U-boats on the Red Sea, the Persian Gulf, the Arctic Ocean or

32. *Ibid.*, p. 8478.
33. *Ibid.*, pp. 8507 f.

wherever the swashbuckling, irresponsible, and erratic Secretary of the Navy may send them, even at the cost of life itself.

Make no mistake about it, Mr. President, the passage of the pending joint resolution would be more than permission to arm merchantmen; it would be more than permission to send American merchant ships into war zones; it would be the approval of the evasion and violation of statutes by the executive and administrative branch of the Government; it would be tantamount to a declaration of war; and would be hailed as a mandate for more and further war steps, and the next step would be to send an expeditionary force. I have charged, and I repeat the charge, that the enactment of such legislation means war. Believing that, I shall oppose it; I shall fight it; I shall vote against it. . . .

Mr. President, we know it is war. We know that the passage of the pending measure means war. No Member of Congress can go back to his constituents and say that he did not mean it, because editorials from one end of the country to the other have said it, and will continue to say it. Any Senator who votes for the pending measure is voting for war; and it will do no good for him to try to deceive his people into thinking that he is not doing so, because he will not succeed. He will not fool them as they have been fooled with respect to other laws. When any Member of Congress thinks he is deceiving the people, he is only "kidding" himself.[34]

When President Roosevelt signed, on November 17, 1941, the Joint Resolution amending the Neutrality Act, the intellectual and moral appearances of things presented many anomalies. For months the Administration had been proceeding under the theory that supplying munitions to the belligerents at war with the Axis Powers, using American war vessels to convoy ships carrying munitions to those belligerents, and shooting at German submarines during attacks on convoys were not acts of war. All these acts, it was maintained by the Administration, were measures of self-defense.

Nevertheless during the same months, the President and his high officials had also been proclaiming again and again formulas that indicated the possibility of American involve-

34. *Ibid.*, pp. 8532 ff.

ment through an attack: War is coming nearer and nearer. The American people must wake up to this fact. Hitler is bent on nothing less than the conquest of the Western Hemisphere and the rest of the world. There is an unbridgeable gulf between the brutal despotism of the Nazi regime and the democratic system of the United States. By the enactment of the Lend-Lease Act in March, 1941, Congress has bound the country to the defeat of the Axis Powers and the President is rightfully taking the "defensive" actions necessary to assure the victory of the Allies.

In reply to these formulas from Administration quarters, opponents of President Roosevelt's measures employed other formulas.[35] The supplying of munitions to belligerents, using the American Navy to convoy ships to belligerents, and shooting at German submarines, are acts of war, in purpose and in reality. They will and are intended to carry the United States into full and open war. It is hypocrisy to maintain otherwise. It is flagrant deception to tell the American people that they can keep out of war and avoid sending their boys to fight outside of the Americas, while committing these acts of hostility with increasing abandon. It is mockery to assert that this "shooting war" is waged only for the defense of the United States, to keep war away from American shores. It is chicanery to pretend that the United States is neutral and that retaliations of German ships of war against American naval vessels are unprovoked and unwarranted "attacks" on the United States. It is a fraud of deepest dye to insist that the aggressive measures taken under color of the Lend-Lease Act are not "warlike acts"—are merely acts in defense of the United States. It is make-believe to protest that the Administration does not in fact want to engage the United States in the war, is not deliberately maneuvering the country into war. Such was the position taken by opponents of President Roosevelt's conduct of foreign affairs during the months preceding Pearl Harbor.

35. For the use of these formulas by the opposition, see above Chap. II (lend-lease), and pp. 165 ff. of this Chapter.

And how did President Roosevelt and high officials in his Administration characterize their opponents? In his message of January 6, the President warned the country against appeasers and selfish men: "We must always be wary of those who with sounding brass and a tinkling cymbal preach the 'ism' of appeasement. We must especially beware of that small group of selfish men who would clip the wings of the American eagle in order to feather their own nests." Some of his critics the President treated as well-meaning, but as suffering from illusions, and in fact aligned, if not in purpose, on the side of "appeasers" and "dupes." He bore down heavily on others as willing tools of Hitler, ready to profit by "doing business" with him, at the expense of servitude for the American people. Many pointed questions regarding his intentions and activities, the President dismissed with jocular gestures.

An excellent example of the President's manner of characterizing the opposition is provided by the following extract from his address before the Governing Board of the Pan-American Union at the White House, on May 27, 1941: [36]

There is, of course, a small group of sincere, patriotic men and women whose real passion for peace has shut their eyes to the ugly realities of international banditry and to the need to resist it at all costs. I am sure they are embarrassed by the sinister support they are receiving from the enemies of democracy in our midst—the Bundists, and Fascists, and Communists,[37] and every group devoted to bigotry and racial and religious intolerance. It is no mere coincidence that all the arguments put forward by these enemies of democracy—all their attempts to confuse and divide our people and to destroy public confidence in our Government—all their defeatist forebodings that Britain and democracy are already beaten—all their selfish promises that we can "do business" with Hitler—all of these are but echoes of the words that have been poured out from the Axis bureaus of propaganda. Those same words have been used before in other countries—to scare

36. Funk, *op. cit.*, p. 401.
37. At this time Stalin and Hitler were allies, and American Communists, calling the European war an "imperialist war," were denouncing President Roosevelt as a "warmonger."

them, to divide them, to soften them up. Invariably, those same words have formed the advance guard of physical attack.

With the lines of the verbal contest between the President and his critics so fixed and emphasized, the month of November, 1941, drew to a close. Despite contentions of war advocates that shootings in the Atlantic constituted the "attacks" which released the President from the antiwar platform of the Democratic party and warranted his calling upon Congress for a declaration of war against Germany, he made no such appeal to the national legislature. If, indeed, he had contemplated a direct request for war power on this ground, the design had been exploded before the country; for the Senate Committee on Naval Affairs and the newspapers had publicly exposed his misrepresentations of the alleged attacks.[38]

As a matter of fact, the President's management of this series of complicated moves in the Atlantic had been repeatedly denounced by his opponents as plain evidence of the duplicity against which they had long been inveighing, and had been criticized even by some of his ardent supporters eager for war. The large vote in both houses of Congress against the resolution riddling the Neutrality Act, as well as the speeches for and against it, clearly indicated that a call from the President for a declaration of war at anytime near the middle of November would precipitate a prolonged conflict in the House and the Senate and that, even if the appeal was successful, it would fail to achieve national solidarity—to silence the large antiwar party. Nobody in the country knew this better than President Roosevelt and Secretary Hull.[39]

With the prospects for an all-out war in the Atlantic beclouded by crimination and recrimination, the President and the Secretary now gave special attention to the conversations with Japan which, it was publicly known, were in a state of high tension about the middle of November.

38. See above, Chap. V.
39. See below, Chap. XVII, p. 529.

CHAPTER VII

Appearances of Relations with Japan

IN many substantial respects the relations of the United States with Japan differed from those with Germany and Italy in 1941. Japan was, no doubt, regarded as an associate of Hitler and Mussolini. Indeed, since September 27, 1940, Japan had been united with Germany and Italy in a treaty which bound the three powers, among other things, to aid one another if any one of them was attacked by any power not then involved in the European war—obviously the United States. Furthermore, the Japanese Government, since 1931, had been flouting the American doctrine of the Open Door for China and had been guilty of aggressions and depredations in that country; and after the fall of France in the summer of 1940 the Japanese Government had extended its imperialist operations to French Indo-China. All this time, American sympathy in general had been on the side of China.

Nevertheless, while the diplomatic relations of the United States with Germany and Italy had become merely nominal, those with Japan had been actively maintained. At the opening of 1941, therefore, some kind of adjustment with the Japanese Government appeared to be probable as well as possible. Moreover, American attitudes to Japan were not such as to preclude such an adjustment. Most Americans had little definite knowledge of Far Eastern affairs. Nor were they, being mainly European in origin, so extensively and deeply enlisted by sympathies or bitterness in the fortunes of Japan, China, and other Far Eastern countries as in the fortunes of Great Britain, France, Germany, and other European nations.

Hence the involvement of the United States in a war with Japan was not as passionately desired by any large group of Americans as involvement in war with Germany and Italy; nor as vigorously opposed by other groups. For the majority of those Americans who were openly or covertly advocating war, Hitler, not Hirohito, was "the" enemy, and to many of them avoidance of war with Japan was highly desirable, since it would permit the concentration of American energies on the defeat of Hitler and his European allies. In short, it was war against Germany, not Japan, that formed the main objective of the American war advocates. This was undoubtedly true even though some American imperialists, who had long had their eyes on the Far East, and some Christian missionaries to China were then desirous of having the United States "settle old scores with Japan" by arms.

Numerous Americans labored under the impression that Japan could be brought to her knees by an economic boycott in one form or another, without war, and favored that kind of "strong policy" or "firm hand" with Japan; but by no means all who advocated a boycott wanted to push that policy to the point of a two-front war, with the Japanese on the one side and the Germans and Italians on the other. Besides, high officers in the American Army and Navy, who would have to fight the two-front war if it came, urged cautious dealings with Japan in efforts to postpone, at least, an armed conflict in the Pacific.[1] Accordingly, American interests engaged in promoting war against Japan were less powerful than those aligned for the drive in the Atlantic.

Whatever the peculiarities of the situation with regard to Far Eastern affairs, the peace pledges of the Democratic platform and of President Roosevelt applied to the Orient as well as to Europe. The party's antiwar plank forbade the sending of American armed forces to fight outside the Americas, "except in case of attack," and hence pertained to the Far East no less than to Europe. And it was in reply to Republican charges that President Roosevelt was maneuvering in the direction of a war with Japan that he had declared, on November 2, 1940, "this country is not going to war."

Undoubtedly, many times during the year 1941 President Roosevelt, Secretary Hull, Undersecretary Welles, Secretary Stimson, and Secretary Knox warned the country that a

1. See below, Chap. XIV.

World War was going on, that America was in danger, that the Axis Powers planned to subjugate the United States, and that extraordinary measures for defense were necessary. And in the midsummer, the President began to apply drastic sanctions to Japan. But such words and actions did not imply that the peace promises of the Administration in respect of Japan were thereby explicitly or automatically canceled.

As a matter of fact, the application of economic sanctions to Japan, including the freezing of Japanese assets in the United States on July 25, 1941, was widely if not generally viewed in the United States, particularly by many professional advocates of peace, as pacific in purpose and probable consequences. This was one of the outstanding ideas in the armory of propagandists who held that the foreign policy of the country should be dedicated to the prevention of war everywhere, in Asia as well as in Europe.[2] It was an idea which Henry L. Stimson, as Secretary of State, had sought to "implement" in 1931 and 1932 in his efforts to checkmate Japan in Manchuria, only to be checkmated himself by President Hoover, who informed his entire Cabinet that economic and military sanctions "are the roads to war."[3] Doubtless, Mr. Stimson, as Secretary of War in 1941, still clung to his "doctrine" of 1931, although he had been informed by his former chief, President Hoover, that it was a way to war. Yet in his Executive Order of July 25, President Roosevelt merely declared that it was "designed among other things to prevent the use of the financial facilities of the United States and trade between Japan and the United States, in ways harmful to national defense and American interest, to prevent the liquidation in the United States of assets obtained by duress and conquest, and to curb subversive activities in the United States."[4] Such at least was President Roosevelt's intention as disclosed to the public on July 25, 1941.[5]

Nor at any time during the months preceding December

2. Beard, *op. cit.*, p. 197.
3. *Ibid.*, pp. 133 ff.
4. Funk, *Roosevelt's Foreign Policy, 1933-1941*, p. 442.
5. It was made known in 1946, at a hearing of the Congressional Committee on Pearl Harbor that President Roosevelt had asked the opinion of Admiral Stark

7, 1941, did President Roosevelt announce to the public that negotiations with Japan were in a hopeless deadlock, that an appeal to Congress for authority to employ war power was contemplated by his Administration, or that diplomatic relations with Japan were so disrupted as to indicate a necessary imminence of war. Even as late as December 2, 1941, the President stated at a press conference that "the United States is at peace with Japan and perfectly friendly, too." [6]

Nevertheless, it was generally known that relations with Japan had reached a point of strain in July, 1941. Thereafter, judging by official statements in various forms, including those at press conferences, the conversations or negotiations with Japan which were highly critical in nature fell into three stages, each marked by special features though not sharply divided: from July 24 to the Atlantic Conference; from the Atlantic Conference to the end of October; and after November 1.

FROM JULY 24, 1941, TO THE ATLANTIC CONFERENCE

DURING the first six months of 1941, according to official statements, relations with Japan, while far from promising,

on the application of embargoes to Japan. On July 22, 1941, Admiral Stark wrote to Mr. Welles in the State Department that he had prepared a memorandum for the President, that the President was pleased with it, and that the President had proposed sending a copy to Mr. Hull. In this memorandum prepared by Admiral Turner and initialed by Admiral Stark, the President's naval advisers informed him: (1) the effect of an embargo would be to hamper Japanese war effort, though not immediately, and not decisively; (2) "an embargo would probably result in a fairly early attack by Japan on Malaya and the Netherlands East Indies. . . . If war in the Pacific is to be accepted by the United States, actions leading up to it should, if practicable, be postponed until Japan is engaged in a war in Siberia"; (3) an embargo on exports "is almost certain to intensify the determination of those now in power [in Japan] to continue their present course. Furthermore, it seems certain that, if Japan should then take military measures against the British and Dutch, she would also include military action against the Philippines, which would immediately involve us in a Pacific war." CJC, Part 5, pp. 2379-2384. Admiral Stark testified before the Navy Court in 1944, in respect of an oil embargo, that, after the imposition of economic sanctions upon Japan, she would go somewhere and take oil and that if he were a Japanese he would do it himself. *Ibid.*, p. 2379 f. In short, when President Roosevelt began his program of economic sanctions in the midsummer of 1941, he had been advised by his naval experts that such actions should be postponed and that, if taken, they would almost certainly inflame the war party in Japan and probably result in a fairly early attack by Japan in the Pacific.

6. *New York Times*, December 3, 1941.

were conducted by President Roosevelt with a view to preventing war in the Pacific. Such was the impression given by the President in a speech on July 24 to members of the Volunteer Participation Committee then engaged in organizing civilian defense. Taken in their context his remarks on that occasion seemed to be directed to American citizens who were discontented because the President had not been drastic enough in imposing economic embargoes on Japan, often under the impression that such measures would bring Japan to book without incurring the risk of shedding American blood in the process. But the President's words on that occasion could be interpreted as evidence that he had been trying to prevent war in the Pacific.

Near the close of his address on July 24, the President said:

There is a World War going on, and has been for some time —nearly two years. One of our efforts, from the very beginning, was to prevent the spread of that World War in certain areas where it hadn't started. One of those areas is a place called the Pacific Ocean—one of the largest areas of the earth. . . .

It was very essential from our own selfish point of view of defense to prevent a war from starting in the South Pacific. So our foreign policy was—trying to stop a war from breaking out down there. . . . It was essential for Great Britain that we try to keep the peace down there in the South Pacific.

All right. And now here is a nation called Japan. . . . If we had cut the oil off, they probably would have gone down to the Dutch East Indies a year ago, and you would have had war.

Therefore, there was—you might call it—a method in letting this oil go to Japan, with the hope—and it has worked for two years—of keeping war out of the South Pacific for our own good, for the good of the defense of Great Britain, and the freedom of the seas. . . .[7]

Although President Roosevelt did not say explicitly on July 24 that he had quit trying to prevent war in the Pacific, his use of the past tense in his speech of that day lent color to such an interpretation of his words. Journalists, always on the

7. Funk, *op. cit.*, p. 441.

watch for a shift in his policy, raised the issue at a press conference on the next day, July 25. Thereupon the President, in an evasive manner, merely hinted at growing dangers in "the world situation," and left the journalists and the public guessing about his designs and maneuvers—as the following report of the conference in the *New York Times* shows:

The conference opened with a question whether the President's use of the past tense yesterday in describing the policy of appeasement toward Japan indicated that the period of appeasement was over. The President replied that he was only pointing out what had happened up to the time he spoke.

The question was repeated with the assertion that his language strongly suggested his discussion of that policy was a sort of swan song, but he insisted that he had said nothing about that and would say nothing about it.

A questioner wanted to know what the Japanese situation meant to our neutrality, because that was the question uppermost in the minds of many citizens. That, the President said, was a terribly iffy question.

The interrogator repeated that it was a valid question, to which every American wanted the answer. The President replied that so many things haven't happened. Then he was asked, "So many horrible things are looming?"

The President replied that he knew, but he could not talk about things that have not happened yet. If there was some one definite line we could bank on as going to happen, then perhaps we could talk about it. But that's not the situation, he added.

The President declined to answer a question whether the repeated use of the word "duress" in the strong Japanese statement made yesterday by Mr. Welles did not provide a legal policy backing for freezing of Japanese credits in this country. Mr. Roosevelt said he had not heard reports that there were only four Japanese ships left in American harbors. He declined again to state whether his remarks to the committee yesterday indicated an end or a continuance of the appeasement policy.

The President was asked whether he thought the American public was aware of the international situation in the Far East, to which he replied that they were no more so than they were sufficiently aware of the international situation in the West.

It was disclosed that yesterday he received reports from persons who have been around the country—a newspaper man, two magazine writers, a Cabinet officer and two others, all of whom had been across the continent in March or April and again more recently.

All came the same day and all of them agreed, the President said, that there had been a tremendous change since March or April, that the people are far more cognizant of international danger and of the world situation, and increasingly so. Mr. Roosevelt added that he didn't think they were sufficiently aware yet, but there had been a very marked change in three months.

Asked what could be done to sharpen their awareness, the President cited one example out of a dozen, the Volunteer Participation Committee which called at the White House yesterday. He had told its members, he said, of the need for this awareness, and with five members from each corps area, and hundreds of committees under them, he was hopeful that they would reach every home with the message of the situation's urgency.

Would you say, he was asked, that events in the Far East had sharply accentuated the dangers of the international situation? The President replied that he would put it this way: that events in the Far East were bringing greater awareness on the part of the public to the dangers of the world situation.[8]

Journalists and newspaper readers left guessing as a result of the press conference on July 25 received very soon some concrete information on the state of affairs with Japan. By an Executive order, that day, President Roosevelt froze Japanese assets in the United States and brought trade between the two countries to a halt. That action was, of course, open to various interpretations. It could mean an effort to keep peace or prevent war in the Pacific by the use of economic pressure, with the expectation that Japan would yield rather than fight. Or it could be taken as implying that President Roosevelt was traveling the Stimson road [9]—to war, if sanctions failed. But as to his intentions or hopes in this respect, the President also left the public wondering.

8. *New York Times*, July 26, 1941.
9. Beard, *op. cit.*, pp. 133 ff.

Under date lines August 1, 2, 3, 4, 5, 6, and 7, dispatches in the *New York Times* from Tokyo, Saïgon, Chungking, Shanghai, Manila, Washington, and London indicated that the situation in the Far East was growing more strained, that Great Britain and the United States were closely coöperating in the Pacific, that no more crude oil was to be exported to Japan, and that the Japanese Government was complaining against what it called "encirclement."

At a press conference on August 8, the matter of encirclement and British-American joint action in the Far East was presented to Secretary Hull. The Secretary's treatment of the subject was reported by the *New York Times* as follows:

If Japan imagines she finds herself dangerously encircled she has accomplished that encirclement herself, Secretary of State Cordell Hull said today at his press conference.

His comment was prompted by dispatches from Toyko declaring that the Japanese Government felt that the United States, Britain, China and the Netherlands Indies were "encircling" Japan militarily, politically and economically.

Mr. Hull said he knew nothing about this supposed encirclement proposition. If any country thinks it is about to be encircled, he added, it can find lawful areas where it can go and avoid giving the suggestion by itself that it is about to be encircled.

State Department officials said this evening that they had no comment to make at this time concerning London reports that discussions were actually under way between this country and Britain concerning a joint stern warning to Japan designed to curb her policy of expansion in the Far East. . . .[10]

THE ATLANTIC CONFERENCE AND AFTER

WHEN President Roosevelt and Prime Minister Churchill held their meetings in the Atlantic in August, American citizens, except those who, as the President said on July 24, had not read the newspapers or listened to the radio "carefully," knew that affairs in the Pacific were approaching a point of high pressure. Official statements to the press in Washington, veiled

10. *New York Times*, August 9, 1941.

and vague though they were, had left no doubt of that. Accordingly, expectations of reporters were keyed up when the President returned home from his voyage to sea. Had anything been decided at the conference with regard to Japan? The President at his press conference on August 16 spoke only in general terms. The *New York Times* reported him as saying that he and the Prime Minister had "discussed the situation on every continent. Every continent you ever heard of, he had added facetiously." Since Asia had been "heard of," evidently the Far East had been considered at the Atlantic Conference but the President's nebulous statement threw no light on the commitments he had made, if any, with reference to the Far East. On August 18, however, in his report to congressional leaders, he declared that the chief danger of early involvement in a "shooting war," as he saw it, lay in the situation in the Far East, where, he intimated, chances were about even that Japan would start new aggressions.[11]

Although at his press conference immediately after the Atlantic meetings with Mr. Churchill, President Roosevelt said that they had discussed "every continent you ever heard of," he gave no indication to the public at the time that Japan had been one of the chief items on the agenda for discussion with the Prime Minister. Nor between August 17, after his return to Washington, and the end of August, did he report to the American people that as an outcome of the conference any special memorandum on vital relations with Japan had been handed to the Japanese Ambassador in Washington. Judging by outward appearances, relations with Japan after the conference seemed to follow the indefinite course of the previous weeks, as if nothing signifying a new stage in Japanese affairs had been reached or acted upon.

Reporting on the day of August 17, 1941, in Washington, the *New York Times* stated that the President and Secretary Hull had held a long conference and that, it was believed, the principal subject discussed was the repatriation of 100 Ameri-

---

11. For the President's public statements on the Atlantic Conference, see above, Chap. IV.

can citizens detained by the Japanese Government.[12] On leaving the White House, Secretary Hull gave reporters no details. Indeed, he merely indulged in one of his customary generalizations: "It was a general exchange of information in which we were bringing each other up to date on the international situation; we discussed all phases of the international situation in which either of us was interested." At his press conference the next day, Secretary Hull, speaking of the White House conference of the previous day, August 17, told correspondents that he had then considered with the President the Far Eastern situation; and, in a vein unusually light for Mr. Hull, he cautioned correspondents that he and the President had "talked about every part of the geography of the planet. Every geographical area, he emphasized, was discussed to a greater or lesser extent." [13] Such was the official information given to the American public on foreign affairs for August 17, 1941.[14]

At his conference with congressional leaders on August 18, the President referred to the possibility of "shooting" troubles in the Far East, but he told them that no "new commitments" had been made at the Atlantic Conference. Furthermore, he apparently gave them no hint that relations with Japan were at, or approaching, a danger point. On the contrary, the *New York Times*, in its account of this meeting, said: "The result of the President's report to the Congressional group was a lifting of spirits among some of them, who had thought that the Roosevelt-Churchill conference meant early steps that would take this country near to the brink of war." [15]

During the period immediately following the Atlantic Conference, newspaper dispatches, dated at various points in the world, asserted that negotiations with Japan were proceeding feverishly, with the United States pressing for some kind of culmination. A few examples from among hundreds follow. Tokyo, August 19: Relations with Japan were reported to

12. *New York Times*, August 18, 1941.
13. *Ibid.*, August 19, 1941.
14. For the momentous day of August 17, 1941, see below, Chap. XVI, pp. 486 ff.
15. *New York Times*, August 19, 1941.

be near the breaking point after a long conference between Ambassador Grew and Foreign Minister Toyoda; for Mr. Grew warned Mr. Toyoda that unless Japan made fundamental alterations in her foreign policy, American pressure on Japan would be intensified. Chungking, August 18: A survey of the Burma road has been made for the United States Government and traffic is increasing over the line to the Chinese war capital. London, August 20: Authoritative quarters were rejecting the idea of appeasing Japan. Hyde Park, August 22: American changes in the tariff on crab meat strike a severe blow at one of Japan's important and far-flung enterprises. London, August 24: Prime Minister Churchill declared in his speech on the Atlantic Conference that, if President Roosevelt's negotiations with Japan ended in trouble, "we shall of course range ourselves unhesitatingly at the side of the United States."

Speculations on the new course of American-Japanese affairs since the Atlantic Conference, Japan's complaints about "encirclement," and Prime Minister Churchill's offer to join the United States in war with Japan, if it came, were treated in a statement by Secretary Hull, on August 25. As far as press reports went, nothing new had been brought up in the form of an American note to Japan. The United States was still standing for the principles of 1937 and what Mr. Hull was fond of calling "international morality"; and, if his statement was comprehensive, President Roosevelt in his latest exchanges with the Japanese Government was merely emphasizing the doctrine of the Kellogg Pact of 1928, the revision of treaties by peaceful methods, and respect for international law. Such at least was the impression conveyed by the *New York Times* report of Secretary Hull's conference on August 25:

Secretary of State Cordell Hull declared today that conversations with Japan have been purely informal and emphasized that any settlement of difficulties with Japan would have to be based upon the fundamental principles he enunciated in 1937.

These include renouncement of the use of force as a national policy and revision of treaties by peaceful methods and a respect for international law as a sound basis for international dealings.

The Secretary of State thus denied London reports that the United States was seeking an agreement with Japan upon the basis of neutralization of Siam and Indo-China. He made clear that the fundamental position of this government in relation to Japan had not altered.

Mr. Hull made his statements today when asked in a press conference whether he cared to comment upon the assertions made in a speech yesterday by Prime Minister Winston Churchill to the effect that, while the United States is seeking a friendly settlement with Japan, in the event of trouble in the Far East, Britain would range herself at the side of the United States.

The Secretary refused to comment directly upon Mr. Churchill's speech, remarking that, while he always was prepared to pay the highest tribute to the remarkable addresses of the British Prime Minister, he did not care to take up or analyze any particular point in this speech.

Asked specifically about Mr. Churchill's statement that the United States was seeking to arrive at "a fair and amicable settlement that would give Japan the utmost reassurances regarding her legitimate interests," Mr. Hull stressed that the informal conversation he had on Saturday with Admiral Kichisaburo Nomura, the Japanese Ambassador, was typical of the kind of talks that were going on.

The Secretary of State refused to answer a point-blank question as to whether this government had received definite proposals for a settlement of differences from Japan, either through Joseph C. Grew, American Ambassador in Tokyo, or Admiral Nomura.

The impression gained by many reporters was that the conversations with Japan were at a delicate stage and that the Secretary was reluctant to discuss them, but did not want a wrong impression to get abroad about this government's attitude.[16]

By August 29 it was known that Ambassador Nomura had delivered to President Roosevelt a personal letter from the Japanese Premier, Prince Konoye. This information was interpreted by journalists to mean that Japan, now in desperate economic straits, was striving to achieve a settlement with the United States by negotiations between the two highest author-

16. *Ibid.*, August 26, 1941.

ities in their respective governments. Would President Roosevelt seize this occasion to attempt an adjustment of some kind? At a press conference on August 29, he took up the question. As the *New York Times* reported the discussion:

President Roosevelt announced at his press conference today that he would send a reply to the personal letter he had received from Prince Fumimaro Konoye, the Japanese Premier, in connection with the conversations that seek an improvement in relations between the United States and Japan.

In view of the delicacy of the situation, Mr. Roosevelt confined his definite comment on the discussions to that one statement. . . .

Mr. Roosevelt gave no intimation of the nature of the reply that he would make to the Premier nor of the time when it would be sent. The text of the letter from Prince Konoye continued to be held in confidence though it was generally understood to be conciliatory in tone and to urge conversations looking to an adjustment of differences.

The situation was admittedly delicate, and for that reason President Roosevelt discouraged questions on it at his press conference.

"Could you say whether you believe that war can be averted in the Pacific?" he was asked.

He would not be led into a discussion on that question, dismissing it with the remark that the Pacific was too wide to merit a response. Generally, he volunteered, all that could be said about the Pacific situation was that there was no news today.[17]

Secretary Hull was equally uncommunicative in commenting publicly on Premier Konoye's personal and friendly letter urging a settlement of troubles in the Pacific by direct consultation. In a style already made familiar by usage for more than eight years, the Secretary employed many words to say little; conversations were in a preliminary, exploratory stage and nothing definite could be revealed at the moment:

Without minimizing the importance or the seriousness of the diplomatic conversations with Japan that were marked by the delivery to President Roosevelt of the personal letter of Prince Fumimaro Konoye, the Japanese Premier, Secretary of State

17. *Ibid.*, August 30, 1941, pp. 1, 4.

Cordell Hull made clear at his press conference today that the conversations were only in the preliminary stage and that no definite conclusions had been reached or were yet possible.

His remarks, made in response to questions of newspaper correspondents, were directed to reports in the Far East and elsewhere of programs, understandings or virtual agreements that already had been made.

Asked whether Prince Konoye had made any specific proposals in his message to the President, Mr. Hull said that the conversations were exploratory and would not reach the stage contemplated in the question unless or until they had passed beyond into the phase of negotiations. He made the same reply in response to further questions concerning some Tokyo reports that a basic understanding already had been reached.

Then he went further in minimizing the present status of the conversations in response to a question as to whether he felt there was any reason for concern on the part of other interested powers in the Far East that the so-called united front in that area might collapse.

When he said that an exploration was being conducted in the nature of an inquiry into relations between Japan and the United States, he said he meant that casual conversations were taking place on the whole question to determine just what they might reveal. This, he added, did not signify that the discussions had taken on the character of negotiations.[18]

At length Premier Konoye's letter to President Roosevelt was reported by the *New York Herald Tribune* to be a proposal for a personal conference between the President and the Premier "somewhere in the Pacific" for the purpose of adjusting difficulties between the two governments and making a general settlement. The report was, however, soon quashed by an official statement given out at the White House, September 3. As reported in the *New York Times:*

White House Secretary Stephen Early denied today that Premier Prince Fumimaro Konoye of Japan had invited President Roosevelt to confer at a conference in the Pacific.[19]

18. *Ibid.*, August 31, 1941.

19. As a matter of fact, on August 17, the Japanese Ambassador informed President Roosevelt and Secretary Hull that Premier Konoye proposed direct

Mr. Early made this statement after discussing with Mr. Roosevelt the New York Herald Tribune's report that such an invitation had been extended.

"1. The President has no invitation.

"2. If the Herald Tribune had seen fit to check with the White House before the publication of the story I would have told them that.

"3. The only plan the President has involving a trip on the water in the immediate future is a cruise from Annapolis on the Chesapeake Bay and on the Potomac River.

"If the Herald Tribune cares to follow the President to Annapolis, they will readily see the falsity of this story."

Responding to a question, Mr. Early added that he did not believe "Premier Prince Konoye would be coming up Chesapeake Bay." [20]

Mr. Early's statement of September 3, based on instructions from President Roosevelt, may have seemed amusing to him and the correspondents present; but news, other than official communications from the White House and State Department, indicated that the situation was grave and that Premier Konoye had sought to discuss it directly with the President in some manner. Journalists whose profession demanded efforts to obtain from official sources comments on news reports from various parts of the world, including Japan, sought an official explanation of the "Konoye affair," but were completely baffled.

Concerning the actual nature of this "affair," so momentous in the history of American relations with Japan, journalists learned little or nothing definite at the press conferences held at the White House and the State Department in September and October. [21] What were the terms and conditions offered by Premier Konoye? What action, if any, was the

consultation at a meeting in the Pacific; and on August 28, the Japanese Ambassador handed to the President a message from Premier Konoye urging a meeting between the heads of the governments of the United States and Japan to discuss all important problems of the Pacific. CJC, *Report*, p. 23; *Peace and War: United States Foreign Policy, 1931–1941* (July, 1943), pp. 712 f.

20. *New York Times*, September 4, 1941.

21. See below, Chap. XVI.

American Ambassador in Tokyo, Joseph C. Grew, urging upon President Roosevelt and Secretary Hull? What responses were the President and the Secretary making to Japanese overtures? With regard to these primary questions journalists in Washington received no concrete information whatever.

Two extracts from the *New York Times* reports of press conferences during this critical period fairly illustrate the kind of expositions which Secretary Hull and President Roosevelt regarded as fulfilling their obligations to the American people while then conducting foreign affairs of the gravest significance to the Republic:

Sept. 6. Secretary of State Cordell Hull said today that he was wondering what had happened to the exploratory conversations President Roosevelt was supposed to be conducting with the Japanese.

No developments have been announced since Admiral Kichisaburo Nomura, the Japanese Ambassador, last week delivered to the President the personal letter from Prince Fumimaro Konoye, the Japanese Premier. This circumstance led newspaper correspondents to remark at Mr. Hull's press conference that they were wondering what had happened to the conversations. Secretary Hull replied that he was wondering, too.

He had nothing new to communicate to the correspondents, he said, but when he was asked whether something was being awaited from Japan he countered vaguely by saying that it really depended on the viewpoint.

President Roosevelt was also uncommunicative at his press conference. He referred questions on the conversations to Mr. Hull, who pleaded that he could not go into details at this time. An answer would be sent by the President to Prince Konoye in due course, he said, adding that the matter of a reply was not being overlooked in any way.

Asked whether a continuation of the conversations was awaiting dispatch of the reply to the Premier, Mr. Hull again countered by saying that both sides would be consulted before that question was answered.[22]

Sept. 10. Recurring reports, particularly in Tokyo, that a pre-

22. *New York Times*, September 7, 1941.

liminary agreement looking to an adjustment of relations between the United States and Japan was to be expected momentarily were regarded as premature today in view of a brief oral reply made by Secretary of State Cordell Hull to questions at his press conference today.

Mr. Hull said that he had no advices that a statement was imminent. He did not define what he considered was covered by the term "imminent," but it was assumed that he was expecting nothing in this category within the next few days or perhaps longer. This is apart from what Prince Fumimaro Konoye, the Japanese Premier, may say in Tokyo.[23]

AFTER OCTOBER 16, 1941

MANY reports of events in the press after the fall of the Konoye Cabinet on October 16 seemed to indicate that intransigent militarists were in power at Tokyo and that an explosion into war might happen at any time. From Manila, October 16, came a dispatch in which Francis Sayre, American Commissioner in the Philippines, was reported as saying that the United States was moving close to the brink of war and that the Axis would be smashed. From Tokyo, on the same day, Otto Tolischus reported to the *New York Times* that the Director of Japanese Naval Intelligence had declared that the relations of the United States and Japan were "now approaching the final parting of the ways." From Shanghai, October 16, came a dispatch stating that the Central China *Daily News*, organ of the Japanese-sponsored regime in Nanking, had asserted that war between Japan and the United States "is inevitable."

The news was alarming but negotiations or at least conversations between the United States and Japan continued after the substitution of the Tojo Cabinet for the Konoye Cabinet in Tokyo. For a time, however, there was a lull in reports of official comments at Washington bearing on relations with the Japanese Government. Between October 16 and November 15 little more than speculations appeared in the dispatches

23. *Ibid.*, September 11, 1941.

from Washington to the *New York Times*. Few of them were substantial or illuminating as to actual propositions and counterpropositions. On November 15, however, a break in the uniformity of press reports came with the announcement that Saburo Kurusu had arrived in Washington as a special agent from Tokyo to assist Ambassador Nomura and that he was "hoping for peace," in renewed attempts at a meeting of minds. Then a brief period of official reticence ensued during which, the public supposed, exchanges of views or exploratory conversations were going on.

A few days after his arrival notice was served on Mr. Kurusu that the United States was ready for war—in a dispatch to the *New York Times* from Washington, dated November 19, written by Arthur Krock, who often spoke with authority for the State Department. Mr. Krock asserted that the familiar thesis—the United States cannot defend the Philippines—had been challenged by two factors. "One is the naval alliance [24] with Great Britain, joining for all practical purposes the fleets of the two nations in the Pacific." The other was the extension of lend-lease to the Soviet Union with a view to opening up terminal points in Siberia for American fighting planes flown from Manila. Mr. Krock then turned directly to the Japanese special agent, saying that Mr. Kurusu might learn of these circumstances officially before he left Washington or by "reading this dispatch." As if possessing secrets of the United States Government, Mr. Krock added that supporting details for his statements were locked up in the War and Navy Departments.[25]

Reports from Washington, dated November 20 and 22, alleged that each official conference with Ambassadors Nomura and Kurusu had been held at the request of the Japanese; they also noted that the State Department was being extremely proper in its public statements on the negotiations but that "it is now clear that the United States is not prepared to appease the Japanese even on minor points." November 22, Washing-

24. Perhaps this was news to the United States Senate itself.
25. See below, Chap. XIV on "Secret War Decisions and Plans."

ton date line, a dispatch announced that Secretary Hull had conferred with the representatives of Great Britain, China, Australia, and the Netherlands. According to a Washington date-line message, November 24, Secretary Hull was having conferences with these diplomats and no progress was being made in negotiations with Japan. The following day a *New York Times* dispatch reported discussions with representatives of Great Britain, China, and the Netherlands, separately, at the White House and conferences of top officials in preparation for a major move in the Far East.

Two Associated Press dispatches, dated Washington, November 26, revealed that an impasse had been reached in the negotiations with the Japanese representatives. First, Japan faced a showdown and must negotiate on American principles or take the consequences of resuming her forward movement in the waters of southeastern Asia. Second, "The United States tonight handed Japan a blunt statement of policy, which, informed quarters said, virtually ended all chance of agreement between the two countries on explosive Far Eastern issues." On November 28, the *New York Times* published a special article from Washington, dated November 27, to the effect that United States officials were satisfied that they had exhausted all efforts at a solution of Pacific problems and had, for that reason, restated "basic principles." From Tokyo, Otto Tolischus reported to the *Times* that the Japanese Government now saw an end of the negotiations as a result of the United States memorandum of November 26.

The record of news as presented day by day in the press dispatches was amplified, if not confirmed in all respects, by reports of press conferences at the White House and the State Department.[26] The following extracts, from the *New York*

26. In the absence of official reports of press conferences, such as appear in President Roosevelt's *Public Papers and Addresses* for the years before 1941, reliance must be placed on newspaper accounts. In reply to a letter from me, dated September 11, 1946, the Director of The Franklin D. Roosevelt Library at Hyde Park, said, on September 19, 1946, that the official minutes of President Roosevelt's press conferences for 1941 "are not available to public inspection at this time."

Times, illustrate the reserved, uncommunicative, and noncommittal nature of statements by President Roosevelt and Secretary Hull.

November 14, 1941, President Roosevelt:

Mr. Roosevelt answered in the affirmative a question as to whether he believed that "the American people realized the seriousness of the Far Eastern situation." He raised his voice to emphasize that he sincerely trusted not, when asked "whether there will be war right away in the Far East."

"Can war with Japan be avoided?" a reporter bluntly inquired. The Executive answered that question slowly after a moment's pause. If he replied no, he said, the answer would be subject to widespread interpretation. If he answered yes, that would be a pure guess. No interpreter of the national scene knows the answer, he continued.

Asked whether the United States was prepared to make certain that the Burma Road would be kept open, the President said this problem was related to too many others to be answered. Questioned thereafter as to whether he cared to comment upon widely credited reports that Japanese insistence on concessions in China had hampered American-Japanese negotiations, the President indicated that he thought the question and any answer ill-advised at this time.[27]

November 20, 1941, State Department:

The Japanese envoys, Saburo Kurusu and Admiral Kichisaburo Nomura, having received "new advices" from Tokyo, returned today to the State Department, where they continued to discuss with Secretary of State Cordell Hull the possibilities of reaching a general settlement in the Pacific.

At the conclusion of the forty-five-minute meeting State Department officials said that the meeting was held to discuss the international situation and was still "exploratory" in nature.

No further appointments have been made, the officials said, although they added that it was "expected" that the Japanese envoys would return to discuss a readjustment of United States–Japanese relations.

Although both parties have been reticent in their statements

27. *New York Times,* November 15, 1941.

about the tone and substance of the conversations, it is known that Mr. Hull has made perfectly clear to the Japanese envoys that no settlement between the two nations is possible on the basis of Premier Hideki Tojo's statement Monday before the Japanese Diet.[28]

November 21, 1941, Secretary Hull and President Roosevelt:

Mr. Hull met with his Far Eastern advisers in the State Department this morning and was prepared to see the Japanese officials after the Cabinet meeting, this afternoon or tonight. However, the Japanese spent the day in conferences at their embassy going over the situation in the light of yesterday's meeting, and were not prepared to go ahead at the State Department. The precise nature of the snag was not revealed by the embassy.

In the meantime Secretary Hull sought to dispel assumptions that the meetings were being held only as the Japanese requested. He explained at his press conference that the talks were being arranged by mutual agreements. He reiterated that the conversations still were of an exploratory nature.

President Roosevelt, when asked at his press conference whether he had any cause for optimism over the negotiations dismissed the subject by replying that the question was like asking if a man had stopped beating his wife.[29]

November 22, 1941, State Department:

After tonight's conference between Mr. Hull and the two Japanese envoys, a State Department spokesman said their talk was an expansion of previous discussions and that talks would continue next week.[30]

November 23, 1941, State Department:

Official silence was maintained again today at the State Department. Officials said that the Japanese envoys, Saburo Kurusu and Admiral Kichisaburo Nomura, had not talked to any United States official since their conversations with Secretary of State Cordell Hull last night.[31]

28. *Ibid.*, November 21, 1941.
29. *Ibid.*, November 22, 1941.
30. *Ibid.*, November 23, 1941.
31. *Ibid.*, November 24, 1941.

November 24, 1941, Secretary Hull:

At this press conference this morning Secretary Hull insisted that the Far Eastern conferences in the main had thus far been confined to talk and added that discussions had not yet given way to decisions.[32]

November 25, 1941, Secretary Hull:

At a press conference this afternoon, Mr. Hull was not prepared to go into details, but he said he probably would meet with the Japanese envoys very soon. Pressed for some light on how the conversations were proceeding, he replied that it was too early for a basis of negotiation to have been reached and that further talks would be necessary before he would know that such a basis could be reached. Thus far, he said, the discussions have related mainly to the pros and cons of first one question and then of another.

Mr. Hull professed not to be in a position at this time to predict the outcome, but it was believed in usually well-informed diplomatic circles that the conversations would come to a climax before very long and that they would not drag on interminably.[33]

November 26, 1941, State Department and Secretary Hull:

The Japanese representatives were handed for their consideration a document that is the culmination of conferences back and forth during recent weeks. It is unnecessary to repeat what has been said so often in the past that it rests on certain basic principles with which the correspondents should be entirely familiar in the light of many repetitions.[34]

On November 26, 1941, the day that Secretary Hull handed to the Japanese Ambassadors the memorandum that was to prove fateful in history, the *New York Times* reported the action under the headline: United States Gives Terms to the Japanese; Plan Clings to "Basic Principles." In this report the *Times* included the official statement given above. It added that proposals looking to the readjustment of relations

---

32. *Ibid.*, November 25, 1941.
33. *Ibid.*, November 26, 1941, p. 1.
34. State Department to newspaper correspondents. *Ibid.*, November 27, 1941, p. 1.

between Japan and the United States were handed by Secretary Hull late today to Mr. Nomura and Mr. Kurusu; and that this action marked the culmination of the first phase of the conversations that have been in progress since the arrival of Mr. Kurusu ten days ago.

Although no detailed explanation of the proposals was vouchsafed [the report continued], it was assumed that they embraced a plan for permitting further discussions of the problems between the two nations. . . . It was observed that as they [the Japanese Ambassadors] emerged from Mr. Hull's office that they were beaming. The State Department contented itself with a statement to newspaper correspondents to the effect that the United States was adhering to basic principles. From this it was assumed that the peace proposal enunciated by Mr. Hull on July 16, 1937, was being kept in mind.[35]

The Associated Press dispatch of November 26, from Washington, on the memorandum handed to the Japanese was laconic. In substance it declared: the United States and Japan have failed to find a formula for a peaceful settlement of their differences after seven months of diplomatic negotiations, it was learned authoritatively tonight, and peace or war in the Far East may hinge on Japan's next move; informed diplomatic headquarters predicted that Japan, faced with a showdown on her militantly proclaimed objectives, must now decide to negotiate on the basis of American principles or face the consequences of resuming her armed march southward.[36]

More definite was the United Press dispatch, dated Washington, November 26, 1941. By some process the author of that report had succeeded in discovering the essential terms of Secretary Hull's memorandum and the realities of the situation—as distinguished from the generalities offered by Secretary Hull which supposedly left open the door for "further discussions" with Japan, "looking to the readjustment of relations between the United States and Japan." The United Press dispatch read:

35. *Ibid.*, November 27, 1941.
36. *Ibid.*

The United States handed Japan a blunt statement of policy which, informed quarters said, virtually ended all chances of an agreement between the two countries on the explosive Far Eastern issues. The United States Government is reported to be demanding, as the price of any concessions it grants, that Japan abandon plans for future aggression, pull her armies out of China and French Indochina, restore the "open door" policy in China, and substitute peaceful negotiations for the sword in achieving her so-called co-prosperity sphere.[37]

In a special dispatch from Washington to the *New York Times*, dated November 26, 1941, its correspondent, Bertram Hulen, gave what was to all appearances the State Department's "line," namely, that basic principles had been handed to Japan, that the door to further negotiations was still open, and that all depended on Japan's reply. Mr. Hulen said: "All this does not mean that the negotiations have been completed. Everything now depends upon the Japanese reaction. The next move is up to them." He then dwelt at some length on the opposition of China to any agreement between the United States and Japan which did not conform to Chinese views of the interests of that country. Having some inside information, Mr. Hulen stated that the Tokyo Government was believed prepared to give assurance against aggressive actions in the future, and perhaps in some measure to treat its agreement with the Axis as a dead letter in return for assurance of peace in the Pacific for the present and some modification of American economic restrictions. But, also in line with the State Department, Mr. Hulen added that "a big question concerned the bona fides"—would or could Japan abide by "the terms of an agreement."[38]

AFTER NOVEMBER 27, 1941

STATEMENTS from the White House and the Department of State subsequent to those of November 26, and they were

---

37. *Ibid.*, November 27, 1941.
38. *Ibid.*

numerous, altered in no fundamental respect the situation as described in previous communications to the public or the line disclosed in Mr. Hulen's dispatch. Such statements continued to indicate an increasing tension in relations with Japan, but they represented President Roosevelt and Secretary Hull as waiting day after day for the Japanese reply to the memorandum of November 26, with some prospects of a peaceful adjustment in sight, up until the final day of the Japanese attack on Pearl Harbor. There were in the official communications, it is true, strong notes of concern over the continued southward movement of Japanese forces in the Far East and over the possibility of a breakdown in relations with Japan; but there was no hint that a call upon Congress for authority to take strong action was contemplated, that peaceful relations with Japan were de facto at an end, or that even the possibility of a pacific settlement of troubles in the Far East was now, for all practical purposes, out of the question.

The following extracts from the *New York Times* reports on official statements after November 27, 1941, illustrate the essentials of the position taken by President Roosevelt and Secretary Hull in their communications to the American public on relations with Japan during this critical period.

November 28, 1941, President Roosevelt:

All that President Roosevelt would say in a long press conference this morning was that he might have to return from Warm Springs, Ga., for which he departed at 3 P.M. today, because of the Japanese situation, and that, under existing circumstances, American merchant vessels in the Pacific would not be armed. He added that this decision, made by the State and Navy Departments and the Maritime Commission, might be altered by events at any time.

Mr. Roosevelt stressed the words "under existing circumstances" and a correspondent asked: "Mr. President, how long do you expect existing circumstances to continue?" It would be much better, Mr. Roosevelt replied, to ask that question in Tokyo than in Washington.[39]

39. *Ibid.*, November 29, 1941.

November 29, 1941, Secretary Hull:

As for the conversations between Japan and the United States, Secretary Hull maintained at his press conference that there was nothing to be said until the Tokyo government indicated its attitude on the communication he gave last Wednesday to Admiral Kichisaburo Nomura and Saburo Kurusu, the Japanese envoys. He described it as a communication to get some basis, a basis presumably looking to a readjustment of relations, through the suggestions he incorporated in applying American principles to specific matters.

Mr. Hull referred to the Army and Navy a question as to whether a Japanese move from French Indo-China into Thailand at this time would result in a major conflict in the Pacific. The armed services had no views to offer on the subject.

However, Secretary Hull took pains at his press conference to point out as important the presidential ruling against arming American merchant ships for the present on routes not only in the Pacific but to ports of Portugal, Spain and adjacent islands. He emphasized that this applied to both areas, not to the Pacific alone.[40]

November 29, 1941, President Roosevelt:

With tension high in Washington, President Roosevelt during his brief vacation at Warm Springs, Ga., took advantage of the occasion to make a short address that hinted at war, but vaguely and inconclusively. Mr. Merriman Smith, veteran press representative at presidential conferences and on presidential trips, has described the scene. The President's "speech began in customarily hackneyed channels: 'Glad to be back . . . my other home . . . always inspired to be here.' He interjected a few gentle wisecracks, but with an imperceptible change of direction, moved into a discussion of the war. The newspaper men knew this sudden change in the tone of his remarks was intended for them rather than the polio patients." After speaking briefly about the plight of oppressed peoples in Europe, the President indicated that the people of the United States might not be at peace by the next Thanks-

40. *Ibid.*, November 30.

giving. "The newspaper men knew that something ominous and world-shaking was about to be said. The Roosevelt build-up to a smashing remark was unmistakable." After another side reference, about the Army-Navy football game that day, President Roosevelt declared that American boys at naval and military academies might be actually fighting some time in the near future. Thereupon newspaper men made a wild dash for the telegraph office: "Flash—Warm Springs, Georgia—Roosevelt says we may be fighting within a year." [41]

The exact order and wording of President Roosevelt's indirect statement to the American public on November 29, as reported in newspapers, varied slightly, although there was no difference as to the significance of his declaration respecting the possibility that the United States might be at war soon. In the *New York Times* the following report of the address appeared:

"I think we can offer up a little silent prayer that these people will be able to hold a Thanksgiving more like an American Thanksgiving next year. That is something of a dream, perhaps.

"In days like these it is always possible that our boys at the military and naval academies may actually be fighting for the defense of these American institutions of ours."

The President said in his talk he had thought much during the past weeks while dealing with international problems in Washington, about the possibility that another year might see American boys at war.

The American people had reason for thanksgiving, he continued, since "We're one of the largest nations of the world and nearly all other large nations are at war or defending themselves or conquered or else the lives they used to live have been completely blotted out." [42]

Whatever the exact language employed by the President in his address on November 29, he had, as reported, made two

41. A. M. Smith, *Thank You, Mr. President: A White House Notebook* (Harper, 1946), pp. 107 ff. The President left Washington on November 28 and arrived at Warm Springs the following morning, November 29, Saturday. The address at Warm Springs was on Saturday after dinner.
42. *New York Times*, November 30, 1941.

statements bearing on the possibility of war. The first was: "In days like these it is always possible that our boys at the military and naval academies may actually be fighting for the defense of these American institutions of ours." In form and substance this statement was not out of harmony with his campaign pledges of 1940 and with views which he had often expressed publicly, namely, that military preparations were for the defense of the United States and that the country would fight in case of attack. Here was nothing novel in the long list of his public pronouncements on foreign policy since he became a candidate for the presidency in 1932.

President Roosevelt's second statement, as reported in the press, though tentative and speculative, seemed to have, however, a different ring. It ran to the effect that while dealing with international problems during the past weeks he had thought much about "the possibility that another year might see American boys at war." On its face there was nothing new about this statement either. There had always been a possibility that American boys might be at war within a year, in case of attack.

But taken in the context of news of disturbances throughout the world in November, 1941, this statement by the President could be considered a broad hint that war might be coming at least within a year. Here, at all events, was the shadowy appearance of a presidential declaration that the policy of defense for the United States might not keep the country out of war, that war might come, after all that had been said and done about the defense and peace of the United States.[43] Yet the President's statement, if intended to be a war warning, was so casual, cryptic, and hypothetical in character that it conveyed no definite impression to Congress or the American people. Besides, three days later, he declared publicly that "the

43. In my personal papers is a letter from a distinguished newspaper man who attended the President's press conferences and public meetings for many months and heard the President's address on November 29. In this letter the journalist, who had been an assiduous student of President Roosevelt's public pronouncements, informs me that the statement above cited contained the first hint from the President that war might actually be at hand.

United States is at peace with Japan and perfectly friendly, too."

December 2, 1941, President Roosevelt:

An occasion for the new reference to peace and friendship with Japan in this critical period was another report on the southward movement of Japanese forces in Indo-China. If numerous press dispatches from various points in the world were correct, it was the continued advance of those forces which was to bring Great Britain, the United States, and the Netherlands into war with the Japanese Empire.[44] Yet in a statement to the press on December 2, 1941, President Roosevelt treated this ominous event as if it was an incident in American relations with Japan, about which he had directed an inquiry to the Japanese Government—not an ultimatum with a time limit—in the course of conversations which were still peaceful and friendly in nature. Such was the statement as reported by the *New York Times:*

President Roosevelt announced that he formally asked the Japanese Government today why it was sending so many military, naval and air forces into Indo-China. The President insisted that his request did not represent an ultimatum.

Asked about the inquiry, the President replied as follows:

Since April the United States Government has been discussing with the Japanese Government some method of arriving at the objective of permanent peace in the whole Pacific area. It seemed for a time as if progress were being made and, during the period until late June, this government assumed that there would be no act contrary to the desired end of peace.

The United States Government was, therefore, somewhat surprised when, at the end of June, the Japanese Government sent troops—the President thought a limited number—into French Indo-China after brief negotiations with the French Vichy Government. At the conclusion of these negotiations the Vichy Government let it be understood rather clearly it had agreed because it was powerless to do otherwise.

Some time thereafter Japanese-American conversations were resumed and for a time seemed to make progress. Again it was under-

44. See below, Chap. XIV.

stood clearly no additional territory should be taken by any one during the negotiations. The other day this government got word from various sources that there already were in Indo-China large additional Japanese forces—naval, air and land—and that other forces were on the way. Even without the arrival of forces in transit, Japanese strength greatly exceeded the original limitation agreed to by the French, and forces on the way are many times greater.

The question, therefore, has been asked of the Japanese Government, at the President's request, of what intention the Japanese Government has as to the future, eliminating the possibility that the forces might be for the policing of Indo-China, which is a very peaceful spot. The President hopes to get a reply very shortly.

"Was any time limit set for the reply?" a reporter asked.

That was a silly question, Mr. Roosevelt answered in replying in the negative. Those tactics were employed in the last century, but not in this. The United States is at peace with Japan and perfectly friendly, too, he added.[45]

December 3, 1941, Secretary Hull:

The following day, December 3, Secretary Hull gave, at his press conference, a view of the situation that differed slightly from the President's version on the previous day. The Secretary, as if awaiting information on Japanese reactions to his statement of basic principles on November 26, said that the continuation of conversations with Japan depended on her answers to inquiries about Japanese troop movements and to his memorandum of November 26. Since he did not then know exactly when Japan's reply would be forthcoming, Mr. Hull indicated that he "was, therefore, not in a position to predict whether there would be further conversations with the Japanese envoys." He once more reviewed American principles of international morality but he spoke as if he thought that a stage for considering "a basis for wider conversations relating to a peaceful settlement in the Pacific" might yet be reached.

On this press conference of December 3, the *New York Times* reported:

45. *New York Times,* December 3, 1941. pp. 1, 5.

Secretary of State Cordell Hull outlined at his press conference the course of the exploratory conversations with Tokyo's envoys.

Whether the conversations will continue will depend upon Japan's answers concerning her garrison in Indo-China and secondly, on the document Mr. Hull gave Ambassador Kichisaburo Nomura last Wednesday.

Mr. Hull did not know when Tokyo would reply to the President's request for information or to his own document. He was, therefore, not in a position to predict whether there would be further conversations with Japanese envoys.

The Secretary viewed Japan's policies as based on force, in contrast to the American policy of following peaceful means and observing doctrines based on law, justice and morals. All phases of the subject had been taken up in the exploratory conversations, he said, including scores of minor phases and numerous major ones.

Mr. Hull considered his outline of the conversations illuminating on the more important aspects of the situation and a statement of the fundamentals of the situation, as he described it, looking both ways.

He recalled that, since last Spring, there had been, from time to time, purely exploratory discussions between Admiral Nomura and his embassy staff and Secretary Hull and his associates in the State Department, as well as occasionally between President Roosevelt and the Ambassador. These conversations were held to ascertain whether a basis could be reached for negotiations looking to a readjustment of relations in the Pacific area.

While these discussions were in progress, Mr. Hull indicated their exploratory nature to representatives of other interested governments in the Pacific area, such as Great Britain, Australia, the Netherlands and China. Those governments understood that if a stage could be reached where there would be something fundamental, from their viewpoint, it would afford a basis for wider conversations relating to a peaceful settlement in the Pacific. That area, Mr. Hull pointed out, included all the continents and islands and seas and populations, covering nearly one-half the earth.

The really basic questions that came up during these conversations, he explained, were two.

One related to a course based on the doctrine of force as an instrument of policy—political, economic, social and moral—both at home and in connection with populations that might be conquered. That embodied, he emphasized, a twin doctrine of conquest of territory belonging to others and subjugation of the peoples, with the establishment of a military despotism in the most arbitrary manner over the whole political, economic and social and moral affairs of conquered peoples.

There are examples of it, he declared, in Europe under Reichsführer Hitler's policies, and in China.

The opposing view of government and government policy, Secretary Hull said, included the basic doctrines of law, justice, and morals and equality of treatment among nations, especially in relation to commercial opportunities, commercial life and peaceful settlement of matters in controversy rather than their settlement by force.

This and the other basic provisions of the so-called fourteen peace points that he enunciated and sent to all governments in July, 1937, he declared, represented the other viewpoint, as this government understood it, preached and practiced it.

So, he explained, all the exploratory conversations revolved around one phase or another of these two opposing basic policies and principles of government. No more advanced stage of determined questions had been reached, Mr. Hull said, even in a preliminary way. During the many months, he went on, there were casual and informal conversations, unofficial talks in the main about scores of minor phases raised by the discussions and numerous major phases.

His friends representing the Japanese Government, Mr. Hull intimated, presented only in partial form during the exploratory and informal conversations a document on the subject. So he deemed it natural and logical after months of discussion and increasing confusion growing out of utterances and actions of other governments and partial suggestions, as compared with a broad basic settlement, that he should undertake to bring the whole basic phases of the situation up to date by handing the Japanese a document that was comprehensive and basic.

In response to questions, Mr. Hull said he understood the British were keeping this government informed of the reinforcement of naval power at Singapore and that the Netherlands was similarly giving information concerning military preparations in the Netherlands Indies.[46]

46. *Ibid.*, December 4, 1941, pp. 1, 4.

As the early days of December passed, news dispatches from Washington and other points in the world continued to intimate the approach of a real crisis in the relations of the United States with Japan, preparations for coöperative action against Japan by the United States, the British Commonwealth of Nations, the Netherlands, and China, and the imminence of war. But official communications from the White House and Department of State, as reported in the press, indicated that relations with Japan, if strained, were still intact and "perfectly friendly," as President Roosevelt said on December 2, and that the President and Secretary Hull were awaiting, as if otherwise uninformed, new official statements from the Government of Japan respecting its intentions, particularly the reply of Tokyo to the American memorandum of November 26.

According to the appearances reflected in the press dispatches expressing their views, President Roosevelt and Secretary Hull regarded the situation as critical but were still of the opinion that Japan might shrink from war, might come back with proposals for new conversations looking toward the maintenance of peace in the Pacific. Even President Roosevelt's appeal to the Japanese Emperor for peace and coöperation in overcoming "the deep and far-reaching emergency," broadcast on Saturday night, December 6, seemed to show that, while the President thought the outlook for a pacific settlement was dark, he did not consider it as hopeless.[47]

47. For actualities of the situation see Chap. XVII.

CHAPTER VIII

The Attack—Official Explanation

THE attack which was to release President Roosevelt
from his numerous commitments to neutrality and
peace for the United States and to meet "the challenge of
critics," [1] came on December 7, 1941. It came not from German ships of war in the Atlantic, which the President's supporters and advocates of war had been watching with expectancy, but from Japanese bombers in the Pacific, on the
strategic American outpost in Hawaii. Moreover, it came with
such a terrific burst of fire power that it brought disaster to
the American fleet in Pearl Harbor and inflicted appalling
losses on American armed forces and civilians.

Although the extent of the catastrophe was not officially
revealed for many months, enough was soon disclosed by
American newspapers to make it plain that the United States
had suffered a major defeat; that the Navy was badly crippled
for prosecuting an effective war against Japan immediately;
that this nation confronted a long and grueling struggle to
overcome the Japanese. As if to make the conflict global,
Germany and Italy, four days later, December 11, declared
war on the United States and thus the country became engaged
in a two-front war, handicapped initially by the devastation
at Pearl Harbor.

On the following day, December 8, President Roosevelt
went before Congress to call for a declaration that a state
of war had "existed" since the attack. In support of the call,
he said:

Yesterday, December 7, 1941—a date which will live in infamy—
the United States of America was suddenly and deliberately attacked by naval and air forces of the Empire of Japan.

1. Arthur Krock's phrase. See above, p. 147.

The United States was at peace with that nation and, at the solicitation of Japan, was still in conversation with its Government and its Emperor looking toward the maintenance of peace in the Pacific. Indeed, 1 hour after Japanese air squadrons had commenced bombing in Oahu, the Japanese Ambassador to the United States and his colleague delivered to the Secretary of State a formal reply to a recent American message. While this reply stated that it seemed useless to continue existing diplomatic negotiations, it contained no threat or hint of war or armed attack.

It will be recorded that the distance of Hawaii from Japan makes it obvious that the attack was deliberately planned many days or even weeks ago. During the intervening time the Japanese Government has deliberately sought to deceive the United States by false statements and expressions of hope for continued peace. . . .

Japan has, therefore, undertaken a surprise offensive extending throughout the Pacific area. . . .

I ask that the Congress declare that since the unprovoked and dastardly attack by Japan on Sunday, December 7, a state of war has existed between the United States and the Japanese Empire.[2]

In a radio broadcast to the nation, December 9, 1941, President Roosevelt again characterized the Japanese attack as a

2. For the quotations given on this and following pages from President Roosevelt's addresses and messages in December, 1941, see Senate Document No. 148 and House Document No. 458, 77th Congress, First Session, 1941. President Roosevelt's official thesis that the United States was at peace with Japan on December 7, 1941, was engaged in peace conversation with Japanese envoys at the moment, and was completely surprised by the Japanese attack on Pearl Harbor has become a part of a growing literature to that effect. It has even found expression in a judicial opinion: The United States Circuit Court of.Appeals, Tenth Circuit, November 6, 1946, said in the case of The New York Life Insurance Company *vs.* Louise Bennion (p. 2): "When the attack [on Pearl Harbor] was launched, we were not only at peace with Japan, but were actually engaged in a peace conference with her envoys. It was deliberately and strategically planned, and while recognized as a possibility in view of our strained relations, came as a complete surprise to our civil, military, and naval authorities. About one hour after the commencement of the attack . . . the Japanese envoys in Washington delivered a note to our State Department informing our Government of the severance of diplomatic relations." Insofar as this statement is a part of the judicial reasoning necessary to sustain the decision of the court, the "official thesis" may be regarded as incorporated in "the law of the land."

sudden, unexpected, treacherous act committed while relations between the two countries were peaceful.

He said:

The sudden criminal attacks perpetrated by the Japanese in the Pacific provide the climax of a decade of international immorality. . . . The Japanese have treacherously violated the long-standing peace between us. . . .

I can say with utmost confidence that no Americans today or a thousand years hence, need feel anything but pride in our patience and our efforts through all the years toward achieving a peace in the Pacific which would be fair and honorable to every nation, large or small. And no honest person, today or a thousand years hence, will be able to suppress a sense of indignation and horror at the treachery committed by the military dictators of Japan, under the very shadow of the flag of peace borne by their special envoys in our midst.[3]

In a special message to Congress, December 15, 1941, President Roosevelt reviewed the historical relations of the United States with the Far East, including Japan. He referred to the Japanese proposal for a modus vivendi on November 20 and declared:

Such a proposal obviously offered no basis for a peaceful settlement or even for a temporary adjustment. The American Government, in order to clarify the issues, presented to the Japanese Government on November 26, a clear-cut plan for a broad but simple settlement. . . . In the midst of these conversations, we learned that new contingents of Japanese armed forces and new masses of equipment were moving into Indo-China. Toward the end of November these movements were intensified. . . . I promptly asked the Japanese Government for a frank statement of the reasons for increasing its forces in Indo-China. I was given an evasive and specious reply. . . . We did not know then, as we know now, that they had ordered and were even then carrying out their plan for a treacherous attack upon us. I was determined, however, to exhaust every conceivable effort for peace. With this

3. Funk, *Roosevelt's Foreign Policy, 1933–1941*, pp. 559 ff.

in mind, on the evening of December 6 last, I addressed a personal message to the Emperor of Japan. . . . Japan's real reply, however, made by Japan's war lords and evidently formulated many days before, took the form of the attack which had already been made without warning upon our territories at various points in the Pacific. There is the record, for all history to read in amazement, in sorrow, in horror, and in disgust! We are now at war. We are fighting in self-defense. We are fighting in defense of our national existence, of our right to be secure, of our right to enjoy the blessings of peace. . . .[4]

Indications that the United States was at peace with Japan on December 7, when the attack came, and that conversations looking toward the maintenance of peace in the Pacific were still going on, were given in two official releases on December 7—one by the State Department and the other by Secretary Hull. The first was worded as follows:

On November 26 the Secretary of State handed to the Japanese representative a document which stated the principles governing the policies of the Government of the United States towards the situation in the Far East and setting out suggestions for a comprehensive peaceful settlement covering the entire Pacific area.

At 1 P.M. today the Japanese Ambassador asked for an appointment for the Japanese representatives to see the Secretary of State. The appointment was made for 1:45 P.M. The Japanese representatives arrived at the office of the Secretary of State at 2:05 P.M. They were received by the Secretary at 2:20 P.M. The Japanese Ambassador handed to the Secretary of State what was understood to be a reply to the document handed to him by the Secretary of State on November 26.

Secretary Hull carefully read the statement presented by the Japanese representatives and immediately turned to the Japanese Ambassador and with the greatest indignation said:

"I must say that in all my conversations with you [the Japanese Ambassador] during the last nine months I have never uttered one word of untruth. This is borne out absolutely by the record. In all my fifty years of public service I have never seen a document that was more crowded with infamous falsehoods and dis-

4. *Ibid.,* pp. 595 ff.

tortions—infamous falsehoods and distortions on a scale so huge that I never imagined until today that any Government on this planet was capable of uttering them."

Secretary Hull's statement read:

Japan has made a treacherous and utterly unprovoked attack on the United States.

At the very moment when representatives of the Japanese Government were discussing with representatives of this government at the request of the former, principles and courses of peace, the armed forces of Japan were preparing and assembling at various strategic points to launch new attacks and new aggressions upon nations and peoples with which Japan was professedly at peace, including the United States.

I am now releasing for the information of the American people the statement of principles governing the policies of the Government of the United States, and setting out suggestions for a comprehensive peaceful settlement covering the entire Pacific area, which I handed to the Japanese Ambassador on November 26, 1941.

I am likewise releasing the text of a Japanese reply thereto which was handed to me by the Japanese Ambassador today.

Before the Japanese Ambassador delivered this final statement from his government, the treacherous attack upon the United States had taken place.

This government has stood for all the principles that underlie fair dealing, peace, law and order, and justice between nations, and has steadfastly striven to promote and maintain that state of relations between itself and all other nations.

It is now apparent to the whole world that Japan in its recent professions of a desire for peace has been infamously false and fraudulent.

The tenor of the official thesis on the coming of war with Japan was maintained in the documents relative to the coming of war with Germany and Italy. After Germany and Italy, on the morning of December 11, 1941, had declared war on the United States, President Roosevelt sent the following message to the Congress of the United States:

On the morning of December 11 the Government of Germany, pursuing its course of world conquest, declared war against the United States.

The long known and the long expected has thus taken place. The forces endeavoring to enslave the entire world now are moving toward this hemisphere.

Never before has there been a greater challenge to life, liberty, and civilization.

Delay invites greater danger. Rapid and united effort by all the peoples of the world who are determined to remain free will insure a world victory of the forces of justice and of righteousness over the forces of savagery and of barbarism.

Italy also has declared war against the United States.

I therefore request the Congress to recognize a state of war between the United States and Germany and between the United States and Italy.

FRANKLIN D. ROOSEVELT.

THE WHITE HOUSE,
    December 11, 1941.

The two resolutions of Congress recognized the existence of war with Germany and Italy and stated that the governments of those countries had "formally declared war against the Government and the people of the United States of America" and added that "the state of war between the United States" and those governments "which has thus been thrust upon the United States is hereby formally declared." The resolutions authorized and directed the President to employ the armed forces and the resources of the United States to carry on the war against Germany and Italy.[5]

HAWAIIAN COMMANDERS OFFICIALLY DESIGNATED AS RESPONSIBLE FOR THE PEARL HARBOR DISASTER

AT LAST, with constitutional authority from Congress, the United States was at war; and the nation, with slight dissent, was united in the prosecution of the contest to a triumph at arms over the Axis Powers. But in the midst of the alarms and

5. For the war documents, see Senate Document No. 148, 77th Congress, First Session, 1941.

tensions of the armed conflict, pertinent questions were asked persistently in Congress and outside. How did it happen that such a disaster befell American forces at Pearl Harbor? Was it due to the fact that the United States, at peace with Japan and "still in conversation with" the Japanese Government and Emperor "looking toward the maintenance of peace in the Pacific," was suddenly without forewarning caught off guard by the attack? Or had there been lack of alertness and incompetence somewhere in the chain of command from Washington to the high officers in charge at Hawaii—General Walter C. Short and Admiral Husband E. Kimmel?

Although the need of secrecy and precaution in time of war and the requirements of war were undoubtedly paramount considerations, such questions were widely discussed in the country. On Capitol Hill the possibility of a congressional investigation was suggested but discarded for the moment. While Senators and Representatives confined their wonderment to speculations on the subject, President Roosevelt acted. At the earliest possible moment, he sent Secretary Knox to Hawaii to inquire into the disaster and report to him. On the return of the Secretary in a few days, a brief statement on the catastrophe was made public but, for the purpose of withholding information on the losses at Pearl Harbor from the enemy powers and sustaining national morale, the report was brief, cautiously worded, and noncommittal as to responsibilities for the degree of success attained by the Japanese attack.

By an Executive order signed December 18, 1941, President Roosevelt appointed a commission of five men—two Army officers and two Navy officers, headed by Owen J. Roberts, Justice of the United States Supreme Court—to conduct an inquiry into the catastrophe at Pearl Harbor. In his order, the President instructed them:

to ascertain and report the facts relating to the attack made by Japanese armed forces upon the Territory of Hawaii on December 7, 1941.

The purposes of the required inquiry and report are to provide bases for sound decisions whether any derelictions of duty or errors of judgment on the part of United States Army or Navy personnel contributed to such successes as were achieved by the enemy on the occasion mentioned; and, if so, what these derelictions or errors were, and who were responsible therefor.

The investigation was to be in the nature of an inquest and judicial proceeding, ending in a verdict of some kind. This fact was evident not only in the President's instructions but also in an action of Congress which supplemented the Executive order by granting to the commission power to summon witnesses and examine them under oath.

Besides being delimited in other important respects, the duty of the commission was restricted to an inquiry into and report on derelictions of duty and errors of judgment on the part of the United States Army and Navy personnel which might have contributed to the successes of the Japanese attack. In other words, the commission was apparently excluded from inquiring and reporting with regard to the responsibilities of the civilian authorities anywhere for the catastrophe at Pearl Harbor.

After conducting investigations in Washington and Hawaii, the Roberts Commission presented a "report" to the President, dated January 23, 1942, and made public the next day.[6]

With reference to responsibilities for the catastrophe at Pearl Harbor, the Conclusions of the Roberts Report, though numbered *seriatim*, fell into three parts.

The first part exculpated high officials in Washington of responsibility as follows: [7]

1. Effective utilization of the military power of the Nation is essential to success in war and requires: First, the coordination of the foreign and military policies of the Nation; and, second, the coordination of the operations of the Army and Navy.

2. The Secretary of State fulfilled his obligations by keeping

6. The text of the Roberts Report used here is that of Senate Document No. 159, 77th Congress, Second Session 1942, which had been pronounced correct except that the word "distinct" in line 5, p. 12, should read "distant." There is at least one other error in it.

7. But see below, pp. 219 ff.

the War and Navy Departments in close touch with the international situation and fully advising them respecting the course and probable termination of negotiations with Japan.

3. The Secretary of War and the Secretary of the Navy fulfilled their obligations by conferring frequently with the Secretary of State and with each other and by keeping the Chief of Staff and the Chief of Naval Operations informed of the course of the negotiations with Japan and the significant implications thereof.

4. The Chief of Staff and the Chief of Naval Operations fulfilled their obligations by consulting and cooperating with each other, and with their superiors, respecting the joint defense of the Hawaiian coastal frontier; and each knew of, and concurred in, the warnings and orders sent by the other to the responsible commanders with respect to such defense.

5. The Chief of Staff of the Army fulfilled his command responsibility by issuing a direct order in connection with his warning of probable hostilities, in the following words: "Prior to hostile Japanese action you are directed to undertake such reconnaissance and other measures as you deem necessary."

6. The Chief of Naval Operations fulfilled his command responsibility by issuing a warning and by giving a direct order to the commander in chief, Pacific Fleet, in the following words:

"This despatch is to be considered a war warning."
and
"Execute an appropriate defensive deployment preparatory to carrying out the tasks assigned."

The second part of the Conclusions placed responsibilities on General Short and Admiral Kimmel, the commanders at Hawaii, charged them with derelictions of duty and errors of judgment, and declared that their errors of judgment were "the effective causes for the success of the attack." These Conclusions were as follows:

7. The responsible commanders in the Hawaiian area, in fulfillment of their obligation so to do, prepared plans which, if adapted to and used for the existing emergency, would have been adequate.

8. In the circumstances the responsibility of these commanders was to confer upon the question of putting into effect and adapting their joint defense plans.

9. These commanders failed to confer with respect to the warnings and orders issued on and after November 27, and to adapt and use existing plans to meet the emergency.

10. The order for alert No. 1 of the Army command in Hawaii was not adequate to meet the emergency envisaged in the warning messages.

11. The state of readiness of the naval forces on the morning of December 7 was not such as was required to meet the emergency envisaged in the warning messages.

12. Had orders issued by the Chief of Staff and the Chief of Naval Operations November 27, 1941, been complied with, the aircraft warning system of the Army should have been operating; the distant reconnaissance of the Navy, and the inshore air patrol of the Army, should have been maintained; the antiaircraft batteries of the Army and similar shore batteries of the Navy, as well as additional antiaircraft artillery located on vessels of the fleet in Pearl Harbor, should have been manned and supplied with ammunition; and a high state of readiness of aircraft should have been in effect. None of these conditions was in fact inaugurated or maintained for the reason that the responsible commanders failed to consult and cooperate as to necessary action based upon the warnings and to adopt measures enjoined by the orders given them by the chiefs of the Army and Navy commands in Washington.

13. There were deficiencies in personnel, weapons, equipment, and facilities to maintain all the defenses on a war footing for extended periods of time, but these deficiencies should not have affected the decision of the responsible commanders as to the state of readiness to be prescribed.

14. The warning message of December 7, intended to reach both commanders in the field at about 7 A.M. Hawaiian time, December 7, 1941, was but an added precaution, in view of the warnings and orders previously issued. If the message had reached its destination at the time intended, it would still have been too late to be of substantial use, in view of the fact that the commanders had failed to take measures and make dispositions prior to the time of its anticipated receipt which would have been effective to warn of the attack or to meet it. . . .

16. The failure of the commanding general, Hawaiian Department, and the commander in chief, Pacific Fleet, to confer

and cooperate with respect to the meaning of the warnings received and the measures necessary to comply with the orders given them under date of November 27, 1941, resulted largely from a sense of security due to the opinion prevalent in diplomatic, military, and naval circles, and in the public press, that any immediate attack by Japan would be in the Far East. The existence of such a view, however prevalent, did not relieve the commanders of the responsibility for the security of the Pacific Fleet and our most important outpost.

17. In the light of the warnings and directions to take appropriate action, transmitted to both commanders between November 27 and December 7, and the obligation under the system of coordination then in effect for joint cooperative action on their part, it was a dereliction of duty on the part of each of them not to consult and confer with the other respecting the meaning and intent of the warnings, and the appropriate measures of defense required by the imminence of hostilities. The attitude of each, that he was not required to inform himself of, and his lack of interest in, the measures undertaken by the other to carry out the responsibility assigned to each other under the provisions of the plans then in effect, demonstrated on the part of each a lack of appreciation of the responsibilities vested in them and inherent in their positions as commander in chief, Pacific Fleet, and commanding general, Hawaiian Department.

18. The Japanese attack was a complete surprise to the commanders, and they failed to make suitable dispositions to meet such an attack. Each failed properly to evaluate the seriousness of the situation. These errors of judgment were the effective causes for the success of the attack.

The third group of the Conclusions presented in the Roberts Report (15, 19, 20, and 21) dealt with responsibilities or failures in Washington and the conduct of subordinate officers and enlisted men in Hawaii. These Conclusions read:

15. The failure of the officers in the War Department to observe that General Short, neither in his reply of November 27 to the Chief of Staff's message of that date, nor otherwise, had reported the measures taken by him, and the transmission of two messages concerned chiefly with sabotage which warned him not to resort

to illegal methods against sabotage or espionage, and not to take measures which would alarm the civil population, and the failure to reply to his message of November 29 outlining in full all the actions he had taken against sabotage only, and referring to nothing else, tended to lead General Short to believe that what he had done met the requirements of the warnings and orders received by him. . . .

19. Causes contributory to the success of the Japanese attack were:

Disregard of international law and custom relating to declaration of war by the Japanese and the adherence by the United States to such laws and customs.

Restrictions which prevented effective counterespionage.

Emphasis in the warning messages on the probability of aggressive Japanese action in the Far East, and on antisabotage measures.

Failure of the War Department to reply to the message relating to the antisabotage measures instituted by the commanding general, Hawaiian Department.

Nonreceipt by the interested parties, prior to the attack, of the warning message of December 7, 1941.

20. When the attack developed on the morning of December 7, 1941, the officers and enlisted men of both services were present in sufficient number and were in fit condition to perform any duty. Except for a negligible number, the use of intoxicating liquor on the preceding evening did not affect their efficiency.

21. Subordinate commanders executed their superiors' orders without question. They were not responsible for the state of readiness prescribed.

To the readers of headlines in the newspapers and casual listeners at radios, indeed to casual readers of the Roberts Report itself, the Conclusions released to the public probably meant what they appeared to mean, namely, that high officials in Washington, from Secretary Hull down to the Chief of Staff and the Chief of Naval Operations had fulfilled their obligations; that General Short and Admiral Kimmel had been guilty of derelictions of duty; and that errors of judgment on their part "were the effective causes" of the catastrophe at Pearl Harbor.

OFFICIAL ARRAIGNMENT OF THE HAWAIIAN COMMANDERS

AFTER the Report of the Commission on Pearl Harbor was completed President Roosevelt went over it with Justice Roberts, the chairman, and decided that it should be made public. But the action of releasing to the press this state paper so significant for the problem of how war came, the President assigned to his secretary, Stephen Early. After handing copies out to journalists on January 24, 1942, Mr. Early, according to the *New York Times* report, said that the President had spent two hours over it with Justice Roberts and had expressed "his gratitude for a most painstaking and thorough investigation."

Having thus indicated that the Report had been approved by President Roosevelt, Mr. Early clearly and yet carefully intimated that, owing to the gravity of the pronouncements on General Short and Admiral Kimmel, the two commanders would have to face military tribunals, for he declared that "further action was under study. Because of the 'dereliction of duty' charge, it is believed certain that Admiral Kimmel and General Short would be court-martialled." [8] The *New York Herald Tribune* account of this White House conference on the Roberts Report, while varying a little in details, was of the same tenor as the *Times* report.[9]

Secretary Early's comments to newspaper correspondents on the treatment to be accorded to the two commanders were somewhat cryptic. He did not say that the President had approved the indictment and would proceed with preparations to bring them to trial. But he did say that "further action was under study," and, without definitely committing the President, he conveyed the impression that General Short and Admiral Kimmel were to be court-martialed.

For a time, other comments in Washington lent support to the idea broached by Secretary Early at the White House conference on January 24. A United Press dispatch of that

8. *New York Times*, January 25, 1942.
9. *New York Herald Tribune*, January 25, 1942.

day stated that some congressional leaders demanded "summary treatment" for the commanders, and quoted Representative Dewey Short as saying: "It's high time we were getting rid of those incompetents. . . . We've got a lot of gold braiders around here who haven't had a new idea in twenty years. . . . They should be court-martialed!" Commenting on the Roberts Report the next day, Senator Alben Barkley was enthusiastic; he said that it was "a comprehensive and admirable view of the facts and the people are justified in believing that nothing will be kept from them." The Senator added that suspicion should be ended "now that everybody knows what happened." [10]

But neither the Roberts Report nor the idea that General Short and Admiral Kimmel were actually guilty as charged was approved wholesale in Congress. Senator Walsh declared that there were important facts with which the Report did not deal and that "the public will demand to be informed." [11] Senator Gerald Nye uttered warnings against being too hasty and said: "Certainly, I would want an opportunity for these two men to be heard." Senator LaFollette insisted that some of the blame lay right here in Washington, and several members of Congress asserted that "the War and Navy Departments were as much to blame" as General Short and Admiral Kimmel. [12]

Meanwhile criticism of the Roberts Report and its allocation of responsibility for the catastrophe at Pearl Harbor began to come from quarters highly favorable to the foreign policies and measures of President Roosevelt. In an editorial on January 26, 1942, the *New York Times* flatly stated: "However grave the responsibilities of each of these commanders may have been, the conclusions of the Roberts Commission seem too sweeping in exculpating their superiors in Washington from blame and in too easily finding that each of these 'fulfilled his obligations.'" On the same day, the *New York Her-*

10. *Ibid.*, January 26, 1942.
11. *New York Times*, January 26, 1942.
12. *New York Herald Tribune*, January 26, 1942.

ald Tribune, speaking editorially, objected to the complete exoneration of Washington and asserted: "The want of foresight at Pearl Harbor was paralleled higher up." It was revealed that, while some men, including Andrew J. May, chairman of the House Committee on Military Affairs, were calling for quick and drastic action against General Short and Admiral Kimmel, the idea of exculpating superiors in Washington and penalizing the commanders was not being universally accepted; indeed, it was being challenged as untenable, with intimations of troubles ahead for the Roberts Report and its official sponsors.

On January 27, 1942, the *New York Times* carried a report from Washington that an inquiry on Hawaii was being urged in Congress by some members of both parties and that Republicans were "most vocal" in claiming that officials in Washington had been remiss in failing to make sure that the commanders were preparing for any eventuality. "A number of Democrats," the *Times* report added, "privately voiced similar criticism." Inquiries at the War and Navy Departments developed no information as to whether Secretary Stimson and Secretary Knox would act in the case of the court-martial mentioned at the White House three days previously.[13]

With a political storm of no small proportions brewing,[14] journalists were insistent in their demands to know what was to be done with General Short and Admiral Kimmel. At a press conference on January 27, newspaper representatives asked Mr. Early whether any further White House action was

13. Representative Hamilton Fish, vigorous opponent of President Roosevelt and of involvement in war, declared that Secretary Knox should be removed from office: "In any other country the head of the Navy would have been removed for the disaster on December 7. Knox, who has been the leading war maker in the Cabinet and who was openly for war on two oceans and has assured the American people how invincible the American Navy was, ought to take the blame." *New York Times*, January 27, 1942.

14. While Anne O'Hare McCormick was sure that Secretary Hull and the State Department had done the right thing all along (*ibid.*, January 26) as the Roberts Report argued, Arthur Krock and Hanson Baldwin, in their columns, raised fundamental questions respecting the insufficiency of the Roberts Report. *Ibid.*, January 28 and January 29, 1942. See also the *Times* editorial of January 28, "The Chain of Responsibility," which questioned the exculpations and indictments of the Roberts Report.

pending in the case of the two commanders. Mr. Early did not think "it is done that way."

In the course of his exposition of the case that day, Secretary Early let it be known that the matter of further proceedings on the charges against General Short and Admiral Kimmel had been shifted from the President to Secretary Stimson and Secretary Knox (both of whom proved to be then uncommunicative on the subject). He said: "If the judge advocate general of either the Army or the Navy finds any charge in the Roberts Report, either the Secretary of War or Navy can order a court martial at the direction of the President. By direction of the President is just a form phrase. I don't know of any action here [the White House]. The Secretaries of War and Navy have copies of the Roberts Report. They administer the Army and Navy for the President." [15] The next day at his press conference, President Roosevelt, in response to questions, stated that he had been studying the Roberts Report again and would have another conference with the Secretaries of War and the Navy. He added that he had talked with them previously. [16]

Efforts of Republicans in Congress, with some aid from Democrats, to force a new investigation of Pearl Harbor immediately came to an end, temporarily, on January 29, 1942, when the Committee on Naval Affairs of the House of Representatives by a vote of fourteen to six defeated a resolution for an inquiry of some kind. The Republican sponsor of the proposal, Representative Maas, expressed regret over the defeat and declared: "The Roberts Report settled nothing fundamental. It fixed the local blame, but not the cause of the Pearl Harbor disaster. I had hoped that the committee would make a study to find the underlying factors in our politics, both military and foreign. Obviously, simply the removal of two individuals who were carrying out a system does not correct the faults of that system." [17] In its report of the defeat

15. *New York Times*, January 27, 1942.
16. *Ibid.*, January 28, 1942.
17. *New York Herald Tribune*, January 30, 1942.

meted out to the movement for a congressional investigation, the *New York Times* stated that the vote was on party lines, and said that it was indicated elsewhere at the Capitol that the Administration had intervened to head off the inquiry.[18]

By the first of February it was patent to the most persistent journalists that there was to be no further official inquiry into the Pearl Harbor disaster and that the White House, the War Department, and the Navy Department did not intend to give out any specific information respecting courts-martial for General Short and Admiral Kimmel until the President and the two Secretaries were ready to announce their decision in the case. On February 8, 1942, the *New York Times* reported that the two commanders had asked for retirement, to which they were entitled by virtue of their years of service. The dispatch stated that the decision as to the acceptance of their applications was represented as resting entirely with the President as Commander in Chief; and that Army and Navy officers (unnamed) had "pointed out that acceptances of the applications for retirement would not preclude of itself the possibility of future court-martial proceedings." On this report Senator Reynolds, chairman of the Military Affairs Committee of the Senate commented: "If I were in their places, I would not want to retire under a cloud without a chance to explain my side; I would ask for a court-martial." [19] For many days the affair of the two commanders dragged on inconclusively.

Suddenly on February 28, 1942, Secretary Stimson and Secretary Knox issued statements to the press accepting the retirement of General Short and Admiral Kimmel on identical conditions; and at the same time they announced that the preparation of charges for trials on dereliction of duty by courts-martial had been ordered—trials not to be held until such time as the public interest and safety would permit. According to the *New York Times*, the War and Navy Departments stated that the commanders "*are to be tried by courts*

18. *New York Times*, January 30, 1942.
19. *Ibid.*, February 8, 1942.

martial at such time 'as the public interest and safety' permits"; [20] but the official text of each release contained no *guarantee* of trial, for it read as follows:

The Secretary of War announced today the acceptance effective February 28, 1942, of the application for retirement of General Walter C. Short, "without condonation of any offense or prejudice to any future disciplinary action."

The Secretary of War announced at the same time that, based on the findings of the report of the Roberts' Commission, he had directed the preparation of charges for the trial by court-martial of General Short, alleging dereliction of duty. The Secretary of War made it clear, however, that the trial upon these charges would not be held until such time as the public interest and safety would permit.

The release given to the press by Secretary Knox announced the retirement of Admiral Kimmel, effective March 1, 1942, in the same terms that Secretary Stimson applied to the case of General Short.

Thus, after five weeks of unexplained delay, from January 24 to February 28, 1942, the War Department and the Navy Department, not the President, retired the commanders under imputations of guilt; and so things stood officially, as far as the American people knew, for two years and nine months— until December 1, 1944.[21] According to appearances the Report of the President's Commission on Pearl Harbor was valid; Secretary Hull, Secretary Stimson, Secretary Knox, General Marshall, Admiral Stark, and, by implication, President Roosevelt were free from responsibility; but General Short and Admiral Kimmel were guilty of committing derelictions of duty and errors of judgment which were the effective causes of the success of the Japanese attack. By innuendo, if not definite intimation, from the White House as of January 24, 1942, they were guilty and awaiting trials by courts-martial, but from that source had come no guarantee that they would in fact ever be brought to trial and given a chance, at least, to be

20. *Ibid.*, March 1, 1942. (Italics supplied.)
21. See below, Chap. XI.

heard. By innuendo, if not by definite intimation, from Secretary Stimson and Secretary Knox, the two commanders were to expect trials by courts-martial when the public interest and safety would permit; but from those sources had come no guarantee that the alleged offenders would ever be granted such a hearing of their cause.

Judging by the appearances reflected in official communications to the public the record was clear. General Short and Admiral Kimmel had been derelict in the discharge of their duties at Pearl Harbor and incompetent besides. Their blunders, willful and witless, had been the effective causes of the American catastrophe at Pearl Harbor, which crippled the armed forces of the nation for the prosecution of the war and meant prolonging indefinitely the bloody and costly struggle to overcome the enemy. After the disaster they had been relieved of their commands; and then, with guilt hanging over their heads, they had taken advantage of the law and their years of service to ask for retirement on pension. President Roosevelt, Secretary Stimson, and Secretary Knox had granted their application, on condition that none of their offenses were to be condoned and that at the proper time they might face trial by courts-martial on charges alleging derelictions of duty. Thus the two commanders, publicly branded as unfaithful to duty and pilloried before the nation, were to await their doom; the justice of the Republic was to be vindicated— when, in the opinion of the President of the United States, the public interest and safety would permit. Such were the appearances created by Executive announcements.

A SEMIOFFICIAL CONFIRMATION OF THE OFFICIAL THESIS ON PEARL HARBOR

IN THE summer of 1942, the thesis which cleared the Roosevelt Administration of all responsibility for Pearl Harbor was confirmed by two eminent journalists at the White House and State Department, Forrest Davis and Ernest K. Lindley, in *How War Came: An American White Paper* (1942), a volume official in nature but yet not official in terms of responsibility, done in the mode of communication to the people often employed by the Roosevelt Administration.[22] In this work, the President and the Secretary of State were represented (pp. 315 f.) as having fulfilled their obligations to the uttermost:

. . . The danger that the Japanese would attack anywhere, or several places simultaneously, was not overlooked. The most remote possibilities, as well as the probabilities, had been weighed again and again by the responsible officials in Washington. The President and Secretary Hull had kept the Army and Navy fully informed of the gravity of the trend of events. Both had every reason to believe that our armed forces in the Pacific were on the alert and ready, in so far as their strength permitted, to meet any contingency. The defenses of the Philippines were known to be weak—although it was not anticipated that the Japanese would succeed in destroying two thirds of our air forces there on the ground in one afternoon, hours after the assault on Oahu. In the Hawaiian Islands, our naval and air and ground forces were ample to throw back any attack which the Japanese could launch.

Although at other points in their work Davis and Lindley dismissed the Roberts Report as giving the superficial reasons for the disaster at Pearl Harbor and placed the real blame on the smug and ignorant Americans—especially the isolationists, in this passage, they accepted the Report's verdict on the Administration as in effect valid. The danger that the Japanese would attack *anywhere* had not been overlooked. The President and Secretary Hull had kept the Army and Navy [23]

22. For the nature of the Davis and Lindley exploit, see Beard, *op. cit.*, pp. 25 ff.
23. From a careful study of the use of the words "the Army and the Navy," as employed in congressional hearings and debates, official documents, newspapers, and popular writings, I find great discrepancies in practice. The Secretaries of War and the Navy are sometimes included and sometimes excluded. Often the Army and the Navy are treated as if they were autonomous bodies that stand outside or over against the civilian officials, although the position of the President as Commander in Chief is recognized and usually vaguely defined. Is the Commander in Chief, by virtue of his office, to be regarded as belonging to the Army and the Navy? From what source do the Army and the Navy derive their organization, their duties, and their responsibilities? Do their uniforms, insignia, and technical operations establish sharp lines between them and their "civilian" superiors?

fully informed of the *gravity* of the *trend* of *events*. They had *reason* to believe that American armed forces in the Pacific were *ready* and *alert*. Presumably owing to the energy and competence of the Administration, our *naval* and *air* and *ground* forces were *ample to throw back any attack the Japanese could launch at the Hawaiian Islands*. In short, as wise and farseeing statesmen, President Roosevelt and Secretary Hull had fulfilled all their obligations in safeguarding the interests of the smug and ignorant nation. For what had gone wrong, the people, especially the isolationists and the Hawaiian commanders, were to bear the blame at the bar of history.

PART II

UNVEILING REALITIES

CHAPTER IX

The Beginning of Revelations

ACCORDING to appearances reflected in official statements, the situation on the eve of the Japanese attack on December 7, 1941, seemed to be about as described by President Roosevelt in his message of the next day, his broadcast of December 9, and his message to Congress on December 15. The United States was then "at peace with that nation," Japan; and "at the solicitation of Japan" the United States "was still in conversation with its Government and its Emperor looking toward the maintenance of peace in the Pacific." At the very end, the President was determined, as he said, "to exhaust every conceivable effort for peace," in addressing a personal message to the Emperor of Japan.

Meanwhile, according to the official explanation, Japan had been deliberately planning war and had "deliberately sought to deceive the United States by false statements and expressions of hope for continued peace." Even the Japanese reply to Secretary Hull's memorandum of November 26, delivered by the Japanese Ambassador and special envoy about two o'clock on December 7, "contained no hint or threat of war or armed attack." In carrying out this program of premeditated deceit, the President explained, the Japanese undertook "a surprise offensive," "treacherously violated the long-standing peace between us," and commenced to bomb Oahu an hour before the Japanese representatives in Washington handed to Secretary Hull their document, "crowded with infamous falsehoods and distortions," as the Secretary characterized it. Such, the President declared, was "the treachery committed by the military dictators of Japan, under the very shadow of the flag of peace borne by their special envoys in our midst." In this record of Japanese duplicity, the President found his warrant for exclaiming: "no honest person, today or a thousand years hence, will be able to suppress a sense of indignation and horror" at the treachery displayed by Japanese militarists.

Not long after the Japanese attack on Pearl Harbor the publication of official documents and statements on the course of affairs during the previous months and years enlarged the available information respecting the negotiations and activities that eventuated in the climax at Hawaii. As months and years passed, more and more secret information relative to the coming of war was brought to light in varying circumstances. At last in 1945–46, a Joint Committee of Congress investigated the complicated moves prior to Pearl Harbor, and produced from the records of the United States Government new evidence bearing on the official thesis respecting the conduct of foreign affairs in 1941 and the backgrounds of the war.[1]

Indeed, late in the day of December 7, 1941, as if to show how in conversations looking toward the maintenance of peace in the Pacific, he had stood by American principles, Secretary Hull released to the public his memorandum of November 26, 1941, to the Japanese Government—a document

1. As soon as I heard, in the afternoon of December 7, 1941, the news of the American catastrophe at Pearl Harbor, I was convinced that here was no mere accident or incident of war but a culmination in more than a hundred years of American diplomatic negotiations and activities in respect of the Far East, and the opening of a new and dangerous age for the Republic. Studies of diplomatic history, started under the guidance of that great master, Professor John Bassett Moore, at the beginning of the century, and continued during the intervening years, led me to believe that in time to come far more would be known about the foreign policies and the conduct of foreign affairs which eventuated in the attack at Pearl Harbor. What had happened as a result of opening up diplomatic archives after World War I seemed to forecast probable lines of historical investigation during the next twenty-five or fifty years. Consequently, I then began the collection of materials on events relative to the attack on Pearl Harbor, not merely as a momentous occurrence in history, but as presenting to mankind perhaps a revolutionary phase of Great History. In this and succeeding chapters I have employed these materials and sought to treat them as summarily as the multitudinous facts of the record will permit. This, as students of general history know, is only a part of the history of war origins; for secret documents from the archives of Europe and Asia, when published, will provide materials for recasting the official views of war origins in Europe and Asia from 1938 to 1941, inclusive; for example, the documents revealing the real nature of the Hitler-Stalin pact of August, 1939, and of Stalin's subsequent demands on Hitler for a larger share of the spoils wrung from other countries in their joint war of aggression.

hitherto held confidential.[2] Now for the first time the American people had available the exact language of the "principles" that President Roosevelt had firmly espoused in the last fateful days. Then, the question could be properly asked: Is this the foreign policy, the official program of the United States for the Far East, in support of which Americans are to pour out blood and treasure? In publishing the document Secretary Hull appeared to be giving an affirmative answer.

American citizens who had any knowledge of American diplomatic history and foreign affairs worthy of mention could readily detect the significance of the memorandum as soon as it was published. Its historical insignia, despite the phraseology of the new "international morality," stood out starkly in the text—as starkly as if Secretary Stimson had shared in writing it.[3] First of all, it revealed that President Roosevelt and Secretary Hull had categorically rejected a Japanese proposal in November for a modus vivendi—a truce which might have been used to postpone the war until American forces were better prepared to fight, and, perhaps, to avoid a two-front war entirely. The memorandum made it patent that they had not chosen to follow the methods long recognized in diplomacy as calculated to arrive at a modus vivendi; in other words, they had not limited the issues to primary and essential terms, which, if rejected by Japan, would have given them a pointed *casus belli* to be presented to Congress and the country. In any case, in deciding upon the substance of the memorandum they had refrained from directing the main emphasis to the recent southward movements of Japanese troops which menaced the Philippines, as well as British and Dutch possessions in that area.

At no time in the history of American diplomatic relations with the Orient, if published records are to be trusted, had the Government of the United States proposed to Japan such a

2. Text in Funk, *Roosevelt's Foreign Policy, 1933–1941*, pp. 539 ff. When the document was published, it could be seen that, by some process, the author of the United Press dispatch of November 26, 1941, had managed, on that very day, to get hold of the substance of the memorandum. See above, p. 198.

3. Beard, *op. cit.*, pp. 133 ff.

sweeping withdrawal from China under a veiled threat of war and under the pressure of economic sanctions likely to lead to war.[4] Not even the most brazen imperialist under Republican auspices had even ventured to apply this doctrine officially in the conduct of relations with Japan. Moreover there was nothing in platforms of the American political parties,— Democratic or Republican, or in the popular decisions at the polls, between 1900 and November 26, 1941, which gave any color of approbation to the inference or presumption that the American people generally should or would support a war against Japan merely for the purpose of enforcing in the Far East the sweeping proposals of Secretary Hull's memorandum.

Americans with long memories who could place in historical context and perspective the flaming headlines and the documents of the day could recall the solemn asseverations of the Democratic party respecting the imperialist program of the Republicans in 1900:

We hold that the Constitution follows the flag and denounce the doctrine that an Executive or Congress, deriving their existence and their powers from the Constitution, can exercise lawful authority beyond it, or in violation of it. We assert that no nation can long endure half republic and half empire, and we warn the American people that imperialism abroad will lead quickly and

4. Such a threat backed by the imposition of economic sanctions had been urged by Henry L. Stimson, as Secretary of State under President Hoover, with a view to breaking Japan's hold on Manchuria in 1931; but President Hoover rejected both economic sanctions and the very idea of a war for any such purpose in Asia. On the other hand, in 1933, President Roosevelt had privately come to an agreement with Mr. Stimson on what was known as "the Stimson doctrine"; in June, 1940, he had made Mr. Stimson, then seventy-four years old, his Secretary of War; and he had begun in July, 1940, to apply economic embargoes to Japan. The following partial list of President Roosevelt's measures in this respect is indicative: July 26, 1939, denunciation of the Japanese trade treaty of 1911, to go into effect at the end of six months, freeing the Administration for unilateral restrictions on commerce between the United States and Japan. January 26, 1940, United States–Japan trade treaty at an end. March 7, 1940, United States loan of $20,000,000 to China authorized. July 5, 1940, embargo on export of numerous strategic products except under official license. September 25, 1940, additional loan of $25,000,000 to China. September 26, 1940, embargo on shipment of iron scrap outside this hemisphere, except to Great Britain. July 25, 1941, Japanese assets in the United States frozen.

inevitably to despotism at home . . . we are not willing to surrender our civilization, or to convert the Republic into an empire. . . . The greedy commercialism which dictated the Philippine policy of the Republican administration attempts to justify it with the plea that it will pay, but even this sordid and unworthy plea fails when brought to the test of facts. . . . We are in favor of extending the Republic's influence among the nations, but believe that influence should be extended not by force and violence, but through the persuasive power of a high and honorable example. The importance of other questions now pending before the American people is in nowise diminished . . . ; but the burning issue of imperialism, growing out of the Spanish war, involves the very existence of the Republic and the destruction of our free institutions. . . . We oppose militarism. It means conquest abroad and intimidation and oppression at home. It means the strong arm which has ever been fatal to free institutions. It is what millions of our citizens have fled from in Europe. It will impose upon our peace-loving people a large standing army, an unnecessary burden of taxation, and would be a constant menace to their liberties. . . . The Republic has no place for a vast military establishment, a sure forerunner of compulsory military service and conscription. . . . We denounce it as un-American, undemocratic, and unrepublican and as a subversion of the ancient and fixed principles of a free people.

Nor by American citizens of long memories who read the published memorandum of November 26, 1941, could it be forgotten that some Republican statesmen of distant days had joined the Democrats in warning the Republic of dangers that lurked in the imperialist adventure in the Orient; Senator George F. Hoar, for example. Speaking in the Senate on the annexation of Hawaii in 1898, Senator Hoar said:

If this be the first step in the acquisition of dominion over barbarous archipelagoes in distant seas; if we are to enter into competition with the great powers of Europe in the plundering of China, in the division of Africa; if we are to quit our own to stand on foreign lands; if our commerce is hereafter to be forced upon unwilling peoples at the cannon's mouth; if we are ourselves to be governed in part by peoples to whom the Declaration of Independence is a stranger; or, worse still, if we are to govern subjects and vassal States, trampling as we do it on our own great Charter which recognizes alike the liberty and the dignity of individual manhood, then let us resist this thing in the beginning, and let us resist it to the death.[5]

Against a vast historical background of the American past, the memorandum which Secretary Hull, with the approval of President Roosevelt, handed to Japan on November 26, 1941, became easily identifiable. Instead of limiting it to the protection of the Philippine Islands, for which the United States still had the obligation assumed after the Spanish War, or even to the minimum terms necessary to protect the British and Dutch imperial possessions against Japanese aggression, the President and the Secretary had presented to Japan what amounted to the maximum terms of an American policy for the whole Orient. They called upon Japan to withdraw "all military, naval, air and police forces from China and Indochina"; to recognize only the Chungking Government; to make additional concessions of a similar nature; to observe in China the political and economic practices once covered by the apparently righteous phrase, the Open Door—the old Republican formula for American intervention in China; [6] and

5. G. F. Hoar, *Autobiography of Seventy Years* (Scribner, 1903), II, 310 f.

6. This old phrase used by Republicans to justify the intervention of the Government of the United States in Oriental affairs on behalf of economic interests was never more than a kind of shibboleth. Various powers, including Japan, had agreed to observe or respect it, but none of them, not even the United States, had undertaken to guarantee it by political and military action. That profound student of American policy in the Far East, Tyler Dennett, writing in 1922, said of it (as of 1899): "The United States merely demanded an open door for trade in that part of China in which American merchants were already interested, viz., the area westward from Kwangtung on the South to Manchuria on the North. . . . And as for those parts of the traditional Chinese Empire in the extreme South where France had already carved out an empire, or along the Amur where Russia had begun the partition of China in 1860, the United States never murmured a protest. . . . It seems clear that the United States would not have taken up arms either to enforce assent to the open door policy, or to prevent the partition of the Empire. On the other hand, had the dismemberment of China been started, there would have been a very strong sentiment in the United States against remaining aloof from the division of the spoils." *Americans in Eastern Asia* (Macmillan, 1922), pp. 648 f.

henceforth to abide by Secretary Hull's program of international morality.

Such was the memorandum of November 26, 1941, given to the public shortly after the Japanese attack, December 7.[7] As then applied to Japan, it represented also, in sum and substance, an expansion of the Stimson doctrine [8] to cover all China, Indo-China, and indeed almost any part of the Orient— the very doctrine which ten years previously President Hoover, despite the urging of his Secretary of State, Henry L. Stimson, had firmly refused to support by economic sanctions and war in respect of Manchuria. In 1931 President Hoover had solemnly informed his Cabinet, in a statement amazingly prophetic, that, deplorable as they were, the actions of Japan in Manchuria, "do not imperil the freedom of the American people, the economic or moral future of our people. I do not propose ever to sacrifice American life for anything short of this. If that were not enough reason, to go to war means a long struggle at a time when civilization is already weak enough. To win such a war is not solely a naval operation. We must arm and train Chinese. We would find ourselves involved in China in a fashion that would excite the suspicions of the whole world." President Hoover fully approved the idea that the United States should coöperate with the rest of the world and the League of Nations in the field of moral pressures. "But," he added, "that is the limit. We will not go along on war or any of the sanctions either economic or military for those are the roads to war." [9]

Read in the light of such history, the memorandum of November 26, 1941, made it plain that President Roosevelt had

7. For a fuller analysis of the memorandum and its significance, see below, Chap. XVII. As if aware that this memorandum and President Roosevelt's relation to it were crucial to the coming of the war, Alden Hatch in his eulogy of President Roosevelt says that the President was "uncertain" whether he had "done the right thing in allowing Secretary Hull to present" it to Japan, and that the President feared that Japan would not "desist in China." *Franklin D. Roosevelt: An Informal Biography* (Holt, 1947), p. 289.

8. Beard, *op. cit.*, pp. 133 ff.

9. R. L. Wilbur and A. M. Hyde, *The Hoover Policies* (Scribner, 1937), pp. 600 ff.

done what Republican imperialists had shrunk from doing: He had supported with drastic economic sanctions the dangerous and shadowy shibboleth of the Open Door and in his conversations with Japan he had pushed his insistence on a maximum program to the point of an explosion into a frightful two-front war. Anti-imperialists, Democrats and Republicans alike, could readily discern in the memorandum the substance of old imperialism in a new garb of phraseology. Republicans and Democrats who had supported President Hoover in his refusal to travel Henry L. Stimson's road to war in 1931 and 1932 would have been less than human and logical if they had not inferred that Secretary Hull's final manifesto to Japan represented comprehensive designs of power politics which had no support in the antiwar pledges of President Roosevelt and the Democratic party during the campaign of 1940 or in the official explications of his policies and intentions during the previous months of 1941.

Moreover, it required no profound knowledge of Japanese history, institutions, and psychology to warrant two other conclusions respecting the memorandum of November 26, 1941. First, that no Japanese Cabinet, "liberal" or "reactionary," could have accepted the provisions of the memorandum as a basis of negotiating a settlement without incurring the risk of immediate overthrow, if nothing worse. Second, that every high official in the State Department, especially in the division concerned with Far Eastern affairs, must have been aware, while the memorandum was being framed, that the Japanese Government would not accept it as a program for renewed conversations "looking toward the maintenance of peace in the Pacific." Nor was it to be supposed that President Roosevelt and Secretary Hull were so unfamiliar with Japanese affairs as to imagine, on November 26, 1941, that Tokyo would accept the terms of the memorandum or that the delivery of the document to Japan would prove to be otherwise than a prelude to war.

At all events, as soon as the memorandum was published after the Japanese attack, American citizens with any discernment at all could see immediately the pertinence of two leading questions that bore on the coming of the war: Had the Roosevelt Administration actually become entangled in a desperate armed conflict in efforts to enforce the sweeping program of the memorandum for a quick and drastic reordering of affairs in the Orient? [10] If not, what other considerations and expectations did President Roosevelt and Secretary Hull then have in mind?

Notwithstanding its limited nature, the Report of the President's Commission on Pearl Harbor, released January 24, 1942, had a distinct relation to the conduct of foreign affairs as illustrated by the delivery of Secretary Hull's memorandum, November 26, and raised queries about the extent to which President Roosevelt and his high officials were really astonished by the "surprise offensive" undertaken by Japan on December 7. The Roberts Report declared that the American outpost commanders had been duly warned of coming war as early as November 27, the day after Secretary Hull had delivered his memorandum to the Japanese representatives, and that an additional war warning had been sent out by General Marshall at least two hours before the Japanese attack on Pearl Harbor.

Thus the Report clearly implied that President Roosevelt and Secretary Hull were so certain of a Japanese refusal to accept the proposals of the memorandum that, without waiting for the Japanese reply, they authorized a war warning to the American outpost commanders the next day after the document had been handed to the Japanese representatives. This very implication connoted an inquiry: Were President

10. The "settlement" of affairs in Manchuria, China, Hongkong, Indo-China, and elsewhere in the Far East after World War II did not exactly conform to the proposals made to Japan by President Roosevelt and Secretary Hull in the memorandum of November 26, 1941. President Roosevelt's action in conceding to Russia, at the expense of China, a favored position in Manchuria, akin to the position from which Japan was ousted by arms, certainly presented a strange contrast to the grand principles incorporated in the memorandum. If the realization of those principles was in fact the primary purpose for which war was waged in the Pacific by the United States, then the consequences of the great decision on November 26, 1941, were miscalculated by President Roosevelt and Secretary Hull.

Roosevelt and Secretary Hull fairly sure that a Japanese attack might come anytime after November 27? If so, how could they have been really surprised by the attack when it came on December 7?

Three days after the release of the Roberts Report, the British Prime Minister, Winston Churchill, made a speech in the House of Commons, January 27, 1942, which brought in question the official thesis on how war came for the United States. About four months previously President Roosevelt had declared with reference to the Atlantic Conference of August, 1941, that he had entered into no new commitments there and that as a result of the proceedings the United States was no closer to war.[11] But Mr. Churchill on January 27, 1942, gave a different version of certain transactions at the Atlantic meeting. He spoke of the difficulties Great Britain confronted in dealing singlehanded with Japanese movements in the Far East and added that, since the Atlantic Conference, some of the fears had been relieved. To quote his exact words:

On the other hand, the probability, since the Atlantic Conference, at which I discussed these matters with Mr. Roosevelt, that the United States, even if not herself attacked, would come into a war in the Far East, and thus make final victory sure, seemed to allay some of these anxieties. That expectation has not been falsified by the events. It fortified our British decision to use our limited resources on the actual fighting fronts. As time went on, one had greater assurance that if Japan ran amok in the Pacific, we should not fight alone. It must also be remembered that over the whole of the Pacific scene brooded the great power of the United States Fleet, concentrated at Hawaii. It seemed very unlikely that Japan would attempt the distant invasion of the Malay Peninsula, the assault upon Singapore, and the attack upon the Dutch East Indies, while leaving behind them in their rear this great American fleet.[12]

Mr. Churchill's address of January 27, 1942, made plain three points that had previously been obscure or unknown.

11. See above, p. 121.
12. *Voices of History, 1942–43* (Gramercy Publishing Co., 1943), Franklin Watts, ed.

First, the issue of war with Japan had been seriously discussed at the Atlantic Conference. Second, from his conversations with President Roosevelt, the Prime Minister had derived the conclusion that there was a probability that the United States would come into a war in the Far East, even if not herself attacked. Third, as time went on, as negotiations with Japan proceeded, Mr. Churchill had grown more assured that if Japan "ran amok" the British would not have to fight the war alone. So strongly was Mr. Churchill convinced on these points that he felt justified in the decision to use the limited British resources on the actual fighting fronts, thus relying heavily on the "probability" that the United States, "even if not attacked," would come into the war in the Far East. To say the least, this was a revealing commentary on the realities of the Atlantic Conference and the official explanations of the "surprise" attack.

In a flush of triumph over Americans guilty of "smugness" and "ignorance," especially the "isolationists," who had opposed sending American boys to fight in foreign wars and treated as binding President Roosevelt's pledges to that effect in 1940, Davis and Lindley, in *How War Came*,[13] unwittingly contributed to popular skepticism respecting the official thesis on war origins. In this volume they gave the American people in the summer of 1942 startling "inside" information on the conduct of foreign affairs prior to December 7, 1941, which did not square with official pronouncements to the public between the Atlantic Conference and Pearl Harbor; nor with interpretations expounded by President Roosevelt on December 8, 9, and 15, 1941. If they had been trained in the niceties of diplomatic formulations for public consumption, Davis and Lindley might have been more cautious in their revelations. But their enthusiasm for war exceeded their ministerial discretion and in several passages on war origins they disclosed some grim realities behind the appearances created by Presi-

13. See above, p. 227. Undersecretary Welles testified before the Congressional Committee on Pearl Harbor that he and other officials in the State Department had held many conversations with Davis and Lindley and in effect given them inside information. CJC, Part 2, p. 501.

dent Roosevelt for the education of the people between August 1 and December 15, 1941. These passages may be summarized as follows:

At the Atlantic Conference, "The crisis in the Far East claimed first attention, resulting . . . in Churchill's agreement to the President's policy of *delaying hostilities* [14] without invoking a 'dead line' " (p. 267).

Premier Churchill wanted to meet the Japanese issue head on, but President Roosevelt said: "Leave that to me. I think I can baby them along for three months" (p. 10).

President Roosevelt was not without hope that something more than a temporary respite might be achieved by negotiations with Japan (p. 10 n.).

The English people hoped that Churchill would be able at the Atlantic Conference to get the United States into the war and were less concerned with the Atlantic Charter than with war (p. 275).

"For the first time in their century and a half of separate existence the United States and Great Britain had been joined in a written alliance"—at the Atlantic Conference (p. 270).

President Roosevelt and Premier Churchill avoided the blunder of Woodrow Wilson who "did not understand—power politics and economics," and put too much trust in a league of nations; "Roosevelt and Churchill realistically assumed the burden of disarming the aggressors after this war and of themselves policing the peace [15] until such time as a genuine association of self-governing nations might be established" (p. 273).

The question perplexing many high officials [at Washington, late in November] was how, in the absence of a direct Japanese attack on the American flag, to summon the nation, divided as it then was on questions of foreign policy, to the strong action which they believed essential. . . . In planning how best to protect American interests, officials were hampered by political dissen-

14. Italics supplied.
15. "Policing the world" was the phrase actually used by President Roosevelt at the Atlantic Conference. See below, Chap. XV.

sions within the nation. It was commonly supposed that the Japanese were too smart to solve this problem for the President by a direct assault on the American flag—especially at Hawaii, which even the extreme isolationists recognized as a bastion of our security (p. 315).

Having revealed, with startling directness, many of the hidden transactions of the months preceding Pearl Harbor, Davis and Lindley took up another phase of the official thesis—the business of responsibility for that catastrophe. Instead of lending support to the conclusions of the President's Commission on Pearl Harbor, published in the previous January, they took another tack. Like the Roberts Commission, they completely exculpated the President and Secretary Hull. Yet, as if aware that more was needed for the occasion, they asked the question: "Why were the Japanese able to perpetrate so immense and crushing a surprise?" Instead of answering the question they dismissed it curtly: "The answers, being largely subjective,[16] will be endlessly debated." [17]

But what of the Conclusions reached by the President's Pearl Harbor Commission on this subject? For citizens who believed in the integrity of the Roosevelt Administration, the fact-finding capacity of the commission, and in the justice of the treatment meted out to General Short and Admiral Kimmel by President Roosevelt, Secretary Stimson, and Secretary Knox earlier in the year, the Roberts Report had provided sufficient answers, not subjective speculations as to responsibility for Pearl Harbor. Now, in the summer of 1942, such citizens confronted a destructive blast from Davis and Lindley, semi-official spokesmen of the Administration: "There are, of course, all the surface reasons [for the Pearl Harbor disaster] set forth in the Roberts report (p. 316)." So, after all, the

16. How "largely"? In a sense all questions and answers are "subjective," for intellectual operations take place in the mind, not outside of it. This, however, is a highly technical matter in historiography. See *Introduction à la philosophie de l'histoire*, by R. Aron; especially sections "Esprit objectif et réalité collective"; "La Connaissance historique"; "La Compréhension des faits"; "Les limites de l'objéctivité historique"; "La pluralité des modes de considération."

17. At another point in their work, Davis and Lindley placed the blame for Pearl Harbor on the American people, especially the isolationists (pp. 316 f.).

appearances, not the real reasons, for Pearl Harbor and what it signified were to be found in the Roberts Report.[18]

About five months after the Davis and Lindley explanation of how war came was published and advertised as "a report to the American people," the Department of State, as if also recognizing the right of the people to be informed in matters of foreign relations, released to the press and the public, January 2, 1943, an official précis on *Peace and War: United States Foreign Policy, 1931–1941*.[19] In most respects this document conformed to the expectations of students who were acquainted with the nature and functions of white, blue, orange, and red books; but in some respects it illuminated the conversations "looking toward the maintenance of peace in the Pacific," to which President Roosevelt had referred in his war message of December 8, 1941.

After the Japanese representatives, Ambassador Nomura and Special Agent Mr. Kurusu, had read the memorandum of November 26, 1941, in Secretary Hull's office, according to the account in *Peace and War*, Mr. Kurusu "said that when this proposal of the United States was reported to the Japanese Government, that Government would be likely to 'throw up its hands'; that this response to the Japanese proposal could be interpreted as tantamount to the end of the negotiations." In other words, the Japanese agent regarded the American memorandum as a kind of ultimatum.[20] This much at least Secretary Hull knew on November 26.

It is true that the précis reported on conversations of the President and the Secretary of State with the Japanese agents after November 27, but simply represented them as coming to nought.

Immediately after the State Department's report on the conversation with the Japanese representatives, November

18. Davis and Lindley place the blame for the disaster on the ignorance and smugness of the American people, particularly the isolationist opponents of President Roosevelt's leadership. See Beard, *op. cit.*, pp. 25 ff.

19. For comments on this brochure and documents later attached to it, see Beard, *op. cit.*, pp. 28 ff.

20. *Peace and War*, p. 137.

26, as given in *Peace and War*, came a statement of the highest historical significance for the amplification of the President's war message of December 8, and also for the question of responsibility for Pearl Harbor. The statement was headed "Japan May Move Suddenly" and read as follows: "On November 25 and on November 28 [1941], at meetings of high officials of this Government, Secretary Hull emphasized the critical nature of the relations of this country with Japan. He stated that there was *practically no possibility of an agreement* being achieved with Japan; that in his opinion *the Japanese were likely to break out at any time* with new acts of conquest by force; and that the matter of safeguarding our national security *was in the hands of the Army and the Navy.* The Secretary expressed his judgment that any plans for our military defense should include an assumption that the Japanese might make *the element of surprise a central point in their strategy* and also might attack at various points simultaneously with a view to demoralizing efforts of defense and of coordination for purposes thereof." [21]

Under the same heading, the State Department's account in *Peace and War* added: "On November 29, 1941, Secretary Hull conferred with the British Ambassador. The Secretary said that 'the diplomatic part of our relations with Japan was virtually over and that the matter will now go to the officials of the Army and Navy.'" The Secretary also warned the British Ambassador that it would be a serious mistake for this country and other countries interested in the Pacific situation to make counterplans without reckoning with the possibility of surprise attacks by the Japanese over considerable areas.[22]

In a subsequent conversation with the Japanese representatives in Washington, on December 1, 1941, Secretary Hull told them that he had not heard one whisper of peace from Japanese military leaders, "only bluster and bloodcurdling threats"; that "this Government had no idea of trying to bluff Japan and that he saw no occasion for Japan's trying to bluff

21. *Ibid.*, p. 138. (Italics supplied.)
22. *Ibid.*

us; he emphasized that 'there is a limit beyond which we cannot go.' " At a later conference with the Japanese representatives, on December 5, Secretary Hull was informed by Mr. Kurusu "that if an agreement could be reached on temporary measures, we could proceed with the exploration of fundamental solutions; that what was needed immediately was a temporary expedient." To this statement Secretary Hull responded briefly in closing the discussion: "The Secretary said that we could solve matters without delay if the Japanese Government would renounce its policy of force and aggression. He added that we were not looking for trouble but that at the same time 'we were not running away from menaces.' " [23]

In thus making his own case for history, Secretary Hull, in 1943, seemed out of line with President Roosevelt's version of how war came as a "surprise offensive," while the United States was engaged in conversation with Japan looking toward the maintenance of peace in the Pacific. If diplomatic negotiations were virtually over several days before Pearl Harbor, and the matter of safeguarding national security was in the hands of the Army and Navy, was the United States actually "at peace" with Japan during the days immediately preceding December 7 and carrying on conversations looking to the maintenance of peace? If Secretary Hull had informed high officials on November 25 that the Japanese might break out at any time, how could the attacks of December 7 have constituted the surprise to which President Roosevelt had referred on December 8 in his war message to Congress?

On July 1, 1943, the State Department cast some more light on how war came, in a portly volume bearing the same title as its précis of January 2 and purporting to present "a record of policies and acts" by which the United States sought to promote conditions of peace and world order and to meet the dangers resulting from Japanese, German, and Italian aggressions. In Chapter I of this work, called "The Fateful Decade," the State Department announced that in fact President Roose-

23. *Ibid.*, pp. 138–140.

velt and Secretary Hull had "early" broken with the line of nonintervention in European and Asiatic wars and had chosen a course away from neutrality, that is, in the direction of war, if not to war.[24] This announcement from the State Department in July, 1943, gave warrant for asking the question: Just when in their communications to the American public did President Roosevelt and Secretary Hull openly declare that their commitments to the policy of neutrality and peace in 1940 and previous years had been discarded and the new policy—a different policy—substituted? At all events, before the year 1943 closed, official explanations of affairs during "the fateful decade" had begun to disclose realities that deviated from the appearances as described in the official thesis on how war came to the United States.

24. So, at least, I interpret the English used by the authors of this chapter, which, owing to its prolixity and obscurity, is difficult to translate into the English of ordinary discourse. Beard, *op. cit.,* pp. 28 ff.

CHAPTER X

The Official Thesis Challenged in Congress and the Press

MEMBERS of Congress, under the Constitution,[1] had inescapable duties to perform in connection with the charges filed against the Hawaiian commanders by the Roosevelt Administration, with legislation governing the armed forces, and with making investigations into the enforcement of statutes by the Executive.[2] For the loyal discharge of these duties Representatives and Senators were accountable to the American people, for whom they spoke, by whom they were periodically subjected to scrutiny at elections. Among the constant duties of Congress was that of passing upon measures relative to the organization and management of the Army and Navy, through the agency of its committees on military and naval affairs and in searching discussions of such measures on the floors of the House and the Senate.

In the discharge of their duties members of Congress acquired information about war origins and the disaster at Pearl Harbor other than that furnished to them by the White House, the State Department, and semiofficial spokesmen of the Administration. Representatives and Senators who served as members of committees on military and naval affairs had opportunities to question military and naval officers behind

1. As a reminder to those who might overlook the constitutional obligations of Congress, the following provisions of that document bearing on the armed forces, war, and international law deserve attention. The Constitution vests in Congress, not the President, the power to lay and collect taxes, to appropriate money to pay all the costs of the government, to regulate commerce with foreign nations, to define and punish . . . offenses against the law of nations, to declare war . . . and make rules concerning captures on land and water, to raise and support armies, but no appropriation of money to that use shall be for a longer term than two years, to provide and maintain a navy, to make rules for the government of the land and naval forces.

2. The investigation of the Executive branches of the government by standing and special committees had been undertaken early in the history of Congress as a phase of its constitutional obligations and a long line of precedents had established the right of investigation beyond all cavil.

closed doors and to speak with them confidentially about the state of affairs and the ordering of armed forces prior to and on the day of Pearl Harbor. As the months of 1942 and 1943 passed, the amount of information on responsibility for the catastrophe gathered by members of Congress was steadily augmented in volume and portent.

Shortly after the Japanese attack on December 7, many members of Congress were convinced that when the time came for a thorough investigation of Pearl Harbor, the inquiry should be made by an independent committee created by act of legislation.[3] They held that the Roberts Commission, set up and appointed by the President, was an ex parte body employed by the Executive to investigate derelictions in the Executive Department itself and that any new investigating board, if established by War or Navy Departments on their own authority, would likewise be an ex parte body. But to propose a congressional inquiry or to engage in extensive discussions of the Pearl Harbor case seemed, even to critics of the Roberts Report in Congress, inappropriate while the final outcome of the war appeared to be uncertain.

PROVISIONS FOR A NEW INVESTIGATION ON JUNE 5, 1944

IN JUNE, 1944, however, an imperative duty brought the Pearl Harbor case before both houses of Congress. Under federal law, as it stood on December 7, 1941, when the alleged offenses of General Short and Admiral Kimmel, if any, were committed in connection with Pearl Harbor, persons charged with such offenses had to be tried within a period of two years. When this term expired in December, 1943, Congress extended it for six months by special act. When this six months' extension was at an end in June, 1944, a further extension was necessary, if the accused were to be accorded the trials by courts-martial which they demanded for the sake of their honor, and unless the whole question of responsibility for Pearl Harbor was to be dismissed, as far as the statute of limitations was concerned. Now, as the issue of extension came

3. See above, p. 224.

up in Congress in June, 1944, the course of the war indicated a final victory for the Allied Powers and some consideration of the Pearl Harbor problem seemed unavoidable. At all events, discussion occurred; a resolution of extension in a new form easily passed both houses; and it was signed by the President on June 13, 1944.

By its very terms the Joint Resolution approved June 13, 1944, showed a dissatisfaction in Congress with regard to the restraints put on the Roberts Commission by President Roosevelt in his instructions of December 18, 1941, and a determination to have a more extended inquiry into "the facts" of the Pearl Harbor disaster. The resolution was indeed sweeping in its scope. It covered all "statutes, resolutions, laws, articles, and regulations" affecting the possible prosecution of persons sharing responsibility for the Pearl Harbor catastrophe. Furthermore it applied to all persons "in military or civil capacity involved in any matter in connection with the Pearl Harbor catastrophe." It peremptorily ordered the Secretary of War and the Secretary of the Navy to proceed forthwith in making an investigation "into the facts surrounding the catastrophe" and to commence such proceedings against persons found guilty of offenses as the facts may justify.

The text of the law follows:

Resolved by the Senate and House of Representatives of the United States of America in Congress assembled, That effective as of December 7, 1943, all statutes, resolutions, laws, articles, and regulations, affecting the possible prosecution of any person or persons, military or civil, connected with the Pearl Harbor catastrophe of December 7, 1941, or involved in any other possible or apparent dereliction of duty, or crime or offense against the United States, that operate to prevent the court martial, prosecution, trial or punishment of any person or persons in military or civil capacity, involved in any matter in connection with the Pearl Harbor catastrophe of December 7, 1941, or involved in any other possible or apparent dereliction of duty, or crime or offense against the United States, are hereby extended for a further period of six months, in addition to the extension provided for in Public Law 208, Seventy-eighth Congress.

SEC. 2. The Secretary of War and the Secretary of the Navy are severally directed to proceed forthwith with an investigation into the facts surrounding the catastrophe described in section 1 above, and to commence such proceedings against such persons as the facts may justify.

Approved June 13, 1944.

The appearance of, and the ensuing debates over, the Resolution in Congress *directing* the Secretary of War and the Secretary of the Navy to proceed *forthwith* with a new investigation of Pearl Harbor and to commence such proceedings against such persons as the facts might justify naturally disturbed the Roosevelt Administration despite the fact that Democrats controlled Congress. Why a new investigation? Had not the President's Commission, headed by Justice Owen J. Roberts, made an inquiry, cleared the Administration, and named the culprits in its Report, dated January 23, 1942? Why endanger the war unity of the country? Why not wait until the war is over, when the public interest will permit the trial of the accused by courts-martial? Why should good Democrats allow Republican politicians to raise difficulties for the Administration and make capital out of the case for the coming presidential campaign?

Certainly these questions seemed reasonable enough, from the point of view of war unity, as well as Democratic strategy for the approaching campaign. Besides, the Democrats controlled both houses of Congress and could block the proposed investigation, although they could not prevent Republicans from bringing up the issue. But things are not always what they seem to be on Capitol Hill, at least as judged by the *Congressional Record* and the press reports of proceedings in the House and the Senate. By the summer of 1944 Democratic members of committees, as well as Republican members, at hearings attended by military and naval officers, had learned many things about Pearl Harbor which were unknown to the people at large, even to the "intellectuals" who instructed the nation on public affairs. Some of these Democrats were shrewd enough to realize that some day an investigation was almost certain to come and, as Republicans had often declared that the protective tariff, if revised, should be revised by its friends, so Democrats concluded in 1944 that, if Pearl Harbor was to be investigated anew, the inquiry should be in the hands of friends of the Administration. They knew also that the apparently exigent words "proceed forthwith" did not necessarily mean that anything serious would have to be done before the election in November.

Even so, after the Resolution had passed, the question of a veto by President Roosevelt was anxiously considered in Administration circles. The discussions of this point in those circles were not then known to the public but, since the secret documents bearing on them were later brought to light by the Congressional Committee on Pearl Harbor,[4] reference is made to them here, at the risk of breaking the chronological story of "appearances."

Early in June, 1944, Attorney General Biddle told Judge Samuel Rosenman, President Roosevelt's confidential agent in political matters, "that considering the possibility of criticism that the President might be subjected to if he did veto it, it was his personal view that the President ought to think pretty carefully before he did decide to veto it." To the Assistant Solicitor General, Hugh Cox, the Judge Advocate General, Myron Cramer, said, June 8th, that "many people" were "very keen about a veto on it," but Mr. Cox replied that he had the impression that Judge Rosenman "would be very reluctant to have him [the President] veto it." Mr. Cox, with a B.A. acquired at Christ Church, Oxford, England, whose knowledge of the American Constitution may have been slighter than his knowledge of the English Constitution, added, in his communication to the Judge Advocate General:

4. See CJC (1946), Part 19, pp. 3914 ff., for documents bearing on the history of the Resolution of June 13, 1944; as to the bill, the veto proposal, and action under the law, pp. 3925 ff.

"I don't think Congress has got the right to tell you to go ahead forthwith with an investigation but they've done it and it's a question I suppose for the President of weighing an impropriety against the criticism that might come from vetoing the thing." [5]

At any rate President Roosevelt signed the bill. Shortly, General McNarney, who had served with Justice Roberts on the President's Commission on Pearl Harbor, telephoned to the Judge Advocate General that the President had signed the Resolution on the understanding that it was not to interfere with the war effort, "which approves our going ahead with *some sort of an investigation.*" (Italics supplied.)

During the debates in Congress on the Resolution for an extension of the time for the trials of General Short and Admiral Kimmel and for a new investigation, in its original form and with proposed amendments, Representatives and Senators revealed various attitudes toward the matter of responsibility for the disaster at Pearl Harbor and put before their respective chambers a number of new facts, real or alleged, which had not been disclosed by the Report of the Roberts Commission.[6] In respect of attitudes, the language used by the speakers was sufficient evidence. In support of the "new facts," little or no documentary evidence was introduced and on the whole their validity depended at the moment upon the authority of the speaker who presented them during the debates.

Early in the debates in the House, J. Bayard Clark, Democrat from North Carolina, who later served faithfully as a member of the Congressional Committee on Pearl Harbor, took the position of unquestioning loyalty to President Roosevelt and made the issue one of confidence in his Administration. Mr. Clark said on this subject:

5. June 15, 1944, Cornelius H. Bull, Special Assistant to the Judge Advocate General of the Navy Department, wrote to General John Weir that, if Admiral Gatch recommended a court-martial for Admiral Kimmel: "We both know that the President would, in all probability, just put the matter in his files ('under consideration') certainly until after the Elections." *Ibid.*, p. 3932.

6. The debates on the Resolution occurred on June 5, 1944, and the extracts and account given here are all from the *Congressional Record* of that day (daily issue).

. . . what I particularly wish to call to the attention of the House is that section 2 of the bill peremptorily instructs the Secretary of War and the Secretary of the Navy. It reads: "The Secretary of War and the Secretary of the Navy are severally directed to institute court-martial proceedings on all charges against any persons" who may be at fault in connection with the Pearl Harbor disaster. This applies, I believe, to civilian as well as military personnel. . . .

I know there is a disposition in this body and elsewhere to try to find fault in some way with the manner in which the war is being prosecuted. Speaking for myself, I have complete confidence in the way the war is being handled from the Chief Executive right on down the line, and to my mind when the Congress undertakes or finds it necessary to instruct the Secretary of War and the Secretary of the Navy as to what they shall do and how they shall conduct their official duties, it is virtually tantamount to a vote of lack of confidence in these men at the head of our military machine at this time of crisis. I have no doubt whatever the reasons may be that our military personnel have good reasons for what they are doing. . . .

I have not tried to find out why no courts martial have been instituted. I am satisfied in my own mind that whatever the reasons may be they are good ones and that the adoption of this resolution in place of aiding in the war effort will put us in the ridiculous attitude of almost censuring the heads of our War and Navy Departments. I suppose it is inevitable, but nevertheless it is regrettable, that the unity we once had in this Chamber on war measures has so completely disappeared. I do not particularly like to say this, I wish it were otherwise, but from what I have seen and heard and observed I am bound to feel that there are many on the minority side of this Chamber who will be disappointed if they do not find something badly wrong with the prosecution of the war. I am going to go far enough to say in concluding my remarks that too many people in the United States and here in this Chamber apparently are not taking the war seriously enough.

Immediately after Mr. Clark had concluded his address, Harold Knutson, Republican from Minnesota, exclaimed: "Oh, shame! shame!" Then Hamilton Fish, Republican from New York, got the floor and said:

Mr. Speaker, I have the highest regard for the gentleman from North Carolina, who just addressed the House. I do not believe, however, any speech I have heard recently in the House could create more disunity than the remarks of the gentleman from North Carolina. As he well knows, our armed forces are composed of Republicans and Democrats; our sons are fighting all over the world; they are united and determined to beat the enemy, Germany and Japan, as quickly as possible and to get the war over with. To give the impression that there is any Member of the Congress, or anybody in the minority party who is trying to throw monkey wrenches into the war machinery or to impede our war effort is both unfair and untrue.

Mr. Speaker, it seems to be apparent that there are those Members of the House who take the position that the minority has no right even to criticize or talk about the foreign or domestic policies of the administration. . . .

After all, Mr. Speaker, we are the elected Representatives of the American people, and we are speaking here in their behalf. All this resolution seeks to do is to give the facts to the American people whose sons are doing the fighting and the dying; and they are entitled to have all the facts regarding the greatest naval disaster in the history of America. There has already been too much delay and shadow-boxing by the administration in order to avoid telling the whole truth to the American people and in holding all those responsible for the Pearl Harbor catastrophe strictly accountable. . . .

Mr. Speaker, I am going to read an editorial taken from the World-Telegram, a Scripps-Howard paper in New York. . . . This paper is one of the largest in the city of New York and the same editorial was probably circulated widely over the country by the Scripps-Howard syndicate. It is entitled, "Kimmel, Short, Roosevelt, Hull":

"The administration is plainly resolved to postpone the Pearl Harbor trials until after the election. The Japs have long known exactly what they did to us in that most disgraceful disaster ever yet suffered by American arms. To hold the trials now would tell them nothing they don't already know.

"But it is widely believed that the trials would force to light evidence connecting high Washington officials with orders to Kimmel and Short to take the No. 1 alert (readiness for sabotage from within), instead of the No. 3—readiness for anything—

which might have turned Pearl Harbor into a victory for us and shortened the Pacific war. These orders might have been urged by Mr. Hull, or sent by Mr. Roosevelt.

"If such orders were sent, the Administration is determined to keep the American people from knowing who sent them until after the election. Politics, and politics alone, is the cause of this procrastination."

. . . Mr. Speaker, in view of the fact that the Administration has failed, up to now, to court martial either General Short or Admiral Kimmel, all we are seeking, at the present time, is for the Congress to exert its influence 2½ years after Pearl Harbor to be assured of a speedy trial. I am surprised that there has not been more forceful language used in the Congress long before at the request of the American people and the mothers and fathers of the 3,000 American boys who were killed at Pearl Harbor, in a demand to know exactly what the facts are and who was responsible right up to the very top. It is not surprising that this matter should come before the House at this late date in view of the delay and failure of the administration to act.

Later in the debate in the House, Emanuel Celler, Democrat from New York, made a renewed appeal for war unity in the following terms:

I do not think that the perilous times involved during the war should make a suitable setting for any trial of this character. We should not at this critical juncture in our affairs deal in any Pearl Harbor fiasco. There is danger. There is danger of impairment of national security.

Awhile ago I said that there was a Commission authorized by the President to delve into the circumstances attendant upon the dastard Pearl Harbor attack. Justice Owen J. Roberts and his colleagues made a report which was painstaking. It was fair and unbiased. It was erudite. I have it right here before me. I have read it most carefully. It involved 127 witnesses, 1,887 pages of testimony, and a review of 3,000 pages of documents. For the time being, until the war is ended, that Commission's report should satisfy the Nation and the Members of this body. It is not complete, yet it is comprehensive. It is a dignified common-sense report. . . .[7]

7. See below, Chap. XIII.

Any public court martial now, I say would indeed be a sort of grist to Goebbel's mill and would give aid and comfort to Emperor Hirohito.

We are going through an unusual test. It is without precedent. We are fighting a global war on scores of fronts, and in addition we are going through a Presidential campaign . . . A Short-Kimmel court martial would intensify the passions and furies rampant in the political arena. England has a political truce agreed upon by all parties. We are for political warfare unabated. Some abettors of the pending bill would add prussic acid, I would say, to the daily political fare. Some would seek political advantage through this measure. They would use the court martial as a petard by which to climb to power. They would use the court martial as a bludgeon to strafe Roosevelt and the Secretaries of War and of the Navy.

Certain publications and bitterly partisan commentators, like Arthur Krock, of the New York Times, and George E. Sokolsky, of the New York Sun, are already pulling all stops of their organ of hate. Their evil effusions concerning this attempted court martial would undermine the confidence in the over-all commands of our armed forces. With them and others it seems that anything goes.

We cannot and should not dispute the judgment of the high commands of the Army and the Navy. Admiral King said it would be dangerous to take the men from the battle fronts. We also have the word of the Secretary of War and the late Secretary of the Navy, Mr. Knox. It is the word of Admiral King that says, "Let us not take these men away from their important duties and bring them here or anywhere else as witnesses in this court martial."

On the whole the discussion of the resolution in the Senate was far less partisan than in the House. In truth it was not partisan at all in a strict sense; it reflected a matured conviction that General Short and Admiral Kimmel were to be regarded as innocent until proved guilty, and that responsibility for the Pearl Harbor catastrophe was far more complicated than the question of their innocence or guilt. Shortly after Carl Hatch, Democrat from New Mexico, had called for a consideration of the Resolution, Bennett Clark, Democrat from Missouri, said:

Mr. President, I did not object to consideration of the joint resolution . . . I think the procedure has been a disgraceful one.
General Short and Admiral Kimmel have not been brought to
trial. I have heretofore expressed myself on that subject on this
floor. Apparently some of the higher-ups in the Government are
afraid of the nature of the defense which might be made by
Admiral Kimmel and General Short.

Recently I have seen in the public press a demand on the part
of Admiral Kimmel that he be brought to trial. We all know that
if the time limit is extended for a year,[8] we might as well recognize
the fact that these men will never be brought to trial, or, if they
are brought to trial, that the trial will be held after some of the
witnesses are dead and after much of the evidence has been dis-
sipated. If we are to extend the time limit for a year, the whole
proceedings might as well be dismissed. . . .

We all know that Pearl Harbor is one of the most disgraceful
episodes in the history of the United States. We know that the
disaster of Pearl Harbor was not due to any lack of armament or
any lack of equipment or any lack of personnel, but was due to
the fact that the ordinary precautions in the service of security,
which should have been taken in peacetime, were flagrantly dis-
regarded. Someone should be court-martialed for that. Someone
should be court-martialed while the evidence is fresh. If it was
not the fault of Kimmel and Short, they are entitled to be brought
to trial and given the opportunity to show upon whom the responsibility rests.

Senator Albert Chandler, Democrat from Kentucky, expressed a similar opinion of the case:

I remind the Senate that up to the present time no charges have
been filed against either of them. . . .

In my judgment, what we propose to do is perfectly innocuous.
I do not believe it means anything. I believe that any man who is
charged with a serious offense against his country which involves
a court martial is entitled to trial. Admiral Kimmel has demanded
a trial. However, thus far no charges have been filed against him,
and I am not certain that any real charges can be filed against him

8. As originally proposed, the Resolution extended the time of trial for Pearl
Harbor offenders for a full year, until June 7, 1945. By amendment the period was
reduced to six months.

which would support a court martial. The Army and Navy had a right to believe that the President, by appointing a special commission, took the case out of their hands. It is perfectly foolish to assume that the Army has a right to investigate the Executive offices, the State Department, the F.B.I., the Federal Communications Commission, and various other commissions which may have to be investigated in order to ascertain the full facts and circumstances surrounding what happened at Pearl Harbor. . . .

I do not agree with the statement that we were ready for war at Pearl Harbor. We were not ready for war. I should not like to see these two officers made scape-goats because of the failure of many others to estimate the seriousness of the situation and take steps which would have prevented what happened. . . .

Although I should like to see Admiral Kimmel tried, personally I do not believe that he has committed any offense against the American people. He was in the American Navy for 40 years, and reached the highest rank in the Navy. I do not believe that he has committed any wrong. However, time will tell. In the meantime, he carries the burden of suspicion that he has betrayed the American people in an important public trust. I do not believe he did so. However, he must stand trial, and in the suspicion and heat of the day he must remain on the side lines. . . .

Mr. CLARK OF MISSOURI. The Senator from Kentucky said that the Navy Department and the War Department cannot investigate other departments. I wish merely to ask the Senator if it is not a fact that the War Department gave out information with a great flourish of trumpets that General Short would be court martialed, and with a great flourish of trumpets information was given out that Admiral Kimmel would be court martialed,[9] and yet neither has been brought to trial. Kimmel now comes along and says, "I demand to be tried. I demand to be tried while the evidence is available." I express no opinion as to whether either Admiral Kimmel or General Short is guilty, or whether both of them are guilty, but if they are to be tried at all, I assert that they should be tried while the evidence is available. I have heard intimations made repeatedly that the reason they have not been tried is that higher authorities were apprehensive about the nature of their defense.

Mr. CHANDLER. Mr. President, I am quite sure that those who

9. See above, p. 221.

made statements in the heat of debate and without knowing the facts, that certain ones should be shot or court martialed, probably now regret such statements.

A great tragedy has stricken the American people and they do not know who was responsible for it. After 40 years of service Admiral Kimmel was allowed to retire. General Short was removed from his post. The finger of suspicion has been pointed toward each of those men ever since, and many of the American people think to this hour that those men were derelict in their duty. However, no charges have been filed against either of them. According to American justice, they have a right to believe that the presumption of innocence goes with them until they are confronted with charges, know the nature of them, and have an opportunity to present witnesses in their defense, and to be considered innocent until they are proved guilty.

Homer Ferguson, Republican from Michigan, maintained that secret maneuvers were involved in the case and that the time had come to explore the records of the Executive Department:

I think it is well that the Senate should know that up until the day of the hearing before the resolution was reported the War Department made no attempt to obtain the facts to ascertain whether or not anyone was guilty other than General Short or Admiral Kimmel. Therefore, they had no facts in their files from which they could charge anyone else with dereliction of duty. Consequently, they obtained a waiver only from General Short and Admiral Kimmel because the President of the United States and the Secretary of War had stated that they alone were derelict in their duty from the facts disclosed in the Roberts report.

I think it is well that the Senate should know also that the report of Mr. Justice Roberts was filed about the 23d of January 1942. That was before the white paper was published in 1943. The Roberts report and those who were on the Roberts commission did not have the facts which are now contained in the white paper as to whether or not higher-ups were guilty of dereliction of duty to the American people.

I, for one, believe that the Army of the United States and the Navy of the United States and those in charge should ascertain all the facts. For that reason I was satisfied with paragraph 2 of the resolution as now amended. I believe that they should obtain the facts in order to ascertain who is guilty, if anyone, and, then, after a reasonable time, I believe it is the duty of this body to ascertain, in executive session if necessary—for no one wants to give any aid to the enemy—what the Army and Navy have been able to ascertain, and if the State Department and other departments, the Interior Department and even the Executive, fail to give to the Army and Navy officials all the facts so that they can perpetuate those facts for the future of America, then this body should step in and exercise its power to ascertain what the facts are.

That a wider investigation than contemplated by the Resolution was necessary, Senator Hatch and Senator David Walsh agreed:

MR. HATCH. Mr. President, the Committee on the Judiciary considered this joint resolution most carefully and realized all the complicating legal and other questions involved. The subcommittee and the full committee were practically unanimous in agreeing that at this time about the only thing we could do would be to pass the pending joint resolution, extending the period of time.

The question of a congressional investigation was discussed in the committee. I am sure there was no member of the committee who sought or desired to cover up anything. The thought of a congressional investigation received favorable consideration in the committee. We even discussed the possibility of adding an amendment to the joint resolution now pending requiring a congressional investigation of all the incidents. But we realized that was a matter which should be considered by itself. . . .

I repeat, in behalf of the committee, not a member of the committee desired to cover up anything or shield any person whatever. We met the legal situation and we made the recommendation unanimously from the committee that this joint resolution be passed. . . .

MR. WALSH OF MASSACHUSETTS. Mr. President, I should like to ask the Senator from New Mexico a question. From what I have been able to learn about this case, there are two issues involved. So far as Short and Kimmel are concerned, the issue would be, what knowledge did they have, and what, if anything, did they fail to do which they should have done, in view of the knowledge they possessed? That is a real issue which could well be tried by a court martial.

From what I have further heard—and a good deal of it is rumor and not authenticated—the defense of these officers is that other persons had knowledge which, if they had possessed it, would have resulted in a different situation at Pearl Harbor, and that it was the failure of other persons, higher up in the chain of command to transmit knowledge which they possessed, that was largely responsible for conditions at Pearl Harbor.

If that is the situation, certainly we should not ask the Secretary of the Navy and the Secretary of War to investigate themselves, or to investigate their own Departments. It seems to me that sooner or later, if we are to know the whole story of Pearl Harbor, which the American people have a right to know sometime, that will have to be brought about by an investigation through some committees of the Congress.

Mr. Hatch. Mr. President, those were largely the sentiments expressed in our committee. There are many other considerations against either of these departments fully investigating itself, but the investigation authorized by the pending committee amendment is more in the nature of an investigation to secure the facts and to preserve and have ready for use the testimony.

Near the close of the Senate debate on June 5, 1944, Senator Robert A. Taft of Ohio, read into the *Record* a series of searching questions relative to Pearl Harbor, which Arthur Krock had asked in the *New York Times* on May 31, 1944, that is, about a week before the debate occurred. Among these questions the following had a particular bearing on the matter of overhead responsibility for the catastrophe at Pearl Harbor:

1. Why was a fleet concentrated in the harbor waters in the presence of a crisis which the Secretary of State, Cordell Hull, had twice reported to the War Council (that included the Secretaries of War and Navy) and as much as 10 days before had described as requiring an alert against simultaneous Japanese attacks at several points "anywhere in the Pacific area"?

2. Why was the Pacific Fleet based on Hawaii instead of on the west coast of the United States?

3. Why were so many fleet units dispatched into the Atlantic

before, after, and during the time when the Secretary of the Navy, the late Col. Frank Knox, was warning the Secretary of War, Henry L. Stimson, of a possible Japanese air attack in the Pacific, specifically at Pearl Harbor?

4. In what degree was there correlation between State Department intelligence and War and Navy Department instructions to field commanders?

5. What were the circumstances surrounding the selections of General Short and Admiral Kimmel for their commands, and what if any were their liaisons?

6. Why did the Army in Hawaii continue tolerant policies toward those Japanese in Hawaii whom the Navy wished to arrest for violation of the foreign agents registry law?

7. Why did the Navy shore officer fail to call for alert No. 3 after a two-man Japanese submarine was discovered and sunk shortly before the air attack?

8. Why was the Army command in Washington silent after receiving on November 29 General Short's report that he had only instituted alert No. 1, or, if it sent a correcting message before the new attack, what became of that message which is said never to have been received?

9. Why did Washington's orders to Pacific commanders concentrate on sabotage of airplanes on the ground; and why did they emphasize the Southwest Pacific as the point of possible attack when Mr. Hull had predicted simultaneous assaults everywhere in that ocean? Was this emphasis the explanation of what happened at Manila when the Navy was ordered away in time and General MacArthur kept his planes massed on Nichols Field?

10. In general, what is the share the Washington administration should have in culpability for the success of the Japanese attacks?

THE QUESTION OF SECRET CORRESPONDENCE (1939–1941)
BETWEEN PRESIDENT ROOSEVELT AND WINSTON
CHURCHILL RAISED IN THE SENATE

IF THE Joint Resolution signed June 13, 1944, and the debate in Congress that had accompanied its passage were startling to defenders of the official thesis on the coming of the war, no less amazing to them was a debate in the Senate of the United States six days later on the subject of secret communications between President Roosevelt and Winston Churchill alleged to have been opened in September, 1939, if not earlier. The occasion for this debate was a dispatch from London, passed by the British censor on June 16, 1944, dealing with a debate in the House of Commons on that day in respect of the arrest and imprisonment, in 1940, of Captain A. H. M. Ramsay, a member of the House of Commons, and Tyler Kent, a code clerk in the American Embassy at London.[10] At the time of their arrest, Mr. Kent had been charged with purloining certain messages from the American diplomatic bag and with disclosing some of the contents to Captain Ramsay, who was accused of being antiwar and anti-Semitic in his views, and to a woman of Russian origin, Anna Wolkoff, whose designs in the case were obscure.

Using the dispatch from London on the Ramsay-Kent affair as his text, Senator Hendrik Shipstead brought the case to the attention of the Senate and started a long exposition of views in which opponents and defenders of President Roosevelt's conduct of foreign affairs took part. The Senator said at the outset that the dispatch "reflects upon the integrity not only of the Government of the United States, but also, to some extent, upon the integrity of the Government of Great Britain." He quoted the headline of the dispatch: "Commons told F. D. R. pledged aid before war—M. P. says Churchill got promise." Then he proceeded with an analysis of the dispatch.

Extracts from the debate as printed in the *Congressional Record*, June 19, 1944, follow:

MR. SHIPSTEAD. . . . I intend to refer to a matter which in my opinion is of such great importance that it ought to be called to the attention of the Congress of the United States. It deals with a newspaper dispatch from London, England, which has passed through the British censor. It deals with the debate in the Parliament of

10. The text of this debate in the House of Commons is to be found in 400 *House of Commons Debates*, June 16, 1944. My transcript of this debate covers fifteen typewritten pages.

Great Britain. That debate was participated in by members of the three parties represented in the British Parliament, and it is of such a grave character that it reflects upon the integrity not only of the Government of the United States, but also, to some extent, upon the integrity of the Government of Great Britain. I am amazed that the British censor should pass it, but because the British censor has passed it, I assume that it has the imprimatur of the British Government. . . .

I read from the dispatch:

"London, June 16.—President Roosevelt promised Prime Minister Churchill before Britain entered the war that America would come to her aid. This accusation was made today in the House of Commons by John McGovern, an independent Laborite.

"In a debate on regulation 18-B, in which the minister of home security is given authority to detain in prison without trial any person he suspects to be dangerous to the war effort, McGovern asked whether the reason for the continued detention of Capt. A. H. M. Ramsay, a member of Parliament, was that he might make sensational disclosures about pre-war negotiations between Churchill and Roosevelt.

"McGovern linked the detention of Ramsay to the arrest of Tyler Kent, American embassy clerk, whose mother, a resident of Washington, D.C., has been fighting for his release for 4 years. Kent was sentenced to 7 years' imprisonment in camera on a charge of disclosing embassy secrets. He was a code clerk and had access to diplomatic correspondence."

I quote the words of the member of Parliament, Mr. McGovern:

"I have been told that Captain Ramsay is not in because he is a Fascist," McGovern said, "but because Tyler Kent took copies of letters from a diplomatic bag between the Prime Minister and the President of the United States. The Prime Minister was soliciting military aid in the event this country was going to war and preparations were made and promises given by the President of the United States through the diplomatic bag."

That was done when the present Prime Minister was not Prime Minister.

I continue to quote the words of the member of Parliament:

"I am told that while the present Prime Minister was First Lord of the Admiralty under the late Neville Chamberlain—"

That was when the present Prime Minister was head of the British admiralty, and when Chamberlain was Prime Minister and head of the British Government—

"he still was carrying on this campaign behind the back of his Prime Minister—"

I am quoting the words of a member of the British Parliament— "engaging in the exchange of letters through the diplomatic bag in order to find out the strength of American support and whether America could be depended upon to come into the war."

That was before Winston Churchill was Prime Minister. . . .

I quote further from the words of the Member of the British Parliament:

"It is said that if Ramsay were released—"

Ramsay was a member of Parliament, and is now in jail— "it would be extremely dangerous and difficult for him to be going around substantiating these things and stating that they are true, and therefore that he is being held because the Prime Minister does not want him to be liberated." . . .

Mr. WHEELER. . . . My understanding is that no foreigner is allowed to use the American code. It is my understanding that at the time under discussion Mr. Churchill was the First Lord of the Admiralty in Mr. Chamberlain's cabinet. He could not use the British code. In other words, he would not dare to use the British code, if the information which came to me from Mrs. Kent is correct.

Mr. SHIPSTEAD. He could not use the code without the consent of Chamberlain. . . .

Mr. CONNALLY. Mr. President, I regret very much that the distinguished Senator from Minnesota should pay so much attention to a mere hearsay statement of a member of the House of Commons. It will be recalled that in the quotation the Senator stated in several places that this member of the House of Commons— I forget his name—made the statement, "I have been told so and so and so," or, "It is understood so and so and so and so and so. . . ."

The fact that it passed the British censor does not bear much significance because statements made on the floor of the House of Commons are public property, there is general knowledge as to what is said and what occurs there. I see no reason why they should not pass it and let us hear about it. . . .

Mr. Shipstead. Mr. President, will the Senator yield?

Mr. Connally. I yield.

Mr. Shipstead. . . . There is nothing here to indicate that any member of the Parliament denied the charges that were made by the honorable member who discussed the matter. It was discussed as a fact. No question was raised as to the facts in the case. The only question was, "What are we to do about it?"

Mr. Connally. The Senator says no one denied some statement. Does the fact that no one denied it make it true?

Mr. President, since this matter has arisen on the floor, let me say that I have had some contacts with the legal officer in the Department of State, and I find this to be the case about this matter: Young Kent was an employee of the American Embassy. He became involved with a little group in England, member of Parliament Ramsay, a Russian woman, and others who were conspiring to violate and did violate English law. It was not alone a breach of trust to the Government by which he was employed, but in his activity in connection with this group in England he was violating the British law, the Defense of the Realm Act. The British have laws dealing not only with the extraction of documents, but the conveying of information concerning the documents to British citizens, and in that way the young man violated the British law.

The State Department says that the British Government before prosecution submitted the documents to the United States Government, and before the prosecution was begun our Government examined the documents and concluded that Kent ought to be prosecuted, and waived his diplomatic immunity. If we had desired we could have invoked diplomatic immunity in this case and perhaps have prevented it from being prosecuted in the British courts.

But here was a conspiracy. One prong of it was a boy working for the American Embassy; another prong was a member of the British Parliament, and a third prong was a person from Russia.

All of them were engaged in enterprises which under the British law were inimical to the safety of the British realm. Why not try them all in the same jurisdiction where the facts were available, where the crime was committed, especially when our Government, knowing the facts, was willing that that course should be pursued? That is my answer to these charges. . . .

Mr. President, I regret the political tinge that the Senator from

Oregon [Mr. Holman] tried to interject into this matter. We are in a great war. This is not an individual war of President Roosevelt. It is not an individual war of Mr. Winston Churchill. It is not an individual war of Mr. Stalin or of Chiang Kai-shek. It is a war of all the people of these four great countries. Why do we in the midst of it have to have these slings and slurs constantly cast at Mr. Churchill. I hold no brief for Mr. Churchill. Why do we have to have these slings continually at the President of the United States? I have never been an unconditional supporter of the President in his domestic policies; but I have favored his foreign policies, and I expect to continue to follow them so long as they go along the course they have taken in recent years.

Mr. President, this war is not helped, it is not aided, its successful prosecution is not furthered, its cause is not advanced by things of this sort—picking up a newspaper somewhere and reading that John Smith said that Bill Jones told him that the Widow McCafferty told him that Mr. Roosevelt told Churchill before ever he was Prime Minister that we were going to help him militarily. I do not know whether Mr. Churchill invoked the President's aid. Everyone in this Chamber knows that Mr. Roosevelt could not send a soldier, he could not send a dollar of military supplies to Mr. Churchill or his Government or any other government until the Congress of the United States authorized such action.

Mr. President, why can we not have unity until the war is over? Why cannot we stop this sniping and shooting behind the lines? Why can we not do away with sabotage until this struggle is over? When it is, then turn loose your dogs of war, bring on your political organizations and your militaristic groups representing this faction and that faction. But in the name of common sense, during time of war let us remain united. . . .

The subject of communications between President Roosevelt and Winston Churchill prior to 1940,[11] when Mr. Churchill became Prime Minister, was not novel in June, 1944, to American students of English and American history; nor indeed to readers of the London *Times* and the *New York Times*. The matter had been touched upon in both of these great newspapers as early as 1940, the year in which Captain

11. See note at end of this Chapter.

Ramsay and Mr. Kent were arrested and imprisoned.[12] The following citations of "news" establish this fact:

New York Times, August 25, 1940. Report on the arrest of Captain Ramsay. The article charged Captain Ramsay with being "strongly anti-Communist, anti-Semitic, and pro-Hitler," and added: "Informed American sources said that he had sent to the German Legation in Dublin treasonable information given him by Tyler Kent, clerk in the American embassy in London."

London *Times*, October 24, 1940. Report of the opening of the trial of Tyler Kent, accused of offenses contrary to the Official Secrets Act.

London *Times*, November 8, 1940. Report on close of the trial of Tyler Kent.

London *Times*, July 18, 1941. Report on the opening of a lawsuit filed by Captain Ramsay against the New York Times Company, charging the company with slandering him in its issue of August 25, 1940.

London *Times*, July 19, 1941. Report on Captain Ramsay's action against the *New York Times*, with extracts from the Law Report of July 18.

London *Times*, July 26, 1941. Report on further hearings of Captain Ramsay's action against the *New York Times*.

London *Times*, August 1, 1941. Report of the conclusion of the case of Captain Ramsay against the *New York Times*. Judgment was rendered against the *New York Times* in favor of Captain Ramsay, but the damages were assessed at only one farthing in each of the cases—against the New York Times Company of New York City and the Times Company, Limited, of London, respectively.

New York Times, August 1, 1941. Report on the Ramsay case in London and the awarding of "contemptuous" damages against the *New York Times*. Statement that Valentine Holmes, counsel for the *Times*, called Captain Ramsay a

12. The charge that President Roosevelt had entered into secret agreements with other countries in respect of war was made during the campaign of 1940 and denied. Beard, *op. cit.*, pp. 303 f.

"traitor" and an "associate of thieves and felons." Further statement: "Almost every leading British newspaper tonight expressed congratulations to the *New York Times* on the result of the case."

374 *House of Commons Debates*, October 16, 1941, Col. 1509. Mr. McGovern asked the Home Secretary about the nature of the telegrams, cables, or messages stolen or alleged to have been shown to Captain Ramsay and "the name of the British subject who had sent these messages to President Roosevelt and for what purpose." The Home Secretary declined in "the public interest" to reply.

374 *House of Commons Debates*, November 11, 1941, Col. 2042. Mr. Stokes asked the Home Secretary about the messages exchanged by President Roosevelt and "the British subject" and added: "Were any of these cablegrams or messages sent by the Prime Minister [Mr. Churchill] behind the back of the then Prime Minister [Mr. Chamberlain]?" The Home Secretary declined to give information on the subject.

Washington Times-Herald, November 12, 1941. Article by Arthur Sears Henning on the discussion in the House of Commons on the previous day. Mr. Henning noted that the reference in the House of Commons was confined to messages sent by Mr. Churchill as First Lord of the Admiralty in the Chamberlain Cabinet, and said that the White House, in response to an inquiry, professed to have no information on the subject. Mr. Henning made a number of allegations respecting the contents of the messages that passed between President Roosevelt and Mr. Churchill. He alleged that the messages touched upon a more vigorous prosecution of the war by Premier Chamberlain and the possibilities of the United States taking an active part in the support of Great Britain. Mr. Henning also charged President Roosevelt with having previously permitted, if not encouraged, William C. Bullitt and other American diplomats abroad to offer promises of American aid to France and Poland if they got into the war.

At length on September 2, 1944, the State Department issued a long release to the press, taking note "of recent inquiries and newspaper reports regarding the case of Tyler Kent," and giving its official account of the case. In this release the department stated that Mr. Kent, when his room was searched, had in his possession "copies of Embassy material totalling more than 1500 individual papers." It did not describe the nature of these papers; nor did it refer to the allegation that they included messages exchanged between President Roosevelt and Mr. Churchill. Nor did the department deny that such exchanges had taken place. It devoted most of its report to justifying the action that had been taken against Mr. Kent on the part of the British Government as well as the Government of the United States.[13]

Such are a few of the numerous public references to the Roosevelt-Churchill correspondence and the Tyler Kent case.

THE SEPTEMBER, 1944, DEBATE ON PEARL HARBOR

DURING the summer of 1944 a number of events conspired to create an excitement over the Pearl Harbor case in Army, Navy, and political circles. Inquiries were being carried on by War and Navy boards established under the Act of June 13, 1944. At hearings held by the military and naval affairs committees and other committees of Congress on this and related matters, information respecting responsibility for the catastrophe was developed; and members of the Republican minorities of these committees acquired inside knowledge under the seal of secrecy. Indeed, as Senator Hatch had remarked during the June 5 debate in the Senate, the judiciary committee of that chamber had then given favorable consideration to a congressional investigation of the whole Pearl Harbor case.[14] And Republicans were saying that in the hidden facts of the Pearl Harbor disaster lay information that would put entirely new aspects on President Roosevelt's conduct of foreign affairs prior to the catastrophe.

A temper already growing warm was fanned to white heat in the latter part of August, 1944, by Senator Harry S.

13. See Note at the end of this Chapter.
14. See above, p. 263.

Truman, then candidate for Vice President on the Democratic ticket. In *Collier's* magazine Senator Truman, in the course of an argument for the unification of the armed forces, took advantage of the occasion to bring up the Pearl Harbor affair and by direct statement and implication to lay responsibility for the disaster on the lack of coöperation between the Army and the Navy. In the article also was the following insinuation: "In Hawaii, General Short and Admiral Kimmel could meet, if they happened to be on speaking terms, or exchange cables and radiograms." Whether so intended or not, Senator Truman's attack on the two commanders could be and was interpreted to mean that the charges of the Roberts Report against them were well founded, that responsibility for the disaster lay on the commanders, and that President Roosevelt, as well as other high officials in Washington, stood free and clear, as represented by the Report.

Admiral Kimmel was incensed by Senator Truman's insinuations. For more than two years and a half he had remained under the cloud spread by the Roberts Report over his honor and conduct, privately pleading for a trial, for an opportunity to be heard, for the right accorded to the meanest criminal under the principles of American jurisprudence. His position was made more unbearable for the reason that the Navy Department had filed no formal charges against him calling for a trial and he could do nothing about the conclusions of the President's Commission that had designated him as one of the two men responsible for the American disaster.

Under the lash of Senator Truman's criticism, Admiral Kimmel now broke his long silence and made public the following sharp retort:

My dear Senator Truman: In an article appearing under your name in Collier's magazine of August 26, 1944, you have made false statements concerning my conduct as commander in chief of the Pacific Fleet at Pearl Harbor prior to the Japanese attack.

Your innuendo that General Short and I were not on speaking terms is not true. Your statements alleging failure to cooperate and coordinate our efforts are equally false. General Short and I, as well as our subordinates, coordinated the efforts of our commands in close, friendly, personal, and official relationships.

The real story of the Pearl Harbor attack and the events preceding it has never been publicly told. This has not been my decision. For more than two and a half years I have been anxious to have the American people know all the facts.

The Roberts report, upon which you rely, does not contain the basic truths of the Pearl Harbor catastrophe. This is evident from the fact that no official action has ever been taken upon the basis of that report. The Congress of the United States, of which you are a Member, has recognized the inadequacy of the Roberts report by directing that the War and Navy Departments undertake a full investigation of the Pearl Harbor disaster.

Until I am afforded a hearing in open court, it is grossly unjust to repeat false charges against me, when, by official action, I have been persistently denied an opportunity to defend myself publicly.

I suggest that until such time as complete disclosure is made of the facts about Pearl Harbor, you refrain from repeating charges based on evidence that has never met the test of public scrutiny.

I ask for nothing more than an end to untruths and half truths about this matter, until the entire story is given to our people, who, I am convinced, will be amazed at the truth.

I am releasing this letter to the press in the belief that the historic American sense of fair play will approve this action.

Very truly yours
H. E. KIMMEL,
Rear Admiral,
United States Navy (Retired).[15]

In response to this letter from Admiral Kimmel, Senator Truman contented himself with stating that he had at his command documentary evidence to support his charge and then withdrew from the controversy over it. But instead of quenching a smoldering fire, the Democratic candidate for Vice President had poured oil on it and helped to make Pearl Harbor an issue in the presidential campaign.[16] He also defied the critics who were then alleging that President Roosevelt had made

15. *Congressional Record,* August 21, 1944, p. A3958.
16. See below, pp. 288 ff., for an estimate by David Lawrence.

inadequate preparations at Hawaii to cope with the consequences of his own actions in the conduct of affairs with Japan.

Republicans would have been less than human, certainly less
than political, in their sensibilities, if they had not taken advantage of the opportunity afforded by the controversy started
by the Democratic candidate for Vice President. Besides they
now had in their possession a public declaration from Admiral
Kimmel, one of the parties to the case of responsibility for
Pearl Harbor, that the "real story" of the disaster had not
been told, that the Roberts Report did not contain the basic
truths of the business, and that a "complete disclosure" had
not yet been made.

On September 6, 1944, Hugh D. Scott, Republican from
Pennsylvania, raised in the House of Representatives the matter of responsibility for Pearl Harbor, made certain definite
statements on the subject, and asked "some of the questions
which are now being freely discussed in Washington and elsewhere." Among the questions were the following: Did not
President Roosevelt remove Admiral Richardson for refusing
to keep the American fleet bottled up in Pearl Harbor and substitute Admiral Kimmel? Is it not a fact that the splitting of the
fleet and the sending of a part to the Atlantic were opposed by
many naval authorities? Did the President not order all naval
vessels to prepare for action against Axis surface craft on July
30, 1941? Were these not the "shooting orders" reported by
the President to the public for the first time on September 11,
1941? Had not Admiral Kimmel been promised 300 reconnaissance planes and received only 50, as against 250 appor-
tioned to Great Britain by Harry Hopkins of the Munitions
Assignment Board? Did not a high ranking naval official ask
permission to get the fleet out of Pearl Harbor between
September and November, 1941? Did not the Government of
the United States on December 6, 1941, learn from the Australian Government that the Japanese fleet was steaming toward Pearl Harbor? Was not the warning message of
December 7 sent by slow "commercial cable" to the com-

manders in Hawaii (instead of immediately by the swift Army or Navy radio)?

Concerning the advance notice of the Japanese attack vaguely referred to in the Roberts Report, Mr. Scott confined himself mainly to asking questions:

On November 29, 1941, Secretary Hull conferred with the British Ambassador. The Secretary said that " the diplomatic part of our relations with Japan was virtually over and that the matter will now go to the officials of the Army and Navy," adding that "Japan may move suddenly and with every possible element of surprise and spread out over considerable areas and capture certain positions and posts before the peaceful countries interested in the Pacific would have time to confer and formulate plans to meet these new conditions"—Peace and War, page 138.[17] Did the fleet remain in Pearl Harbor and was any change in the alert ordered by the Commander in Chief?

On December 6, 1941, the President went over the heads of the Japanese Government and telegraphed a personal message to the Emperor of Japan. This message appears to have been sent without any notice to the Emperor's representatives here or to the Emperor's Government. On the same date as the President's message to the Emperor, did not the Australian Government learn that a Japanese fleet was steaming toward Pearl Harbor and did it not on the night of December 6–7 inform our Government at Washington? Did not our Government transmit the information to naval and military authorities at Pearl Harbor at or about 6:30 A.M., on December 7—Hawaiian time—by commercial cable and was not the message received 7 hours after the attack?

But with regard to the problem of equipment for air defense at Hawaii, Mr. Scott made a positive assertion that it was inadequate:

Reverting to September 1941, there were 50 Consolidated Navy PBY's—seaplanes—available for the protection of Pearl Harbor. Had not Admiral Kimmel as commander in chief, Pacific Fleet, been promised 300 PBY's in all? Upon the completion of the ad-

17. See above, p. 247.

ditional 250 PBY's by Consolidated, the arrangement to send them to Pearl Harbor was canceled and all 250 were sent by Harry Hopkins, of the Munitions Assignment Board, to Great Britain. In the absence of these planes, the Navy was unable to conduct, for the protection of the fleet, an adequate 360° reconnaissance of the area around the Hawaiian Islands. We were, therefore, left with a number of blind spots in this essential survey. The Commander in Chief vested the power to make this decision in Harry Hopkins, who had had no naval or military experience, and in the Munitions Assignment Board. Mr. Hopkins is not subject to court martial.

Attacking President Roosevelt's policy of basing the fleet at Pearl Harbor, Mr. Scott said:

About the beginning of 1941, numerous complaints were forwarded to high administration sources by merchants, business interests, and others in the Hawaiian Islands that the fleet was being kept out of Pearl Harbor and at sea too much. Did not the President send for Admiral James O. Richardson, then Commander in Chief of the Pacific Fleet, who had then served but 1 year of his normal 2-year tour of duty at this time? Did the President advise Admiral Richardson that the fleet should be kept in Pearl Harbor more often and particularly on week ends, as there had been complaints from Hawaii that the absence of the fleet was bad for business, or words to that effect? Did not Admiral Richardson, who had flown to Washington from Hawaii, demur to the suggestion and return to the Pacific? These questions are being asked among Members of Congress and in the press. If they are not true, why not have an investigation or court martial promptly and make all the facts known—after nearly 3 years—to the American public?

Subsequently, was not Admiral Richardson again summoned from Hawaii to the White House and was he not told in more peremptory fashion that the fleet must be kept in Pearl Harbor more frequently? At this point did not Admiral Richardson state, in effect, that as long as he was commander of the Pacific Fleet he would be compelled to use his own judgment and would do what was best for the security of the fleet, adding that, of course, the President had the power to remove him? After this inconclusive conference, did not Admiral Richardson fly back to Hawaii and was he not then or shortly thereafter relieved of his command by Admiral Kimmel, who had been jumped about 50 numbers—over other admirals—and given the assignment? Did not Admiral Kimmel then comply with administration orders and keep the fleet in Pearl Harbor much more frequently than before? In fact, after the negotiations began with the Japanese special envoy, Kurusu, was not the fleet definitely kept in Pearl Harbor during these negotiations? Naval officers present at the time have informed me that the concentration in Pearl Harbor during the time shortly before the disaster was greater than any concentration they had ever known.

September 11, 1944, Forest A. Harness, Republican from Indiana, member of the Military Affairs Committee, delivered a long address in the House of Representatives on the subject of Pearl Harbor. Before coming to his main points, he charged the Roosevelt Administration with throwing a blanket of secrecy over the whole affair and indicated, without saying it in so many words, that he had some acquaintance with General Short's documentary file of "more than 250 pages," which "General Short believes will completely vindicate him of unfounded charges." As a member of the Military Affairs Committee Mr. Harness may have had access to General Short's files or at least have heard the whole matter of responsibility discussed by other members of the committee and representatives of the armed forces who from time to time appeared before the committee. This is highly probable. Yet Mr. Harness was himself under a seal of secrecy and could not give the actual sources upon which he relied for his contentions. He confessed, "Let me repeat here that I have no personal knowledge of the facts related here, but they come to me from a source that I believe to be thoroughly reliable and trustworthy."

Taking up the charge that General Short was responsible for the failure to complete the permanent installation of aircraft warning apparatus in Hawaii and that he had not taken proper precautions in view of the warning messages received from Washington, Mr. Harness said:

This evidence, I am informed, will show that General Short was in charge of the Pearl Harbor defenses from February of 1941 until he was relieved of that post about December 20, 1941, a few days after the Pearl Harbor attack; that on numerous occasions General Short asked the War Department for additional men and equipment, and for priorities and critical supplies, in view of the imminence of danger, in his opinion. These requests were denied and no satisfaction was given to his pleas. For example, on June 10, 1941, he sent a wire to the War Department with reference to the aircraft warning system in Honolulu.

In the wire, Short stated that this project of building such system was, in his opinion, the most important single project in the islands. He asked for immediate priority in order that the work could be started on this and completed at the earliest possible moment. The response that he received from the War Department, and subsequent correspondence shows that up to the time of the attack the project had not been completed. This evidence will further show that on November 27, 1941, as a result of communications passing between General Short and Washington, Short put into effect in the Hawaiian Islands one of three very extensively planned alerts. This was alert No. 1, and was called principally for general vigilance against sabotage. Simultaneously with putting this into effect, he informed the Chief of Staff in Washington that he had done so. The Chief of Staff, by return wire, confirmed the propriety of this alert and by very clear intimation in this confirmation indicated that it was the proper one of the three alerts, and that the other two were properly held in abeyance for the moment. The other two were more drastic, the third one being the alert that was to announce preparation for an immediate attack. Short had no information on which to judge that the No. 3 alert was the proper one.

In respect of an additional advanced notice of the Japanese attack, Mr. Harness spoke with assurance, though he furnished no documentary proof:

There appears to be an abundance of evidence to show that 72 hours before the attack on Pearl Harbor, the Australian Government advised the American Government in Washington that an aircraft carrier task force of the Japanese Navy had been sighted by Australian reconnaissance headed toward Pearl Harbor; that our Government was again notified 48 hours before the attack that this Japanese task force was still in progress toward Hawaii, and the same notification was sent 24 hours before Pearl Harbor. None of this information was, I am informed, given to General Short.

When he came to the explosive subject of the last warning message sent "about noon" on December 7, which the Roberts Report vaguely mentioned, Mr. Harness declared categorically:

The wire was sent by commercial radio instead of the usual more rapid direct military means. General Short will contend that this information was extremely significant because of the instructions to destroy the code which is only a last resort. General Short believes that if this message had been telephoned him at 1:30 A.M., he would have been sufficiently alerted by that information and would have been much better prepared when the attack occurred.[18] This evidence will further show that at 9 P.M., December 6, 1941, the night before the attack, the Army dispatched 12 B-24 bombers from San Francisco to Honolulu for use in the general defense of the islands. These bombers were sent with their defense equipment completely inoperative, and arrived that way in Honolulu. All of the machine guns and small cannon were in their original wrappings and cosmoline, were not sighted in, and none of the ammunition was in position to be used. These planes arrived about half an hour after the attack started, and in the midst of it several of them were shot down and the crews killed. Fortunately the planes carried only skeleton crews. It is shown that the Army had been flying bombers from San Francisco to Honolulu in this same manner prior to this date, and General Short had vigorously protested against the flights being made without proper defense mechanism, but his protests were unheeded.

After presenting his case to the House of Representatives, Mr. Harness ventured to put the responsibility for the Pearl Harbor disaster on high officials in Washington:

On whom rests the responsibility for Pearl Harbor if it is not the Commander in Chief? Can the President as Commander in Chief claim credit for all victories and escape responsibility for our defeats? It is clear that the President would like the country to hold

18. As to the opposite contention by the Roberts Report, see above, p. 218.

General Short and Admiral Kimmel responsible, and thereby escape criticism himself. His refusal to bring them to trial is proof of that. You know, of course, that Mr. Roosevelt placed both of these officers in command at Pearl Harbor and they were under command of the President. Who had the inside information if it was not the State Department, the White House, the Secretary of War, and the Secretary of the Navy?

On September 21, 1944, John W. McCormack, Democratic majority leader in the House of Representatives, took notice of charges that had been made by Mr. Harness and characterized them as unfortunate, incorrect, and in the nature of scandalmongering. He devoted special attention to the claim made by Mr. Harness that the United States Government had received from the Australian Government warnings long in advance about the Japanese fleet steaming toward Pearl Harbor, and called it "a vicious and false rumor." Mr. McCormack read into the *Record* statements from the War and Navy Departments which denied any knowledge of such warning from the Australian Government and expressed the belief that "there is no foundation whatever for the charge that such a message was sent." He also reported that the State Department had made a similar denial and, in response to a special inquiry, had received from the Australian Government the following message: "This is pure invention. Our cables had no data regarding the Japanese Fleet." Mr. McCormack then branded the "rumor" on which Mr. Harness had based his allegation as "a lie according to this incontrovertible evidence."

When Representative Ralph Church, Republican from Illinois, remarked that Mr. McCormack had only quoted the Secretary of War, the Secretary of the Navy, and the State Department, and went further by saying, "He has not yet quoted nor has he yet inquired . . . ," Mr. McCormack exclaimed: "I think that is contemptible. That shows the gentleman's state of mind . . . I think the gentleman ought to be ashamed of himself in view of this evidence."

Mr. McCormack thereupon made an eloquent appeal for nonpartisanship and national unity:

There would appear to be a bottomless cavern wherein cheap politics beget unforgivable war rumors. Over 300,000 American fighting men have suffered casualties in this war. Death has knocked at the door of thousands upon thousands of families who before Pearl Harbor were content to live their lives in the space they now so prayerfully yearn. Thousands of permanently disabled veterans will carry their cross of war throughout life as potent evidence of their love of country. Men did not so suffer to protect slanders and vilifiers of the Government for which in the idealism of youth and the realism of manhood they offered their all for liberty of mankind. They believed in freedom of speech but not license of tongue, nor irresponsibility of position and trust.

What does it profit anyone to gain a vote through the tears of bereaved mothers, fathers, wives, other loved ones, because they, with unwarranted faith, believe in the political effulgence of their elected representative in Congress who spends his time castigating the Commander in Chief of our armed forces because he happens to be a candidate for President of these United States?

In war, when the national effort is consecrated to victory and integrity in public life is an essential of national unity, the unfounded stories of unbridled imagination purloined from the lips of those who lack the courage to manfully proclaim the facts, are injurious, speaking mildly, of the war effort. . . .

Yet Mr. McCormack was not prepared to declare that Admiral Kimmel and General Short were actually guilty of the charges lodged against them by the President's Commission on Pearl Harbor. When a colleague interposed to say that everybody shared the conviction that the two commanders were guilty, Mr. McCormack replied that he would not go that far, that his mind was still open on the point, and that the burden of proof was on those who sought to win a conviction.

Later in the day, September 21, Mr. Church, whose inquiry to the effect that President Roosevelt might know about the mysterious message which had been denounced by Mr. McCormack as "contemptible," took the floor and replied to the majority leader. Mr. Scott had asked leading questions. Mr. Harness had made statements on the basis of sources which he claimed to be reliable and trustworthy. Mr. Church now made positive allegations and introduced names and dates.

Reaffirming the contention that the Roosevelt Administration had received from some quarter an advance notice respecting Japanese intentions to attack Pearl Harbor on December 7, 1941, Mr. Church said:

The distinguished gentleman from Massachusetts states that he has checked with the State Department, Navy Department, and the War Department, and that they each authorized him to make certain statements. But the gentleman did not mention the White House. Apparently the gentleman from Massachusetts, who, as majority leader, is the administration's spokesman on this floor, accepted a statement from the War and Navy Departments that denied only that a message was received from the Australian Government. The gentleman from Massachusetts does not state that either the War Department, the Navy Department, or the White House have denied that they had information, 3 days before Pearl Harbor, from sources other than Australia, that Japan was to attack the United States.

Apparently the majority leader does not know that Lt. Comdr. A. D. Kramer, U.S.N.R., now serving in the Pacific, was on duty in the Navy Department on Saturday night, December 6, and that he delivered a message to the State Department about 10 A.M. the following Sunday morning, which would be 4:30 A.M. Pearl Harbor time. He commented to the group at the State Department that "This looks like a sunrise attack at Pearl Harbor and midnight attack at the Philippines." He then went to the White House and delivered the message.

The gentleman from Massachusetts will probably say "rumor, just a rumor." But the gentleman is not willing to have an investigation made to ascertain whether the facts I have just recited are true. The able majority leader cannot dismiss the whole matter simply by replying "rumor, mere rumor." The burden is on him to prove it to be a rumor. Why, Mr. Speaker, why does the administration so violently oppose an investigation? Is there any objection to having Lieutenant Commander Kramer testify before a committee of Congress?

To support specifically the claim that an advance notice had come from the Australian Government, Mr. Church laid before the House of Representatives sworn testimony on the subject, which, it is to be noted, did not sustain the particular charge made by Mr. Harness:

The distinguished gentleman contends that the stories which have been circulating about Pearl Harbor are false. He claims, for example, that there is no truth in the statements made by the gentleman from Indiana that Australia knew well in advance of the Japanese attack that such an attack was to be made on December 7.

Let me read to my friend and colleague an affidavit executed by Mr. Sidney C. Graves, a reliable citizen residing in the District of Columbia, who was present at a dinner when the Australian Minister to the United States, Sir Owen Dixon, stated that Australia knew about the coming attack. Is it perhaps not without significance, Mr. Speaker, that Sir Owen Dixon has been recalled to Australia? Has he been guilty of telling the truth?

I now read the affidavit:

To Whom It May Concern:

On December 7, 1943, I attended a dinner in Washington. Among those present were Sir Owen Dixon, then serving as Australian Minister to the United States on duty here in Washington, Senator Homer Ferguson, Mr. Frank C. Hanighen, 1737 H Street NW., Washington, D.C., and others whom I do not remember.

After the dinner the Australian Minister stated to myself and the others mentioned above in substance, as follows:

Shortly after the outbreak of war in 1939, I left my judgeship to assume control of coastal shipping in Australian waters. About 72 hours before Pearl Harbor, I received a flash warning from my naval intelligence that a Japanese task force was at sea and Australia should prepare for an attack; 24 hours later this was further confirmed with a later opinion of intelligence that the task force was apparently not aimed at Australian waters and perhaps was directed against some American possession. Finally, on December 7, 1941, my intelligence stated "We are saved, America is in the war, Pearl Harbor has been bombed."

The Australian Minister was questioned by one of the guests as to whether this information was available to American authority and he stated in substance that it was if requested.

I certify that the above is a substance of the statement made by Sir Owen Dixon on the aforesaid date.

SIDNEY C. GRAVES
Washington, D.C.

DISTRICT OF COLUMBIA,
Washington, D.C. ss:
Sworn to before me a notary public this 21st day of September 1944.
[Notarial seal] EDNA W. HERBERT,
Notary Public Washington, D.C.

. . .

MR. MCCORMACK. There is nothing in that affidavit which states that our Government was notified. Is that correct?

MR. CHURCH. That is correct.

But the gentleman said nothing in his speech with regard to the message being delivered to the White House. I have given him the name and rank of the naval officer who delivered the message, the time delivered, and his interpretation of it.

In reply to another inquiry from Mr. McCormack, Mr. Church gave his reasons for believing that the issue should be and could be cleared up soon without injury to war needs and war unity:

MR. MCCORMACK. Will the gentleman read what I said about our War, Navy, and State Departments?

MR. CHURCH. That is simply the statement of interested parties. There are others who have a contrary opinion. What is the truth? What are the real facts? That is all the American people ask. They want to know, not from me nor from the distinguished gentleman from Massachusetts, what may be our respective ideas on the Pearl Harbor catastrophe; but they want to know the facts upon which they may form their own opinion as to who should be held responsible for the Japanese success in surprising our forces at Pearl Harbor.

If what the distinguished gentleman has said is correct, an impartial investigation made by a committee of Congress will factually sustain him in his views. Such an investigation will stop the stories and rumors he alleges to be false, if false they are. Let me remind the majority leader that one of the reasons there are so many

rumors and stories concerning Pearl Harbor, about which he bitterly complained today, is the fact that the administration he represents has taken such pains to prevent a public investigation.
Those who oppose an investigation of their acts and deeds are not
above suspicion. If the majority leader is correct in his contentions,
then the administration he represents has everything to gain and
nothing whatsoever to lose by seeing that the facts pertaining to
Pearl Harbor are brought to light by an investigation in which the
people have confidence.

It has been almost 3 years since Pearl Harbor, but Admiral Kimmel and General Short have never been given so much as the opportunity to defend themselves. The American people want to
know why the delay. The administration first answered that to
hold a court martial would reveal to the enemy the extent of the
damage at Pearl Harbor and reveal valuable military information.
But the Pearl Harbor incident was 3 years ago. The damage done
has been repaired and the whole military and naval situation has
changed. The administration now argues that the court martial
of Admiral Kimmel and General Short would necessitate bringing
back to the United States military and naval leaders needed in the
theaters of operations. That argument will not stand analysis. It is
not even an argument, it is an excuse. But even assuming its validity,
what legitimate reason is there for not having a congressional investigation? Such an investigation need not concern itself with
military and naval details, the technicalities of military and naval
operations, but will serve a real purpose if it looks into the controversial question as to the extent of the knowledge in Washington
and at Pearl Harbor of the imminent attack on Pearl Harbor. It
will serve a great purpose if it resolves these many questions in the
minds of our people.

Although the Democratic majority leader appeared willing
to let the troublesome business rest, President Roosevelt was
moved to make a public statement on the issue of advance
notice from the Australian Government. A press report of
this statement ran as follows: [19]

Anyone who has information that this government knew 72
hours in advance of the Pearl Harbor attack that a Jap task force

19. *New York World-Telegram*, September 22, 1944.

was steaming toward the Hawaiian Islands should submit that information to the military boards now investigating the entire Pearl Harbor case, President Roosevelt said today.

He told a news conference that there would be lots of things like that—referring to charges that information about the Jap naval activity had been submitted to this government in advance of the attack—circulating day and night from now until Nov. 7 [election day].

Asked if he intended to order courtmartial trials at any time soon for Army and Navy leaders at Pearl Harbor at the time of the attack, Mr. Roosevelt replied that there were two committees or boards working on that now and that it would be just as well to wait to hear from them. He referred to the Army and Navy boards which are investigating all circumstances surrounding the attack.

Meanwhile, Secretary of State Cordell Hull revealed that Australian Minister Sir Owen Dixon had denied to the State Department that he had any advance information the Japs planned to attack American territory. Sir Owen previously had denied to reporters that he had any such information, as was charged in the House yesterday by Representative Ralph E. Church (R., Ill.).

Sir Owen, who is departing to take a seat on the Australian Court, was drawn into the running Pearl Harbor debate between Republicans and Democrats when Mr. Church read to the House an affidavit quoting Sir Owen as saying he had advance information of Jap plans to attack.

During the months immediately preceding the election, Washington buzzed with conversations about responsibility for Pearl Harbor and about probable action by directors of the Republican campaign in springing secret information that would put the onus squarely on President Roosevelt, then seeking reëlection on his record. In the *United States News* of August 24, 1944, David Lawrence, a veteran news hunter in Washington, described at length the background and strategy of the conflict between Democrats and Republicans with reference to the ticklish subject:

WASHINGTON, August 24, 1944.—Maybe SENATOR HARRY TRUMAN, Democratic Vice Presidential nominee, has unwittingly done the Nation a service by bringing on at this time a discussion of the true responsibility for the tragedy of Pearl Harbor—something that has been concealed from the public now for more than 2½ years.

When SENATOR TRUMAN wrote his article for Collier's magazine and made certain charges against Admiral Kimmel and General Short, he was obviously speaking with a background of confidential information obtained in his position as a member of the Senate committee investigating the war effort. Admiral Kimmel has indignantly denied the charges and innuendoes in a public letter but the Missouri Senator insists that when the court-martial proceedings are held his charges in the article will be correct.

This raises at once the question of why the court martial has been delayed and what reason SENATOR TRUMAN had for taking the initiative in airing in a magazine article something that the Roosevelt administration has thus far so effectively kept from the public by postponing the court-martial proceedings again and again.

The official reason given for the delay is that it would be prejudicial to the war effort to try the case now. But the Republicans in the Senate also have been in possession of certain information about it and succeeded recently in forcing an Army-Navy board to begin an inquiry on what happened at Pearl Harbor. These proceedings, however, are secret and conclusions reached will not be available till after the Presidential campaign.

Meanwhile, Governor Thomas E. Dewey, Republican Presidential nominee, who has a bit of experience in prosecutions, might decide to try the case in public. Certainly SENATOR TRUMAN has given him the cue.

For a long time Army and Navy officers, retired and otherwise, have been gossiping about the Pearl Harbor tragedy and have been asking many question, as for instance:

1. Why were all our battleships in harbor in Hawaii on December 7, 1941, instead of out at sea, and who in Washington gave the orders to keep them there, especially at a time of tension in the relations between Japan and the United States?

2. What admiral recommended that the ships be sent from Hawaii and what happened to the admiral who made such a recommendation, and was he relieved of his command at his own request or through the initiative of someone higher up?

3. Why, in view of the tense relations between Japan and the United States after the November 26 note was sent to Japan by the State Department and prior to December 7, were no mobilization orders sent to the fleet by Admiral Stark, then Chief of Naval Operations, thus putting the fleet on a war basis?

4. Why was the report of Justice Roberts confined wholly and specifically to circumstances and events happening in Hawaii, and why were the official acts of commission or omission at Washington in the War and Navy Departments excluded from the scope of the Roberts inquiry, so that the public got only part of the story?

There are many other collateral questions which a congressional inquiry rather than a court martial could get at.

Inasmuch as President Roosevelt is running for reelection on the argument that he has been Commander in Chief of the armed services "for more than 11 years," as he expressed it in his letter to Chairman Hannegan, of the Democratic National Committee, the Republicans feel they have a right to pin the responsibility for Pearl Harbor on the Commander in Chief who knew all the facts about our relations with Japan and was in a position to order the mobilization of the fleet or else to send it away from Pearl Harbor. The American people, including the mothers and fathers of the more than 3,000 boys who were killed at Pearl Harbor, are entitled now to all the facts that SENATOR TRUMAN had when he wrote his magazine article and to all other facts that bear on the tragedy.

One point congressional investigators of Pearl Harbor want cleared up is why President Roosevelt, as Commander in Chief, relieved Admiral James O. Richardson as Chief of Naval Operations, after 1 year instead of the normal 2 years of service, following Admiral Richardson's protest against concentration of the United States Fleet in Pearl Harbor on the ground that this concentration was dangerous and offered the Japanese an opportunity to destroy much of the Navy at a single blow.[20]

Mr. Lawrence's statement that Governor Thomas Dewey, the Republican candidate for President, might decide to try the case of Pearl Harbor in public, had some foundation in collateral rumors. If these rumors were to be believed many documents bearing on Pearl Harbor had come into the hands

20. *Congressional Record*, September 6, 1944, p. 7670.

of Republicans; these documents completely demolished the Roberts Report and the Administration's thesis as to responsibility for the disaster on December 7, 1941; they had been or were to be turned over to Governor Dewey, with the hope or expectation that he would use them to demonstrate the duplicity and incompetence of President Roosevelt in the management of foreign affairs prior to and after Pearl Harbor. Whatever may have been the truth of the business, however, Governor Dewey, for some reason, did not make use of such inside information during his campaign.[21]

Writing on Governor Dewey's dilemma, after the campaign was over, Arthur Krock in his column for the *New York Times*, December 5, 1944, confirmed the reports afloat as early as August of that year:

. . . as Governor Dewey discovered during the recent Presidential campaign, this [getting the facts relative to Pearl Harbor] is almost a hopeless enterprise in time of war. He had other experiences to prove how great is the handicap of candidacy against an incumbent of the White House in the midst of desperate and dubious battle, when no citizen worthy of his birthright can imperil the security of the armed services or success against the enemy by revelations which the High Command asserts are likely to do both. But Mr. Dewey's decision to keep Pearl Harbor out of the campaign in so far as he was concerned was the best illustration of that handicap.

It is reported that to the Republican nominee were brought what were represented to be facts about Pearl Harbor which would, if published and *sustained*, have had these effects: they would have laid the primary blame for the fatal concentration of naval and air units, and for the surprise element which swelled the disaster to heavy proportions, to high places in Washington. They

21. Governor Dewey's reason may have been the secret protest presented to him by General Marshall, Chief of Staff, in September, 1944, based on the alleged necessity of preserving certain war secrets in the national interest. General Marshall's first letter to Governor Dewey, dated September 25, 1944, opened: "I am writing you without the knowledge of any other person except Admiral King (who concurs) because we are approaching a grave dilemma in the political reactions of Congress regarding Pearl Harbor." General Marshall's account of his negotiations with Governor Dewey—which furnishes basic materials for a study of the relations of war and the armed forces to politics—is to be found in the Hearings of the Congressional Committee on Pearl Harbor, December 6, 1945, Part 3, pp. 1127 ff.

would have further explained why Secretary Hull's two explicit warnings of imminent Japanese attack "simultaneously and at all points in the Pacific" were ineffective, although he delivered them in the presence of War and Navy authorities and well in advance of the raids on Pearl Harbor and the Philippines. They would have tended to silence hereafter the excuse that Japanese "treachery" instead of high official policy was the cause of that unpreparedness for air attack which accounted for the degree of the calamity.[22]

But the explanation, as offered to Mr. Dewey, is said to have included a certain statement which high military authority asserts still to be unknown to the Japanese. And this information, it is also contended in the same quarters, has since been most serviceable in the prosecution of the Pacific war and will continue to be. Since no case against even higher authorities could have been documented without this evidence, and since Mr. Dewey was informed that to produce it would have been to invite a charge of imperiling security and the prospects of the Pacific war, the issue was left out of the campaign.

The account above was given to this correspondent by very responsible persons who he has reason to believe are stating the facts as they understand them. He has no information to support their view that the high military officials who bar publication of this evidence on security grounds agree that it would fully explain the surprise at Pearl Harbor, and establish the culpability of Washington personages not thus far involved in responsibility. But there seems to be no doubt the publication would have been assailed by them as lending aid to the enemy.

While charges and countercharges as to responsibility for Pearl Harbor were being exchanged, in September and October, 1944, news came out that the cloud of guilt which had long been hanging over Admiral Kimmel and General Short was soon to be dispelled, despite the Roberts Report and everything else that had been said and done in their case. On October 3, 1944, a special writer learned from "Navy circles" that the Navy board had about completed its investigation and would soon report that it had unearthed no evidence that warranted the filing of charges against Admiral Kimmel. From "Army" sources the same correspondent discovered that the Army

22. See above, p. 211.

board would report a similar conclusion in respect of the charges against General Short.[23]

Mrs. Eleanor Roosevelt added some tinder to the Republican fire on October 8, 1944. In a special article entitled "Just a Little Job," based on an interview with Mrs. Roosevelt about her experiences as First Lady of the Land, the following statement from her about the "surprise" in connection with the Japanese attack on December 7, 1941, appeared in the *New York Times* Magazine Section of October 8, 1944, pp. 40–41:

One of the memories she [Mrs. Roosevelt] will take with her when she leaves the White House, no matter what the date of her ultimate departure, is its relatively normal atmosphere on Dec. 7, 1941. Actually, she recalls, there was only a little more commotion than usual, following receipt that morning by the President of the historic message from Pearl Harbor. Within those walls tenseness and apprehension had hung heavy for nearly a year previous, with the realization that an explosion might come in the international situation at any time.

Hence, she adds, "Dec. 7 was just like any of the later D-days to us. We clustered at the radio and waited for more details—but it was far from the shock it proved to the country in general. We had expected something of the sort for a long time."

Time passed and yet there was no sign of any report from the Army and Navy boards engaged in the new investigation of Pearl Harbor; and some political leaders were restless over the delay. About the middle of October, 1944, John W. Bricker, Republican candidate for Vice President, accused President Roosevelt of intending to conceal "the black story of Pearl Harbor" until after the election.[24] Speaking at St. Paul, October 19, Melvin J. Maas, Republican member of Congress from Minnesota, demanded the publication of the Navy Report on Pearl Harbor, and charged the Roosevelt

23. *New York Herald Tribune*, October 4, 1944. This is one among many illustrations of the interesting fact that ingenious journalists often unearth the truth about inside business in Washington days, months, or years before it is made public officially. Although, as students of history have learned from experience, the use of newspapers as "sources" may be highly dangerous, it is safe to say that the student of history who neglects them, while examining official documents, is in peril of self-deception.

24. *Ibid.*, October 19, 1944.

Administration with the intention of holding back the report until after the election. Mr. Maas also asserted that high officials in Washington had news of the coming Japanese attack six hours in advance and had sent a message to the Hawaiian commanders by commercial telegraph, too late. Mr. Maas added a sidelight by declaring that Justice Owen J. Roberts, after closing the hearings in Hawaii, had congratulated Admiral Kimmel on his conduct on the fateful day of December 7, 1941, and had said to the Admiral: "I am glad that you are in the clear"—thus giving an apparent confirmation to what had been intimated in Congress, namely, that the Roberts Report was at bottom an *ex parte* document.[25]

After accounts of Mr. Maas' charges had come out in the press, President Roosevelt declared at a press conference that "he knew nothing about" the claim that the Navy Report would be withheld until after the election. A reporter put to him a question relative to Mr. Maas' call upon him to deny that the Administration had advance notice of the Japanese attack "hours" in advance, and had failed to notify the Hawaiian commanders promptly. On this point "Mr. Roosevelt said he knew nothing about it." [26]

At all events, the reports of the Army and Navy boards were withheld from the public until after the election day in November, 1944, although they had been filed with the Secretary of War and the Secretary of the Navy respectively about two weeks before that day. Not until December 1, 1944, did the two Secretaries make public statements with regard to the findings of the boards and not until August 29, 1945, were the main parts of their reports laid before the country for examination.[27]

Note to Chapter X

THE first indisputable evidence that President Roosevelt had initiated an exchange of messages with Mr. Churchill at least as

25. AP Dispatch, St. Paul, October 20, 1944. *New York World-Telegram.*
26. UP Dispatch, Washington, October 20, 1944. *Ibid.*
27. See below, Chap. XI. After December 1, 1944, and still more after August 29, 1945, it required no vivid imagination on the part of Republicans to discover

early as September, 1939, while Mr. Churchill was first Lord of the British Admiralty, and that the exchanges had continued until the President's death in April, 1945, became public in April, 1945. This indisputable evidence was revealed by Mr. Churchill himself in his eloquent tribute to President Roosevelt at the great memorial meeting held in London. The opening passages of this address as given in the London *Times*, April 18, 1945, follow: [28]

My friendship with the great man to whose work and fame we pay our tribute today began and ripened during this war. I had met him, but only for a few minutes, after the close of the last war, and as soon as I went to the Admiralty in September, 1939, he telegraphed, inviting me to correspond with him direct on naval or other matters if at any time I felt inclined. Having obtained the permission of the Prime Minister, I did so. Knowing President Roosevelt's keen interest in sea warfare I furnished him with a stream of information about our naval affairs and about the various actions, including especially the action of the Plate River, which lighted the first gloomy winter of the war.

When I became Prime Minister and the war broke out in all its hideous fury, when our own life and survival hung in the balance, I was already in a position to telegraph to the President on terms of association which had become most intimate and, to me, most agreeable. This continued throughout all the ups and downs of the world struggle until Thursday last when I received my last message from him. These messages showed no falling off in his accustomed clear vision and vigour upon perplexing and complicated matters.

I may mention that this correspondence which, of course, greatly increased after the United States entry into the war, comprises, to and fro between us, over 1,700 messages. Many of these were lengthy messages, and the majority dealt with those more difficult points which come to be discussed upon the level between heads of Governments only after official solutions had not been reached at other

---

political reasons for withholding official information respecting the two reports until after the election of 1944 was safely over.

28. There are certain discrepancies in Mr. Churchill's address as reported in the *Manchester Guardian*, the *New York Times*, and the *New York Herald Tribune*. One of the most significant bore on the line, "About that same time he devised the extraordinary measure of assistance called Lend-Lease." Mr. Churchill undoubtedly, it seems, used the word "he" or the words "the President" (*Manchester Guardian*, April 18, 1945); but the *New York Times*, April 18, 1945, gave the line as reading: "About that same time we devised the extraordinary measure of assistance called Lend-Lease." The London *Times* report appears to be the most complete of the four reports. All texts agreed on the statement about the exchanges of approximately 1,700 messages.

stages. To this correspondence there must be added our nine meetings—at Argentia, three in Washington, Casablanca, Teheran, two at Quebec, and, last of all, at Yalta, comprising in all about 120 days of close personal contact, during a great part of which I stayed with him at the White House or at his home at Hyde Park, or in his retreat in the Blue Mountains which he called Shangri-la.

I conceived an admiration for him as a statesman, as a man of affairs, and as a war leader. I felt the utmost confidence in his upright, inspiring character and outlook—and a personal regard—affection, I must say—for him beyond my power to express today. His love of his own country, his respect for its constitution, his power of gauging the tides and currents of its mobile public opinion—all this was evident, but added to this were the beatings of that generous heart, which was always stirred to anger and stirred to action by spectacles of aggression and oppression by the strong against the weak. It is a loss indeed, a bitter loss, to humanity that those heart-beats are stilled forever. . . .

With the text of Mr. Churchill's address and other materials (including transcripts of the parliamentary debates) bearing on the subject of the messages exchanged with President Roosevelt before me, and desirous of learning more about the methods of the American State Department in dealing with citizens who ask for information relative to the conduct of the nation's foreign affairs, I directed on August 27, 1945, the following letter to the Secretary of State:

New Milford, Conn., August 27, 1945.

My dear Sir:

For several years I have been studying the *methods* employed by the Government of the United States in conducting foreign affairs. In the course of my inquiry I have come across the allegation that President Roosevelt entered into personal communications with Mr. Winston Churchill in the autumn of 1939, before Mr. Churchill became Prime Minister, and exchanged many messages with him, while Mr. Chamberlain was the head of the British Government (*Congressional Record*, June 19, 1944).

I have examined with care the State Department's release to the press on the Tyler Kent case, September 2, 1944, and I find in it no denial that such an exchange of messages took place between the President and Mr. Churchill during the period mentioned (September, 1939, and May, 1940).

If it is compatible with the public interest, I should be grateful if you will answer two questions that have arisen in my mind:

1. Did President Roosevelt exchange messages with Mr. Churchill between September, 1939 and May, 1940?

2. If so, is it not unusual for the President of the United States to exchange such messages with a member of a foreign government who is not the head of that government or in charge of foreign affairs for that government?

Thanking you in advance for your consideration, I am,

Faithfully yours,

Charles A. Beard

Presumably, the State Department, if properly informed on such matters of current public interest, was aware of Mr. Churchill's own public statement that the messages in question had in fact been exchanged. But in replying to my letter, the Assistant Secretary, William Benton, with perfect courtesy, avoided answering both of my questions. Here is the text of his letter:

DEPARTMENT OF STATE
WASHINGTON

October 19, 1945

My dear Dr. Beard:

I regret very much that your letter of August 27, 1945, concerning the allegation that President Roosevelt entered into personal communications with Mr. Winston Churchill in the autumn of 1939, has not been replied to before this time.

The Department has been endeavoring to obtain the information which would be of assistance to you. The late President's papers were removed from the White House and impounded immediately after his death. It is my understanding that President Roosevelt's papers are to be made available to the Congressional Committee investigating the events leading up to Pearl Harbor. At this time perhaps answers to your question may become available.

Sincerely yours,

William Benton
Assistant Secretary

Charles A. Beard, LL.D.,[29]
New Milford,
Connecticut.

29. This honorific title, which I did not use in my letter to the State Department, was added by Mr. Benton. Perhaps the Assistant Secretary had my name looked up in *Who's Who* and added this decoration as befitting the tenor of his letter.

CHAPTER XI

Army and Navy Boards Undermine the Official Thesis

AFTER the election of 1944 was over, the Secretary of War and the Secretary of the Navy faced the problem of what to do about the reports of the Army and Navy boards appointed under the Act of Congress in the previous June; for the press had disseminated, during the campaign, news to the effect that the two boards had reported to the Secretaries in October and had exonerated the Hawaiian commanders from the grave charges of the President's Commission headed by Justice Roberts. At length, on December 1, 1944, Secretary Stimson and Secretary Forrestal broke their silence by issuing brief statements to the press on this subject. These statements were, to say the least, startling to citizens who had accepted the Roberts Report of January 23, 1942, as valid.

What did the statements of the two Secretaries contain? Terse mention of the ways in which the Army and Navy boards' inquiries had been conducted. Assurances that the principal documents in the case must still remain secret, on account of "relation to national security." Declarations that the evidence produced by the boards did not justify a trial of anybody by court-martial. Secretary Stimson's formula was: "Under all the circumstances the evidence now recorded does not warrant the institution of any further proceedings against any officer in the Army." Secretary Forrestal's formula was: "The evidence now available does not warrant and will not support the trial by general court martial of any person or persons in the naval service." Secretary Forrestal did not mention Admiral Kimmel by name in his statement. Secretary Stimson made some criticism of General Short's operations at Hawaii but added that the relief of the General from command status was sufficient action against him, in view of his "long record of excellent service."

The passages from Secretary Stimson's statement of December 1, 1944, bearing on the point of Army responsibility follow:

The Army Pearl Harbor Board, although it recommended no disciplinary or other action, concluded that *there were several officers in the War Department who did not perform their duties with the necessary skill or exercise the judgment which was required under the circumstances.* On the recorded evidence, *I agree with some but not all of the board's conclusions.*

So far as the commanding general of the Hawaiian Department is concerned, *I am of the opinion that his errors of judgment were of such a nature as to demand his relief from a command status.* This was done on Jan. 11, 1942, and in itself is a serious result for any officer with a long record of excellent service, and conscientious as I believe General Short to be. *In my judgment on the evidence now recorded, it is sufficient action.*

Furthermore, I am satisfied that proper steps were taken to correct such inadequacies of either personnel or organization as were shown to exist either in the War Department or in the field at the time of the Pearl Harbor disaster. *My conclusion is that under all the circumstances the evidence now recorded does not warrant the institution of any further proceedings against any officer in the Army.*[1]

For the Department of the Navy, Secretary Forrestal spoke on the subject of Navy responsibility as follows:

The net result of the findings of fact and opinion of the Pearl Harbor Court of Inquiry, as reviewed by the Judge Advocate General of the Navy, and the Commander in Chief, U.S. Fleet, and Chief of Naval Operations, and by the Secretary of the Navy, *is that the evidence now available does not warrant and will not support the trial by general court martial of any person or persons in the naval service.*

The Secretary, *in his findings upon the evidence* before the Court of Inquiry and all the other proceedings in the matter to date, *has found that there were errors of judgment on the part of certain officers in the naval service, both at Pearl Harbor and at Washington.*

1. *New York Times*, December 2, 1944. (Italics supplied.)

The Secretary *is not satisfied that the investigation has gone to the point of exhaustion of all possible evidence.* Accordingly, he has decided that *his own investigation should be further continued until* the testimony of every witness in possession of material facts can be obtained and all possible evidence exhausted.[2]

Since, however, the two Secretaries referred to continuation of investigations, their statements of December 1 left various issues hanging in mid-air. What was the status of Admiral Kimmel and General Short on and after December 1, 1944? Charles B. Rugg, counsel for Admiral Kimmel declared, "the statement of Secretary of the Navy Forrestal means that Admiral Kimmel has been cleared." [3] General Short, in response to an inquiry, said that out of a sense of loyalty to our country he had refrained from making any statement about Pearl Harbor, that in the interest of national security he was prevented from stating his position at the moment, and that "when the entire story is unfolded, I am certain of complete vindication in the eyes of the American people." But what was the official position? The *New York Times* reported: "At both The Pentagon and the Navy Department, officers protested against statements that General Short and Admiral Kimmel had been 'absolved,' the fact actually being, they said, that nothing had been found to justify the courts-martial." [4]

Comments by members of Congress on the Secretaries' statements varied. Senator Ferguson demanded—in vain—that the evidence collected be submitted to Congress. Representative May, chairman of the House Military Affairs Committee, and a steadfast supporter of the Roosevelt Administration, opposed such action and said that as far as he was concerned, "the Army-Navy decision ended the matter." Senator Connally, chairman of the Foreign Relations Committee declared: "I have always felt that the Army and Navy com-

2. *Ibid.* (Italics supplied.)

3. Comments on the Secretaries' reports given here are from the *New York Times* of December 2, 1944.

4. This statement from official quarters appears in a copy of the *Times* of December 2, 1944, bought at New Milford, Conn., on that day. The version of the dispatch regarding Short and Kimmel differed in some respects in a copy of the *Times* bought in Washington on that same day.

manders in Hawaii were negligent in not taking measures to detect and prepare to repel the attack on Pearl Harbor." Representative Sumners, of the House Judiciary Committee, called for a renewed extension of the statute of limitations for Pearl Harbor courts-martial, thus indicating dissatisfaction with the present state of affairs. Representative Hancock, ranking Republican member of the House Judiciary Committee, expressed the opinion that the people would never be satisfied until there was a congressional investigation of Pearl Harbor. Senator Edwin Johnson, Democratic member of the Senate Military Affairs Committee, insisted that there was a contradiction between the Army-Navy reports and the Roberts Report and said that "they ought to tell us who was responsible for the disaster at Pearl Harbor."

In his column in the *New York Times* of December 5, 1944, Arthur Krock reviewed the situation as to responsibility for Pearl Harbor under the caption: "Unsatisfactory Status of Pearl Harbor Case." Mr. Krock, in opening, remarked that there was a fundamental conflict between the Report of the Roberts Commission and the recent reports from the War and Navy Departments. He then dwelt upon the confusion that resulted from this contradiction, and expressed the opinion that, unless the conflict was overcome as a result of additional investigations under the direction of Secretary Stimson and Secretary Forrestal, Congress could be expected to "try to find out the facts for the public and itself."

After the outburst of discussion that greeted the cautious statements by Secretary Stimson and Secretary Forrestal respecting the secret reports of the Army and Navy boards, public interest in the possibility of revelations to come seemed to decline from the high peak reached during the presidential campaign. The rising tempo of the war on all fronts and the concentration of national energies on the armed conflict were too absorbing to permit the kind of debate that marked the campaign year. But, reports and articles published in many newspapers, particularly the *Chicago Tribune*, the *Washington Times-Herald*, and the *New York Daily News*, aided by the Hearst press, often brought the issue to the attention of their readers throughout the period. Moreover, the reports that the Administration's indictments of General Short and Admiral Kimmel in January and February, 1942, were already quashed continued in circulation and aroused widespread curiosity about what might be found in the secret pages of the Army and Navy boards' reports.

Great events contributed to a rekindling of public interest in war origins as the autumn of 1945 drew near. The death of President Roosevelt in April, the unconditional surrender of Germany in May, and the collapse of Japan in August released many restraints on differences of opinion in the country. Friends of General Short and Admiral Kimmel now argued that, since the war was at an end, grounds of national safety could no longer be properly used in delaying the public hearings which had been denied to them since their arraignment in January, 1942; and, indeed, the American sense of fair play, manifest in Congress and outside, demanded that at last the two officers be given opportunities to state their sides of their cases publicly.

But the Administration, the War Department, and the Navy Department knew privately that their competent lawyers had gone on record as contending that the charge of dereliction of duty filed by the Roberts Commission against the commanders could not be sustained. Secretary Stimson had publicly admitted as much with regard to General Short on December 1, 1944; and Secretary Forrestal had practically conceded the point as far as Admiral Kimmel was concerned. Leaders of the Democratic party knew that the Army and Navy boards' reports were full of "political dynamite," which, if set off, would produce a great uproar over war origins. A few Democrats in high places maintained that the people should "forget Pearl Harbor," but most Democratic members of Congress did not share that view or at least did not believe that it could prevail.

RELEASE OF THE ARMY AND NAVY REPORTS

EARLY in August, 1945, as the Japanese war lords staggered toward their doom, the demand for action in the Pearl Harbor case became insistent, if not irresistible, and rumors were current to the effect that President Truman would soon release to the public the reports of the Army and Navy boards. In his column of August 20, in the *New York Daily News*, John O'Donnell announced that, "within the week, possibly within a few days," President.Truman would give out "the true story" of Pearl Harbor and that the reports of the Army and Navy boards were being placed in the hands of the chairmen of the appropriate committees in the Senate. Mr. O'Donnell also stated that Justice Owen J. Roberts, chairman of the President's Commission on Pearl Harbor, had visited the White House on August 20, and interpreted this visit as having a connection with the probable action of President Truman with regard to forthcoming Pearl Harbor revelations.

At one o'clock, August 29, President Truman did in fact release to the public two sets of Pearl Harbor documents. The first consisted of the Report of the Army Pearl Harbor Board (with one section omitted),[5] accompanied by a memorandum from Secretary Stimson, taking exceptions to parts of the board's Report. The second set of documents embraced the Report of the Navy Court of Inquiry and "endorsements," or comments, from the Judge Advocate General, Rear Admiral Gatch, from Admiral King, Chief of Naval Operations, and from James Forrestal, Secretary of the Navy. All the documents were in mimeograph form and filled about four hundred typewritten pages. Newspaper correspondents present rushed to the high pile of documents on the table before them and with copies in hand dashed from the White House to spread the news throughout the land.

5. This section (Chap. V) was released by the War Department after the Congressional Committee on Pearl Harbor had been established. Certain "Top Secret" documents and the supporting evidence for the Army and Navy boards' reports were likewise withheld from the public until after the committee got under way. See CJC, Parts 22–39.

The statement by President Truman in releasing the documents follows:

I have here reports on the Pearl Harbor disaster. One is from the Army and one is from the Navy. The Navy report gives a "Finding of Facts" by a Navy Court of Inquiry. Attached to this Finding of Facts are indorsements by the Judge Advocate General of the Navy, Rear Admiral T. L. Gatch; Admiral E. J. King, Chief of Naval Operations, and the Secretary of the Navy. You will find a summation of the findings in the final indorsement by the Secretary of the Navy at the end of the document.

From the Army we have the report of the Army Pearl Harbor Board, and, bound separately, a statement by the Secretary of War. Certain criticisms of the Chief of Staff, General Marshall, appear in the report of the Army Pearl Harbor Board. You will notice in the Secretary's statement, beginning on page nineteen, that he takes sharp issue with this criticism of General Marshall, stating that the criticism "is entirely unjustified." The conclusion of the Secretary of War is that General Marshall acted throughout this matter with his usual "great skill, energy and efficiency." I associate myself wholeheartedly with this expression by the Secretary of War.

Indeed I have the fullest confidence in the skill, energy and efficiency of all our war leaders, both Army and Navy.

The headlines of the newspapers indicated the emphasis given to the reports by the respective news editors. The *New York Sun* on the evening of that date, August 29, blazed across the front page in letters an inch high, "Pearl Harbor Report Criticizes Marshall; Truman Defends Him." The next morning the *New York Times* carried on its front page the headline: "Army, Navy Report on Pearl Harbor; Marshall, Hull and Stark Censured." The story also made the front page of the *New York Herald Tribune:* "Pearl Harbor Reports Broaden the Blame, Marshall and Hull Are Included in the Criticism." General Marshall, Admiral Stark, and Secretary Hull had been explicitly absolved from blame in the report of the President's Commission in January, 1942; now top authorities in Washington had sprung into the headlines. Judging by editorial protests on the one side and editorial jubilation on the other, the issue of responsibility for Pearl Harbor had entered a new phase: the official thesis of how war came in the Pacific had been radically altered, if not reversed, by boards representing the Army and the Navy—the armed forces of the United States. Politicos had been brought to book by men of arms.

If the newspaper headlines and the amount of column space given to the Army and Navy reports may be taken as the criteria, the country was profoundly disturbed by the revelations and charges. Evidently President Truman was shaken by the repercussions. While he defended General Marshall when he released the reports and expressed faith in the Army and the Navy, he gave at that moment no intimation of seeing in the reports any "political angles." In fact, he had not read the documents before he gave them to the press.[6]

By some process, however, President Truman quickly learned that the Army and Navy reports contained information and political implications that traversed the official thesis set forth by officials in charge of affairs in Washington before and after Pearl Harbor. The very next day after he had released the reports, August 30, 1945, he took the extraordinary step of holding a "press and radio conference" on the subject. At this conference he declared that Pearl Harbor was "the result of the policy which the country itself pursued," and that every time President Roosevelt had made an effort to get a preparedness program through Congress, it had been stifled. Thus he mentioned the President in connection with Pearl Harbor, attacked Congress, and shifted the onus from high officials in the Executive Department, including President Roosevelt, to the American people and their representatives in the national legislature.

In presenting his case to the country President Truman admitted that he had not read the Army and Navy reports when

6. *New York Times*, August 31, pp. 1, 6. Here too is to be found President Truman's admission that as Senator he had made a mistake a year previously when he had intimated in *Collier's* weekly that Admiral Kimmel and General Short were not on speaking terms. Evidently he had been mistaken when he had declared, in reply to Admiral Kimmel, that he had evidence to prove his charges. See above, p. 275.

he made them public the previous day but now a day later he claimed that in the meantime he had read them "very carefully." Considering the bulk of the two documents and the highly technical matters discussed in them, this "careful" reading on the part of the President in so short a time was certainly an intellectual feat. In any event he easily caught the political drift of the reports and the conclusions, and swiftly formulated a countercharge which exonerated President Roosevelt and his high officials.

President Truman's statement of August 30, 1945, follows:

I have read it (the Pearl Harbor reports) very carefully, and I came to the conclusion that the whole thing is the result of the policy which the country itself pursued. The country was not ready for preparedness. Every time the President made an effort to get a preparedness program through the Congress, it was stifled. Whenever the President made a statement about the necessity of preparedness, he was vilified for doing it. I think the country is as much to blame as any individual in this final situation that developed in Pearl Harbor.

ACCUSATIONS IN THE REPORTS

THE Army and Navy reports released on August 29, 1945, although unaccompanied by the hundreds of pages of testimony and documents on which they rested, evoked alarms among faithful Democrats who had been clinging to the official thesis on how war came in the Pacific. There could be differences of opinion as to the meaning and upshot of various passages and conclusions contained in the reports but certain indisputable items stood out in the record now laid before the American people.

First of all, the Army and Navy boards traversed the grave indictment lodged against General Short and Admiral Kimmel by the President's Commission in January, 1942, and by the Administration later, in retiring the two commanders—the indictment which charged these men with derelictions of duty and failures to act which were "the effective causes" of the disaster at Pearl Harbor—offenses warranting trials by courts-martial.[7] The Army board found that General Short had failed to take proper steps in enumerated particulars but, with regard to any procedure against him or any other person, it stated: "Recommendations: NONE." The Navy Court of Inquiry, in respect of Admiral Kimmel and other naval officers said: "Finally, based upon the facts established, the Court is of the opinion that no offences have been committed nor serious blame incurred on the part of any person or persons in the naval service. The Court recommends that no further proceedings be had in the matter."

American citizens could, therefore, legitimately ask: Why had General Short and Admiral Kimmel been publicly arraigned in January and February, 1942, and kept as if under indictment for more than three years and six months?

In the second place, and this was more adverse to the official thesis of war origins in the Pacific, the Army and Navy boards reversed the tables and brought charges against, and raised grave questions respecting the performances of, certain high authorities in Washington who had been expressly exonerated by name in the report of President Roosevelt's Commission in January, 1942.

The Roberts Commission had declared that the Chief of Naval Operations, Admiral Stark, had fulfilled his obligations in the warnings and orders sent to Admiral Kimmel.[8] Now, in its Report, completed on October 19, 1944, and released on August 29, 1945, the Navy Court of Inquiry said that Admiral Stark had, in fact, "failed to display the sound judgment expected of him," in not transmitting to Admiral Kimmel in 1941 important information, including information to the effect "that an attack in the Hawaiian area might be expected soon."

The Roberts Commission had declared in January, 1942, that the Secretary of War and the Chief of Staff had fulfilled

7. See above, Chap. VIII.
8. It is to be noted that the Roberts Commission to some extent qualified its exculpations by its Conclusion 19. See above, p. 219.

their obligations in respect of preparedness at Pearl Harbor. Now the public could discover that the Army board in its Report, signed October 20, 1944, and released August 29, 1945, had rendered a different judgment. It had declared that "the extent of the Pearl Harbor disaster was due primarily to two causes." It placed first the failure of General Short adequately to alert his command for war; but it immediately coupled with this the second "cause" which, for practical purposes, canceled the first "cause." The second cause, the Army board said, was: "The failure of the War Department, with knowledge of the type of alert taken by the Commanding General, Hawaiian Department, to direct him to take an adequate alert, and the failure to keep him adequately informed as to the development of the United States–Japanese negotiations, which in turn might have caused him to change from the inadequate alert to an adequate one." In short, the Army board brought serious charges against the management of the War Department.

Under the head, "Responsibilities," the Army board, while enumerating particulars in which General Short had failed at Hawaii, specifically declared that "the Chief of Staff of the Army, General George C. Marshall, failed in his relations with the Hawaiian Department" in enumerated particulars. The Army board also named Major General Leonard T. Gerow, Chief of the War Plans Division, War Department General Staff, and then enumerated four particulars in which he had failed in his duties.

Under the head of "Responsibilities," the Army board also referred to the memorandum delivered by "the Secretary of State—the Honorable Cordell Hull"—to the Japanese on November 26, 1941, and then stated: "To the extent that it [this action] hastened such attack [by the Japanese] it was in conflict with the efforts of the War and Navy Departments to gain time for preparations for war."

In the third place, the Army and Navy reports, besides bringing Secretary Hull, General Marshall, General Gerow, the War Department, Admiral Stark, and the Navy Department into the network of responsibilities, did more. They placed on the public record numerous facts about transactions in Washington relative to Pearl Harbor which were hitherto unknown to the American public. In this respect, the Report of the Army Board was fuller than that of the Navy Court and more direct in its accusations and implications.

The Army Board Report, although it did not mention President Roosevelt in its chapter of "Conclusions," did by implication bring him into the "chain" of responsibilities.[9] In referring to Secretary Hull, it must have known very well that, under the statutes of the United States, the Secretary was merely an agent of the President in the conduct of foreign affairs and did not hand his memorandum of November 26, 1941, to the Japanese without authorization of the President. In the main body of its Report the Army Board gave detailed descriptions of the structure and operations of the "War Cabinet" under the direction of the President and mentioned him by name in several places as participating in crucial decisions (for example, mimeograph copy, pp. 116, 119, 121, 219, 220, 222, 224). In gross and in detail, the revelations of the Army Board Report stood in strange contrast to the descriptive pages of the Report by the President's Commission on Pearl Harbor, January 23, 1942.

In their memoranda accompanying the Army and Navy reports, the political heads of the War and Navy Departments, Secretary Stimson and Secretary Forrestal, commented on certain facts and conclusions presented in the reports. In his memorandum, Secretary Stimson reprinted passages from his statement of December 1, 1944, indicated that General Short had had enough punishment, and renewed his declaration that the evidence now recorded did not warrant the institution of "any further proceedings against any officer in the Army." But, Secretary Stimson criticized the Army Report in several aspects and warmly defended General Marshall against its

9. By an analytical study of the language used by the Army Board in its Report, I came to the conclusion that its authors had sharp differences of opinion as to the responsibilities of the Roosevelt Administration and that their final draft was more moderate in tone than the facts cited could have warranted.

charges. On the whole, the Secretary of War did his best to keep intact the old record provided by the President's Commission on Pearl Harbor, on January 23, 1942, and in so doing wrote a new chapter in the history of his own operations in connection with the Pearl Harbor disaster from the beginning. Secretary Forrestal declared that Admiral Kimmel and Admiral Stark (both retired) should not hold any positions in the Navy which required "the exercise of superior judgment."

VARIETIES OF PRESS OPINIONS

As was to be expected, the reception accorded by the press to the releases of the Army and Navy reports on August 29, 1945, varied more or less roughly with the presuppositions of the newspaper editors. A large number of clippings of editorials taken at random from papers in widely scattered sections of the country display an extraordinary interest in the revelations, conclusions, and recommendations of the Army and Navy boards and highly conflicting opinions as to their value and significance.[10] Of these editorial views three are here reprinted as representing three main types of opinion.

The *New York Times*, August 30, 1945:

THE PEARL HARBOR REPORTS

Since Dec. 7, 1941, one of the most controversial subjects for public discussion has been responsibility for the naval and military disaster we suffered in the Japanese attack of that date on Pearl Harbor and other installations in the Hawaiian Islands. On the plea of military secrecy, a full report was withheld until after the completion of the war. Now, only a week after the cease-fire order and before the war with Japan is officially at an end, President Truman has made public the lengthy findings of the Army and Navy boards that were appointed to assess the responsibility.

The Army board, headed by Lieut. Gen. George Grunert, finds grounds for criticism of Maj. Gen. Walter C. Short, the Hawaiian Area commander in 1941; Gen. George C. Marshall,

10. For a carefully selected collection of editorials, from which certain types of opinion highly critical in nature were omitted, see *New York Times*, August 31, 1945.

then and now Army Chief of Staff; Lieut. Gen. Leonard T. Gerow, former chief of war plans, and Cordell Hull, then Secretary of State. Secretary of War Stimson and the President dispute the findings as to the responsibility of General Marshall. Mr. Stimson also disputes the Army board's comments on Mr. Hull's handling of the diplomatic negotiations. The Navy board of inquiry, headed by Vice Admiral Henry K. Hewitt, finds responsibility for the complacency and lack of readiness that made the attack possible shared by Rear Admiral Husband E. Kimmell and Admiral Harold C. Stark, respectively the Pacific Fleet Commander and the Chief of Naval Operations of that date. The Army board makes no recommendations. The Navy board recommends that court-martial proceedings not be instituted on the grounds there was insufficient basis for such action.

The reports are in considerable detail—100,000 words in the Army report and 27,000 words in the Navy report. Admittedly, neither is complete. Both were prepared before the final Japanese surrender and speak of information available in Washington that was not transmitted to our commanders in the Hawaiian Islands. There probably will be a clarification later of exactly what is referred to in those passages. Otherwise the reports seem as clearly stated as it is possible to present the matter for public understanding. Because of all that has been said on the subject of the Japanese attack, much of it misleading and some of it colored by political thinking, the reports should be given the widest possible circulation and, what is more important, the most judicial study by all thinking Americans. Many probably will reach the same conclusion as some of the investigators, that Pearl Harbors are inevitable in a society where there are powerful aggressor nations and unprepared peace-loving democracies, and that it is impossible for the one to guard entirely against the hostile actions of the other. It is comforting for the future to remember that we did rally and go on from Pearl Harbor to complete victory.

Whether the record as now set forth will be acceptable to those Army and Navy commanders involved is for them to decide. If they desire open courts-martial, whether or not promises have been made to them, it would be in the American tradition to give them that opportunity.[11]

11. Subsequently the *Times* warmly defended Secretary Hull against the charges of the Army board. See below, p. 317 ff.

The *New York Herald Tribune*, August 30, 1945:

PEARL HARBOR

The exceptionally voluminous reports on the Pearl Harbor disaster obviously call for far more careful digestion than can be given to them in a few hours. A frank first impression, however, derived from the summaries and conclusions, is that they still contain a regrettably high content of policy, politics and white-wash—ingredients which at this late date it seems might have been reduced to somewhat more rigid minimums.

General of the Army Marshall is an officer who has unquestionably rendered the highest possible services to the country in the last four years. It is that very fact which engenders skepticism over the haste with which Secretary Stimson and President Truman rush to defend him against certain specific criticisms leveled by the Army board. Admiral Stark, on the other hand, is given a staggering blow between the eyes, uncushioned by higher indorsement. Perhaps it is deserved; but, if so, why did the Navy Department, which now demolishes his whole professional career, retain him for three years after the fact as its commander in chief in European waters? One is not impressed by the care with which Secretary Forrestal, after commenting severely upon the "failure" at Pearl Harbor of the system of joint command, goes on to explain that this is no argument for a single service. Perhaps it is not; but that issue of Navy Department policy hardly deserves a place in this supposedly judicial finding, and it is not reassuring to find it there.

The Navy points to serious dereliction within its bureaucracy and solemnly finds that no officer was to blame and that no action should now be taken. The Army board, which conveys an impression of somewhat greater courage, names a few names. It specifically censures General Gerow, for example, then in the War Plans Division; again, however, there is no suggestion of action. General Short was summarily "broken"; General Gerow was ultimately promoted and appointed to the command of the 15th Army in Europe. The public, while it will, no doubt, be glad that it could profit by General Gerow's abilities despite any lapse in 1941, will find it very difficult to make sense out of such results, to say nothing of justice.

It will find it more difficult still to make sense out of reports which, while conveying a vivid impression of over-all confusion, unawareness and "buck-passing" in the Army, the Navy, the State Department and the White House, have nothing to say about the President, hastily suppress an inferential criticism of the Secretary of State and leave it to be supposed that it was just an accident of fate that we were caught in December, 1941, with divided command, an inadequate intelligence service, a radar warning system at Pearl Harbor that was ineffective (the British had established their first coastal net long before 1939 and had made all their secrets available to us in 1940) and too few planes at our major naval base to fly long-distance patrol! As has been said, the reports must be examined with care before final conclusions may be drawn. One suspects, however, that the reports will never answer ethical issues as to culpability; these will have to be determined by each individual for himself; but out of the facts conveyed in this sea of words we may be able to shape military and diplomatic policies adequate to prevent a repetition of such a catastrophe.

The *New York Daily News*, August 31, 1945:

ROOSEVELT WAS RESPONSIBLE

Three documents, totaling 130,000 words, have been released by President Truman giving the purported facts leading up to the disaster of Pearl Harbor on December 7, 1941. The disaster cost us eight battleships, numerous planes ashore and the lives of more than 3,000 sailors, marines and soldiers. The three voluminous reports consist of findings by an Army Board of Inquiry, a Navy Court of Inquiry and an exhaustive statement by 74-year-old Secretary of War Henry L. Stimson, reading like a Supreme Court Justice's opinion in a finding for the defense. The "defendants" cleared by Stimson are former Secretary of State Cordell Hull and Gen. George C. Marshall, Chief of Staff. He concurred with the Army report making Lieut. Gen. Walter C. Short a scapegoat again as did the investigation headed by former Justice Owen J. Roberts of the Supreme Court.

The Navy Court of Inquiry, likewise following the lines of the Roberts commission, tagged another guilty count on Admiral Husband E. Kimmel, bracketing him with Short, and bringing a new figure into the picture—Admiral Harold R. Stark, chief of naval operations at the time of Pearl Harbor. He is alleged to have neglected to do the things necessary to prevent the disaster. With Secretary of the Navy James Forrestal concurring, the Navy court recommended that neither Kimmel nor Stark should ever again be placed in posts requiring superior judgment. Both are in retirement as is also Short. Secretary of the Navy Frank Knox is dead and so cannot give his version.

With all their wordage and painstaking—if not painful—adherence "to the book," the three documents tell the American public little it did not know or at least surmise of the obvious facts leading up to Pearl Harbor. Of course, Hull was wrong. Of course, Stimson was wrong. Or course, Marshall was wrong. They were wrong because the whole system in Washington was wrong. The whole system was wrong because it was centered in, and dominated by, one man, Franklin D. Roosevelt. He "was" the War Department, the Navy Department and the State Department.

It was Roosevelt, as we know, who was responsible for Pearl Harbor. The 130,000 words all point up that fact—some by significant inference when they have reached certain high levels of Washington officialdom, others by gratuitous defense of F.D.R. as in the case of Stimson. The Army report itself came as near as it dared to the White House in a section summarizing "Responsibilities in Washington." Speaking of Hull and his handling of the powder keg situation in late November of 1941, it said:

"The responsibility apparently assumed by the Secretary of State (and we have no other proof that any one else assumed the responsibility finally and definitely) was to determine when the United States would reach an impasse with Japan. It was the Secretary of State who was in charge of the negotiations with the Japanese. . . . He was the contact man and the responsible negotiator."

Hull remains silent so far as the present investigations are concerned. The 74-year-old Tennessean was probably the closest man to F.D.R. in the Roosevelt Cabinet.

Only a full dress Congressional investigation could bring Hull's story into the open along with the necessary revelations of F.D.R.'s relationships with Hull, Stimson, Knox, etc., etc. Hull's testimony is vital if the American public is to get the real truth of Pearl

Harbor. A Congressional inquiry could also summon key figures of the Roosevelt secretariat.

For the good or the evil that will come out of this war—and it may take some years to assess those factors—Roosevelt, in our opinion, planned and sent us into the war. He will get the blame or the praise that follows. His big ambition was the European war—the war with Japan being subsidiary. He wanted to help Great Britain. He committed eight of our battleships to the Atlantic for convoy duty, escorting vast supplies to England and on a smaller scale to Russia. We had then a 17-battleship Navy with one battleship undergoing repairs. Roosevelt split it, thus violating a cardinal principle laid down by Admiral Mahan, great naval authority. Eight of our battleships were on duty in the Pacific, and tied up snugly in pairs like sitting ducks in Pearl Harbor when the Japs sprang their attack. If the Japs had been smart they would have landed a few divisions of troops and captured the islands.

Roosevelt exploited the role of Commander-in-Chief of the War and Navy and State Departments to the full. He continually accented the role and guided his policies accordingly. It was a one-man decision that sent us into the European war as it was a one-man decision that started Napoleon off on the invasion of Russia.

The Pearl Harbor investigations haven't yet gone high enough. The blame doesn't rest with subordinates at the level of the Marshalls, the Starks, the Shorts, the Kimmels—even the Hulls. Let us get at the facts with a complete wide open Congressional investigation.

The very mention of Secretary Hull and General Marshall in the Army Board Report was resented by their loyal supporters. With alacrity, Secretary Stimson sprang to the defense of Secretary Hull and General Marshall; the Department of State, "on orders from Secretary Byrnes," came to the aid of the former Secretary, Mr. Hull; and many Democratic newspapers joined in treating the Army board's criticism of Secretary Hull and General Marshall as a kind of outrage.

In Chapter IV of its Report, entitled "Responsibilities in Washington," the Army board devoted a section (3) headed

"Secretary of State" to Mr. Hull and the memorandum handed to the Japanese on November 26, 1941.[12] There the board said:

The responsibility apparently assumed by the Secretary of State (and we have no other proof that anyone else assumed the responsibility finally and definitely) was to determine when the United States would reach the impasse with Japan. It was the Secretary of State who was in charge of the negotiations with the Japanese. . . . He was the contact man and the responsible negotiator. He was doubtless aware of the fact that no action taken by him should be tantamount to a declaration of war. That responsibility rests with Congress. . . . Undoubtedly the Secretary of State had been frequently advised through the meetings of the War Council of the inadequate status of the defenses of the United States. Our Army and Navy were not ready for war, and undoubtedly the Secretary of State had been fully advised of that fact. . . . Apparently on the 26th in the morning, Mr. Hull had made up his mind not to go through with the proposals shown the day before to the Secretary of War containing the plan for the "Three Months' Truce." Evidently the action "to kick the whole thing over" was accomplished by presenting to the Japanese the counter proposal of the "Ten Points" which they took as an ultimatum. It was the document that touched the button that started the war, as Ambassador Grew so aptly expressed it. . . . Apparently the Secretary of War was not advised by the Secretary of State that he had handed this so-called ultimatum to the Japanese. . . . It seems well established that the sending of this "Ten Point" memorandum by the Secretary of State was used by the Japanese as the signal for starting the war by the attack on Pearl Harbor. The Japanese attacking force departed from Tankan Bay on the 27–28 November for its attack on Hawaii. It also appears that the delivery of the 14-point reply of the Japanese to this memorandum was contemporaneous with the attack.[13]

As if aware that Secretary Hull's action in presenting the memorandum to the Japanese on November 26, 1941, was a crucial performance in the history of the coming of war in

12. CJC, Part 39, pp. 135 ff.
13. See below, Chap. XVII.

the Pacific, the editors of the *New York Times* were indignant over the Army board's references to the Secretary of State and, on September 1, 1945, published the following editorial entitled "The So-Called Ultimatum":

In whatever future consideration the Pearl Harbor reports receive, whether official or unofficial, it will be an excellent thing for all concerned if the word "ultimatum" is dropped, once and for all, as a description of Secretary Hull's now famous note of Nov. 26, 1941. "Ultimatum" is the term that has been used time and again in the last few days to describe this message. The official Army Board report speaks of it as "the document that touched the button that started the war." In the light of all this a visitor from Mars might be forgiven if he drew the conclusion that the Government of the United States had deliberately provoked Japan into war with a highhanded and arbitrary challenge, and that Japan had made the only possible answer to this "ultimatum" by hitting us at Pearl Harbor.

For the sake of restoring some perspective to this fantastic picture, let us recall the circumstances and the character of the Hull note which has prompted all this talk about an "ultimatum":

Diplomatic conversations were held in Washington with emissaries of the Japanese Government in November, 1941, with a view to considering the critical problems which had arisen between that Government and our own. What was the situation at that time? Japan had just invaded Indo-China. Great Japanese armies had been landed there. Great Japanese naval forces had assembled in Cam Ranh Bay. They were obviously on their way either to the Philippines or Singapore. Other great Japanese armies were still ravaging and pillaging China, to the maintenance of whose territorial integrity the United States had pledged itself by solemn treaty.[14] Still other great Japanese armies were massed on Russia's eastern frontier. German armies had driven deep into Russia from the west. At this moment they stood at the very gates of Moscow. And Japan had just concluded, with Germany and Italy, an offensive-and-defensive military alliance which made her a full-fledged member of the Axis triumvirate that had as its

14. The United States never pledged itself by treaty to the maintenance of the territorial integrity of China. It bound itself to respect that integrity, not to uphold it against other powers and certainly not to maintain it by the blood of American citizens.

clear goal the destruction of British and American power and the conquest of the world.

What was the proposal made by the Japanese emissaries in Washington, at this critical juncture, as a means of improving the relations between Japan and the United States?

In a note addressed to our Government on Nov. 20, the Japanese offered to change none of the policies which were threatening the peace of the Orient and the security of the United States. Instead, they proposed that the United States agree forthwith to supply Japan with as much oil as she wanted. And they demanded simultaneously that the United States cease giving any aid to China.[15]

This was the note to which Secretary Hull sent his now famous reply of Nov. 26. In it he did what any self-respecting American would have done. He refused to be bullied into the abject humiliation of his country and the complete betrayal of its ally, China. He told the Japanese that they could not have their oil and that we would not turn quitters on our promises to China. But he did not slam the door on further discussions. He did not threaten the Japanese with war. He did not threaten them with anything save the further loss of American respect and friendship if they persisted in the bare-faced aggression on which they had embarked. And, as a means of keeping alive at least some hope of a peaceful settlement, he offered the Japanese a program which contained a restatement of principles which had long been basic in this country's foreign policies, with the request that "further effort be made to resolve our divergences of views in regard to the practical application of these fundamental principles."

Was this an "ultimatum"? It was an "ultimatum" if it is an "ultimatum" for a man with a pistol at his head to say no when a thug demands his pocketbook.

Adverse opinions respecting the Army and Navy reports were also expressed by Mrs. Eleanor Roosevelt, long an expositor and defender of the President's policies and measures. In her column, headed "Futile Criticism," published in the *New York World-Telegram*, September 1, 1945, Mrs. Roosevelt said:

15. This paragraph was a gross simplification of the facts in respect of the modus vivendi. See below, Chap. XVII.

Hyde Park, Friday—I have just been reading the Army and Navy reports on Pearl Harbor, as well as the innumerable newspaper comments. It all seems to me rather futile. Perhaps the simplest thing for us all to do would be to say that, in varying degrees, every one of us has been to blame. Our joint feelings, beliefs and actions had an effect on some of those in places of authority, and the division of blame is an extremely difficult thing to assess.

How often, for instance, was Congress asked for more appropriations to fortify Wake and Guam? Do we blame Congress for not listening to these requests? They were deaf because they did not think their constituents would consider that money wisely spent.

* * *

Are we going to censure Gen. Marshall today even if he didn't send explicit enough directions to Gen. Short in Pearl Harbor in 1941, and forget the magnificent record which he has made during the past four years? Are we going to take away the credit for the achievements of Gen. Gerow and Adm. Stark even if they did fall short in some specific way in the Pearl Harbor situation?

If we had been clamoring for preparedness as a nation, we would not have allowed certain writers and papers and radio speakers to hurl the epithet of "warmonger" at the many people who warned us in the years before Pearl Harbor that war might be coming. Secretary Stimson's diary shows that President Roosevelt warned the Japanese might attack on a certain day. Yet that wasn't the first warning he had given that we should prepare for war—and some of you may remember what certain newspapers in this country said about those warnings.

* * *

Is Secretary Hull, after his years of patient, wise leadership, now to be censured because he decided the time had come to take certain diplomatic steps as regards Japan? He was exercising his best judgment, and it would be well if we remembered how easy it is to be wise when you look back after events have occurred and how extremely difficult it sometimes is to gauge what those events will be.

It is very human to do little straight thinking about our own shortcomings. We want to accuse and punish our good loyal public servants who have worked themselves to the point of ill health, and some of them even to death. Instead of marveling at the few mistakes they made, we harp upon those mistakes and give scant praise for all the years where they worked successfully and well. Yet we do not turn on our real enemies—the propagandists, writers and speakers who kept us unaware of danger, who tried to divide us and weaken us, and who are in our midst today, untouched and as dangerous to our peace efforts as they were to our war efforts.

Recriminations will not bring back our dead. Instead of recriminations, it would be safer and wiser if we determined in the future never again to be a flabby and ill-prepared people.

Whatever the appearances of the situation created by the release of the Pearl Harbor documents and President Truman's statements relative to them, as viewed from distant editorial sanctums, the realities presented grave difficulties to Democratic managers in the National Capital, especially in Congress. A more than impressionistic sketch of the situation was presented in an editorial of the *Washington Post*, reprinted in the *New York Times* of August 31, 1945. The *Post*, though Republican, had faithfully supported the conduct of foreign affairs by President Roosevelt and yet was moved to speak critically respecting the administration of affairs in 1941:

The report shows the real villain was the bureaucratic mind. The picture presented is a veritable masterpiece of snafu. The Navy knew a Japanese task force was at Jaluit, but General Short was not informed. More fantastic was the War Department habit of keeping vital information from Short. . . . Notwithstanding the confusion, Short's inadequacies, General Marshall's aberrations and Secretary Hull's intransigence, it is certain almost classical fatality pervades the whole story.

In the tumult of clashing opinions raised by the Army and Navy boards' reports, many disputants seemed obsessed by attention to the personalities involved in the Pearl Harbor catastrophe. Among these personalities, of course, President Roosevelt and Secretary Hull were central figures; and, in final analysis, President Roosevelt was the major figure. The President had been Chief Executive and Commander in Chief of the armed forces; while Mr. Hull had been, under the law, merely his agent in the conduct of affairs leading up to the catastrophe and all it signified. If there was one thing that faithful Democrats and original advocates of involvement in the global war could not bear at all, it was flat statements, even insinuations, from Republican or any other quarters, that the President had dissembled in the conduct of affairs which led to war, after making solemn pledges in 1940 that "the country is not going to war," or that either by incompetence or by deliberate resolve he had involved the United States in the war. Doubtless, John W. McCormack, the majority leader in the House of Representatives, had expressed the sentiment of all the faithful when he told Representative Church on the floor during the debates in September, 1944, that a reference to President Roosevelt's probable responsibilities "is contemptible . . . I think the gentleman should be ashamed of himself." [16]

In this obsession with personalities on both sides of the party line, newspaper commentators on the Report of the Army Board paid little or no attention to a few pages in that board's document which had an enduring significance for the American people and constitutional government, and transcended mere controversies over the character of President Roosevelt and his associates in the Cabinet. The board said in Chapter II of its Report:

For a long period of time prior to the war the public was reluctant even to consider a war. There was a distinct lack of a war mind in the United States. Isolationist organizations and propaganda groups against war were powerful and vital factors affecting any war action capable of being taken by our responsible leadership. So influential were these campaigns that they raised grave doubts in the minds of such leadership as to whether they would be supported by the people in the necessary actions for our defense by requisite moves against Japan. Public opinion in the early stages had to be allowed to develop; in the later stages it ran ahead of

16. See above, p. 282.

preparation for war. There was little war spirit either amongst the general public or in the armed forces, due to this conflicting opinion having its influence. *The events hereinafter recited must be measured against this important psychological factor.*[17]

After describing the confusion that prevailed in "the Administration, State, War, and Navy Departments" on the eve of Pearl Harbor and the "conference method" of conducting affairs which resulted in mismanagement, the Army board in effect seemed to think that responsibility for this situation belonged to the people of the United States, by declaring: "That was the product of the time and conditions due to the transition from peace to war in a democracy." [18]

In and between its lines the Army Board Report intimated that a kind of inexorable fate due to the muddleheadedness of democracy, at bottom, accounted for the disaster at Pearl Harbor, even though the board ascribed responsibilities to Secretary Hull, General Marshall, and General Gerow, and by association to President Roosevelt. Central to its reasoning, the board placed the inability of the Administration, in such circumstances, to take "the necessary actions for our defense by requisite moves against Japan." [19] This meant, if it meant anything, that democracy was inimical to unity and strength in conducting foreign affairs and that, owing to the lack of power to wage war without a declaration of war by Congress—to strike Japan by an overt act of war when and where he deemed it most advantageous—President Roosevelt was handicapped in taking "necessary actions for our defense." [20]

It is scarcely believable that the three officers on the Army board were so unfamiliar with military and political history as to be unaware of what they were pleading for or, at all events, suggesting in Chapter II of this Report, namely, that, in an age of Power Politics and *Blitzkriege*, democratic processes

---

17. CJC, Part 39, pp. 28 f. (Italics supplied.)
18. *Ibid.*, p. 28.
19. *Ibid.*, p. 29.
20. This, in some respects, fitted into the official thesis of the Roosevelt Administration in 1941 as set forth semiofficially by Davis and Lindley in *How War Came*. See above, p. 244.

and constitutional methods of government in relation to war are outmoded. To military history there was nothing new in the proposition that the power to conduct foreign affairs must be supported by the power to strike the enemy first in his weakest spot and at the most advantageous moment, without regard to "democratic processes" or the will or vagaries of any legislative body.

But the idea was doubtless distressing to some Americans who read this chapter of the Army Board Report after it was released in August, 1945. It was indeed particularly disturbing in view of the fact that President Truman himself, after releasing the document, put the blame for Pearl Harbor on the country and on the Congress which had "stifled" President Roosevelt's programs for preparedness.

Chapter II of the Army Board Report was, of course, grist to the mill of many Republicans and Antiwar Democrats.[21] For them, it posed pointed questions, for example, who had contributed more to the "lack of war mind," to the widespread belief of the American people that the United States should and could keep out of war, than President Roosevelt, by his categorical antiwar promises? When, in 1941, despite his numerous speeches on war dangers, had he declared his peace promises obsolete and informed the country that war was certainly at hand, if not desirable or necessary in the changing circumstances? In intimating that historic practices of conducting foreign affairs and war under the Constitution were archaic and unadapted to the new age of diplomacy and warfare, did the Army War Board represent any considerable opinion in the Administration and the War Department?

The situation created by the release of the Army and Navy

---

21. Senator Ferguson and Senator Brewster, the minority of the Congressional Committee on Pearl Harbor, took note of the Army board's contentions respecting "democracy" (CJC, *Report*, p. 564). Representative Keefe, although he signed the majority report, concluded that "secret diplomacy was at the root of the tragedy" (pp. 266-T and 266-W) and declared: "In the future the people and their Congress must know how close American diplomacy is moving to war so that they may check its advance if imprudent and support its position if sound." Thus, although he did not refer to the Army Board Report in this connection, Mr. Keefe repudiated its assumptions.

boards' reports and public discussion of their conclusions presented certain features not to be ignored by political leaders. Republicans, as a matter of course, prepared to take full advantage of it. To Democrats who cherished, for numerous reasons, the tradition inherited from President Roosevelt and naturally were eager to avoid shattering it, the state of affairs offered more than one dilemma. The President's Commission on Pearl Harbor had, on January 23, 1942, simplified matters by exculpating the high officials in Washington and laying the primary guilt for Pearl Harbor on General Short and Admiral Kimmel, technicians of the Army and the Navy. Now the technicians of the Army and the Navy themselves, represented in the Army and Navy boards, besides clearing General Short and Admiral Kimmel of the grave sin of dereliction ascribed to them by the President's Commission and by the Administration, had brought into the picture President Roosevelt and his liaison officers in the Army and Navy Departments—General Marshall and Admiral Stark—and had laid blame on Secretary Hull, the President's agent in the conduct of foreign affairs. In other words, the technicians had shifted the major part of the responsibility from the Hawaiian commanders to their political and semipolitical superiors in Washington. So, at least, things seemed to stand after August 29, 1945.

Perhaps inadvertently, President Truman made additional trouble by his statement of August 30, 1945; for he then brought President Roosevelt into the controversy by saying that Congress had regularly blocked his preparedness programs; and he also shifted the blame for Pearl Harbor to the country—almost.[22] In transferring a part of the burden of guilt to Congress, President Truman also struck at the loyalty and conduct of the Democratic majority who had controlled both houses since 1933. They could easily point to their record and demonstrate by citations of cold figures that they had voted more money for preparedness between 1933 and

22. See text of his statement above, p. 306.

1941 than the President had proposed.[23] Accordingly, Democratic Senators and Representatives had two good reasons for being discontented with "the situation": The Army and Navy boards had challenged President Roosevelt's thesis on the coming of war in the Pacific and President Truman had criticized Congress as well as the people.

23. Beard, *op. cit.*, pp. 35 ff.

CHAPTER XII

A Congressional Committee Probes the Records and Reports

IN September, 1945, the question of a new Pearl Harbor inquiry passed from the Executive Department to the Legislative Department. This was in accordance with the necessities of the American constitutional system. Had the President desired to settle the issue himself, he possessed no sole power to say the final word, whatever the members of his Cabinet and other counselors might have urged upon him. The division of governmental authority under the Constitution and the powers vested in Congress by that national charter made such an action on his part impossible.

For the Democrats in Congress, the issue of a new Pearl Harbor inquiry raised many considerations. Having majorities in the House and the Senate, formally they could have ignored it or buried it under silence. But that action, they knew, would result in consequences to be immediately weighed. It would have left standing as the last word, so far, the reports of the Army and Navy boards, which had impeached the Conclusions of President Roosevelt's Commission on Pearl Harbor, the former attributing responsibilities to high members of his civil and military administration, including no less a personage than his Secretary of State, Cordell Hull. Besides, in any case, suppressing the issue could have been only nominal and temporary and, in any event, confined to party councils. Under the explicit terms of the Constitution, inexorably as the earth turned, new congressional elections were bound to come, the first in the very next year, 1946; and if Democratic Representatives and Senators had wanted to keep Pearl Harbor out of the campaign, the two-party system and freedom of the press, both constitutionally beyond their reach, would have estopped the realization of that wish.

Nor, under the provisions of the Constitution relative to the organization and procedure of Congress, were the Democrats able, had they so desired, to prevent Republicans from calling for a new Pearl Harbor inquiry and to block another, even more tempestuous, debate on the subject than had raged in the House of Representatives in September, 1944.[1] That Republicans in Congress were being urged to act by the party press was evident to anybody who could read the English language. For example, the *New York Herald Tribune*, an unqualified supporter of the war, had in effect called for an inquiry, in a leading editorial in August, 1945. The editorial said that the public would find it "more difficult still to make sense out of [the Army and Navy boards'] reports which, while conveying a vivid impression of over-all confusion, unawareness, and 'buck-passing' in the Army, the Navy, the State Department, and the White House, have nothing to say about the President, hastily suppress an inferential criticism of the Secretary of State, and leave it to be supposed that it was just an accident of fate that we were caught in December, 1941," without adequate preparations—intelligence, military, and naval.

It was then, for practical purposes, in full view of hawk-eyed journalists and through them of the American public, that Democratic leaders in Congress carried on their secret sessions respecting the action to be taken on the issue of the new Pearl Harbor inquiry. They were not a few commissars sitting with a Chief Executive behind the massive barricades of a Kremlin preparing orders for obedient subjects. If the walls of their conference rooms were opaque, they knew full well, as astute Representatives and Senators well schooled in the American system of government and liberty, that every move they made was under nation-wide observation, perhaps under the eye of eternity.

SENATOR BARKLEY, MAJORITY LEADER, CALLS FOR AN
INVESTIGATION

ON SEPTEMBER 6, 1945, after the prayer had been offered and a little routine business transacted, Senator Barkley forestalled

1. See above, pp. 273 ff.

the Republican demand for an inquiry by securing unanimous consent to make a brief statement and introduce a concurrent resolution. By way of introduction, he referred to the various reports that had been made on Pearl Harbor, beginning with that of the President's Commission, headed by Justice Roberts. He emphasized the fact that these documents contained confusing and contradictory statements. He acknowledged that there was widespread suspicion among the American people and members of Congress. Consequently, he said, Congress should make a thorough, fearless, and impartial investigation of the facts, conditions, and circumstances prevailing prior to and at the time of the attack on Pearl Harbor.

Such an inquiry, the Senator declared, "should produce the facts and all the facts, so far as it is humanly possible to produce them. . . . It should be conducted without partisanship or favoritism toward any responsible official, military, naval, or civilian, high or low, living or dead." With becoming gravity, he warned his colleagues that the inquiry should proceed on a high level of judicial responsibility, not with any design of vindicating or aspersing any person, high or low, living or dead, but solely for the purpose of ascertaining "the cold, unvarnished, indisputable facts so far as they are obtainable." Its purpose, the Senator explained, should be twofold: first, "fixing responsibility, whether that responsibility be upon an individual or a group of individuals, or upon a system under which they operated or cooperated, or failed to do either"; and, second, to ascertain whether, in view of what happened at Pearl Harbor, before or subsequently, anything might be developed that would be useful to Congress in legislating with reference to the armed forces and the executive departments "having control of them, or which are supposed to work with them."

The Joint Resolution to accomplish this twofold purpose, amended slightly after a brief discussion, was couched in terms broad enough to satisfy the most scrupulous critics. It provided for a committee of ten members—five from the Senate and five from the House of Representatives, appointed by the President of the Senate pro tempore and the Speaker of the House respectively. Betraying the mark of party management, it further provided that not more than three of the Senators and three of the Representatives from the two chambers should be "members of the majority party." Thus the idea of a committee composed of an equal number of Democrats and Republicans, broached in certain quarters, was by clear intimation rejected in favor of a committee controlled by a majority of Democrats. The Resolution as amended passed the Senate without a dissenting vote and the House quickly concurred.

CRITICS PLEAD FOR NONPARTISAN PROCEDURES

In his column for the *New York Times*, dated Washington, September 6, 1945, and published the next day, Arthur Krock discussed the general situation before the new committee and the country under the heading "Standards for Investigation of Pearl Harbor." Owing to the fact that Mr. Krock cannot be dismissed as an "isolationist" and that he possessed extraordinary knowledge of inside affairs in Washington, certain passages from his report deserve quotation as providing a background for evaluating the spirit of the inquiry and results produced by the methods employed:

A joint committee of Congress is soon to begin an inquiry into the disaster at Pearl Harbor. . . . Since the record of Congressional investigations is spotty with reference to fairness and ability of procedure, concentration on the main point and the exclusion of partisan and personal animations, the forthcoming inquiry begins under a handicap. But by its procedure and the nature of its report the joint committee can dispel that, and the gravity and importance of the task require it.

Senator Barkley, moving with the approval of the President, laid down an admirable set of standards for the committee in his remarks today. . . .

The principal questions it must determine are these, and, if all testimony is directed and held to lines leading straight to the answers, the report should be clear and satisfactory:

1. What factors, human and material, military and political,

were responsible, directly or indirectly, for the highly successful time element of surprise in the attack; for the general unpreparedness of the base, even if there had been several hours of warning; for the concentration of the fleet in the harbor, the airplanes on the ground and the ammunition under lock and key?

2. Was high policy, or military and administrative incompetence or neglect—or all of them in combination—the chief cause of the poor liaisons among high officials in Washington who were fully informed of the Japanese crisis and the equally poor liaisons between the Washington headquarters of the services and their commanders in the field?

3. Who were the individuals most responsible for these poor liaisons?

4. To what degree was high policy responsible for the military lapses of the commanders in Hawaii at a time which, despite poor liaisons, common report revealed as critical and the verge of war?

5. To what extent were these lapses, and those attributed to Washington authority by the Army and Navy boards, the result of the public's anti-war state of mind?

There are other questions, but they are in the category of subdivisions. If the Congressional inquiry concentrates on the five major points, gets the available testimony efficiently and fairly, and sifts it by the same methods, the answers will be clear, and Pearl Harbor can be relegated to history except for such partisan and personal ammunition as it may supply for a while. But if the committee, or its majority, or even any individual members sets out to protect or defend any individual proved to have been concerned, or obviously connected, then the inquiry will resemble certain others which have damaged the reputation of Congress and confused, hoodwinked or disgusted the public.

The committee if it chooses can take up the issue of why or how the United States got into World War II. Yet to achieve its real purpose it will not need to concern itself over whether the diplomatic negotiations with Japan were well or ill handled in Washington or in Tokyo. . . .

The argument of the previous Administration that the "people" must bear a large share of blame for a military disaster, at a scene commanded by professionals, has been revived. The Army board asserted that the Army "was influenced by public opinion * * * and the state of the public mind." Echoing this, President Truman commented, "I think the country is as much to blame as any individual in this final situation that developed at Pearl Harbor."

But the committee is instructed to inquire into the particular development. And surely unusual talents will be required to prove that the civilian state of mind prevented Government authorities from keeping one another informed, units of the War Department from keeping others informed and commanders from invoking sound defense measures at an outpost. . . .

On the morning of Pearl Harbor [the public] had read a report of Secretary Knox that the Navy was never more powerful. In the . . . campaign of 1940 it had been assured by both Presidential candidates that each would be more likely to keep the nation out of war. In 1941 it was solemnly told that lend-lease, which actually made war inevitable,[2] was a move to assure exactly the reverse. And in the fiscal year ending in June, 1941, the public, through Congress, had assigned more than $20 billions additional to national defense.

The editors of the *New York Times*, on September 8, greeted the establishment of the new committee with moderate satisfaction. They admitted the need for such an inquiry and stated that Senator Barkley had laid down the proper standards for the conduct of the investigation. They declared that politics should be kept out of the inquiry—"Democratic politics" and "Republican politics." But this would be difficult the editors granted, and they were disturbed by the possibility that unregenerate "isolationists" would inject politics into the inquiry. The *Times* paragraph on political troubles ahead follows:

The problem will be to keep politics out of the inquiry—Democratic politics, Republican politics and the politics of that small but unregenerate group of pre-war isolationists which is still hoping to justify its own past blindness and its own poor advice by using a Pearl Harbor investigation to prove somehow that despite Japan's aggressive actions on the Continent of Asia and despite Japan's alliance with Hitler aimed directly at the United States and despite the fact that our own territory was invaded by the

2. See above, pp. 150 ff., for Mr. Krock's statement in November, 1941.

enemy and our own men killed and our own ships destroyed, President Roosevelt "plunged the country into war."

The Congressional inquiry will perform a useful purpose, and carry conviction with the public, to the extent that it sticks to "the cold, unvarnished, indisputable facts" for which Senator Barkley calls.

Under the title: "Pearl Harbor Inquiry: Open, Fearless Investigation Urged to Glean Data of Value for Future," Hanson Baldwin, specialist in military and naval affairs for the *New York Times*, set forth his views in the edition of Sunday, September 9, 1945. Mr. Baldwin contended that a bipartisan civilian commission should have been appointed, and that politics would not be kept out of the inquiry "unless the caliber of the Congressional Committee is extraordinary." Appreciating the fact that the management of the armed forces at Pearl Harbor had profound significance for popular government and citizenship, aware that a broad range of events had to be covered, and anxious about the prospects of partisanship, Mr. Baldwin proposed a constructive program of operations:

(1) The committee should consist of an equal number of Democrats and Republicans.

(2) Its members should be chosen for their intellectual and judicial capacity and their ability to discard partisanship.

(3) The date set for reporting the committee's findings—Jan. 3, 1946—should be postponed, possibly to next March or April; [3] the intervening period is far too short to permit a comprehensive investigation without back-breaking work.

(4) All hearings and all committee meetings should be open to the public. As a start, the full texts of the Army and Navy investigations and the full text of the Roberts Commission report and testimony, with supporting documents (none of them yet published in full), should be released.

(5) The hearings and the testimony should be prepared by competent committee counsel, and these should be selected with great care and should include one or more leading lawyers or judges, newspaper men and Army and Navy officers.

3. The term of the committee was, in fact, later extended by Congress.

(6) The investigation should be unlimited in scope. It must not only consider the attack upon Pearl Harbor and the events that led up to and followed it; it must investigate the whole course of American foreign policy and military policy in the pre-war and initial war period, and it should determine whether or not these policies were mutually supporting. It should also consider the events in the first disastrous Philippine campaign, including the loss of our B-17's in the surprise attack upon Clark Field, and the friction that developed between Admiral Thomas C. Hart, then commander of the Asiatic Fleet, and General of the Army Douglas MacArthur. The investigation must be without fear or favor.

An investigation of such scope and sincerity is essential—not only in justice to men whose reputations already have been clouded—but because of the importance to the future of the lessons learned. Already some of the lessons of Pearl Harbor are being misread in the light of incomplete and, in some cases, misleading facts. Pearl Harbor can be not only the "date that will live in infamy," but a sign-post to a better organized Government and a more responsible citizenry—but only if its full lessons are carefully and impartially analyzed.

ORGANIZATION AND MANAGEMENT OF THE COMMITTEE

THE Joint Committee on Pearl Harbor as organized consisted of five Senators: three Democrats—Alben Barkley of Kentucky, Walter F. George of Georgia, and Scott W. Lucas of Illinois; and two Republicans—Owen Brewster of Maine and Homer Ferguson of Michigan; and five Representatives: three Democrats—Jere Cooper of Tennessee, J. Bayard Clark of North Carolina, and John W. Murphy of Pennsylvania; and two Republicans—Bertrand W. Gearhart of California and Frank B. Keefe of Wisconsin. Two Democrats were chosen to preside: Senator Barkley as chairman and Representative Cooper as vice chairman. From November 15, 1945, to May 31, 1946, the committee held open hearings on seventy days, took testimony, and collected exhibits of papers and documents. At the end the committee reported that its record encompassed approximately 10,000,000 words. A one-volume Report presenting the findings and conclusions of the committee was completed by July 20, 1946, handed to the Senate and House, and released to the press that day. The testimony and supplementary records were published later—in October, 1946.

Although the investigation brought to light a multitude of "cold, unvarnished, indisputable facts" hitherto secret, it left many avenues of inquiry still closed. By a party vote, as a rule, the majority members decided disputed points as to the witnesses to be summoned, access to documents, and procedures. They denied to minority members the right to carry on individual searches in the files and records of the Executive Departments, even if accompanied by one of the committee's counsel.

The committee heard none of the principal parties to the case, except Secretary Hull. President Roosevelt was dead; his personal papers were in the hands of his former secretary, Miss Grace Tully, and the majority of the committee allowed her to decide which, if any, of those papers were pertinent to the purposes of the investigation. Secretary Knox was dead. Harry Hopkins died shortly after the committee began its work—before he could be called upon to give testimony. Owing to illness, the Secretary of War, Mr. Stimson, was not able to appear and endure the strain of cross-examination; but he prepared a statement for the committee, allowed portions of his *Diary* to be entered in the record, and answered in writing, in his own way, a number of written questions framed by Senator Ferguson. Secretary Hull filed a long statement giving his version of affairs and answered several questions directed to him by counsel; but the hearings at which Mr. Hull appeared were so managed that he was not required to undergo the stress of a cross-examination by any of the minority members. He did, however, answer, in his own way, a number of questions formulated by Senator Ferguson and transmitted to him in writing.

Whatever may be the long-term judgment of specialists in law, morals, and technology on the controversies between the Democrats and the Republicans in the committee meetings

American citizens will always have grounds for being grateful to the Democratic majority in Congress and the committee for permitting such an extensive exploration of archives on the political, diplomatic, and military history of the United States. To come down to practical cases, Americans who care at all how the government and foreign affairs of the United States are actually conducted will be thankful for the thousands of pages of documentary materials which the majority of the committee, persistently prodded by the minority, placed on public record. For this service citizens are entirely indebted to the often maligned Congress of the United States. Now they may explore to a considerable extent the realities behind the appearances of 1940–41.

When the committee closed its hearings in May, 1946, it confronted transcripts of testimony, exhibits, and documents astounding in volume and complexity. On the basis of this mountainous mass of evidence it was bound to discharge its duty, as explained by Senator Barkley in his address in the Senate on September 6, 1945.[4] Even to hurried readers of newspaper reports of the hearings it was plain that the committee, Congress, and the people of the United States had before them new and startling information respecting the conduct of foreign and military affairs by the Roosevelt Administration for months, even years, before December 7, 1941. It was also plain that the official explanation of how war came did not exactly correspond to the facts now brought to light from sources which had been hidden to the American people until the committee had brought them into the open. If dazed by the magnitude of their task, members of the committee knew that the records unearthed and indeed the committee itself, stood before the bar of history; that its decisions, and conclusions would be subjected to the judgment of historical scholarship in years to come, unless forsooth critical scholarship was to disappear in some future cataclysm, moral and political.

From all that had transpired in the committee's closed meet-

4. See above, pp. 327 ff.

ings and in open hearings since they began, it was fairly certain at the end that the Report of the committee would not be unanimous. Taking the language of the Democratic resolution and Senator Barkley's exposition of September 6, 1945,[5] literally, all the Republican members had insisted that "no person, high or low, living or dead" would be spared from unrestricted scrutiny in the search for "the cold, unvarnished, indisputable facts." Yet the Republicans had struggled in vain for the privilege of seeing President Roosevelt's file of secret papers bearing on the conduct of foreign affairs in respect of war origins, for the right to cross-examine the two great living principals, Secretary Hull and Secretary Stimson, and to secure testimony from certain subordinates in the Foreign Service of the United States who were presumed to know about the policies and decisions of President Roosevelt and Secretary Hull.

The resolve of the Democratic members to block such Republican efforts, generally voiced courteously at the public hearings but sometimes contemptuously, had been patent from the outset. In addition, at the open hearings, clashes had occurred between the Democrats and the Republicans over types of questions to be asked in the examination of witnesses, over Republican insistence on searches for more documents, over the admission and interpretation of evidence. Hence at the close of the hearings, in May, 1946, it seemed likely that there would be a strict party division over the conclusions drawn from the testimony and papers before the committee.

The division that occurred in the committee at the end and the document called the Report of the committee did not conform to such expectations. All Democrats agreed, it is true, on one long document, including a section of Conclusions and Recommendations and Appendices. This document they all signed. One Republican Representative, Mr. Gearhart, signed it, apparently without reservations. The other Republican Representative, Mr. Keefe, also signed it, but with "Additional Views" which amounted, in fact, to a dissenting opinion re-

5. See above, p. 328

specting most of the fundamental declarations to which the Democratic members and Mr. Gearhart affixed their names. The two Republican Senators, Mr. Ferguson and Mr. Brewster, openly dissented from the majority's statement and filed a separate statement bearing the title of "Minority Views." The documentary outcome of this division of opinion, which in reality amounted to three separate "reports," was entitled: *Report of the Joint Committee on the Investigation of the Pearl Harbor Attack/Congress of the United States/ . . . And Additional Views of Mr. Keefe/Together with Minority Views of Mr. Ferguson and Mr. Brewster.*

THE MAJORITY REPORT

As THEY prepared to draw up their Conclusions the Democrats on the committee faced a primary problem which had been set for them by Senator Barkley in his statement of September 6, 1945, when he introduced the resolutions creating the committee. They could easily ascribe to Republican partisanship, and hence ignore, the claim that Secretary Stimson had accurately characterized the conduct of affairs immediately prior to Pearl Harbor as the operation of maneuvering the Japanese into the position of firing the first shot "without allowing too much danger to ourselves." They could also dismiss on the same ground the further claim that in the records of the committee were documents which supported this contention and put the ultimate responsibility for the disaster on the Administration in Washington. But they could not, in view of the committee's obligation to clear up confusions in previous reports,[6] so easily pass over a specific contradiction presented by certain major documents in the record before them—particularly the Roberts Report on Pearl Harbor, on the one side, and the reports of the Army and Navy boards on the other.[7]

In these reports was a contradiction which could not be

6. See Senator Barkley's statement in introducing the resolution for the inquiry, above, p. 328.
7. See above, Chaps. VIII and XIII.

resolved or avoided without making trouble for the Democrats on the committee. If General Short and Admiral Kimmel had received adequate orders and information from their Washington superiors and had failed to do their duty under the orders, they were guilty of derelictions of duty as charged by the President's Commission; the complaints filed against them publicly by the Roosevelt Administration in January and February, 1942, were well founded; appropriate members of the Administration were to be completely absolved from responsibility for the catastrophe at Pearl Harbor; and evidence to support court-martial trials for the two commanders was available. If, on the other hand, General Short and Admiral Kimmel were to be exculpated from derelictions of duty, as the Army and Navy boards had recommended, then some official or officials in Washington had failed to discharge their duties properly; some share of responsibility for the catastrophe, yet to be determined, lay on members of the Roosevelt Administration, and the treatment accorded to General Short and Admiral Kimmel was to be characterized as inexcusable, if indeed, not dishonorable.

In these reports also was another irksome contradiction to be resolved by the majority of the committee. That was the contradiction between the Roberts Report, which exculpated by name high authorities in Washington and by implication President Roosevelt, and the Army Pearl Harbor Board Report, which traversed the Roberts Report, recommended no action against General Short and filed complaints against General Marshall, General Gerow, and Secretary Hull, including by implication President Roosevelt. In addition Admiral Kimmel had been cleared by the Navy Court.[8]

With these contradictions, the Democratic members of the committee, fully supported by Mr. Gearhart, Republican Representative, dealt forcefully in their conclusions as to responsibilities. Following the line of the Roberts Report, they exculpated by name, and gave high praise to, the President, the Secretary of State, the Secretary of War, and the Secretary

8. See above, Chap. XI.

of the Navy. They ascribed a list of specific failures to General Short and Admiral Kimmel but immediately added: "The errors made by the Hawaiian commands were errors of judgment and not derelictions of duty." [9] Thus the high political officers in Washington and the Hawaiian commanders won a great victory. The majority, in addition, reversed the judgment of the Army Pearl Harbor Board and of the Navy Court of Inquiry in vital respects by putting the blame squarely on the Army and the Navy. Thus the politicos settled their account with the men of arms. The majority's "Conclusions with Respect to Responsibilities" follow:

1. The December 7, 1941, attack on Pearl Harbor was an unprovoked act of aggression by the Empire of Japan. The treacherous attack was planned and launched while Japanese Ambassadors, instructed with characteristic duplicity, were carrying on the pretense of negotiations with the Government of the United States with a view to an amicable settlement of differences in the Pacific.

2. The ultimate responsibility for the attack and its results rests upon Japan, an attack that was well planned and skillfully executed. Contributing to the effectiveness of the attack was a powerful striking force, much more powerful than it had been thought the Japanese were able to employ in a single tactical venture at such a distance and under such circumstances.

3. The diplomatic policies and actions of the United States provided no justifiable provocation whatever for the attack by Japan on this Nation. The Secretary of State fully informed both the War and Navy Departments of diplomatic developments and, in a timely and forceful manner, clearly pointed out to these Departments that relations between the United States and Japan had passed beyond the stage of diplomacy and were in the hands of the military.

4. The Committee has found no evidence to support the charges, made before and during the hearings, that the President, the Secretary of State, the Secretary of War, or the Secretary of the Navy tricked, provoked, incited, cajoled, or coerced Japan into attacking this Nation in order that a declaration of war might be more easily obtained from the Congress. On the contrary, all

9. See below, Chap. XIII.

evidence conclusively points to the fact that they discharged their responsibilities with distinction, ability, and foresight and in keeping with the highest traditions of our fundamental foreign policy.

5. The President, the Secretary of State, and high Government officials made every possible effort, without sacrificing our national honor and endangering our security, to avert war with Japan.

6. The disaster at Pearl Harbor was the failure, with attendant increase in personnel and material losses, of the Army and the Navy to institute measures designed to detect an approaching hostile force, to effect a state of readiness commensurate with the realization that war was at hand, and to employ every facility at their command in repelling the Japanese.

7. Virtually everyone was surprised that Japan struck the Fleet at Pearl Harbor at the time that she did. Yet officers, both in Washington and Hawaii, were fully conscious of the danger from air attack; they realized this form of attack on Pearl Harbor by Japan was at least a possibility; and they were adequately informed of the imminence of war.

8. Specifically, the Hawaiian commands failed—

(*a*) To discharge their responsibilities in the light of the warnings received from Washington, other information possessed by them, and the principle of command by mutual cooperation.

(*b*) To integrate and coordinate their facilities for defense and to alert properly the Army and Navy establishments in Hawaii, particularly in the light of the warnings and intelligence available to them during the period November 27 to December 7, 1941.

(*c*) To effect liaison on a basis designed to acquaint each of them with the operations of the other, which was necessary to their joint security, and to exchange fully all significant intelligence.

(*d*) To maintain a more effective reconnaissance within the limits of their equipment.

(*e*) To effect a state of readiness throughout the Army and Navy establishments designed to meet all possible attacks.

(*f*) To employ the facilities, matériel, and personnel at their command, which were adequate at least to have greatly minimized the effects of the attack, in repelling the Japanese raiders.

(g) To appreciate the significance of intelligence and other information available to them.

9. The errors made by the Hawaiian commands were errors of judgment and not derelictions of duty.

10. The War Plans Division of the War Department failed to discharge its direct responsibility to advise the commanding general he had not properly alerted the Hawaiian Department when the latter, pursuant to instructions, had reported action taken in a message that was not satisfactorily responsive to the original directive.

11. The Intelligence and War Plans Divisions of the War and Navy Departments failed:

(a) To give careful and thoughtful consideration to the intercepted messages from Tokyo to Honolulu of September 24, November 15, and November 20 (the harbor berthing plan and related dispatches) and to raise a question as to their significance. Since they indicated a particular interest in the Pacific Fleet's base this intelligence should have been appreciated and supplied the Hawaiian commanders for their assistance, along with other information available to them, in making their estimate of the situation.

(b) To be properly on the *qui vive* to receive the "one o'clock" intercept and to recognize in the message the fact that some Japanese military action would very possibly occur somewhere at 1 P.M., December 7. If properly appreciated, this intelligence should have suggested a dispatch to all Pacific outpost commanders supplying this information, as General Marshall attempted to do immediately upon seeing it.

12. Notwithstanding the fact that there were officers on twenty-four hour watch, the Committee believes that under all of the evidence the War and Navy Departments were not sufficiently alerted on December 6 and 7, 1941, in view of the imminence of war.

After dealing with failures on the part of the Army and Navy, the majority of the committee presented five recommendations and twenty-five explicit conclusions in respect of "Supervisory, Administrative, and Organizational Deficiencies in Our Military and Naval Establishments Revealed by the Pearl Harbor Investigation." With remarkable skill and comprehensiveness, the majority summarized the hundreds of pages of evidence before the committee and maintained that confusion, neglect of elementary precautions, failures to coöperate, delays in the dissemination of crucial information as to Japanese designs, the use of loose and equivocal language in instructions and orders to subordinates, maladministration, and shocking incompetence (as distinguished from willful derelictions) had accompanied the conduct of affairs along "the chain of command" from authorities in Washington down to Army and Navy subordinates in Hawaii. In their formulation of the twenty-five headings and in the citation of proof, the majority, although they compiled no list of "culprits," high or low, by name, spared neither the War Department nor the Navy Department, nor by implication any high officials responsible for the administration of the two departments.

No one can spend laborious weeks and months studying the recommendations of the majority, the sound principles of military and naval administration prescribed by them, and the volumes of documentation upon which they relied for their facts, without being convinced that the majority had thoroughly mastered the record before them and its meaning with regard to over-all administrative responsibility for the catastrophe. That much appears to be certain—amid all the differences of opinion in the committee over the propriety of the conduct of foreign affairs prior to Pearl Harbor.[10]

Such was, indeed, the judgment of the experienced Washington observer and journalist, David Lawrence. In a column written shortly after the Report of the committee came out, he presented the following explanation of the significance and

10. For an extended treatment of the position taken by the majority of the Congressional Committee, with reference to particulars and overhead responsibility for Pearl Harbor, see the challenging book by George Morgenstern, *Pearl Harbor: The Story of the Secret War* (Devin-Adair, 1947), which is based on a meticulous study of the committee's records.

upshot of the majority's "Conclusions and Recommendations":

The American people are indebted to the special Senate and House committee which investigated the Pearl Harbor disaster. Despite the impressions which the concluding part of the [majority] report seeks to establish, the headings of the document fix responsibility as plainly as if names had been called.

The [majority] report is ingeniously developed. It states factually what occurred and subdivides each important section with a heading. Future historians cannot fail to read those telltale headings, for each one states an impersonal conclusion out of which only one inference can be made—namely, that the persons who had the responsibility for each task and did not perform it efficiently are being blamed.

Thus, there is language in the conclusion of the report itself, signed by the majority, which absolves certain individuals, but there is no such evasiveness in the headings. Here, for instance, are some of the committee's own headings which subdivide the conclusions and recommendations of the report:

"1. Operational and intelligence work requires centralization of authority and clear-cut allocation of responsibility.

"2. Supervisory officials cannot safely take anything for granted in the alerting of subordinates.

"3. Any doubt as to whether outposts should be given information should always be resolved in favor of supplying the information.

"4. The delegation of authority or the issuance of orders entails the duty of inspection to determine that the official mandate is properly exercised.

"5. The implementation of official orders must be followed with closest supervision.

"6. The maintenance of alertness to responsibility must be insured through repetition.

"7. Complacency and procrastination are out of place where sudden and decisive action is of the essence.

"8. The co-ordination and proper evaluation of intelligence in times of stress must be insured by continuity of service and centralization of responsibility in competent officials.

"9. The unapproachable or superior attitude of officials is fatal.

There should never be any hesitancy in asking for clarification of instructions or in seeking advice on matters that are in doubt.

"10. There is no substitute for imagination and resourcefulness on the part of supervisory and intelligence officials.

"11. Communications must be characterized by clarity, forthrightness and appropriateness."

There are in all twenty-five of these headings. Particularly significant are Nos. 17, 23, 24 and 25. Here they are:

"17. An official who neglects to familiarize himself in detail with his organization should forfeit his responsibility.

"23. Superiors must at all times keep their subordinates adequately informed and, conversely, subordinates should keep their superiors informed.

"24. The administrative organization of any establishment must be designed to locate failures and to assess responsibility.

"25. In a well-balanced organization there is close correlation of responsibility and authority." [11]

Having set forth a logical exposition of the majority's findings, Mr. Lawrence ventured upon some prophecy as to the verdict which historians in coming times will render on the committee's Pearl Harbor Report, including the majority and minority views:

All that the historian of tomorrow needs to do is find out who, on December 7, 1941, was Chief of Staff of the Army, Chief of Naval Operations, and in command of subordinate positions in the War and Navy departments and who was Commander in Chief of the Army and Navy and then read the main headings of the report on Pearl Harbor. He will find that Republicans and Democrats were unanimous about the headings, but politeness, courtesy and deference caused the omission of the names of the personalities involved, in the case of the majority who signed the report, whereas the minority just named those responsible. It's really a unanimous report on what happened [in respect of the catastrophe at Pearl Harbor].

Mr. Lawrence's contention respecting the powers and responsibilities of the President as Chief Executive and as Commander in Chief was, of course, sound and supported by evi-

11. David Lawrence's column, *New York Sun*, July 23, 1946.

dence before the Congressional Committee, especially Secretary Stimson's statement and *Diary*, and by ample precedents in American military history. Undoubtedly President Roosevelt had enjoyed through all the years immediately preceding Pearl Harbor full authority to order unification, under his own direction, in the field of over-all policy-making and to force, also under his own direction, the coördination of the activities and decisions of the Secretary of State, the Secretary of War, and the Secretary of the Navy with the activities and decisions of the Chief of Staff and the Chief of Naval Operations and vice versa. Few if any specialists in the domain of government, administration, and constitutional law knew this better than the majority and minority of the Congressional Committee on Pearl Harbor.

For some reason not yet established beyond argument, Representative Gearhart, a Republican, signed the findings, Conclusions, and Recommendations of the majority. Early in the history of the committee's inquiry, Mr. Gearhart had attacked the methods employed by the majority, charging them with attempting to block many lines of investigation; and he had demonstrated by his questioning of witnesses that he was in complete sympathy with his Republican colleagues in their determination to bring out documents and evidence which the majority were loath to see introduced. It was claimed at the time the Report was made public in July, 1946, that Mr. Gearhart, who represented a close district in the House, had been intimidated by threats of Democratic constituents to defeat him in the November election of 1946 if he joined in any adverse criticism of the great party leader, the late President Roosevelt; but Mr. Gearhart indignantly denied such allegations in public. At all events, his signature appears immediately after the names of the Democrats at the end of the Conclusions and Recommendations.

REPRESENTATIVE KEEFE'S ADDITIONAL VIEWS

ALTHOUGH some Democratic newspapers jubilantly hailed the fact that Representative Keefe, from the Republican ranks, had signed the statement agreed to by the Democratic majority, a careful comparison of Mr. Keefe's report with the majority report on the one side and the minority report on the other shows that the jubilation could not have been based on a study of Mr. Keefe's Additional Views. As far as the printed words of the three reports are concerned, it is difficult to see why Senator Barkley and his Democratic colleagues wanted Mr. Keefe to sign their document or why Mr. Keefe did not offer a separate report of his own or sign the minority report, with Additional Views. It is evident from the text of Mr. Keefe's statement that he agreed with certain of the Conclusions and Recommendations framed by the majority, especially those showing that the catastrophe at Pearl Harbor had been largely due to maladministration on the part of high Washington authorities. Indeed, the Republican minority did not dissent with this view of responsibility; on the contrary they upheld it in their report.[12] The minority, however, refused to join the majority in exculpating by name President Roosevelt, Secretary Hull, Secretary Stimson, and Secretary Knox; and they insisted that President Roosevelt, as Chief Executive and as Commander in Chief of the Army and Navy, had possessed full and ample power to cure, between 1933 and 1941, the evils of maladministration which the majority described in their report. Moreover, the minority refused to join the majority in making recommendations to overcome such administrative defects and took the position that such defects could not be cured by legislation. Indeed, the matter of recommendations seems to have been one of the leading points of difference between the majority and the minority; and on this point at least it appears from the text of his Additional Views that Mr. Keefe agreed with the majority.[13]

In fact, at the opening of his statement, Mr. Keefe said that he was "in agreement with most of these conclusions and recommendations," but his Additional Views constitute an

12. See below, pp. 358 ff.
13. In response to an inquiry, Mr. Keefe courteously informed me in a letter dated March 13, 1947, that he gave his "full support to the recommendations that were finally worked out"—by the majority.

arraignment of the Roosevelt Administration's management of affairs during the months before December 7, 1941, which is, in many ways, sharper in tone than the "Propositions" filed by the two Republican Senators, Mr. Ferguson and Mr. Brewster. Indeed, in phrasing, Mr. Keefe's statement is even more like an indictment than the essentially historical Conclusions advanced by the minority. At any rate, it was certainly based on an independent, searching, and thoughtful examination of the record before the committee and, in sum and substance, went to the roots of the most of the central issues before the committee.

In the second paragraph of his statement, Mr. Keefe gave "in a general way" his "fundamental objection" to the majority report: "I feel that facts have been marshaled, perhaps unintentionally, with the idea of conferring blame upon Hawaii and minimizing the blame that should properly be assessed at Washington." While thus genially conceding that the directing bias of the Democratic members was "perhaps" unintentional, Mr. Keefe proceeded to file a brief, supported by citations of evidence, which flatly contradicted many prime Conclusions of the majority, without challenging their Recommendations.[14]

Mr. Keefe's statement drew a picture of the Pearl Harbor "Fortress" and the matériel allotted to Commanders Short and Kimmel, which made "preparedness" there look farcical—as if the statesmen and war planners in Washington had been foolish as well as negligent.

Mr. Keefe listed vital Japanese messages, intercepted, decoded, and translated by Army and Navy Intelligence, which gave President Roosevelt and his War Cabinet definite infor-

14. Conceivably the majority had not read Mr. Keefe's report when they accepted his signature, which *ipso facto* gave them an appearance of another supporter from the Republican side; for all of his statement, except a fairly pleasant introductory paragraph, is published as an insert in the committee's Report between pages 266 and 267, as pages 266-A to 266-W, evidently after the majority's document had been paged in some form. The minority made no "recommendations" for they took the position that legislation was not needed to correct errors of judgment such as those made by the Roosevelt Administration prior to Pearl Harbor.

mation days before December 7, 1941, to the effect that a
Japanese attack on the United States was immediately imminent—information withheld from the Hawaiian commanders.

Mr. Keefe's brief scored General Marshall for several crucial errors; for example, for failure to put General Short on a
definite war alert and for failing to respond to General Short's
report on November 27, 1941, that he had alerted his forces
for sabotage only. Passages were quoted from the testimony
before the committee showing that General Marshall, after
much parrying, admitted that a "tragic mistake had been
made" in this respect and acknowledged his "responsibility"
for not setting General Short right with an order for a full
war alert.

The Additional Views contained passages from the evidence before the committee to the effect that President Roosevelt had secretly authorized more than one warlike move in
the Pacific before the Japanese attack came on December 7,
1941.

Employing documentation from records of the committee,
Mr. Keefe condemned the methods employed by the Roberts
Commission. He declared that it by-passed the secret Japanese
war warnings known to President Roosevelt and his War
Cabinet; that it "nearly buried" the truth about Pearl Harbor;
and that it provided incomplete evidence for its "indictment"
of the Hawaiian commanders.

Having paid his critical respects to the Report of the Roberts Commission and to President Roosevelt as parties to the
case, Mr. Keefe, on the basis of indisputable evidence in the
Congressional Committee's records, described the secret negotiations in Washington, directed by President Roosevelt
personally, through which Secretary Stimson, Secretary
Knox, Attorney General Biddle, and "military officials" managed the retirement of General Short and Admiral Kimmel,
and shaped the accompanying publicity for the press in such
a way as to place them before the American people as condemned men "solely responsible" for Pearl Harbor.[15]

15. See below, Chap. XIII.

Not yet finished with the War Department and the Navy Department, Mr. Keefe, again well within the limits of evidence, showed that Secretary Stimson and Secretary Forrestal in 1944 had striven to keep General Short and Admiral Kimmel under a pall of guilt after the Army and Navy boards had cleared them of derelictions of duty. In this regard, Mr. Keefe accused those departments of affecting adversely "the morale and integrity of the armed services."

Turning sharply on the Democratic majority, with whom he had nominally associated himself by signing their statement, Mr. Keefe reminded them that "we have been denied much vital information," listed some of it, and told them that the mistakes of judgment on the part of General Short and Admiral Kimmel mentioned in their Conclusions were directly related to the failures in Washington. Taking account of charges, repeated by President Truman after making public the Army and Navy boards' reports in August, 1945, that the American people and Congress were to blame for what happened at Pearl Harbor, Mr. Keefe denied the charge and cited facts and figures in support of his denial.

Near the close of his statement, Mr. Keefe dealt with what he evidently regarded as the supreme issue before the committee, and concluded that "secret diplomacy was at the root of the tragedy." The majority had asserted, in their Conclusion 6, that the President, the Secretary of State, the Secretary of War, and the Secretary of the Navy "discharged their responsibilities with distinction, ability, and foresight, and in keeping with the highest traditions of our fundamental foreign policy." Without mentioning this passage, Mr. Keefe declared that President Roosevelt had made numerous warlike commitments prior to Pearl Harbor and that Secretary Stimson had described the Administration's tactics "succinctly" when he recorded in his *Diary* that the question considered by the President and members of the War Cabinet shortly before Pearl Harbor was how to maneuver the Japanese into firing the first shot without allowing too much danger to ourselves.

"In the future," Mr. Keefe concluded, "the people and their Congress must know how close American diplomacy is moving to war so that they may check its advance if imprudent and support its position if sound. . . . To prevent any future Pearl Harbor more tragic and damaging than that of December 7, 1941, there must be constant close coordination between American public opinion and American diplomacy."

THE MINORITY REPORT

Two members of the committee, Senator Ferguson and Senator Brewster, Republicans, declared themselves unable to concur with the findings and conclusions of the majority's report because "they are illogical, and unsupported by the preponderance of the evidence before the committee. The conclusions of the diplomatic aspects are based upon incomplete evidence." Accordingly they filed a separate statement, or, report, "setting forth the conclusions which we believe are properly sustained by evidence before the Committee."

While the majority had been at great pains to indicate that the foreign policy as well as the methods pursued by President Roosevelt and Secretary Hull in the conduct of foreign affairs had been entirely correct and proper, the minority said that the question of the wisdom of the course followed by the Government of the United States in respect of diplomacy "is excluded by the terms of the Committee's instructions." They took as binding on them Senator Barkley's exposition of the first purpose of the investigation, in the Senate on September 6, 1945, as that of "fixing responsibility" for the Pearl Harbor disaster upon "an individual, or a group of individuals, or a system." With this purpose as their guide Senator Ferguson and Senator Brewster devoted their attention to this basic problem before the committee.

"Of necessity," the minority report reasoned, "as used in relation to the obligation of this committee, responsibility means responsibility for failure on the part of individual officers or groups of officers or civilian officials to do their full official duty" in preparing for meeting the Japanese attack on Pearl Harbor. As if noting that "duty" undefined is nebulous and vacuous, the minority emphasized the fact that, in the business before the committee, the word meant duty according to the Constitution, laws, and established administrative practices under which all officials and officers were bound to operate before and on the day of the Japanese attack.

After dwelling on the adverse rulings of the majority which estopped the members of the committee from getting at highly important documents and on the "incompleteness of the record," the minority turned to the main issue before the committee, as they had described it. They asked questions which they treated as going to the substance of the committee's obligations. Did the high authorities in Washington secure, before 10 o'clock A.M. (E.S.T.) December 7, 1941, information respecting Japanese designs and intentions of such a nature as to convince them beyond all reasonable doubt that war with Japan was immediately imminent? If so, did these high authorities give the Hawaiian commanders clear and definite orders to be fully alert for defense against the attack? Was Hawaii adequately equipped for defense against the attack? Did the Hawaiian commanders take appropriate measures required by their orders from Washington, their official duties, the information in their possession and the resources at hand to cope with the attack?

The minority of the committee, in providing their answers to these questions, summed up their case in the form of twenty-one Conclusions, which were first given seriatim and then repeated item by item, each accompanied by citations of supporting evidence. Their "Conclusions of Fact and Responsibility," which mainly take the form of historical statements, follow:

1. The course of diplomatic negotiations with Japan during the months preceding December 7, 1941, indicated a growing tension with Japan and after November 26 the immediate imminence of war.

2. By November 7, 1941, President Roosevelt and his Cabinet had reached the unanimous conclusion that war tension had reached such a point as to convince them that "the people would back us up in case we struck at Japan down there (in the Far

East)." They then took under consideration "what the tactics would be" (Tr., Vol. 70, p. 14415). Unless Japan yielded to diplomatic representations on the part of the United States, there were three choices on tactics before the President and the Cabinet; they could wait until Japan attacked; they could strike without a declaration of war by Congress; or the President could lay the issue of peace or war before Congress (Tr., Vol. 70, p. 14415 ff.).

3. So imminent was war on November 25, that the President in a conference with Secretary Hull, Secretary Knox, Secretary Stimson, General Marshall, and Admiral Stark, "brought up the event that we were likely to be attacked perhaps (as soon as) next Monday" (December 1); and the members of the conference discussed the question "How we should maneuver them (the Japanese) into the position of firing the first shot without allowing too much danger to ourselves" (Tr., Vol. 70, p. 14418).

4. Having considered without agreeing upon the proposition that a message on the war situation should be sent to Congress, the President and the Secretary of State, the Secretary of War, and the Secretary of the Navy, pursued from November 25 to December 7 the tactics of waiting for the firing of "the first shot" by the Japanese.

5. The appropriate high authorities in Washington had the organization for working in such close cooperation during the days immediately prior to the Japanese attack on December 7 that they had every opportunity to make sure that identical and precise instructions warranted by the imminence of war went to the Hawaiian commanders.

6. Through the Army and Navy Intelligence Services extensive information was secured respecting Japanese war plans and designs, by intercepted and decoded Japanese secret messages, which indicated the growing danger of war and increasingly after November 26 the imminence of a Japanese attack.

7. Army and Navy information which indicated growing imminence of war was delivered to the highest authorities in charge of national preparedness for meeting an attack, among others, the President, the Secretaries of State, War, and Navy, and the Chief of Staff and the Chief of Naval Operations.

8. Judging by the military and naval history of Japan, high authorities in Washington and the Commanders in Hawaii had good grounds for expecting that in starting war the Japa-

nese Government would make a surprise attack on the United States.

9. Neither the diplomatic negotiations nor the intercepts and other information respecting Japanese designs and operations in the hands of the United States authorities warranted those authorities in excluding from defense measures or from orders to the Hawaiian commanders the probability of an attack on Hawaii. On the contrary, there is evidence to the effect that such an attack was, in terms of strategy, necessary from the Japanese point of view and in fact highly probable, and that President Roosevelt was taking the probability into account—before December 7.

10. The knowledge of Japanese designs and intentions in the hands of the President and the Secretary of State led them to the conclusion at least 10 days before December 7 that an attack by Japan within a few days was so highly probable as to constitute a certainty and, having reached this conclusion, the President, as Commander in Chief of the Army and Navy, was under obligation to instruct the Secretary of War and the Secretary of the Navy to make sure that the outpost commanders put their armed forces on an all-out alert for war.

11. The decision of the President, in view of the Constitution, to await the Japanese attack rather than ask for a declaration of war by Congress increased the responsibility of high authorities in Washington to use the utmost care in putting the commanders at Pearl Harbor on a full alert for defensive actions before the Japanese attack on December 7, 1941.

12. Inasmuch as the knowledge respecting Japanese designs and operations which was in the possession of high authorities in Washington differed in nature and volume from that in the possession of the Pearl Harbor commanders it was especially incumbent upon the former to formulate instructions to the latter in language not open to misinterpretation as to the obligations imposed on the commanders by the instructions.

13. The messages sent to General Short and Admiral Kimmel by high authorities in Washington during November were couched in such conflicting and imprecise language that they failed to convey to the commanders definite information on the state of diplomatic relations with Japan and on Japanese war designs and positive orders respecting the particular actions to be taken—orders that were beyond all reasonable doubts as to the need for

an all-out alert. In this regard the said high authorities failed to discharge their full duty.

14. High authorities in Washington failed in giving proper weight to the evidence before them respecting Japanese designs and operations which indicated that an attack on Pearl Harbor was highly probable and they failed also to emphasize this probability in messages to the Hawaiian commanders.

15. The failure of Washington authorities to act promptly and consistently in translating intercepts, evaluating information, and sending appropriate instructions to the Hawaiian commanders was in considerable measure due to delays, mismanagement, noncooperation, unpreparedness, confusion, and negligence on the part of officers in Washington.

16. The President of the United States was responsible for the failure to enforce continuous, efficient, and appropriate cooperation among the Secretary of War, the Secretary of the Navy, the Chief of Staff, and the Chief of Naval Operations, in evaluating information and dispatching clear and positive orders to the Hawaiian commanders as events indicated the growing imminence of war; for the Constitution and laws of the United States vested in the President full power, as Chief Executive and Commander in Chief, to compel such cooperation and vested this power in him alone with a view to establishing his responsibility to the people of the United States.

17. High authorities in Washington failed to allocate to the Hawaiian commanders the material which the latter often declared to be necessary to defense and often requested, and no requirements of defense or war in the Atlantic did or could excuse these authorities for their failures in this respect.

18. Whatever errors of judgment the commanders at Hawaii committed and whatever mismanagement they displayed in preparing for a Japanese attack, attention to chain of responsibility in the civil and military administration requires taking note of the fact that they were designated for their posts by high authorities in Washington—all of whom were under obligation to have a care for competence in the selection of subordinates for particular positions of responsibility in the armed forces of the United States.

19. The defense of Hawaii rested upon two sets of interdependent responsibilities: (1) The responsibility in Washington in respect of its intimate knowledge of diplomatic negotiations, wide-

spread intelligence information, direction of affairs and constitutional duty to plan the defense of the United States; (2) the responsibility cast upon the commanders in the field in charge of a major naval base and the fleet essential to the defense of the territory of the United States to do those things appropriate to the defense of the fleet and outpost. Washington authorities failed in (1); and the commanding officers at Hawaii failed in (2).

20. In the final instance of crucial significance for alerting American outpost commanders, on Saturday night, December 6, and Sunday morning, December 7, the President of the United States failed to take that quick and instant executive action which was required by the occasion and by the responsibility for watchfulness and guardianship rightly associated in law and practice with his high office from the establishment of the Republic to our own times.

21. The contention coming from so high an authority as President Truman on August 30, 1945, that the "country is as much to blame as any individual in this final situation that developed in Pearl Harbor," cannot be sustained because the American people had no intimation whatever of the policies and operations that were being undertaken.

In the first group of Conclusions, the minority dealt with a leading issue relative to the over-all question of responsibility for Pearl Harbor: Were high officials in Washington (President Roosevelt, Secretary Hull, Secretary Stimson, and Secretary Knox) so lacking in knowledge of Japanese war intentions that they were truly surprised by the Japanese attack and could properly be excused for sending no unequivocal orders to the Hawaiian commanders, General Short and Admiral Kimmel putting them on full war-alert for defense against an immediate attack? In other words, did President Roosevelt correctly describe the situation in his war message of December 8, 1941, when he stated that the United States was at peace with Japan on December 7, 1941, and was conducting negotiations with the Japanese Government looking toward the maintenance of peace in the Pacific, and that the Japanese note of December 7, 1941, "contained no threat or hint of war or armed attack"? Or did these high officials have secret information of Japanese designs and actually believe that war with Japan was imminent? The minority cited, from the testimony and documents before the committee, evidence bearing on this over-all question. Of the minority's factual citations, the following are illustrative:

On October 8, 1940, President Roosevelt said to Admiral J. O. Richardson, then in charge of the fleet at the Hawaiian base, that "sooner or later they [the Japanese] would make a mistake and we would enter the war." At the Atlantic Conference in August, 1941, President Roosevelt expressed the belief that, by adopting the course there agreed upon with Prime Minister Churchill, further moves of aggression on the part of the Japanese "which might result in war could be held off for at least thirty days." "So imminent was war on November 25," the minority said, quoting from Secretary Stimson's *Diary*, "that the President, in a conference with Secretary Hull, Secretary Knox, Secretary Stimson, General Marshall and Admiral Stark 'brought up the event that we were likely to be attacked perhaps (as soon as) next Monday [December 1]'; and members of the conference then discussed the question, 'How we should maneuver them [the Japanese] into the position of firing the first shot without allowing too much danger to ourselves.' " Through intercepts of messages passing between the Japanese Government and its agents in various parts of the world, President Roosevelt and his high officials had in their possession before December 7 secret information with regard to Japanese intentions which showed them that war was only days or even hours ahead; and about ten o'clock, December 6, in the evening before the Japanese attack, President Roosevelt declared to Harry Hopkins, in the presence of the officer who brought him the first thirteen parts of the intercepted Japanese message to be delivered to Secretary Hull the next day, December 7: "This means war."

In short, the minority cited and quoted passages from the evidence before the committee to support the conclusion that President Roosevelt and his high officials, days and hours before Pearl Harbor, knew that war was at hand—immediately at hand.

Did President Roosevelt and his high officials know that the attack was to be on Pearl Harbor, as they were engaged in maneuvering the Japanese into firing the first shot? The minority could not cite direct evidence to that effect. But they argued that every rule of sound sea war strategy should have warned the President and his officials that the Japanese would not dare to move far southward toward the East Indies, while leaving the powerful American fleet poised at Hawaii to strike them on their left flank and life lines.[16] Moreover, in pursuing this argument, the minority cited intercepts of Japanese secret messages which demonstrated that Japanese agents in Hawaii had been sending to Tokyo precise information on the disposition of American ships and other armed forces in the Hawaiian area—intercepts which indicated that the Japanese Government knew more about the state of American preparedness at Pearl Harbor on December 6 than President Roosevelt and his officials in Washington knew. Hence, the minority reasoned, if Washington authorities did not adequately prepare for an attack on Pearl Harbor they were lacking in the discernment and prudence to be expected of men occupying such responsible posts of trust in the Government of the United States.

Possessing voluminous knowledge of Japanese war designs and intentions and expecting war daily and finally hourly, did the high authorities in Washington definitely put the Hawaiian commanders on an all-out alert for war? In Conclusion 13, the minority, still citing evidence from the records before the committee to support it, stated: "The messages sent to General Short and Admiral Kimmel by high authorities in Washington during November were couched in such conflicting and imprecise language that they failed to convey to the commanders definite information on the state of diplomatic relations with Japan and on Japanese war de-

16. For Mr. Churchill's view, see above, p. 242.

signs and positive orders respecting the particular actions to be taken [at Pearl Harbor]—orders that were beyond all reasonable doubts as to the need for an all-out alert. In this respect the said high authorities failed to discharge their full duty." Furthermore, the minority maintained, there was no excuse for the failure of General Marshall and Admiral Stark themselves to be on the alert early Sunday morning, December 7, and to reach General Short and Admiral Kimmel by the swiftest possible means with a final warning message, based on the latest information and designed to put the commanders on special guard against an immediate attack.

What about the allocation to General Short and Admiral Kimmel of the war matériel which they had more than once demanded from the War Department and the Navy Department as necessary for reconnaissance and defense? The minority dwelt at length on the evidence as to deficiencies in the allotments of matériel to the commanders and concluded: "The fatal error of Washington authorities in this matter was to undertake a world campaign and world responsibilities without first making provision for the security of the United States, which was their prime constitutional obligation."

The minority heartily agreed with the statements of the majority to the effect that proceedings in Washington as well as in Hawaii prior to Pearl Harbor were marked by confusion, conflicts, lack of coöperation, and general mismanagement.[17] They went further, however, and dealt with the responsibility for that state of affairs as having a necessary relation to the lack of alertness and preparedness on the part of the Hawaiian commanders. Who had the legal power, and hence the duty, to correct such maladministration in Washington and Hawaii prior to the Japanese attack? The minority turned to the Constitution and laws of the United States for their answer; they pointed out that the Constitution vested the Executive power in the President of the United States and that acts of Congress empowered the President to issue orders directly to the Secretary of War and to the Secretary of the Navy and

17. See above, pp. 242 ff.

also directly to the Chief of Staff and the Chief of Naval Operations.

The minority called attention to additional facts. Under the Constitution, President Roosevelt was Commander in Chief of the armed forces of the United States. Secretary Hull, Secretary Stimson, and Secretary Knox were President Roosevelt's own appointees, subject to his orders. President Roosevelt had appointed, with the consent of the Senate, the Chief of Staff and the Chief of Naval Operations, General Marshall and Admiral Stark. He had assigned General Short and Admiral Kimmel to their posts of duty in Hawaii. "The President of the United States," the minority held, "was responsible for the failure to enforce continuous, efficient, and appropriate cooperation" among his high officials, "in evaluating information and dispatching clear and positive orders to the Hawaiian commanders as events indicated the growing imminence of war. . . ."

Besides placing on President Roosevelt the responsibility for the mismanagement that contributed so materially to the disaster at Hawaii, the minority made the President personally responsible for the failure to take the quick and instant action for alerting the Hawaiian commanders in the final hours before Pearl Harbor. They referred to testimony about his statement on Saturday evening, on receipt of the intercepted thirteen parts of the Japanese message to be handed to Secretary Hull the next day, as proof of his knowledge that "this means war." They cited information about Japanese designs that came to him on Sunday morning at least two hours before the Japanese attack. Thus forewarned, they claimed, it was then the President's bounden duty to put his own war Administration in Washington on war alert and, through his agents in that Administration, also to put all the American outpost commanders on full war alert. Owing to the fact that General Marshall and Admiral Stark could remember nothing about their actions on the evening and night of December 6, however, Senator Ferguson and Senator Brewster were unable to discover just what President Roosevelt then tried to do in the way of alerting outpost commanders; but they cited evidence to show that he did not force the immediate dispatch of new messages to the outpost commanders in the final hours before the Japanese attack.

Having presented this line of historical statements and inferences, with citations from the committee's record, the minority declared: "We find the evidence supports the following final and ultimate conclusion:

The failure of Pearl Harbor to be fully alerted and prepared for defense rested upon the proper discharge of two sets of *interdependent* responsibilities: (1) the responsibilities of high authorities in Washington; and (2) the responsibilities of the commanders in the field in charge of the fleet and of the naval base. (See Conclusion No. 19.)

The evidence clearly shows that these two areas of responsibilities were inseparably essential to each other in the defense of Hawaii. The commanders in the field could not have prepared or been ready successfully to meet hostile attack at Hawaii without indispensable information, matériel, trained manpower and clear orders from Washington. Washington could not be certain that Hawaii was in readiness without the alert and active cooperation of the commanders on the spot.

The failure to perform the responsibilities indispensably essential to the defense of Pearl Harbor rests upon the following civil and military authorities:

> FRANKLIN D. ROOSEVELT—President of the United States and Commander in Chief of the Army and Navy.
> HENRY L. STIMSON—Secretary of War.
> FRANK KNOX—Secretary of the Navy.
> GEORGE C. MARSHALL—General, Chief of Staff of the Army.
> HAROLD R. STARK—Admiral, Chief of Naval Operations.
> LEONARD T. GEROW—Major General, Assistant Chief of Staff of War Plans Division.

The failure to perform the responsibilities in Hawaii rests upon the military commanders:

> WALTER C. SHORT—Major General, Commanding General, Hawaiian Department.

HUSBAND E. KIMMEL—Rear Admiral, Commander in Chief of the Pacific Fleet.

Both in Washington and in Hawaii there were numerous and serious failures of men in the lower civil and military echelons to perform their duties and discharge their responsibilities. These are too numerous to be treated in detail and individually named.

Secretary of State, CORDELL HULL, who was at the center of Japanese-American negotiations bears a grave responsibility for the diplomatic conditions leading up to the eventuality of Pearl Harbor but he had no duties as a relevant link in the military chain of responsibility stemming from the Commander in Chief to the commanders at Hawaii for the defense at Pearl Harbor. For this reason and because the diplomatic phase was not completely explored we offer no conclusions in his case.

In respect of most Conclusions presented by the minority, there was no conflict with the Additional Views of Representative Keefe, whose name was appended to the majority's Conclusions and Recommendations. That Senator Ferguson and Senator Brewster had some or all of Mr. Keefe's document before them as they wrote their report is suggested by the fact that inserted in their statement (p. 571) is a whole paragraph from Mr. Keefe's Additional Views, without quotation marks. What then were the grounds of disagreement between Mr. Keefe and the minority? In the absence of inside information, only conjectures are possible but an examination of the texts of the two documents side by side shows disagreement on only a few crucial points in the two statements.

DIFFERENCES WITHIN THE COMMITTEE OVER THE CHARGES AGAINST THE HAWAIIAN COMMANDERS

AMONG the Conclusions reached by Senator Barkley and his colleagues of the majority was this summation: "the errors made by the Hawaiian commands were errors of judgment and not derelictions of duty." This was certainly among the Conclusions of the majority to which Mr. Keefe subscribed; and it must have been a disappointment to loyal defenders of

President Roosevelt's Administration. President Roosevelt had appointed the members of the Roberts Commission which charged General Short and Admiral Kimmel with derelictions of duty and errors which were, they said, the "effective causes" of the disaster; he had accepted the Roberts Report; and he had been the director of the arrangements which forced General Short and Admiral Kimmel into retirement, accompanied by carefully formulated publicity, as culprits awaiting trial by courts-martial—perhaps.[18] Furthermore Justice Roberts, at a committee hearing in 1946, admitted that he had been uninformed about vital matters, when his report was prepared; he treated his own ignorance with an unbecoming levity; and he was forced by Senator Brewster to concede that the Roberts Report was incorrect with regard to a crucial point.

Senator Brewster and Senator Ferguson knew these things for they had taken an active part in the hearings at which the facts were developed. Mr. Keefe knew about them and he evidently looked upon the actions of President Roosevelt and his high officials associated with him in the public indictment of General Short and Admiral Kimmel as nothing less than shameful.[19]

Nevertheless, although they criticized the Roberts Report and put an over-all responsibility on President Roosevelt, the Republican minority report left General Short and Admiral Kimmel under the stigma put upon them by the Roberts Report and the subsequent action of President Roosevelt. After placing primary responsibility for Pearl Harbor upon the President and his high officials, the minority flatly declared that "the commanders in the field were left with sufficient responsibility which they were under obligation to discharge as field commanders of the major outpost in the Pacific defense of the United States. There is adequate and sufficient evidence to show that they failed to discharge that responsibility."

In this statement the minority asserted in effect that Gen-

18. See above, pp. 221 ff., and below, Chap. XIII.
19. See above, p. 348.

eral Short and Admiral Kimmel had *sufficient responsibility as commanders of the Hawaiian outpost*—apparently to be prepared for and to beat off the Japanese attack. If not that, then what responsibility? Having made this assertion and listed failures on the part of the two commanders, the minority treated the failures in Washington as providing "extenuating circumstances" for the failures of the two commanders in Hawaii. Thus after distinctly emphasizing the failures of General Short and Admiral Kimmel, the minority characterized the failures of Washington as if merely diminishing or attenuating the responsibilities of the commanders in Hawaii.

With regard to the primary point at issue in respect of responsibility for the success attained by the Japanese attack at Pearl Harbor, therefore, the Report of the Congressional Committee, considered as a whole, presented a sharp contradiction. Were General Short and Admiral Kimmel guilty of derelictions of duty and were their errors "the effective causes" of the catastrophe which befell American forces on December 7, 1941? The majority, composed of the six Democrats and two Republicans, Representative Gearhart and Representative Keefe, specifically agreed that the errors of the two commanders *were not derelictions of duty*. Thus they repudiated the charge of the President's Commission on Pearl Harbor and passed over any contradiction that appeared between such a clearing of the commanders and the complete vindication of their highest superiors in Washington by name.

On the other hand, the minority not only let stand unchallenged the grave charges filed against the two commanders by the President's Commission and the Administration in January and February, 1942, but they contended that the two commanders "nevertheless" had "sufficient responsibility"—presumably "sufficient" to some end, namely, to be fully alert and meet the Japanese attacks successfully; in which case there might have been no catastrophe to American arms for the committee to investigate.

Moreover, while the majority of the committee took great pains in their attempt to give a plausible explanation of the mistreatment accorded to General Short and Admiral Kimmel and the anguish of spirit they suffered under the indictment that had been lodged against them by the Roberts Commission and the Roosevelt Administration in January and February, 1942,[20] the minority passed over this subject without pronouncing judgment. As far as the conclusions of Senator Ferguson and Senator Brewster are concerned, General Short and Admiral Kimmel are still guilty of derelictions of duty and errors which were called by the President's Commission "the effective causes" of the disaster at Pearl Harbor.[21] On the other hand, by the verdict of the Democratic majority, supported by the two Republican Representatives, the two commanders were cleared of the grave charges which had kept them standing before the country for years as culprits awaiting actions by courts-martial.

WAS THE JAPANESE ATTACK A SURPRISE TO THE HIGH AUTHORITIES IN WASHINGTON? [22]

AT A meeting of his War Cabinet at noon, November 25, 1941, President Roosevelt "brought up the event that we were likely to be attacked perhaps (as soon as) next Monday [December 1], for the Japanese are notorious for making an attack without warning." [23] Was the Japanese attack on the

20. See below, Chap. XIII, pp. 383 ff.

21. Persons unacquainted with history and the meaning of "dereliction of duty" and other terms employed in the Roberts Report and Executive statements respecting the "guilt" of the commanders may be inclined to regard the above discussion as quibbling over words, but others interested in efforts to get the truth of the business will note with advantage that the Judge Advocate General of the War Department, learned in the law of the case, on January 27, 1941, informed the Chief of Staff, for the benefit of Secretary Stimson, that "the offenses charged against General Short are offenses of omission or nonfeasance which require a much stronger showing to justify a trial than those involving misfeasance or malfeasance." Testimony, Part 7, p. 3145. The Judge Advocate General thought that General Short had been finished off on account of "the lack of confidence which the public now has in him" (as a result of the kind of publicity given to his case by the Roosevelt Administration), and he warned the Administration against promising trial by court-martial in General Short's case. See below, Chap. XIII. President Roosevelt's secretary, Stephen Early, in giving out the Roberts Report had indicated that the charge of dereliction of duty warranted trial by court-martial. See above, p. 221.

22. See above, Chap. VIII.

23. See below, pp. 517 ff.

United States Sunday, December 7, 1941, a surprise to these high authorities in Washington? Or to state the question in another way, did these authorities have substantial grounds for expecting that the Japanese would attack the United States (including Pearl Harbor), on or about Sunday, December 7?

This question in some form was regarded as crucial to the determination of responsibility for the Pearl Harbor disaster by the men in charge of the various inquiries into that subject. For instance, the Roberts Commission touched upon it in its Report to the President, January 23, 1942; the Army Pearl Harbor Board probed for an answer to it; and the Congressional Committee on Pearl Harbor gave extended consideration to it. Hundreds of pages of testimony and documents bear directly upon this issue of the expectations of Washington authorities as to the time and place of the Japanese attack which they believed to be imminent.

After a review of evidence bearing on expectations of and preparations to meet a Japanese air attack at Hawaii, the Army Pearl Harbor Board stated:

In view of the foregoing, the estimate of the situation showed that an all-out attack by air was the judgment of the best military and naval minds in Hawaii. Under established military doctrine, that called for preparation for this worst eventuality.[24] . . . We must therefore conclude that the responsible authorities, the Secretary of the Navy and the Chief of Staff in Washington, down to the Generals and Admirals in Hawaii, *all expected an air attack before Pearl Harbor* [the board's italics]. As a general statement, when testifying after the Pearl Harbor attack, they did not expect it. Apparently the only person who was not surprised was the Secretary of War, Mr. Stimson, who testified: "Well, I was not surprised." [25]

The Congressional Committee on Pearl Harbor, in command of the materials provided by previous inquiries, went into the problem of expectations in Washington with regard

24. The Army board also dealt with the failure of Washington to meet the calls of the Hawaiian commanders for matériel to cope with the eventuality of a Japanese air attack.
25. CJC. Part 39, pp. 76 f.

to the Japanese attack, in general and in particular, on Pearl Harbor about one o'clock, December 7, 1941 (Washington time); and it added hundreds of pages of testimony and documents to the already voluminous record relative to the subject. The Democratic majority of the committee reviewed this evidence and set forth their Conclusions in their report, which was signed by the Republican Representatives, Mr. Gearhart and Mr. Keefe—the latter with Additional Views.

In dealing with the question of expectations as to the time of the Japanese attack, the majority laid stress on the so-called "one o'clock" Japanese message which specified the time for the delivery of the Japanese reply to Secretary Hull's memorandum of November 26. This message was intercepted by a Navy monitoring station at 4.37 A.M., December 7; it was available in the Navy Department about 7 A.M.; it was sent to the War Department for translation because there was no translator on duty in the Navy Department at the time; copies of the translation were at the Navy Department about 9 A.M.; a copy came into the hands of General Marshall some time between 11.15 and 11.30 when he arrived at his office late, owing to a delay in finding him. The message from Tokyo instructed the Japanese Ambassador in Washington to deliver the reply to the United States "at 1:00 P.M. on the 7th, your time."

Respecting the delivery of this one o'clock message to other Washington authorities, the majority said:

Captain Kramer testified that upon his return to the. Navy Department at 10:20 A.M. he found the "one o'clock" message and thereafter, between 10:30 and 10:35 delivered it to the office of the Chief of Naval Operations, where a meeting was in progress. Delivery was then made within approximately 10 minutes to an aide to Secretary Hull at the State Department and thereafter within roughly another 10 minutes, to a Presidential aide at the White House. In the course of delivery to the office of the Chief of Naval Operations and to Secretary Hull's aide mention was made of the fact that 1 P.M., Washington time, was about dawn at Honolulu and about the middle of the night in the Far East. *No mention was made that the time indicated an attack at Pearl Harbor* [majority's italics].[26]

Speaking of another message intercepted about the same time as the one o'clock message, namely, instructions ordering the Japanese Embassy in Washington to destroy its remaining code machine, the majority of the Congressional Committee said that the code message added little to what was already known. On the other hand, with regard to the one o'clock message, the majority stated: "We believe, however, that the 'one o'clock' intercept should have been recognized [in Washington] as indicating the distinct possibility that some Japanese military action would occur somewhere at 1 P.M., December 7, Washington time. If properly appreciated, this intercept should have suggested a dispatch to *all* Pacific outpost commanders supplying this information, as General Marshall attempted to do immediately upon seeing it." [27]

The majority further stated: "He [General Marshall] testified that he and the officers present in his office were certain the hour fixed in the 'one o'clock' message had 'some definite significance'; that 'something was going to happen at 1 o'clock'; that 'when they specified a day, that of course had significance, but not comparable to an hour'; and, again, that it was 'a new item of information of a peculiar character.' " [28]

In other words, in the opinion of the majority, the one o'clock message (which, but for inexcusable delays in the Navy and War Departments, should have been available to all the responsible high authorities in Washington by 8 A.M. on December 7, 1941, and was made available to most of them before 11 A.M.) should have been recognized as indicating the distinct possibility of a Japanese attack on the United States somewhere about 1 P.M. Also, in the opinion of the majority, this message, properly appreciated (as it was by some officers, including General Marshall) should have sug-

26. CJC, *Report*, p. 223.
27. *Ibid.*, p. 228.
28. *Ibid.*, pp. 223 f.

gested a new warning dispatch to all Pacific outpost commanders.

With regard to other Japanese messages intercepted which showed that the Japanese spies in Hawaii had reported meticulously to Tokyo on American ship berthing and movements, on military and naval installations and preparations, the majority of the Congressional Committee were positive in their conclusion. They declared:

We are of the opinion, however, that the berthing plan and related dispatches [on American preparedness in Hawaii] should have received careful consideration [in Washington] and created a serious question as to their significance. Since they indicated a particular interest in the Pacific Fleet's base this intelligence should have been appreciated and supplied the commander in chief of the Pacific Fleet and the commanding general of the Hawaiian Department for their assistance, along with other information and intelligence available to them, in making their estimate of the situation.[29]

In other words, the majority, to this extent, indicted Washington authorities for failure to appreciate in advance the danger of an attack by the Japanese about one o'clock, Sunday, December 7, 1941, on Pearl Harbor, as well as on other American outposts.

Yet the majority also declared: "The evidence reflects that virtually everyone in Washington was surprised Japan struck Pearl Harbor at the time she did. Among the reasons for this conclusion was the apparent Japanese purpose to move toward the south—the Philippines, Thailand, the Kra Peninsula; and the feeling that Hawaii was a near-impregnable fortress that Japan would not incur the dangers of attacking." [30]

29. *Ibid.*, p. 233. For documents relative to American thinking and planning for the defense of Hawaii against a possible Japanese attack before December 7, 1941, and reports of Japanese spies on American preparedness and unpreparedness at Hawaii, see CJC, Part 12, Exhibits 2, 3, Part 13, Exhibits 8, 8-A, 8-B, 8-C, 8-D, Part 14, Exhibits 10, 14, 15, 32, 35, Part 15, Exhibits 44, 55, 56, 57, 59, 60, 63, 64, 69, 84, Part 16, Exhibit 89, Part 17, Exhibits 117, 117-A, 118, 120, 122, Part 18, Exhibits 129, 130, 138, 141, 154.

30. CJC, *Report*, p. 234. As to the "near-impregnable fortress" the Congressional Committee had before it a mass of evidence showing that the Washington

In his Additional Views, which followed his signature at the bottom of the majority Report, Mr. Keefe said:

It [the majority report] correctly states that both Washington and Hawaii were surprised by the attack upon Pearl Harbor. It is apparently agreed that both Washington and Hawaii expected the initial attack to come in the Asiatic area. . . . Despite the elaborate and labored arguments in the [majority] report and despite the statements of high ranking military and naval officers to the contrary, I must conclude that the intercepted messages received and distributed in Washington on the afternoon and evening of December 6 and the early hours of December 7, pointed to an attack on Pearl Harbor.

This statement Mr. Keefe then followed by citations from these messages and an extended criticism of Admiral Stark and General Marshall for failing to act upon this information promptly and give proper instructions to General Short and Admiral Kimmel in Hawaii.[31]

In their report, the Republican minority, Senator Ferguson and Senator Brewster, took the position that in terms of sea-power strategy an attack on the American Fleet at Pearl Harbor was necessary from the Japanese point of view, was in fact highly probable, and "President Roosevelt was taking the probability into account—before December 7." The minority dealt extensively with the intercepts of Japanese messages relative to espionage in Hawaii and with Japanese secret reports, both meticulous and numerous, on American military and naval installations and preparedness. Respecting opinions in Washington about Pearl Harbor as a point of at-

---

authorities had again and again been informed about the vulnerability of the Pacific Fleet at Pearl Harbor, the shortage of war matériel there from long-range reconnaissance planes to antiaircraft guns. Whatever the American public knew about the "fortress," Washington authorities had long been warned by Army and Navy men that the "fortress" was not equipped to maintain the continuous long-distance reconnaissance necessary to detect the approach of Japanese carrier-ships and smash the Japanese attack at its inception in the Pacific Ocean. Nor did the majority of the committee give a comprehensive judgment on the evidence as to expectations in Washington *before* December 7, 1941, as distinguished from the "surprise" in Washington *after* the Japanese attack had fallen with such disastrous effect.

31. *Ibid.*, pp. 266-A, 266-F.

tack, the minority said: "None of the Army and Navy witnesses before the committee admitted they had neglected the possibility—or the probability—of a Japanese attack on Pearl Harbor during the period prior to December 7. On the contrary, they testified that they had consistently reckoned with the possibility, even when they minimized the probability. (Tr., for example, Vol. 12, p. 2111, Vol. 13, pp. 2162, 2167, 2172, 2173, Vol. 14, p. 2341.)" [32]

The statements of the Democratic majority and the Republican minority in respect of expectations of a Japanese attack on Pearl Harbor deserve special consideration in the light of the evidence furnished by the committee's record.

The majority said: "The evidence reflects that virtually everyone in Washington was surprised Japan struck Pearl Harbor at the time she did."

The minority said: "None of the Army and Navy witnesses before the committee admitted they had neglected the possibility—or the probability—of a Japanese attack on Pearl Harbor during the period prior to December 7. On the contrary they testified that they had consistently reckoned with the possibility, even when they minimized the probability."

It is obvious that the majority's statement is vague. "The evidence *reflects that virtually everyone* in Washington was surprised. . . ." (Italics supplied.) The "virtually" allows for exceptions, indeed, indicates that there were exceptions. Secretary Stimson had told the Army Pearl Harbor Board that he was not surprised. Were General Marshall, Admiral Stark, President Roosevelt, Secretary Hull, and Secretary Knox surprised and if so why in view of all the secret information which they had with regard to Japanese war intentions?

The real function of the Congressional Committee was to inquire into responsibility for the American catastrophe and that inquiry involved, not only the commanders in Hawaii, but also their superiors in Washington. It did not involve "virtually everyone in Washington"; and if it did how and by what method did the majority discover what virtually

32. *Ibid.*, p. 523.

everyone in Washington thought about the matter before December 7, 1941? [33] Granting the truth of the majority's contention about the opinion of virtually everyone in Washington, which is evasive, uninformative, and irrelevant, and coming down to cases, the evidence bearing on what a few high authorities in Washington actually knew about Japanese war intentions before December 7, 1941, 1 P.M. Washington time was the evidence material to the committee's duty and obligation under the statute creating it; and this evidence, if reviewed by the majority, was not cited by the majority to support the conclusion on "virtually everyone."

In contrast to the allegation of the majority, the statement of the minority was definite and conveyed information that was correct.

The problem of expectations in Washington was embarrassing to Army and Navy officers—and it must be remembered that none of their civilian superiors was subjected to free examination before the Congressional Committee.[34] Early in its sessions and during the course of its hearings, the Congressional Committee spread on the public record documents and testimony showing: (1) Army and Navy plans for the defense of Hawaii, including expectations of a Japanese air attack and preparations of some kind to meet it; (2) Exhibit 1, pp. 1–253, selected Japanese secret diplomatic messages and Exhibit 2, secret Japanese messages on American military installations, ship movements, and kindred matters; and (3) miscellaneous papers respecting war designs and plans—Japanese and American. These papers in the hands of the Congressional Committee posed for Army and Navy officers a dilemma.

The papers showed conclusively that Army and Navy officers had, for years prior to December 7, 1941, and especially

---

33. It is to be noted that the majority's statement on this point applies only to the attack on Pearl Harbor, not the attack in general. In view of the evidence in the record and many specific statements in their report the majority knew that the highest authorities in Washington were aware of the immediate imminence of war. See above, pp. 365 ff.

34. See above, pp. 334 ff.

during the preceding months, consistently taken into their calculations the possibility and probability of a Japanese attack in general and specifically on Hawaii. Indeed, if they had not done exactly this, they would have been guilty of a dereliction of duty far more serious than the dereliction charged against General Short and Admiral Kimmel by the President's Commission on Pearl Harbor in 1942.

On the other hand, if the Army and Navy officers had admitted to the Congressional Committee that they had fully expected a Japanese attack and prepared for it, they would have incriminated themselves for failure to furnish to General Short and Admiral Kimmel not only more specific war warning orders for a high-tension alert but also additional information on the known approaching breach in relations with Japan. In fact the Democratic majority, in their report, criticized the Washington officers for failing to inform the Hawaiian commanders about the concentration of Japanese spying on Hawaiian installations and preparedness and about the significance of the fateful one o'clock message, indicating the probability of an attack on the morning of December 7 (Honolulu time).[35]

In this painful dilemma, Army and Navy officers did just what the Republican minority said they did: "They testified that they had consistently reckoned with the possibility [of a Japanese attack on Pearl Harbor], even when they minimized the probability."

With regard to the Japanese attack in general, high Army and Navy officers were in possession of the Japanese secret messages and other information which indicated the immediate imminence of war. General Marshall and Admiral Stark, as members of the War Cabinet, also knew that their immediate superiors were expecting a Japanese attack for many days before it came. They could not have been surprised when the attack came.[36]

What were the expectations of the high authorities superior

35. See above, pp. 366 ff.
36. See below, pp. 517 ff.

to the Army and Navy officers who appeared before the Congressional Committee?

Secretary Stimson testified before the Army Pearl Harbor Board that he was not surprised by the Japanese attack—on Pearl Harbor.[37]

Secretary Hull told Secretary Stimson and Secretary Knox as early as November 27 that relations with Japan were at an end and that the matter was in the hands of the Army and the Navy.[38] Secretary Knox received intercepts of secret Japanese messages which revealed to him the war designs of the Japanese Government.[39] He was a member of the War Cabinet and present on November 25, 1941, when the problem of maneuvering the Japanese into firing the first shot was discussed.[40]

Indeed according to evidence from his own hand Secretary Knox was not surprised himself. Rather he was surprised that authorities in Washington were surprised. In his secret report to President Roosevelt after his return from a visit to Hawaii in December, 1941, shortly after the Japanese attack, Secretary Knox stated: *"Neither Short nor Kimmel,* at the time of the attack, had any knowledge of *the plain intimations* of some surprise move, *made clear in Washington,* through the interception of Japanese instructions to Nomura, in which a surprise move of some kind was clearly indicated by the insistence upon the precise time of Nomura's reply to Hull, at one o'clock on Sunday." [41]

As this one o'clock message had been made available to all the high authorities in Washington before eleven o'clock on December 7, including President Roosevelt,[42] Secretary Knox was plainly saying to the President in his report that none of these authorities should have been surprised by the Japanese attack—even on Pearl Harbor. The majority of the Con-

37. See above, p. 365.
38. See above, p. 247.
39. See below, p. 388.
40. See above, p. 364.
41. CJC, Part 5, p. 2338. (Italics supplied.)
42. See above, p. 366.

gressional Committee said as much and this was also a point on which the minority agreed.[43]

President Roosevelt, as Chief Executive and Commander in Chief of the Army and Navy, had received intercepted and translated messages showing Japanese war designs and, besides, had hundreds of secret documents in his personal files (not yet, 1947, opened to the public). It was his official duty to scrutinize and master all the information bearing on the possibility and probability of a Japanese attack; for, as Secretary Stimson has cogently said: The President

must constantly watch, study, and estimate where the principal or most dangerous attack is most likely to come, in order that he may most effectively distribute his insufficient forces and munitions to meet it. . . . For all these reasons he is compelled to give constant and close attention to the reports from all his intelligence agencies in order that he may satisfactorily solve the innumerable problems which are constantly arising in the performance of the foregoing duties.[44]

President Roosevelt expressed to the members of his War Cabinet, many days before December 7, 1941, his conviction that war with Japan was immediately imminent and he was expecting a Japanese attack upon the United States.[45] Therefore, President Roosevelt was not surprised by the Japanese attack when it came on December 7.[46]

43. See above, pp. 354 ff.

44. Statement to the Congressional Committee (mimeograph, pp. 32 f.)

45. See below, Chap. XVII, pp. 517 ff. Admiral Stark testified that President Roosevelt told him in the summer of 1944 that "he [the President] was surprised at the attack on Pearl Harbor." As Admiral Stark had recently testified before the Navy Court of Inquiry (in 1944) to the same effect, he found "some comfort" in having the President "reiterate it." CJC, Part 5, p. 2272.

46. For supporting evidence, see Chaps. XIV–XVII. For the declaration of Mrs. Eleanor Roosevelt that the residents of the White House had been expecting a Japanese attack for many days before it came, see above, p. 293.

PART III

REALITIES AS DESCRIBED BY THE PEARL HARBOR DOCUMENTS

CHAPTER XIII

Engineering the Official Thesis of Guilt

CENTRAL to the official explanation of how war came was the official thesis that the responsibility for the disaster at Pearl Harbor rested upon General Short and Admiral Kimmel, the high officers of the Army and the Navy in charge of defending that outpost in the Pacific against the Japanese.[1] Although both the majority and the minority of the Congressional Committee dealt in their respective reports with that part of the official thesis which put the primary blame for the catastrophe on the Hawaiian commanders, with the exception of Mr. Keefe they treated it gingerly and with circumlocution.[2] By acquitting General Short and Admiral Kimmel of derelictions of duty, the Democratic members with the support of Representatives Gearhart and Keefe exploded a main point in the Roberts Report. Thereby they conceded that an injustice had been done to the two commanders. They also went so far as to express regret that the General and the Admiral had endured "suffering and mental anguish" as a result of false charges. On their part the Republican minority refrained from admitting even this much. Hence only the fringes of this crucial and delicate matter were touched by the committee in what is called its Report.

The Congressional Committee, however, produced a huge mass of evidence bearing on the operations of the Roberts Committee and the maneuvers of President Roosevelt and other high officials in making use of that indictment to brand the Hawaiian commanders in January and February, 1942, as culprits awaiting trials by courts-martial.[3] This evidence con-

1. See above, Chap. VIII.
2. Representative Keefe, in his Additional Views, scored the Roberts Report and President Roosevelt's handling of the retirement of the commanders. CJC, *Report*, pp. 266-P ff.
3. See above, Chap. VIII, pp. 221 ff.

sists of testimony, letters, memoranda, legal opinions, and other documents entered in the permanent record of the committee. An examination of these documents takes the reader behind the appearances of the official operations in December, 1941, and in January and February, 1942, behind the words of the Congressional Committee, to ultimate historical sources which describe realities in the process by which the Roberts Report came into being and was subsequently used by President Roosevelt and his official entourage.

Revelatory information respecting the creation of the President's Commission on Pearl Harbor was put on record at a hearing of the Congressional Committee on January 28, 1946.[4] This information was contained in letters from Secretary Stimson to President Roosevelt, dated December 16, 1941. According to the first of these letters, President Roosevelt had asked Secretary Knox and Secretary Stimson for their suggestions relative to the selection of members to serve on his "investigating board" for Pearl Harbor. Secretary Stimson proposed Justice Roberts, as "civilian head," and General Frank R. McCoy and General Joseph T. McNarney, as representatives of the War Department. Presumably Secretary Knox also complied with the President's request and proposed the names of men to represent the Navy Department.

This recommendation of a Justice of the Supreme Court to serve as head of a special administrative body created by the President to conduct an inquest, as if he were a kind of chief prosecuting attorney, was an extraordinary action on the part of Secretary Stimson. As a lawyer he knew or should have known that it is a violation of the spirit, if not the letter, of the Constitution for a Justice of that Court to abandon his duties in that tribunal for the purpose of carrying on nonjudicial activities of an inquisitory, administrative, and political nature at the behest of the President. For Justice Roberts to accept the commission was still more extraordinary. He knew the legal position of his own tribunal,[5] and he knew also

4. CJC, Part 7, pp. 3260 ff.
5. For instance, *Hayburn's Case* (1792), 2 Dallas, 409.

that he was chosen, not to hear a case at law arising under the Constitution and laws of the United States, but to engage in a search for derelictions of official duty which in the necessity of things involved politics, even partisanship.

Without waiting for definite information respecting misconduct, if any, on the part of General Short and Admiral Kimmel at Pearl Harbor, Secretary Stimson, in his letters dated December 16, 1941, nine days after Pearl Harbor, informed the President that the department was immediately sending out two officers to relieve General Short and General Martin, the Army Air Commander at Hawaii. Not content with the management of his own department, Secretary Stimson expressed to the President his opinion that "the housecleaning" in his department, "should be synchronized with a similar housecleaning in the Navy Command and all announced at the same time." The action taken by Secretary Stimson for the War Department and the action suggested by him to the President for duplication by the Navy Department were announced to the public. Thus the twofold "housecleaning" was accomplished.[6]

6. The texts of the two letters from Secretary Stimson to President Roosevelt follow:

"Personal and Confidential

"December 16, 1941

"Dear Mr. President: Knox tells me that you would like our suggestions as to the investigating board this morning.

"1. My suggestion for the civilian head is Justice Roberts. No less a man in my opinion should be asked and Roberts, by his action in investigating and prosecuting the Teapot Dome scandal and in deciding the Black Tom case more recently, has an outstanding reputation among our people for getting down to the bottom of a factual situation. I think his appointment would command the confidence of the whole country. I believe Knox agrees with me.

"2. For the War Department representatives I suggest Major General Frank R. McCoy, Retired, and Brigadier General Joseph T. McNarney of the Air Corps.

a. McCoy you know personally. He has the most outstanding record of any man in the Army for such an appointment, requiring as it does breadth of view, superlative character, and wide similar experience. As a member of the Lytton Commission which investigated the Japanese in Manchuria, he won a very high reputation among all nations involved for his balance and tact. It was due to him more than any other member that the report of that Commission was unanimous.

b. McNarney I recommend as the best air man we have for that purpose. I think there must be an air man on the board because the duties and alleged

Secretary Stimson's expectations in suggesting Justice Roberts to head the President's Commission on Pearl Harbor were not disappointed. Charged by the President with the duty of inquiring merely into derelictions and errors of judgment on the part of the Army and Navy personnel, the commission took pains to declare (Conclusions 2–6) that the Secretary of State, the Secretary of War, the Secretary of the Navy, the Chief of Staff of the Army, and the Chief of Naval Operations had fulfilled their obligations in relation to Pearl Harbor— had committed no breaches of duty. The commission also provided a sanction for the twofold "housecleaning" operation in the War and Navy Departments—by designating General Short and Admiral Kimmel as the real offenders at Pearl Harbor.

Three days after the Report of the President's Commission came out, Secretary Stimson wrote to Justice Roberts, whom he had proposed as "civilian head," a letter of appreciation: "This is just a hasty line to tell you what an admirable job I think that you and your colleagues have done in your difficult task of drawing the report on the disaster at Pearl Harbor"— the Report in which it was stated that Secretary Stimson had

---

derelictions were in air protection. . . . McNarney has a reputation which commands the respect of everybody. As you know, he was Chief of Staff for Chaney in London, was on the recent Staff conferences with the British, went to Moscow, and is familiar with British technique in respect to air defense. Marshall and I think he is the most competent man we have at the present time on air and ground joint requirements.

"Marshall and I united on all the foregoing suggestions after very careful consideration by each of us.

"Most confidentially we are sending to Hawaii two men to relieve Short and Martin, the present Army Commander and Air Commander. Lieutenant General Emmons, our present Air Combat Commander, will relieve Short. Brigadier General Tinker will relieve Martin. They are starting at once and I think nothing should be said about it until they arrive to take command. . . .

"Faithfully yours,

"Henry L. Stimson.
"Secretary of War.

"The President.
"*The White House.*"

"My opinion is that the housecleaning which I describe in the last paragraph should be synchronized with a similar housecleaning in the Navy Command, and all announced at the same time." CJC, Part 7, p. 3260.

"fulfilled" his "obligations" in respect of the affair. In this letter, Secretary Stimson called the commission's Report "a masterpiece of candid and accurate statement based upon most careful study and analysis of a difficult factual situation." To Secretary Stimson's letter of appreciation, Mr. Justice Roberts replied in grateful terms.[7]

On the insistence of Senator Ferguson and Senator Brewster, the Congressional Committee summoned Justice Roberts to a hearing—January 28, 1946. In the course of his testimony, certain findings in the Report of the President's Commission and the processes by which it had arrived at its Conclusions, bearing on the subject of responsibility, were explored. Thus, the "masterpiece of candid and accurate statement" was subjected to public scrutiny.

For example, an inquiry was made about General Marshall's final warning message of December 7 to General Short, which reached him after the Japanese attack had ended. Speaking of this message, the President's Commission had stated in its Report: "*Every effort* was made to have the message reach Hawaii *in the briefest possible time,* but *due to conditions beyond the control of anyone concerned* the delivery of this urgent message was delayed until after the attack." (Italics supplied.) The sentence "every effort was made to have the message reach Hawaii in the briefest possible time" was read to Justice Roberts at the hearing of the Congressional Committee. Justice Roberts was then asked, in effect, by Senator Brewster whether this statement was correct and the Justice conceded that "probably" it was not correct. Evidence brought before the committee established the fact that it was not correct, that there had been inexcusable delay in sending it, and that the immediate responsibility for the delay rested on the War Department and General Marshall.[8]

Another crucial fact established at the examination of Justice Roberts was related to the kind of documents used by the

7. For the texts of these letters, see *ibid.,* p. 3261.

8. For example, see CJC, *Report,* pp. 266-F ff. (with citations); CJC, Part 9, pp. 4517 ff.; and *ibid.,* Part 39, pp. 139 ff., for the Army Pearl Harbor Board's condemnation of the delay.

President's Commission in framing its Report and Conclusions. Among the documents reposing in the files of the War and Navy Departments while the commission was at work were hundreds of secret messages exchanged between the Japanese Government and its agents in Washington and other parts of the world between July 1, and December 8, 1941. The messages had been intercepted by Army and Navy intelligence, decoded, and translated for the information of the President and other high officials. They disclosed detailed information respecting Japanese intentions, designs, and movements prior to the attack on Pearl Harbor.[9] From these messages the President and high officials in his Administration derived special knowledge in respect of Japanese reactions to its proposals and of Japanese war plans and maneuvers—information which was not transmitted by the War and Navy Departments to the American outpost commanders at Hawaii. In official circles in Washington, at the time, they were called "magic," or "magic messages."

At the hearing of the Congressional Committee, Justice Roberts testified that his commission were "never shown one of the magic messages." He was asked: "Were you ever shown the substance of the magic messages?" He answered: "No, sir."

Under questioning, Justice Roberts disclosed the nature of the information and the mental operations employed by the President's Commission in exculpating Washington officials and drawing up the indictment of General Short and Admiral Kimmel. For instance, the Justice was asked where he got the knowledge on which rested the commission's declaration that Secretary Hull had fulfilled his obligations by keeping the War and Navy Departments fully advised as to the course and probable termination of negotiations with Japan. The Justice answered that he went to see Secretary Hull, that Secretary Hull gave him the information, and that General Marshall and Admiral Stark said that they had received ample warning from Secretary Hull.

9. For example, CJC, Part 12, Exhibit 1, pp. 1–253.

Did Justice Roberts know that the President, the Secretary of State, the Secretary of War, the Secretary of the Navy, the Chief of Staff, and the Chief of Naval Operations had been furnished with the magic messages? The Justice replied: "I did not know it and I would not have been interested in it."

Asked whether the Conclusions of the President's Commission were derived from sources which did not include "the magic," Justice Roberts states: "The magic was not shown to us. I would not have bothered to read it if it had been shown to us." The Justice then went on to say that the messages to the Hawaiian commanders gave them ample warning.[10]

GENERAL MARSHALL AND ADMIRAL STARK ON THE TREATMENT OF THE COMMANDERS

THE specific subject of General Short's retirement and treatment by the Administration was taken up at an examination of General Marshall by the Congressional Committee, December 13, 1945.[11] As a result of questioning by Senator Ferguson, General Marshall presented the following facts. In relation to the "relief" of General Short, General Marshall had been consulted by the Secretary of War. The consultation came after the return of Secretary Knox from his brief visit to Hawaii. Secretary Stimson discussed the matter with General Marshall after Secretary Knox had returned to Washington. General Short was relieved of his command and ordered to report to the United States, presumably to the War Department. Thereafter the question before the War Department was whether General Short should be given another assignment or retired. Referring to the retirement, General Marshall said: "I believe [it] was at his request; I do not recall that."[12] Had General Marshall been consulted on the question whether General Short be given another assignment?

10. On this, see above, p. 361, and below, pp. 523 ff.
11. CJC, Part 3, pp. 1528 ff.
12. See below, pp. 392 ff. All of General Marshall's testimony before the Congressional Committee should be contrasted with the War Department documents in the case, see below, pp. 393 ff., especially General Marshall's own memoranda of January–February, 1942.

General Marshall replied simply: "I do not recall that, sir."

The order relieving General Short, dated December 16, 1941, had read, "By direction of the President." Had General Marshall conferred with the President? The General could not recall. What conversation did General Marshall have with Secretary Stimson as to why General Short should be relieved of his command? General Marshall: "I do not recall the conversation." His recollection was that, after his return from Hawaii to Washington, Secretary Knox consulted with Secretary Stimson and they reached a decision to relieve both General Short and Admiral Kimmel. Whether they had a meeting with President Roosevelt, General Marshall did not know.

Senator Ferguson asked General Marshall for the specific reasons on which General Short's removal was based. General Marshall did not recall any specific statement of the reasons; nor did he have any "clear recollection." Was the reason for General Short's removal his "disobedience to the alert order of the 27th [November]"? General Marshall: "I could not say that, sir." [13] It was, General Marshall thought, the general status of affairs in Hawaii as viewed, presumably, by Colonel Knox. Did General Marshall have reason to believe that Colonel Knox brought from Hawaii "the cause of the removal"? "That," replied General Marshall, "is my vague recollection of what occurred." Did General Marshall base the order removing General Short on his own findings or on what somebody else found? The General replied that he based it on the direction of the Secretary of War. Did Secretary Stimson give to General Marshall his reasons for removing General Short? General Marshall: "I do not recall that, sir. I mean he undoubtedly did, and undoubtedly I gave him an opinion. . . ." Did General Marshall recall any of the reasons which Secretary Stimson gave him as grounds for the removal of General Short? General Marshall replied: "I do not, sir." [14]

Senator Ferguson's questions on this occasion bore on the

13. For additional light on this crucial point, see above, p. 348.
14. CJC, Part 3, pp. 1528 ff.

relieving of General Short from his command at Hawaii, not on the retirement of General Short, with accompanying publicity, which came later—in February, 1942. But certain facts had been entered by General Marshall in the record. After his brief trip to Hawaii, Secretary Knox consulted Secretary Stimson, as well as President Roosevelt. General Marshall was thereupon directed by Secretary Stimson to relieve General Short from his command. What were the reasons for relieving General Short? General Marshall could not recall them. The presumption was that there had been some reasons for this quick and summary action against General Short, but General Marshall could not remember them.[15]

At an examination of Admiral Stark, on January 5, 1946, Senator Ferguson, by steady questioning, brought out some of the Admiral's recollections respecting the retirement of Admiral Kimmel. The Senator asked whether Admiral Stark was familiar with Admiral Kimmel's retirement. Admiral Stark replied: "Well, I knew that he had retired; yes, sir." With whom had Admiral Stark consulted and conferred in this matter? He had been "directed" by Secretary Knox with regard to the detachment or relief of Admiral Kimmel. Admiral Stark had read the report of Secretary Knox to President Roosevelt on his visit to Hawaii; had he found in the memorandum anything critical that called for Admiral Kimmel's removal? The answer was: "No, sir." When had Secretary Knox first talked with Admiral Stark about the removal or detachment of Admiral Kimmel? Shortly after he had returned from Hawaii and had discussed matters with President Roosevelt, Secretary Knox directed that Admiral Kimmel be relieved of his command, December 16, 1941. Did Admiral Stark receive any information as to the cause of Admiral Kimmel's removal? He was not consulted beforehand; he received his orders to act against Admiral Kimmel, and the Commander had been removed with the "permission" or "O.K." of the President.

15. Was this what Secretary Stimson called "the housecleaning" in his letter to President Roosevelt on December 16, 1941? See above, p. 380.

Did Admiral Stark consult with Admiral Kimmel about his resignation or retirement? Admiral Stark recalled writing something on the subject to Admiral Kimmel. He had discussed the matter from one angle or another; he had remarked to Admiral Kimmel that he was not trying to influence the Commander; he had reported to Admiral Kimmel that General Short had requested retirement, and had suggested to the Admiral that he also might or might not want to parallel General Short's action; and the Admiral had asked to be advised. Did Admiral Stark confer with Secretary Knox on this matter? He had consulted the Secretary, but was not certain [in 1946] whether the suggestion as to retirement came from the Secretary or was his own idea. Did Admiral Kimmel retire "on your suggestion"? Admiral Stark replied that Admiral Kimmel retired "on his own volition.[16] We did not force him at all as I remember it. I never knew of a man to put up a manlier, straighter, finer front than did Admiral Kimmel in this entire picture at that time. His whole bearing was exemplary and what I would have expected of him."

Would Admiral Kimmel have been removed if he had not retired on his own volition? Admiral Stark did not know what action would have been taken in that case. Senator Ferguson asked: "You felt that he would do it on the suggestion?" Admiral Stark replied: "He did it. He did do it, I think, after sizing up all the considerations. . . . Now, if I am mistaken in that he can correct it and I would abide by anything that he stated with regard to it." Had Secretary Knox consulted the President in respect of Admiral Kimmel's retirement? Admiral Stark imagined that such a consultation had taken place.[17]

With reference to the relief and retirement of General Short and Admiral Kimmel, the recollections of General Marshall and Admiral Stark, the immediate superiors, were meager in 1945–46. Apparently the Chief of Staff and the Chief of Naval Operations had issued their orders on direc-

16. For documents and other testimony to the contrary, see below, pp. 389 ff.
17. CJC, Part 5, pp. 2429 ff.

tions from above and they could not recall the reasons, if any, which had been officially assigned as grounds for actions against the two commanders. Secretary Knox, after his brief visit to Hawaii, had presented a memorandum on the disaster to President Roosevelt but the memorandum had contained no critical charges carrying proposals for drastic action against the commanders. After a conference with the President, Secretary Knox consulted Secretary Stimson and, "perhaps," General Marshall and Admiral Stark; orders had quickly been issued relieving General Short and Admiral Kimmel from their commands. Later, it seemed to be remembered by General Marshall and Admiral Stark that General Short and then Admiral Kimmel had asked to be retired, and their requests had been granted—in due form and with the public announcements which represented the two men as if awaiting disciplinary actions to come—courts-martial in fact.[18]

Recognizing as material to this specific line of inquiry, the personal report of Secretary Knox to President Roosevelt, after the Secretary's inspection of the state of things at Pearl Harbor immediately following the Japanese attack, Senator Ferguson had earlier asked Admiral Stark to read the report into the record.[19] The document contained no charges of dereliction of duty on the part of General Short and Admiral Kimmel; nor any hint that they should be relieved, retired, and brought to trial for any negligence, nonfeasance, or dereliction on their part before or on December 7, 1941. The report of Secretary Knox was primarily factual in nature and even noted that neither of the commanders had any knowledge of the plain intimations of a surprise move by the Japanese which had been made known in Washington by interceptions of Japanese secret messages.[20] Thus Secretary Knox implied that in some respects Washington had been at fault. The opening passages of the Secretary's report to the President follow:

18. See above, pp. 383, 386.
19. CJC, Part 5, pp. 2338 ff.
20. See above, p. 382.

The Japanese air attack on the Island of Oahu on December 7th was a complete surprise to both the Army and the Navy. Its initial success, which included almost all the damage done, was due to a lack of a state of readiness against such an air attack, by both branches of the service. This statement was made by me to both General Short and Admiral Kimmel, and both agreed that it was entirely true.

Neither Army or Navy Commandants in Oahu regarded such an attack as at all likely, because of the danger which such a carrier-borne attack would confront in view of the preponderance of the American naval strength in Hawaiian waters. While the likelihood of an attack without warning by Japan was in the minds of both General Short and Admiral Kimmel, both felt certain that such an attack would take place nearer Japan's base of operations, that is, in the Far East. Neither Short nor Kimmel, at the time of the attack, had any knowledge of the plain intimations of some surprise move, made clear in Washington, through the interception of Japanese instructions to Nomura, in which a surprise move of some kind was clearly indicated by the insistence upon the precise time of Nomura's reply to Hull, at one o'clock on Sunday.

A general warning had been sent out from the Navy Department on November 27th, to Admiral Kimmel. General Short told me that a message of warning sent from the War Department on Saturday night at midnight, before the attack, failed to reach him until four or five hours after the attack had been made.

Both the Army and the Navy command at Oahu had prepared careful estimates covering their idea of the most likely and most imminent danger. General Short repeated to me several times that he felt the most imminent danger to the Army was the danger of sabotage, because of the known presence of large numbers of alien Japanese in Honolulu. Acting on this assumption, he took every possible measure to protect against this danger. This included, unfortunately, bunching the planes on the various fields on the Island, close together, so that they might be carefully guarded against possible subversive action by Japanese agents. This condition, known as "Sabotage Alert" had been assumed because sabotage was considered as the most imminent danger to be guarded against. This bunching of planes, of course, made the Japanese air attack more effective. There was, to a lesser degree, the same lack of dispersal of planes on Navy stations, and although the possibility of sabotage was not given the same prominence in Naval minds, both arms of the service lost most of their planes on the ground in the initial attack by the enemy. There were no Army planes in the air at the time of the attack and no planes were warmed up in readiness to take the air.

The Navy regarded the principal danger from a Japanese stroke without warning was a submarine attack, and consequently made all necessary provisions to cope with such an attack. As a matter of fact, a submarine attack did accompany the air attack and at least two Japanese submarines were sunk and a third one ran ashore and was captured. No losses were incurred by the Fleet from submarine attack. One small two-man submarine penetrated into the harbor, having followed a vessel through the net, but because it broached in the shallow water it was immediately discovered by the *Curtis* and was attacked and destroyed through the efforts of that vessel and those of the destroyer *Monaghan*. This submarine fired her torpedoes which hit a shoal to the west of Ford Island.

The Navy took no specific measures of protection against an air attack, save only that the ships in the harbor were so dispersed as to provide a field of fire covering every approach from the air. The Navy morning patrol was sent out at dawn to the southward, where the Commander-in-Chief had reason to suspect an attack might come. This patrol consisted of ten patrol bombers who made no contacts with enemy craft. At least 90% of Officers and enlisted personnel were aboard ship when the attack came. The condition of readiness aboard ship was described as "Condition Three," which meant that about one-half of the broadside and anti-aircraft guns were manned, and all of the anti-aircraft guns were supplied with ammunition and were in readiness. . . .

ADMIRAL KIMMEL AND GENERAL SHORT ON THEIR "RETIREMENT"

ON JANUARY 15, 1946, Admiral Kimmel was at last accorded the public hearing denied to him since January, 1942—before the Congressional Committee on Pearl Harbor.[21] Under questioning from the committee's counsel the Admiral described

21. CJC, Part 6, pp. 2561 ff.

the circumstances of his retirement and treatment after December 7, 1941. On December 17, 1941, he was relieved of his command and later ordered to the West Coast, stopping in San Francisco, where he waited "for whatever disposition they wished to make." Shortly after the Roberts Report came out in January, Admiral Kimmel was informed by a circuitous route through the naval establishment that the Acting Secretary of the Navy (in fact, Secretary Knox) had a message to the effect that General Short had submitted a request for retirement.[22]

Thereupon Admiral Kimmel, who had hitherto not considered the idea of submitting a request for his retirement, decided that he would not stand in the way of action by the Navy Department; and so he submitted his own request for retirement. A few days later he was assured that the information about General Short's retirement had not been intended to influence him and that he was free to do as he thought best. Subsequently letters about the subject were exchanged by Admiral Stark and Admiral Kimmel which revealed a queer state of affairs in the Navy Department with regard to just what was being done in the case of the Administration *vs.* Admiral Kimmel.

On January 28, 1942, Admiral Kimmel wrote a second letter to the Navy Department about his retirement. He said that his first letter had been submitted after he had been officially informed by the department that General Short had requested retirement. The Admiral added: "I was officially informed today [January 28, 1942] by the Navy Department that my notification of General Short's request was not intended to influence my decision to submit a similar request. I desire my request for retirement to stand, subject only to determination by the Department as to what course of action will best serve the interests of the country and the good of the service."

About three weeks later, February 22, 1942, Admiral Kim-

22. For the truth of this allegation, see below, pp. 392 ff.

mel wrote a letter to Admiral Stark in which he gave several passages from the history of his case:

. . . I submitted my [first] request for retirement because I was notified that Short had done so and took that notification as a suggestion for me to do likewise. I submitted this request solely to permit the department to take whatever action they deemed best for the interests of the country. I did not submit it in order to escape censure or punishment.

When I was notified that the notification in regard to Short was not meant to put pressure on me, I submitted my second letter on the subject.

When the fact that Short and I had submitted requests for retirement was published to the country, I was astounded that the department would put Short and me in such light before the country.

On February 19, I received notification by the Secretary that I would be placed on the retired list on March 1, 1942. Paragraph 2 of this letter states, "This approval of your request for retirement is without condonation of any offense or prejudice to future disciplinary action."

I do not understand this paragraph unless it is to be published to the country as a promise that I will be disciplined at some future time.

Then Admiral Kimmel made the following statement of his position:

I stand ready at any time to accept the consequences of my acts. I do not wish to embarrass the government in the conduct of the war. I do feel, however, that my crucifixion before the public has about reached the limit. I am in daily receipt of letters from irresponsible people over the country taking me to task and even threatening to kill me. . . .

I feel that the publication of paragraph two of the Secretary's letter of February 16 [19] will further inflame the public and do me a great injustice.

I have kept my mouth shut and propose to continue to do so as long as it is humanly possible.

I regret the losses at Pearl Harbor just as keenly, perhaps more keenly than any other American citizen. I wish that I had been smarter than I was and able to foresee what happened on December 7. I devoted all my energies to the job and made the dispositions which appeared to me to be called for. I cannot now reproach myself for any lack of effort.

I will not comment on the Report of the Commission, but you probably know what I think of it. . . .

All this I have been willing to accept for the good of the country out of my loyalty to the Nation, and to await the judgment of history when all the factors can be published.

But I do think that in all justice the department should do nothing further to inflame the public against me. . . .[23]

When General Short was at last given his day in court before the Congressional Committee, on January 22, 1946, the question of the circumstances of his "retirement" was raised by Senator Brewster. Then occurred a long series of questions and answers, during which many documents were introduced into the record. The report of the testimony and the documents fill many pages. The essential facts brought to light were as follows:

When, on January 25, 1942, he read in the newspapers the findings of the President's Commission on Pearl Harbor that charged him and Admiral Kimmel with grave offenses, General Short was "completely dumbfounded." He immediately telephoned General Marshall and asked whether he should retire. General Marshall replied: "Stand pat but if it becomes necessary I will use this conversation as authority." But after the telephone conversation was ended, General Short thought that it was not quite fair to General Marshall to leave the matter merely in the form of a conversation.

General Short then wrote out a formal application for retirement and enclosed it in a personal letter to General Marshall. In the letter, General Short said that he appreciated General Marshall's advice not to submit a request for retirement at the present time, that he preferred to remain on the active list, and that he submitted his request for retirement to

23. CJC, Part 6, p. 2562.

be used if deemed desirable any time in the future. General Marshall never replied to this letter. Later General Short's retirement was announced to him and the press.[24]

In connection with the testimony about the retirement of General Short and Admiral Kimmel many documents hitherto secret were read into the record of the Congressional Committee on Pearl Harbor and other documents, also hitherto secret, brought from the files of the War Department and the Navy Department, were included in the Exhibits of the committee.[25] Taken collectively the testimony and the official papers in the Exhibits present an authentic account of the way in which General Short and Admiral Kimmel were "retired" and publicized before the country as men under the grave charge of dereliction of duty awaiting trials by courts-martial. In some respects the cases of the two men were handled separately by the War and the Navy Departments but the principal actions in the two cases were carefully "synchronized," to use Secretary Stimson's verb, and the two operations were controlled by a common policy in all fundamental matters.

SUMMARY OF THE ADMINISTRATION'S OPERATIONS AGAINST
GENERAL SHORT AND ADMIRAL KIMMEL

1. From about December 16, 1941, when the decision was made to relieve the two commanders of their duties in Hawaii, until February 28, 1942, when their retirement under a stigma of guilt was publicly announced, the case was under advisement and consideration by the Administration. The subject was discussed at least once in a meeting of the Cabinet, and during proceedings which lasted from January 13, 1942, until February 28, 1942, the following high officials took part in making the decisions and devising the formulas of public announcement: President Roosevelt, Secretary Stimson, Secretary Knox, General Marshall, Attorney General Biddle, Gen-

24. *Ibid.*, Part 7, pp. 3133 ff., and see above, p. 225, for the public announcement. Previously General Marshall had testified before the Congressional Committee that "The procedure in General Short's case was handled by the Secretary of War." See *ibid.*, Part 7, p. 3135, where this statement is repeated.
25. CJC, Part 17, Exhibit 121; Part 18, Exhibit 140; Part 19, Exhibit 170.

eral Cramer (Judge Advocate General), and General J. H. Hilldring (Assistant Chief of Staff).

2. January 13, 1942, by telegraphic orders, the War Department instructed General Short to proceed to Oklahoma City "on temporary duty" and, on receipt of further notice, to report to Washington for "further temporary duty"—as if the War Department contemplated giving him a new assignment in the armed services.

3. January 13, 1942, that is, the day the above instructions went out to General Short, Secretary Stimson wrote an office memorandum on the case of General Short: "This is to be held for a few days to await the cooling down of the situation."

4. January 25, 1942, General Short wrote to General Marshall a covering letter for his application for retirement. He expressed his appreciation of General Marshall's advice over the telephone to the effect that such an application should not be submitted then. In this letter, General Short, perhaps unfortunately for himself, raised an embarrassing issue for General Marshall: a group of the War Department's airplanes arrived at Hawaii, with guns cosmolined and without ammunition, in the midst of the Japanese attack.[26] Surely the War Department was not expecting a Japanese attack and agreed with General Short that sabotage was the most dangerous thing to be guarded against in Hawaii?

5. January 26, 1942. General Marshall advised Secretary Stimson that General Short's application for retirement be accepted "quietly without any publicity at the moment."

6. Secretary Stimson sought the opinion of the Judge Advocate General: whether the acceptance of General Short's retirement, on the understanding that this action would not preclude later trial by court-martial, would be valid at law.

7. January 27, 1942. The Judge Advocate General warned General Marshall and Secretary Stimson that the charges lodged against General Short were grave and would require a strong showing for conviction; that the result of any trial

26. For General Marshall's lame explanation of that strange event, see CJC, Part 3, p. 1121.

could not be predicted with certainty; that the War Department might be accused of "persecuting" if General Short was convicted; or, if he was acquitted, of "whitewashing." After reviewing the applicable law, the Judge Advocate General declared, in effect, that official promises of trial by court-martial would be dubious, if not dangerous, for the Administration.

8. January 31, 1942. The Judge Advocate General responded to a second inquiry from Secretary Stimson: whether a subsequent court-martial could be validly brought if the War Department announced an understanding that the acceptance of General Short's application for retirement would not preclude a future court-martial. The Judge Advocate General answered favorably, as a matter of law, namely, that the retirement at the discretion of the President would not involve passing judgment on the officer's past services or a condonation of prior offenses which would preclude subsequent court-martial; but he advised the Secretary of War to make sure that General Short's retirement be made subject to his prior acceptance of the condition that it did not constitute a condonation of his offenses, "if any," or bar future trial by court-martial, "in case such a trial should be deemed advisable."

9. February 13, 1942. Discussion of the retirement of General Short and Admiral Kimmel at a Cabinet meeting. Later in the day Secretary Stimson wrote to General Marshall that he had taken this matter up with Secretary Knox after the Cabinet meeting, and that, "roughly," the formula devised by President Roosevelt, as reported by Secretary Knox, was as follows: "Provided it is agreed by you [General Short and Admiral Kimmel] that this is no bar to be used legally or otherwise to subsequent court martial proceedings."

10. February 14, 1942. Memorandum from Secretary Stimson to President Roosevelt, stating that he and Secretary Knox had considered the subject since the Cabinet meeting and had agreed to accept the requests of the two commanders for retirement, subject to the following condition: "Is ac-

cepted, effective ———, without prejudice to future action in the interest of the Government." To this memorandum, were added in handwriting two formulas of Secretary Stimson's own wording: "without condonation of any offense or prejudice to future action on behalf of the Gov't," and "without condonation of any offense or prejudice to any future disciplinary action."

The formulas, Secretary Stimson said, had been approved "as safe" by the Attorney General by telephone, February 16. Notation at the bottom, "Green copy never on file."

11. February 14, 1942. Memorandum from General J. H. Hilldring, Assistant Chief of Staff to Attorney General Biddle. This document gives the various formulas for the conditions to be imposed on the retirement of the two commanders and states: "The President has requested that you express your judgment as to which of the suggestions offered is preferable, and whether or not the preferable wording serves the legal purpose for which it is intended. . . . In view of the fact that the President desires to reach a decision in regard to this matter on Monday morning, the Secretary of War has directed me to request that you make available to him your decision before the end of this week end."

12. February 14, 1942. Memorandum from Attorney General Biddle to Secretary Stimson. Mr. Biddle found objection to making any reference to "court martial" and also to using the words "without condonation of any offense," in the formula to be applied to the retirement of the two commanders. Reference to court-martial "would indicate to the officers concerned that such action was definitely planned for a future date, and would move one or both of them to insist that such proceedings be had immediately. Similarly, the reference to an offense may suggest to these officers that we felt that an offense had been committed, and thus might lead them to an insistence that the question of whether or not they were guilty of an offense be immediately determined by appropriate proceedings." Mr. Biddle then stated that he regarded as the

preferable formula a noncommittal line: "is accepted, effective ————, without prejudice to future action in the interest of the Government."

This memorandum by Attorney General Biddle is especially significant for the inside history of the Administration's proceedings against General Short and Admiral Kimmel. In his opening paragraph Mr. Biddle said that he had read the opinions and other documents that accompanied General Hilldring's memorandum of that day (see above, No. 11). Hence he had before him a fairly full record of the case up to that day, when he warned the Administration against indicating *that court-martial was definitely planned* for a future date and against giving the commanders an opportunity to demand an immediate hearing. Mr. Biddle also objected to going on public record as saying "that we felt that an offense had been committed." Evidently he was under the impression that the Administration's representatives in the case were not sure, as of February 14, that an offense had actually been committed by either or both of the commanders.

13. February 14, 1942. Letter from Secretary Stimson to Secretary Knox: "Here is my own revised suggestion as to the saving clause to be inserted in the acceptance of the retirement: 'without condonation of any offense or prejudice to any action on behalf of the Government.' " Mr. Stimson went on to say: "*Any reasons we want to give for our action can be said to the press. I am in favor of leaving the acceptance itself in this language if the Attorney General says that it is sufficient to keep open the power to court martial.*" (Italics supplied.)

14. Undated memorandum by General Marshall stating that the revised formula offered by Secretary Stimson had been agreed upon by the Secretary of War, the Secretary of the Navy, and the Attorney General.

15. February 17, 1942. Memorandum by General Hilldring presenting to the Adjutant General, at the direction of Secretary Stimson, a detailed schedule of the steps to be taken

in retiring General Short and committing him in advance to the conditions of the formula as at last agreed upon by the Secretary of War, Secretary Knox, and Attorney General Biddle.

16. February 25, 1942. Brief note, which the Congressional Committee on Pearl Harbor called a "blind memo." and reproduced as follows: "February 25, 1942. The President intends to ask for a court-martial on the issue of whether as stated in the report of the Roberts' Commission, there was a dereliction of duty on the part of Admiral Kimmel and General Short: the court to be held as soon as the public interest permits. It is the privilege of the officers themselves to ask for such a court-martial."

17. February 26, 1942. On the morning of this day, the Judge Advocate General personally handed to General Marshall a memorandum giving advice against promising the commanders a court-martial at any specified time and stating that at such a trial "the defense would certainly attempt to pass *part of the blame to the War Department*," thus tending to discredit the department and the men in charge of war operations. The Judge Advocate General also pointed out that no charges had as yet been preferred against the commanders, that certain procedure was necessary to present such charges, that *there was no law authorizing General Short to request a court-martial*, and that it was *inadvisable for the President to announce in advance of preferring charges a trial of the officers concerned, for it would give them an opportunity* to allege that "the President is the accuser" and to charge that the court convened by him "is not an impartial body." (Italics supplied.)

Such in substance is the intellectual, moral, and legal history of the secret negotiations carried on by President Roosevelt, Secretary Stimson, Secretary Knox, Attorney General Biddle, Judge Advocate General Cramer, and General Marshall, which eventuated in the identical statements respecting the retirement of General Short and Admiral Kimmel, released to the press, with supplementary announcements by Secretary

Stimson and Secretary Knox, February 28, 1942.[27] The statement was guarded and terse: the applications of the commanders had been accepted, "without condonation of any offense or
prejudice to any future disciplinary action."

The announcement accompanying the statement about each
officer contained no promise of trial by court-martial, but
informed the public that preparation of charges for trial by
court-martial had been ordered on the basis of the Roberts Report "alleging" dereliction of duty. Protecting themselves
against any clamor for an immediate action against the two
commanders or any demand on their part for a trial, the two
Secretaries made it clear that no trial upon these charges would
be held until "such time as the public interest and safety would
permit"—a time that might never come, that never came.
Moreover they required the commanders to waive their rights
to a trial at any given time, as a condition of the settlement.[28]

It is not surprising, therefore, that the Democratic majority
of the Congressional Committee on Pearl Harbor, with the
documents pertaining to these negotiations and other testimony in the voluminous record before them, were moved to
conclude in their report released to the press and the radio on
July 20, 1946, this statement: "The errors made by the Hawaiian commands were errors of judgment and not derelictions of duty"; while declaring at the same time that the
President, the Secretary of State, the Secretary of War, and
the Secretary of the Navy had "discharged their responsibilities [in respect of Pearl Harbor] with distinction, ability,
and foresight and in keeping with the highest traditions of our
fundamental foreign policy." But why had General Short
and Admiral Kimmel been kept so long disgraced before the
country as a result of the report by the President's Commission on Pearl Harbor, made public January 24, 1942, and the
official statements and announcements between January 24
and February 28, 1942?

27. See above, p. 225.
28. Had the commanders stood fast on demanding an immediate hearing, the
members of the Administration, as they well knew, would have been placed in an
awkward position.

THE DEMOCRATIC MAJORITY OF THE CONGRESSIONAL COMMITTEE AND THE "MENTAL ANGUISH" OF THE TWO COMMANDERS

THE "moral problem" created for the Democratic members of the Congressional Committee by the testimony and documents bearing on the treatment accorded to General Short and Admiral Kimmel by high officials in Washington before and after the release of the Report of the President's Commission on Pearl Harbor, January 24, 1942, was undoubtedly difficult to resolve. From certain quarters they were urged to sustain the charge of dereliction of duty and thus validate the Roberts Report.[29] But they rejected this advice; they declared that the failures of the commanders were errors of judgment, not derelictions of duty; and, having done this, they prepared a statement on the subject, which is a marvelous display of rhetorical ingenuity. This statement appears in brief passages of the Report placed under the heading: "Prior Inquiries Concerning the Pearl Harbor Attack." [30]

It was in this statement that the six Democratic members of the committee, presumably supported by Representative Gearhart and perhaps to some extent by Representative Keefe from the Republican side,[31] conceded that General Short and Admiral Kimmel had undergone mistreatment and suffered mental anguish as a result of the position in which they had been placed between their removal from command in December, 1941, and the close of the Congressional investigation in 1946. It was here that Democratic members of the committee dealt with the injustice suffered by the two commanders. In their efforts to cope logically with the moral problem

29. This statement that the Democratic members were urged to validate the Roberts Report is based on information from good authority, which I am not at liberty to disclose. The application of the canons of historical criticism to the majority's passages on General Short and Admiral Kimmel suggests that several hands were engaged in shaping and giving final form to the sentences so constructed as to fit relevant facts in the record, and to produce a self-consistent pronouncement on the misfortunes of the two commanders.

30. CJC, *Report*, pp. 246 f.

31. In his report, Mr. Keefe dissented from most, though not all, of their views. See above. pp. 345 ff

the members ran into a veritable maze of contradictions—in the previous reports on Pearl Harbor and in their own attempts to square their unequivocal exoneration of high authorities in Washington with their conclusion to lift from the Hawaiian commanders the stigma of dereliction placed upon them by the Roosevelt Administration.

The Democratic members did not untie the knot; they cut it with one swift stroke: "We have not presumed to pass judgment on the nature of or charges of unfairness with respect to seven prior inquiries and investigations of the Pearl Harbor attack." Why not, since clearing up confusions, as Senator Barkley had said, was one of the prime reasons for the establishment of the committee? The answer of the Democratic members was, we feel "that by conducting a full and impartial hearing our report to the Congress along with the committee's record would present to the American people the material and relevant facts of the disaster."

Then, after some remarks on the nature of the Congressional Committee's inquiry, the Democratic members took up the issue of the treatment accorded to General Short and Admiral Kimmel. The two paragraphs dealing directly with this problem read:

Shortly after the disaster both Admiral Kimmel and General Short were retired from active duty. Consideration was thereafter given by the War and Navy Departments to the question of whether the errors made in Hawaii justified proceedings by court martial. Admiral Kimmel and General Short were requested in the interest of the Nation's war effort to waive their rights to plead the statute of limitations in bar of trial by general court martial for the duration of the war and 6 months thereafter.[32] Both these officers properly and commendably did so waive their rights. It was the duty of the Offices of the Judge Advocate General of the Army and the Navy to consider the facts of the disaster as relating to the responsibilities of the Hawaiian commanders, even though after inquiry and deliberation it was determined

32. See committee Exhibits 170, 171. Also see above, pp. 393 ff. for facts respecting their retirement in February, 1942.

that the errors were errors of judgment and not derelictions of duty.

On the morning of December 7, 1941, Admiral Kimmel and General Short were catapulted by the Empire of Japan into the principal roles in one of the most publicized tragedies of all time. That improper and incorrect deductions were drawn by some members of the public, with consequent suffering and mental anguish to both officers, cannot be questioned, just as erroneous conclusions were made by others with respect to the extent and nature of responsibility in Washington. But this is the result of the magnitude of public interest and speculation inspired by the disaster and not the result of mistreatment of anyone. The situation prevailing at Pearl Harbor on the morning of December 7 in the wake of the Japanese attack cast everyone, whether immediately or remotely concerned, beneath the white light of world scrutiny.

In view of the whole record before the Congressional Committee, and especially the pages upon pages of the testimony and documents bearing on the subject matter, these two paragraphs prepared by the Democratic members, with or without aid from the two Republican Representatives, are wonders in the history of ethics, jurisprudence, and the descriptive sciences, as the following analysis shows:

"Shortly after the disaster [at Pearl Harbor] both Admiral Kimmel and General Short were retired from active duty." The statement is correct; but how, in what circumstances, by whom, and by what methods?

"Consideration was *thereafter* given by the *War and Navy Departments* to the question of whether the errors made in Hawaii justified proceedings by court martial." (Italics supplied.)

Consideration of whether the errors of the commanders justified proceedings against them by court-martial was not given merely *after* the retirement of General Short and Admiral Kimmel. It was also given *before* they were officially retired, in immediate connection with the devising of a formula to accompany notice of their retirement; and the departments were warned by legal counsel that proving the case against the commanders would be a dubious undertaking and that a public promise of trial by court-martial was inadvisable.

Consideration of whether the errors of the commanders justified proceedings against them by court-martial was given not only by the War and Navy Departments. The whole question was also given "consideration" by President Roosevelt, Secretary Stimson, Secretary Knox, General Marshall, and Attorney General Biddle in close collaboration. These members of the Administration knew at the time of their consideration that their case against General Short and Admiral Kimmel was so dubious, indeed so unsupported by evidence, that in finally deciding upon the legal and public formula for retiring the commanders under the stigma of guilt, they did not dare to promise "proceedings by court martial." [33]

To summarize this "consideration" by the highest authorities in the Roosevelt Administration: After a Cabinet meeting at the White House, on February 13, 1942, Secretary Stimson took up with Secretary Knox the retirement of General Short and Admiral Kimmel. President Roosevelt had evidently been discussing the matter with Secretary Knox, and had supplied to Mr. Knox a formula to accompany the retirement. "The language of the President roughly," wrote Secretary Stimson to General Marshall, "as given me by Knox, was as follows: 'provided that it is agreed by you [General Short or Admiral Kimmel] that this is no bar to be used legally or otherwise to subsequent court martial proceedings.' " So President Roosevelt as well as officials in the War and Navy Departments, devoted "consideration" to the question of court-martial proceedings against the commanders and President Roosevelt gave Secretary Knox a formula which, if it had been adopted and used, would have conveyed to the public a clear impres-

33. Their moral problem was "solved," however, by comments accompanying the announcement of the formulas, which Secretary Stimson and Secretary Knox made for the benefit of the press to the effect that they had directed "the preparation of charges for trial by court martial . . . , alleging dereliction of duty." See above, Chap. VIII, p. 226. Yet those charges were never formally prepared and lodged against the two commanders.

sion that proceedings by court-martial were to be expected in due time.

If the Democratic members of the Congressional Committee had coupled these relevant facts with their statement about the consideration given by the War and Navy Departments to retirement and court-martial proceedings, they would have brought immediately into the center of the secret negotiations in January and February, 1942, the name of President Roosevelt who had suggested a harsher formula than that found tenable by the Attorney General and the legal advisers of the Army and the Navy.

In the records before them the Congressional Committee also had evidence that the legal advisers of the War and Navy Departments had, while the retirement of General Short and Admiral Kimmel was under "consideration," reported against promising trials by court-martial in that connection. To this point the Democratic members referred as follows: "It was the duty of the Offices of the Judge Advocate General of the Army and the Navy to consider the facts of the disaster as relating to the responsibilities of the Hawaiian commanders, *even though* after inquiry and deliberation it was determined that the errors were errors of judgment and not derelictions of duty." (Italics supplied.) Why "even though"? Was it not the plain and obvious duty of those officers, when the issue was duly presented to them by their superiors, to make a judicial inquiry into the facts and the law of the case and to report *whether* the errors were errors of judgment *or* derelictions of duty warranting proceedings by court-martial? In truth, the legal advisers of the War and Navy Departments warned President Roosevelt, Secretary Stimson, and Secretary Knox *before* the retirement of General Short and Admiral Kimmel that the grave charges made against them by the Roberts Commission would be difficult if not impossible to sustain and should not be publicly pressed.

Having in their manner disposed of the retirement of General Short and Admiral Kimmel and the business of dereliction of duty and court-martial proceedings against them, the Democratic members of the Congressional Committee came to the fact that the retirement of the commanders and the official announcements accompanying it had imposed intolerable suffering upon the commanders, had disgraced them before the country, and had long kept them in ignominy. What now was to be said in full view of the negotiations, decisions, and acts of will on the part of President Roosevelt, Secretary Stimson, Secretary Knox, General Marshall, Admiral Stark, and Attorney General Biddle which resulted in this tragedy for the commanders? Was any blame to be attached to these high officials for the tragedy of the commanders? This question must have given the Democratic members of the committee anxious hours.

How had the two commanders been placed in a position of disgrace before the American people? The Democratic members offered a curious explanation. First, they "were catapulted by the Empire of Japan into the principal roles in one of the most publicized tragedies of all time." Had the Empire of Japan inspired the charges brought by President Roosevelt's Commission against the commanders, given these charges to the public, and retired the commanders with official announcements in Washington which imputed guilt to them? Doubtless the majority did not intend to imply as much in their reference to the catapulting act performed by the Empire of Japan; but their formula, to say the least, was scarcely comprehensive.

Concretely, who in the United States brought the "suffering and mental anguish" to the commanders? To this question the Democratic members replied by putting the blame on "some members of the public"—the old and favorite recourse in such dilemmas. "Some members of the public" had drawn "improper and incorrect deductions." From what could the careless or evil persons have drawn their deductions except from the official pronouncements of the Roosevelt Administration which had charged the two commanders with grave offenses and had broadcast news of their retirement with a clear imputation of guilt?

Could the "suffering and mental anguish" of General Short and Admiral Kimmel have been due in some measure at least to actions of high authorities of Washington in respect of the "housecleaning" and the charges brought against them? Here was, indeed, the crux of the matter. The majority vaulted it by saying that while the personal tragedy of the commanders could not be questioned, "this is the result of the magnitude of public interest and speculation inspired by the disaster and not the result of mistreatment of anyone." As if to lighten the load for the two commanders the majority, in this connection, referred to "erroneous conclusions" that "were made by others with respect to the extent and nature of responsibility in Washington."

The upshot, in the opinion of the Democratic members, appeared to be: High authorities in Washington had also endured suffering and mental anguish as a consequence of erroneous deductions drawn by some people; General Short and Admiral Kimmel had been caught in this remorseless web of errors; but the misfortune of the two commanders, as of their superiors in Washington, "was not the result of mistreatment of anyone." So, if the distress of the General and the Admiral was not wholly assuaged by the findings of the Democratic members, they could take consolation in the thought that President Roosevelt, Secretary Hull, Secretary Stimson, Secretary Knox, General Marshall, and Admiral Stark, and perhaps Attorney General Biddle, had likewise been misunderstood and that yet nobody had been mistreated, presumably by anybody, except, possibly, by some anonymous members of the public. Transcending this flight of causational reasoning and philosophical eloquence seemed scarcely possible to the Democratic members of the Joint Committee on the Investigation of the Pearl Harbor Attack.[34]

34. The Republican minority of two avoided that problem in evidence by the simple expedient of ignoring, in their dissenting views, the question of the validity of the Roberts Report on this point and the question of the treatment accorded to General Short and Admiral Kimmel by the Roosevelt Administration.

CHAPTER XIV

Secret War Decisions and Plans

AT what point in time, if any, did President Roosevelt decide that the United States would, deliberately or of necessity, enter or become involved in the war and begin to make plans with this issue in view? [1] Since he never called upon Congress for a declaration of war, until after the Japanese attack, or publicly announced such a decision on his part, this subject will long remain open to debate.[2]

The problem, however, is by no means academic. Indeed it presents many practical aspects—political, ethical, and constitutional, and is intrinsic to a determination of how war came. Former associates of President Roosevelt and writers of a eulogistic bent have recognized it as basic to the exaltation of his leadership. If the President was driven into war by the overt acts of aggressors and in no manner contributed to bringing on the war, he was a victim, not a maker, of history; he did not lead the nation into war for reasons of world morality but was forced into it or drawn into it or compelled to take up arms against his will, by circumstances beyond his control. From this point of view, the President does not appear in the heroic role of the farsighted leader, in advance of his people, battling for the Four Freedoms against enemies of mankind.

1. It is needless to point out to anyone given to precision in the use of language how elusive are such phrases as "war was inevitable," "drawn into war," "compelled to take up arms," "forced into war," and "America has been wantonly attacked." They connote a determinism of events for the United States, as if President Roosevelt was a mere agent of "forces" beyond his initiation or control, not an active agent in a conjuncture of circumstances which he had helped to create by deliberate actions on his own part. Of course, it may be assumed that the whole world drama has been determined from the beginning of human time and that all the men and women who have taken part in it have been mere actors, mere puppets speaking lines and acting roles assigned to them by fate or "the nature of things." If so, so-called human virtues of courage, prescience, wisdom, and moral resolve are to be reckoned as phantoms.

2. What the papers in President Roosevelt's personal files will show, if ever opened to the public, must remain for the present a matter of conjecture. See below, p. 543 ff.

On the other hand, if the President did at some time before the Japanese attack decide that the United States should and would enter the war, and conducted his "complicated moves" in that direction, difficulties obvious in the historical record arise for consideration. More than a year before Pearl Harbor, President Roosevelt made his campaign pledges of 1940. After Pearl Harbor, he said: "The United States was at peace with that nation [Japan, on December 7] and, at the solicitation of Japan, was still in conversation with its Government looking toward the maintenance of peace in the Pacific. . . . Japan has, therefore, undertaken a surprise attack throughout the whole Pacific area."

For members of the Congressional Committee on Pearl Harbor the question of any kind of war decision had concrete pertinence to the issue of responsibility for the disaster. The Democratic members confronted something like a paradox. If the President did not decide at any time before the Japanese attack that war was actually at hand, how could it be claimed that General Short and Admiral Kimmel had been given orders specific enough, in terms of time and action, to sustain the charges lodged against them by the Roberts Commission? On the other hand, if President Roosevelt and Secretary Hull knew well in advance that Japan had resolved to break off relations and that involvement in war was immediately imminent, the official thesis of December 8 on the coming of war as a surprise took on the form of a contradiction.

Aware of the relation between the time of a war decision and responsibility for Pearl Harbor, Senator Ferguson sought by questioning Secretary Hull to find out the day and the hour of decision. In written questions the Senator asked the Secretary just *when* the Administration decided that war was immediately imminent, definitely informed the Army and Navy of the fact, and transferred the duty of defending American interests to the armed forces of the United States. Secretary Hull ingeniously avoided making an informative answer.[3]

3. See below, Chap. XVII, pp. 563 ff.

Recognizing the significance of the time question, the majority of the Congressional Committee on Pearl Harbor dealt with it as follows: "The Secretary of State fully informed both the War and Navy Departments of diplomatic developments and, *in a timely and forceful manner, clearly pointed out* to these Departments that relations between the United States and Japan had passed beyond the stage of diplomacy and *were in the hands of the military*." [4] By using the word "timely," the majority refrained from coping with Senator Ferguson's call for the day, but, in stating that Secretary Hull's notification of the War and Navy Departments was "timely," they clearly indicated that the time was on some day before December 7, 1941. Their indication thus cut across the official thesis of the President's war message of December 8, 1941.

As if fully sensitive to the fact that this question of time has a decisive bearing on President Roosevelt's antiwar pledges in 1940 and preceding years, as well as on the process by which the United States actually became involved in war, former officials of the Roosevelt Administration and other expositors of its measures have undertaken to meet the challenge. Referring to it in a review of my *American Foreign Policy in the Making, 1932–1940*, Adolf Berle, Jr., Assistant Secretary of State, 1938–44, and presumably possessing inside knowledge, said in 1946: "Somewhat rhetorically, on p. 45, it is asked, 'At what point in time of [during] these "fateful years" did the President and the Secretary (Hull) decide that the policy of neutrality and isolationism . . . was untenable and announce to the public that another foreign policy—one opposed to it—was in the best interest of the United States?' " [5]

Then Mr. Berle gave what he apparently regarded as an answer to the question: "The date when war was considered probable rather than remotely possible was shortly after the Munich conferences [1938]—up to which time the President

4. CJC, *Report*, p. 251. (Italics supplied.)

5. *Tomorrow*, November, 1946. My words "fateful years," if "rhetorical," were based on the State Department's title for Chap. I, "The Fateful Decade," *Peace and War, 1931-1941* (July, 1943 ed.), pp. 1-3.

and Secretary were hoping against hope that Europe at least would find a balance and solve its own problems. General disarmament after Munich was to be the acid test." When did the President announce to the country that the policy of neutrality and isolation had been abandoned for another policy? On this point Mr. Berle remarked:

This reviewer [Mr. Berle] would have thought that the records of the President and Mr. Hull were clear. Notable among the relevant documents are President Roosevelt's "quarantine speech" in 1937 [the year before Munich] and repeated warnings by Mr. Hull (many of which the author [Beard] omits) that Axis aggression, if continued, would endanger the safety of the United States as well as of the rest of the world. The growing and ever blunter expressions to foreign governments, instinct with American apprehension, plainly indicated the coming development. Historians may argue that clearer statements could have been made. Perhaps. But the country did not misunderstand.

Mr. Berle appeared to fix the date of the turn from neutrality and isolationism at some time in 1938 and cited President Roosevelt's quarantine speech of October 5, 1937, the previous year, as among the relevant documents. If October 5, 1937, is to be taken as the date of the turn, then it is to be noted that President Roosevelt at a press conference the following day, October 6, 1937, when asked whether the quarantine speech was "a repudiation" of the Neutrality Act, replied: "Not for a minute. It may be an expansion." [6] If the date of the turn is to be fixed "shortly after" the Munich conferences in 1938, then what may be said of numerous reaffirmations of their adherence to peace and neutrality for the United States made publicly by President Roosevelt and Secretary Hull in 1939 and 1940? [7]

Among the other "relevant documents" mentioned by Mr. Berle, in addition to the quarantine speech of October 5, 1937, were "repeated warnings" about Axis aggressions, and "the growing and ever blunter expressions to foreign governments"

6. Beard, *op. cit.*, pp. 188 ff.
7. *Ibid.*, pp. 223–323 *passim.*

which "plainly indicated the coming development." But Mr. Berle cited no specific warning or expression that could be dated and analyzed with a view to discovering whether it "plainly indicated" a turn from or repudiation of the anti-war and proneutrality pledges of President Roosevelt and the Democratic party in 1939 and 1940.[8] As if appreciating intellectual difficulties of explication, Mr. Berle stated that "historians may argue that plainer statements could have been made. Perhaps." Then he added: "But the country did not misunderstand." [9]

As a matter of fact a careful examination of every sentence in all these addresses and speeches in the nature of warnings and ever blunter expressions yields no information on the point of time at which President Roosevelt had decided to abandon the policy of neutrality and announce that another foreign policy—one pointed in the direction of war—was in the best interest of the United States.[10] Yet, for what it is worth and means, Mr. Berle's statement may be taken to imply that in 1937 or 1938 or thereabouts, President Roosevelt had decided that "war was considered probable," and hence that the maintenance of neutrality and peace for the United States was improbable. Such at least seems to be the upshot of Mr. Berle's effort to enlighten "historians," if not "the country" on the point at issue. Even so, it is no answer to the question I posed.

In respect of this chronological problem, Sumner Welles, former Undersecretary of State, said in 1946:

As I have earlier written, President Roosevelt since the autumn of 1936 had become ever more deeply engrossed with foreign policy. No matter how urgent the problems of domestic reform and recovery might be, he had long since recognized that neither re-

8. Mr. Berle may be sure that the country did not misunderstand, but a study of the debates in Congress on the Lend-Lease Bill and the amendment of the Neutrality Act in 1941 "plainly indicates" that Democratic members of Congress did misunderstand or misrepresent the purport of President Roosevelt's policy if it was as apparently described by Mr. Berle. See above, Chaps. II and VI.

9. See above, Chap. I.

10. Beard, *op. cit.*, pp. 28 ff.

covery nor reform could be enduring in a world so rapidly rushing toward war. He was already obsessed with the dangers by which the United States was confronted. By the summer of 1941 *the dangers had become imminent. . . .* By the summer of 1941 the overwhelming issue was his need *to obtain the support of the people of the United States, and of their Congress,* for those measures which were indispensable if the United States *was to be prepared to defend herself should she be drawn into war* and if, in the meantime, she was to be able to render such assistance as was available to the British people then fighting alone against the Axis. Isolationist sentiment was still widespread. . . .[11]

Another document furnished by Mr. Welles was more specific in respect of President Roosevelt's decision about the coming of war for the United States. After Mr. Welles had testified before the Congressional Committee on Pearl Harbor in November, 1945, a copy of his confidential memoranda of conversations at the Atlantic Conference was secured from the State Department and entered in the records of the committee.[12] Many passages of these memoranda were relative to the point of President Roosevelt's attitude toward war for the United States in August, 1941, about four months before Pearl Harbor, and one in particular bore on his expectations as to the time of the outbreak of war with Japan. In his memorandum for the morning of August 11, 1941, Mr. Welles recorded that the President, referring to the agreement with Prime Minister Churchill on parallel warnings to Japan, "expressed the belief that by adopting this course any further move of aggression on the part of Japan which might result in war could be held off for at least thirty days." [13]

11. *Where Are We Heading?* (Harper & Brothers, 1946), p. 3. (Italics supplied.) This statement, like the above-quoted passage from Mr. Berle, is couched in the elusive style employed by President Roosevelt and members of his Administration in their speeches of 1941 referring to war "dangers," as if the involvement of the United States in war would be due in no way to actions of the President, including the use of the American Navy in patrolling, convoying, and shooting. See above, Chaps. III and V. The style is to be characterized as naturally turgid or deliberately ambiguous.

12. See below, Chap. XV.

13. Davis and Lindley, in *How War Came*, reported the President as saying facetiously with regard to this point, "I think that I can baby them [the Japanese]

That President Roosevelt had made the fateful decision before the summer of 1940 was intimated by Mr. Justice Frankfurter in his memorial address at Harvard University in April, 1945:

But there came a time when he [the President] could no longer doubt that he had to shift from the task of social reform to war leadership, in order not only to maintain our spiritual heritage but to assure opportunities for further progress as a free society.

There came a moment when President Roosevelt was convinced that the utter defeat of Nazism was essential to the survival of our institutions. That time certainly could not have been later than when Mr. Sumner Welles reported on his mission to Europe [March, 1940]. Certainly from the time that the fall of France seemed imminent, the President was resolved to do everything possible to prevent the defeat of the Allies. Although confronted with the obvious danger of attack by the Axis upon us, there came that series of bold and triumphant measures which Mr. Churchill authoritatively summarized in his recent moving speech to the House of Commons—the shipment of arms to Great Britain, the stab-in-the-back speech, the base-destroyer deal, lend-lease, the smoothing of the difficult ways of the Allied purchasing missions, the encouragement of Mr. Willkie's trip to England,[14] the assistance in a hundred ways of British economic warfare, the extraordinarily prompt and cordial support of Russia. Moreover, while engaged in this series of complicated moves, he so skilfully conducted affairs as to avoid even the appearance of an act of aggression on our part.

---

along for three months." That fixed the date line of war near the middle of November. As to time at least, the Lindley and Davis account was more accurately predictive than the less rhetorical account in Mr. Welles' memorandum. As a result of his conversations with President Roosevelt at the Atlantic Conference, Mr. Churchill decided to make dispositions of British matériel and fighting forces on the expectation that the United States, even if not attacked, would enter the war. CJC, Part 14, p. 1283, and see below, Chap. XV. Also, p. 242.

14. After the campaign was over, President Roosevelt invited Mr. Willkie to the White House for a conference. The next day he talked to Frances Perkins, Secretary of Labor, about Mr. Willkie's visit, and said to her: "You know he [Mr. Willkie] is a good fellow. He has lots of talent. I want to use him somehow . . . I don't want him right around with us. . . . But I'd like to use him, and I think it would be a good thing for the country, it would help us to a feeling of unity." In the same conversation the President expressed a low opinion of Mr. Willkie's talents as a politician and campaigner. *The Roosevelt I Knew* (Viking, 1946), pp. 117 f.

And so, in the hour of national disaster on that Sunday afternoon after Japan had struck, when the President had gathered about him his cabinet and his military chiefs, the most experienced statesman among his advisers, after watching the President's powerful and self-possessed control of the situation, could say to himself, "There is my leader." [15]

The question of the time when President Roosevelt accepted "the probability that the United States would have to enter the approaching European war" is treated by Alden Hatch in his *Franklin D. Roosevelt: An Informal Biography* (1947). Owing to the laudatory and imaginative nature of Mr. Hatch's work, any of his statements not otherwise supported by authentic documents, may, of course, be discounted by critics, but Mr. Hatch secured information from a number of distinguished persons, "intimates" of President Roosevelt in the prewar years; for example, Mrs. Roosevelt, Admiral William D. Leahy, Vice-Admiral Ross T. McIntire, Samuel I. Rosenman, Franklin D. Roosevelt, Jr., Josephus Daniels, Justice Felix Frankfurter, and Ernest K. Lindley.

Mr. Hatch states that Vice-Admiral McIntire was convinced that the President accepted "the probability that the United States would have to enter the approaching European war if the democratic way of life were to be saved," for the first time, just after he had received news of the Hitler-Stalin Pact in August, 1939. Mr. Hatch concedes that the President did not then say positively that such was his decision but Mr. Hatch declares this to be a reasonable assumption based on what the President actually said. This opinion, Mr. Hatch says, he checked with other advisers of the President—in addition to Vice-Admiral McIntire—and put to them the question: "When do you think that the President decided that the United States would probably have to enter the war?" In every instance, he reports, "the reply fixed the

15. Like Mr. Berle and Mr. Welles, Mr. Justice Frankfurter seems to be saying that at some point in time President Roosevelt abandoned his peace pledges to the people and decided that the country was going to war; but like Mr. Berle and Mr. Welles, Justice Frankfurter avoided saying just that in decipherable language.

time within a few weeks of that day [August 23, 1939, the date of the Hitler-Stalin Pact]." [16]

Respecting President Roosevelt's calculations as to the probability of war in the Pacific, Admiral James O. Richardson was quite precise in his testimony before the Congressional Committee on Pearl Harbor in November, 1945. Admiral Richardson had been Commander in Chief of the Pacific Fleet from May 4, 1940, until relieved on February 1, 1941, by the designation of Admiral Husband E. Kimmel.[17] Occupying this responsible position during those months, Admiral Richardson was anxious to learn whether war or peace was the policy in Washington. On May 22, 1940, he raised the question with his superior in the Navy Department, Admiral Stark, Chief of Naval Operations; for he felt unable to make any rational disposition of the naval forces under his command unless he knew the purposes of policy he was supposed to serve: "Are we here primarily to influence the actions of other nations by our presence? . . . Are we here as a stepping-off place for belligerent activity? If so, we should devote all our time and energies to preparing for war. . . . If we are here to develop this area as a peacetime operating base, consideration should be given to the certain decrease in the efficiency of the Fleet. . . ." [18]

On October 8, 1940, Admiral Richardson had a long conversation with President Roosevelt at the White House. This was nearly a month before the President declared at Buffalo, with particular reference to a possible conflict with Japan, "Your President says this country is not going to war." At that White House conference, Admiral Richardson testified, "I took up the question of returning to the Pacific Coast all of the fleet except the Hawaiian detachment." In reply, "the President stated that the fleet was retained in the Hawaiian

16. Hatch, Foreword, and pp. 250 ff.
17. Apparently Admiral Richardson was removed from his command of the Pacific Fleet by President Roosevelt on the ground that he opposed basing the fleet at Pearl Harbor. Admiral Richardson was convinced that this policy was dangerous to the security of the United States, as, in fact, it proved to be, tragically.
18. CJC, Part 1, p. 259.

area in order to exercise a restraining influence on the actions of Japan." With respect to the "restraining influence," Admiral Richardson commented forthrightly: "Mr. President, I still do not believe it, and I know that our fleet is disadvantageously disposed for preparing for or initiating war operations." Subsequently during the conversation Admiral Richardson "asked the President if we were going to enter the war." [19]

This was President Roosevelt's response to the question, according to Admiral Richardson's testimony:

He [the President] replied that if the Japanese attacked Thailand, or the Kra Peninsula, or the Dutch East Indies, we would not enter the war, that if they even attacked the Philippines he doubted whether we would enter the war, but that they could not always avoid making mistakes and that as the war continued and the area of operations expanded sooner or later they would make a mistake and we would enter the war.[20]

That Admiral Richardson was not trusting to his memory in testifying that President Roosevelt had said to him on October 8, 1940—"the Japanese would make a mistake and we

19. *Ibid.*, pp. 265 f.
20. *Ibid.*, p. 266. In his version of President Roosevelt's statement to Admiral Richardson, Alden Hatch represents the Admiral as asking "abruptly," "Are we going to war?" and the President as pondering the question and answering carefully: "Not now, even if the Japs attack Thailand, the Kra Peninsula, or the Dutch East Indies. But they can't always avoid making mistakes, and if they start this thing and then make a mistake that arouses American opinion, we will go to war." *Franklin D. Roosevelt: An Informal Biography*, p. 274. What authority did Mr. Hatch have for giving this altered form to President Roosevelt's statement? In his Foreword, Mr. Hatch stated that he received information from Admiral William D. Leahy on some matters. Admiral Leahy was present at the White House with Admiral Richardson when the President's statement was made. Was Admiral Leahy responsible for this altered version? Mr. Hatch does not say that he was. Could Admiral Leahy have been responsible for it? If so then consider what Admiral Leahy said about Admiral Richardson's conversation with the President when he testified before the Congressional Committee in 1945. President Roosevelt's statement to Admiral Richardson as quoted above was read to Admiral Leahy by Senator Ferguson who then asked whether the incident occurred. Admiral Leahy could not remember whether it had or not, but he thought that the quotation as read "would not have been in disaccord" with the President's ideas, and added, "I should think it would have been in accord with his thoughts." CJC, Part 1, pp. 356 f. If Mr. Hatch was not resorting to license in his "informality," what authority did he have for his version of President Roosevelt's statement as reported by Admiral Richardson?

would enter the war"—was made manifest by other evidence laid before the Congressional Committee on Pearl Harbor. On his return West, the Admiral wrote a letter, dated at the United States Navy Yard, Bremerton, State of Washington, October 22, 1940, to Admiral Stark, in the City of Washington, D.C. In this letter Admiral Richardson said that on the occasion of his visit to Washington, D.C., early that month, he gained a distinct impression: ". . . it now appears that more active, open steps aimed at Japan are in serious contemplation and that these steps, if taken now, may lead to active hostilities." Thereupon Admiral Richardson presented to Admiral Stark the outline of what he deemed a new "realistic" plan, adapted to meeting the contingencies envisaged in relation to the "more active, open steps aimed at Japan."

Admiral Richardson was certainly convinced that war with Japan was envisaged by President Roosevelt in October, 1940, and that this meant a revolution in the war policy of the government upon which older war plans of the Navy rested. For, in his letter of October 22, 1940, he informed Admiral Stark that on an earlier visit to Washington, in July, 1940, he had received three distinct impressions: *"First.* That the Fleet was retained in the Hawaiian area solely to support diplomatic representations and as a deterrent to Japanese aggressive action; *Second.* That there was no intention of embarking on actual hostilities against Japan; *Third.* That the immediate mission of the Fleet was accelerated training. . . ." Yet after October 8, 1940, the Admiral was so sure "we would enter the war" that he urged a thorough overhauling of naval plans to meet the consequences of the shift in the President's views.[21]

21. Admiral Richardson's letter and outline of plans are in CJC, Part 14, Exhibit 9. More than incidentally it is to be noted that in a memorandum to Mr. Knox, Secretary of the Navy, dated September 12, 1940, Admiral Richardson warned the Secretary against Navy publicity indicating that "The Fleet is fully manned, fully trained and ready to fight at the drop of a hat," and other misleading extravagances of the kind. The Admiral said to the Secretary: "The type of publicity mentioned above is wrong in that it tends to lull the public into a false sense of security. It tends to weaken their moral fibre and to create an unhealthy national morale in a country which may be drawn into war on very short notice." This warning, however, did not keep Secretary Knox from declaring repeatedly to the American people: "The Navy is ready." *Ibid.,* pp. 957 f.

Information on President Roosevelt's opinions and decisions in respect of American involvement in a war with Japan is provided by extracts from the *Diary* of the Secretary of War, Henry L. Stimson, which were placed in the records of the Congressional Committee on Pearl Harbor.[22] Summaries of a few of the entries which Secretary Stimson made from day to day in November follow in chronological order:

November 6, 1941. President Roosevelt suggested to Mr. Stimson that he might propose a truce with the Japanese for six months. Mr. Stimson filed objections to this.

November 7. President Roosevelt took a vote of his full Cabinet on the proposition whether the country would back up the Administration if it struck at the Japanese in the southeastern Pacific area; and the Cabinet was "unanimous in feeling the country would support us."

November 21. Mr. Stimson had a talk with President Roosevelt about preparations to use poison gas in the Philippines in case the Japanese began to use it. The President agreed with Mr. Stimson that preparations should be made at once; and on his return to the War Department the Secretary issued instructions to General Gerow "to look up all the facts and get ready for the possible shipments with the idea that it should be done so that it would not come out in the press."

November 25. Conference of the President, Secretaries Hull, Stimson, and Knox, General Marshall, and Admiral Stark (the "War Cabinet") at the White House. President Roosevelt brought up the idea that the United States was likely to be attacked by the Japanese perhaps as soon as next Monday, December 1. Then the question before the conference was "how we should maneuver them [the Japanese] into the position of firing the first shot without allowing too much danger to ourselves."

22. The extracts from Mr. Stimson's daily notes (here called, for convenience, *Diary*), which he submitted to the Congressional Committee on request, appear in CJC, Part 11, pp. 5431 ff. Each reference to Mr. Stimson's *Diary* in this volume may be found there under the heading of the day. But my quotations are from the mimeographed copy as presented to the Congressional Committee in its original form.

November 26. Secretary Stimson called up Secretary Hull with regard to a truce with Japan then pending and Mr. Hull "replied . . . that he had about made up his mind to give up the whole thing in respect to a truce and to simply tell the Japanese that he had no further action to propose."

November 27. Secretary Hull told Secretary Stimson that he had broken off the whole matter of the truce or *modus vivendi* with the Japanese. He said to Mr. Stimson: "I have washed my hands of it and it is now in the hands of you and Knox—the Army and the Navy." [This day, war warning notices of a kind went from the War and Navy Departments to commanders of American outposts.]

November 28. War Cabinet meeting. "It was agreed that if the Japanese got into the Isthmus of Kra, the British would fight. It was also agreed that if the British fought, we would have to fight." The idea of a message to Congress and a letter of appeal to the Japanese Emperor was discussed. "The President asked Hull and Knox and myself to draft such papers."

December 7—about 2 P.M. After hearing from the President about the Japanese attack at Pearl Harbor, Mr. Stimson wrote in his *Diary:* "Now the Japs have solved the whole thing by attacking us directly in Hawaii. . . . My first feeling was of relief that the indecision was over and that a crisis had come in a way which would unite all our people. . . . I feel that this country united has practically nothing to fear; while the apathy and divisions stirred up by unpatriotic men have been hitherto very discouraging." [23]

Whatever conclusion may be drawn from such evidence in respect of the point of time at which President Roosevelt decided that the United States should become involved in the war and began to act on this decision, one thing is indisputable. By the middle of November, 1941, he was not saying privately to his official entourage what he had declared publicly in 1940, such as, "Your President says this country is not going to war." On the contrary, by the middle of November, 1941, he was

23. For fuller treatment of events and views recorded by Secretary Stimson in a broader setting with regard to decisions, see below, Chaps. XVI and XVII.

making statements to his official entourage which were pointed in one direction—war. And it is equally certain that President Roosevelt, Secretary Hull, Secretary Stimson, Secretary Knox, and Undersecretary Welles, in their war danger speeches in previous months of 1941, never said to the American people anything equivalent to what was being said in the White House behind the curtain of secrecy in November, 1941.

ADMIRAL STARK'S LETTERS ON THE PROGRESS OF WAR PLANS AND ACTIVITIES, JANUARY–SEPTEMBER, 1941

OFFICIAL, concrete, and informative in respect of war origins for the United States are the letters of Admiral Harold R. Stark to Admiral Kimmel and other naval commanders in 1941, which were placed in the open record of the Congressional Committee on Pearl Harbor.[24] Admiral Stark was in a strategic position to find out what was going on in President Roosevelt's mind as to war intentions and activities. Owing to the technical responsibility of Admiral Stark, the President had to be more explicit in communicating information to him than to his political subordinates. As Chief of Naval Operations, the Admiral was charged with making plans for naval actions pointed in the direction of war and for issuing orders to the naval officers who had to do the patrolling, convoying, shooting, and fighting—the waging of war, undeclared at first and finally declared. All along Admiral Stark, therefore, was in close contact with the President, personally and as a member

24. I have used here the *mimeographed* copy of Admiral Stark's letters, entitled "Admiral H. R. Stark's Letters to Admiral H. E. Kimmel" (166 pages) as presented to the committee in its original and complete form. For reasons of its own, the management of the Congressional Committee did not print every one of Admiral Stark's letters in its "Section A: Admiral H. R. Stark's Letters to Admiral H. E. Kimmel" in its Exhibit No. 106, CJC, Part 16. For example, it omitted his letter of April 3, 1941, in which Admiral Stark said: "The question as to our entry into the war now seems to be *when*, and not *whether*" (see below, p. 425). It is true that this letter was sent to the commanders of the Asiatic Fleet and the Atlantic fleets as well as to Admiral Kimmel but it appears—marked "*SECRET*"—in the mimeographed edition and is entitled "Observations on the present international situation." Students of history should be on guard against basing conclusions solely on the voluminous *printed* record of the Congressional Committee on Pearl Harbor.

of the war group that met frequently at the White House; hence he had access to many of the inmost secrets of the War Cabinet.[25]

It is true that Admiral Stark, as his letters show, often had difficulty in getting definite statements from President Roosevelt on designs and intentions relative to war and that he was at times apparently nonplussed, not to say impatient and provoked, by signs of indecisiveness on the part of the President. But the Admiral was loyal to his Commander in Chief and eager to get into the war as soon as feasible. And since it was the Navy that had to do the shooting and bear the first brunt of war when, as, and if it came, President Roosevelt had ample reason for keeping Admiral Stark well informed on crucial tendencies and decisions respecting war prospects and projects. Indeed, the Admiral's letters demonstrate that the President was rather free in communicating with him throughout the year.

Accordingly, Admiral Stark's letters and instructions to Admiral Kimmel and other naval officers are a primary source of concrete information bearing on President Roosevelt's war moves and on the realities of how war came for the United States—as distinguished from appearances. Inasmuch, however, as these letters are too voluminous for comprehensive treatment within the small compass of this book,[26] only extracts from the particularly explicit letters are given here under the successive dates.

January 13, 1941. Admiral Stark to Admiral Kimmel:

In my humble opinion, we may wake up any day with some mines deposited on our front doorstep or with some of our ships bombed, or whatnot, and find ourselves in another undeclared war, the

25. For Admiral Stark's relations to war projects from September to December 7, 1941, see Chaps. XVI and XVII, below.

26. Sometime, it is probable, a student of history with ample space at his disposal will combine in a single treatise a survey of Admiral Stark's letters and instructions, including those to Admiral J. O. Richardson, predecessor of Admiral Kimmel at Hawaii and all other documents relative to the development of American war plans and activities. See CJC, Part 14, Exhibit 9 and *Index of Exhibits*. But it is to be noted that this Exhibit does not include all the letters. It is entitled "Selected Letters." See note above, p. 420.

ramifications of which call for our strongest and sanest imagination and plans.

I have told the Gang here for months past that in my opinion we were heading straight for this war, that we could not assume anything else and personally I do not see how we can avoid, either having it thrust upon us or our deliberately going in, many months longer. And of course it may be a matter of weeks or of days. I would like to feel that I could be perfectly complacent if some day some one opens the door of my office and reports that the war is on. I have been moving Heaven and Earth trying to meet such a situation and am terribly impatient at the slowness with which things move here. Even though I know much has been accomplished, there still remains much to be done.

My estimate of the situation— . . . —which I presented to the Secretary and Rainbow 3, both of which you should have, will give you fairly clearly my own thoughts. Of course I do not want to become involved in the Pacific, if it is possible to avoid it. I have fought this out time and time again in the highest tribunals but I also fully realize that we may become involved in the Pacific and in the Atlantic at the same time; and to put it mildly, it will be one H— of a job, and that is one reason why I am thankful that I have your calm judgment, your imagination, your courage, your guts and your good head, at the seagoing end. Also your CAN DO— rather than *can't*.

In [Admiral] King, I believe you have the very best possible man to handle the situation in the Atlantic and that we can give him a free rein. He will lick things into shape and he knows the game from every standpoint. . . .

February 10, 1941. By this time the tension with Japan had reached such a point that a contest over the subject of commitments in the Pacific had been waged in the White House during the previous week. Admiral Stark fought against commitments and dispositions that would involve the country on two fronts and against sending more combatant ships to the Far East. In this contest, as reported by Admiral Stark, Secretary Hull took a contrary position and held to it tenaciously, as if unafraid of a war in the Pacific as well as in the Atlantic. Moreover, the Admiral represented President Roosevelt as then hesitant about asking Congress for more men, although willing to approve an authorization if Admiral Stark could secure it, as his letter of February 10, 1941, reveals:

. . . I continue in every way I possibly can to fight commitments or dispositions that would involve us on two fronts and to keep from sending more combatant ships to the Far East. I had a two hour struggle (please keep this absolutely secret) in the White House this past week and thank God can report that the President still supports my contentions. You may be amused to know that the Secretary of War, Colonel Stimson, has been a very great assistance to me in this connection in recent conferences. Mr. Hull never lets go in the contrary view and having fought it so many times I confess to having used a little more vehemence and a little stronger language than was becoming in fighting it out this last week for the nth time. Present were the President, Stimson, Knox, Marshall and myself. I mention this just to show you that the fight is always on and that some day I might get upset. But thank God, to date at least, the President has and continues to see it my way.

. . . I am struggling, and I use the word advisably, every time I get in the White House, which is rather frequent, for additional men. It should not be necessary and while I have made the case just as obvious as I possibly could, the President just has his own ideas about men. I usually finally get my way but the cost of effort is very great and of course worth it. I feel that I could go on the Hill this minute and get all the men I want if I could just get the green light from the White House. As a matter of fact what we now have, was obtained by my finally asking the President's permission to go on the Hill and state our needs as I saw them at that time and his reply was "go ahead, I won't veto anything they agree to." However, the struggle is starting all over again and just remember we are going the limit, but I cannot guarantee the outcome.

February 11, 1941. Memorandum from Admiral Stark to President Roosevelt on the possibility of sending a naval detachment to the Philippines as a kind of "bluff" to the Japanese, although it involved the possibility of a Japanese attack:

Since your thought yesterday morning of the possibility of sending a detachment to the Philippines via the southern route consisting of approximately 4 cruisers, a squadron (9) of destroyers and carriers and perhaps to permit a leak that they were going out there just for a temporary visit and then return, I confess to having pondered a good deal on it last night during the wee small hours because, as you know, I have previously opposed this and you have concurred as to its unwisdom. Particularly do I recall your remark in a previous conference when Mr. Hull suggested this and the question arose as to getting them out and your 100% reply, from my standpoint, was that you might not mind losing one or two cruisers [27] (we have 2 out there now), but that you did not want to take a chance on losing 5 or 6. Frankly, I breathed a great sigh of relief and thought the issue pretty definitely closed.

You also called it a "bluff" and questioned it from that standpoint. Obviously, if we permitted a leak about their coming back, there would be even less, if any, bluff, and again if we did not permit a leak with regard to their coming back, we would then certainly look like turning tail and running if something happened and we did come back. I believe it pretty thoroughly agreed that we do not want that force in the Philippines in case of sudden attack, and that even were we to consider in emergency increasing our forces in the Far East, we would not send them to Manila Bay but rather to the southward or into Dutch East Indies where they would be better supported and not so open to attack.

Continuing his report to the President in the same letter, Admiral Stark expressed the opinion that sending a small force into the Far Pacific would probably act as no deterrent to Japan or hamper the Japanese in advancing southward. He further said:

There is a chance that further moves against Japan will precipitate hostilities rather than prevent them. We want to give Japan no excuse for coming in in case we are forced into hostilities with Germany who we all consider our major problem. . . . If we are forced into war our main effort as approved to date will be directed in the Atlantic against Germany. . . . If we send part of the Fleet to the Asiatic now, we may show our hand and lose the value of any strategic surprise.

April 3, 1941. Writing personally and confidentially to Admiral Kimmel at Hawaii, Admiral Stark said:

27. Presumably as the result of a Japanese attack.

I am more and more of opinion that Japan will hesitate to take further steps, perhaps even against Indo-China, so long as affairs do not go too badly for Britain. What the effect on her would be were the United States to transfer a large part of the Pacific Fleet to the Atlantic can, as yet, be only surmised. In any case we shall rigidly avoid making any indication that we contemplate such a transfer until the last possible moment. The question as to our entry into the war now seems to be *when*, and not *whether*. Public opinion, which now is slowly turning in that direction, may or may not be accelerated. My own personal view is that we may be in the war (possibly undeclared) against Germany and Italy within about two months, but that there is a reasonable possibility that Japan may remain out altogether. However, we can not at present act on that possibility.

April 4, 1941. Admiral Stark to Admiral Kimmel:

I am enclosing a memo on convoy [28] which I drew up primarily to give the President a picture of what is now being done, what we would propose to do if we convoyed, and of our ability to do it. . . . I feel it is only a matter of time before King is directed to convoy or patrol or whatever form the protective measures take. . . . The situation is obviously critical in the Atlantic. In my opinion, it is hopeless except as we take strong measures to save it. . . . Our officers who have been studying the positions for bases in the British Isles have returned, and we have decided on immediate construction of 1 destroyer base and 1 seaplane base in Northern Ireland. We are also studying Scotland Iceland bases for further support of the Protective force for shipping in the northward approaches to Britain.

The memorandum to which Admiral Stark thus referred dealt with "Ocean Escort in Western Atlantic" and showed that the American Navy had been for some time and was then engaged in coöperating with the British in the "escort" of "convoys" in the Western Atlantic.[29]

April 19, 1941. In a letter to Admiral Kimmel, Admiral Stark spoke of the difficulties he encountered in the White

---

28. See above, Chap. III, for President Roosevelt's statement on April 25, 1941, to the effect that only "patrolling" was in operation at that time.

29. Text of memorandum on ocean escort in Western Atlantic, CJC, Part 16, pp. 2162 f.

House with regard to the use of the Navy as an instrument of policy in the conduct of relations with Japan. Apparently President Roosevelt, supported by the State Department, wanted to employ American naval vessels for the purpose of keeping "the Japs guessing," by "popping up here and there." The President did not make clear what objective he hoped to gain by such maneuvers but it was again evident that the State Department was pertinacious in its demand for demonstrations of force against Japan, despite the fact, or on account of it, that a war incident might occur at any stage of such "tactics."

Extract from Admiral Stark's letter of April 19, 1941:

. . . I wrote you about the Australian Detachment. The President said (and incidentally when I open up to you this way I don't expect you to quote the President and I know there is nobody who can keep things secret better than you can); "Betty, just as soon as those ships come back from Australia and New Zealand, or perhaps a little before, I want to send some more out. I just want to keep them popping up here and there, and keep the Japs guessing." This, of course, is right down the State Department's alley. To my mind a lot of State Department's suggestions and recommendations are nothing less than childish (don't quote me) and I have practically said so in so many words in the presence of all concerned, but after 13 months they finally got it going. Of course I recognize some merit, if exercised with some discretion—and that is where Navy has to count on F. D. R. for reserve; so we did not have to send ships into Singapore and we did keep them on a flank to be in position to go to work or to retire if something broke. . . .

To that extent, namely, more or less in position if something broke, I acquiesced in the Australian Cruise with far more grace than I would have otherwise. I am not insensible to the advantages of a cruise of this sort, as well as to the disadvantages of interruption in training.

Now when the question of "Popping up everywhere" came and having in mind keeping on the flank, I said to the President: "How about going North?" He said: "Yes, you can keep any position you like, and go anywhere."

There was a little method in my madness as to the Northern cruise; I thought for once, if I could, I would give the State Department a shock which might make them haul back, and incidentally, that Northwest cruise has many good points. It still conforms to the flank, and a detachment on an occasional sortie up in an unexpected direction might be good ball, and if you even want to make such a cruise yourself of your own initiative, don't hesitate to ask. Of course you can see what a striking force of the composition I gave you, and known to the Japs, would mean to them, in view of their unholy fear of bombing. This striking detachment would have been right in position for most anything.

I had a broad inward smile when the State Department in effect said: "Please, Mr. President, don't let him do it"; or words to that effect. It was a little too much for them. . . .

I had hoped that with the passage of the Lend-Lease Bill we could look forward to some unity on Capitol Hill but just at present there seems to be far from that desired unity on vital issues. What will be done about convoy and many other things, and just how much a part of our Democratic way of life will be handled by Mr. Gallup, is a pure guess. From that you might think I am getting a little bit cynical, but believe it or not, that is not the case, and I am sawing wood as usual and am still cheerful.

April 26, 1941. Admiral Stark to Admiral Kimmel:

This is just to get you mentally prepared that shortly a considerable detachment from your fleet will be brought to the Atlantic.

May 14, 1941. Admiral Stark to the Commandants of twelve Naval Districts, including Admirals King (Atlantic), Kimmel (Hawaii), and Hart (Far East). Admiral Stark was still of the opinion that the question of war for the United States was "a case of only WHEN?" He transmitted speculations as to June and July and added: "It continues to be just 'Around the corner.' " Extracts follow:

You will recall my previous letter of 3 October 1940, in which I stressed readiness and not to be taken aback should somebody suddenly start depositing mines on our front doorstep, etc. etc.

I might add that I have no inside information as to what is going to happen or when, but it seems to me now, as it did then, that it is a case of only

WHEN?

The trend of events, and public opinion certainly all tend increasingly this way.

If and when we do get in, my hunch is that Hitler would certainly, in one way or another, attack our shipping wherever he thought it would be profitable, either from a material or psychological standpoint. . . .

This is just again to remind you all of the seriousness of the present situation and of the necessity of our being ready, to the utmost extent, to use what we have or what we can improvise, should the issue suddenly be drawn.

Plans and machinery for convoy are pretty well in hand but here, too, there may be hitches or slips which, in the last analysis, may only be found by actual practice. However, convoy games on paper by those who must handle the details should be good mental exercise, and may bring to light certain correctable deficiencies. . . .

I might add that some months ago (and less than that) our studies here in the Department indicated that if we did not get into this war by March we would be fairly well off in the local defense picture; later it was put at April with assurances that in any case I could feel fairly comfortable by the first of May. Now I am told the latter part of May or maybe some time in June or the first of July. It continues to be just "Around the corner." I think the time is here now for even more personal strenuous effort by all of us, in responsible positions. . . .

May 24, 1941. Admiral Stark to Admiral Kimmel:

Day before yesterday afternoon the President gave me an overall limit of 30 days to prepare and have ready an expedition of 25,000 men to sail for, and take the Azores. Whether or not there would be opposition I do not know but we have to be fully prepared for strenuous opposition. You can visualize the job particularly when I tell you that the Azores recently have been greatly reinforced. The Army, of course, will be in on this but the Navy and the Marines will bear the brunt.[30]

30. See below, Chap. XV for the secret proceedings relative to this matter at the Atlantic Conference.

July 7, 1941. Admiral Stark to Admiral Kimmel, giving the Commander of the Pacific Fleet "not an order, but just a thought which I wanted to transmit to you." The "thought" was that if a foreign man-'o-war told the Dutchman to stop, "I would tell the Dutchman to disregard the order," and "Moreover I would lay my ship fairly close to the Dutchman and between the Dutchman and the foreign man-'o-war and let the latter do his worst."

July 31, 1941. Admiral Stark to Captain Charles M. Cooke, with a copy for Admiral Kimmel. In this letter, Admiral Stark represented himself as pressing the President to "announce and start escorting immediately," urging that war psychology be speeded up, although as yet uncertain whether an incident in the Atlantic would result in war soon:

. . . Within forty-eight hours after the Russian situation broke, I went to the President, with the Secretary's approval, and stated that on the assumption that the Country's decision is not to let England fall, we should immediately seize the psychological opportunity presented by the Russian-German clash and announce and start escorting immediately, and protecting the Western Atlantic on a large scale; that such a declaration, followed by immediate action on our part, would almost certainly involve us in the war and that I considered every day of delay in our getting into the war as dangerous, and that much more delay might be fatal to Britain's survival. I reminded him that I had been asking this for months in the State Department and elsewhere, etc. etc. etc. I have been maintaining that only a war psychology could or would speed things up the way they should be speeded up; that strive as we would it just isn't in the nature of things to get the results in peace that we would, were we at war.

The Iceland situation may produce an "incident." You are as familiar with that and the President's statements and answers at press conferences as I am. Whether or not we will get an "incident" because of the protection we are giving Iceland and the shipping which we must send in support of Iceland and our troops, I do not know. Only Hitler can answer.

The Far Eastern situation has been considerably changed because of the entrance of Russia into the picture.

Personally, I threw into the arena that we consider along with the British a joint protectorate over the Dutch East Indies, as a move calculated to prevent further spread of war in the Far East. It is a debatable question. Certainly there can be no joy in our camp over the occupation of Indo-China . . .

August 22, 1941. Admiral Stark to Admiral Kimmel:

"There is much doing in the Atlantic in the formative stage. Thank God we should have things in full swing before long and with plans fairly complete. It has changed so many times—but now I think we at last have something fairly definite—maybe." This letter was accompanied by a long memorandum, dated August 19, 1941, on the situation and technical matters of preparations for war.

September 22, 1941. Admiral Stark to Admiral Thomas Hart, Commander of the Asiatic Fleet:

In this letter Admiral Stark described the situation in the Atlantic, briefly explained the methods of convoying employed and declared that "we are all but, if not actually, in it:"

. . . So far as the Atlantic is concerned, we are all but, if not actually, in it. The President's speech of September 11, 1941 put the matter squarely before the country and outlined what he expected of the Navy. We were ready for this; in fact, our orders had been issued.[31]

In addition to the incidents cited by the President, other and probably equally compelling reasons lay behind his decision. For some time, the British have found the problem of getting supplies across the Atlantic a difficult one. They have never had enough ships suitable for escort duty. Their forces are thinly spread and, as a result of casualties, the spreading has had to be thinner and thinner as the campaign has progressed. If Britain is to continue, she has to have assistance. She will now get it openly. King's forces, too, are thinly spread, working as he is from 20 South to the Iceland area.

In a nutshell, we are now escorting convoys regularly from the United States to points in the Iceland area, where these convoys are picked up by the British and escorted to the British Isles. In addition to our own escort vessels, the Canadians are participating.

31. See above, pp. 139 ff.

Both forces (Canadian and our own) are operating under King's direction. . . .

September 23, 1941. Admiral Stark to Admiral Kimmel on the "shooting orders" for the Atlantic and the Southeast Pacific sub-area:

. . . At the present time the President has issued "shooting orders" only for the Atlantic and Southeast Pacific sub-area.

The situation in the Pacific generally is far different from what it is in the Atlantic. The operations of raiders in the Pacific at present are not very widespread or very effective. Most of the merchantmen in the Pacific are of United States or Panamanian flag registry. Instituting any steps toward eliminating raiders outside of waters close to the continents of North and South America, might have unfavorable repercussions, which would not be worth the cost to the United States in the long run. The longer we can keep the situation in the Pacific in status quo, the better for all concerned. . . .

In reply to question (a) your existing orders to escorts are appropriate under the present situation. They are also in accordance with Art. 723 U.S. Navy Regulations; no orders should be given to shoot at the present time, other than those clearly set forth in this article. I believe there is little possibility of an Italian or German raider molesting a naval ship, but there might be another "Robin Moore" incident in the Pacific, in which case the President might give orders for action in the Pacific similar to those now in effect in the Atlantic; but that is something for the future. . . .

Regarding question (b), we have no definite information that Japanese submarines have ever operated in close vicinity to the Hawaiian Islands, Alaska or our Pacific Coast. They may have been near Wake recently. The existing orders, that is not to bomb suspected submarines except in the defensive sea areas, are appropriate. If conclusive, and I repeat conclusive, evidence is obtained that Japanese submarines are actually in or near United States territory, then a strong warning and a threat of hostile action against such submarines would appear to be our next step. Keep us informed . . .

November 7, 1941. Admiral Stark to Admiral Hart.

Events are moving rapidly toward a real showdown, both in the Atlantic and in the Pacific. The Navy is already in the war of the

Atlantic, but the country doesn't seem to realize it. Apathy, to the point of open opposition, is evident in a considerable section of the press. Meanwhile, the Senate is dragging out the debate with reference to the arming of the merchantmen. Whether the country knows it or not, *we are at war.*[32]

PLANS FOR AMERICAN NAVAL OPERATIONS IN THE ATLANTIC

FOR the belief that the United States was headed in the direction of war, which he expressed in various ways and many times to naval officers between January and September, 1941, Admiral Stark had grounds other than mere conversations with President Roosevelt on war prospects. From January 29 to March 27, 1941, he was engaged in conferences with British and American Army and Navy officers, at Washington, on the task of drawing up over-all war plans for coöperation with the British Commonwealth of Nations in war, "should the United States be compelled to resort to war."[33] On April 4, he prepared for President Roosevelt a memorandum on convoys, giving him a picture of what was being done and what might be done "if we convoyed." Far more significant, however, for the actual involvement of the United States in war were Admiral Stark's preparation and execution, under the President's direction, of plans for patrolling, convoying, intervening, and "shooting" in the Atlantic, between April and November.

Although much was publicly known about warlike activities in the Atlantic between June and November, 1941, the origins and nature of these activities were obscure, at least as officially explained.[34] Had the "shootings" reported in the press opened with flagrant attacks by German warcraft, as represented on two critical occasions by President Roosevelt in impassioned addresses to the nation?[35] Or had they occurred in connection with operations undertaken by the American Navy in the execution of plans or orders drawn

32. CJC, Part 5, p. 2121. (Admiral Stark's italics.)
33. See below, pp. 442 ff. "Compelled" by what or whom, and how?
34. See above, Chaps. III and V.
35. See above, Chap. V.

and put into effect at the direction of the President? Revelations made by the American press and by the Senate Committee on Naval Affairs had indicated in October and November that the "shootings" bore some relation to the enforcement of plans authorized by President Roosevelt,[36] but the dates and precise terms of such plans remained among the secrets of the Navy Department, until they were brought into the open by the Congressional Committee on Pearl Harbor in 1945–46.

At a hearing of the committee, in January, 1946, Representative Gearhart raised with Admiral Stark the question of how the "shooting war" in the Atlantic came into being.[37] Thereupon in the course of a colloquy that ensued Admiral Stark presented to the committee a summary or digest of the plans for American naval operations in the Atlantic between April and October, 1941, in the chronological order of their development.

The colloquy ran as follows:

MR. GEARHART. Now, you testified in your written statement that the Navy was in the war in the Atlantic on the 7th day of November 1941. You remember that testimony?

ADMIRAL STARK. Yes, sir.

MR. GEARHART. If we were at war on the 7th day of November of 1941, in the Atlantic when did that war begin?

ADMIRAL STARK. I would like to say as to that statement that we were at war that it should be interpreted as in effect. We were not belligerents, we did not have the right of belligerents, but when we had orders to shoot any German or Italian on the high seas to the westward of the twenty-sixth meridian and when they in turn were attacking us and we were endeavoring to sink their attacking vessels and they were endeavoring and had wounded our vessels at that time, we were in effect engaging them and to that extent we were at war, and so far as the high seas were concerned when we actually entered the war there wasn't much change in that particular case.

On the other hand, there was at one time a request come to me to apprehend a certain vessel, a German vessel which was, we

36. See above, Chap. V.
37. CJC, Part 5, pp. 2292 ff.

found, approaching Germany with rubber and we refused to do it because of the fact that we did not have belligerent rights.

On the other hand, again as regards being in war, we were in the position of having command of Canadian vessels or they might have of ours, or we might under certain circumstances under the shooting order command British vessels, Britain being at war with Germany, or a British officer might have command of ours, so in effect I made the statement we were at war. There were certain belligerent rights technically and the thing had not been openly declared, but in the ways which the President had defined and of which he had informed the country in his speech in September,[38] there was war on the sea for any Axis power that came within that limit.

MR. GEARHART. Now, you described the conditions as existing on the 7th day of November 1941 as indicating a condition of war. Now, I am asking you when did the condition come into being?

ADMIRAL STARK. I think perhaps I might read a brief which I had made up thinking it might be of use to the Committee—primarily I wanted it for myself to get the sequence—of the hemispheric defense orders. . . .

MR. GEARHART. Was there an order commanding commanders of American ships in the Atlantic to fire upon German submarines or surface ships under any conditions?

ADMIRAL STARK. There was.

MR. GEARHART. Who issued that order?

ADMIRAL STARK. I did, by direction of the President.

MR. GEARHART. And when was it issued?

ADMIRAL STARK (reading):

"On October 8, 1941 by despatch 082335 the Chief of Naval Operations ordered the above outlined plan executed at 1400 G.C.T."

that is Greenwich Civil Time—

"11 October 1941. The plan remained in effect until December 11, 1941, at which time the Chief of Naval Operations by despatch 111550 ordered the above outlined plan cancelled and replaced by WPL 46, Navy Basic War Plan Rainbow No. 5."

I think it might be helpful if I would read this correspondence which lays down the sequence and is a brief.

38. See above, p. 139.

THE CHAIRMAN. Go ahead and read it, Admiral.

MR. GEARHART. I will be glad to have you do that, Admiral, with permission of the chair.

ADMIRAL STARK. It is six pages long.

MR. GEARHART. Go ahead.

ADMIRAL STARK. But it gives the picture and consolidation of a good many pages.

MR. GEARHART. All right.

The digest of war orders, or instructions, promulgated secretly between April 21, 1941, and September 26, 1941, which was presented to the Congressional Committee by Admiral Stark disclosed realities that offered a strange contrast to many statements made publicly by President Roosevelt earlier in the year, to the allegations made by sponsors of the Lend-Lease Bill in Congress, and to the amendments to the bill in respect of convoying.[39] For example, on January 21, 1941, the President dismissed the idea of convoying supplies to Great Britain as if out of consideration; on March 5, 1941, he said: "I am glad to reiterate the assurance that the policy under which the measure [Lend-Lease] would be operated would not be a war policy but the contrary"; and at his press conference on April 25, 1941, he "denied that the Government was considering Naval escorts for convoys" and had described his policy of "patrolling" in terms which brought it within the limitations of international law and a peace policy.[40]

Admiral Stark's digest of war orders, or instructions, between April 21, 1941, and September 26, 1941, may be summarized as follows:

I. The first plan described by Admiral Stark, promulgated, at the direction of the President, April 21, 1941, and made effective in the Atlantic on April 24, if cautious and limited in form, was explicit in its direction. It did not declare that German and Italian naval vessels and aircraft entering the Western Hemisphere as *ipso facto* hostile, but "as actuated *by a possibly unfriendly intent toward territory or shipping*

39. See above, Chaps. II and III, *passim.*
40. See above, pp. 22, 97.

within the Western Hemisphere" (italics supplied) thus covering territory and shipping belonging to other countries with possessions in this hemisphere as well as the United States. The plan, by the use of particular phraseology, ordered the American Navy to "trail" German and Italian naval vessels and aircraft and broadcast "in plain language their movements at four hour intervals, or oftener if necessary." The American Navy was to prevent interference with United States flag shipping by belligerents, to avoid intervening in or interfering with the armed engagements of belligerents, and to give the execution of the plan "the appearance of routine exercises where departure of units from port are being made."

The text of Admiral Stark's digest of this project follows:

Navy Hemisphere Defense Plan #2 (WPL–49), promulgated April 21, 1941, issued by the Chief of Naval Operations at the direction of the President, was based on the general concept:

"Entrance into the Western Hemisphere by Naval vessels and aircraft of belligerent Powers, other than of those Powers which have sovereignty over Western Hemisphere Territory, will be viewed as actuated by a possibly unfriendly intent toward territory or shipping within the Western Hemisphere."

The General Task assigned the Navy was:

". . . warn Western Hemisphere Powers against possible impending danger, and defend United States flag shipping against attack."

The specific tasks assigned the Naval Operating Forces were:

"(a) Trail naval vessels and aircraft of belligerent Powers (other than of those Powers which have sovereignty over Western Hemisphere Territory), and broadcast in plain language their movements at four hour intervals, or oftener if necessary.

"(b) Trail merchant vessels of belligerent Powers (other than of those Powers which have sovereignty over Western Hemisphere Territory) if suspected of acting as supply vessels for, or otherwise assisting the operations of, the naval vessels or aircraft of such belligerents. Report the movements of such vessels to the Chief of Naval Operations.

"(c) Prevent interference with United States flag shipping by belligerents.

"(d) Avoid intervening in or interfering with the armed engagements of belligerents."

The above plan became effective in the Atlantic on April 24, 1941, the dispatch placing it into effect stated "The execution of this plan shall give the appearance of routine exercises where the departure of units from port are being made." (Chief of Naval Operations Dispatch 211520 of April, 1941, to Holders of WPL–49.)

II. The second plan listed by Admiral Stark, called Hemisphere Defense Plan #4 (WPL–51), was issued on July 11, 1941, at the direction of the President. The major portion of it was ordered in execution on July 26 and the remainder was not to be executed until necessary arrangements had been made. Plan #4 repeated the statement of Plan #2 that the entrance of German and Italian naval vessels and aircraft would be regarded as actuated by a "possibly" unfriendly intent toward territory and shipping within the Western Hemisphere. It incorporated passages from President Roosevelt's message to Congress respecting the occupation of Iceland.[41] After these passages came a list of general and specific tasks to be executed, as follows:

The General Tasks assigned the Navy were within the Western Hemisphere and were as follows:

"(a) Insure the safety of communications with United States strategic outposts;

"(b) Insure the adequate defense of Iceland;

"(c) Defend United States and Iceland flag shipping against hostile attack or threat of attack: and

"(d) Warn Western Hemisphere Powers against possible impending danger."

When the order to execute this plan was issued, Change #1 had been incorporated. The Tasks assigned to the Atlantic Fleet were:

"(a) Protect United States and Iceland flag shipping against hostile attack, by escorting, covering, and patrolling, as required

41. See above, p. 113.

by circumstances, and by destroying hostile forces which threaten such shipping.

"(b) Escort convoys of United States and Iceland flag shipping [including shipping of any nationality which may join such convoys, between United States ports and bases and Iceland].[42]

"(c) Provide protection and sea transportation for the initial movements and continued support of United States overseas garrisons.

"(d) Trail naval vessels and aircraft of belligerent Powers (other than of those Powers which have sovereignty over Western Hemisphere Territory and other than belligerent vessels and aircraft involved in encounters in executing a, b, and c): and broadcast in plain language their movements at four hour intervals, or oftener if necessary. Amplify such broadcasts by encrypted despatch to the Chief of Naval Operations.

"(e) Trail merchant vessels of belligerent Powers (other than those Powers which have sovereignty over Western Hemisphere Territory), if suspected of acting as supply ships for, or otherwise assisting the operations of, the naval vessels or aircraft of such belligerents. Report the movements of such vessels to the Chief of Naval Operations. . . ."[43]

The plan stated that Canada had made available Shelburne and Halifax as operating bases for United States Naval vessels and patrol planes, and Sydney for United States Naval vessels in case of necessity.

The Chief of Naval Operations would exchange information on movements of British and Canadian convoys and Naval forces and United States Naval forces and United States and Iceland flag shipping with the British and Canadian authorities.

On July 25, 1941, the Chief of Naval Operations by dispatch 251600 ordered the above outlined plan executed at 1200 (GCT) July 26th, except that only United States and Iceland flag shipping was to be escorted, i.e., the words in Task (b), "including shipping of any nationality which may join such convoys, between United States ports and bases, and Iceland," were not to be executed until necessary arrangements had been made.[44]

42. This clause enclosed in brackets was put into effect on September 16, 1941. See below, p. 439.

43. (e) was cancelled September 13, 1941, and superseded by broad provisions for escorting and convoying.

44. See III, 1, below.

III. By a number of changes in war projects, listed by Admiral Stark, the following steps were taken in expanding the operations of the Navy:

1. August 13, 1941, instructions for the operation of convoys and escorts in the North Atlantic which were to become effective when the escort of convoys including ships of nationality other than those of United States and Iceland was ordered.[45]

2. August 25, Admiral Stark, as Chief of Naval Operations, ordered the Commander in Chief of the Atlantic Fleet to interpret previous orders as requiring Atlantic Fleet forces to destroy surface raiders which attacked shipping along the sea lanes between North America and Iceland or approached these lanes sufficiently close to threaten such shipping.

3. August 28, provisions made for destruction of "surface raiders which attacked or threatened to attack United States flag shipping in the Southeast Pacific Sub-area." Instructions to the effect: "The approach of surface raiders," in the Panama Naval Coastal Frontier and the Sub-area, was to be interpreted as a threat to United States flag shipping.

4. September 3, instruction that hostile forces will be deemed to threaten United States or Iceland flag shipping "if they enter the general area of the sea lanes which lie between North America and Iceland or enter the Neutrality Zone in the Atlantic Ocean described in the Declaration of Panama of October 3, 1939."

5. September 13, effective September 16, convoy system broadened to include, besides United States and Iceland shipping, the "shipping of any nationality which may join such convoys, between United States ports and bases, and Iceland"—an "execute" for section (b) "Tasks assigned to the Atlantic Fleet," Plan #4, see above, p. 437. This order put into force "the detailed instructions for the operations of convoys and escorts" in a wide area of the North Atlantic routes.

6. September 13, Chief of Naval Operations informed the Commander in Chief of the Atlantic Fleet that "the President

45. September 13, 1941, see No. 5, below.

had modified previous instructions regarding convoy and escort, and that the United States Naval vessels could escort
convoys in which there was no United States or Iceland flag
vessels and that United States flag vessels could be escorted by
Canadian ships."

IV. September 26, 1941, a new Western Hemisphere Defense Plan #5 (WPL–52) was issued, superseding Plan #4.
This plan was to be put into effect by the Chief of Naval
Operations after the Commander in Chief of the Atlantic
Fleet had submitted a readiness report. On October 8 it was
ordered in force as of October 11, 1941, and remained in effect until December 11, 1941, when the United States was
involved in "lawful" war in the Atlantic and the Pacific. Then
#5 was superseded by the Navy Basic War Plan, Rainbow
No. 5, which had long been reposing in the secret files of the
Navy Department, awaiting eventualities. Admiral Stark's
digest of Plan #5—WPL–52, issued September 26, and in
force from October 11, to December 11, 1941, follows:

Western Hemisphere Defense Plan #5 (WPL–52), issued September 26, 1941, superseded Western Hemisphere Defense Plan
#4. It was to be placed into effect by the Chief of Naval Opera-
tions after Commander-in-Chief, Atlantic Fleet, had submitted a
readiness report.

It stated that approximately 60 Royal Navy and Royal Canadian Navy destroyers and corvettes would be engaged in escorting
convoy in the Western Atlantic Area under the strategic direction of the United States. It quoted extracts from the President's
speech of September 11, such as:

"Upon our Naval and air patrol—now operating in large
numbers over a vast expanse of the Atlantic Ocean fell the duty
of maintaining the American policy of freedom of the seas—
now. That means . . . our patrolling vessels and planes will protect all merchant ships—not only American merchant ships, but
ships of any flag—engaged in commerce in our defensive
waters. . . .

"From now on, if German or Italian vessels of war enter the
waters, the protection of which is necessary for American defense,
they do so at their own peril. 'The orders which I have given as

Commander-in-Chief of the United States Army and Navy are to carry out that policy—at once.' "

It is stated in the Concept of the Plan:

"It must be recognized that, under the concept of this plan, the United States is not at war in the legal sense, and therefore does not have any of the special belligerent rights accorded under United States law to States which are formally at war.

"The operations which will be conducted under this plan are conceived to form a preparatory phase for the operations of Navy Basic War Plan Rainbow No. 5 (WPL–46)" [for open and declared war].

The Tasks assigned the Atlantic Fleet were:

"(a) Protection against hostile attack United States and foreign flag shipping other than German and Italian shipping by escorting, covering, and patrolling as circumstances may require, and by destroying German and Italian Naval, Land, and Air Forces encountered.

"(b) Insure the safety of sea communications with United States and strategic outposts.

"(c) Support the defense of United States Territory and Bases, Iceland, and Greenland.

"(d) Trail merchant vessels suspected of supplying or otherwise assisting operations of German and Italian naval vessels or aircraft. Report the movements of such vessels to the Chief of Naval Operations."

On October 8, 1941, by dispatch 082335, the Chief of Naval Operations ordered the above outlined plan executed at 1400 (GCT) October 11, 1941. This plan remained in effect until December 11, 1941, at which time the Chief of Naval Operations by dispatch 111550 ordered the above outlined plan cancelled and replaced by WPL–46 (Navy Basic War Plan, Rainbow No. 5).

After Admiral Stark had finished reading Plan #5, Mr. Gearhart resumed his questioning:

MR. GEARHART. Now, is this the order that you made pursuant to the direction of the President under which the Navy began to wage war in the Atlantic?

ADMIRAL STARK. It is the order under which we operated and under which we told the Germans, and Italians in the later stages, that if they came to the westward of the 26 Meridian, as I recall, that their intent would be regarded as hostile and they would be dealt with accordingly, and regarding which the President had previously informed the country.

MR. GEARHART. Then pursuant to this order shells were exchanged by American surface warships carrying American flags and German submarines?

ADMIRAL STARK. Yes, sir; we attacked German submarines under this order. . . .

PLANS FOR COÖPERATION IN A GENERAL WAR

IN PREPARATION for implementing President Roosevelt's conceptions of war eventualities and contingencies in a global conflict, officers of the United States Army and Navy, in coöperation with military and naval representatives of the British Commonwealth and the Netherlands, developed at special conferences technical plans for joint action in war, when and if it came, or to use the American form of reservation "should the United States be compelled to resort to war." [46] These plans did not bind the United States to enter the war on any given contingency or set of contingencies. Such an agreement would have been in the nature of an alliance, and hence under the provisions of the Constitution called for ratification by the Senate. In form they were, the majority of the Congressional Committee on Pearl Harbor stated, the result of "technical discussion on a staff level"—"nonpolitical" in nature; practically they served as the basis for collective action in diplomacy and war.

The first of these military and naval conferences for joint action in war was opened at Washington on January 29, 1941, while the Lend-Lease Bill was pending, and closed on March 27, 1941, after the bill had been enacted into law. It was initiated by Admiral Stark, Chief of Naval Operations, and attended by American and British Army and Navy officers.[47] At this meeting, a plan for coöperation in respect of war in the

46. CJC, *Report*, p. 169.
47. Admiral Stark testified before the Congressional Committee that he initiated this meeting and did not notify the President until after he had done it. *Ibid.*, pp. 169 ff.

Atlantic and war in the Pacific—a report known as ABC–1—was perfected. The purpose of the conversations, as officially described by American authorities, was "to determine the best methods by which the armed forces of the United States and British Commonwealth, with its present allies, could defeat Germany and the Powers allied with her, should the United States be compelled to resort to war."

In April, 1941, a second series of staff conversations was held at Singapore, referred to as ADB. This meeting was attended by military and naval representatives of the United States, Great Britain, and the Netherlands. Although this meeting was also technical in nature, the report which emerged from it contained some agreements which Admiral Stark and General Marshall regarded as having political implications, and hence they did not give it their formal approval. The Admiral and the General, however, adopted one of the Singapore proposals and jointly recommended it to President Roosevelt. This recommendation stipulated that military counteraction should be undertaken in the event that Japan attacked or directly threatened the territory or mandated territory of the United States, the British Commonwealth, or the Netherlands East Indies, or if the Japanese moved forces into Thailand west of 100° East or south of 10° North, Portuguese Timor, New Caledonia, or the Loyalty Islands.[48] This general recommendation, Admiral Stark and General Marshall incorporated in joint memoranda to the President on November 5, and again on November 27, 1941. In fact, it fitted into the diplomatic negotiations which the United States had been and was then carrying on with Great Britain, the Netherlands, and Japan.

The American-British Naval and Military conferences of January–March and April, 1941, were continuations of such discussions for coöperation in the Far East, in case of a war with Japan, begun many years previously. It had long been a part of American imperialist strategy in respect of the Orient to break the Anglo-Japanese alliance of 1902 (subsequently

48. *Ibid.*, p. 170.

renewed) and to draw Great Britain into the American line of policy against Japan. At the Washington Conference in 1921–22, the American representatives succeeded in destroying the Anglo-Japanese alliance, but as the American Secretary of State under President Hoover, Henry L. Stimson, later learned in his efforts to commit Great Britain to his scheme for collective action against Japan on account of her seizure of Manchuria in 1931, the British Government was still loath to see Japan destroyed as a makeweight in the conflict of the great Powers in Asia. Nevertheless, in spite of Secretary Stimson's defeat in 1931–32, American advocates of a "strong policy" in respect of Japan, as well as advocates of "peace" by "collective security," were unwilling to give up the idea of enlisting the help of Great Britain against Japan as hopeless.

When Franklin D. Roosevelt, as President-elect, committed himself to "the Stimson doctrine" for the Far East at a luncheon with Mr. Stimson at Hyde Park, on January 9, 1933, he had taken a fateful step leading in the direction of Pearl Harbor. His close personal adviser, Raymond Moley, who subsequently served for a time under him as Assistant Secretary of State, and Rexford Tugwell, who remained in his official family almost continuously to the end, raised with Mr. Roosevelt in January, 1933, the issue of the peril involved in his commitment to Mr. Stimson's doctrine. Writing of this doctrine later, Mr. Moley declared: "It endorsed a policy that invited a major war in the Far East—a war which the United States and England might have had to wage against Japan had England not refused to go along with Stimson." [49] But after he became President, Mr. Roosevelt reckoned with this exigency.

As early as December, 1937, shortly after his quarantine speech at Chicago, President Roosevelt sent Captain Royal E. Ingersoll, an officer in the Navy war planning division, to London for the purpose of discussing with British authorities American policy in the Far East and exploring the nature of

49. For a neglected chapter in the history of President Roosevelt's commitments, see Beard, *op. cit.*, pp. 133 ff., and sources there cited.

the aid which might be given by Great Britain in case the United States became involved in war with Japan.[50]

The documents on the continuance of Anglo-American military conversations, if any, between 1938 and 1940 are not yet available. With reference to any understanding reached at such conferences, Admiral Richardson was under the impression early in 1940 that it was one-sided, that it "has little value as it affords us the use of a base in exchange for an obligation to protect about two and one-half continents."[51] The Admiral admitted that there might have been "some slight exaggeration" in his estimate, but he was evidently of the opinion that the United States was not a good bargainer.

Although the results of earlier Anglo-American conversations still remain largely matters of conjecture, the outcome of the secret Anglo-American military and naval conferences of January–March and April, 1941, is a matter of the public record provided by the Congressional Committee on Pearl Harbor.[52] So, also are the report of the January–March conference and the underlying assumptions on which American and British officers proceeded. As to these assumptions, the report reads:

The Staff Conference assumes that when the United States becomes involved in war with Germany, it will at the same time engage in war with Italy. In those circumstances, the possibility of a

50. During the public discussion of President Roosevelt's "big battleship bill," initiated in January, 1938, it was charged that Captain Ingersoll had effected some kind of naval agreement with Great Britain in London and the charge was criticized in Administration quarters. In a dissenting report, the Republican minority of the Naval Affairs Committee of the House of Representatives declared that the bill disclosed a purpose on the part of the President to pursue power politics in Asia and uphold the obsolete British-Mahan sea-power doctrine. Beard, *op. cit.*, pp. 212 ff. The bill as enacted woefully neglected the role of air power in modern sea war.

51. CJC, Part 1, p. 308; Part 14, pp. 924 ff. In a letter to Admiral Hart, Commander in Chief of the Asiatic Fleet, dated December 12, 1940, Admiral Stark authorized Admiral Hart to conduct staff conversations with the British and Dutch Supreme Commanders respecting war plans, on the assumption that there might be a war between the United States and Japan, Germany, and Italy, and that the United States, the British, and the Dutch would be Allies in such a war. Admiral Hart was warned to keep the conversations secret and to take care lest the Japanese become aware of his contact with the Dutch. *Ibid.*, Part 4, pp. 1929 ff.

52. CJC, Part 15, Exhibits 49, 50, 51.

state of war arising between Japan, and an association of the United States, the British Commonwealth and its Allies, including the Netherlands East Indies, must be taken into account. . . . Since Germany is the predominant member of the Axis Powers, the Atlantic and European area is considered to be the decisive theatre. The principal United States Military effort will be exerted in that theatre, and operations of United States forces in other theatres will be conducted in such a manner as to facilitate that effort.[53]

On the basis of the Anglo-American military and naval understandings, the Army and Navy of the United States drew up a joint war plan in contemplation of coöperation with the British Commonwealth and its associates in a worldwide war, when, as, and if. This joint plan was approved by the Secretary of War and the Secretary of the Navy, and by the President, "except officially."[54] The spirit, purpose, and design of the joint plan were tersely set forth by Admiral Richmond K. Turner, War Plans Officer for the Chief of Naval Operations, in his testimony before the Hart Inquiry in 1944 as follows:

It was intended against the Axis Powers: Germany, Italy, Japan, and the Powers that were allied with those principal Powers. It did not include any particular participation for the purpose of the plan by the Government of China. . . . I believe it envisaged war in which either Germany and her European Allies were the sole enemies, or in which Japan was also engaged. The main basis of the plan, however, was a global war in which both Germany and her European Allies and Japan were at war with the United States, the British Commonwealth, and the Netherlands East Indies. . . . The plan contemplated a major effort on the part of both the principal associated Powers against Germany, initially. It was felt in the Navy Department, that there might be a possibility of war with Japan without the involvement of Germany, but . . . it was determined that in such a case the United States

---

53. CJC, Part 15, pp. 1489 ff.
54. *Ibid.*, Part 26, p. 264. Admiral Stark testified before the Congressional Committee: "I do know the President, except officially, approved of it, although it shows he was not willing to do it officially until we got into the war." *Ibid.*, Part 5, p. 2391.

would, if possible, initiate efforts to bring Germany into the war against us in order that we would be enabled to give strong support to the United Kingdom in Europe. We felt that it was encumbent on our side to defeat Germany, to launch our principal efforts against Germany first, and to conduct a limited offensive in the Central Pacific, and a strictly defensive effort in the Asiatic.[55]

Recommendations based on coöperative action by Great Britain, the United States, and the Netherlands in given contingencies were set forth in a memorandum to President Roosevelt from Admiral Stark and General Marshall on November 5. They read as follows:

The Chief of Naval Operations and the Chief of Staff are in accord in the following conclusions:

(a) The basic military policies and strategy agreed to in the United States–British Staff conversations remain sound. The primary objective of the two nations is the defeat of Germany. If Japan be defeated and Germany remain undefeated, decision will still have not been reached. In any case, an unlimited offensive war should not be undertaken against Japan, since such a war would greatly weaken the combined effort in the Atlantic against Germany, the most dangerous enemy.

(b) War between the United States and Japan should be avoided while building up defensive forces in the Far East, until such time as Japan attacks or directly threatens territories whose security to the United States is of very great importance. Military action against Japan should be undertaken only in one or more of the following contingencies:

1. A direct act of war by Japanese armed forces against the territory or mandated territory of the United States, the British Commonwealth, or the Netherlands East Indies;

2. The movement of Japanese forces into Thailand to the west of 100 degrees East or south of 10 degrees North; or into Portuguese Timor, New Caledonia, or the Loyalty Islands.

(c) If war with Japan cannot be avoided, it should follow the strategic lines of existing war plans; i.e., military operations should be primarily defensive, with the object of holding territory, and weakening Japan's economic position.

55. *Ibid.*, Part 26, pp. 264 f.

(d) Considering world strategy, a Japanese advance against Kunming, into Thailand except as previously indicated, or an attack on Russia, would not justify intervention by the United States against Japan.

(e) All possible aid short of actual war against Japan should be extended to the Chinese Central Government.

(f) In case it is decided to undertake war against Japan, complete coordinated action in the diplomatic, economic, and military fields, should be undertaken in common by the United States, the British Commonwealth, and the Netherlands East Indies.

The Chief of Naval Operations and the Chief of Staff recommend that the United States policy in the Far East be based on the above conclusions.

Specifically, they recommend:

That the dispatch of United States armed forces for intervention against Japan in China be disapproved.

That the material aid to China be accelerated consonant with the needs of Russia, Great Britain, and our own forces.

That aid to the American Volunteer Group be continued and accelerated to the maximum practicable extent.

That no ultimatum be delivered to Japan.[56]

In a memorandum of November 27, 1941, to President Roosevelt, General Marshall and Admiral Stark presented another version of the coöperative war project, with a new set of recommendations, as follows:

The most essential thing now, from the United States viewpoint, is to gain time. Considerable Navy and Army reinforcements have been rushed to the Philippines but the desirable strength has not yet been reached. The process of reinforcement is being continued. Of great and immediate concern is the safety of the Army convoy now near Guam, and the Marine Corps' convoy just leaving Shanghai. Ground forces to a total of 21,000 are due to sail from the United States by December 8, 1941, and it is important that this troop reinforcement reach the Philippines before hostilities commence. Precipitance of military action on our part should be avoided so long as consistent with national policy. The longer the delay, the more positive becomes the assurance of re-

56. CJC, *Report*, pp. 173 f.

tention of these islands as a naval and air base. Japanese action to the south of Formosa will be hindered and perhaps seriously blocked as long as we hold the Philippine Islands. War with Japan certainly will interrupt our transport of supplies to Siberia, and probably will interrupt the process of aiding China.

After consultation with each other, United States, British, and Dutch military authorities in the Far East agreed that joint military counteraction against Japan should be undertaken only in case Japan attacks or directly threatens the territory or mandated territory of the United States, the British Commonwealth, or the Netherlands East Indies, or should the Japanese move forces into Thailand west of 100 degrees East or south of 10 degrees North, Portuguese Timor, New Caledonia, or the Loyalty Islands.

Japanese involvement in Yunnan or Thailand up to a certain extent is advantageous, since it leads to further dispersion, longer lines of communication, and an additional burden on communications. However, a Japanese advance to the west of 100 degrees East or south of 10 degrees North, immediately becomes a threat to Burma and Singapore. Until it is patent that Japan intends to advance beyond these lines, no action which might lead to immediate hostilities should be taken.

It is recommended that:

Prior to the completion of the Philippine reinforcement, military counteraction be considered only if Japan attacks or directly threatens United States, British, or Dutch territory, as above outlined;

In case of a Japanese advance into Thailand, Japan be warned by the United States, the British, and the Dutch Governments that advance beyond the lines indicated may lead to war; prior to such warning no joint military opposition be undertaken;

Steps be taken at once to consummate agreements with the British and Dutch for the issuance of such warning.[57]

Late in 1941, Admiral Hart, Commander in Chief of the American Asiatic Fleet, and Admiral Phillips, British Far Eastern Naval Commander, held meetings with a view to developing the ADB report and arrived at arrangements for counteracting the probable moves of the Japanese in the Far East. Admiral Hart's report of these conversations reached the

57. *Ibid.*, pp. 174 f.

Navy Department in Washington about 11 P.M., December 6, 1941, and were ordered in effect by the Chief of Naval Operations on December 7, after the Japanese "surprise offensive" had begun.[58]

With reference to these secret military and naval understandings between the United States, the British Commonwealth, and the Netherlands, the majority of the Congressional Committee on Pearl Harbor stated:

There is no evidence to indicate that Japanese knowledge of the "ABC" and "ADB" conversations was an inducing factor to Japan's decision to attack the United States. . . . Indeed, the idea of attacking us at Pearl Harbor was conceived before these conversations were initiated. Manifestly any estimate which the Japanese made of American probable action was based on this country's long standing Far Eastern policy and the course of diplomatic negotiations, and not on nonpolitical, technical discussions on a staff level.[59]

"Manifestly" this statement by the majority was pure conjecture, for the committee did not have possession of papers from the Japanese archives to support it. While, as far as records go, there is no evidence that the Japanese Government was informed about the precise terms of these contingent war plans, there is ample proof that it was acquainted with the fact that conversations were going on between the United States, Great Britain, and the Netherlands.[60] Associated Press and United Press dispatches from Japan, China, Australia, and other points in the Pacific, published in New York newspapers, freely advertised such coöperative undertakings to the general public. For example, an Associated Press dispatch dated Tokyo, November 17, 1941, reported that, in a speech to the Japanese Diet, the Japanese Foreign Minister had said that Great Britain and the United States were taking leadership in "encircling" Japan and exerting economic pressure against her. Again, an Associated Press dispatch from

58. *Ibid.*, p. 170; see also below, Chap. XVII.
59. CJC, *Report*, p. 171.
60. CJC, Parts 12 and 13 especially.

Chungking, on the same day, reported the Chinese Foreign Minister, Quo Tai-chi, as saying that "all signs point to an ABCD alliance to resist Japan."

Beyond all question, the Japanese Government knew that the United States and Great Britain were coöperating in the making of military plans, as well as in the application of economic sanctions and diplomatic pressures. Indeed, as if it had no relation to what they had said on page 171 of their Report, the majority stated on the very next page (172):

While no binding agreement existed [among the ABD Powers], it would appear from the record that the Japanese were inclined to the belief that the United States, Britain and the Netherlands would act in concert. . . . A message of December 3 which was intercepted from the Washington Embassy to Tokyo related: "Judging from all indications, we feel that some joint military action between Great Britain and the United States, with or without a declaration of war, is a definite certainty, in the event of an occupation of Thailand." [61]

As a matter of fact, Arthur Krock, in November, 1941, had served public notice on the Japanese special agent in Washington, Mr. Kurusu, that the United States had a "naval alliance with Great Britain, joining for all practical purposes the fleets of the two nations in the Pacific." [62] And, while President Roosevelt and Secretary Hull, with the support of the other members of the War Cabinet, were maneuvering the Japanese into firing the first shot,[63] they were well aware that war would bring the ABD war plans into immediate application.

61. CJC, *Report*, p. 172.
62. See above, Chap. VII, p. 193.
63. See below, Chap. XVII, pp. 517 ff.

CHAPTER XV

Actualities of the Atlantic Conference

BESIDES lifting the curtain of appearances,[1] which had hidden the war decisions and plans of President Roosevelt,[2] the Congressional Committee on Pearl Harbor opened up many of the realities in the transactions at the Atlantic Conference of August, 1941. On his return from that meeting with Prime Minister Churchill, President Roosevelt had publicly announced that arrangements for expediting operations under the Lend-Lease Act had been developed, that dangers to world civilization had been considered, and that an agreement had been reached on a statement of principles, later called the Atlantic Charter;[3] at the same time the President had assured the people and Congress that no "new commitments" had been made in the name of the United States and that the country was no closer to war, as a result of the Atlantic Conference.

But the Congressional Committee insisted on going behind these appearances, on getting at, if possible, the actual agreements reached at the Atlantic Conference. In November, 1945, the committee called to an open hearing the one man then available to it who could give, out of first-hand, personal knowledge, factual information on discussions and agreements of the conference. That man was Sumner Welles. Mr. Welles had been Undersecretary of State in 1941; he had served as the President's chief civilian aide at the conference; he had participated in sessions of the conference; and he had kept minutes of certain formal discussions and agreements at the conference, other than those of a military nature. At the hearing, the Congressional Committee wrung some informa-

1. See above, Chaps. II and III.
2. See above, Chap. XIV.
3. See above, Chap. IV.

tion on the conference from Mr. Welles, but not much.[4] Going beyond with the results of this examination, the committee secured from the State Department and placed on record, December 18, 1945, the memoranda of discussions and agreements at the conference, which Mr. Welles had prepared at the time for the archives of the department.[5]

As reported by Mr. Welles in his memoranda, four basic agreements were reached by President Roosevelt and Prime Minister Churchill at the Atlantic Conference: (1) an agreement on parallel and ultimative action in respect of Japan; (2) an agreement as to the occupation of the Azores by the armed forces of the United States in coöperation with British armed forces; (3) an understanding as to a kind of world policy to be pursued, presumably, by the United States and Great Britain during and after the war—a policy incorporated in the document later known as the Atlantic Charter; and (4) an agreement on the form and language of the joint announcement to be made public by the President and the Prime Min-

---

4. See below, Chap. XVI, pp. 489 ff.

5. These memoranda do not cover, of course, any personal understandings reached by President Roosevelt and Mr. Churchill privately. For one of these, see above, Chap. IX, p. 242. For texts of the memoranda, see CJC, Part 4, pp. 1784 ff. American citizens who are interested in the methods employed by the State Department in "educating" the public will derive instruction from a comparison of Mr. Welles' secret memoranda on the Atlantic Conference with the version made public by the department in 1943. In the department's report to the public on "policies and acts" 1931–41, entitled *Peace and War: United States Foreign Policy, 1931–1941*, released to the press January 2, 1943, 9 P.M., the section dealing with the Atlantic Conference, headed "Atlantic Charter," was exceedingly brief. Most of the page and a half given to the conference was taken up by the text of the Charter and a slight reference to the President's message on the subject to Congress, August 21, 1941. As to other decisions, agreements, and understandings reached by President Roosevelt and Prime Minister Churchill on that occasion, the State Department's account merely said: "At this Conference they examined the whole problem of the supplying of munitions of war, as provided by the Lend-Lease Act, for the armed forces of the United States and for the countries actively engaged in resisting aggression." In its collection of documents for the period, issued in July, 1943, also called *Peace and War*, the State Department was equally uncommunicative with regard to what was actually decided upon at the Atlantic Conference. In other words, the State Department's report for the information of the American people left them completely in the dark as to the actual agreements and understandings concluded by the President and the Prime Minister at the Atlantic Conference, and thus matched in ingenuity the best of white papers issued by foreign chancelleries.

ister at the close of the conference—a brief statement giving to the public an enigmatic version of what had transpired at the conference. It was around drafts of these commitments and problems that official discussions at the conference mainly centered, and Mr. Welles' memoranda provide minutes of conversations connected with each of the four agreements. An examination of the record of the proceedings provided by Mr. Welles' memoranda follows:

I. AGREEMENT ON PARALLEL ACTION IN RESPECT OF JAPAN [6]

AT THE President's dinner on August 9, 1941, the subject of "proposed parallel and simultaneous declarations" by the United States and British Governments relating to Japanese policy in the Pacific was discussed by the President, the Prime Minister, Sir Alexander Cadogan, and Mr. Welles. The following day, Sir Alexander told Mr. Welles that he had made tentative drafts of these declarations. The draft of the parallel declaration to be made by the United States, as prepared by Sir Alexander for subsequent consideration, read:

1. *Any further encroachment* by Japan in the Southwestern Pacific would produce a situation in which the United States Government would be compelled to take counter measures even though these might lead to war between the United States and Japan.

2. If *any third power* becomes the object of aggression by Japan in consequence of such counter measures or of their support of them, *the President would have the intention to seek authority from Congress to give aid to such power.* (Italics supplied.)

Sir Alexander's draft of the declaration for the United States Government was followed by similar drafts of declarations to be made to Japan by the British Government and

6. There was much haggling in the Congressional Committee over the exactness of the term "parallel," but if British action did not precisely parallel that of the United States, there can be no doubt as to use of the words "parallel and simultaneous declarations" in connection with the agreement at the Atlantic Conference.

the Netherlands Government. The draft of the British Government's project read:

Declaration by His Majesty's Government that:

1. Any further encroachment by Japan in the Southwestern Pacific would produce a situation in which His Majesty's Government would be compelled to take counter measures even though these might lead to war between Great Britain and Japan.

2. If any third Power becomes the object of aggression by Japan in consequence of such counter measures or of their support of them, His Majesty's Government would give all possible aid to such Power.

Keep the Soviet Government informed. It will be for consideration whether they should be pressed to make a parallel declaration.

As Mr. Welles was about to leave the British ship, Mr. Churchill held a brief conversation with him. Mr. Churchill said that the President had copies of the documents and in urgent language he told Mr. Welles that "such a clear-cut declaration" by the United States seemed necessary to prevent a war between Great Britain and Japan. To quote Mr. Welles' report:

He [Mr. Churchill] impressed upon me his belief that some declaration of the kind he had drafted with respect to Japan was in his opinion in the highest degree important, and that he did not think there was much hope left unless the United States made such a clear-cut declaration of preventing Japan from expanding further to the south, in which event the prevention of war between Great Britain and Japan appeared to be hopeless. He said in the most emphatic manner that if war did break out between Great Britain and Japan, Japan immediately would be in a position through the use of her large number of cruisers to seize or to destroy all of the British merchant shipping in the Indian Ocean and in the Pacific, and to cut the lifelines between the British Dominions and the British Isles unless the United States herself entered the war. He pled with me that a declaration of this character participated in by the United States, Great Britain, the Dominions, the Netherlands and possibly the Soviet Union would definitely restrain Japan. If this were not done, the blow to the British Government might be almost decisive.

At a meeting on the morning of August 11, Mr. Churchill brought up the subject of the declaration to Japan which he wanted the President to make in conjunction with Great Britain and other governments, including the proposition that in a certain contingency the President would request from Congress authority to assist the British and Dutch Governments in their defense against Japanese aggression. Evidently the President was unwilling to accept the proposed declaration. Mr. Welles says nothing precise about this point in his account of this meeting but merely records that the President gave Mr. Churchill copies of the two statements handed to Secretary Hull by the Japanese Ambassador on August 6. After some discussion of these notes and the situation in the Far East, the President said "he felt very strongly that every effort should be made to prevent the outbreak of war with Japan."

Thereafter the President presented his plan. His project excluded the necessity of making any request to Congress for authority to act against Japan in case Great Britain went to the aid of the Netherlands East Indies in efforts to ward off Japanese aggression. But it provided that if Japan would not agree to abide by certain proposals respecting the abandonment of further military expansion, he would let the Japanese Government know "that in such event in his belief various steps would have to be taken by the United States notwithstanding the President's realization that the taking of such further measures might result in war between the United States and Japan."

Commenting on the President's suggested procedure against Japan, Mr. Churchill said that "it had in it an element of 'face-saving' for the Japanese and yet at the same time would constitute a flat United States warning to Japan of the consequences involved in a continuation by Japan of her present course." Later in the session, the Prime Minister stated that if negotiations or conversations actually took place between the United States and Japan on the basis which had been formulated, there was "a reasonable chance that Japanese policy might be modified and that a war in the Pacific might be averted." His confidence in the power of the United States to avert a war was apparently greater than that of the President who thought the crisis could be held off "for at least thirty days."

At all events, Mr. Churchill and President Roosevelt had agreed upon a definite line of diplomatic action against Japan; and the President had committed himself to paralleling British policy in that relation and to warning Japan directly in a statement, diplomatic in form, but unequivocal in its implications.

After Mr. Churchill had declared that the President's proposal for procedure appeared to cover the situation very well, Mr. Welles expressed the opinion that the ground of action against Japan should be broadened to include her policy of aggression in the entire Pacific region, "regardless whether such policy was directed against China, against the Soviet Union or against the British Dominions or British colonies, or the colonies of the Netherlands in the Southern Pacific area." Both the President and Mr. Churchill agreed to this. Following a discussion of the parallel statements, "The President expressed the belief that by adopting this course any further move of aggression on the part of Japan *which might result in war could be held off for at least thirty days.*" [7] (Italics supplied.)

7. This may be the origin of the statement ascribed to President Roosevelt by Davis and Lindley (p. 10): "I think I can baby them [the Japanese] along for three months." However, the limit as fixed by Mr. Welles was "at least thirty days." The statement of President Roosevelt to the Japanese Ambassador on August 17, 1941, read: ". . . this Government now finds it necessary to say to the Government of Japan that if the Japanese Government takes any further steps in pursuance of a policy or program of military domination by force or threat of force of neighboring countries, the Government of the United States will be compelled to take immediately any and all steps which it may deem necessary toward safeguarding the legitimate rights and interests of the United States and American nationals and toward insuring the safety and security of the United States." *Foreign Relations of the United States: Japan, 1931–1941*, II, 556 f. Thus the declaration to Japan, conceived in the spirit of the agreement of August [1]

Text of Mr. Welles' Memorandum on Conversations Relative to Parallel Action in Respect of Japan

As I was leaving the ship [August 10, 1941] to accompany the President back to his flagship, Mr. Churchill said to me that he had likewise given the President copies of these documents. He impressed upon me his belief that some declaration of the kind he had drafted with respect to Japan was in his opinion in the highest degree important, and that he did not think that there was much hope left unless the United States made such a clear-cut declaration of preventing Japan from expanding further to the south, in which event the prevention of war between Great Britain and Japan appeared to be hopeless. He said in the most emphatic manner that if war did break out between Great Britain and Japan, Japan immediately would be in a position through the use of her large number of cruisers to seize or to destroy all of the British merchant shipping in the Indian Ocean and in the Pacific, and to cut the lifelines between the British Dominions and the British Isles unless the United States herself entered the war. He pled with me that a declaration of this character participated in by the United States, Great Britain, the Dominions, the Netherlands and possibly the Soviet Union would definitely restrain Japan. If this were not done, the blow to the British Government might be almost decisive.

The Prime Minister then [August 11, 1941] said that he desired to discuss the situation in the Far East. He had with him a copy of a draft memorandum, of which he had already given the President a copy and which suggested that the United States, British and Dutch Governments simultaneously warn Japan that further military expansion by Japan in the South Pacific would lead to the taking of counter measures by the countries named even though such counter measures might result in hostilities between them and Japan, and, second, provided that the United States declare to Japan that should Great Britain go to the assistance of the Netherlands East Indies as a result of aggression against the latter on the part of Japan the President would request from the Congress of

---

was in the nature of a statement which, in the language of diplomacy, was "ultimative" and yet rested the case at least nominally on the rights and interests of the United States. If Mr. Welles' account is comprehensive, the possibility of action in case of a Japanese movement against the Philippines was not specifically considered.

the United States authority to assist the British and Dutch Governments in their defense against Japanese aggression.

The President gave Mr. Churchill to read copies of the two statements handed to Secretary Hull by the Japanese Ambassador on August 6.

The Prime Minister read them carefully and then remarked that the implication was that Japan, having already occupied Indochina, said that she would move no further provided the United States would abandon their economic and financial sanctions and take no further military or naval defensive measures and further agree to concessions to Japan, including the opportunity for Japan to strangle the Chinese Government, all of which were particularly unacceptable.

The President replied that that was about the picture as he saw it, that he felt very strongly that every effort should be made to prevent the outbreak of war with Japan. He stated that what he intended to do was to request Secretary Hull by radio to inform the Japanese Ambassador that the President would return to Washington next Saturday or Sunday and desired to see the Ambassador immediately upon his return. The President stated that in that interview he would inform the Japanese Ambassador that provided the Japanese Government would give the commitment contained in the first paragraph of the proposal of the Japanese Government of August 6, namely, that the Japanese Government "will not further station its troops in the Southwestern Pacific areas, except French Indochina, and that the Japanese troops now stationed in French Indochina will be withdrawn," specifically and not contingently, the United States Government, while making it clear that the other conditions set forth by the Japanese Government were in general unacceptable, the United States would, nevertheless, in a friendly spirit seek to explore the possibilities inherent in the various proposals made by Japan for the reaching of a friendly understanding between the two Governments. The President would further state that should Japan refuse to consider this procedure and undertake further steps in the nature of military expansions, the President desired the Japanese Government to know that in such event in his belief various steps would have to be taken by the United States notwithstanding the President's realization that the taking of such further measures might result in war between the United States and Japan.

Mr. Churchill immediately declared that the procedure suggested appeared to him to cover the situation very well. He said it had in it an element of "face-saving" for the Japanese and yet at the same time would constitute a flat United States warning to Japan of the consequences involved in a continuation by Japan of her present course.

There was then discussed the desirability of informing Russia of the steps which would be taken as above set forth and of possibly including in the warning to Japan a statement which would cover any aggressive steps by Japan against the Soviet Union.

I stated that in my judgment the real issue which was involved was the continuation by Japan of its present policy of conquest by force in the entire Pacific region and regardless whether such policy was directed against China, against the Soviet Union or against the British Dominions or British colonies, or the colonies of the Netherlands in the Southern Pacific area. I said it seemed to me that the statement which the President intended to make to the Japanese Government might more advantageously be based on the question of broad policy rather than be premised solely upon Japanese moves in the Southwestern Pacific area.

The President and Mr. Churchill both agreed to this and it was decided that the step to be taken by the President would be taken in that sense.

The question then arose as to the desirability of the President's making reference in his proposed statement to the Japanese Ambassador to British policy in the Southern Pacific region and specifically with regard to Thailand. The President said that he thought it would be advantageous for him to be in a position at that time to state that he had been informed by the British Government that Great Britain had no aggressive intentions whatever upon Thailand. Mr. Churchill said that in this he heartily concurred.

I asked whether it would not be better for the President to be in a position to state not only that Great Britain had no intentions of an aggressive character with regard to Thailand, but also that the British Government had informed the United States Government that it supported wholeheartedly the President's proposal for the neutralization of Indochina and of Thailand.

Mr. Churchill stated that he agreed that it would be well to make an all-inclusive statement of that character with respect to British policy, that he trusted that the President would, therefore, inform the Japanese Ambassador that he had consulted the British Government, and that the British Government was in complete accord with the neutralization proposal, and that it had likewise informed the President that it would in no event undertake any initiative in the occupation of Thailand.

It was agreed that Sir Alexander Cadogan, after further consultation with Mr. Churchill, would give me in writing a statement which the British Government was prepared to make with regard to this issue.

The President expressed the belief that by adopting this course any further move of aggression on the part of Japan which might result in war could be held off for at least thirty days. Mr. Churchill felt that if negotiations or conversations actually took place between the United States and Japan on the basis which had been formulated, there was a reasonable chance that Japanese policy might be modified and that a war in the Pacific might be averted.

II. OCCUPATION OF THE AZORES

THE second commitment made by President Roosevelt and Mr. Churchill at the Atlantic Conference pertained to combined naval and military operations in connection with a proposed occupation of the Azores by the armed forces of the United States.

This project had long been under consideration although no official announcement had been given to the public. In his testimony before the Pearl Harbor investigating committee, January 4, 1946, Admiral Harold R. Stark stated that on May 22, 1941, President Roosevelt ordered him to have the Navy ready to occupy the Azores on thirty days' notice. Our government, he explained, feared that Germany would go into Spain and Portugal, seize the Azores, and thus threaten communications. The Admiral, however, added that, although he had prepared the plans, he had not been called upon to carry them out.[8]

According to Mr. Welles' account, the issue of the Azores

8. CJC, Part 5, pp. 2309 f. See above, p. 428.

was raised at the Atlantic Conference on August 11, by President Roosevelt. The President read to Mr. Churchill a letter he had received from the Prime Minister of Portugal which, it was agreed, "made possible without any difficulty the carrying out of arrangements for the occupation of the Azores as a means of assurance that the islands would not be occupied by Germany."

Thereupon Mr. Churchill referred to "a highly secret operation" to be undertaken by the British Government in occupying the Canary Islands. He described the situation in respect of Spain and Portugal, and explained that the British Government could not conveniently assist in the defense of the Azores.

"It was therefore agreed" that, on his return to London, Mr. Churchill would notify Dr. Salazar of the British position and inform him that the British Government "desired him to request the United States for such assistance." The President agreed that, upon receipt of notification from the Prime Minister of Portugal, the United States "would send the necessary forces of occupation to the Azores" and would ask the Brazilian Government to join in dispatching at least a token force to take part in the expedition.

A supplementary agreement was then made relative to the occupation of the Cape Verde Islands. The President informed Mr. Churchill that the United States was not in a position to undertake the protection of those islands. The Prime Minister replied that the British Government could occupy the islands on the understanding that the task of protecting them would be turned over to the United States when it was in a position to assume it. Mr. Churchill further agreed that the British Navy would assist the United States in the occupation of the Azores by maintaining a large force between the mainland and the Azores while the United States was carrying out its landing operations, to protect the Americans against a possible German expedition from the mainland.

Text of Mr. Welles' Memorandum of Conversations on the Occupation of the Azores

DATE:
Monday, August 11, 1941
At Sea.

SUBJECT: British-American Cooperation
PARTICIPANTS: The President.
The British Prime Minister.
Sir Alexander Cadogan, British Permanent Under
Secretary of State for Foreign Affairs.
The Honorable Harry Hopkins.
The Under Secretary of State.

The President received Mr. Churchill this morning on the *Augusta* at 11:00 A.M. There were present at the meeting Sir Alexander Cadogan, Harry Hopkins and myself.

I

The conference commenced with the subject of Portugal. The President read to Mr. Churchill the letter addressed to the former by the Prime Minister of Portugal. It was agreed by both that the contents of the letter were highly satisfactory and made possible without any difficulty the carrying out of arrangements for the occupation of the Azores as a means of assurance that the islands would not be occupied by Germany.

Mr. Churchill stated that a highly secret operation had been decided upon by the British Government, namely, the occupation of the Canary Islands during the days immediately after the September full moon. This date, as Mr. Churchill remembered it, would be about the 15th of September. The British Government were undertaking this operation with full knowledge that the islands had been recently heavily fortified and that a very large number of German officers were engaged there in the training and preparation of the Spanish troops. It was undertaken with the further realization that this step would almost inevitably involve a Spanish attack either in conjunction with or upon the instigation of German military forces and that such attack would render untenable by the British Navy the harbor of Gibraltar. The British Government, however, had decided upon the step in view of its belief that the situation in Spain from the British standpoint was going from bad to worse and that Hitler almost inevitably would undertake the occupation of Spain and Portugal with the subsequent penetration of North Africa if any collapse took place on the part of the Russian Army or even if a winter stalemate resulted. In that event, Mr. Churchill stated Gibraltar would be isolated anyway and the occupation by Great Britain of the Canary Islands was of the utmost importance in guarding a Southern Atlantic convoy route into the British Isles.

In view of this operation, the British Government would not be in a position conveniently to carry out the commitment they had made to the Portuguese Government to assist in the defense of the Azores.

In view of the contents of Dr. Salazar's letter to the President, it was therefore agreed that the British Government immediately upon the return of Mr. Churchill to London would notify Dr. Salazar that the British Government could not conveniently undertake to assist in the defense of the Azores and would further inform Dr. Salazar that they therefore desired him to request the United States for such assistance. It was agreed on the part of the President that immediately upon the receipt of such notification from Dr. Salazar the United States would send the necessary forces of occupation to the Azores and that the Brazilian Government would be simultaneously requested to send at least a token force to take part in the expedition.

The President stated to Mr. Churchill that in view of our present military situation if the United States undertook to occupy the Azores it would not be in a position in the near future at least to undertake the protection of the Cape Verde Islands. Mr. Churchill stated that the British Government would be in a position to occupy the Cape Verde Islands with the understanding that it would later turn over the protection of those islands to the United States at such time as the United States was in a position to take those measures. Mr. Churchill further stated that during the time that the United States was landing the necessary forces in the Azores, the British Navy would maintain a large force between the Azores and the mainland of Portugal in order to render impossible the sending of any German expeditionary forces should Portugal at that time be already occupied by Germany.

III. AMERICAN AND BRITISH WORLD POLICY—"THE
ATLANTIC CHARTER"

THE third item on which President Roosevelt and Mr. Churchill agreed at the Atlantic Conference was the policy which they were to pursue in connection with the overthrow of Nazi tyranny and the peace settlement to follow.

The discussion of this issue at the conference turned in part on the fifth proposition in Mr. Churchill's draft of a joint declaration of principles to be issued after the meetings came to an end. As Mr. Churchill had framed it, the proposition read: "Fifth, they seek a peace which will not only cast down forever the Nazi tyranny but *by effective international organization* will afford to all States and peoples the means of dwelling in security within their own bounds and of traversing the seas and oceans without fear of lawless assault or need of getting burdensome armaments." (Italics supplied.)

A discussion of this matter occurred at the morning meeting on August 11, 1941. Mr. Churchill inquired "whether the President would not agree to support some kind of 'effective international organization' as suggested by the Prime Minister in his original draft of the proposed joint declaration." The President replied "that he did not feel that he could agree to this," and gave two reasons for his dissent. In the first place, it was "because of the suspicions and opposition that such a statement on his part would create in the United States." In the second place, the President said that he himself "would not be in favor of the creation of a new Assembly of the League of Nations, at least until after a period of time had transpired and *during which an international police force composed of the United States and Great Britain* had had an opportunity of functioning." (Italics supplied.)

Coupled with the discussion of the fifth proposition in Mr. Churchill's original list, relative to an effective international organization, was a consideration of a seventh proposition, the exact form and fulness of which are not disclosed in Mr. Welles' memorandum presented to the Congressional Committee on Pearl Harbor. In his entry for the afternoon of August 11, Mr. Welles says that the seventh proposition contained a clause "declaring for the disarmament of nations which undertook aggression outside their frontiers."

During their sessions on the morning of the 11th, Mr. Churchill said "that he did not feel that he would be candid if he did not express to the President his feeling that point seven would create a great deal of opposition from the extreme internationalists." President Roosevelt replied "that he realized that, but that he felt that the time had come to be realistic and that in his judgment the main factor in the seventh point was complete realism." Apparently Mr. Churchill himself had little regard for the opinions of "extreme internationalists," for he immediately "remarked that, of course, he was wholeheartedly in favor of it [point seven] and shared the President's view."

At a meeting on the afternoon of August 11, Sir Alexander Cadogan stated to Mr. Welles that the Prime Minister felt very strongly—"perhaps exaggeratedly"—about the opposition which would be created on the part of a certain pro-League of Nations group in England to the contents of point seven. Six Alexander, however, said that there would not be the amount of opposition which the Prime Minister anticipated. But Sir Alexander

nevertheless thought that *it would be a tragic thing to concentrate solely upon* the transition period after the war was ended *when some kind of joint police power* would have to be exercised by the British and by the United States Governments and *omit any reference to the need of the creation of some effective and practicable international organization which would function after the transition period was concluded.* (Italics supplied.)

With this view Mr. Welles expressed himself as "in full agreement" but that "the matter would have to be determined by the President."

Subsequently, on the afternoon of August 11, Mr. Welles had a long conversation with President Roosevelt, in the course of which the President's world policy for the period following the war was explored. Mr. Welles raised a question with regard to the proposed declaration that it is essential that aggressor nations be disarmed, and suggested that this declaration might raise "a very considerable opposition on the part of extreme isolationists in the United States." Mr. Welles then explained his grounds for this opinion:

I said that if a great Power like the United States publicly declares that something is essential, *the inference is that the Power is going to do something itself about it.* I said it appeared to me more than likely that the isolationists will insist that this public statement by the President meant that the United States would go to war in order to disarm not only Germany but even possibly Japan and *theoretically, at least, even the Soviet Union if that country should later once more embark upon aggression on its neighbors.* (Italics supplied.)

President Roosevelt apparently did not share Mr. Welles' view that isolationists and the people of the United States would infer from the clause relative to disarming aggressors that the United States was going into the war in order to achieve that disarmament. To Mr. Welles' reasoning the President replied

that the whole intent of point seven, as he saw it, was to make clear what the objective would be *if the war was won* and that he believed people in the United States would take that point of view. He further said he felt the realism inherent in article seven was one which would be apparent to the enormous majority of the American people and that they would enthusiastically support the need for the disarmament of aggressor nations. (Italics supplied)

Evidently the President did not think that the language of the point in question would be interpreted at home as meaning that the United States was going to war in order to achieve that end; or, if he did, Mr. Welles made no record of any statement to that effect.

Then Mr. Welles took up with the President the issue of a world organization and the policing of the world by the

United States and Great Britain during a transition period of uncertain duration. Mr. Welles said to the President: "I also had been surprised and somewhat discouraged by a remark that the President had casually made in our morning's conference—if I had understood him correctly—which was that nothing could be more futile than the reconstitution of such a body as the Assembly of the League of Nations." With reference to the President's idea of a transition period "during which Great Britain and the United States would undertake the policing of the world," Mr. Welles entered a mild dissent:

It seemed to me that it would be enormously desirable for the smaller Powers to have available to them an Assembly in which they would all be represented and in *which they could make their complaints known* and join in *recommendations* as to the policy to be pursued by the major Powers who were doing the police work. I said it seemed to me that an organization of that kind would be *the most effective safety value* that could be devised. (Italics supplied.)

To Mr. Welles' conception of a league assembly which would allow the smaller powers to voice their complaints and make recommendations as to policies, President Roosevelt offered no objections. On the contrary he "agreed fully" and explained that by his remark during the morning session he intended to make clear his belief "that a transition period was necessary and that during that transition period *no organization such as the Council or the Assembly of the League* could undertake the powers and prerogatives *with which they had been entrusted during the existence of the League of Nations.*" (Italics supplied.)

Mr. Welles still insisted that some kind of hearing or voice should be accorded to some of the smaller powers. He agreed that "*the United States and Great Britain were the only Powers which could or would exercise the police trusteeship.*" But he was of the opinion that "it would be impossible if such a trusteeship were set up to exclude therefrom the other American republics, or, for that matter, the countries at present oc-

cupied such as Norway, the Netherlands, and even Belgium."
(Italics supplied.)

Apparently the President was somewhat impressed by Mr.
Welles' argument but not enough to warrant altering his
general conclusion as to committing to the United States and
Great Britain the function of policing the world during the
transition period and excluding therefrom any such bodies as
the Council or Assembly of the League of Nations. He noted
the difficulty raised by Mr. Welles and said "he felt that a
solution for this difficulty could probably be found through
the *ostensible* joining with Great Britain and the United
States of those Powers" mentioned by Mr. Welles. He
added, however: "But it would have to be recognized that
it would only be ostensible since none of the nations mentioned would have the practical means of taking any effective
or, at least, considerable part in the task involved." (Italics
supplied.) At this point evidently Mr. Welles surrendered,
for he recorded no further discussion of the delicate topic.

*Text of Mr. Welles' Memorandum of Conversations on
British-American World Policy—The Atlantic Charter*

[At the meeting, Sunday, August 10, Sir Alexander Cadogan presented to Mr. Welles a draft of a proposed joint declaration to be made public by the President and the Prime
Minister at the end of the Atlantic Conference. The draft
read as follows:]

"The President of the United States of America and the Prime
Minister, Mr. Churchill, representing His Majesty's Government
in the United Kingdom, being met together to resolve and concert the means of providing for the safety of their respective
countries in face of Nazi and German aggression and of the dangers to all peoples arising therefrom, deem it right to make known
certain principles which they both accept for guidance in the
framing of their policy and on which they base their hopes for a
better future for the world.

"First, their countries seek no aggrandizement, territorial or
other;

"Second, they desire to see no territorial changes that do not accord with the freely expressed wishes of the peoples concerned;

"Third, they respect the right of all peoples to choose the form of government under which they will live; they are only concerned to defend the rights of freedom of speech and of thought without which such choosing must be illusory;

"Fourth, they will strive to bring about a fair and equitable distribution of essential produce not only within their territorial jurisdiction but between the nations of the world.

"Fifth, they seek a peace which will not only cast down forever the Nazi tyranny but by effective international organization will afford to all States and peoples the means of dwelling in security within their own bounds and of traversing the seas and oceans without fear of lawless assault or need of getting burdensome armaments."

I [Mr. Welles] then gave the President [morning session, August 11], Mr. Churchill and Sir Alexander Cadogan copies of a redraft which I had made this morning of the proposed joint declaration before Mr. Churchill had arrived and had had an opportunity of going over it with the President, and the latter had approved it. Mr. Churchill then commenced to read it. He suggested that there be inserted in the text of the third point before the word "self-government" the words "sovereign rights and." This was agreed upon.

Mr. Churchill then read the fourth point which ran as follows: "Fourth, they will endeavor to further the enjoyment by all peoples of access, without discrimination and on equal terms, to the markets and to the raw materials of the world which are needed for their economic prosperity."

He immediately inquired whether this was meant to apply to the terms of the Ottawa agreements. I replied that, of course, it did, since the policy which the United States Government had been pursuing for the better part of nine years had been addressed primarily towards the removal of all of those artificial restrictions and controls upon international trade which had created such tragic havoc to world economy during the past generation. I said I understood fully the immediate difficulties which this occasioned him, but I pointed out that the phraseology was "they will endeavor to further" and that this naturally did not imply a formal and immediate contractual obligation on the part of his Government. The President stated that he believed the point was of very great importance as a measure of assurance to the German and Italian peoples that the British and the United States Governments desired to offer them, after the war, fair and equal opportunity of an economic character.

The Prime Minister said that, of course, he was without any power himself to agree upon this point. He set forth in considerable detail the position of the United Kingdom vis-à-vis the Dominions and emphasized his inability, without the agreement of the Dominions, to enter into the proposed declaration insofar as this point was concerned. He said that insofar as he himself was concerned the issue was one with which his own personal life history was connected. He referred to the days at the outset of the century when Joseph Chamberlain first brought up the proposal for Empire preferences and the predominant part which this issue had played in the political history of Great Britain during the past forty years. He said that he felt that the proposal as now phrased would have the enthusiastic support of all the liberals everywhere. He said that he himself was heartily in accord with the proposal and that he himself had always been, as was well known, emphatically opposed to the Ottawa agreements. He said, however, that it would be at least a week before he could hope to obtain by telegraph the opinion of the Dominions with regard to this question.

Harry Hopkins then suggested that Sir Alexander Cadogan and I be requested to draft new phraseology which would take care of these difficulties and prevent the delay of which Mr. Churchill spoke. He said it was inconceivable that the issuance of the joint declaration should be held up by a matter of this kind.

I said that in my own judgment further modification of that article would destroy completely any value in that portion of the proposed declaration. I said that it was not a question of phraseology, that it was a question of a vital principle which was involved. I said that if the British and the United States Governments could not agree to do everything within their power to further, after the termination of the present war, a restoration of free and liberal trade policies, they might as well throw in the sponge and realize that one of the greatest factors in creating the present tragic situation in the world was going to be permitted to continue unchecked in the post-war world. I said that the trade policies of the British Empire during the latter portion of the nineteenth century had, I felt, contributed enormously to the sane and prosperous condition of the world at that time, and that, of course, I realized that the tariff policies pursued by the United States and many other countries during that period had played an important part in the creation of the evils which had sprung up after the last war. I said, however, that it seemed to be imperative that we try to agree now upon the policy of constructive sanity in world economics as a fundamental factor in the creation of a new and better world and that except through an agreement upon such a policy by our two governments there would be no hindrance whatever to a continuation later to the present German practices of utilizing their trade and financial policies in order to achieve political ends.

Mr. Churchill agreed very emphatically to this policy. He and Sir Alexander Cadogan both agreed that it was not a question of phraseology, but that they were up against a material obstacle which Mr. Churchill had already indicated. The Dominions would have to be consulted. It might well be that an agreement could not be had from the Dominions and that consequently the proposed joint declaration could only be issued some time after news of the meeting between the President and the Prime Minister had been given out. Mr. Churchill suggested that the inclusion before the phrase "they will endeavor to further" of the phrase which would read "with due regard for our present obligations" might ease the situation.

The President suggested, and Mr. Churchill agreed, that the latter would try and draft some phraseology which would make that situation easier, and it was arranged that I would call later in the afternoon upon the Prime Minister and Sir Alexander Cadogan to go over with them such redraft as they might have in mind.

Mr. Churchill was in entire accord with points five and six.

He then read point seven and after discussion at the meeting of this point it was agreed that the phrase "to use force" be replaced by the word "aggression" in the second sentence of the seventh point.

Mr. Churchill said that, of course, he was heartily and enthusiastically in favor of this point seven, which had been initiated by the President. He inquired, however, whether the President would not agree to support some kind of "effective international organization" as suggested by the Prime Minister in his original draft of the proposed joint declaration.

The President replied that he did not feel that he could agree to this because of the suspicions and opposition that such a statement on his part would create in the United States. He said that he himself would not be in favor of the creation of a new Assembly of the League of Nations, at least until after a period of time had transpired and during which an international police force composed of the United States and Great Britain had had an opportunity of functioning. Mr. Churchill said that he did not feel that he would be candid if he did not express to the President his feeling that point seven would create a great deal of opposition from the extreme internationalists. The President replied that he realized that, but that he felt that the time had come to be realistic and that in his judgment the main factor in the seventh point was complete realism. Mr. Churchill then remarked that of course he was wholeheartedly in favor of it and shared the President's view.

The meeting then broke up and I arranged with the President that I would drop by to see him after my conference later in the afternoon with the Prime Minister. The latter stated that he would not be able to leave until at least 5:00 P.M., tomorrow, August 12 and that as he felt it of importance to reach a complete meeting of minds with the President upon all of the issues involved, that he would be willing to spend an additional twenty-four hours should that be necessary.

I [Mr. Welles] went by arrangement to see Sir Alexander Cadogan on the PRINCE OF WALES this afternoon [August 11, 1941]. He gave me to read memoranda which he had already completed on the conference between the Prime Minister and the President this morning and, with a few changes which I indicated, they appeared to be a correct presentation of the discussion and of the agreements reached.

With regard to the draft of the joint declaration, Sir Alexander told me that the Prime Minister had already radioed to London the text of the proposed joint declaration incorporating therein modifications of points four and seven. Sir Alexander gave me the revised text to read. Inasmuch as the Prime Minister's draft of point four was far broader and more satisfactory than the minimum which the President had instructed me, after our conference of the morning, to accept, I raised no objection thereto, and with regard to the proposed change in point seven I stated that while it was completely satisfactory to me and entirely in accord with my own way of thinking I had no idea what the President's decision might be. I said that I would have to submit it to him.

Sir Alexander stated that the Prime Minister felt very strongly—perhaps exaggeratedly—the opposition which would be created on the part of a certain pro-League-of-Nations group in England to the contents of point seven declaring for the disarmament of nations which undertook aggression outside of their frontiers. He went on to say that while he believed there would not be the amount of opposition which the Prime Minister anticipated he nevertheless thought that it would be a tragic thing to concentrate solely upon the transition period after the war was ended when some kind of joint police power would have to be exercised by the British and by the United States Governments and omit any reference to the need of the creation of some effective and practicable international organization which would function after the transition period was concluded. I said that as I had already indicated while I was in full agreement with his own views the matter would have to be determined by the President.

We discussed the desirability of informing the Chinese Government of the steps which the United States Government in the person of the President was taking with regard to Japan. I said that while I felt very definitely that every effort should be made to keep China closely informed of what was being done in her interest by Great Britain and by the United States I wondered whether telling China of what the President intended to state to the Japanese Government at this particular moment would not mean that the Government at Chungking for its own interests would make public the information so received. If publicity resulted, I stated I feared that the extreme militaristic element in Tokio and that portion of the Tokio press which was controlled by Germany would immediately take advantage of the situation so created to inflame sentiment in Japan to such an extent as to make any possibility remote, as it might anyhow be, of achieving any satisfactory result through negotiation with Japan. Sir Alexander said he was entirely in accord and would be governed by those views. He said, of course, I realized how terribly persistent the

Chinese were and that the present Ambassador in London, Dr. Wellington Koo, would undoubtedly press him day in and day out to know what had transpired at the meeting between the Prime Minister and the President with regard to China. He said that he felt that the best solution was for him merely to say in general terms that the two governments had agreed that every step should be taken that was practicable at this time for China and its defense and avoid going into any details.

I subsequently went to see the President. The President said that he was entirely in accord with the redraft of point four which was better than he had thought Mr. Churchill would be willing to concede. He also accepted without question the amendment made by Mr. Churchill to point seven and the President said that it seemed to him entirely desirable since the amendment made it clear that once the war was over a transition period would have to take place and that the permanent international organization would only be set up after that experimental period had passed. He had jotted down certain minor changes in the text of the proposed joint declaration, most of which were merely verbal changes for the purpose of clarification.

I said I felt it necessary for me to ask him whether he did not believe that a very considerable opposition on the part of extreme isolationists in the United States would result from that portion of point seven which declares in the judgment of the United States that it is essential that aggressor nations be disarmed. I said that if a great Power like the United States publicly declares that something is essential, the inference is that the Power is going to do something itself about it. I said it appeared to me more than likely that the isolationists will insist that this public statement by the President meant that the United States would go to war in order to disarm not only Germany but even possibly Japan and theoretically, at least, even the Soviet Union if that country should later once more embark upon aggression on its neighbors. The President replied that the whole intent of point seven, as he saw it, was to make clear what the objective would be if the war was won and that he believed people in the United States would take that point of view. He further said he felt that realism inherent in article seven was one which would be apparent to the enormous majority of the American people and that they would enthusiastically support the need for the disarmament of aggressor nations.

I said I also had been surprised and somewhat discouraged by a remark that the President had casually made in our morning's conference—if I had understood him correctly—which was that nothing could be more futile than the reconstitution of a body such as the Assembly of the League of Nations. I said to the President that it seemed to me that if he conceived of the need for a transition period upon the termination of the war during which period Great Britain and the United States would undertake the policing of the world,[9] it seemed to me that it would be enormously desirable for the smaller Powers to have available to them an Assembly in which they would all be represented and in which they could make their complaints known and join in recommendations as to the policy to be pursued by the major Powers who were doing the police work. I said it seemed to me that an organization of that kind would be the most effective safety valve that could be devised.

The President said that he agreed fully with what I said and that all that he had intended by the remark he made this morning was

9. Mr. Welles' memorandum containing this reference to the "policing of the world" by Great Britain and the United States during a transition period after the war proved to be somewhat embarrassing to defenders of President Roosevelt, when released to the public late in 1945. Representatives of the Russian Government in the United States probably heard about it in Washington. It evidently troubled Mr. Welles himself, for in his book, "*Where Are We Heading?*" (Harper and Brothers, 1946), he offers an explanation: "It will, of course, be noted that the President made no reference to the Soviet Union. But it must be remembered that in the early days of August, 1941, the Soviet Union had only just been invaded by the Nazi armies. The highest military authorities were continually advising the President not only that the Soviet Union could resist the German onslaught for but a brief period, but also that the occupation of the whole of Russia west of the Urals was inevitable. It must also be remembered that relations between the United States and the Soviet Union, particularly during the period of the German-Soviet agreement, had been practically nonexistent. Our knowledge of the views of the Kremlin about the future establishment of world order or, for that matter, about any other aspect of Russian foreign policy was very slight" (pp. 5 f.). Chap. I of this volume by Mr. Welles deals with the Atlantic Conference. Since the Congressional Committee on Pearl Harbor had forced the publication of his memoranda on conversations and agreements at the conference, he evidently felt moved to enter into certain elucidations. Whether his explanation of the failure of President Roosevelt and Mr. Churchill to bring the Soviet Union into the work of "policing the world" after the war mollified any of the feelings or suspicions the Russian Government may have had on the subject must be left to further exploration when and if Russian archives are ever opened to students. Mr. Welles says (p. 18) that some of the statements in his memoranda have been lifted out of their context and used "to charge that the President was *at heart* an isolationist." (Italics supplied.) Since the context is reproduced in this Chapter, readers may form their own judgments.

to make clear his belief that a transition period was necessary and that during that transition period no organizations such as the Council or the Assembly of the League could undertake the powers and prerogatives with which they had been entrusted during the existence of the League of Nations.

I further said that while from the practical standpoint I was in agreement that the United States and Great Britain were the only Powers which could or would exercise the police trusteeship and that it seemed to me that it would be impossible if such a trusteeship were set up to exclude therefrom the other American republics or for that matter the countries at present occupied such as Norway, the Netherlands, and even Belgium. The President said that he felt that a solution for this difficulty could probably be found through the ostensible joining with Great Britain and the United States of those Powers, but it would have to be recognized that it would be ostensible since none of the nations mentioned would have the practical means of taking any effective or, at least, considerable part in the task involved.

I said that it seemed to me that now that the text of the joint declaration had been agreed upon, since I assumed from what Mr. Churchill had told me that the British Government would support his recommendations with regard thereto, all that was left to do in the way of drafting was the preparation of the brief statement which would be issued simultaneously in London and at Washington announcing that the President and the Prime Minister had met, referring to the discussions under the Lease-Lend Act and the inclusion at the termination thereof of the text of the joint declaration. I said that Mr. Churchill had told me that he had cabled his Government that he was not leaving Argentia until Wednesday afternoon and said it seemed to me that everything could be definitely agreed upon and cleared up by 1:00 P.M. tomorrow, and I could see no practical reason for waiting another twenty-four hours. The President agreed and said that he would try and get a decision reached in that sense when he saw Mr. Churchill this evening.[10]

10. According to Elliott Roosevelt, who was at the Atlantic Conference as his father's son (*As He Saw It* [Duell, Sloan & Pearce, 1946], Chap. II), sharp, even bitter, conflicts occurred there between the President and the Prime Minister; the President attacked the British Empire on the ground that its colonial peoples, as a result of British policy, were backward; he also declared that they could not fight a war against fascist slavery and at the same time "not work to free people

IV. FORM AND LANGUAGE OF THE JOINT
ANNOUNCEMENT

BESIDES framing agreements and commitments, President Roosevelt and Prime Minister Churchill had to consider the form and language in which their respective announcements to the public were to be couched. This task was made easier after Mr. Churchill agreed to omitting any reference to an "effective world organization" and substituting the words "the establishment of a wider and permanent system of general security." But the Prime Minister remembered that the British people were asking "How soon is the United States coming into the war" and expecting from him something more than a statement of fine principles unsupported by any definite commitments on the part of President Roosevelt.[11] To meet this situation, delicate at best, Mr. Churchill, in his original draft of the preamble to the joint declaration had proposed to announce that the President and he

being met together *to resolve and concert the means of providing for the safety of their respective countries in face of Nazi and German aggression and of the dangers to all peoples arising therefrom*, deem it right to make known certain principles *which they both accept for guidance in the framing of their policy* and on which they base their hopes for a better future for the world. (Italics supplied.)

While Mr. Churchill "dreamed of, aimed at, and worked for" a union of the United States and the British Commonwealth of Nations in the war, as he said later,[12] he was familiar with the American constitutional system which imposed limits on the power of the President to take the country directly and

---

all over the world from a backward colonial policy" (p. 37). As the son reported the contest, the Prime Minister was "a real old Tory, of the old school" (p. 38), and the President was bent on raising the standard of life for all oppressed peoples in the colonial world. Interested citizens of the United States will doubtless want to test the accuracy of Elliott Roosevelt's reporting against the methodical account supplied by Mr. Welles' memoranda.

11. See above, Chap. IV, p. 131.
12. Mr. Churchill's broadcast, February 15, 1942. *Voices of History, 1942–1943,* pp. 143 ff.

openly into the armed conflict by personal action. The nature of this system Mr. Churchill recognized when, in his draft of parallel communications to Japan, he wrote: "If any third Power becomes the object of aggression by Japan in consequence of such counter measures or of their support of them, the President would have the intention to seek authority from Congress to give aid to such power." Though he was unable to obtain the President's consent to follow that course, Mr. Churchill, nevertheless, felt the desirability, if not the necessity, of having some definite gains to report at home after the Atlantic Conference had come to an end.

But as soon as he brought up for discussion, on the morning of August 11, the proposed joint declaration to be made public at the conclusion of the conference, President Roosevelt presented his own plan which differed in important respects from the Prime Minister's project. According to Mr. Welles' memorandum, the President then said "he believed the best solution of this problem" would be "an identic statement" to be made in London and the United States,

to the effect that the Prime Minister and the President had met at sea, accompanied by the various members of their respective staffs; that these members of the two Governments had discussed the question of aid under the terms of the Lease-Lend Act to nations resisting aggression, and that *these military and naval conversations* had in no way involved *any future commitments between the two Governments, except as authorized under the terms of the Lease-Lend Act;* that the Prime Minister and the President had between them discussed certain principles relating to a better future for the world and had agreed upon a joint declaration which would then be quoted verbatim. (Italics supplied.)

The Prime Minister was evidently disturbed by the President's limited proposal for, as Mr. Welles' recorded, "Mr. Churchill dissented very strongly from *the form* in which the President had desired to make it clear that *no future commitments had been entered into*." (Italics supplied.) After all they had, in fact, reached agreements as to the occupation of the Azores and the Cape Verde Islands and parallel diplomatic actions in respect of Japan. It is true that the President's proposed form of statement excluded these commitments, for they had not been made at the "military and naval conversations" but at conversations which could be regarded as diplomatic in nature, although they involved military and naval operations. But Mr. Churchill apparently overlooked the distinction.

At all events, President Roosevelt was insistent. He replied to Mr. Churchill's dissent by declaring that "that portion of the proposed statement was of extreme importance *from his standpoint* inasmuch as a statement of that character would make it impossible for extreme isolationist leaders in the United States to allege that *every kind of secret agreement had been entered into during the course of these conversations.*" (Italics supplied.)

In reply "Mr. Churchill said that he understood that side of the question, but that he believed that any categorical statement of that character would prove deeply discouraging to the populations of the occupied countries and would have a very serious effect upon their morale. He likewise made it clear that a similar effect would be created by British public opinion." Taking cognizance of the President's desire to keep the public statement within the limits of the authority granted to him by the Lease-Lend Act, Mr. Churchill "asked if the statement could not be worded in such a way as to make it *positive rather than negative,* namely, that *the members of the staffs* of the Prime Minister and of the President had *solely discussed questions relative to the furnishing of aid to the countries resisting aggression under the terms of the Lease-Lend Act.*" (Italics supplied.)

Mr. Churchill's countersuggestion met President Roosevelt's requirements. "The President replied that he believed that the statement could be drawn up in that way and that *if we were then queried in the United States he need merely reply that nothing had been discussed or agreed upon other than that which had already been indicated in his public statement.*" (Italics supplied.)

As a result of the discussions of the President's problems a compromise was reached as to the form of the public statement to be issued at the close of the conference. Mr. Churchill's objections were met by omitting the President's formula "that these military and naval conversations had in no way involved future commitments between the two Governments, except as authorized under the terms of the Lease-Lend Act." President Roosevelt's needs were met by omitting certain phrases from Mr. Churchill's original proposal (see above, p. 478) and by confining the opening passages of the joint statement to matters respecting the problem of supply as provided by the Lend-Lease Act, the dangers of Axis policies to world civilization, and steps taken for the safety of the United States and Great Britain in the face of these dangers.[13] As far as the text of the final formula was concerned, President Roosevelt felt that he could properly say when queried in the United States that "no new commitments" had been made.

Text of Mr. Welles' Memorandum of Conversations on the Form and Language of the Joint Announcement

Mr. Churchill then said [after the agreement on Far Eastern policies on the morning of August 11] that he desired to bring up for discussion the proposed joint declaration by the President and himself.

The President said that he believed the best solution of this problem was for an identic statement to be made in London and in the United States, probably on Thursday, August 14, to the effect that the Prime Minister and the President had met at sea, accompanied by the various members of their respective staffs; that these members of the two Governments had discussed the question of aid under the terms of the Lease-Lend Act to nations resisting aggression, and that these military and naval conversations had in no way involved any future commitments between the two Governments, except as authorized under the terms of the Lease-Lend Act; that the Prime Minister and the President had between them discussed certain principles relating to a better

13. For the opening passages of the joint statement see above, p. 119.

future for the world and had agreed upon a joint declaration which would then be quoted verbatim.

Mr. Churchill dissented very strongly from the form in which the President had desired to make it clear that no future commitments had been entered into. The President stated that that portion of the proposed statement was of extreme importance from his standpoint inasmuch as a statement of that character would make it impossible for extreme isolationist leaders in the United States to allege that every kind of secret agreement had been entered into during the course of these conversations.

Mr. Churchill said that he understood that side of the question, but that he believed that any categorical statement of that character would prove deeply discouraging to the populations of the occupied countries and would have a very serious effect upon their morale. He likewise made it clear that a similar effect would be created by British public opinion. He asked if the statement could not be worded in such a way as to make it positive rather than negative, namely, that the members of the staffs of the Prime Minister and of the President had solely discussed questions relative to the furnishing of aid to the countries resisting aggression under the terms of the Lease-Lend Act. The President replied that he believed that the statement could be drawn up in that way and that if he then were queried in the United States he need merely reply that nothing had been discussed or agreed upon other than that which had already been indicated in his public statement.[14]

14. See President Roosevelt's public statements in August, 1941, in respect of the Atlantic Conference, above, Chap. IV.

CHAPTER XVI

"Complicated Moves" in Relations with Japan

WHAT Mr. Justice Frankfurter described as President Roosevelt's "complicated moves" "so skilfully conducted as to avoid even the appearance of an act of aggression on our part" seem comparatively simple in respect of Japan, at least as revealed by the documentation made available to the American people by the State Department and the Congressional Committee on Pearl Harbor. To be sure the documentation is far from complete. The Democratic majority of the committee so skillfully conducted their complicated moves that the President's own papers, including the personal messages exchanged with Mr. Churchill from September, 1939, until long after Pearl Harbor, were kept from the prying eyes of the Republican minority and likewise from the scrutiny of the American people. As to its part in the secret negotiations or "conversations" with Japan, the British Government has seen fit to maintain a guarded reticence; and concerning Japanese archives bearing on the subject, which survived the destruction of the war, relatively little has been made known to the American public by the American Army of Occupation.[1]

Moreover, the Democratic majority of the Congressional Committee conducted its affairs so skillfully that, on account of the state of Mr. Hull's health, members of the Republican minority had no opportunity to examine him orally at the hearings. Thus several of the Administration's complicated moves in relation to Japan remain obscure, despite the thousands of selected pages composing the record published by Secretary Hull and the State Department. Hence, it may be years before every specific exchange between the United

---

1. See, for example, CJC, Part 18, Exhibits 132, 132-A; and Part 20, Exhibit 173, "Memoirs of Prince Konoye." What German, Italian, Russian, and United States archives will yield, if ever fully opened, remains a matter of conjecture.

States and Japan, from August to December, 1941, can be treated in the light of full documentation. But there is now available extensive evidence pertaining to the final program presented to Japan, November 26, 1941, by Secretary Hull, the methods employed in implementing it, and its connection with the historic policy of the United States in the Orient (see above, Chap. IX).

There is also now available sufficient evidence respecting two primary questions with which my inquiry is particularly concerned: (1) How did the secret actions of the Roosevelt Administration bearing on relations with Japan from August 17 to December 7, 1941, as described in official documents now available, square with official representations of the Administration to the American people at the time—realities with appearances? (2) Do these official documents sustain the official thesis respecting relations with Japan presented to Congress and the people by President Roosevelt's message to Congress on December 8, 1941?

On that occasion, the President said—to repeat, for convenience—that on December 7, 1941, the United States was at peace with Japan, that at the solicitation of Japan it was still in conversation with the Japanese Government and Emperor, looking toward the maintenance of peace in the Pacific, and that on that day Japan had undertaken a planned "surprise offensive," of which the attack on Pearl Harbor was a phase. Did the course of American-Japanese affairs as conducted during the months preceding Pearl Harbor, however it "looked," actually point in the direction of peace with Japan? Were those affairs in such a state at any time during this period that the President actually expected them to eventuate in the maintenance of peace in the Pacific? Did the Japanese Government make any proposals during this period which looked to the possibility of maintaining peace in the Pacific? And, if so, how did Secretary Hull and President Roosevelt treat these proposals with a view to the maintenance of peace? Did the President think that the Japanese final memorandum delivered to Secretary Hull on December 7 actually constituted no threat or hint of an armed attack? Was the Japanese offensive really a surprise to the Administration? With reference to these questions there are some answers in the documents now available.

As early as October 8, 1940, during the campaign of that year while he was still making peace pledges to the country, President Roosevelt had become convinced that Japan would make a mistake and that the United States would enter a war in the Pacific. He expressed this conviction to Admiral J. O. Richardson, Commander in Chief of the Fleet in the Pacific, whose duty it was to prepare plans for the war thus foretold by the President.[2] The development of an American war plan, based on arrangements made with the British Commonwealth and the Netherlands in the spring of 1941, contemplated a general war in which the United States would participate when and if it came [3]—a plan which President Roosevelt approved, "except officially," to use Admiral Stark's ingenious phrase.

On December 14, 1940, the American Ambassador in Tokyo, Joseph Grew, wrote a long letter to President Roosevelt on American-Japanese relations, in the course of which he said that, unless the United States was prepared to withdraw bag and baggage from the entire sphere of Greater East Asia and the South Seas, "(which God forbid), we are bound eventually to come to a head-on clash with Japan." President Roosevelt replied, January 21, 1941, "I find myself in decided agreement with your conclusions"; and went on to say that "our strategy of self-defense must be a global strategy which takes account of every front and takes advantage of every opportunity to contribute to our total security." [4] In other words, in January, 1941, President Roosevelt envisaged a head-on clash with Japan as a phase of assistance to Great Britain in a world of inseparable spheres of interest. This conclusion squared with the conviction he had expressed to Admi-

2. See above, p. 416.
3. See above, pp. 442 ff.
4. Joseph C. Grew, *Ten Years in Japan* (Simon & Schuster, 1944), pp. 359 ff.

ral Richardson on October 8, 1940: Japan will make a mistake and we will enter the war.

Concerning the course of specific transactions in official relations between the United States and Japan from the opening of the Atlantic Conference until December 7, 1941, the American people knew little at the time. Those who read the newspapers learned from reports of the President's meetings with representatives of the press that, at the Atlantic Conference, no new commitments had been made, that the country was no closer to war, that arrangements for operations under the Lend-Lease Act had been developed, that a list of grand principles, soon known as the Atlantic Charter, expressing hopes for a better world, had been promulgated over the names of the President and the Prime Minister, and that relations with Japan were dangerously strained. From the President's quip that he and Mr. Churchill had discussed affairs in all the continents of the earth, newspaper readers possessed of the slightest imagination could conclude that affairs in the Far East had in some manner been reviewed at the Atlantic Conference.[5]

PRESIDENT ROOSEVELT'S WARNING NOTE TO JAPAN ON AUGUST 17, 1941

BUT the American people had no official information until 1945 that Japanese affairs had come up first in the proceedings of the Atlantic Conference, that there the President made a definite commitment to Mr. Churchill's proposal for joint action in respect of Japan. It is true that after the United States had been involved in war for several months, two journalists, Forrest Davis and Ernest K. Lindley, permitted to make a "scoop" from secret information which had been conveyed to them by the White House and the State Department, published a story that approached a correct, if in many respects inadequate, account of the transactions relative to Japan at the Atlantic Conference.[6] Yet, after all, Davis and Lindley were

5. See above, Chap. IV.
6. See above, p. 121, and Beard, *op. cit.*, pp. 25 ff.

simply journalists whose report could be repudiated as unofficial or unreliable by any defender of the Roosevelt Administration, if their allegations made trouble for its high officials. Hence, it is proper to say that nothing like the real truth about the discussions of Japanese affairs at the Atlantic Conference in August, 1941, was revealed to the American people until December, 1945, when an official record of certain proceedings at the conference made by the Undersecretary of State, Sumner Welles, was placed among the exhibits in the documentation of the Congressional Committee on Pearl Harbor.[7] What does that record show?

Japanese affairs, it was learned from the Welles' memoranda, were taken up by the principal parties to the Atlantic Conference on the evening of August 9 and they received close attention subsequently until agreement was reached on a program of parallel warnings to Japan. President Roosevelt rejected Mr. Churchill's proposal that he strengthen his warning to the Japanese Government by adding a declaration of his intention to seek authority from Congress to aid any power attacked by Japan in the Southwestern Pacific. But the President agreed to send a stiff note to Japan—a note in the nature of an ultimatum—after he had returned to Washington.

Although Mr. Churchill said that, as a result of the warning agreed upon, there was a reasonable chance of avoiding war in the Pacific, President Roosevelt expressed no such hope. On the contrary, he remarked that by taking this course "any further move of aggression on the part of Japan which might result in war could be held off for at least thirty days." Hence, it now appears, President Roosevelt did not think, on August 11, 1941, that the warning he was about to give to Japan would go very far in the direction of the "maintenance of peace in the Pacific."

On August 17, 1941, after his return from the Atlantic Conference, President Roosevelt called the Japanese Ambassador to the White House and told him point-blank, among other things:

7. See below, p. 489, and above, Chap. XV.

. . . this Government now finds it necessary to say to the Government of Japan that if the Japanese Government takes any further steps in pursuance of a policy or program of military domination by force or threat of force of neighboring countries, the Government of the United States will be compelled to take immediately any and all steps which it may deem necessary toward safeguarding the legitimate rights and interests of the United States and American nationals and toward insuring the safety and security of the United States.

Such was the formula of the President's warning as recorded in the State Department's *Peace and War*, published in July, 1943 (p. 714).[8]

To the Japanese Ambassador, familiar with the language of diplomacy, the statement could have had only one meaning. Although the President did not even hint that he would appeal to Congress for a declaration of war if the Japanese Government failed to heed his warning, he did indicate that if that government took any further steps in the direction of dominating neighboring countries, by force or threat of force, the United States would do something besides send another diplomatic memorandum to Tokyo.

Long historical practice justified this interpretation of his note on August 17. When on July 31, 1914, for instance, the German Ambassador in Paris asked the French Foreign Minister what France would do in case of a war between Germany

8. I searched the files of the *New York Times* and the *New York Herald Tribune* from August 17 to August 31, 1941, for references to press releases or statements from the White House and the State Department bearing on the delivery of this warning notice to Ambassador Nomura and found no such reference. Later I had two independent searches made of these files by two scholars trained in historical research and neither of them found even a hint that this note had been delivered to the Japanese Ambassador. On December 16, 1946, I wrote to the State Department asking whether the department had issued any statement or press release on the note of August 17, 1941, and received a reply dated January 3, 1947, which did not constitute an answer. In a letter dated January 7, 1947, I directed this question to the State Department: "Did the Department of State issue on or after August 17, 1941, any press release or statement to the press notifying the public that the important memorandum of August 17, 1941, had been delivered to the Japanese Ambassador in Washington on that day?" In a letter dated January 21, 1947, the State Department said: "the records of the Department indicate that a press release was not issued on the subject to which you refer."

and Russia, the latter replied: "France will have regard to her interests"; and that meant France would fight. When President Roosevelt informed Japan on August 17, 1941, that, in case of any more aggressive moves on her part against her neighbors, the United States would safeguard its interest, he meant that the United States would, sooner or later, take effective action to stop such moves. This interpretation of the President's intention is supported by evidence produced by the Congressional Committee on Pearl Harbor.

At a hearing of the Congressional Committee on November 23, 1945, when the former Undersecretary Welles appeared as a witness, the Assistant Counsel, Mr. Gesell, first offered as Exhibit 22, two telegrams and a draft of a proposed communication to the Japanese Ambassador brought to the State Department by Mr. Welles after the Atlantic Conference. After the documents had been put on record, Mr. Gesell asked Mr. Welles to indicate briefly his position in the State Department during the years 1940 and 1941. The following dialogue ensued: [9]

MR. WELLES. During those years my time and attention were primarily given to relations between the United States and the other American republics and, to a considerable extent, to our relations with European governments. I had no participation in the diplomatic discussions which went on between Secretary Hull and the Japanese Government representatives and only at certain times, when the Secretary was away on a much needed vacation or was not in the Department and I had to act as Acting Secretary of State did I take any active part.

MR. GESELL. You were present, were you not, during the meeting in the Atlantic between President Roosevelt and Prime Minister Churchill?

MR. WELLES. I was.

MR. GESELL. *Did you at that time participate in any discussions between President Roosevelt and Prime Minister Churchill concerning Japan or developments in the Far East?*

MR. WELLES. *No. During the meeting at Argentia the President delegated to me the work which had to do with the drafting*

9. CJC, Part 2, pp. 458 ff.; see also Part 14, Exhibit 22. (Italics supplied.)

of the Atlantic Charter. My conversations were almost entirely taken up with talks with the British Under Secretary of State for Foreign Affairs, Alexander Cadogan, and those conversations related solely to the drafting of the Atlantic Charter text and to one of the diplomatic negotiations, *none of which had to do with Japan.* (Italics supplied.)

MR. GESELL. Did you receive any information at that meeting as to any agreement or arrangement or understanding that had been arrived at, if there was any, between President Roosevelt and Prime Minister Churchill concerning joint action of the United States and Great Britain in the Pacific?

MR. WELLES. When I left the President, since he was due to return to Washington before myself, he told me that he had had a conversation, or several conversations, with Mr. Churchill with regard to the Japanese situation and the increasing dangers in the Far East; that Mr. Churchill had suggested to him that the two Governments, as a means which might be of some effect, should take parallel action in issuing a warning to the government of Japan.

As I recall it, the President stated that what Mr. Churchill had suggested was that the Government of the United States should state to the Government of Japan that if Japan persisted in her policy of conquest and aggression the United States, in the protection of its legitimate interests and in order to provide for its own security, would have to take such acts as were necessary in its own judgment.

The President also asked me to tell Secretary Hull that he wished to see the Japanese Ambassador immediately upon his return and that warning which had been suggested as a parallel action by Mr. Churchill was communicated to the Japanese Ambassador by the President on August 17 of that year.

MR. GESELL. Were you present at the meeting?

MR. WELLES. I was not. You mean the meeting between the President and the Japanese Ambassador?

MR. GESELL. Yes.

MR. WELLES. No.

MR. GESELL. Now, the Exhibit 22 which has just been introduced includes as the first document a document dated August 10, 1941, reading as follows:

DRAFT OF PARALLEL COMMUNICATIONS TO THE JAPANESE GOVERNMENT

Declaration by United States Government that:

"1. Any further encroachment by Japan in the South West Pacific would produce a situation in which the United States Government would be compelled to take counter measures even though these might lead to war between the United States and Japan.

"2. If any third Power becomes the object of aggression by Japan in consequence of such counter measures or of their support of them, the President would have the intention to seek authority from Congress to give aid to such Power."

Declaration by H. M. G.

"Same as above, mutatis mutandis, the last phrase reading:

'. . . their support of them H. M. G. would give all possible aid to such Power.' "

Declaration by Dutch Government.

"Same as that by H. M. G.

"Keep the Soviet Government informed. It will be for consideration whether they should be pressed to make a parallel declaration."

Do you recall ever having seen this document?

Mr. WELLES. I do not remember having seen that document.[10] I remember seeing the draft, however, which I took from Argentia to Washington and which is one of the exhibits itself in this collection.

Mr. GESELL. Well, now, did you prepare that draft or do you know who prepared it?

Mr. WELLES. As I recall it that was prepared after discussions between the President and myself the last day of the Argentia meeting.

Mr. GESELL. The last paragraph of that draft reads:

"The Government of the United States, therefore, finds it necessary to state to the Government of Japan that if the Japanese Government undertakes any further steps in pursuance of the policy of military domination through force or conquest in the Pacific region upon which it has apparently embarked, the United

---

10. Paragraphs 1 and 2 were contained in Mr. Welles' memorandum of August 10, 1941. See above, p. 454.

States Government will be forced to take immediately any and all steps of whatsoever character it deems necessary in its own security nothwithstanding the possibility that such further steps on its part may result in conflict between the two countries."

Was that, in essence, your understanding of the agreement between President Roosevelt and Prime Minister Churchill concerning the notice or threat which should be given to the Japanese?

Mr. Welles. That is correct.

Mr. Gesell. Now, referring to Volume 2, Foreign Relations of the United States with Japan 1931–1941, where the conversations between President Roosevelt and the Japanese Ambassador on August 17, 1941 is reported.

At page 556 I find in the paragraph beginning at said page what appears to be a somewhat different statement. This is the oral statement handed by the President to the Japanese Ambassador. It reads:

"Such being the case, this Government now finds it necessary to say to the Government of Japan that if the Japanese Government takes any further steps in pursuance of a policy or program of military domination by force or threat of force of neighboring countries, the Government of the United States will be compelled to take immediately any and all steps which it may deem necessary toward safe-guarding the legitimate rights and interests of the United States and American nationals and toward insuring the safety and security of the United States."

That statement that I have just read is a somewhat watered down version of the one you brought back, is it not, Mr. Welles?

Mr. Welles. That is correct.

Mr. Gesell. Is it your opinion that the statement that I have just read from Volume II is, in fact, the statement which was made at this meeting rather than the statement that you brought back?

Mr. Welles. The statement was handed by the President, I understood, to the Japanese Ambassador in writing, as an aide-mémoire, and that is the statement to which you refer.

Mr. Gesell. Have you any information as to what accounted for the watering down process?

Mr. Welles. I am not informed on that point, beyond the fact that the papers I brought back were given to Secretary Hull and he discussed them with the President before the President handed them to the Ambassador.

So much for Mr. Welles' accounting to the Congressional Committee on what happened at the Atlantic Conference with regard to the warning message handed to the Japanese Ambassador on August 17, 1941. At its hearing on December 18, 1945, about three weeks after the examination of Mr. Welles, Mr. Gesell placed in the records of the Congressional Committee three documents which had been secured from the State Department.[11] These documents, entered as Exhibits 22-B, 22-C, and 22-D, were memoranda, dated August 10–11, 1941, of conversations at the Atlantic Conference. These memoranda set down by Mr. Welles' own hand put in a curious perspective his sworn statements to the Congressional Committee in November. Either Mr. Welles' memory had been faulty on November 23, 1945, or his understanding of the English language differed from that which generally prevails among persons less experienced in diplomatic usages.

Mr. Welles, on November 23, 1945, had said "No," when asked whether he had participated in any discussions between President Roosevelt and Mr. Churchill concerning Japan or developments in the Far East. But, according to Mr. Welles' memorandum for August 10, 1941, a conversation on the subject of a warning to Japan actually was held by President Roosevelt, Mr. Churchill, Sir Alexander Cadogan, and Sumner Welles at dinner on the evening of August 9. Sir Alexander made tentative drafts of proposed parallel and simultaneous declarations by the British and the United States Governments relating to Japanese policy in the Pacific, to be presented to Japan by the President and the Prime Minister at the close of the Atlantic meeting.[12] The next day, August 10, Sir Alexander handed drafts of the proposed declarations to Mr. Welles; and on August 11, the subject was taken up at a meeting attended by the President, Mr. Churchill, Sir Alexander, Harry Hopkins, and Sumner Welles, and discussed. As a re-

11. See above, Chap. XV.
12. For Mr. Welles' account of these meetings, written for the State Department, see Chap. XV.

sult, a general formula was agreed upon, to be finally shaped up by Sir Alexander and Mr. Welles.

Out of the conversations and arrangements at the Atlantic Conference, with Mr. Welles acting as the President's agent in draftsmanship, emerged a text or draft of a warning note to Japan. This text or draft Mr. Welles took to the State Department on his return. It represented in substance the formula upon which the President and the Prime Minister had agreed at the conference. That formula as outlined by the President at the conference had met the approval of Mr. Churchill, who said that "it had in it an element of 'face saving' for the Japanese and yet, at the same time would constitute a flat United States warning to Japan of the consequences involved in a continuation by Japan of her present course." The text or draft dated August 15, 1941, taken by Mr. Welles to the State Department was sharper than the note of August 17 delivered to the Japanese Ambassador by the President. The draft of August 15 read:

The Government of the United States, therefore, finds it necessary to state to the Government of Japan, that if the Japanese Government undertakes any further steps in pursuance of the policy of military domination through force or conquest in the Pacific region upon which it has apparently embarked, the United States Government will be forced to take immediately any and all steps of whatsoever character it deems necessary in its own security notwithstanding the possibility that such further steps on its part *may result in conflict between the two countries*.[13]

In the memoranda made by Mr. Welles on the meetings at the Atlantic Conference it is patent that the notice given by President Roosevelt to the Japanese Ambassador on August 17, 1941, was intended to be in the nature of a war warning. It is true that in the final form given to the notice, two points

13. CJC, Part 14, Exhibit 22, pp. 1256 ff. (Italics supplied.) In the "watering down" process referred to by Assistant Counsel Gesell, it will be noted, the area in which Japan was to attempt no further domination was narrowed from "the Pacific region" to "neighboring countries" in a final draft presented to the Japanese Ambassador on August 17.

brought up at the Atlantic Conference had been eliminated or softened. Mr. Churchill's suggestion that the President inform Japan that he intended to seek authority from Congress to implement his notice was rejected. Also eliminated from the draft dated August 15, 1941, were the words: "notwithstanding the possibility that such further steps on its [Japan's] part may result in conflict between the two countries"; for these words were substituted a formula more veiled, but scarcely any less meaningful to Ambassador Nomura and the Government of Japan.

Nevertheless, Secretary Hull, who was present when President Roosevelt delivered this warning to the Japanese Ambassador on August 17, 1941, refused to concede in 1946 that the President's statement implied warlike action if Japan refused to heed. In May, 1946, Senator Ferguson, as a member of the Congressional Committee on Pearl Harbor, directed a written question to Secretary Hull, inquiring whether the Japanese warlike movements between November 30 and December 6, 1941, in the Southeastern Pacific, constituted a challenge to the United States to implement the position it had taken in its note of August 17, 1941, to Japan. Secretary Hull replied in a statement that looks queer when put beside Undersecretary Welles' account of the agreement concerning action against Japan reached by President Roosevelt and Mr. Churchill at the Atlantic Conference.

Secretary Hull's statement of May, 1946, read:

The purpose of the United States in making the statement of August 17 under reference was to tell Japan *in a friendly* way that if she kept encroaching upon *our rights and interests, we would defend ourselves.* This Government at that time was acutely concerned over Japan's refusal to agree to our proposal for the neutralization of Indochina, to abandon her jumping-off place there, and otherwise to desist from the menace she was creating to us and other peace-minded nations. It *wholly misrepresents the attitude of the United States* in the period after August 17 to allege that this Government *was planning any step other than that*

of pure defense in the event the Japanese should attack. Other
aspects of this question, for example, where, when, and how we
would resist the Japanese, *were essentially a military matter.*[14]

THE JAPANESE GOVERNMENT'S PROPOSAL FOR A
PACIFIC CONFERENCE REJECTED

WHILE the Japanese Government was considering President
Roosevelt's stern warning of August 17, with a diplomatic
postulate of implementation, it was seeking to develop a proposal to the President, which, at least on its surface, looked in
the direction of maintaining peace in the Pacific. Indeed, the
very day that Ambassador Nomura called at the White House
and received his warning, he drew from his pocket an instruction from his Government to the effect that the Prime Minister, Prince Konoye, felt strongly and earnestly about preserving peaceful relations with the United States and would
be disposed to meet the President somewhere in the Pacific for
the purpose of talking the matter out "in a peaceful spirit." [15]

Subsequently, the Japanese project for a Pacific Conference
was explored by exchanges of views between the two governments, over the merits of which students of diplomatic history
will probably differ for years to come. These diplomatic exchanges continued for nearly two months—until the fall of
the Konoye Cabinet in Tokyo on October 16, 1941. Whatever the justification for the position finally taken by President Roosevelt and Secretary Hull on the Japanese proposal,
the methods they employed during this period were dilatory,
and from start to finish they pursued the usual policy of
secrecy.[16] Numerous "leaks" in Washington, noncommittal
releases from the Department of State, and rumors kept the
American public in expectancy—and confusion. In fact, at
one time, when it was openly said in newspaper circles that arrangements had been made for a meeting of President Roosevelt and Premier Konoye, this "rumor" was brushed aside

14. CJC, Part 11, pp. 5406. (Italics supplied.)
15. *Peace and War*, pp. 712 f.
16. See above, pp. 183 ff.

humorously by the President's Secretary, Stephen Early, at the White House.[17]

Although, during the tortuous exchanges of notes on the proposed conference in the Pacific, the American public remained in the dark with regard to the nature of the various offers and counteroffers, documents made available since December 7, 1941, have partly disclosed the nature of the tactics employed by President Roosevelt and Secretary Hull in conducting those exchanges. For example, in July, 1943, the State Department published *Peace and War, 1931–1941*, which contained many papers on relations with Japan; and in the same year it issued two bulky volumes, *Foreign Relations with Japan, 1931–1941*, with a prefatory note to the effect that additional documents were to come. In 1944, Joseph Grew, former American Ambassador at Tokyo, published his *Ten Years in Japan*,[18] which illuminated the official documents released by the State Department. Additional evidence unearthed by the Congressional Committee on Pearl Harbor amplified the accounts of the Department and Ambassador Grew.

The strategy pursued by the President and the Secretary of State during these conversations on the Japanese Premier's proposal for a peace conference in the Pacific was, in brief, as follows. The President and the Secretary expressed to Japan a willingness to consider favorably the idea of a Pacific Conference, but insisted that the Premier should first agree upon certain principles in advance, with a view to assuring the success of the conference.

The Premier of Japan, on September 6, 1941, informed the American Ambassador in Tokyo that he subscribed fully to the four great principles of American policy laid down in Washington.[19] Then President Roosevelt and Secretary Hull declared that this was not enough, that agreements on more principles and formulas was necessary, that the replies of the Japanese Government were still unsatisfactory; but they re-

17. See above, p. 189.
18. See especially, pp. 416 ff.
19. *Peace and War*, pp. 733 ff.

frained from saying in precise language just what it was they demanded in detail as fixed conditions for accepting the Japanese invitation to a conference in the Pacific. To meet their obvious distrust of Japanese authorities and especially the Japanese militarists, Premier Konoye assured them that he had authority for bringing with him to the conference high army and naval officers as evidence that his commitments would have the support of the Army and the Navy of Japan. Still the President and the Secretary continued adamant in their tactics of prolonging the conversations as if they were merely playing for time, "babying the Japanese along."

It may be said that President Roosevelt and Secretary Hull thus chose a course well within their discretion, and demonstrated wisdom in so doing. That militarists in the Japanese Government and outside had been engaged in barbaric practices in China for many years and were rattling the sabers in the autumn of 1941, was a matter of general knowledge in the United States. That the Roosevelt Administration had long been opposed to Japan's policies and measures was, at least, equally well known. Still, if keeping out of war in the Pacific was a serious issue for the United States, then the primary question for President Roosevelt and Secretary Hull was: Did the Japanese proposal offer an opportunity to effect a settlement in the Pacific and were the decisions they made in relation to it actually "looking" in the direction of peace?

Immediately pertinent to this question, and necessary to an informed judgment on it, is a report by Ambassador Grew to Secretary Hull and thus to the President, dated Tokyo, September 29, 1941, after discussions of the Japanese Conference proposal had been dragging along for more than a month.[20] Mr. Grew had been the American Ambassador in Japan for about ten years. He was well acquainted with Japanese institutions, politics, party interests, and the bitter struggle between conciliatory citizens of Japan and the bellicose militarists. He and his secretaries were in intimate and constant touch with the Japanese Premier and Foreign Office from the

20. Grew, *op. cit.*, pp. 436 ff., *Foreign Relations with Japan*, II, 645 ff.

beginning of the controversy over the proposed peace conference in the Pacific. To say that Mr. Grew had more first-hand knowledge about the possibilities of these negotiations looking in the direction of peace in the Pacific and about the probable outcome of a conference, if held, than did President Roosevelt and Secretary Hull is scarcely an overstatement. Hence, the advice given to them by their representative in the Japanese capital has an immediate bearing on how war came.

In his report to Washington, September 29, Ambassador Grew laid stress on the growing eagerness of the Japanese Government to bring about a peace conference with the President. He expressed the hope that "so propitious a period" be not permitted to slip by without laying a new foundation for a better order in Japan and her relations to the United States. Japan, he said, had joined the Italo-German Axis to obtain security against Russia and avoid the peril of being caught between the Soviet Union and the United States and was now attempting to get out of this dangerous position. The Ambassador considered that the time had arrived for the liberal elements to come to the top in Japan. He saw a good chance that Japan might fall into line if a program of world reconstruction could be followed as forecast by the joint declaration of President Roosevelt and Mr. Churchill at the Atlantic Conference. The United States, Mr. Grew thought, could choose one of two methods in dealing with Japan: progressive economic strangulation or constructive conciliation, "not so-called appeasement." If conciliation failed, he reasoned, the other method—coercion and war—would always be available. He believed that a failure of the United States to use the present opportunity in the interest of conciliation would result in adding to the chances of an armed conflict.

While admitting that there were risks in any course of dealings with Japan, Ambassador Grew offered "his carefully studied belief" that there would be substantial hope of preventing the Far Eastern situation from becoming worse, and perhaps of insuring "definitely constructive results, if an agreement along the lines of the preliminary discussions were brought to a head by the proposed meeting of the heads of the two Governments." The Ambassador then raised "the question whether the United States is not now given the opportunity to halt Japan's program without war, or an immediate risk of war, and further whether, through failure to use the present opportunity, the United States will not face a greatly increased risk of war. The Ambassador stated his firm belief in an affirmative answer to these two questions." Mr. Grew conceded that certain elements in Japan or the United States might so tend to inflame public opinion in the other country as to make war unavoidable; and he recalled the cases of the *Maine* and the *Panay*. But he solicitously advised President Roosevelt and Secretary Hull to accept the offer of the Japanese Premier to discuss the situation directly, especially since the Premier had taken important steps in showing evidences of good faith.

Aware that in negotiations with the Japanese Ambassador in Washington, President Roosevelt and Secretary Hull were insisting upon further explorations of the Japanese proposal and that more than a month had passed in these "exploratory" operations, Mr. Grew warned them against this procedure. He told them that if the United States expected or awaited "clear-cut commitments" which would satisfy the United States "both as to principle and as to concrete detail," the conversations would be drawn out indefinitely and unproductively "until the Konoye cabinet and its supporting elements desiring rapprochement with the United States will come to the conclusion that the outlook for an agreement is hopeless and that the United States Government is only playing for time." [21] In this case, the Ambassador continued, the Konoye Government would be discredited. "The logical outcome of this will be the downfall of the Konoye cabinet and the formation of a military dictatorship which will lack either the disposition or the temperament to avoid colliding head-on with the United States."

[21]. Did this mean that the Japanese would suspect that President Roosevelt's intention was "to baby them along," as Davis and Lindley represented his designs at the Atlantic Conference? *How War Came*, p. 10.

If Premier Konoye was sincere in his intentions why could he not give President Roosevelt and Secretary Hull clear-cut commitments as to details before the conference? To this central question Ambassador Grew gave serious attention and provided for the President and the Secretary an answer based on his knowledge of the critical situation in Tokyo. Mr. Grew knew that a "liberal" government in Japan, or indeed any government inclined to keep peace with the United States, was beset by the militarist and chauvinist press, always engaged in frightening and inflaming the Japanese public by war-mongering. He knew also, what had recently been demonstrated many times, that the head and members of any such government were likely to be assassinated in cold blood by desperate agents of "patriotic" societies. He knew and so did Premier Konoye that Axis secret agents and Japanese enemies of peace with the United States were boring within the Konoye Government and watching with Argus eyes every message or communication sent from Tokyo to Washington. In other words, Premier Konoye could not be sure that any note he dispatched to Washington, no matter how guardedly, would escape the vigilance of his enemies on every side in Japan.

This situation Ambassador Grew went into at length in his report of September 29, 1941, to Secretary Hull and President Roosevelt. He had been in close and confidential communication with Premier Konoye. On the basis of very intimate knowledge, he informed them that the Japanese Government was ready to undertake commitments other than those set down in the communications which had already passed. He reported, if in cautious language as befitted a diplomat, that he had been told that "Prince Konoye is in a position in direct negotiations with President Roosevelt to offer him assurances which, because of their far-reaching character, will not fail to satisfy the United States." Mr. Grew added that he could not determine the truth of this statement, but he said definitely that while the Japanese Government could not overtly renounce its relations with the Axis Powers, it "actually has shown a readiness to reduce Japan's alliance adherence to a dead letter by its indication of willingness to enter formally into negotiations with the United States."

Thereupon Mr. Grew presented the alternatives as he saw them from his point of vantage in Tokyo. The Japanese military machine and army could be discredited by wholesale military defeat. That was one alternative. On the other hand the United States could place a "reasonable amount of confidence" in

the professed sincerity of intention and good faith of Prince Konoye and his supporters to mold Japan's future policy upon the basic principles they are ready to accept and then to adopt measures which gradually but loyally implement those principles, with it understood that the United States will implement its own commitments *pari passu* with the steps which Japan takes.

This was the alternative which the American Ambassador commended to President Roosevelt and Secretary Hull as "an attempt to produce a regeneration of Japanese thought and outlook through constructive conciliation, along the lines of American efforts at present."

As to the alternatives, Mr. Grew closed his plea by inquiring "whether the better part of wisdom and of statesmanship is not to bring such efforts to a head before the force of their initial impetus is lost, leaving it impossible to overcome an opposition which the Ambassador thinks will mount inevitably and steadily in Japan." In Mr. Grew's opinion it was evidently a question of now or never, though he ended by paying deference to "the much broader field of view of President Roosevelt and Secretary Hull" as compared with "the viewpoint of the American Embassy in Tokyo."

While the negotiations over the proposed meeting between President Roosevelt and Premier Konoye were still dragging along, the Japanese Foreign Minister, Toyoda, discussed with the British Ambassador in Tokyo, Sir Robert Craigie, various problems in the then delicate relations between Japan and the United States. At the same time, he asked Ambassador Grew to speak to Ambassador Craigie and later he learned

that the British and American Ambassadors had held a conference on these questions. On October 3, 1941, Minister
Toyoda sent to Ambassador Nomura in Washington information respecting the Japanese-British-American transactions
in Tokyo and said to Ambassador Nomura: "Subsequently,
according to absolutely unimpeachable sources, Ambassador
Craigie cabled Foreign Secretary Eden and Ambassador Halifax, explaining the importance of having the United States
and Japan come to an immediate agreement to hold a conference." [22]

In a supplementary message to Ambassador Nomura, Tokyo
furnished him with "the gist of Craigie's opinions" expressed
in messages to Anthony Eden and Lord Halifax, with a warning to keep the information strictly secret. According to Minister Toyoda's summation, Ambassador Craigie presented the
following views to his government in London and his colleague, Lord Halifax, in Washington. First, with the resignation of former Foreign Minister Yosuke Matsuoka "the
chances of turning away from the Axis policy and toward
the democracies, has been considerably enhanced." Second,
to Japan the speeding up of the conference between President
Roosevelt and Premier Konoye is important for the reason
that undue delay would place the Konoye Cabinet in a precarious position owing to the opposition in Japan to a reversal of relations with the Axis. Third,

by pursuing a policy of stalling, the United States is arguing about
every word and every phrase on the grounds that it is an essential
preliminary to any kind of an agreement. It seems apparent that
the United States does not comprehend the fact that by the nature
of the Japanese and also on account of the domestic conditions in
Japan, no delays can be countenanced. It would be very regrettable indeed if the best opportunity for the settlement of the Far
Eastern problems since I assumed my post here, were to be lost
in such a manner. . . . Both the U.S. Ambassador in Japan and I

22. CJC, Part 12, Exhibit 1, p. 50. This was a secret message intercepted, decoded, and translated by American Naval Intelligence, October 4, 1941, for the
information of appropriate officials in Washington.

are firmly of the opinion that it would be a foolish policy if this superb opportunity is permitted to slip by assuming an unduly suspicious attitude.

Fourth, British retaliatory economic measures should be continued until "the Konoye principles actually materialize." [23]

Nevertheless, President Roosevelt and Secretary Hull rejected the advice of their Ambassador in Japan and prolonged the "explorations" until the Konoye Cabinet fell about two weeks later, October 16, 1941. Why? Records now available provide no answer. As far as the President was concerned, the question remains open, save for such inferences as may be drawn from collateral documents. Secretary Hull's answer is to be sought in many words spread over many pages, and, owing to the fact that he was the President's agent in the conduct of foreign affairs, his answer, by inference, may be treated as that of the Administration. When Secretary Hull's prolix and involved explanations as yet presented to the American public are all analyzed, compared, and tabulated, they amount to this: The Japanese had a long record of barbaric deeds; Prince Konoye was not much better, if any, than the bloodthirsty militarists; the promises and proposals of the Konoye Government were not to be trusted as offering any hope of peace to the "peace-loving nations of the world," as represented by the United States.

If this summation is regarded as too simple, then resort may be had to Secretary Hull's own summation. Although the state of Secretary Hull's health did not permit him to undergo a cross examination by any Republican members of the Congressional Committee on Pearl Harbor during its proceedings

23. *Ibid.*, p. 51. These and other intercepted Japanese secret messages in Exhibit 1, a volume of 253 pages, amply warn American students of diplomatic history against even attempting to write any kind of "balanced" and "objective" history of American-Japanese relations in 1941 until British, Japanese, and American archives are opened. They should also put a stop to the vulgar saying: "The United States was raking British chestnuts out of the fire." I venture the opinion that when these archives are opened, it will become apparent that the British Government, while seeking American coöperation, also sought to exert a moderating influence on the development of American Far Eastern policy in 1941, until, and in fact after, November 26, the day Secretary Hull handed his memorandum to Tokyo.

of 1945–46, he answered in his own way certain questions formulated by Senator Ferguson and submitted to him in writing on April 5, 1946.

In Questions 71 and 72, Senator Ferguson dealt with conversations relative to the Japanese proposal for negotiations looking to the maintenance of peace in the Pacific. Senator Ferguson referred to the message of the Japanese Foreign Minister on the resumption of conversations in mid-August transmitted to Washington with a covering note by Ambassador Grew. He quoted from the Ambassador's covering note in which he urged "with all the force at his command, for the sake of avoiding the obviously growing possibility of an utterly futile war between Japan and the United States, that this Japanese proposal be not turned aside without every prayerful consideration." Senator Ferguson also reminded Secretary Hull of Ambassador Grew's words that the proposal was "unprecedented" in Japanese history, and had been made with the approval of the Emperor and the highest authority of Japan. "That is correct, is it not?" The Senator asked.

Secretary Hull replied that there was no controversy about the contents of the documents in question and then said:

The President and I, together with our Far Eastern advisors,[24] were looking at the situation with the benefit of all the world-wide information available to us in Washington. We judged that the Japanese Government had no serious expectation of reaching an understanding at the proposed meeting [in the Pacific] unless the American Government surrendered its basic position while Japan rigidly adhered to and went forward with its policy of aggression and conquest. We had fully tested out the Japanese Government by preliminary inquiries and found it adamant in its position.[25]

24. With reference to this point it is to be noted that the Far Eastern Division of the State Department late in the following November was advising Secretary Hull to meet another Japanese proposal for a settlement in the Pacific by a plan of adjustment and conciliation. See below, p. 511. Also that Secretary Hull himself considered, even if he did not believe in it, a plan for a modus vivendi and possible settlement with Japan. See below, pp. 509 ff.

25. CJC, Part 11, pp. 5389 f.

In other words, the President and Secretary Hull regarded the Japanese proposal for a Pacific Conference as essentially dishonest, as if a kind of subterfuge to deceive the Government of the United States while Japan went on with aggression and conquest.

It is at present impossible to determine the parts played by President Roosevelt and Secretary Hull respectively in the final decision to reject the Konoye proposal, as it is in the case of their action on the memorandum of November 26, 1941 (see below, p. 559). According to Premier Konoye's Memoirs (CJC, Part 20, Exhibit 173), the President was at first enthusiastic about the idea of a conference in the Pacific but Secretary Hull was at the outset cool and at length resolute in pursuing the course which, as Ambassador Grew had warned him in effect, would end in failure and war.

Nor is it possible now to discover whether, if the Pacific conference had been held, Premier Konoye could have carried out his intentions as communicated to the President and Secretary Hull. It is easy, of course, to take passages from Premier Konoye's Memoirs, and other fragmentary documents at present available, for the purpose of making an argument for or against American acceptance of his proposal; but, as Ambassador Grew informed the President and Secretary Hull at the time, the alternative of war would remain open to the United States if the conference had not fulfilled expectations. The "solution" of this insoluble "problem," however, lies outside the purposes and limitations of my inquiry (see above, p. 484).

THE JAPANESE PROPOSAL OF A MODUS VIVENDI REJECTED IN FAVOR OF AN ULTIMATIVE NOTICE

Though the Konoye Cabinet in Tokyo had been succeeded by what was regarded as a "strong" government headed by General Hideki Tojo, supposed to be an irreconcilable militarist, the Japanese did not break off conversations "looking to the maintenance of peace in the Pacific." On the contrary, the Japanese Government early in November dispatched to Ambassador Nomura two proposals for new discussions to be taken up with President Roosevelt and Secretary Hull and sent a special agent, Saburo Kurusu, to assist the Ambassador in further explorations. The first of these proposals, called proposal "A," was plainly a document for bargaining; the second, proposal "B," was more conciliatory and had the signs of being the last offer the Japanese Government might make to the United States—"a last effort to prevent something happening." Was this move on the part of Japan just another evidence of what Secretary Hull called Japanese trickery, a desire to prolong negotiations and to deceive the Government of the United States?

On their face the two proposals, as finally presented to the State Department, might have been so regarded by Secretary Hull. But as a matter of fact, having previously broken the Japanese code, American Navy and Army Intelligence had intercepted, translated, and made available to the Administration, before either of the projects had been laid before Secretary Hull, the substance of the two documents as sent in code from Tokyo to Ambassador Nomura. It had done more. It had intercepted accompanying messages from Tokyo to the Ambassador which indicated, in the first place, that the Tojo Cabinet was anxious to reach some kind of settlement with the United States; and, in the next place, that the second proposal was, to use the language of the Japanese dispatch containing it, "advanced with the idea of making a last effort to prevent something from happening." If the opinion often expressed by Secretary Hull to the effect that the Japanese were chronic liars be accepted as correct, still it is hardly to be presumed that the Japanese Government was lying to its. Ambassador when, in secret messages intended for his eyes alone, it informed him that a settlement was urgently desired in Tokyo and that proposal "B" was to be offered in a last effort to prevent something from happening—that is, doubtless, an open break and war.[26]

In short, Secretary Hull knew in advance, on November

26. CJC, Part 12, Exhibit 1, for the two proposals, pp. 94–97; for various relevant Japanese messages, intercepted and translated by American Intelligence, pp. 90 ff.

4, 1941, that the Japanese proposals were coming to him, that the Tokyo Government had expressed to Ambassador Nomura anxiety to reach some settlement with the United States, that it had fixed November 25 as a dead line, that failure to achieve a settlement or truce meant drastic action, if not war, on the part of the Japanese Government. On November 1, Secretary Hull had asked the Army and Navy whether they were ready to give support to new warnings to Japan, and expressed the opinion that there was no use to issue any additional warnings "if we can't back them up." [27] On November 5, General Marshall and Admiral Stark addressed to President Roosevelt a memorandum in which they strongly objected to military action against Japan at the moment and urged the postponement of hostilities in order to allow the Army and Navy as much time as possible to effect better preparations for war.[28] It was in this state of affairs that Secretary Hull undertook to deal with Ambassador Nomura when he presented a sketch of proposal "A," November 7, 1941.

As history long ago recorded, explorations of the Japanese proposal "A" came to nothing. On the afternoon of November 7, the day Ambassador Nomura laid the proposal before Secretary Hull, the President, at a meeting of his Cabinet, took a poll on the question "whether the people would back us up in case we struck at Japan down there and what the tactics should be." The vote was a solid yea. Such are the facts as recorded by Secretary Stimson in his *Diary*

27. At a meeting of the Joint Board of the Army and Navy, November 3, 1941, General Marshall and Admiral Stark present, among others, Captain R. E. Schuirmann, liaison officer between the Office of Naval Operations and the State Department, reported on actions at the State Department meeting on November 1. Captain Schuirmann "pointed out that on August 17, following the President's return from the meeting at sea with Mr. Churchill, the President had issued an ultimatum to Japan that it would be necessary for the United States to take action in case of further Japanese aggression. . . . Mr. Hull was of the opinion that there was no use to issue any additional warnings to Japan if we can't back them up, and he desired to know if the military authorities would be prepared to support further warnings by the State Department." CJC, Part 14, p. 1063. The Japanese dead line was later moved to November 29. CJC, Part 20, p. 165.

28. CJC, Part 12, Exhibit 1; Part 14, Exhibits 16, 18.

for his own eyes. He also added that Secretary Hull made a good presentation of the general situation and that he narrowed it down, following steps already taken to show "what needed to be done in the future." Secretary Stimson likewise noted that "the thing would have been much stronger if the Cabinet had known—and they did not know except in the case of Hull and the President—what the Army is doing with the big bombers and *how ready we are to pitch in.*" [29]

With reference to the conduct of foreign affairs, it is enlightening to compare the record of this Cabinet meeting as entered in Secretary Stimson's secret *Diary* with Secretary Hull's public statement describing the meeting to the Congressional Committee on Pearl Harbor in November, 1945. Mr. Hull then said that the President at the outset asked him whether he had anything on his mind and that he thereupon took about fifteen minutes in describing the dangers of the international situation. Mr. Hull stated that relations were extremely critical and that "we should be on the lookout for a military attack anywhere by Japan at any time." When he had finished, Mr. Hull continued, "the President went around the Cabinet. All concurred in my estimate of the dangers." The Cabinet agreed that some speeches should be delivered in order that "the country would, if possible, be better prepared for such a development." Four days later, November 11, 1941, Secretary Knox and Undersecretary Welles carried out the mandate. They served notice on the people of the United States. Secretary Knox called their attention to the dangers in the Pacific; and Mr. Welles informed them that "at any moment war may be forced upon us." [30]

It was with this matured conviction secretly maintained in the Cabinet and the notice given to the public by Secretary Knox and Mr. Welles in circulation, that Secretary Hull began to explore proposition "B" with the Japanese Ambassador and Mr. Kurusu. This Japanese proposal, slightly modified as

29. Stimson, *Diary*, for November 7, 1941. (Italics supplied.)
30. CJC, Part 2, p. 429.

they presented it on November 20, embraced five principal points as follows:

1. Both the Governments of Japan and the United States undertake not to make any armed advancement into any of the regions in the Southeastern Asia and the Southern Pacific area excepting the part of French Indochina where the Japanese troops are stationed at present.

2. The Japanese Government undertakes to withdraw its troops now stationed in French Indochina upon either the restoration of peace between Japan and China or the establishment of an equitable peace in the Pacific Area.

In the meantime the Government of Japan declares that it is prepared to remove its troops now stationed in the southern part of French Indochina to the northern part of the said territory upon the conclusion of the present arrangement which shall later be embodied in the final agreement.

3. The Government of Japan and the United States shall cooperate with a view to securing the acquisition of those goods and commodities which the two countries need in Netherlands East Indies.

4. The Governments of Japan and the United States mutually undertake to restore their commercial relations to those prevailing prior to the freezing of the assets.

The Government of the United States shall supply Japan a required quantity of oil.

5. The Government of the United States undertakes to refrain from such measures and actions as will be prejudicial to the endeavors for the restoration of general peace between Japan and China.[31]

When President Roosevelt and Secretary Hull were called upon to make decisions with regard to the Japanese program for a kind of modus vivendi looking to a general settlement in the Pacific, they confronted a fateful choice and they knew it. From secret Japanese messages intercepted by the Army and Navy Intelligence, they had learned that this proposal was the final offering from the Japanese Government. They confronted the urgent appeal from General Marshall and Admiral Stark to postpone hostilities with Japan on the ground

31. *Ibid.*, p. 431.

that the Army and Navy were not ready for war. Should at least a truce of some form be attempted if only to give the United States more time to prepare for war? The idea of a truce had been taken up by the President with Secretary Stimson as early as November 6, two days after the secret Japanese message on the negotiations had been intercepted.[32] And Mr. Stimson had strongly objected to the idea.[33]

Despite Secretary Stimson's objections, however, the President apparently decided that a truce or modus vivendi might and should be attempted; for he sent an undated note to Secretary Hull, giving his suggestions for the terms of such a temporary or preliminary adjustment with Japan. The President's note contained the following points:

6 Months

1. United States to resume economic relations—some oil and rice now—more later.

2. Japan to send no more troops to Indo-China or Manchurian border or any place South (Dutch, Brit. or Siam).

3. Japan to agree not to invoke tripartite pact even if the U.S. gets into European war.

4. U.S. to introduce Japs to Chinese to talk things over but U.S. to take no part in their conversation.

* * *

Later in Pacific agreements.[34]

In addition to President Roosevelt's suggestions for a modus vivendi, Secretary Hull had for his consideration, in arriving at a decision, a long memorandum on the subject from his experts in the Far Eastern Division of the State Department. This document, dated November 11, 1941, contained a draft of principles and details to be applied in efforts to arrive at some kind of middle course in handling the now tense relations with Japan. The authors of the memorandum called Mr. Hull's attention to the difficulties involved in an attempt at

---

32. See above, pp. 507 f.
33. Stimson, *Diary*, for November 6, 1941.
34. CJC, Part 14, p. 1109.

the moment to reach a comprehensive settlement "covering the entire Pacific area," and then stated:

Such a prospect prompts the question whether it might not be possible to propose some tentative or transitional arrangement the very discussion of which might serve not only to continue the conversations pending the event of a more favorable situation, even if the proposal is not eventually agreed to, but also to provide the entering wedge toward a comprehensive settlement of the nature sought providing the proposal is accepted by Japan and provided further that China is able to obtain satisfactory terms from Japan.[35]

While working at his reply to the "last effort" of Tokyo to reach an adjustment, Secretary Hull had, besides the President's proposals and the memorandum from the Far Eastern Division, a strong recommendation from the senior officers of the Far Eastern Division relative to a project for a Pacific settlement, not a mere truce. This recommendation from his specialists in Far Eastern affairs, dated November 19, grew out of an outline for "a proposed basis for agreement between the United States and Japan," prepared by the Secretary of the Treasury, Henry Morgenthau, Jr. It took the form of a covering note to Secretary Hull initialed by Maxwell Hamilton, Chief of the Division. Mr. Hamilton pronounced the proposal offered by the Secretary of the Treasury "the most constructive I have seen," and added that all the senior officers in his Division concurred in his judgment. Therefore, he urged Secretary Hull to give it prompt and careful consideration and suggested a conference with General Marshall and Admiral Stark on the proposal.

During this period, as the testimony, documents, and exhibits procured by the Congressional Committee on Pearl Harbor abundantly demonstrate, hectic negotiations and conversations went on in Washington, with foreign ambassadors, ministers, and special agents, as well as American citizens and members of the Cabinet bringing pressures to bear on the

35. For this and other documents on the modus vivendi, see CJC, Part 14, Exhibit No. 18.

President and Secretary Hull—some for war and others for peace. Insiders knew that the die was about to be cast, and some outsiders knew it too. If newspapers reflected the state of popular opinion, thousands of American citizens, utterly uninformed as to the nature of the inner transactions of the Administration, were aware of an approaching crisis. If they believed Undersecretary Welles' speech of November 11, they feared that war might at any moment be "forced upon us." Those who recalled the President's peace pledges of 1940, which still stood in the record, may have hoped that he could or would, in spite of the crisis, keep the country out of war.

It was amid complicated circumstances that Secretary Hull worked at the problem raised by the Japanese proposal for a truce or modus vivendi. He knew from intercepts of secret Japanese messages, that this was regarded in Tokyo as the "last effort" on the part of the Japanese Government. Should he make a blunt reply or resort to supreme diplomatic ingenuity in an attempt to keep conversations going in the hope of peace in the Pacific or at least postponing war for a time until the American Army and Navy were better equipped to fight it? He knew that on August 17, 1941, President Roosevelt had served a warning notice on Tokyo to the effect that in case of any further Japanese encroachments on their neighbors, the United States would take steps that meant war. He knew that during all the explorations since August, the position then taken had been firmly maintained, that the war plans for coöperation with Great Britain, the Netherlands, and Australia were all predicated upon joint action against Japan if she moved southward beyond definite boundary lines. Secretary Hull was well aware that General Marshall and Admiral Stark had been and were pressing for more time in which to prepare the Army and Navy for war. Was it not for him a matter of supreme statesmanship to prevent, if humanly possible, a two-front war for the United States—a war in the Pacific as well as the "shooting war" in the Atlantic?

As far as the documentary record goes, Secretary Hull for a few days at least considered a modus vivendi with Japan desirable and feasible. From November 22 to November 26, the Secretary, in consultation with the President and the highest military authorities, worked over proposals and plans for some kind of adjustment with Japan on the basis of the Japanese note of November 20.[36] In this connection the project was discussed with representatives of Great Britain, Australia, the Netherlands, and China. The principles of the final draft were approved by Secretary Stimson, who declared that it adequately safeguarded "American interests."

Alarmed lest the Government of the United States make something like a truce or temporary standstill with Japan, with a view to further negotiation actually looking to the maintenance of peace in the Pacific, Chinese diplomatic and special agents, supported by powerful American interests, made a storm over the proposed modus vivendi with Japan. In this operation, they were ably led by the Chinese Ambassador, Dr. Hu Shih, a liberal, wise in the ways of the West and the East, once well marked by the dread police of the Chiang Kai-shek Government, now serving it in the United States where "liberalism" was an asset. From day to day, hour to hour, the Chinese and their agents bombarded Secretary Hull so heavily with protests against any truce with Japan that the situation in Washington became almost hysterical.

This state of affairs was later described by Secretary Hull himself. The Secretary, in a subsequent statement relative to the pressures then brought to bear on him by the Chinese, declared that Chiang Kai-shek "has sent numerous hysterical cable messages to different cabinet officers and high officials in the Government other than the State Department, and sometimes even ignoring the President, intruding into a delicate and serious situation with no real idea of what the facts are." Secretary Hull further said that "Chiang Kai-shek had his brother-in-law, located here in Washington, disseminate damaging reports at times to the press and others, apparently

36. Various drafts of the proposed modus vivendi with Japan are to be found in *ibid.*, along with other relevant documents. For a digest of Mr. Hull's account, see CJC, *Report*, pp. 33 ff.

with no particular purpose in mind." Besieged by Chinese agents in London, Prime Minister Churchill, instead of supporting his Ambassador in Washington, Lord Halifax, who was eager for a truce in the Pacific, intervened by sending a confusing message as if trying to support the Chinese side of the dispute with the Government of the United States.

Disturbed by the vacillations introduced by Mr. Churchill's intrusion into American affairs, Secretary Hull exclaimed that

it would have been better if, when Churchill received Chiang Kai-shek's loud protest about our negotiations here with Japan, instead of passing the protest on to us without objection on his part, thereby qualifying and virtually killing what we knew were the individual views of the British Government toward these negotiations, he had sent a strong cable back to Chiang Kai-shek telling him to brace up and fight with the same zeal as the Japanese and the Germans are displaying instead of weakening and telling the Chinese people that all of the friendly countries were now striving primarily to protect themselves and to force an agreement between China and Japan, every Chinese should understand from such a procedure that the best possible course was being pursued and that this calls for resolute fighting until the undertaking is consummated by peace negotiations which Japan in due course would be obliged to enter into with China.[37]

In other words, while the negotiations over the Japanese proposal for a modus vivendi were proceeding, Secretary Hull was disgusted with the operations of Chinese agents. He was convinced that the tentatives of the proposal should be explored and efforts be made to reach some kind of basis for further explorations in the direction of a settlement in the Far East. He was likewise convinced that in the proceedings along this line the real interests of China could be protected by the United States, indeed advanced, until, at least, the willingness of Japan to come to decent terms could be probed to the bottom. So, at least, it seems.

But for reasons which are nowhere explicit, despite the thousands of words on the subject that appear in the Pearl

37. CJC, Part 14, pp. 1194 ff.

Harbor documents and testimony, Secretary Hull, after consulting President Roosevelt, suddenly and completely abandoned the project and on November 26, 1941, handed the Japanese Ambassador and Mr. Kurusu, the historic memorandum which the Japanese Government treated as an ultimatum.[38] When the Japanese representatives in Washington read the document, Mr. Kurusu assured the Secretary that the Japanese Government, after examining it, would be likely to throw up its hands. When, the next morning, Secretary Stimson asked Secretary Hull what had been done about the modus vivendi project, the Secretary replied that "he had broken the whole matter off." He then added: "I have washed my hands of it and it is now in the hands of you and Knox—the Army and the Navy." [39]

38. For the nature and significance of this memorandum, see above, Chap. IX; and for the upshot of the decision to send it, see below, pp. 555 ff.

39. Alden Hatch, who claims to have inside information from prominent persons close to President Roosevelt at the time, seems to ascribe this momentous decision mainly to Secretary Hull, for he says: "Roosevelt was uncertain if he had done the right thing in allowing Hull to present his ten-point program to Japan on November 26. Though it offered them great economic concessions, and the access to the goods of the Indies that they desired, it called on them to desist in China. He feared they would never do that." *Franklin D. Roosevelt: An Informal Biography*, p. 289.

CHAPTER XVII

Maneuvering the Japanese into Firing the First Shot

AS a matter of fact, President Roosevelt and his War Cabinet were far from convinced that Secretary Hull's memorandum of November 26 and the desultory conversations with the Japanese which followed actually looked toward the maintenance of peace in the Pacific. On November 25, the day before this ultimative note was delivered to Japan, Secretary Stimson told Secretary Hull that even the milder proposal for a modus vivendi [1] would not be accepted by the Japanese "because it was so drastic." [2] Moreover, at noon that day, while decision on the modus vivendi was presumably pending, the President and his War Cabinet discussed war, not prospects of peace, and dealt with the question of how the war might start.

November 25, 1941. An inside account of this meeting of the President and his War Cabinet is provided by Secretary Stimson, a leading and pertinacious actor in the affairs of the time, in his *Diary* for November 25, 1941, as follows:

Then at 12 o'clock we (*viz.*, General Marshall and I) went to the White House, where we were until nearly half past one. At the meeting were Hull, Knox, Marshall, Stark, and myself. There the President, instead of bringing up the Victory Parade,[3] brought up entirely the relations with the Japanese. He brought up the event that we were likely to be attacked perhaps (as soon as) next Monday, for the Japanese are notorious for making an attack without warning, and the question was what we should do. The question was how we should maneuver them into the position of firing the first shot without allowing too much danger to ourselves.

1. See above, pp. 510 ff.
2. *Diary*, for November 25, 1941.
3. "This was an office nickname for the General Staff strategic plan of national action in case of war in Europe." [Mr. Stimson's note.]

It was a difficult proposition.[4] Hull laid out his general broad propositions on which the thing should be rested—the freedom of the seas and the fact that Japan was in alliance with Hitler and was carrying out his policy of world aggression. The others brought out the fact that any such expedition to the South as the Japanese were likely to take would be an encirclement of our interests in the Philippines and cutting into our vital supplies of rubber from Malaysia. I pointed out to the President that he had already taken the first steps towards an ultimatum in notifying Japan way back last summer that if she crossed the border into Thailand she was violating our safety and that therefore he had only to point out (to Japan) that to follow any such expedition was a violation of a warning we had already given. So Hull is to go to work on preparing that. When I got back to the Department I found news from G-2 that an (a Japanese) expedition had started. Five divisions have come down from Shantung and Shansi to Shanghai and there they had embarked on ships—30, 40, or 50 ships—and have been sighted south of Formosa. I at once called up Hull and told him about it, and sent copies to him and to the President of the message from G-2.[5]

In a statement to the Congressional Committee on Pearl Harbor in 1946, Secretary Stimson elaborated his views respecting the problem of the tactics pursued by the Administration in maneuvering the Japanese into firing the first shot. The War Cabinet knew very well in November, 1941, that

4. "See statement, pp. 11 and 14. Our military and naval advisers had warned us that we could not safely allow the Japanese to move against British Malaysia or the Dutch East Indies without attempting to prevent it." [Mr. Stimson's note.]

5. Secretary Stimson's statement that the question was one of maneuvering the Japanese into the position of firing the first shot made much trouble for the Democratic members of the Congressional Committee. See above, Chap. XII. Senator Scott Lucas asked Admiral Stark whether there was "any one man or group of men who maneuvered the Japanese crisis so as to deliberately invite the Pearl Harbor attack." Admiral Stark replied in the negative and declared that "on the contrary we were trying to maintain peace in the Pacific." CJC, Part 5, p. 2271. In their Conclusions, the majority denied that "the President, the Secretary of State, the Secretary of War, or the Secretary of Navy tricked, provoked, incited, cajoled, or coerced Japan into attacking this Nation in order that a declaration of war might be more easily obtained from the Congress." (CJC, *Report*, p. 251). They refrained from using in this sentence the word "maneuvered."

none of the official announcements issued by the White House or the Department of State had revealed anything definite about the diplomatic situation as of November 25, 1941, and that the American people were sharply divided over war involvement in the Pacific or in the Atlantic. Hence, as Mr. Stimson later told the Congressional Committee in 1946, the War Cabinet confronted a delicate situation on November 25, 1941:

One problem troubled us very much. If you know that your enemy is going to strike you, it is not usually wise to wait until he gets the jump on you by taking the initiative. In spite of the risk involved, however, in letting the Japanese fire the first shot, *we realized that in order to have the full support of the American people it was desirable to make sure that the Japanese be the ones to do this so that there should remain no doubt in anyone's mind as to who were the aggressors. We discussed at this meeting the basis on which this country's position could be most clearly explained to our own people and to the world, in case we had to go into the fight quickly because of some sudden move on the part of the Japanese.* We discussed the possibility of a statement summarizing all the steps of aggression that the Japanese had already taken, the encirclement of our interests in the Philippines which was resulting and the threat to our vital supplies of rubber from Malay. I reminded the President that on August 19th [17th] he had warned the Japanese Ambassador that if the steps which the Japanese were then taking continued across the border into Thailand, he would regard it as a matter affecting our safety, and suggested that he might point out that the moves the Japanese were now apparently on the point of making would be in fact a violation of a warning that had already been given.[6] (Italics supplied.)

At a hearing of the Congressional Committee on April 9, 1946,[7] Senator Ferguson asked General Marshall, who had been present at the War Cabinet meeting on November 25, 1941, to explain what was meant by maneuvering the Japa-

6. Stimson, Statement (Mimeograph), pp. 14 f.
7. CJC, Part 11, pp. 5187 ff. April 9, 1946.

nese into the position of firing the first shot. The questioning and answering ran as follows:

SENATOR FERGUSON. General Marshall, you have read Secretary Stimson's memorandum. I want to go to page 12 and ask you if you were notified of this—quoting the Secretary of War:

"The President at the meeting undertook to take an informal vote of the Cabinet as to whether it was thought the American people would back us up if it became necessary to strike at Japan, in case she should attack England in Malaya, or the Dutch in the East Indies. The Cabinet was unanimous in the feeling that the country would support such a move."

That comes from the diary as of November 7.

Were you advised as to that vote?

GENERAL MARSHALL. I have no recollection of it, but I am pretty certain he must have told me, because he was telling me the results of those meetings.

SENATOR FERGUSON. Then I go to page 27 (page 46) of his memorandum. This is on November 25. This is the day before the Secretary of State sent his message to the Japanese. He is quoting the President:

"Then, at 12 o'clock, General Marshall and I went to the White House where we were until nearly half-past one. At the meeting were Hull, Knox, Marshall, Stark, and myself. There the President, instead of bringing up the Victory Parade . . . brought up entirely the relations with the Japanese. He brought up the event that we were likely to be attacked perhaps (as soon as) next Monday, for the Japanese are notorious for making an attack without warning, and the question was what we should do. The question was how we should maneuver them into the position of firing the first shot without allowing too much danger to ourselves. It was a difficult proposition."

Do you recall that discussion with the President?

GENERAL MARSHALL. Yes, sir.

SENATOR FERGUSON. How was it thought that we could maneuver them into firing the first shot? Was that discussed?

GENERAL MARSHALL. I don't recall the details of that particular phase of the matter.

SENATOR FERGUSON. This takes place before we sent the message of the 26th.

GENERAL MARSHALL. Yes, sir.

SENATOR FERGUSON. Or before you had sent your message to General Short on the 27th.

GENERAL MARSHALL. Yes, sir.

SENATOR FERGUSON. What were we going to do to maneuver them into firing the first shot? What was the plan of operation?

GENERAL MARSHALL. You are talking, I take it, about diplomatic procedure?

SENATOR FERGUSON. Yes.

GENERAL MARSHALL. I am assuming that it is the diplomatic procedure that is being discussed at the present time. We knew our resources. We knew our deployment. It was impossible to change that on any brief notice. We were committed to deployment thousands of miles away from the United States.

So far as the war plan goes, the concern was whether or not the final alert should be given.

I took a discussion of this kind—at least I take it now—was a discussion of the diplomatic procedure involved, having in mind that it was the accepted thought in all of our minds at that time, that if we were forced to take offensive action, immediate offensive action, that it would be a most serious matter as to its interpretation by the American people, whether we would have a united nation, or whether we would have a divided nation in getting into a world conflict.

SENATOR FERGUSON. But this—

GENERAL MARSHALL. The planning they are talking about is the discussion that came later, as I understood.

SENATOR FERGUSON. You would take it that Mr. Stimson has in mind that we were going to maneuver diplomatically into a position where they would be compelled to fire the first shot?

GENERAL MARSHALL. No, I don't mean to imply that. I mean the expression he is using relates to what would be the diplomatic procedure we would follow, so we would not find ourselves in a dangerous position where we had to do something initiating a fight. He was not trying to provoke the Japanese to fight.

SENATOR FERGUSON. Let's take his language:

"The question was how we should maneuver them into the position of firing the first shot without allowing too much danger to ourselves."

GENERAL MARSHALL. That is exactly what I said, sir. When you are sitting back and the other man is doing all of the maneuvering, you are in a very dangerous position. The question and the desire at that time was to delay in every way possible a rupture in the Pacific.

Now, if they were going to attack, it was very important—

SENATOR FERGUSON. Right there, General, may I interrupt to ask, were we of the opinion at that time that they were going to attack?

GENERAL MARSHALL. That was the general opinion, that they were going to attack, definitely, in the Southwest Pacific.

SENATOR FERGUSON. And we wanted to lay our course diplomatically so that we would make sure that they would fire the first shot?

GENERAL MARSHALL. So that we would make sure that we would not be in such a dangerous position that we would be forced to fire the first shot ourselves. That is another way of putting it, but that is what he is talking about.

SENATOR FERGUSON. That is one of the things that led to this restricted language in the message of the 27th [to General Short in Hawaii].

GENERAL MARSHALL. So far as the first shot is concerned; yes, sir.

SENATOR FERGUSON. And also as to—well, the first overt act is the same thing as the first shot.

GENERAL MARSHALL. Yes.

SENATOR FERGUSON. And that was leading up to that message; is that correct?

GENERAL MARSHALL. No, this was leading up, as I understood it, and as I recall it, to what the diplomatic procedure was to be. The alert, to a certain extent, you might say, is a routine. Not in one sense that alert for war is ever routine, but the arranging, the phrasing of that alert to fight. What the diplomatic and political situation was, was another matter.

SENATOR FERGUSON. Now, was this discussed at the same meeting?

Mr. Stimson said, at the bottom of page 47:

"I pointed out to the President that he had already taken the first steps toward an ultimatum in notifying Japan way back last summer that if she crossed the border into Thailand, she was violating our safety, and that therefore he had only to point out (to Japan) that to follow any such expedition was a violation of a warning we had already given. So Hull is to go to work on preparing that."

Now, I take it he was talking about the memorandum and the conversation he had on the 27th [17th] of August. That is when the President returned from the Atlantic Conference.[8]

We had taken, as Mr. Stimson defines it, the first step in an ultimatum, and that if America wanted to, we could rely upon that particular message as saying—

We have warned you. Therefore if you do anything you take the first step and fire the first shot.

Is that correct? Is that a fair analysis?

GENERAL MARSHALL. I think that is the rough idea of the thing; yes.

SENATOR FERGUSON. And it says then:

"So Hull is to go to work on preparing that."

What did he mean by "preparing that"? Have you any idea?

GENERAL MARSHALL. You are having me act as both Mr. Stimson and Mr. Hull.

SENATOR FERGUSON. Well, the reason I am asking you, General, is that you were supposed to be at this meeting.

GENERAL MARSHALL. Yes. As I said, they were trying to arrange a diplomatic procedure, rather than firing off a gun, that would not only protect our interests, by arranging matters so that the Japanese couldn't intrude any further in a dangerous way, but also that anything they did do, they would be forced to take the offensive action, and what we were to do had to be prepared for the President by Mr. Hull. It was not a military order. It was not a military arrangement. . . .

November 27, 1941, the day after Secretary Hull had handed his memorandum to the Japanese, the War Department and the Navy Department sent to the American outpost commanders, including General Short and Admiral Kimmel, messages which the Roosevelt Administration, supported by the Roberts Commission, later claimed were sufficient notices to prepare for the coming of war. A comparison of the Army and Navy messages from October 16 to December 7, 1941,

8. See above, p. 486.

including the messages of November 27, demonstrates the truth of what the Army Pearl Harbor Board says of them:

a. That they were conflicting.

b. That the Navy messages were predominant with warnings of a conflict and the Army messages with the idea of avoiding a conflict and taking precautions against sabotage and espionage.[9]

Even the President's own Commission on Pearl Harbor implied that the messages were not clear and precise when it charged General Short and Admiral Kimmel with failure to "consult and cooperate" with respect to necessary action in view of the warnings received, and further declared that "it was a dereliction of duty on the part of each of them not to consult and confer with the other respecting the meaning and intent of the warnings, and the appropriate measures of defense required by the imminence of hostilities." [10] This was, indeed, a definite admission to the effect that the messages were confused and confusing; for, if the Washington superiors of the two commanders had written clear and precise instructions in their messages it would have been unnecessary for General Short and Admiral Kimmel to consult and confer with each other at length for the purpose of finding out what the language of the messages meant.

The majority of the Congressional Committee on Pearl Harbor, while holding that General Short and Admiral Kimmel should have done more in the way of preparations for defense on receipt of the messages of November 27, 1941, cleared the Commanders of derelictions of duty in the matter of semantics and concluded that there had been confusion in Washington as well as Hawaii in this respect.[11] With regard to the messages of November 27, the minority of the Congressional Committee commented on their vagueness and said: "If any candid person has any doubt about their insufficiency to constitute orders for an all-out alert to meet a probable Japanese attack on Pearl Harbor, he can allay his doubt by examining carefully the messages of November 27 to General

9. CJC, Part 39, p. 140.
10. Full text above, pp. 217 ff.
11. CJC, *Report*, Parts 4 and 5.

Short and Admiral Kimmel." The minority then printed them with italics supplied as follows in parallel columns for examination: [12]

To General Short

Negotiations with Japanese appear to be terminated *to all practical purposes with only the barest possibilities that the Japanese Government might come back and offer to continue. Japanese future action unpredictable* but hostile action possible at any moment. If hostilities cannot, repeat can not, be avoided *the U.S. desires that Japan commit the first overt act.* This policy should not, repeat not, be construed as restricting you to a course of action that might jeopardize your defense. Prior to Japanese hostile action you are directed to undertake such reconnaissance and other measures as you deem necessary *but these measures should be carried out so as not, repeat not, to alarm the civil population or disclose intent. Report measures taken.* Should hostilities occur, you will carry out tasks assigned in Rainbow Five as far as they pertain to Japan. *Limit dissemination of this highly secret information to minimum essential officers.*

To Admiral Kimmel

Consider this dispatch a war warning. The negotiations with Japan in an effort to stabilize conditions in the Pacific *have ended.* Japan is expected to make aggressive move within the next few days. *An amphibious expedition against either the Philippines, Thai, or Kra Peninsula or possibly Borneo is indicated by the number and equipment of Japanese troops and the organization of their naval task forces.* You will execute a defensive deployment in preparation for carrying out the tasks assigned in WPL 46 only. *Guam, Samoa and Continental Districts have been directed to take appropriate measures against sabotage. A similar warning is being sent by the War Department.* Inform naval district and Army authorities. British to be informed by Spenavo.

Although the controversy over the nature, meaning, and sufficiency of these so-called war warning messages of No-

12. *Ibid.*, p. 539.

vember 27, 1941, fills pages and pages of the committee's testimony and documentation, the subject pertains to military and naval administration rather than to the conduct of foreign affairs. The point here is that President Roosevelt, Secretary Hull, Secretary Stimson, and Secretary Knox were then convinced that conversations looking to the maintenance of peace in the Pacific were for practical purposes at an end on November 27.

November 28, 1941. In the morning Secretary Stimson took to President Roosevelt a report of facts relative to the latest movement of Japanese southward. They discussed the situation. As Mr. Stimson recorded their conversation, the President's "alternatives were—first to do nothing; second, to make something in the nature of an ultimatum again, stating a point beyond which we would fight; third, to fight at once." Thereupon, Mr. Stimson reports: "I told him my only two were the last two, because I did not think anyone would do nothing in this situation, and he agreed with me. I said of the other two my choice was the latter one," that is, to fight at once.[13]

In a statement to the Congressional Committee on Pearl Harbor in 1946, Secretary Stimson described in stronger terms this conversation with President Roosevelt. He then said that he had told the President on November 28, 1941, that

the desirable thing to do from the point of view of our own tactics and safety was to take the initiative and attack [the Japanese forces moving southward] without further warning. It is axiomatic that the best defense is offense. It is always dangerous to wait and let the enemy make the first move. I was inclined to feel that the warning given in August by the President against further moves by the Japanese toward Thailand justified an attack without further warning,[14] particularly as their new movement southward indicated that they were about to violate that warning. On the other hand, I realized that the situation could be made more clean

13. *Diary*, for November 28, 1941.
14. In other words, make war, without calling upon Congress for a declaration of war.

cut from the point of view of public opinion if a further warning were given.[15]

An immediate attack by the United States, however, was obviously out of line with the tactics of maneuvering the Japanese into firing the first shot which had been discussed at the meeting of the War Cabinet three days before, on November 25, 1941, and more than incidently out of line with the declaration of the Democratic platform of 1940: no war, "except in case of attack." [16]

At noon, November 28, 1941, when the War Cabinet met with the President, the southward movements of Japanese forces were taken under consideration. It was agreed that if the Japanese expedition was allowed to get around the southern point of Indo-China and land in the Gulf of Siam, it would be a terrific blow at Britain, the Netherlands, and the Philippines. All members of the conference, Mr. Stimson recorded in his *Diary*, were of the opinion that "this must not be allowed. Then we discussed how to prevent it. It was agreed that if the Japanese got into the Isthmus of Kra, the British would fight. It was also agreed that if the British fought, we would have to fight."

They considered striking the Japanese force, as it went by, without a warning, but this bold deed was one "which we didn't think we could do." The President brought up the idea of sending a warning letter to the Japanese Emperor. Secretary Stimson offered objections and said that the President should send a message to Congress and the American people, reporting the danger and "what we would have to do if the danger happened." The letter to the Emperor, he thought, should be a separate and "secret thing." The President asked Secretaries Hull, Stimson, and Knox to make drafts of these papers.

Sometime during the day, November 28, 1941—on which the President and his War Cabinet considered anew the tactics of maneuvering—American Army Intelligence intercepted,

15. Stimson, *Statement*, pp. 26 f.
16. See Beard, *op. cit.*, p. 291.

decoded, and translated a startling message from the Japanese Government to its Ambassadors in Washington. This message declared that Secretary Hull's memorandum of November 26 was a "humiliating proposal," that it was "unexpected and extremely regrettable," and that it could not be used as "a basis for negotiations." The message also informed the Ambassadors that a reply to Secretary Hull's memorandum would be sent from Tokyo "in two or three days" and that then "the negotiations will be de facto ruptured. This is inevitable. However, I do not wish you to give the impression that the negotiations are broken off. Merely say to them that you are awaiting instructions. . . . From now on do the best you can." [17] If President Roosevelt and Secretary Hull had actually entertained on November 26 any hope of further conversations looking to peace in the Pacific, this message from Tokyo on November 28 must have put an end to it.

November 29, 1941. Since the President and his War Cabinet had decided on November 28 against committing an overt act by striking the Japanese forces moving southward in the Far Pacific and in favor of other tactics, Secretary Hull, with the aid of Secretary Stimson and Secretary Knox, prepared and sent to the President a draft of a proposed message to Congress. With this draft, Secretary Hull enclosed a memorandum in which he said: "I think we agree that you will not send message to Congress *until the last stage of our relations, relating to actual hostility*, has been reached." (Italics supplied.)

Whether the draft of a proposed message to Congress was for "the record" or not, it proved to be merely one of the documents in the record, for it was never sent to Congress. With regard to a proposed letter to the Japanese Emperor, a draft of which also went with the suggested presidential message, Secretary Hull, on November 29, told the President that sending it to the Emperor would be "of doubtful efficacy. Except

17. CJC, Part 12, Exhibit 1, p. 195. This message, coupled with messages that had been intercepted on previous days, especially November 27, 1941, lent support to the view privately expressed by President Roosevelt on November 25 to the effect that the Japanese might attack as early as Monday, December 1. See intercepted messages, *ibid.*, pp. 172 ff.

for the purpose of making a record it might even cause such a complication as Colonel Stimson and I referred to on yesterday." Asked by Senator Ferguson in 1946 what he meant by the expression "for the purpose of making a record," Secretary Hull said: "The expression, 'for the purpose of making a record,' has reference to the matter of making perfectly clear to both the American and Japanese peoples then and for the future that all the efforts of this Government were directed toward maintaining peace to the very end." [18]

Senator Ferguson, in Question 17, also asked Secretary Hull in 1946 to relate what President Roosevelt had said about the proposal to send a message to Congress discussed on or about November 30. Secretary Hull answered that he had no specific recollection as to that, "but the record is that he did not send the message to Congress."

Question 18. Why did he not send it to Congress?

Answer: The President and I had for some time been communicating to various Members of Congress our views on the imminent dangers in the situation in connection with such matters as neutrality legislation and extension of selective service [back in October and earlier]. A message to Congress during the last few days would have contained very little that was new without giving to the Japanese leaders material which would have enabled them to arouse their people against us all the more, a thing we wished to avoid so long as there was even the slightest possibility of keeping the discussions alive.

Furthermore, the powerful isolationist groups in this country would probably have renewed their oft-repeated charges of "warmongering" and "dragging the nation into foreign wars." The Japanese leaders would then have been in a position to play up the situation as evidencing disunity in the United States in order to gain support in Japan for plunging ahead.[19]

18. CJC, Part 11, pp. 5384 f.
19. *Ibid.*, pp. 5374 f. The majority of the Congressional Committee on Pearl Harbor stated in 1946: "It is indisputable that the President and his Cabinet contemplated presenting the problem to the Congress should our position in the Far East become intolerable." CJC, *Report*, p. 171. If, however, the President and his Cabinet did "contemplate" appealing to Congress, they certainly never laid the problem before Congress and if the position of the United States was not "intolerable" between November 28, 1941, and December 7, 1941, then it would be

On Monday, December 1, the President and members of his War Cabinet received the intercept of a secret message of November 30 from Tokyo to Berlin instructing the Japanese Ambassador there to say to Chancellor Hitler and Foreign Minister Ribbentrop, "very secretly," that "there is extreme danger that war may suddenly break out between the Anglo-Saxon nations and Japan through some clash of arms and add that the time of the breaking out of this war may come quicker than anyone dreams." That day these high officials in Washington also had an intercept of a secret message from Tokyo to the Embassy in Washington giving instructions relative to burning its codes when "faced with the necessity." [20]

Shortly before midnight on December 1, at the direction of President Roosevelt, the Navy Department instructed Admiral Hart, Commander of the American Asiatic Fleet, to charter three small vessels to form a "defensive information patrol," each in command of a naval officer, for the purpose of observing and reporting by radio on movements of Japanese forces in the west China Sea and Gulf of Siam. Admiral Hart was also ordered to report on the nature and effectiveness of Army and Navy reconnaissance in that region by American planes and submarines. [21]

December 2, 1941. Undersecretary Welles, acting for Secretary Hull who was ill and absent from the State Department, called the Japanese Ambassadors to his office and told them that President Roosevelt wanted information from their gov-

---

difficult to imagine a position that would come within any definition of the word. In his draft of a proposed message to Congress, covered by a memorandum to the President, dated November 29, 1941, Secretary Hull wrote: "We do not want war with Japan, and Japan does not want war with this country. If, however, war should come, the fault and the responsibility will be those of Japan." CJC, Part 14, pp. 1201 ff., 1222. For drafts of a proposed message to Congress, drawn by Secretary Knox and Secretary Stimson, see CJC, Part 19, Exhibit 161. None of these drafts went beyond generalities already known to members of Congress and informed observers outside of Congress. They gave no hint that, if he had sent a message based on these drafts, the President would have called upon Congress for a declaration of war in view of the "intolerable" position of the United States.

20. CJC, Part 12, Exhibit 1, pp. 204 ff.
21. CJC, *Report* (Appendix D), p. 414.

ernment on the nature and meaning of the continuing movement and concentration of Japanese forces in Indo-China.[22]

Secretary Stimson advised two Chinese representatives, Alfred Sze and T. V. Soong, to counsel Generalissimo Chiang "to have just a little more patience and then I think all things will be well." [23]

Messages from Tokyo to Ambassador Nomura made available to American officials in Washington on December 2, explained arrangements for secretly communicating information respecting armed clashes or "full-fledged general war" if or when they came.[24]

December 3, 1941. At a press conference, Secretary Hull outlined the course of recent exploratory conversations with Japanese envoys and stated that whether the conversations would continue would depend upon Japan's answers to inquiries respecting her troops in Indo-China, and to the memorandum he had delivered to Ambassador Nomura on November 26.[25]

December 4, 1941. President Roosevelt conferred for two hours with six majority and minority leaders of the Senate and House on the Far Eastern situation. The members of Congress were reported to have left the White House "with the impression that the situation is critical, but will not necessarily come to a show-down" on receipt of Japan's reply on her troop movements in Indo-China.[26]

On December 4, Army Intelligence made available to high officials in Washington the corrected translation of an ominous message from the Japanese Government to its Embassy in Washington and its Embassy in Havana.[27] These messages, dated December 2, 1941, ordered the destruction of certain code machines and machine codes. The messages could have

---

22. CJC, *ibid.*, pp. 415 f.
23. *Diary*, for December 2.
24. CJC, *Report*, p. 418.
25. *New York Times*, December 4, 1941; Secretary Hull then knew that the Japanese answer would mark a de facto disruption of negotiations. See above, p. 528.
26. CJC, *Report*, p. 419, quoting the *Washington Post* of December 5, 1941.
27. CJC, Part 12, Exhibit 1, pp. 215 ff.

only one meaning to anybody informed about the relation of such orders to the immediate imminence of war, as repeatedly demonstrated in diplomatic history.

On December 4 or 5, Admiral Beardall, the Navy Aide to the President, on delivering to President Roosevelt some of the intercepts of Japanese secret messages, called his attention to the message about burning the codes. After reading it, the President asked: "Well, when do you think it will happen?" The Admiral replied: "Most any time." In testifying before the Congressional Committee on Pearl Harbor about four years later, Admiral Beardall said he understood the President to mean: "When is war going to break out, when are we going to be attacked, or something." [28]

December 4, 1941.

On December 4, 1941, information was received through the Navy Department which was sent to Captain Safford which contained the Japanese "winds" message, "War with England, War with America, Peace with Russia." This original message has now disappeared from the Navy files and cannot be found. It was in existence just after Pearl Harbor and was collected with other messages for submission to the Roberts Commission. Copies were in existence in various places but they have all disappeared. . . . This "winds execute" message . . . was last seen by Commander Safford about December 14, 1941, when he collected the papers together with Commander Kramer and turned them over to the Director of Naval Communication for use as evidence before the Roberts Commission.

There, therefore, can be no question that between the dates of December 4 and December 6, the imminence of war on the following Saturday and Sunday, December 6 and 7, was clear-cut and definite.[29]

The above statement is from "Top Secret Report of the Army Pearl Harbor Board" (1944) which was not released to the public until after the Congressional Committee on Pearl Harbor had begun its inquiry.

28. CJC, *Report*, p. 420.
29. CJC, Part 39, pp. 225 f., 229 f.

Like the Army Pearl Harbor Board, the Navy Court of Inquiry, in the course of its investigation came across the problem of the "winds execute" message. In its report (1944, Addendum), the Inquiry declared: "On 4 December an intercepted Japanese broadcast employing this code was received in the Navy Department. . . . This message cannot now [1944] be located in the Navy Department." The Navy Court, however, concluded that "this notification was subject to two interpretations, either a breaking off of diplomatic relations between Japan and the United States, or war," and stated that "this information was not transmitted to the Commander-in-Chief, Pacific Fleet, or to other Commanders afloat." The Navy Court added: "No attempt was made by the Navy Department to ascertain whether this information had been obtained by the Commander-in-Chief, Pacific and by other Commanders afloat. Admiral Stark stated that he knew nothing about it, although Admiral Turner stated that he himself was familiar with it and presumed that Admiral Kimmel had it." [30] Whether the winds execute message was to be taken as meaning a breach in diplomatic relations with Japan or war, it was included in the items of evidence on which the Navy Court cleared Admiral Kimmel of the grave charges filed against him by the President's Commission on Pearl Harbor (1942) and at the same time indicted high authorities in Washington.[30a]

The truth of the statement on the winds execute message made by the Army Pearl Harbor Board signed October 20, 1944, was soon challenged by Secretary Stimson. Evidently impressed by it and other passages in the Report, the Secretary ordered re-investigations of the issues so posed and for that purpose commissioned his own agents. Secretary Stimson's example in this respect was followed by Secretary Forrestal. On the basis of these new inquiries, in the course of which some witnesses changed their previous testimony, a decision was reached in Administration circles to the effect that the winds execute message, at least in the form quoted by the Army

30. *Ibid.*, pp. 324 f.
30a. See above, pp. 306 ff.

Pearl Harbor Board, had not been received and distributed to President Roosevelt and other high officials as contended by the Board. Thus questions of fact, the credibility of witnesses, and the good faith of several parties to the transactions were raised after the release of the board's "Top Secret Report" in December, 1945.

These controversial questions were reviewed by the Congressional Committee on Pearl Harbor at several hearings during which a number of witnesses made strange spectacles of themselves. In their report (Appendix E) the Democratic majority gave a brief survey of the disputed points and the contradictions in the evidence and stated:

From consideration of all evidence relating to the winds code, it is concluded that no genuine message, in execution of the code and applying to the United States, was received in the War or Navy Department prior to December 7, 1941. It appears, however, that messages were received which were initially thought possibly to be in execution of the code but were determined not to be execute messages. In view of the preponderate weight of evidence to the contrary, it is believed that Captain Safford is honestly mistaken when he insists that an execute message was received prior to December 7, 1941. Considering the period of time that has elapsed, this mistaken impression is understandable.[31]

Then the majority of the committee made an extraordinary declaration. The alleged Japanese execute message in question received on December 4, 1941, read: "War with England, War with America, Peace with Russia." The majority's declaration in 1946 was: "Granting for the purposes of discussion that a genuine execute message applying to the winds code was intercepted before December 7, it is concluded that *such fact would have added nothing to what was already known concerning the critical character of our relations with the Empire of Japan.*"[32] Apparently this conclusion concedes that the Administration, after December 4, 1941, was fully aware of Japanese war intentions without the aid of the winds message.

31. CJC, *Report* (Appendix E), p. 486 and pp. 191 f. (Italics supplied.)
32. *Ibid.*

It is also to be noted that the conclusion of the majority is cautiously worded. It reads: "It appears, however, that messages were received which were initially thought possibly to be an execution of the code." Then the majority added: but these messages "were determined not to be execute messages." Determined *when* and *by whom* not to be execute messages? As far as I can discover by a study of the Congressional Committee's record it was not clearly so determined in 1941 by the Navy officers most responsible for receiving and interpreting the "execute" message in December, 1941. Nor was it so determined by the Army Pearl Harbor Board or the Navy Court of Inquiry in 1944. The majority's conclusion in this respect was based on the conflicting, contradictory, and confused evidence brought out by the Congressional Committee *after* the bitter controversy had arisen over the truth of the matter as a result of the release of the Army and Navy boards' reports.[33]

On one point respecting the winds execute message, the Republican minority of the Congressional Committee agreed with the majority, by saying that, if it be discounted, such discounting in no way affected the other evidence with regard to Japanese war intentions which was in the hands of high authorities in Washington in December, 1941. The minority, however, drew attention to testimony of Admiral Royal E. Ingersoll, Assistant Chief of Naval Operations and thus deputy of Admiral Stark, before the Hart Inquiry. Admiral Ingersoll had then been asked whether he recalled a Japanese plan for a weather message, and he replied: "Yes; I do recall such messages." He had then been asked whether he recalled having seen, on or about December 4, 1941, broadcast directions indicating that the Japanese were about to attack both Great Britain and the United States, and to this he responded: "Yes."

After citing Admiral Ingersoll's testimony before the Hart Inquiry, the minority referred to testimony before the Congressional Committee and said that Admiral Ingersoll and Admiral Richmond K. Turner, Chief of the Navy War Plans

33. See above, pp. 532 ff., and below, p. 536.

Division, had stated "they did not know until 1945 about the allegation that there had been no wind execute message." The minority concluded: "Even if the wind execute message they saw was a false one they believed it true at the time and should have acted accordingly"—by sending a new warning message to Admiral Kimmel.[34]

From the vast mass of evidence relative to the winds execute message, what substantial conclusion may be properly drawn? It is, in my opinion, that, despite all confusing testimony educed by the Congressional Committee in 1945–46, high and responsible officers in the Navy Department did have before them on December 4 or 5 a message which they regarded as a winds execute message and at the time did believe that it meant either a breach in diplomatic relations with Japan or war.[35]

During the morning of December 5, 1941, Undersecretary Welles informed the President that the Australian Prime Minister had suggested that his government would welcome a visit from Wendell Willkie if Mr. Willkie could come with the

34. CJC, *Report*, p. 526.
35. My opinion expressed above is based on a careful study of relevant documents and testimony in the case from the Roberts Report of January, 1942, to the enormous record of the Congressional Committee (1946). A full exposition of the materials would fill a volume. Any one who ventures an informed opinion on the subject confronts the task of reviewing (1) the early and direct evidence indicating the existence of the winds execute message; (2) the denials and contradictory evidence educed after Secretary Stimson and Secretary Forrestal, faced by the indictments launched by the Army and Navy boards against high officials in Washington, employed their own special agents to review, if not traverse, previous positive testimony; and (3) efforts of the Democratic majority on the Congressional Committee to minimize the direct evidence and show that no real winds execute message ever existed; while the Republican minority limited itself to stating a few undoubted facts in the case, without denying or affirming the existence of the real execute message. In the course of any comprehensive survey of the evidence and documents, a student encounters witnesses who stuck to one story through all the inquiries; witnesses who told one story early and changed their stories after the controversy became crucial; witnesses who once remembered well and could not remember so well in 1945 or 1946; evidences of records that had strangely disappeared; charges that the special agents of Secretary Stimson and Secretary Forrestal induced witnesses to change their previous testimony and had even prepared affidavits for them to sign; evidence of a luncheon at Admiral Stark's home in September, 1945, at which at least one witness, who changed his testimony, "refreshed" his memory (CJC, Part 9, pp. 4063 f.); and more evidence indicating that pressures had been put on witnesses. See digest in the majority's Report, pp. 469–486; and CJC, Part 18, Exhibits 142, 142-A, 142-B, 142-C, 142-D, 150, and 151, for documents.

President's approval, as a kind of official representative. There-upon President Roosevelt dictated a letter to Mr. Willkie in which he said that an armed clash with Japan might come per-haps in the next four or five days. The President's words were: "There is always the Japanese to consider. The situation is definitely serious and there might be an armed clash at any moment if the Japanese continued their forward progress against the Philippines, Dutch East Indies or Malaya or Burma. Perhaps the next four or five days will decide the matters." [36]

December 5, 1941. The Japanese Ambassadors called on Secretary Hull and replied to the President's recent inquiry about Japanese troop movements in Indo-China, saying that they were "precautionary" in nature. When Secretary Hull expressed doubts on that point, Ambassador Nomura answered that Japan was alarmed over the increasing military prepara-tions of the "ABCD" Powers in the Southwest Pacific. This was an intimation on the part of Mr. Nomura that both sides were maneuvering with a view to a coming clash in that area.[37]

December 5 (Washington time). On February 18, 1946, Admiral Hart, who had been in command of the Asiatic Fleet in December, 1941, testified before the Congressional Com-mittee that he had received a dispatch from Captain John M. Creighton, American Naval Observer then stationed at Singa-pore under the direct orders of the Navy Department, stating that British Air Marshal Brooke-Popham had been advised from London that in certain eventualities the British had been assured of American support. At the moment Admiral Hart could not recall the details of the case.[38]

At a subsequent hearing of the Congressional Committee a copy of the dispatch received by Admiral Hart was placed in the record. The dispatch of December 5 (December 6, Singa-pore time) read:

Brooke-Popham received Saturday from War Department Lon-don Quote "We have now received assurance of American armed support in cases as follows: Affirm we are obliged execute our plans to forestall Japs landing Isthmus of Kra or take action in reply to Nips invasion any other part of Siam XX Baker if Dutch East Indies are attacked and we go to their defense XX Cast if Japs attack us the British XX Therefore without reference to London put plan in action if first you have good info Jap expedition advancing with the apparent intention of landing in Kra second if the Nips violate any part of Thailand Para if NEI are attacked put into operation plans agreed upon between British and Dutch" Unquote.[39]

This dispatch has a crucial bearing on a fundamental question: What military commitments to Great Britain, if any, did President Roosevelt make before December 7, 1941? Recognizing it as such, stout defenders of President Roosevelt's conduct of foreign affairs have attacked it as unfounded, as based on "hearsay" and "rumor," employing in this contention words used by Captain Creighton, from whose office at Singapore, the dispatch was sent to Admiral Hart. But, since these words were used by Captain Creighton in the course of a colloquy, before the Congressional Committee, covering nine pages (CJC, Part 10, pp. 5080–5089), it is necessary, if the truth of the matter be a consideration, to keep them in the context of the Captain's full testimony.

Captain Creighton testified at first that when he heard in 1946 that Admiral Hart had mentioned the dispatch to the Congressional Committee, he could not remember to what Admiral Hart was referring; that he could recall nothing about it; that when he had secured a copy from Admiral Hart's file he had no memory of ever having seen it before; that he hadn't the faintest idea to whom Brooke-Popham had given the information contained in the dispatch or who had repeated Brooke-Popham's report to him (Creighton). Yet later in the examination, Captain Creighton, although he had testified again and again that he could remember nothing about the dispatch, called the information in it "a matter of hearsay." When Chairman Barkley suggested to him that it was "really

39. *Ibid.*, pp. 5082 f.

nothing more than rumor," Captain Creighton quickly responded, "That is right."

Respect for the elementary principles in the law of evidence calls for a question: How could Captain Creighton remember that the information in the dispatch was nothing more than hearsay and/or rumor just a few minutes after he had testified that he could remember nothing whatever about the dispatch and that he did not remember who sent it, on what information it was based, where the information came from, the nature of the information, or whether Brooke-Popham had ever said what was ascribed to him in the dispatch? Given Captain Creighton's total loss of memory with regard to the dispatch in 1946, only one rational conclusion is admissible, namely, that his testimony about the dispatch as hearsay and/or rumor is worthless, that the dispatch is to be taken as it stands for whatever it is worth, and that the authenticity of the information contained in it is to be tested by a huge array of collateral evidence and undoubted facts which have a bearing on it. Although numerous passages in previous chapters and in the preceding and following pages of this chapter are related to this matter of authenticity, a few of the immediately pertinent facts are summarized here as follows:

1. Admiral Hart undoubtedly testified in 1946 that he had received the dispatch in question, although at the moment he could not remember some of the conditions set forth in it (CJC, Part 10, pp. 4802 f.).

2. Later Admiral Hart got possession of a copy of the dispatch and had it in a file (*ibid.*, p. 5081).

3. Subsequently, with Admiral Hart's authorization, Captain Creighton took this copy from Admiral Hart's file and presented it to the Congressional Committee during the course of his testimony in 1946 (*ibid.*, pp. 5080 ff.).

4. Captain Creighton explained to the Committee how busy he had been at Singapore in December, 1941, and said that he could not remember the dispatch or recall the source of the information on which it was based. But he did not deny that the message was sent from his office to Admiral Hart. In fact,

he declared that he had "such a trust in the fidelity of the Navy communications system" that he accepted (identified) the dispatch as a genuine telegram. Captain Creighton also explained to the committee that General Francis G. Brink, not he, "was between us the person to consult Brooke-Popham," and stated that when he left Singapore all the American records in his office, except a small folder, had been burned (*ibid.*, p. 5085).

5. In response to a cabled inquiry from the Congressional Committee, General Brink stated in 1946: "At 3:36 P.M. on 6 December 1941, Singapore time, Capt. John Creighton sent the following message in code to Admiral Hart at Manila:

On Saturday [Friday, December 5, Washington time] Brooke-Popham received from War Department London:
   American armed support has now been assured us [the British] in following cases:
   a. We have to execute our plans to prevent landing Isthmus of Kra by Japs or counteract Jap invasion elsewhere in Siam.
   b. Attack is made on Dutch Indies and we proceed to their defense.
   c. Japs attack US the British. Accordingly, put plan into action without reference to London if you have good information that Jap expedition is advancing apparently with intention of landing in Kra, or if any part of Thailand is violated by the Japs.
   Should NEI be attacked, put the plans agreed upon between Dutch and British into operation." [40]

General Brink, replying to other inquiries, said that he had not discussed the matter with Brooke-Popham and had no personal knowledge respecting the source of the information contained in the dispatch.

6. Air Chief Marshal Sir Robert Brooke-Popham was no obscure or transitory British officer in the Far East. He was a British commander in chief in the Far East and British representative at the Singapore staff conference. Captain Creighton testified (p. 5086) that Brooke-Popham was "the most important military figure in Malaya" and that "it was my housemate's [Colonel Brink's] duty to know him well."

40. CJC, Part 11, pp. 5514 ff. General Brink held the title of colonel in 1941.

7. About the time Admiral Hart received the dispatch from Singapore, he was in conference with the new British Commander in Chief, Admiral Tom Phillips. (CJC, Part 10, p. 4803). At this conference, December 5 (Washington time), Admiral Hart and Admiral Phillips drew up a program for American-British naval coöperation in that area, in case of war. This program, signed by Admiral Hart and Admiral Phillips, was sent to Admiral Stark, Chief of Naval Operations. It arrived in Washington about 11 P.M., December 6. A reply was prepared in the Navy Department in the forenoon of December 7, approving parts of the program provisionally, as in case of all such war plans (see above, Chap. XIV), but the reply was not sent out to Admiral Hart until after the Japanese attack (CJC, Part 4, pp. 1933 ff.).

8. After receiving the message from Singapore, December 6, 1941, Admiral Hart sent to Admiral Stark in Washington the following dispatch: "Learn from Singapore we have assured Britain armed support under three or four eventualities X Have received no corresponding instructions from you" (CJC, Part 14, Exhibit 40, p. 1412).

Given these facts, it is questionable whether a responsible Army or Navy officer of the United States in Singapore would have sent this alarming dispatch to Admiral Hart on December 6, 1941 (Singapore time) on the basis of a mere rumor, without any definite information on which to found it. It is scarcely credible that such a definite commitment on the part of the United States was passed around in British Army or Navy circles in the Far East without any authorization whatever from London. But whether or not the commitment was made by President Roosevelt must await confirmation from the President's secret papers not now (1947) available and/or from British archives still under seal. But it is pertinent to note that the eventualities mentioned in the Singapore dispatch were essentially the eventualities on which President Roosevelt's War Cabinet agreed that "we must fight." [41]

On the evening of that day, December 5, the State Depart-

41. See above, pp. 447 ff., and below, pp. 553 ff.

ment sent a telegram to the American Embassy in Tokyo (for use there and distribution to American representatives at certain other points in the Far East) which dealt with the destruction of American codes, papers, and other documents and the making of other preparations "in the event of sudden emergency." [42]

That same day, December 5, the British Ambassador, Lord Halifax, called on Secretary Hull with a message from Anthony Eden, head of the British Foreign Office, setting forth the British view that "the time had come for immediate coöperation with the Dutch East Indies by mutual understanding." This message was related to the joint action against Japan in a given contingency, to which the United States was tentatively committed by the war plans that had been unofficially approved by the President. [43] Respecting his reply to this notification by Lord Halifax, Mr. Hull recorded laconically: "I expressed my appreciation." [44]

This notification to Secretary Hull about the time for coöperation with the Dutch East Indies was merely one incident in a long chain of events—the development of secret war plans for the coöperation of the United States, Great Britain, and the Dutch—in January–April, 1941 (see above, Chap. XIV). On November 30, 1941, Lord Halifax had asked Secretary Hull point blank: "What the United States Government would do if the British should resist any Japanese undertaking to establish a base on the Kra Isthmus?" Mr. Hull replied that he would lay "all phases of the situation" before the President on his return from Warm Springs. After the President returned to Washington on December 1, he said that he would notify and see Lord Halifax. [45] Concerning the conference between the President and Lord Halifax on American coöperation in case the British resisted the Japanese in that case and the President's commitment, if any, the records unearthed

42. CJC, *Report*, p. 423.
43. See above, Chap. XIV.
44. CJC, Part 11, p. 5472.
45. CJC, Part 14, Exhibit 21, pp. 1249 f.

or at least published by the Congressional Committee on Pearl Harbor offer no conclusions.

Whether President Roosevelt made any military commitment whatever in this instance must be for the present a matter of conjecture. If conjectures one way or the other are to be indulged in, however, the following facts come into consideration.

The first is that the President's immediate military and naval subordinates who testified before the Congressional Committee agreed that the ABD military plans were tentative and conditional and that they had been warned against committing any overt acts of war in the Pacific area, thus distinguishing that region from the Atlantic where an undeclared "shooting war" had long been in progress. Admiral Stark repeatedly testified that he knew nothing about any obligations on the part of the President to join the British and the Dutch in war if Japan attacked them or violated the terms laid down in any ultimative notes sent from Washington to Tokyo.

The second fact is that the record of President Roosevelt's personal communications with foreign governments and their representatives as presented to the Congressional Committee is far from complete. This issue came up in the committee near the close of its hearings. Senator Brewster remarked that all Mr. Grew's *Diary* and all Mr. Stimson's *Diary* had not been made available to the committee and counsel for examination but his motions to have them made available were voted down by the committee. Senator Brewster also said:

The telephone communications between London and Washington during the period before Pearl Harbor is something which we have not been able, apparently, to run down. Miss Tully advises she had no record. It seems to me incredible that communications of that importance between the heads of state were not made a matter of record. If they were not made a matter of record it seems to me that there was serious dereliction. If they were made a matter of record I believe that this committee should have knowledge regarding them. I think that covers some of the items. There are many other unexplored fields in the higher echelons which it seems to me most unfortunate that the committee has not been able to explore and expose.

Senator Barkley replied in general that the committee had made as exhaustive and careful an investigation as any committee had ever made in a similar case. Then he added:

So far as these records of telephone conversations are concerned, I think this committee, and counsel, have felt, and the President of the United States [Mr. Truman], who issued orders with reference to the examination of documents in the State, War, and Navy Departments, and other departments, and in the White House, realized that Miss Tully, who had been in charge of those documents, was a reputable, responsible woman of long experience and high character, I think the committee felt that she had brought to the attention of counsel everything in the President's papers that had any relationship to this investigation.[46]

December 6, 1941, late in the afternoon, President Roosevelt made another complicated move in relation to affairs in the Pacific. At some previous time, Prime Minister Churchill had proposed to the Governments of the British Dominions that they unite with Great Britain in warning the Japanese Government "in the most solemn manner that if Japan attempts to establish her influence in Thailand by force or threat of force she will do so at her own peril and His Majesty's Governments will at once take all appropriate measures. Should hostilities unfortunately result the responsibility will rest with Japan." This warning was to be in the nature of a clear notification to Japan that in the contingency stated Great Britain and the Dominions would resist force or a threat of force by employing force. In effect the declaration was to be

46. CJC, Part 11, pp. 5538 f. The committee members, even accompanied by counsel, at least the Republican members, were not permitted to examine the messages exchanged by President Roosevelt and Mr. Churchill between September, 1939, and December 7, 1941 (see above, Chap. X). With regard to telephone communications between Washington and London, Senator Barkley did not indicate whether, to his knowledge, they had been recorded or not. In the case of an oral commitment by President Roosevelt to the Australian Minister in Washington, Miss Tully said "of course, no record was ever made" of it. See below, p. 548 n.

an ultimatum from the British Empire backed by a definite threat of war action.

A copy of this proposal to the Dominion Governments was sent by Prime Minister Churchill to President Roosevelt accompanied by a note inviting the President's comments. Just when the copy of the proposal and the Prime Minister's note came into the hands of the President is uncertain; [47] but two things are certain. First, the Australian Government made its acceptance of the Prime Minister's proposal "subject to the condition that President gives prior approval to text of warning as drafted and also gives signal for actual delivery of warning." Second, in the afternoon of December 6, Mr. Casey, the Australian Minister in Washington, discussed this subject with President Roosevelt and received from him a commitment as to the procedure to be followed in connection with carrying out the proposal.

The evidence relative to the transaction, which was brought out by the Congressional Committee on Pearl Harbor in the spring of 1946, did not come from the files of the State Department, but from President Roosevelt's personal papers [48] and from records of the Australian Government with the consent of the British Government. The facts are as follows: "Late in the afternoon of December 6," President Roosevelt informed the Australian Minister that he was prepared to follow a given procedure in conjunction with the delivery of the British warning to Japan. That information, accompanied by a description of the procedure, "was dispatched from Washington at 9:30 P.M. on December 6, 1941"; and that evening the Australian Government sent a dispatch from Canberra to the Secretary of State for Dominion Affairs in London informing the Secretary that, in respect of the British proposal for an ultimative warning to Japan, a message just received from the Australian Minister at Washington had described the

47. See below, p. 546.
48. See above, p. 544 n. Miss Grace Tully, who had charge of the papers, regarded these documents as pertinent to the committee's inquiry and so supplied them to the committee.

steps which President Roosevelt would take in supporting the program.

The procedure described by the Australian Minister at Washington in his message of 9:30 P.M. December 6 to the Australian Government was as follows:

1. President has decided to send message to the [Japanese] Emperor.

2. President's subsequent procedure is that if no answer is received by him from the Emperor by Monday evening [December 8, 1941].

> (a) he will issue his warning on Tuesday afternoon or evening [December 9, 1941].
>
> (b) warning or equivalent by British or others will not follow until Wednesday morning, i.e., after his own warning has been delivered repeatedly in Tokyo and Washington.

Only one link in evidence respecting this action by the President remained obscure after Senator Ferguson and Senator Brewster, by persistence, had developed the subject in the proceedings of the Congressional Committee in April, 1946, namely, the exact time when the actual text of Prime Minister Churchill's proposal and an accompanying note were placed in President Roosevelt's hands. These documents, as taken from the President's personal file, were two in number. The first was the note from the Prime Minister asking for the President's comments on the proposal; the second consisted of the text of the proposal. The first sheet, containing Mr. Churchill's request for comments, was a small paper from the British Embassy in Washington which bore at the bottom the date of December 7, 1941. To this sheet was attached two sheets which gave the full text of the Prime Minister's proposal for an ultimative warning to Japan.

During a hearing of the Congressional Committee, Senator Barkley laid emphasis on the date December 7, 1941, at the bottom of the small sheet from the British Embassy and contended: "That was all thrown out the window by what happened at noon Sunday, which must have been not very long after this thing was delivered to the President, because it was delivered to him on the morning of the 7th." But, if as contended, the President did not receive the text of the Prime Minister's proposed warning to Japan until December 7, at least he was informed in the afternoon of December 6, 1941, about the substance of the proposal.

The grounds for this statement are four in number: (1) the Australian Government had made its acceptance of the British proposal "subject to conditions that President gives prior approval to text of warning as drafted and also gives signal for actual delivery of warning"; (2) the Australian Minister at Washington conferred with the President on the subject in the afternoon of December 6; (3) by a dispatch to his Government in Australia, sent at 9:30 P.M. December 6, the Australian Minister informed his Government in respect of the President's commitment to procedure in the matter as described above; and (4) that evening the Australian Government informed the British Government in London about the President's agreement to procedure in the matter.[49]

In any case the facts of the commitment are well established: [50] President Roosevelt agreed, in the afternoon of December 6, 1941, at a conference with the Australian Minister, to send a message to the Japanese Emperor. Furthermore, at the same time he agreed to coöperate with Great Britain and the Dominions in the project for giving Japan an ultimative notification and, if he had received from the Emperor no answer by Monday evening, December 8, to issue his warning on Tuesday afternoon or evening. These agreements were predicated on the understanding that British and other warnings would not be sent until Wednesday morning, December 10—"after his own warning had been delivered repeatedly in Tokyo and Washington."[51]

49. It is to be noted that December 6, 1941, Washington time, was December 7, 1941, Canberra time, for some confusion has arisen as to the date of the completion of the transaction.

50. The documents and other evidence relative to this commitment of December 6, 1941, are in CJC, Part 11, pp. 5164 ff.

51. In a letter dated Washington, April 17, 1946, Miss Grace Tully, who had

What relation, if any, did the President's appeal to the Japanese Emperor on Saturday night, December 6, have to his oral commitment made in the late afternoon that day to the Australian Minister in Washington? The Australian Minister merely stated to his government that "President has decided to send message to Emperor," as a part of the general procedure in connection with the ultimative warning to Japan. Was the President's message framed to meet that commitment or was it an independent action? The answer must be conjectural, not positive, for such a letter had been discussed many days prior to December 6 by the President, Secretary Hull, Secretary Stimson, and Secretary Knox.

Sometime on December 6, the Navy Department made available to high officials in Washington a notice that the Japanese Embassy in Washington had destroyed its codes.[52]

About 3 P.M. on December 6, Army Intelligence delivered at the office of the Secretary of State a translation of an intercepted secret message from the Japanese Foreign Minister to Ambassador Nomura, which stated that the Japanese reply to Secretary Hull's memorandum of November 26 would be sent shortly in fourteen parts and that a later dispatch would inform the Ambassador as to the time the reply was to be handed to Secretary Hull.[53] This was the Japanese message which, Secretary Hull knew from a previous intercept, would mark the de facto rupture of negotiations with the United States.[54]

About 9 P.M. on December 6, the State Department dispatched to Tokyo President Roosevelt's appeal to the Japanese Emperor for aid in restoring traditional amity between the United States and Japan and in preventing further death

---

charge of the papers in President Roosevelt's files, responded to a request from the Congressional Committee for additional information by saying that she could find no other papers relative to the subject in the files and adding: "My feeling about the message from the Australian Minister at Washington, Mr. Casey, is that he and the late President discussed the subject but, of course, no record was ever made of such conversation." *Ibid.*, p. 5510.

52. CJC, Part 12, pp. 236 ff.
53. CJC, *Report*, p. 433.
54. See above, p. 528.

and destruction in the world. In a brief note to Secretary Hull on the appeal, the President said: "Dear Cordell: Shoot this to Grew—I think can go in grey code—saves time—I don't mind if it gets picked up." Secretary Grew testified before the Congressional Committee on Pearl Harbor in 1945 that he first learned of the President's message that evening while listening to a radio broadcast from San Francisco.[55] Hence, it appears, this message to the Emperor was, indeed, quickly "picked up" and broadcast to the world.

Shortly after 9.30 P.M., December 6, 1941, Commander Schulz, assistant to Admiral Beardall, Naval Aide to the President, delivered to President Roosevelt in his study at the White House the first thirteen parts of the Japanese message in reply to Secretary Hull's memorandum of November 26, notice of which had been received earlier in the day. Commander Schulz testified before the Congressional Committee on Pearl Harbor in 1946 that Harry Hopkins was present on that occasion and that the President read the documents and handed them to Harry Hopkins, "who was pacing back and forth slowly."

The following passages from the testimony[56] of Commander Schulz before the Congressional Committee describe the conversation that ensued:

COMMANDER SCHULZ. Mr. Hopkins then read the papers and handed them back to the President. The President then turned toward Mr. Hopkins and said in substance—I am not sure of the exact words, but in substance—"This means war." Mr. Hopkins agreed, and they discussed then, for perhaps 5 minutes, the situation of the Japanese forces; that is, their deployment and—

MR. RICHARDSON. Can you recall what either of them said?

COMMANDER SCHULZ. In substance I can. There are only a few words that I can definitely say I am sure of, but the substance of it was that—I believe Mr. Hopkins mentioned it first—that since war was imminent, that the Japanese intended to strike when they were ready, at a moment when all was most opportune for them—

55. CJC, *Report*, pp. 426–428.
56. *Ibid.*, pp. 434 ff.

THE CHAIRMAN. When all was what?

COMMANDER SCHULZ. When all was most opportune for them. That is, when their forces were most properly deployed for their advantage. Indochina in particular was mentioned, because the Japanese forces had already landed there and there were implications of where they should move next.

The President mentioned a message that he had sent to the Japanese Emperor concerning the presence of Japanese troops in Indochina, in effect requesting their withdrawal.

Mr. Hopkins then expressed a view that since war was undoubtedly going to come at the convenience of the Japanese, it was too bad that we could not strike the first blow and prevent any sort of surprise. The President nodded and then said, in effect, "No, we can't do that. We are a democracy and a peaceful people." Then he raised his voice, and this much I remember definitely. He said, "But we have a good record."

The impression that I got was that we would have to stand on that record, we could not make the first overt move. We would have to wait until it came.

During this discussion there was no mention of Pearl Harbor. The only geographic name I recall was Indochina. The time at which war might begin was not discussed, but from the manner of the discussion there was no indication that tomorrow was necessarily the day. I carried that impression away because it contributed to my personal surprise when the news did come.

Mr. RICHARDSON. Was there anything said, Commander, with reference to the subject of notice or notification as a result of the papers that were being read?

COMMANDER SCHULZ. There was no mention made of sending any further warning or alert. However, having concluded this discussion about the war going to begin at the Japanese convenience, then the President said that he believed he would talk to Admiral Stark. He started to get Admiral Stark on the telephone. It was then determined—I do not recall exactly, but I believe the White House operator told the President that Admiral Stark could be reached at the National Theater.

Mr. RICHARDSON. Now, was it from what was said there that you draw the conclusion that that was what the White House operator reported?

COMMANDER SCHULZ. Yes, sir. I did not hear what the operator said, but the National Theater was mentioned in my presence, and the President went on to state, in substance, that he would reach the Admiral later, that he did not want to cause public alarm by having the Admiral paged or otherwise when in the theater, where, I believe, the fact that he had a box reserved was mentioned and that if he had left suddenly he would surely have been seen because of the position which he held and undue alarm might be caused, and the President did not wish that to happen because he could get him within perhaps another half an hour in any case.

MR. RICHARDSON. Was there anything said about telephoning anybody else except Stark?

COMMANDER SCHULZ. No, sir; there was not.

After receiving the intercept of the Japanese message which he thought meant war between the United States and Japan and having called Admiral Stark by telephone later in the evening,[57] President Roosevelt took no further action in respect of warning the outpost commanders about the immediate imminence of war. Such at least is the only inference that is permissible in view of all the evidence on the point brought to light by the Congressional Committee on Pearl Harbor.

December 7, 1941. In the morning Secretaries Hull, Stimson, and Knox held a conference at the State Department on various matters, including what was to be done about the movements of Japanese forces southward into the zone where war was expected to break out at any moment. Before their conference closed they had available all the fourteen parts of the intercepted Japanese message which was to be delivered soon to Secretary Hull and also the final dispatch saying that the message was to be handed to Secretary Hull at one o'clock that day.[58]

Meanwhile, about 10 A.M., the fourteenth part of the Japanese reply to Secretary Hull's memorandum was delivered by Admiral Beardall to President Roosevelt in his bedroom at the White House.[59]

57. CJC, Part 11, pp. 5543 ff., for final testimony of Admiral Stark.
58. CJC, *Report*, p. 437.
59. *Ibid.*, p. 436.

Sometime before noon on December 7, General Marshall had at hand the latest intercepts of Japanese secret messages, including the notice to Ambassador Nomura that one o'clock was fixed as the hour for his appearance at the State Department with the last Japanese memorandum. General Marshall decided that the outpost commanders must have a new war warning. After strange delays on his own part and that of his immediate associates, General Marshall sent, about noon, the final war warning to General Short at Hawaii—the message which arrived *after* the Japanese attack on Pearl Harbor.[60]

At 1.50 P.M., December 7, the Navy Department received a dispatch from Admiral Kimmel that there had been an air raid on Pearl Harbor.[61]

The President quickly informed Secretary Hull at the State Department about the report that Hawaii had been attacked. Hence the Secretary apparently had news of the attack, as well as a copy of the message soon to be delivered by the Japanese, before 2.05 P.M. when the Japanese Ambassadors arrived at his office. After he had received the Japanese Ambassadors, read their memorandum, and told them what he thought of the document in forcible language, Secretary Hull issued a public statement to the effect that the Japanese had been preparing their "treacherous" attack "at the very moment" when Japan was discussing peace with the United States and the other nations now assailed by Japanese arms. "It is now apparent to the whole world," he said, "that Japan in its recent professions of a desire for peace has been infamously false and fraudulent." [62]

About 2 P.M. Sunday, December 7, 1941, President Roosevelt telephoned Secretary Stimson: "They have attacked Hawaii. They are now bombing Hawaii." Secretary Stimson noted in his *Diary* for the day: "Well, that was an excitement indeed." He wrote a few lines about the conference which he

60. For negligence and bungling with regard to this warning sent too late, see CJC, Part 39, pp. 93 ff.; and above, Chap. XII, pp. 366 ff.
61. CJC, *Report*, p. 439.
62. *Ibid.*, pp. 440 f. All hours given above are Washington time (E.S.T.) on December 7.

had held with Secretary Hull and Secretary Knox that morning and added: "Our efforts this morning in drawing our papers [on the policy to be pursued by the United States] was to see whether or not we should all act together. The British will have to fight if they [the Japanese] attack the Kra Peninsula. We three all thought that we must fight if the British fought. But now the Japs have solved the whole thing by attacking us directly in Hawaii." Mr. Stimson also made the following entry in his *Diary* for December 7: "When the news first came that Japan had attacked us, my first feeling was of relief that the indecision was over and that a crisis had come in a way which would unite all our people. This continued to be my dominant feeling in spite of the news of catastrophes which quickly developed. For I feel that this country united has practically nothing to fear; while the apathy and divisions stirred up by unpatriotic men have been hitherto very discouraging."

Like Secretary Stimson, after the news of the Japanese attack on Pearl Harbor came, President Roosevelt, despite reports of the disaster that befell American forces, felt relieved that the indecision was over and that war had come. For this statement, his Secretary of Labor, Frances Perkins, provided evidence in 1946. She noted that, at the Cabinet meeting in the evening of December 7, 1941, the President, "in spite of the terrible blow to his pride, to his faith in the Navy and its ships, and to his confidence in the American intelligence service, and in spite of the horror that war had actually brought to us, . . . had, nevertheless, a much calmer air. His terrible moral problem had been resolved by the event. As we went out Frank Walker [the Postmaster General] said to me: 'I think the Boss really feels more relief than he has had for weeks.' " [68]

December 7, 1941, evening. Meeting of the Cabinet at 8.30 and of legislative leaders at 9 in the White House. On this occasion, President Roosevelt, besides making a report on the extent of the American disaster at Pearl Harbor, as far as frag-

63. *The Roosevelt I Knew* (Viking Press, 1946), pp. 379 f.

mentary news reports would permit, gave to members of the Cabinet and legislative leaders an exposition of recent events that foreshadowed his statement of the official thesis presented to Congress on the following day.[64] He said that conversations with Japan continued until

about two weeks ago, when we received indications from various sources—Europe and Asia—that the German government was pressing Japan for action under the tripartite pact. In other words, an effort to divert the American mind, and the British mind, from the European field, and divert American supplies from the European theatre to the defense of the East Asia theatre.

About two weeks ago [the President continued], we began to realize that the probability of Japan being in earnest was so slim that it was time to make a final and definite effort to pin them down on the one subject that they had never ever been pinned down on, and that was that they were to agree to cease their acts of aggression, and that they would try to bring the China war to a close. The result was that the Secretary of State sent a message on that point, to find out whether Japan would be willing to discuss or consider that point of nonaggression.[65] That was the 26th of November. From that time on we were getting more and more definite information that Japan was headed for war, and that the reply to the Secretary of State would be in the negative. . . .

And so the thing went along until we believed that under the pressure from Berlin the Japanese were about to do something. . . . And so yesterday I sent a final message to the Emperor. . . .

Of course, it is a terrible disappointment to be President in time of war, and the circumstances [words inaudible] came most unexpectedly. Well, we were attacked. There is no question about that. . . .

The fact is that a shooting war is going on today in the Pacific. We are in it.[66]

Mrs. Charles Hamlin, for many years a close friend of President Roosevelt, was a guest at the White House in November and December, 1941, and made notes respecting his attitudes

64. See above, pp. 209 ff.
65. See below, pp. 555 ff., for the memorandum of November 26.
66. CJC, Part 19, Exhibit 160, pp. 3503 ff. The stenographer notes that at several points the President's remarks were inaudible and so indicates.

and remarks on days following Pearl Harbor—from which the following extracts are taken.[67]

December 9. The President, the night of his broadcast to the nation on the coming of war,[68] "looked relieved, as if a load was off his mind at last, now that fate and the Japanese attack had finally settled everything that had been brewing for so long."

December 10, evening. "The President quipped that 'Hungary, Rumania, and Czechoslovakia have all declared war on us—I told Cordell to take no notice of them and I will not inform the Congress.' His cigarette was tipped at its usual jaunty angle."

December 22. Dinner attended by Lord Halifax and Winston Churchill. The President shook cocktails "with Mr. Churchill standing beside him." Shortly before the dinner ended, the President said: "I have a toast to offer—it has been in my head and on my heart for a long time—now it is on the tip of my tongue—'To the common cause.'"

December 23. Mr. Bernard Baruch was present. "He had brought with him a bottle of special brandy, which the President served at the end of dinner." Mr. Churchill and President Roosevelt made short stirring speeches and the President "appointed the first day of 1942 as a day of prayer, a day of consecration to the tasks of the present. . . . The band played 'God Save the King' and then 'The Star Spangled Banner.' . . . Every night we drink to the health of the United States and Great Britain and then to the common cause."

THE GREAT DECISION

It is evident from the records presented to the public by the Congressional Committee on Pearl Harbor that, as Secretary Hull had repeatedly insisted, the Roosevelt Administration

67. *The New Republic*, April 15, 1945 (Supplement, "Roosevelt: A First Appraisal by Those Who Knew Him").

68. For the President's radio address on December 9, see above, Chap. VIII, p. 210.

had conducted affairs in relation to Japan according to a strong policy, at least from the Atlantic Conference to December 7, 1941—a policy of no compromise with the Japanese Government.

But the policy was broader in demands in November than on August 17. The declaration to Japan, August 17, was the outcome of President Roosevelt's agreement at the Atlantic Conference, after he had heard Prime Minister Churchill's appeal for aid in the Far East. In keeping with that agreement, the declaration was narrowly limited in scope. With a clear threat of counteraction, it warned Japan against taking *"any further steps* in pursuance of a policy or program of military domination by force or threat of force of neighboring countries." [69] It did not order Japan to withdraw entirely from China or Indo-China, to observe the territorial and administrative integrity of China, to practice equality of commercial opportunity in China, to abandon her support of the puppet government in Nanking, or to give up her extraterritorial rights in China.

In short, the American declaration on August 17, 1941, simply demanded that the Japanese Government take no further steps of aggression in the Far East. It did not seek to impose on Japan the whole system of world morality and economic practices set forth as American "principles" by Secretary Hull. In its terms was a narrow basis for negotiations which high officials in Tokyo could carry on without "losing face" or incurring the risk of overthrow or assassination.

In form at least, the Japanese proposal for a modus vivendi on November 20, 1941, offered as a ground for negotiations the possibility of halting "any further steps" of aggression in the Southeast area of Asia. President Roosevelt at first thought that the proposal did offer this possibility for he definitely recognized it in the outline memorandum for adjustments with Japan which he wrote out by hand and sent to Secretary Hull.[70] Officers of the Far Eastern Division in the Department of State arrived at the conclusion that a modus vivendi

69. See above, p. 488. (Italics supplied.)
70. See above, p. 511.

was desirable and prepared a draft of an American proposal for consideration by Secretary Hull.[71] Henry Morgenthau, Jr., Secretary of the Treasury, was evidently convinced that the occasion presented an opportunity for avoiding a two-front war and prepared a plan for concessions to Japan, which was approved by the senior officers of the Far Eastern Division in the State Department and recommended for careful consideration to Secretary Hull by the Chief of the Division.[72]

But the suggestions of President Roosevelt, the Far Eastern Division, and Secretary Morgenthau were rejected by Secretary Hull in favor of the line of action proposed in his memorandum of November 26, which, with the approval of President Roosevelt and without previous consultation with Secretary Stimson, the British Ambassador in Washington, and other high parties to the negotiations, was handed to the Japanese Ambassadors on that day. This action was taken with clear awareness of its significance; for Secretary Hull, the very next day when he told Secretary Stimson that he had "washed his hands" of the matter, added: "it is now in the hands of you and Knox—the Army and the Navy." [73]

It is true that Secretary Hull, in 1946, in response to Senator Ferguson's questions, sought to explain these words away,[74] and insisted that, in his opinion, there had always been a bare chance that the Japanese would not treat the memorandum as an ultimatum and might come back for more conversations. It is true also that he refused all along to acknowledge that he had looked upon the action of November 26 as putting an end to diplomatic processes and bound to result in war. Yet his own statements relative to this crucial decision on November 26, made with the approval of the President, indicate beyond all doubt that his hope for any further negotiations looking toward peace in the Pacific was so slight as to be negligible, if indeed he had any such hope at all.[75]

In any event, whatever may have been the expectations of

71. See documents in CJC, Part 14, Exhibit 18.
72. See above, p. 512.
73. See above, p. 516.
74. See below, p. 563.
75. See below, p. 561.

President Roosevelt and Secretary Hull on November 26, 1941, the document which was handed to the Japanese Ambassadors on that day was sweeping in its terms. It was, to be sure, partly in line with the narrow and simple declaration of August 17, in that it applied to any further steps by the Japanese toward British, Dutch, and American spheres of interest; but it was comprehensive enough in scope to satisfy all Americans who looked upon the Atlantic Charter as furnishing a blueprint for a new world order and also those American imperialists who wanted to employ war as an instrument of policy for enforcing the doctrine of the Open Door in the Far East.[76]

The memorandum of November 26 was skillfully drawn. The first part—the "oral statement"—*suaviter in modo*, referred to conversations carried on in recent months for the purpose "if possible" of arriving at a settlement based upon "the principles of peace, law and order, and fair dealing among nations." It rejected the Japanese proposal for a modus vivendi as not likely to contribute to the objectives of "ensuring peace under law, order and justice in the Pacific area." Then the oral statement alluded to the accompanying plan as "one practical exemplification of a program which this Government envisages as something to be worked out during our further conversations."

Here, in the oral statement, *ex vi termini*, was no ultimatum. It contained no hint that, on the previous day, November 25, the President, Secretary Hull, Secretary Stimson, Secretary Knox, General Marshall, and Admiral Stark had been discussing the problem of how to "maneuver" the Japanese into firing the first shot without allowing too much danger to ourselves.[77] Here was no intimation that Secretary Hull regarded the memorandum as warranting him in saying to Secretary

76. See above, Chap. IX for an analysis of the imperialist nature of the memorandum of November 26, 1941; for "the Stimson doctrine" and President Roosevelt's acceptance of this "doctrine," see Beard, *op. cit.*, pp. 33 ff. For text of the memorandum, see *Foreign Relations of the United States: Japan, 1931–1941*, II, 766 ff.

77. See above, p. 517.

Stimson the next day that the matter is now in the hands of the Army and the Navy.[78]

The second part of the memorandum of November 26, though called "Outline of Proposed Basis for Agreement between the United States and Japan," laid down definite prescriptions for the Japanese. After proposing a joint declaration of liberal policies, it stipulated, among other things, that: "The Government of Japan will withdraw all military, naval, air and police forces from China and from Indo-China. The Government of the United States and the Government of Japan will not support—militarily, politically, economically—any government or regime in China other than the National Government of the Republic of China with capital temporarily at Chungking." This proposition, President Roosevelt and Secretary Hull must have known very well, meant a sudden reversal of policy and action in Tokyo, which the Japanese Government was not likely to make, which was indeed so highly improbable as to warrant no hope of continued negotiations looking toward the maintenance of peace in the Pacific, if that was what the President and Secretary Hull had contemplated at any time after August 17, 1941.

When, instead of reaffirming the declaration of August 17, 1941, President Roosevelt and Secretary Hull, on November 26, made this comprehensive and drastic proposal to the Government of Japan, did they believe that their action would lead to a break in negotiations, if not immediate war? If they made this crucial decision with reference to such consequences, why did they resort to ultimative action in the Pacific rather than in the Atlantic? These certainly are questions necessarily related to the real problem of "how war came." [79]

78. See above, p. 516.

79. Davis and Lindley, in *How War Came*, speaking semiofficially, said in 1942: "The question perplexing many high officials was how, in the absence of a direct attack on the American flag, to summon the nation, divided as it then was on questions of foreign policy, to the strong action which they believed essential. There had been considerable discussion of possible methods. . . . It was commonly supposed that the Japanese were too smart to solve this problem for the President by a direct assault on the American flag—especially at Hawaii, which even the extreme isolationists recognized as a bastion of our security" (page 315).

Since President Roosevelt's personal records, papers, and memoranda were carefully safeguarded against scrutiny by members of the minority in the Congressional Committee and are not yet open to students of diplomatic history, answers to these questions must be sought elsewhere.[80] And chief among other sources are extended statements bearing on the subject by two of the President's most intimate associates in the inner circle of his War Cabinet—Secretary Hull and Secretary Stimson.

Although Secretary Hull's health did not permit him to undergo the strain of a direct cross examination by members of the Congressional Committee on Pearl Harbor, he did answer, in his own way, many of the questions directed to him in writing by Senator Ferguson, of the minority, in April, 1946, through the good offices of the majority. Likewise, Secretary Stimson, though prevented by poor health from appearing before the committee, wrote terse replies to numerous questions presented to him in writing by Senator Ferguson.

Well acquainted with the testimony and exhibits brought forth by the Congressional Committee, Senator Ferguson evidently regarded the decision of President Roosevelt and Secretary Hull to reject the Japanese proposal for a truce or

---

When Davis and Lindley wrote these words, they probably did not have access to the "Magic"—the secret Japanese messages intercepted, decoded, and translated by the American Army and Navy and distributed almost daily among the "high officials" to whom they referred. Nor did they have access, it is also probable, to many of the secret documents in American files which were opened to view by the Congressional Committee on Pearl Harbor in 1945 and 1946.

80. On September 19, 1946, the Director of the Roosevelt Library at Hyde Park, wrote me that "President Roosevelt's press conferences are not available for public inspection at this time." Through the courtesy of a large metropolitan newspaper, I was offered the privilege of examining its rather full stenographic reports of these press conferences, but I could not be allowed to make free use of the Mss. It is an anomaly that a group of journalists are permitted to take notes at the President's press conferences, held presumably for the benefit and information of the public, whereas students of American history are denied access to the official minutes which are supposed to give the authentic version of what was actually said. I was once permitted to read (but not to use) the minutes of Secretary Hull's utterances at a press conference which filled many pages of "flimsy," and compare it with a few paragraphs "on the record," which newspapers were permitted to print. I may say that I was deeply impressed by the vigor of Secretary Hull's language "off the record."

modus vivendi and to substitute the ultimative memorandum of November 26 as highly pertinent to the issue of how war came. At all events, the Senator sought to discover, by questioning Secretary Hull, whether the action was deliberately taken with full knowledge that war would be a consequence so probable as to constitute a practical certainty. In his replies [81] Secretary Hull made the following various statements on the subject:

We knew from Japanese acts and utterances that the Japanese proposal of November 20 was their last word and it was obviously desirable that the record of the American Government's position throughout the conversations be made crystal clear. Therefore, the proposals of November 26 were directed toward making our position utterly clear and toward keeping the door open for further conversations notwithstanding the ultimative character of the Japanese proposal of November 20.

Before and after presenting that proposal [of November 20], Ambassador Nomura and Mr. Kurusu talked emphatically about the urgency of the situation and intimated vigorously that this was Japan's last word and if an agreement along these lines was not quickly concluded ensuing developments might be most unfortunate.

The Japanese proposal of November 20 . . . was of so preposterous a character that no responsible American official could ever have dreamed of accepting it.[82] Nevertheless, I felt that I should not be violent in my comment to the Japanese in regard to it so as to avoid giving them any pretext to walk out on the conversations. . . . Moreover, we wanted to show our interest in peace up to the last split second and at the same time to expose the bad faith of the Japanese.

From November 22 on it was my individual view that Japan was through with any serious conversations looking to a peaceful settlement. From that day I and my associates had reached a stage of clutching at straws in our effort to save the situation.

We had no serious thought that Japan would accept our pro-

---

81. CJC, Part 11, pp. 5367 ff.
82. Accepting it was one thing; using it as a basis for possible adjustment was another thing. President Roosevelt apparently did not regard it as so "preposterous" that it could not be so used. See above, p. 511.

posal of November 26. I said at the time that there was only the barest possibility of her accepting it. She would have proceeded to attack us whether we had presented that proposal or any other proposal—unless it had been one of humiliating and abject surrender. . . .

During this period all the information we received made clearer Japan's purpose to attack unless the United States yielded to them. In other words, Japan had no intention of yielding any part of her plan of conquest by force, but was giving the United States, by its proposal of November 20, a last opportunity to choose between yielding or fighting.

It is my understanding that the main object of the Japanese Government in pressing for a reply to their November 20 proposal was to ascertain beyond any doubt whether this Government would yield to the Japanese or whether this Government was going to stand firm, and if the Japanese had learned that we were standing firm they would continue forward with the attack. Our position of not yielding was as clear as crystal to the Japanese Ambassadors.[83]

On November 29,[84] the Australian Minister called on me and brought up the question of his conferring with the Japanese representative, Mr. Kurusu, and suggesting to Kurusu that Australia would be glad to act as mediator. I offered no objection to his taking such a step, but merely stated my opinion to the Minister that the diplomatic stage was over and that nothing would come of such a move.

Referring to the intercepted message of the Japanese Government on November 28, which announced that negotiations would be de facto disrupted, Secretary Hull said: "This reaction was fully expected in the light of the delivery of the Japanese ultimatum on November 20 and of subsequent developments."

Although Secretary Hull more than once stated categorically that he regarded the American memorandum of Novem-

83. Evidently, then, Secretary Hull understood on November 26 when he presented his memorandum to the Japanese that they would "continue forward with the attack"—would reject his memorandum and attack the United States.

84. CJC, Part 11, p. 5374, gives the date as November 9, 1941, but the original manuscript record of the committee gives the date correctly as November 29.

ber 26 as marking the end of diplomatic relations with Japan, he also sometimes qualified the assertion by referring to a slim chance and a slight possibility that Japan would continue conversations looking toward peace. Apparently the Secretary did not see any contradictions between such statements as "the diplomatic stage was over" and other statements such as "keeping the discussions alive."

Aware of these contradictions in Mr. Hull's statements, Senator Ferguson tried to pin him down to a definite proposition one way or the other by asking him the following questions:

When did you decide that further negotiations were useless and that you were going to turn the matter over to the Army and Navy?

When did you advise either the Army or the Navy that you were turning the matter over to the Army or Navy or both?

What had happened that you told Secretary Stimson you were turning the matter over to the Army and Navy?

Had you conferred with the President on the matter of turning the matter over to the Army and Navy?

Give date and conversation with the President on this.

In his reply, Secretary Hull did not answer these questions squarely one by one. He declined to say when he had decided that further negotiations were useless, when he had turned the matter over to the Army and the Navy. He refused to state when or whether he had conferred with President Roosevelt on the matter of putting the issue of war into the hands of the Army and the Navy. Instead the Secretary dealt generally with the subject in a single reply to Questions 29–33 and 45–47, and gave an explanation which is among the striking curiosities of his intellectual history.

According to Secretary Hull's interpretation in 1946 his statement of November 27, 1941, that "the matter is now in the hands of the Army and the Navy" did not mean that. He said in reply to Senator Ferguson's questions that this

expression . . . as applied in the situation which then arose, does not imply any idea of a transfer from the Department of State to the Departments of War and of the Navy of any part of the Department of State's functions or responsibilities. Nor do I think that there was any misunderstanding on the part of the President or of the Secretaries of War and of the Navy as to the sense in which this expression was used.[85] It seemed self-evident that the Army and the Navy would be our chief reliance in the light of the critical situation known to all of us. It was, of course, the understanding of each of us that the Department of State would continue to function and coordinate its action with that of the Army and Navy, but I emphasized that we could no longer be expected materially to control the situation.[86]

Secretary Hull's resolve to break off "the whole matter" of the modus vivendi, wash his hands of the issue, and refer it to the Army and the Navy, as he originally described the transaction, had necessary pertinence to the coming of war in the Pacific on December 7, 1941. Of this there can scarcely be a doubt. Instead of a note diplomatically calculated to continue conversations looking to the maintenance of peace in the Pacific, the Secretary, with the approval of the President, delivered to Japan a memorandum which they both knew to be, if not an ultimatum, at least so ultimative in character as to offer a trifling chance, if any, of maintaining peace in the Pacific. In a few days war came, bringing disaster to American arms at Pearl Harbor.

Between November 7 and November 25 or 26, 1941, while President Roosevelt and Secretary Hull were coming to their great decision, many impinging circumstances invited their consideration. The President was confronted in those days by what his Secretary of Labor, Frances Perkins, called his "terrible moral problem"—and the dilemma arising out of his campaign pledges in 1940 and especially the declaration of the Democratic platform, which he had endorsed in the campaign, that American armed forces were not to be sent out of this

85. There evidently was a misunderstanding on the part of Secretary Knox, for in his war warning to Admiral Kimmel, on November 27, he declared that negotiations with Japan had terminated. And Secretary Stimson thought on November 27 the statement meant an end to diplomatic negotiations, until he called up Secretary Hull and received a modified version. See above, p. 525.

86. CJC, Part 11, p. 5382.

hemisphere to fight "except in case of attack." The moral problem had been accentuated rather than diminished in October and November, 1941.

The "shooting war" in the Atlantic had not culminated in a full-fledged and duly acknowledged war. Investigations of the *Greer* and *Kearny* cases of "shooting," conducted by the Senate Naval Affairs Committee, under the direction of Senator David Walsh, had so deteriorated the President's declaration of October 27—"America has been attacked"—that this very formula evoked suspicions among many members of the President's own party, while to most Republicans mention of it appeared to be an evidence of duplicity.[87] When, on November 7, the Japanese Ambassador opened the last phase of the negotiations between Japan and the United States, involving at length the modus vivendi, the long contest in Congress over modifications of the Neutrality Act was just coming to a close. During the discussions of the Neutrality Act in the House and the Senate, spokesmen of the Administration had represented it as a design to avoid rather than seek war,[88] and the vote cast in both chambers against the bill on final action was ominously large.[89] When President Roosevelt signed it on November 17, echoes of the angry debate were still ringing in the Capital. Secretary Hull must have remembered all that, for later he declared that had President Roosevelt sent a war message to Congress in the last tense days before Pearl Harbor, "the powerful isolationist groups in this country would probably have renewed their oft repeated charges of 'warmongering' and 'dragging the nation into foreign wars.' "[90]

Thus, the prospects of a full-fledged war in the Atlantic or of a declaration of war in the Pacific by Congress were far from favorable when President Roosevelt and Secretary Hull decided to deliver the memorandum of November 26 to Japan. But, in view of the information which they had gained from

87. See above, Chap. V.
88. See above, Chap. VI.
89. See above, p. 159.
90. CJC, Part 11, p. 5375.

intercepts of messages and other sources, they had reason for believing that the memorandum would be rejected and that the consequent impasse would eventuate in war. Certainly they had little or no ground for expecting anything else.

Such was the conjuncture of circumstances, in which the President and the Secretary made the great decision which, as events demonstrated, transferred the conflict with Japan from the sphere of diplomacy to the sphere of war. Beyond question, according to the evidence produced by the Congressional Committee, the President and the Secretary, before, on, and after making the decision, were expecting if not actively seeking war; and having this expectation they continued to "maneuver" the Japanese and awaited the dénouement, without calling upon Congress for the authority to wage war.

Was it within the legal and moral competence of President Roosevelt in 1941 so to conduct foreign affairs as to maneuver a foreign country into firing the shot that brought on war—indeed, to make war on his own authority? This question was answered in the affirmative by his close associate in the negotiations and maneuvers that preceded Pearl Harbor—by Henry L. Stimson, his Secretary of War. Secretary Stimson's answer was given in a prepared statement sent to the Congressional Committee in the spring of 1946, in response to inquiries directed to him in writing by Senator Ferguson.

The Senator opened his questioning by referring to a previous statement of Secretary Stimson, that "our military advisers had given the President their formal advice that if Japan moved beyond certain lines we would have to fight for the sake of our own security." This reference was to the two memoranda to the President dated November 5 and November 27, 1941, and signed by Admiral Stark and General Marshall.[91] The Senator then asked Secretary Stimson in Question 3: "Was that advice accepted and did it become our Government policy prior to the Pearl Harbor attack?" Secretary Stimson replied by declaring, in effect, that the President possessed plenary powers in matters of policy,

91. See above, pp. 447 ff.

strategy, and war and also full authority for the exercise of these powers by virtue of the Constitution and the Acts of Congress:

It has always been the fixed and permanent policy of the United States Government to defend itself and its possessions. The Congress itself reaffirmed and endorsed this policy on numerous occasions as the dangers to this country from the war which was starting across the world became more acute. It reaffirmed it when the regular size of our ordinary military appropriations were enormously increased by the Congress in May and June 1940, at the time of the fall of France, Belgium, and the Netherlands. It reaffirmed it in September 1940, when it passed the draft law, and by the joint resolution in August 1940, which authorized the total mobilization of the National Guard for large scale maneuvers or training. It reaffirmed it by its passage of the lend-lease legislation to assist in arming the nations who were fighting in the front line against aggression by the Axis and in opening our ports for the repairs of their warships. Each of these extraordinary congressional enactments indicated beyond peradventure a policy to prepare the United States against an immediate impending attack by the Axis nations.

It is the President of the United States who is charged with the execution of that policy, both as Chief Executive and as Commander in Chief of the armed forces. *It was his duty to make the decisions as to how this policy of defense should be best carried out. The adoption of plans for defense are ultimately for his decision and if the adoption of a particular strategy is to be termed policy at all, it is executive policy the decision of which is entirely a matter for the President.* In making this decision, the President receives the advice of numerous advisers, including his military advisers and the members of his Cabinet. Their views and recommendations, however, are purely advisory, *and the final policy and strategy is for the decision of the President and it is his alone.*

As I have already pointed out in my statement, and as my contemporaneous notes indicate, *it was the consensus of opinion of the President's advisers that if the Japanese in the latter part of November should advance beyond a certain point the security of this country demanded that we would have to fight.* It was also the consensus of opinion that a further warning by us to

Japan should be given. *The President was in fact during the early part of December engaged in preparing an address to the Congress which would incorporate such a warning,* and was also considering a special telegram to the Emperor of Japan. *Before the address to the Congress was delivered, however, the Japanese struck on December 7. I do not recollect that the President prior to December 7 formally announced any decision on his part to fight if the Japanese passed the point in question, but he was undoubtedly considering such a decision most seriously, because it was the advice of his best qualified advisers.*

4. If so, what plans were promulgated to carry out that advice?

See answer to question 3.

5. Did you have information from the President that we would fight for the sake of our security upon the happening of that event mentioned in question 1?

See answer to question 3.

6. If so, did you convey that information to General Marshall?

See answer to question 3.

7. Will you state if the Secretary of the Navy had such advice and if he conveyed it, or caused it to be conveyed, to Admiral Stark?

I have no information as to this. . . .

10. On page 12 of the mimeographed statement you speak of the vote of the Cabinet as to whether or not it was thought that the American people would back you up if it became necessary to strike Japan in case she attacked England in Malay or the Dutch East Indies, does this mean that it became the policy of this Government at that time to take such steps?

See answer to question 3.

11. If so, to whom was this policy communicated?

See answer to question 3.

12. Did you advise General Marshall and was he to advise others in the field of this policy?

See answer to question 3.[92]

Such were Secretary Stimson's formulas of law and morals presented in justification of the exercise of illimitable powers by President Roosevelt in framing foreign policy, conducting foreign affairs, and making the commitments that eventuated

92. CJC, Part 11, pp. 5456 ff. (Italics supplied.)

in war. Here were Secretary Stimson's legal and ethical sanctions for the secret decisions and operations during the days preceding Pearl Harbor, which he tersely described as maneuvering the Japanese into the position of firing the first shot.

PART IV
EPILOGUE

CHAPTER XVIII

Interpretations Tested by Consequences

THE discrepancies between official representations and official realities in the conduct of foreign affairs during the year 1941, until the coming of war, stand out starkly in documents already available. Other documents that bear on the subject, running into the thousands, are known to exist, but they are still under the seal of secrecy. What they will reveal, if all of them are ever unsealed, can only be a matter of conjecture for the general public and students of history. But in any event several primary discrepancies are established beyond question by the documents now published.

In the nature of things human and political, these established discrepancies may be and are being turned to account in various ways by politicians, publicists, and commentators. They may be, for example, formulated into a bill of indictment against President Roosevelt and his Administration. Or they may be incorporated in a brief of defense which, like a demurrer in a court of justice, concedes the facts and denies that they make a true case under superior and overriding principles, taken for granted in advance. Or they may appear to reflective minds as furnishing precedents material and relevant to the future and fortunes of constitutional and democratic government in the United States.[1]

1. Assuming that critical historiography will not disappear from the Western civilization, as it did from the western Empire of Rome after the fifth century, A.D., the debate over interpretations of these discrepancies will probably continue indefinitely. For instance, students of history, after the lapse of centuries, still differ over the policy of Nero in relation to conquered Britain as represented by Suetonius and as otherwise represented by Tacitus. R. C. Collingwood, *The Idea of History* (1946), pp. 244 f. For comment on problems of interpretation in contemporary historiography, see R. Aron, *Introduction à la philosophie de l'histoire*, "La pluralité des systèmes d'interprétation," pp. 91 ff.

THE MAIN BRIEF OF DEFENSE—TESTED
BY CONSEQUENCES

For these discrepancies a favorable interpretation has been and is still being offered by many American publicists in the following form. The great end which President Roosevelt discerned and chose justified the means which he employed. As a farsighted statesman he early discovered that unless the United States entered the war raging in Europe, Hitler would be victorious; and the United States, facing alone this monstrous totalitarian power, would become a victim of its merciless ideology and its despotic militarism. According to this interpretation, it was a question of democracy, the Four Freedoms, the noble principles of the Atlantic Charter, and world security on the one side; of totalitarianism, consummate despotism, and military subjugation on the other side. Since the American people were so smug in their conceit, so ignorant of foreign affairs, and so isolationist in sentiment that they could not themselves see the reality of this terrible threat to their own safety and a necessity to meet it by a resort to war, President Roosevelt had to dissemble in order to be reëlected in 1940 as against Wendell Willkie, then the antiwar candidate of the Republicans on an antiwar platform. Furthermore, as members of Congress, Democrats and Republicans alike, continued throughout the year, until December 7, their vigorous opposition to involvement in war, President Roosevelt, in conducting foreign affairs, had to maintain the appearance of a defensive policy until the Japanese attack on Pearl Harbor. But the means which President Roosevelt actually employed in the conduct of foreign affairs were justified by the great end which he, with peculiar clairvoyance, had early discerned and chosen for himself and his country.[2]

Oblique but evident support for this interpretation was provided by the Department of State in Chapter I of its publication, *Peace and War, 1931–1941*, issued in July, 1943,

2. This is, in sum and substance, the official case as presented in the semiofficial work by Davis and Lindley, *How War Came;* Beard, *op. cit.*, pp. 25 ff.

prepared by or for Secretary Hull. In that chapter, the President and the Secretary of State are represented as convinced at some time "early" in that decade that "the idea of isolation as expressed in 'neutrality' legislation" was untenable, as having information about foreign affairs or foreseeing developments in foreign relations of which the public was not aware, and as compelled to move gradually "to a position in the forefront of the United Nations that are making common cause against an attempt at world conquest unparalleled alike in boldness of conception and in brutality of operation." [3]

The interpretation that the end justified the means, like all other interpretations, depends upon the point of view of those who make or accept it; and though it be proclaimed as the settled truth, its validity is nonetheless open to tests of knowledge.[4] Even a cursory examination of the thesis raises questions of time and consequences, foreign and domestic.[5]

When did the end that justified the means actually come? With the surrender of Italy, Germany, and Japan? If not,

3. For an analysis of this chapter in *Peace and War*, see Beard, *op. cit.*, pp. 28 ff.

4. For the use of the test of consequences, we have the very high authority of Sumner Welles. In his book, *The Time for Decision* (Harper, 1944), Mr. Welles says: "The wisdom of any foreign policy can generally be determined only by its results." CJC, Part 2, p. 509.

5. The proposition that President Roosevelt as a perceptive statesman foresaw, in advance of the American people, the great end to be attained and the necessity of America's entrance into war involves questions of chronology and history. When, before December 7, 1941, did President Roosevelt and Secretary Hull decide that war for the United States was desirable and necessary, if they ever did before the Pearl Harbor attack? President Roosevelt's answer to that question of time is not yet forthcoming (see above, Chap. XIV). Secretary Hull, when it was put to him squarely by Senator Ferguson, parried it with the verbal skill of a trained diplomat (see above, pp. 563 f.). The majority of the Congressional Committee on Pearl Harbor eluded it by the use of the word "timely" (see above, p. 339). The conflict of the proposition with the official thesis on the coming of war, established by President Roosevelt on December 8, 1941, is obvious. According to that thesis, the President was seeking peace with Japan and the United States was precipitated into war by the surprise attack launched by the Japanese on December 7. Nor did the United States declare war on Germany and Italy at the request of President Roosevelt. On the morning of December 11, Germany and Italy declared war on the United States. The resolutions of Congress, December 11, 1941, said that a state of war had been "thrust upon" the United States by Germany and Italy and that this state of war "is hereby formally declared." If the state of war had been thrust upon the United States, were President Roosevelt and Secretary Hull merely victims, not makers, of history?

when did it come or is it to come—in what span of time, short or long? By whom and according to what criteria is the question of time to be answered beyond all reasonable doubt?

If the time for the achievement of the end be postponed to some point in the indefinite future, the confirmation of the thesis must likewise be postponed indefinitely. In that case an effort to confirm it now becomes a matter of calculating probabilities, ponderable and imponderable. If, however, the results of the war—foreign and domestic—thus far known be taken into the reckoning, a question both logical and historical may be asked: Does it now appear probable that President Roosevelt did in fact so clearly discern the end—the consequences to flow from his actions in 1941—that he was in truth justified in his choice and use of means?

With regard to consequences in foreign affairs,[6] the noble principles of the Four Freedoms and the Atlantic Charter were, for practical purposes, discarded in the settlements which accompanied the progress, and followed the conclusion, of the war. To the validity of this statement the treatment of peoples in Estonia, Lithuania, Poland, Rumania, Yugoslavia, China, Indo-China, Indonesia, Italy, Germany, and other

6. In respect of the alarming state of foreign affairs for the United States in February, 1947, testimony was given by a high-ranking authority, the Secretary of State, George C. Marshall, in an address at Princeton University, on the 22d of that month. On that occasion, Secretary Marshall said:

"As you all must recognize, we are living today in a most difficult period. The war years were critical, at times alarmingly so. But I think that the present period is, in many respects, even more critical [than during the war years]. The problems are different but no less vital to the national security than those during the days of active fighting. But the more serious aspect is the fact that we no longer display that intensity, that unity of purpose, with which we concentrated upon the war task and achieved the victory. . . .

"We have had a cessation of hostilities, but we have no genuine peace. Here at home we are in a state of transition between a war and peace economy. In Europe and Asia fear and famine still prevail. Power relationships are in a state of flux. Order has yet to be brought out of confusion. Peace has yet to be secured. And how this is accomplished will depend very much upon the American people.

"Most of the other countries of the world find themselves exhausted economically, financially and physically. If the world is to get on its feet, if the productive facilities of the world are to be restored, if democratic processes in many countries are to resume their functioning, a strong lead and definite assistance from the United States will be necessary." *Congressional Record*, March 3, 1947 (Appendix).

places of the earth bears witness. More significant still for the fortunes of the American Republic, out of the war came the triumph of another totalitarian regime no less despotic and ruthless than Hitler's system, namely, Russia, possessing more than twice the population of prewar Germany, endowed with immense natural resources, astride Europe and Asia, employing bands of Quislings as terroristic in methods as any Hitler ever assembled, and insistently effectuating a political and economic ideology equally inimical to the democracy, liberties, and institutions of the United States—Russia, one of the most ruthless Leviathans in the long history of military empires.

Since, as a consequence of the war called "necessary" to overthrow Hitler's despotism, another despotism was raised to a higher pitch of power, how can it be argued conclusively with reference to inescapable facts that the "end" justified the means employed to involve the United States in that war? If the very idea of neutrality with regard to Hitler was shameful in 1941, what is to be said of commitments made in the name of peace and international amity at Teheran and Yalta, where the avowed and endorsed principles of the Atlantic Charter for world affairs were shattered—in commitments which were subsequently misrepresented by President Roosevelt, publicly and privately? [7]

Nor more than two years after the nominal close of the war did the prospects of "reconstruction" in Germany and Japan promise the achievement of President Roosevelt's great end in any discernible time ahead.

In respect of domestic affairs, the consequences of the involvement in the war are scarcely less damaging to the thesis that the end justified the means. Among the many dangers long emphasized by advocates of war in the name of perpetual or durable peace, none was described in more frightening terms than the prospect that Hitler would be victorious in Europe and that the result of his victory would spell disaster for the United States. It would mean the transformation of the

7. For instance, as to Poland, see Jan Ciechanowski, *Defeat in Victory* (Doubleday, 1947).

United States into a kind of armed camp for defense, with all the evils thereunto attached: a permanent conscript army, multiplied annual outlays for armaments, a huge national debt, and grinding taxes. The expansion of American economy, so necessary for domestic prosperity, would be blocked by the impossibility of "doing business with Hitler," that is, by barriers to American commerce in the form of state-fostered cartels and state-controlled economies in Europe. Moreover, the promotion of beneficent reforms at home, from which President Roosevelt had been compelled to turn in military preparations for defense, would be permanently barred. Only by victory over Hitler, it was claimed, could these frightful evils be avoided.

But judging by results of participation in the war, and the prospects of evident tendencies, were these dreadful evils obviated by the victory at arms? While the war was still raging, President Roosevelt recommended to Congress the adoption of conscription as a permanent policy for the United States—under the softer name of universal service; and his successor, President Truman, continued to urge that policy upon Congress even after large-scale fighting had nominally stopped. Furthermore, it was now claimed by former advocates of war that huge armed forces were necessary in "peacetime" to "secure the fruits of victory" and "win the peace"—by extirpating the spirit of tyranny in Germany and Japan and by restraining the expansion of Russian imperial power.

As for military expenditures, they were fixed in 1947 at many times the annual outlays of prewar years, despite the cuts made by the Republican Congress in President Truman's budget demands. To the people of the United States, the war bequeathed a national debt, augmented from about $60,000,-000,000 in 1940 to approximately $279,000,000,000 in 1946, or about $2,000 for every man, woman, and child in the country. To meet the annual interest on the national debt it was necessary in 1947 for the government to raise about $5,000,000,000, or more than the total peacetime outlay of the government for all purposes in any year before 1933—the advent of the New Deal; and the tax rates of 1947 made the tax rates of any year before 1941 look positively trivial in comparison. So stupendous was the debt and so heavy the tax burden that only Communists, looking gleefully to repudiation and a general economic crash, could envisage the future with satisfaction. Nor was the outlook for doing business with Stalin save on his own terms, or for that matter with several other European governments, any brighter than doing business with Hitler in the prewar years had been in fact.

With regard to the Democratic party as the party offering beneficent and progressive reforms, the outcome of the war was little short of disastrous, at least immediately. Though entrenched in every department of the Federal Government and commanding the support of a bureaucracy numbering more than 3,000,000 officers and employees, enjoying all the economic perquisites therewith associated, the party was ousted from power in both houses of Congress by Republicans triumphant at the polls in the congressional elections of 1946.

Deprived of its "indispensable" leader through the death of President Roosevelt in 1945, the Democratic party broke immediately into belligerent factions, while internationalists quarreled over the proceedings, meaning, and utility of the United Nations. On the extreme right, gathered old-line Democrats bent on extinguishing all signs of the New Deal; on the extreme left, rallied the new-line "progressives," headed by Henry Wallace, pledged to innovations more radical, extensive, and costly than those of the New Deal; and in the middle a small number of reformers, claiming to be guardians of the true faith, established the Committee for Democratic Action, with which Mrs. Eleanor Roosevelt was affiliated. Hence, when the fortunes of the Democrats as the unified party of reform were considered, it was academic to raise the question whether the domestic consequences of the war for the new world order justified the means chosen by President Roosevelt to gain the end which he chose for himself and the United States.

Indeed, two years after the nominal close of the war for the end proclaimed, it was almost academic to discuss domestic affairs at all, for they were subordinate to overriding foreign commitments, known and secret, made by President Roosevelt and by his successor, President Harry Truman. In 1947, under President Truman's direction, the Government of the United States set out on an unlimited program of underwriting, by money and military "advice," poverty-stricken, feeble, and instable governments around the edges of the gigantic and aggressive Slavic Empire. Of necessity, if this program was to be more than a *brutum fulmen,* it had to be predicated upon present and ultimate support by the blood and treasure of the United States; and this meant keeping the human power and the economy of the United States geared to the potentials inherent in the undertaking.

In these circumstances, it was impossible for the Government or people of the United States to make any rational calculations as to economy, life, and work at home. Over young men and women trying to plan their future days and years hung the shadow of possible, in fact probable, calls to armed services. Congress could do no more than guess at the requirements of taxation and expenditures, domestic and foreign. Business enterprisers, with prospects of new war demands ahead, could lay out no programs for the production of civilian goods with any degree of assurance as to the future, immediate or remote. In short, with the Government of the United States committed under a so-called bipartisan foreign policy to supporting by money and other forms of power for an indefinite time an indefinite number of other governments around the globe, the domestic affairs of the American people became appendages to an aleatory expedition in the management of the world.

JUDGMENT BY REFERENCE TO THE AMERICAN CONSTITUTIONAL SYSTEM

NEVERTHELESS, if it is still contended that President Roosevelt was justified in his choice and use of means to accomplish his end, there remains to be faced the relation of the means, as actually employed, to the Constitution of the United States and all that it signifies in terms of limited government, consent of the governed, democratic processes, and political ethics. The issue of this relationship rises above political parties and political personalities. It is timeless in its reach for the American people, perhaps for the people of the whole world. In short and plain form this issue is: Given the precedents set by President Roosevelt in the choice and use of means, what is to be the future of representative government under the Constitution of the United States?

When the Constitution, with its provisions for popular government, its limitations and checks on personal and arbitrary government, and its safeguards for the rights of the people, is taken as the standpoint for reviewing the conduct of foreign affairs by President Roosevelt, a more permanent and concrete basis is established for judgment than is furnished by the theory that the end justified the means. According to that standard, the very conception of limited government, which is indubitably anchored in the Constitution, of necessity circumscribes the powers and the means which may be employed by every department of the Government of the United States.

It is true that the Constitution is flexible in many respects but as to the division and limitation of power its language is explicit.[8] Certainly it does not vest in the Congress or the President illimitable power secretly to determine the ends of the government in foreign or domestic affairs and secretly to choose and employ any means deemed desirable by either branch of the government to achieve those ends. The President, members of Congress, and all high officials take an oath to support and defend the Constitution; and unless legal commitments involve no moral commitments and oaths of office are to be belittled as empty formalities, the conduct of for-

8. For an authoritative exposition of this axiom of divided and limited power, see *The Federalist*, Nos. 47–51.

eign affairs is subject to the Constitution, the laws, and the democratic prescriptions essential to the American system of government.

Yet, if the precedents set by President Roosevelt in conducting foreign affairs, as reported in the records of the Congressional Committee on Pearl Harbor and other documents, are to stand unimpeached and be accepted henceforth as valid in law and morals then:

The President of the United States in a campaign for re-election may publicly promise the people to keep the country out of war and, after victory at the polls, may set out secretly on a course designed or practically certain to bring war upon the country.

He may, to secure legislation in furtherance of his secret designs, misrepresent to Congress and the people both its purport and the policy he intends to pursue under its terms if and when such legislation is enacted.

He may, by employing legal casuists, secretly frame and, using the powers and patronage of his office, obtain from Congress a law conferring upon him in elusive language authority which Congress has no constitutional power to delegate to him.

He may, after securing such legislation, publicly announce that he will pursue, as previously professed, a policy contrary to war and yet at the same time secretly prepare plans for waging an undeclared "shooting war" that are in flat contradiction to his public professions.

He may hold secret conferences with the Premier of a foreign government and publicly declare that no new commitments have been made when, in fact, he has committed the United States to occupying, by the use of American armed forces, the territory of a third country and joining the Premier in parallel threats to another government.

He may make a secret agreement with a foreign power far more fateful in consequences to the United States than any alliance ever incorporated in a treaty to be submitted to the Senate for approval.

He may demand, and Congress may pliantly confer upon him, the power to designate at his discretion foreign governments as enemies of the United States and to commit hostile acts against them, at his pleasure, in violation of national statutes and the principles of international law hitherto accepted and insisted upon by the United States.

He may publicly represent to Congress and the people that acts of war have been committed against the United States, when in reality the said acts were secretly invited and even initiated by the armed forces of the United States under his secret direction.

He may, on the mere ground that Congress has made provisions for national defense, secretly determine any form of military and naval strategy and order the armed forces to engage in any acts of war which he deems appropriate to achieve the ends which he personally chooses.

He may, by employing his own subordinates as broadcasters and entering into secret relations with private agencies of propaganda, stir up a popular demand for some drastic action on his part which is not authorized by law, and then take that action, thus substituting the sanction of an unofficial plebiscite for the sanction of the Constitution and the laws enacted under it.

He may, after publicly announcing one foreign policy, secretly pursue the opposite and so conduct foreign and military affairs as to maneuver a designated foreign power into firing the first shot in an attack upon the United States and thus avoid the necessity of calling upon Congress in advance to exercise its constitutional power to deliberate upon a declaration of war.

He may, as a crowning act in the arrogation of authority to himself, without the consent of the Senate, make a commitment to the head of a foreign government which binds the United States to "police the world," at least for a given time, that is, in the eyes of other governments and peoples policed, to dominate the world; and the American people are thereby in honor bound to provide the military, naval, and economic forces necessary to pursue, with no assurance of success, this exacting business.

In short, if these precedents are to stand unimpeached and to provide sanctions for the continued conduct of American foreign affairs, the Constitution may be nullified by the President, officials, and officers who have taken the oath, and are under moral obligation, to uphold it. For limited government under supreme law they may substitute personal and arbitrary government—the first principle of the totalitarian system against which, it has been alleged, World War II was waged—while giving lip service to the principle of constitutional government.

Moreover, in addition to the sanctions provided by these precedents, the theory that the President has the power to determine foreign policy, support his policy by arms, and, without appealing to Congress for war authority, strike a designated enemy, has received approval in certain military, naval, and civilian circles of the United States. To this fact the conduct of General George C. Marshall, as Chief of Staff, and Admiral Harold R. Stark, as Chief of Naval Operations, in 1941, bears witness. It may be claimed, of course, that as loyal officers and subordinates of President Roosevelt, Secretary Stimson, and Secretary Knox, Admiral Stark and General Marshall were bound to accept the rulings, orders, and plans of their civilian superiors. Indeed, for their plans and actions, including the initiation of an undeclared war on German and Italian war vessels in the Atlantic, they had the color of authority in the orders and instructions of President Roosevelt.

Even so, documents made public by the Congressional Committee on Pearl Harbor reveal that General Marshall and Admiral Stark, in giving form to war plans in coöperation with British military and naval officers and making military recommendations to President Roosevelt, took the position that the United States must fight if Japan moved her armed forces beyond certain lines in the direction of British and Dutch possessions in the Far East.

Fortunately for American people who want to know how they are governed, Admiral Stark was a voluminous letter writer and a part, at least, of his immense file was opened by the Congressional Committee.[9] Perhaps it was for this "indiscretion" that Admiral Stark, after services in the war for which he was awarded high honors, was cashiered by Secretary Forrestal, placed in the class of Admiral Kimmel, and publicly discredited by the official declaration that henceforward he should hold no office calling for "superior judgment." In any case, as demonstrated by his letters and testimony before the Congressional Committee, Admiral Stark was a willing and indeed eager servant of the idea that the United States must enter the European war, by clandestine methods if necessary, and that the President had the power to initiate war; and he was a party to the misrepresentations of the alleged "attacks" in the Atlantic as the work of a truculent enemy.[10]

As Chief of Staff of the Army, General Marshall was less involved immediately than Admiral Stark in initiating the secret undeclared war in the Atlantic, but that action was only an expression of a general policy in the making of which he participated actively as a member of the War Cabinet. Admiral Stark consulted him before he invited British naval experts in the fall of 1940 to Washington with a view to framing common naval plans for war.[11] General Marshall participated in the drafting of the British-American war plans which contemplated the opening of war in the Atlantic.[12] Since the Army was to be involved in the occupation of the Azores, he was a party to that design.[13] If Admiral Stark is to be accepted as authority, General Marshall was preparing the Army early in 1941 for the invasion of Europe, as the following colloquy shows:

9. See above, Chap. XIV. General Marshall was apparently more restrained than Admiral Stark in his letter writing.
10. See above, Chaps. III, V, and XIV.
11. CJC, Part 11, p. 5240.
12. See above, Chap. XIV, especially, pp. 442 ff.
13. *Ibid.*

SENATOR FERGUSON. Was it ever contemplated, as far as you know, to come to Congress to declare war on Portugal and take the Azores?

ADMIRAL STARK. I never heard of it, or I never thought of it until this minute.

SENATOR FERGUSON. Well, if you were preparing the fleet, and preparing ships to take the Azores, it wasn't just a drill, was it?

ADMIRAL STARK. We prepared to take the Continent of Europe too.

SENATOR FERGUSON. That early? . . .

ADMIRAL STARK. Well, I dare say that the Army was working on plans, and they were asking for men, and so forth, for a big and huge Army.[14]

As a member of the War Cabinet, General Marshall took part in the business of "maneuvering" the Japanese into firing the first shot. Although in his testimony before the Congressional Committee he insisted that this maneuvering was essentially "diplomatic," he knew very well that diplomatic maneuvering unsupported by war plans and arms was chimerical and that it rested at bottom on the war recommendations of November 5 and November 27 which he had joined Admiral Stark in presenting to the President and War Cabinet.

If all this be discounted, it is to be noted that General Marshall was in accord with the doctrine of presidential power over diplomacy, strategy, and war set forth by Secretary Stimson in the extracts from his *Diary* and in his statement presented to the Congressional Committee. There, Secretary Stimson maintained that, as Chief Executive and Commander in Chief of the Army and the Navy, the President had power to inform a foreign government that, if terms he laid down were not accepted and obeyed, the United States would fight—indeed that the President had the power to order war on that government, without an advance declaration of war by Congress, if it made moves forbidden by the President. During the course of General Marshall's testimony before the

14. CJC, Part 11, p. 5260.

Congressional Committee on April 9, 1946, Mr. Keefe put the following question to him: "So that as a member of the committee I am safe in accepting the statement of Secretary Stimson, together with the memoranda contained in his diary, as being in full accord with your own attitude toward the things and events which he described?" General Marshall answered: "Yes, sir. . . ."[15]

Furthermore, it is to be remembered that Secretary Stimson, in another place, declared, without any reference to the Constitution, that when Congress has provided for a policy of defense by legislation, the President alone has the power to make the decisions as to how this policy is to be best carried out, to adopt plans for national defense, and to determine the particular strategy requisite to effect these plans, including that of maneuvering any designated enemy into firing the first shot.[16] Beyond that, in the boundless realm of power politics, it is scarcely possible for a soaring imagination to go; for Congress regularly makes continuing provision for national defense.

On November 28, 1941, for example, Secretary Stimson discussed with President Roosevelt measures which might be taken against Japan. If anything was to be done, the President suggested: "to make something in the nature of an ultimatum again, stating a point beyond which we would fight; [or] . . . to fight at once." Secretary Stimson favored the latter alternative. In his statement to the committee, Mr. Stimson explained his decision by saying "the desirable thing to do from the point of view of our own tactics and safety was to take the initiative and attack without further warning. It is axiomatic that the best defense is offense. It is always dangerous to wait and let the enemy make the first move. I was inclined to feel that the warning given in August [1941] by the President against further moves by the Japanese toward Thailand[17]

15. *Ibid.*, p. 5195.
16. *Ibid.*, p. 5456 ff.; see also above, p. 517.
17. See above, pp. 447 ff.

justified an attack without further warning, particularly as their new movement southward indicated that they were about to violate that warning."

This utility of limitless presidential power in matters of foreign policy and foreign affairs, and even in waging war, was also expounded, less explicitly but no less forcefully, by the Army Board on Pearl Harbor which was appointed by Secretary Stimson under the Act of Congress, June 13, 1944, and reported to him on October 20 of that year.[18] Although the board was presumably engaged in exploring responsibilities for the catastrophe at Pearl Harbor, it took advantage of the occasion to assert an overriding philosophy of politics and war. In Chapter II of its Report, the board laid heavy emphasis on the handicaps imposed upon the Roosevelt Administration by "isolationists and nationalists who objected to involvement in war," on the difficulties encountered by the State Department in conducting negotiations with Japan without means of enforcing its views by arms, and on the advantages which the Executive of Japan had in its unrestricted power to make a surprise war at its own will, without reference to the Parliament.

The Army Pearl Harbor Board did not claim with Secretary Stimson that acts of Congress providing for national defense ipso facto authorized the President to conduct foreign affairs and make war at will; nor did it attack the Constitution of the United States by name. But it did definitely intimate that the responsibility for the disaster at Pearl Harbor must be ultimately ascribed to the system of checks on arbitrary power provided by the Constitution and by the processes of representative and democratic government as carried on under the Constitution. It declared that the consequences of those processes furnished the background for allocating responsibilities in respect of the catastrophe: "There was a distinct lack of a war mind in the United States. Isolationist organizations and propaganda groups against war were powerful and vital factors affecting any war action capable of being taken by our re-

18. See above, Chap. XI.

sponsible [19] leadership. So influential were these campaigns that they raised grave doubts in the minds of such leadership as to whether they would be supported by the people in the necessary actions for our defense by requisite moves against Japan. Public opinion in the early stages had to be allowed to develop; in the later stages it ran ahead of preparation for war. There was little war spirit either amongst the general public or in the armed forces, due to this conflicting public opinion having its influence. The events hereinafter recited must be measured against this important psychological factor." [20]

With more caution, the Navy Court of Inquiry, in its Report on Pearl Harbor, said of constitutional limitations on the President's power to make war: "In time of peace it is a difficult and complicated matter for the United States to prevent an attack by another nation because of the constitutional requirement that, prior to a declaration of war by Congress, no blow may be struck until after a hostile attack has been delivered. This is a military consideration which gives to a dishonorable potential enemy the advantage of the initiative, deprives the United States of an opportunity to employ the offensive as a mean of defense, and places great additional responsibility on the shoulders of commanders afloat in situations where instant action, or its absence, may entail momentous consequences." [21]

The theory of unlimited power in the Executive over international relations is by no means confined to Army and Navy circles. Close students of international law and foreign affairs who follow the literature of the subject, including articles in law journals, are aware that numerous defenders of President Roosevelt's methods have been for years engaged in stretching political precedents and obiter dicta of Supreme Court justices in an effort to establish two propositions in particular: (1) the President's power in the management of foreign affairs is practically sovereign; and (2) the President may

19. Responsible how and to whom?
20. CJC, Part 39, pp. 27 ff.
21. *Ibid.*, p. 298.

incorporate in an executive agreement with a foreign government—even a secret executive agreement—any commitment he wishes to make in the name of the United States, despite the constitutional provision for the ratification of treaties by the Senate.

Subsidized and powerful private agencies engaged nominally in propaganda for "peace" are among the chief promoters of presidential omnipotence in foreign affairs. They look to the President rather than Congress for assistance in advancing their ideas of America's obligation to join other "peace-loving" nations in ordering and reordering the world. Moreover, as these agencies in turn subsidize professors and "students of international relations" by the hundreds, they thereby help to exalt presidential "leadership" and, correspondingly, degrade the Senate or the House of Representatives or both with regard to their responsibilities in foreign affairs. Consequently, American education from the universities down to the grade schools is permeated with, if not dominated by, the theory of presidential supremacy in foreign affairs. Coupled with flagrant neglect of instruction in constitutional government, this propaganda in universities, colleges, and schools has deeply implanted in the minds of rising generations the doctrine that the power of the President over international relations is, for all practical purposes, illimitable.

The theory of limitless power in the Executive to conduct foreign affairs and initiate war at will, unhampered by popular objections and legislative control, is of course old in the history of empires and despotisms. It was long accepted and practiced by despotic monarchies. It was held and applied by Hitler and Mussolini. It is now the theory, as well as the practice, of totalitarian governments everywhere. But such governments have never been under the delusion that limitless power can be exercised over foreign affairs and war, while domestic affairs and domestic economy are left free and the authority of government over them is constitutionally limited.

Since the drafting of the Constitution, American statesmen of the first order have accepted the axiom that militarism and the exercise of arbitrary power over foreign affairs by the Executive are inveterate foes of republican institutions.[22] It was in part to meet the threatened establishment of a military dictatorship on the ruins of representative government that George Washington took leadership in the formation and ratification of the Constitution.[23] In No. 8 of *The Federalist*, Alexander Hamilton pointed out that any necessity which enhances the importance of the soldier "proportionably degrades the condition of the citizen. The military state becomes elevated above the civil."

But it is contended by some contemporary publicists, whose assurance is often more impressive than their knowledge of human government, that offense is the best defense, that unlimited striking power in the Executive is necessary to survival in an age of "power politics" and "atom bombs." Few of them, it is true, venture to say openly that the Constitution is obsolete and that such a centralization of authority should be, in fact, substituted for the system of limited government fortified by checks and balances. Yet the implication of their arguments is inexorable: constitutional and democratic government in the United States is at the end of its career.

If it be urged that the United Nations organization and American membership in it offer an escape from the dilemma so posed, many countervailing realities become obvious to reflective minds. If the violent differences of opinion among supporters of that organization as to its meaning and prospects furnish no caveats, events certainly do.

Neither the operations of the organization nor the procedures under the prolix and redundant asseverations of peace and human rights incorporated in its charter have indicated discernible alterations in the warlike, revolutionary, and ambitious propensities of politicians, governments, and nations. The ordinary conduct of international relations by separate diplomatic agencies and contests for prestige and supremacy among power-hungry politicians have continued despite the

22. C. A. Beard, *The Republic* (Viking, 1943), pp. 212 ff.
23. *Ibid.*, pp. 22 ff.

existence and nominal functioning of the United Nations organization. Whether the public and often vitriolic debates that occur in the so-called "town meeting of the world," especially with regard to controversial issues arising within and among nations, will produce more peaceful settlements and fewer wars than ordinary diplomatic processes is at best dubious. At any rate, the rights of independence, self-defense, and freedom from outside intervention in internal affairs are explicitly accorded by the charter to all member nations; and the pursuit of what are called "national interests" appears no less vigorous or intransigent than before the United Nations came into existence.

The crisis in constitutional government represented by the present foreign perils and the contest over Executive authority relative to the conduct of foreign affairs, including the war power, has not sprung entirely from physical objects such as atom bombs and rocket planes or from sources entirely outside the United States, beyond the control of the American people. In no small measure it has come from doctrines proclaimed by presidents and political leaders, strongly supported by subsidized propaganda and widely applauded by numerous American citizens since the opening of the twentieth century. Among these doctrines four are especially effective in creating moral and intellectual disorder at home and hostility toward the United States among the nations of the earth.

The first of these doctrines is the jubilant American cry that the United States is now a world power and must assume the obligations of a world power. Undoubtedly the United States is a great power *in* the world and has obligations as such. But the range of its *effective* power supportable by armed forces and economic resources is limited. The further away from its base on the American continent the Government of the United States seeks to exert power over the affairs and relations of other countries the weaker its efficiency becomes; and the further it oversteps the limits of its strength the more likely it is to lead this nation into disaster—a terrible defeat in a war in Europe or Asia beyond the conquering power of its soldiers, sailors, and airmen. If wrecks of overextended empires scattered through the centuries offer any instruction to the living present, it is that a quest for absolute power not only corrupts but in time destroys. A prudent recognition and calculation of the limits on power is a mandate for statesmen and nations that seek to survive in the struggles of "power politics." And, as there are limitations on power to control or obliterate other nations, so there are limitations on the obligation to serve them either morally, physically, or economically.

A second danger to the peace and the security of the United States is the doctrine which runs to the effect that the President of the United States has the constitutional and moral right to proclaim noble sentiments of politics, economics, and peace for the whole world and commit the United States to these sentiments by making speeches and signing pieces of paper on his own motion. The futility of this practice has been demonstrated again and again and again, as the history of the Open Door, the Fourteen Points, the Kellogg Pact, the Four Freedoms, and the Atlantic Charter attests.

But the hazards in it are usually overlooked. Such commitments, even if intended for popular consumption, are often accepted as real, meaningful, and enforceable by some foreigners who share the sentiments of good will, and as easy bargains by foreign governments in dire need of American blood and treasure. In the one case disappointed hopes provoke bitterness against the United States; [24] and in the other case ingratitude for favors received produces similar results. In both cases the United States is opened to the imputation of hypocrisy and in fact often deserves it, with a loss in self-respect and of moral standing among the nations.

The practice of presidents in proclaiming noble sentiments of politics, economics, and peace for the whole world becomes all the more dangerous to the standing and security of the

---

24. A recent and classic example of such promises made by President Roosevelt under the head of world morality but also with some reference to the Polish-American vote in coming elections and secretly broken at Teheran and Yalta, is provided by the former Polish Ambassador, Jan Ciechanowski, *op. cit., passim.*

United States if accompanied by public denunciations of other governments and by unilateral procedures designed to coerce them, such as embargoes and other economic sanctions. A melancholy illustration of this practice is provided by the ill fortune of the Stimson doctrine proclaimed in January, 1932, to the effect that the United States will not admit the legality of any situation, agreement, or treaty brought about by acts of aggression contrary to the Open Door policy, the Nine-Power Treaty of 1922, or the Kellogg-Briand Pact of 1928.[25] With this announcement President Hoover agreed but he differed from Mr. Stimson, his Secretary of State, in that he objected to employing other than moral sanctions to enforce it.

In time Mr. Stimson, however, won the support of President Roosevelt for his doctrine and, as Secretary of War, had the satisfaction of seeing Japan driven out of Manchuria, where the "incident" to which the doctrine was first applied arose in 1931. But in time, Mr. Stimson, in common with the world, also saw Russian imperialist power reëstablished at strategic points in Manchuria (as well as the northern part of Korea) with the sanction of President Roosevelt, who even coöperated in compelling the Government of China to accept the *fait accompli*. Furthermore, Mr. Stimson, in common with the world, saw other gross violations of the doctrine that the United States will not admit the legality of territorial seizures by acts of aggression—violations agreed to by President Roosevelt at Teheran and Yalta, by President Truman at Potsdam, and by the then Secretary of State, James F. Byrnes, in "settlements" reached at various places after the conclusion of the war, as if *sub lege talionis*.[26]

Closely associated with the idea that the President is serving the United States and mankind when he emits grand programs for imposing international morality on recalcitrant nations by American power, alone or in conjunction with that of allies

25. For passages in the history of this ill-fated "doctrine," see Beard, *op. cit.*, pp. 111 ff., 133 ff.
26. For a list of treaty-breaking acts and acts of aggression on the part of Soviet Russia, and President Roosevelt's acquiescence in Russian demands, see William Bullitt, *The Great Globe Itself* (Scribner, 1946).

or associates, is another doctrine which helps to build up public support for Executive supremacy in foreign affairs and to make enemies abroad. This doctrine proudly announces that it is the duty of the United States to assume and maintain "the moral leadership of the world" in the interest of realizing American programs of world reform. Apart from the feasibility of establishing such moral leadership in fact, the assertion of it adds to the discord rather than the comity of nations.

To sensibility, the very idea is repulsive. As ladies and gentlemen who publicly proclaim their own virtues are suspected and resented by self-respecting persons, so the Government and people of the United States, by loudly proclaiming their moral leadership of the world, awaken suspicion and resentment in Great Britain, France, Russia, China, and other countries of the world; and, what may be worse in the long run, contemptuous laughter. Nor, in truth, can American democracy, culture, or ways of life be "sold" to the world over the radio or by any other means of communication.

Not less disturbing to the fostering of decency in international intercourse is an array of opinions pertaining to international commerce. Proponents of these opinions say, for example, international commerce ipso facto promotes peace; it will raise the low standards of life which are "causes" of wars; such commerce, if expanded, will make it unnecessary for "have-not" nations to wage war for economic purposes; lowering trade barriers to international commerce will assure the continuous expansion of the international trade that works for peace and prosperity at home and abroad; and, therefore, the Government of the United States, in its search for world peace, must employ the engines of pressure and money lending in order to insure peace through the establishment of universal prosperity. Separately or collectively, these ideas are supported by powerful economic interests in the United States and if pushed in application will aggravate domestic conflicts, lead to limitless spending of taxpayers' money,[27] and bring on

27. It is well known that bankers and other private investors in the United States, having lost billions in the business of foreign "loans" after the conclusion

collisions with the controlled or semicontrolled economies of foreign countries.

The dangers of evoking foreign antagonisms by the use of the powers of government to promote commerce with other nations were well understood by leading framers of the Constitution. Among the many fictions attacked by Alexander Hamilton were two popular ideas: (1) republics are necessarily pacific and (2) "the spirit of commerce has a tendency to soften the manners of men." [28]

With acumen, Hamilton asked: "Has commerce hitherto done anything more than change the objects of war? Is not the love of wealth as domineering and enterprising a passion as that of power or glory? Have there not been as many wars founded upon commercial motives since that has become the prevailing system of nations, as were before occasioned by the cupidity of territory or dominion? Has not the spirit of commerce, in many instances, administered new incentives to the appetite, both for the one and for the other? Let experience, the least fallible guide of human opinions, be appealed to for an answer to these inquiries." While Washington, under whom Hamilton served in war and peace, favored the fostering of foreign commerce, he warned his fellow countrymen, in the Farewell Address, against forcing it.

It remained for the nineteenth century to produce a full-blown concept for using the engines of state to break and keep channels open for foreign trade and to create spheres of economic interest. Critics dubbed this concept "imperialism." Defenders finally accepted the term and clothed it in moral verbiage as a design for "doing good to them that sit in darkness," that is, have a low standard of life. Rejecting imperialism as motivated by greed and lacking in virtue, other promoters of foreign trade chose more gracious covering phrases but called for the use of government in the process on similar grounds of

of World War I, will not voluntarily finance such schemes of "trade promotion" and that, if the policy of promotion is pressed, these projects must be financed by agencies of the United States Government out of funds derived from taxing and borrowing.

28. *The Federalist*, No. 6.

national and universal interest—raising the standards of life for everybody, everywhere, and giving four or more freedoms to the "common man" throughout the world.

In fact, this new internationalism of commerce does not, as often claimed, rise wholly above special economic interests into the pure empyrean of world welfare. If "greedy" and "purblind" manufacturers for the domestic market are to be found supporting high tariff rates on products that compete with their goods, exporters, importers, producers of raw materials, and manufacturers for the export market are likewise to be discovered using money, influence, and politics on their side.[29]

However that may be, delegating to the President the power to effect commercial treaties with other countries at will and to make loans to politicians temporarily at the head of their governments helps to augment Executive authority in the United States, and to give foreign peoples reasons or pretexts for suspecting the motives and impugning the character of the American Government, rightly or wrongly. At all events, using political engines and public funds in wholesale efforts to promote universal prosperity through free or freer international commerce so called, while in practice sowing the seeds of discord at home and abroad, approaches an impasse in thought and action.[30]

29. A few years ago good Democrats were shocked and made loud outcries when a Republican Senator openly allowed the secretary of a manufacturers' association to help him write certain schedules in a pending tariff bill; but in 1947 good Democrats were deeply pained and highly indignant when a Republican member of the House of Representatives vociferously protested against permitting a rich cotton broker and exporter of cotton to serve as Undersecretary of State and engage in making "reciprocal" trade arrangements.

30. The extent to which government-controlled trade prevails, not only in Russia, where it is an absolute monopoly, but also in Great Britain, where a Socialist government is in power, and in other countries of western Europe, is well known to economic literates. The likelihood of a return to the "free trade" age of Richard Cobden and John Bright seems to be about as remote as a return to the ice age. At the Atlantic Conference in 1941, President Roosevelt and Undersecretary Welles took advantage of Prime Minister Churchill's dire need to press upon him the disruption of preferential trade within the British Empire, but Mr. Churchill was unable to commit the other members of the British Commonwealth and the subject was dismissed with a few vague words in the Atlantic Charter. See above, Chap. XV. Democratic sponsors of the bill for the large

At this point in its history the American Republic has arrived under the theory that the President of the United States possesses limitless authority publicly to misrepresent and secretly to control foreign policy, foreign affairs, and the war power.

More than a hundred years ago, James Madison, Father of the Constitution, prophesied that the supreme test of American statesmanship would come about 1930.

Although not exactly in the form that Madison foresaw, the test is here, now—with no divinity hedging our Republic against Caesar.

"loan" to Great Britain in 1946 defended it by broad and unfounded hints that breaking imperial preference would result from the passage of the bill. This is the use of the engines of government for commercial coercion.

Index

with Germany, 7; German invasion, 317; and Japan, 455–456, 458, 460, 499, 532, 534; Japanese on Russian border, 317; Lend-Lease and, 119–120, 128–129, 193; as postwar power, 577–578, 594; Roosevelt concessions to, 241 n., 594 n.; control of trade, 597; treaty-breaking acts, 594 n.; and U.S. leadership, 595

SAFFORD, CAPTAIN, 532, 534
Salazar, Dr., 462, 464
Salinas, S.S., 148–149
Sanctions, 178, 182, 236, 239–240, 444, 594
Sandburg, Carl, 125
Satterfield, Congressman D. E., 102
Sauthoff, Congressman Harry, 72
Sayre, Francis, 192
Schuirmann, Captain R. E., 508 n.
Schulz, Commander, 549–551
Scott, Congressman Hugh D., 276–279, 283
Selective Service Act, extended, 124, 529
Sheppard, Senator Morris, 54–55
Ship losses, 101
Shipstead, Senator Hendrik, 266–269
Short, Congressman Dewey, 59–60, 222
Short, General Walter C., appointment to Pacific command, 265, 359; precautions against attack, 388–389; removed from post, 262, 379, 383–387, 393; appeals for men and equipment, 280, 354, 358, 365 n.; war warnings to, 525–526, 552; and Pearl Harbor, 265, 283, 287, 319–320, 338, 373, 381, 388–389, 523–524; held responsible for Pearl Harbor, 215, 220, 226, 360, 362–364, 377, 380, 382, 392; condemned by Congressman Short, 222; condemned by Barkley, 222; and Stimson, 245, 393–396; defended, 222–223, 279–281, 302, 377; exonerated by Army Board, 298–300, 310, 312–313, 324; Truman attacks, 274; partial repudiation, 305 n.; and Marshall, 381, 392–394; and retirement, 225–227, 314, 348, 362, 377 n., 390–399, 402, 404; and court-marshal, 221–227, 251, 255, 257–261, 263–264, 282–287, 289, 298, 302, 306–307, 311, 364 n., 394–399, 402–403; Army Board investigation,

292–293, 300–302, 308, 310, 312–313, 324; Joint Committee on Pearl Harbor Investigation, 338–341, 347–349, 353, 355, 357–358, 360–364, 369, 372, 392–406, 408, 521–522, 524–525; Roberts Report, 217–219, 262, 362–363
Siam. *See* Thailand
Siberia, 179 n., 193, 449
Singapore, 130, 207, 242, 317, 426, 449, 539–541
Smith, Senator, 80
—— A. M., 202 n.
—— George H. E., 159 n.
—— Congressman Martin F., 161
—— Merriman, 201
Sokolsky, George E., 259
Soong, T. V., 531
Spain, 201, 461–464
Stalin, Josef, 39, 120, 174 n., 234 n., 270, 414, 579
Stark, Admiral Harold R., 19 n., 550–551; appraisal of, 585; on Azores, 428, 461; on belligerent rights, 433–434; on British and American officer conferences, 442–443; denies convoying, 82; on convoying, 91, 94, 96, 104 n., 427, 430–431; on occupation of Iceland, 113 n.; on investigation of the *Greer*, 140–142; on the *Kearny*, 148; establishes Japan as aggressor, 558; and embargoes to Japan, 178 n., 179 n.; position on war with Japan, 447–449, 508; war with Japan inevitable, 566; accused of war intentions, 116; interpretation of executive powers, 584; instructions to Hart, 427–428, 430–432; approves Hart-Phillips plan, 449–450, 510–513, 541; and parallel war plans, 420–442, 485, 543; before Naval Affairs Committee, 114; opposed to Philippine cruise, 423–424; opposed to split of Navy, 424–425; plan for Northwest cruise, 427; opposed to two-ocean war, 422–424; and Kimmel, 385–387, 390–391, 405, 420; and Richardson, 415, 417; and Roosevelt, 421; and "winds" message, 533, 535, 536 n.; and retirement, 310, 314; discredited, 585; and Pearl Harbor, 290, 370, 372, 374; instructions to Kimmel, 420–422, 424–431; Joint Committee investigation of Pearl Harbor, 344,